Fragonard

Galeries Nationales du Grand Palais, Paris
September 24, 1987–January 4, 1988

The Metropolitan Museum of Art, New York
February 2–May 8, 1988

*F*ragonard

by Pierre Rosenberg

The Metropolitan Museum of Art
New York

Distributed by Harry N. Abrams, Inc., New York

The exhibition "Fragonard" has been made possible by Ann and Gordon Getty, The Sharp Foundation, The Real Estate Council of The Metropolitan Museum of Art and the National Endowment for the Arts. An indemnity has been granted by the Federal Council on the Arts and the Humanities.

This catalogue has been published in conjunction with the exhibition "Fragonard," held at the Galeries Nationales du Grand Palais, Paris, September 24, 1987–January 4, 1988, and at The Metropolitan Museum of Art, New York, February 2–May 8, 1988. Curators of the exhibition: Pierre Rosenberg, Conservateur en Chef, Département des Peintures, Musée du Louvre, Paris, assisted by Marie-Anne Dupuy; and Katharine Baetjer, Curator, Department of European Paintings, The Metropolitan Museum of Art, New York.

Published by The Metropolitan Museum of Art, New York
John P. O'Neill, *Editor in Chief*
Ellen Shultz, *Editor*
Teresa Egan, *Managing Editor*
Gwen Roginsky, *Production Manager,* assisted by Heidi Haeuser and Jean Levitt

Catalogue translated by Jean-Marie Clarke. Chapters VI and VII translated by Anthony Roberts

Assistants on the catalogue: Barbara Cavaliere and Jean Wagner

Design by Bruno Pfäffli, adapted for the English-language edition by Ellen Shultz and Joseph B. Del Valle

Library of Congress Cataloging-in-Publication Data

Rosenberg, Pierre.
    Fragonard / by Pierre Rosenberg.
        p.   cm.
    Bibliography: p.
    Includes indexes.
    ISBN 0-87099-516-2 (MMA)
    ISBN 0-8109-0921-9 (Abrams)
    1. Fragonard, Jean-Honoré, 1732–1806—Exhibitions.
    I. Title.
N6853.F68A4 1988
760'.092'4—dc19   87-30676
                                              CIP

Jacket: *Portrait of the Abbé de Saint-Non.* See catalogue no. 133

Type set by Cardinal Type Service, Inc., New York
Printed and bound by Imprimerie Blanchard, Paris, France

Contents

Author's Acknowledgments

To those individuals whose generous loans have made this exhibition possible, we are very grateful:

Mr. Étienne Ader
Mrs. Gertrude L. Chanler
Mr. and Mrs. George M. Cheston
Duc d'Harcourt
Mr. Akram Ojjeh
Mr. John W. Straus
Mr. and Mrs. Eugene V. Thaw
Baron Thyssen-Bornemisza
Mrs. Jeannette Veil-Picard

and all who prefer to remain anonymous.

Our thanks are due equally to those responsible for the following collections:

Argentina	Buenos Aires, Museo Nacional de Arte Decorativo
Austria	Vienna, Graphische Sammlung Albertina
Belgium	Brussels, Musée d'Ixelles
Brazil	São Paulo, Museu de Arte de São Paulo
Federal Republic of Germany	Berlin-Dahlem, Staatliche Museen Preussischer Kulturbesitz, Kupferstichkabinett
	Frankfurt am Main, Städelsches Kunstinstitut, Graphische Sammlung
	Hamburg, Hamburger Kunsthalle
	Karlsruhe, Staatliche Kunsthalle, Kupferstichkabinett
	Munich, Collection Bayerische Hypotheken- und Wechsel-Bank (on deposit at the Alte Pinakothek)
France	Amiens, Musée de Picardie
	Angers, Musées d'Angers
	Annecy, Musée-Château d'Annecy
	Besançon, Bibliothèque Municipale
	Musée des Beaux-Arts
	Chambéry, Musée des Beaux-Arts
	Chartres, Musée des Beaux-Arts
	Dijon, Musée des Beaux-Arts
	Grasse, Musée Fragonard
	Langres, Musées de Langres
	Le Havre, Museé des Beaux-Arts André Malraux
	Lyons, Musée des Arts Décoratifs
	Marseilles, Musée Borély
	Musée Grobet-Labadie
	Montpellier, Musée Atger, Faculté de Médecine
	Musée Fabre
	Narbonne, Musée d'Art et d'Histoire
	Nice, Musée des Beaux-Arts Jules Chéret
	Orléans, Musée des Beaux-Arts
	Paris, Banque de France
	École Nationale Supérieure des Beaux-Arts

We are grateful to all those individuals who have assisted us in our work—in particular:

D. and O. Aaron, D. Alcouffe, F. Aldao, M. Aldao, C. Alégret, C. Allsopp, M. Arango, A. Arikha, P. Arizzoli-Clémentel, D. Arnaudet, F. Arquié-Bruley, A. Auger, R. Bacou, H. Baderou, K. Baetjer, C. Bailey, M. Barbin, D. Barret, M. Bascoul, B. de Bayser, J. Bean, L. Beaumont, C. Beddington, P. Bérès, R. Beresford, S. Bergeon, F. Bergot, M. Bernascone, S. Bettagno, M.C. Bianchini, N. Bichier, I. Bizot, C. Blanchard, G. Blot, B. de Boisseson, G. Bouchards, A. Brejon de Lavergnée, B. Brejon de Lavergnée, G. Bresc, S. de Breteuil, G. Briganti, D. Bull, J. Cailleux, B. Calabresi, E. Cambo, Y. Cantarel Besson, R.M. Carpier-Bienfait, J. Carter Brown, K. Cederholm, C. Chagneau, M. Charriau, L. Chastel, M. Clarke, R. Cleyet-Michaud, S. Coca, U. Collinet, I. Compin, P. Conisbee, J. Coquelet, O. Cortet, M. Coursaget, H. Coutts, E. Crea, J.P. Cuzin, M. David Roy, Mme Deilhes, F. Delaroche-Vernet, C. Deryabina, J. Desjardin, F. Dijoud, B. Donon, R. Donoso, L. Faillant-Dumas, J. Feray, C. Filhos-Petit, Y. Fischer, H. de Fontmichel, J. Fouace, J. Foucart, E. Foucart-Walter, B. Fragonard, F. Franchini Guelfi, L. Franck, S. Freedberg, E. du Frétay, S. de Fuoni, J.R. Gaborit, A. de Gaigneron, M. Gallet, M.N. de Gary, E. Gavazza, Mlle Gazier, J. Gies, M. Gimpel, G. Grieten, C. Grodecki, P. Grunchec, R. Guardans, J.J. Guerlain, M. Guillaume, J. Guze, C. Haffner, F. Haskell, C. van Hasselt, M. Heugel, V. Huchard, P. Huot, F. Huré, L. Huygue, J. Ingamells, M. Jaffe, C. Jean, P. Jean-Richard, M. Jeune, W. Koschatzky, M. Labbe, M. Laclotte, A. Laguarigue, A. Laing, H. Landais, M. Lapallus, C. de La Rochère, A. Lasson, B. de La Tour, E. Launay, P. de La Vaissière, S. Laveissière, V. Lavergne, P. Le Chanu, O. Lecomte, A. Lefébure, O. Lefuel, C. Legrand, P. Le Leyzour, G. Le Pavec,

R. Lepéletier, A. Levi, S. Loire, A. Lombrail, B. Lossky, J.J. Luna, M.L. Madonna, G. Magnanimi, J.P. Marandel, L. de Margerie, L. Marques, R. May, S. McCullagh, J.F. Méjanès, J. Meyssard, C. Michel, O. Michel, A. Miquel, J. Montagu, J. Montague Massengale, P. Morel, M. Morgan Grasselli, V. Moritz, M. Mosser, B. de Moustiers, E. Munhall, N. Munich, G. Naughton, C. Nicq, M. Normand, A. Okada, Y. Ono, I. Osser, A. Ottani Cavina, H. Oursel, V. Pacelli, R. Pardo, M.F. Pérez, C. Personne, B. and V. Pfäffli, C. Pichois, E. Pillsbury, M. Pinault, M. Polakovits (†), M. Polo, B. Pons, S. Poujade, A. Poulet, H. Pousse, M. Pozuelos, L.A. Prat, M. and H. Prouté, M.F. Ramspacher, C. Ressort, F. Robinson, Mlle Roquet, M. Roland Michel, K. Rorschach, J. Roullet, M.C. Sahut, A. Salz, Mme Samson, H. Samuel, E. Schaar, P. Schatborn, E. Schleier, A. Schnapper, J. Schordans, A. Scottez-Wambrechies, M. Ségoura, A. Sérullaz, M. Sevin, M. Sheriff, D. Sickles, S. Slive, P. Sollers, F. Souchal, Mme Soulié-François, R. Spear, N. Spinosa, T. Standring, E. Starcky, M. Stein, M. Stewart, J. Stock, J.W. Straus, M. Stuffmann, J. Sureda, D. Sutton, G. Touminet-Potelle, S. de Tuoni, N. Turner, C. Urquijo, C. Vasselin, F. Viatte, D. Viéville, D. Vila, L. Vilarasau, N. Villa, H. Vincent, G. Vindry, W. de Virieu, G. de Vogüé, N. Volle, D. Walker, M.A. Wambre, S. Wells-Robertson, A. Wertz, J. Wilhelm, E. Williams, N. Willk-Brocard, S. Wise, M.C. zu Sayn Wittgenstein, I. Woodner, E. Wyckoff, E. Zafran, Y. Zolotov.

We have devoted the Slade Lectures at Cambridge University, during the academic year 1986–87, to Fragonard. We wish to thank warmly all those who shared their observations with us on this occasion, and offered their council.

Foreword

The "Fragonard" exhibition in New York and in Paris provides visitors with the opportunity to see some examples of the artist's most beautiful pictures. The approximately three hundred works, representing Fragonard's production in all its diversity, comprise the first retrospective, of this scope, ever to be organized. Fragonard's works encompass all of the different genres: history and religious painting, portraiture (which includes the *Figures de fantaisie*), landscape, and genre painting (domestic and everyday scenes), as well as *pastiches* after the old masters. His drawings, too, display the same variety.

For more than a century, Fragonard has been one of the most admired of French painters. The freedom of his brushwork, the range of his subjects, the liveliness and humor of his compositions, and the elegiac beauty of his landscapes explain this popularity. The exhibition permits further discoveries: one encounters an artist who knew how to depict both the ardent surge of passion, and the rush of wind through an avenue of cypress trees; maternal tenderness, as well as the awakening of the senses. Fragonard was, indeed, one of the great poets in the history of painting.

New York exhibition-goers are fortunate in being able to see installed at The Frick Collection, just a few blocks away from the Metropolitan Museum, the panels that Fragonard painted for the *Pavillon neuf* of Mme du Barry, at Louveciennes. (In accordance with museum regulations, these masterpieces of French painting—one of the most important decorative ensembles from the eighteenth century—cannot leave the Frick.) This visit is all the more indispensable because the panels have recently been restored.

Lastly, the "Fragonard" exhibition marks the occasion for yet another fruitful collaboration between the Réunion des Musées Nationaux and The Metropolitan Museum of Art.

Philippe de Montebello
*Director, The Metropolitan
Museum of Art*

Olivier Chevrillon
Directeur des Musées de France

I would like to thank all those at The Metropolitan Museum of Art who have contributed to making the "Fragonard" exhibition and its accompanying catalogue possible. Foremost is Katharine Baetjer, Curator, Department of European Paintings, who played an active and invaluable role in every stage of the exhibition, from negotiations for loans to the redaction of the English catalogue. Ms. Baetjer was ably assisted by Bianca Calabresi and Elena Giamatti. The exhibition catalogue was edited by Ellen Shultz and produced under the direction of John P. O'Neill, Editor in Chief and General Manager of Publications. I am also grateful to Emily Rafferty, Vice President for Development; John Buchanan, Registrar; Linda M. Sylling, Assistant Manager for Operations; and Exhibition Designer David Harvey.

Philippe de Montebello
*Director
The Metropolitan Museum of Art*

"Gens, honorez Fragonard!"

"There are so few precise points of reference...that, at the present time, only a comprehensive exhibition and the confrontation of a vast ensemble of works would make it possible to establish a reliable chronology, and to define [Fragonard's] oeuvre" (Thuillier, 1967, pp. 45, 46). Jacques Thuillier's desire has finally been realized. This exhibition has opened its doors—not without difficulties, it must be said, but also not without some rewards.

We were aware of the difficulties of mounting the major "Fragonard" exhibition that the Louvre had been contemplating for a long time when Philippe de Montebello, the director of The Metropolitan Museum of Art in New York, broached the possibility of participating. We knew in advance that the Frick Collection in New York would not be able to lend us the pictures that Fragonard painted for the Louveciennes residence of Mme du Barry, one of the finest decorative ensembles by him (and in all of French art). Nor could the Wallace Collection in London lend its admirable canvases by Fragonard, some of which—*The Swing*, certainly, but also *Le Petit Parc* and the *Fountain of Love*—are irreplaceable. Nor would Baron Edmond de Rothschild part with the Fragonards in his own collection; we have not seen them, but his *Blindman's Buff* and *The Visit to the Nursery* would have been welcome additions, indeed. There were other inaccessible marvels: We were counting on the *Rinaldo in the Enchanted Forest* and the *Rinaldo in the Gardens of Armida* in the Veil-Picard collection, but, unfortunately, we had to forego these two works as well—just as, in some cases, the conditions for the loans were such that a work, however important, could not be shown in both Paris and New York. While this exhibition does have some gaps, it is clear that there is no lack of masterpieces (for example, those lent by the Banque de France, the Gulbenkian museum, and the National Gallery of Art in Washington).

The major question, however, is whether the exhibition fulfills the goals formulated by Professor Thuillier, and whether it provides us with a better understanding of Fragonard, this giant of painting, and of the evolution of his art.

The literature on Fragonard is abundant. We cannot praise too highly the exemplary studies by Roger Portalis (1889) and by Pierre de Nolhac (1906), which served as daily sources of inspiration. The monographs by the Goncourts (1865) and by Jacques Thuillier (1967) analyze, with sensitivity and with admirable germane precision, the work of this artist, who seems to have taken an uncanny pleasure in dissimulation. The catalogue raisonné by Georges Wildenstein (1960), one of Fragonard's most fervent admirers in our century, remains an indispensable reference work, as are the catalogue of the paintings by Daniel Wildenstein and Gabriele Mandel (1972) and the catalogue of the drawings published by Alexandre Ananoff between 1961 and 1970. Without seeming to draw up an honor roll, we would also mention the names of Jacques Wilhelm (whose unpublished monograph was a constant help), Marianne Roland Michel, Mary D. Sheriff, Jean-Pierre Cuzin (whose monograph we impatiently await), Denys Sutton (one of our regrets is not to have seen the Fragonard exhibition that he organized in Tokyo in 1980), Eunice Williams (responsible for the indispensable catalogue of the exhibition of

Fragonard drawings in American collections), Jean Cailleux, Yuri Zolotov, Louis Réau, Georges Wildenstein (for his valuable research on Saint-Non and Bergeret), Sally Wells-Robertson (a Marguerite Gérard specialist), Donald Posner, Charles Sterling, Willibald Sauerländer, Jacques Thuillier, Thomas Crow, Thomas Gaehtgens, Philip Conisbee, Francis Watson, and David Wakefield. Their work, and that of many others has led to a better understanding of Fragonard's multifaceted genius.

Can the present catalogue be considered a definitive summa of the artist? This was never our intention, and it must be confessed that on many points the results of our research have been modest. We will consider ourselves satisfied if this huge volume can be of use to future scholars: Fragonard studies are just in the beginning stages, and there are many discoveries yet to be made.

Our approach consisted in referring as much as possible to eighteenth-century sources: archival documents, the Salons, the rare contemporary texts devoted to Fragonard, sales catalogues, the testimony of people who knew the artist—such as Saint-Non and Bergeret—engravings by, or after, Fragonard, and so on. These sources, however, proved woefully scarce and often disappointing. We have also paid close attention to the short biographies that were published after his death in 1806 (by Landon, Gault de Saint-Germain, Le Carpentier, and Lenoir, who "knew him well"), giving special attention to the testimony of Théophile Fragonard, the artist's grandson. Not only did Théophile communicate information about his grandfather to Frédéric Villot (1855), Charles Blanc (1862), the Goncourts (1865), and Bellier de la Chavignerie (1865), but he also wrote a letter, of supreme importance, to Théophile Thoré [Bürger] on the "9bre" 1847. The actual letter has been lost, but it was published in its entirety by Catherine Valogne in the February 17, 1955, issue of *Les Lettres françaises*. One might object that Théophile, who was born in 1806, never knew his grandfather; this is true, but his grandmother, who died in 1823, spoke of the artist's second trip to Italy in 1773–74 (see Bellier de la Chavignerie), and shared many other memories of Jean-Honoré; his great-aunt, Marguerite Gérard, who died in 1837, no doubt did the same. As for Théophile's father, Alexandre-Évariste (the artist's son), he was twenty-six when Fragonard died, and he himself died only three years after the letter of 1847 was written.

We did not set out to write a book, but an exhibition catalogue, which belongs to a genre that has its own rules, demands, constraints... and rewards. The catalogue is divided into eight chapters corresponding to the main periods in Fragonard's career:

1732–56	The early years
1756–61	The first trip to Italy; Tivoli; and Fragonard's return to France with the Abbé de Saint-Non
1761–65	The temptation of an official career, and accreditation by the Academy
1766–70	The "Figures de fantaisie"—Fragonard between Vice and Virtue
1770–73	The decorations for Mme du Barry and Mlle Guimard
1773–74	The second trip to Italy
1774–91	The allegories of Love; illness and retirement in Grasse
1792–1806	Fragonard as a functionnaire at the Louvre

Each of these chapters is introduced by an essay that analyzes the available information: the man, the vicissitudes of his career, his failures, his successes, the development of his style, the evolution of his art. This is followed by a detailed chronology compiled by Marie-Anne Dupuy, and by the entries. It remains to be seen whether this "preciosity of useless exactitude and of honesty" that Gide (*Journal*, 1955, p. 327, entry for June 11, 1948) so admired in the journal of Charles du Bos will be appreciated. "Useless," it is not; "precious," perhaps; but "exactitude" and "honesty" were the rule.

A last word: The catalogue is too long, too weighty. We offer the assurance that this very lengthy catalogue will be, for us, the last of its kind . . .

Jean-Honoré Fragonard="Gens, honorez Fragonard!"

"At public auctions, when his name was pronounced, some thought that they heard, 'gens, honorez Fragonard' [a play on the sound of Jean-Honoré, meaning, literally, 'People, honor Fragonard!'], and they responded to the entreaty by shouting out loud, 'He well deserves it!'" (Théophile Fragonard, letter of 1847).

Yes—he does, indeed.

Fragonard. *Self-portrait, Seen Full Face*. Catalogue no. 287

Fragonard,
A "Figure de Fantaisie"

I

"Rotund, well fed, lively, always alert, always cheerful..."—this is the popular image of the *"bonhomme* Frago," "red-cheeked," "sparkling-eyed," "tousled, and gray-haired," who was beloved by all. It is known that he was short, just under five and a half feet. He had gray eyes, and pockmarked skin. But was Fragonard really the carefree, ever-smiling old man of legend—"le bon Papa Frago"—who never let adversity get him down, who was always ready for a laugh or a joke, the jovial companion of all, as described by his nineteenth-century biographers?

Surely not; but this portrait of him cannot be entirely false, and it would be foolish to replace it with one of a tormented, "romantic," and misunderstood Fragonard. As the Introductions to the eight chapters of the catalogue, chronicling the artist's life and career, will show, the observations and remarks by his contemporaries that contradict this image are too many to be ignored.

It is true that we have very little information on Fragonard, the man; this has been one of our constant handicaps. He left nothing in writing (if, indeed, he knew how to write), no disclosures. He is but rarely mentioned by his contemporaries. There is no lack of documents about David, who was Fragonard's junior by sixteen years, or about Greuze, who was older by seven years. In Fragonard's case, all that remain are a few documents in the archives, some official correspondence (Natoire's letters are invaluable), some reminiscences of his travels—although his lifelong friend, the Abbé de Saint-Non, with whom he traveled in Italy for more than five months, in 1761, does not mention the artist by name in his journal—some reviews of the Salons, pamphlets, and a few lines in scattered journals and letters. An important source is the texts written after his death, and published between 1808 and 1832 (Landon, 1808, 1832; Lenoir, 1816; Gault de Saint-Germain, 1808, 1819; Le Carpentier, 1821; Vivant-Denon, 1829), by personalities in the arts who knew him in later life.

In reading these texts, one gets a very different image of the artist; he seems to have been a secretive man, lacking in self-confidence, moody, capricious, mysterious, accommodating, indecisive, incapable of finishing his projects. During Fragonard's lifetime, Mariette noted the "timidity" of his "character"; he "erased his works and kept starting over"; while Cochin (1765) spoke of his "excessive self-distrust." Bergeret's harsh criticism (he called him weak, a coward, a Milquetoast, a fake!), written after the artist's second trip to Italy in 1774, is no doubt excessive, and may be attributed to great disappointment or anger—but his testimony is not to be discounted too hastily.

Fragonard was modest—this word comes up several times—and anxious. He lacked self-confidence; shortly after he arrived in Rome in 1756, he experienced a serious artistic crisis that kept him from painting for months. Of the private and official commissions that he received, he completed only two: one has been lost, and the other, for Mme du Barry, was refused. He stopped painting altogether when he no longer felt any encouragement from the public, and retreated into silence.

The Fragonard of legend lacks credibility on two other points: it has been said that he lived a carefree existence, unconcerned with the material side of life (Mme Fragonard, his "treasurer," is supposed to have attended to such matters). This was not true. In 1771, Mme d'Épinay informs us that "he is wasting his time and his talent; he is making money." "In an average year, his talent would earn him 40,000 francs," Landon confirms (1832). If Fragonard died impoverished, it was because he lost his money through imprudent speculation, and was subsequently ruined by the Revolution.

The second point, a hotly debated one to which we will often allude, concerns his supposed love affairs, which gave rise to the most extravagant rumors. He has been depicted as the "Casanova" of the art world (as it happens, he was a friend of Casanova's brother, a talented painter of military subjects). Yet, the cold facts recommend prudence. There is no proof of his alleged love affairs, and if there were a liaison with the dancer Mlle Guimard, or the Colombe sisters, it was conducted with the utmost discretion, without gossip or fanfare—which would have been contrary to the usual behavior of these dancers, who were not averse to publicity.

Finally, we know nothing of Fragonard's political opinions. However, working for the *fermiers généraux* (tax collectors) did not prevent him from also serving the Republic. He had to earn a living, after all.

This portrait of the man may be surprising to some—but is it to be doubted? Nineteenth-century writers, as was their wont, fashioned the artist in the image of his work. Fragonard's paintings were interpreted as so many self-portraits, and he was seen as a "figure de fantaisie" himself. This temptation is understandable, considering how little is actually known about his life. Yet, we are more cautious today. Landon writes that, in later life, Fragonard fell prey to "sadness, discouragement, and fear." Lenoir tells us that he "stopped painting, and died unhappy." The tone is unsettling, and the words have an astonishing ring—but that Fragonard, *too*, was Fragonard.

II

"He tried his hand at all the genres: portraits; everyday scenes and landscapes, which he treated in a superior way; pastiches of the great masters, in which he displayed great skill; miniatures, which he executed with a particular grace and lightness; charming pastels, gouaches, watercolors, and etchings," Frédéric Villot wrote, in his superb essay on Fragonard in the Louvre catalogue of 1855.

This diversity is one of the particularities of Fragonard's genius, and it deserves further discussion. Fragonard was a prolific artist; he experimented with all of the different techniques and with all kinds of subject matter, and this variety is reflected in the choice of works included here.

Certain pastels could not be exhibited because of their fragility. Some three hundred works are represented here, exclusive of the miniatures by

Fragonard, which present a separate problem: the fact that it is difficult to tell them apart from those by his wife, Marie-Anne Gérard, who painted most of the examples that are extant, would have entailed complex discussions, further encumbering the catalogue. We intend, however, to return to this question in the near future.

Several of the "genres" at which Fragonard tried his hand were omitted by Frédéric Villot; one oversight was justified—still life—but not the others: religious and history painting, mythological subjects, and allegories. As far as we know, this pupil of Chardin—who shared with Fragonard the secrets of his craft, before entrusting him to Boucher—did not paint any independent still lifes; an apple here, an urn there—such were Fragonard's contributions to "la vie silencieuse." Very likely, his innate liking for motion was partially responsible for this lack of interest.

Villot's silence on the works that made Fragonard's reputation is revealing. By way of review, we would mention the *Coresus and Callirhoë* (cat. no. 104), and several earlier paintings: the recently rediscovered *Psyche* (cat. no. 9), acquired by the National Gallery, London; the *Christ Washing the Feet of the Apostles* in Grasse, recently restored by the municipality; the *Jeroboam Sacrificing to the Idols* (cat. no. 8), which earned the artist a Grand Prix de Rome; and then, in his moment of glory, the *Visitation* (cat. no. 231), and the *Adoration of the Shepherds* (cat. no. 234); and, lastly, the later allegories, the *Vow to Love*, and the *Sacrifice of the Rose* (cat. nos. 280, 284, 285), after which engravings were often made, ensuring the painter a livelihood.

The Fragonard who was discovered and showered with admiration by Charles Blanc, Thoré, Renouvier, Théophile Gautier, and especially by the Goncourts, was not the creator of great religious paintings or of sensual allegories with too slick a finish. That Fragonard, who had been appreciated by his first biographers, did not reemerge until our own time, with a more complete understanding of his career as an artist.

There is no doubt that he was a great painter of amorous allegories, as well as of religious pictures of a new type. With regard to mythological subjects, in comparison to Boucher's output, the small number by Fragonard is surprising. Considering the erotic possibilities of mythological subject matter, and the tastes of his clientele, its absence from Fragonard's oeuvre is conspicuous.

Villot mentioned portraits first of all, which is curious, for Fragonard would seem to have been unable to equal the outstanding portraitists of the eighteenth century, from Rigaud to David, from Largillière to Ingres—not to mention Maurice-Quentin de Latour, Jean-Baptiste Perroneau, and a number of less famous artists, all of whom could capture not just the intricate details of a face, but also a mood or a gaze. This is true when it came to his ability to render physical likenesses, psychological analyses, or the moral character of his sitters, but it does not mean that there is no place for Fragonard among the portraitists. The *figures de fantaisie*, in transcending the narrow definition of the genre of portraiture, gave it a new dimension. In them, he sacrificed resemblance to rapid execution, so as to capture a fleeting gesture or pose. This paved the way for a new concept of the portrait, whose success is now a part of history.

By familiar scenes, Villot meant the delightful and humorous little vignettes of intimate life that had been so admired a generation before by Le Carpentier: "It would be impossible to introduce more charm and spirit than one finds in these familiar scenes. What grace in the expressions and gestures of these women! What a naïve and child-like aspect he gave to these pretty little babes! The accessories in these pictures are always painted and placed with taste and appropriateness." Le Carpentier was no doubt referring to the erotic scenes; his contemporaries were discreet about them, when they were not severe (or pretending to be). He "has strayed into little-known byways to invent a genre that is more pleasing to the delights of the imagination," one of them wrote in 1785. We know that Cochin had to inform Marigny by letter that if the *Coresus* were not paid for soon enough, Fragonard would "find himself obliged . . . to paint works little suited to his genius" (and yet Cochin could not have ignored the fact that Fragonard's "genius" was not in the area of history painting). It was long thought that Fragonard painted these "erotic compositions" ("it was the fashion, anyway," Vivant-Denon wrote, with the indulgence of a specialist) to "satisfy the demands of the collectors." For a time, they marred the reputation of the painter, who, as a victim of the "taste of the time," was said to have "abandoned noble compositions and serious studies to devote himself to subjects of an inferior kind" (Landon, 1808). However, for reasons both good and bad, they ensured his fame when eighteenth-century painting came back into fashion. No one, in 1860, could have presented a better defense than Paul de Saint-Victor: "Fragonard is the poet of erotic painting: he avoids the indecency of the genre through speed of execution. Art must run over these burning coals; only a slight headiness can excuse the license and the orgies of the brush. The sketch is their modesty and their ideal: indecency begins with finish. The spirited sketch of a libertine fancy is easily excused: but something crude that is slickly painted is unforgivable. It is the *puritas impuritatis* of the ancients. Thus, I prefer by far Fragonard's galant jottings to his famous painting *L'Escarpolette* [*The Swing*], in which everything is emphasized, indicated, underlined. . . . It is not fitting for such a free tale to be so neatly transcribed." These words have a special pertinence for us today, at a time when nothing is hidden.

The last genre that Villot mentions is landscape. For Le Carpentier, and perhaps rightly so, this was the field in which Fragonard demonstrated the most genius, whether he "imitated Ruysdael and other painters of this school to the point of deception," or just painted "simple sketches that one would be tempted to take for beautiful dreams." "Is it possible to have a better understanding of the magic of the skies, which he painted exquisitely, and to capture the wonderful effects that nature presents only after a thunderstorm or when an overcast and cloudy sky lets a few shafts of sunlight shine forth onto the earth?" This poet of the "oaks," pines, and cypress trees of Italy, these "crazy trees, with toppling crowns like snowdrifts" (Bonnefoy, 1983, p. 211), surpassed all the other artists of his time in depicting not the countryside, but a nature that is both grandiose and inviting, exuberant and overwhelming, familiar and mysterious. Fragonard's conception—far removed from the realism of the Barbizon painters, or the romantic vision and spontaneity of the Impressionists—remains unique, and without any real successors. This achievement alone ensures him a place among the greatest masters.

As for the *meaning* of this variety, we know that, in the eighteenth century, paintings were categorized by their subject matter, according to very specific distinctions: history painting—which included both religious subjects and classical history and mythology—the portrait, genre scenes, landscape, and still life. This hierarchy of the genres was questioned by no one, not even Diderot, but no one in the eighteenth century seems to have concerned himself with the problem of classifying the works of Fragonard —who, it should be remembered, was accredited by the Academy as a history painter. His portraits were not really portraits, and his genre scenes, compared to those of a painter like Greuze, did not conform to the type either, while his landscapes seemed to invent nature rather than to depict it. The painter of bulls and of beds was not someone who followed the accepted rules—neither in his subject matter nor in his technique.

Fragonard. *The Bathers*. Detail of catalogue no. 74

III

Reading the sales catalogues from the eighteenth century and the few texts from the period leaves one with the impression that Fragonard's contemporaries were amazed by his technique. What we now consider, unthinkingly, as finished works, often seemed to the eighteenth-century eye, and even to the artist's "rediscoverers" in the mid-nineteenth century, merely sketches, studies, first drafts, preliminary ideas—in other words, works of an inferior order. Thus, in 1777, the expert at the Varanchan de Saint-Geniès sale noted in his foreword to the catalogue, after having sung the praises of Boucher, that "one will be pleased to see many preliminary sketches ["pensées"] by one of his pupils, who has become famous without resembling him" (he was doubtless referring to Fragonard). "Carefully finished pictures may give pleasure in an ordinary way, but there is a certain class of art lovers that finds supreme enjoyment in a single sketch; they look for the thoughts and the soul of the man of genius, which they know how to see and to recognize."

In other words, the artist's brushwork was, understandably enough, a source of surprise. Never, before Fragonard, had the brush so imperiously subjected the canvas to its own laws. The brushwork *became* the painting. Indeed, there was admiration for free execution—for that "fire" attributed to so many artists—and appreciation for the sketches of Rubens, the technique of Rembrandt, and the vigorous, highly visible brushstrokes in Tintoretto's works. Yet, a distinction was made between the sketch—the "première pensée"—and the finished composition. Fragonard abolished this distinction; he raised the sketch to the rank of a finished painting—a work of art in its own right. Fragonard's brushwork was an integral part of the work itself, of the creative process. His virtuosity with the brush was recognized, but there was much more to it than that. The brushstrokes give a work of art its life; his brushwork had to be extremely visible and conspicuous, because the artist wanted its speed to be seen and admired. Rapidity of execution, for Fragonard, was synonymous with vitality, the creative impulse, and the faster he painted, the better he painted. According to the Goncourts (*Journal*, II, p. 170), when the collector Walferdin stood before his many Fragonards, he would exclaim: "He is the dynamic painter." This term caught on—and rightly so—but does it say it all, and can we go further and consider Fragonard as the father of pure painting—even of "action painting"?

No artist before Fragonard had involved the spectator so closely in his craft, had revealed himself so. Fragonard obviously wanted us to admire his technique, to let us in on the execution of a picture, but he never abandoned his subject, not even in his wonderful drawings. Along with Boucher, he was perhaps the most prolific French draftsman of his time, and he drew in black and red chalk; bister wash, in all its nuances; colored pencils; and, more rarely, pen and ink. Often, he used only red chalk or black alone. Sometimes, he mixed different techniques, made his own "cuisine," which was frequently imitated, although inimitable. His favorite combination was chalk and wash, employed in a unique manner, the specifics of which have not been fully understood. Artists before and after Fragonard generally proceeded in two steps: they sketched in the composition in black chalk, and then gave it depth, volume, and tone through the use of wash. The black chalk outlined, described, transcribed, and the brush modeled, completed, and animated the composition.

Fragonard worked in a completely different way: he tried to capture what his eye saw and to hold on to it, before it could vanish or be forgotten. He would rapidly cover the whole paper with a fine network of long, sinuous lines that might seem completely unintelligible. Sometimes the lines formed a closely interwoven pattern; at other times he would pause to indicate or to accentuate a detail. Then, in bister wash laid over and even effacing the underdrawing in black chalk, he would compose the work, and render the subject legible. It was as if Fragonard first *destroyed* the scene that he copied, the better to *re-create* it with his brush, to endow it with life—this life that he sought to capture and that he, better than anyone else, succeeded in transcribing.

Fragonard. *Portrait of M. de La Bretèche*. Detail of catalogue no. 132

IV

When one thinks of Boucher, blue and pink come to mind. Fragonard's color was yellow: he painted every possible shade of yellow, the yellow of eggs, buttercups, straw, lemons, canaries, mimosa, gold, topaz, saffron, and mustard, and yellow-orange, including all varieties of ocher, burnt umber, burnt sienna, and that greenish yellow described at the time as "espagnol malade" ("sick Spaniard"), as well as the "Fragonard blond" mentioned by Patrick Modiano (*De si braves garçons*, 1982, p. 41). Not that he sacrificed the other colors; his paintings contain astonishing cobalt blues, madders, and emerald greens, but yellow, either as color or as light, predominates, and this, for whatever reason, was the case throughout his career.

Light, that "fine intelligence of light" admired by the author of the Vassal de Saint-Hubert collection sales catalogue (1774), served not only to create depth, but also to heighten the colors. Gault de Saint-Germain (1819) tells us that "he was so enchanted by the sparkling effect of a strong light in his compositions that he called it the pistol shot of chiaroscuro." Landon, writing in 1832, was more reticent (which is not surprising for an advocate of Neoclassicism): "in seeking the color of sunlight, he often gave his paintings too even a yellow tonality, which is not the same thing as that golden-toned light that, far from dulling the nearby colors, seems to enrich them even more." For Fragonard, light modeled and modified form and color, and in this context his admiration for La Fosse takes on its full significance (he acquired four sketches by him at the Boucher collection sale in 1771: see pages 295, 300; later, we will quote from the fascinating text published by Ratouis de Limay in 1950). Light is an integral part of a work, and gives it its life.

The paint is so thick, so conspicuous, so "palpable," that sometimes it seems to want to destroy the subject. It does not efface itself before the subject; on the contrary, it tries to efface the subject, or at least to partially take its place. The rapidity of its application is meant to astound, but it still remains at the service of the composition, which Fragonard wanted to endow with the same sense of motion. Nothing stays in place, everything moves, the trees and clouds no less than the individual figures and couples. The "dynamism" of the brushwork—to borrow Walferdin's expression— and of the composition become one and the same.

"Fragonard's technique is original and unlike that of any other contemporary painter," Le Carpentier wrote in 1821—a true enough statement that is not as trite as it sounds. He elaborates further, noting that "everything of his exudes pleasure and happiness." This means the subjects, of course, but also the way in which he handled them. In his palette, the paint, and the craft of painting, Fragonard conveyed a sensuality and an impetuosity, a liveliness and a gaiety, that are to be found in the work of no other painter.

V

We must dispel a misunderstanding concerning Fragonard's artistic background. He lacked the education dispensed by the Academy to young artists preparing for the Prix de Rome competition. In addition to excellent artistic instruction, there were general courses in a variety of subjects (biblical history, geography, and so on). Students were first taught how to draw, and then how to paint, according to tried and tested methods that permitted artists to paint from their own imagination the history subjects that enjoyed such great prestige at the time. Fragonard, who was trained first by Chardin, and then by Boucher, never received this instruction. It is true that he later attended the excellent École royale des élèves protégés, but he lacked this basic, early training. Perhaps it was even one of the reasons for the artist's poor record in completing his official commissions.

His contemporaries did not fail to notice this, and expressed a similar judgment, with more or less understanding (or severity). Landon, writing the day after the artist's death, praised the great *Coresus and Callirhoë*, which had "justified the public's acclaim by the warmth of the composition and the masterful effect," but how unfortunate that Fragonard,

Fragonard. *Portrait of the Abbé de Saint-Non*. Detail of catalogue no. 133

"gifted with a lively imagination and a great facility for painting ... [had abandoned] the path that he had adopted": "His brilliant gifts ... were not supported by a solid educational background."

Although he lacked this facet of a sound education, and perhaps regretted it himself, he possessed another, whose importance was not immediately recognized by his contemporaries: an exceptional artistic background. From the time of his apprenticeship, Fragonard made copies in the churches of Paris; in Italy, of paintings by "Barocci, Solimena, and Tiepolo," and also by Mengs, according to Grimm (1765) and Cochin (1773). He admired the great masters of the Baroque more than those of the Renaissance. Then there were the hundreds of copies drawn for the Abbé de Saint-Non. Back in Paris, he copied works by Rembrandt in the

Crozat collection and by Rubens in the Galerie du Luxembourg, and by Ruisdael (he owned a painting by him), Bourdon (according to Mariette), and La Fosse (and perhaps even Watteau). The voracity of his eye (not to say his hand) knew no bounds. He absorbed and assimilated the most diverse, seemingly contradictory artistic fare, and from each type he learned something. He compensated for the confidence that he lacked by studying the great masters. Hence, as Villot observed, his "extreme skill" as a *pasticheur*. Yet, he always left his own personal stamp on whatever he copied. This quality, greatly appreciated today, was criticized at one time: "It is to be regretted . . . that he did not endeavor to retain the character of the originals. . . . Fragonard substituted his own spirit for that of the master" (Landon).

His exceptional visual intelligence allowed Fragonard to keep something of the original and yet to be himself. All of this copying served him in the creation of his own compositions; there is hardly a picture in which Fragonard did not discreetly—and usually humorously—make some allusion to his illustrious predecessors, thus acknowledging his debt.

Fragonard was a pupil of Boucher, and owed a lot to him—as the Goncourts remarked, "Fragonard recalls Rubens by way of the brilliance of Boucher"—but not as much as is generally believed. The world of Boucher is mainly one of imagination, invention, and artifice. Mythology reigns supreme, and the execution of his works followed the conventional method: preparatory drawings, sketches, then the finished painting (sometimes executed in part by a pupil). The technique was kept discreet, and the brushwork was subordinated to the overall effect. Fragonard, however, did not shrink from expressing himself in the first person. Only exceptionally were his drawings studies for his paintings (we agree with Eunice Williams's premise that most of his so-called preparatory drawings were, in fact, "ricordi" of his painted compositions). Often, his paintings are sketches. He turned the rules around. Fragonard, unlike Boucher, did not have an *atelier*, and his artistic ideals were the opposite of his master's: he painted the everyday world. His figures are young and beautiful and of flesh and blood, they are alive, they breathe, take pleasure in their existence, and play, laugh, and love. Fragonard's work cannot be called realistic—imagination and fancy are integral parts—but his world is the earth, not Mount Olympus. He is close to us; the world he presents us with is our world—or we would like it to be.

It is more difficult to evaluate the influence of Hubert Robert. The two artists met in Rome, and became lifelong friends. In 1791, their names (along with that of the architect Pierre-Adrien Pâris) are mentioned in the will of the Abbé de Saint-Non. The sale of Hubert Robert's collection in 1809 included several oil sketches and a number of drawings by Fragonard. In Rome, their works were very close (the *Bishop Praying in Saint Peter's*—W. 101, pl. 11—is, in fact, by Robert), but afterward they followed different paths. Hubert Robert loved ruins; Fragonard preferred trees. Who led the way is not certain, but Robert's more solid and robust temperament must have made a strong impression on Fragonard. What distinguishes their landscapes is the fact that, while Robert was the painter of the past, of the passage of *time*, Fragonard was the painter of the *instant*, of the intensity of the moment.

Fragonard also met Greuze in Rome: Both became famous in their lifetimes, only to die forgotten. In his family scenes, Fragonard tried to imitate Greuze, or at least sought inspiration from him, but he was not completely successful. He was not suited to the sentimental; for him, art and morality did not rhyme.

Was Fragonard himself imitated in his lifetime? To be sure, he influenced the work of Durameau and Vincent (W. 372, fig. 158; W. 373, fig. 159), Casanova, and Loutherbourg (W. 154, fig. 85 *b*), Leprince (whose 1774 sketch, *L'Amoureux secret* [in Munich], was long attributed to Fragonard), Taraval (W. 65, fig. 45; the sketch *La Femme couchée*, of 1779, in Tours, was for a long time misattributed), Jollain (W. 64, fig. 44), and Berthélemy. Yet, all of these works were correctly attributed in the eighteenth century; the inflation of Fragonard's oeuvre was the work of later periods, including our own.

Fragonard's art was too personal to lend itself to imitation, and it was admired for too little time to be "pastiched." Marguerite Gérard, his best pupil, born in the same year as Boilly, took a completely different direction very early on.

VI

There are no definitive solutions to the problem of the chronology of Fragonard's work—the subject of the most controversy among Fragonard specialists, even today. Fragonard only rarely dated his paintings and drawings, and exhibited at practically none of the Salons. The study of old sales catalogues, while a necessary task, does not always yield the desired results, so vague are the descriptions of the pictures and so unreliable the dimensions. In other words, the points of reference are few, and our attempts at adding to them have not always been successful. Among the authors of monographs on Fragonard, only Georges Wildenstein (1960; 545 entries), and Daniel Wildenstein and Gabriele Mandel (1972; 568 entries) have attempted to establish a chronology for the paintings (Jacques Wilhelm's has not been published), while Alexandre Ananoff, who catalogued 2,700 drawings, opted for a thematic classification. We have tried to date the drawings and paintings that are the subjects of the individual entries. When these works are exhibited together the juxtapositions will challenge some of our hypotheses and also, we hope, solve some longstanding controversies—hence, the usefulness of such exhibitions.

Yet, finally, are discussions of dates so important, after all? What do they tell us about Fragonard? How do they permit us to better understand him? There are artists who build up their work like an architect builds a house: each stone has its place, or else the edifice crumbles. Others repeat themselves, creating the same painting over and over again, throughout their lives. Still others abruptly change direction and turn their backs on their previous efforts, seemingly denying them. Fragonard, however, cannot be fitted into any of these categories. He evolved, while always remaining the same. He changed his manner, according to whether he was painting a landscape or a free study (and, later in his career, for a sketch, as opposed to a finished canvas). In the same period, he could paint in seemingly opposite styles. He was an impulsive artist who undertook a work without too much self-examination. Such is our impression, anyway. He had a vast visual frame of reference, and he called upon his memory and on whatever he currently admired. Attuned to changes in taste, he tried to adapt himself to them, and he did not escape the slow and irresistible rise of Neoclassicism. He was also an anxious and indecisive artist, and did not stick to any particular program. In short, the evolution of Fragonard's art is anything but linear; he could work in several, parallel manners at the same time. There is no special logic to his art; the question is extraordinarily more complex, which is important to realize. For, in this art that appears gratuitous and created for pleasure alone, nothing is really gratuitous.

VII

This is not to say that Fragonard worked in a metaphysical vein. He had no taste either for the heroic or for the sentimental, and avoided both drama and introspection. His art is never grave—or never, except where love is concerned. He was not interested in depicting illness, decrepitude, or old age. Fragonard was neither the painter of melancholy nor of nostalgia, nor of silence or the arrested gesture, nor even of ambiguous feelings. His was a world of *joie de vivre*, of gaiety, openness, happiness, and, especially, of freshness. He was an observer who neither insisted on exactitude nor relied on caricature. He described accurately, with a smile, with rapture, and with a remarkably keen eye. He was the painter of luxuriant and exuberant vegetation, the painter of the elements—air, sky, clouds, wind, rain sometimes, but, especially, water in all of its forms: sprays of water and fountains, cascades and rivers, whose sights and sounds invite us to escape. He was the painter of renewal, of ceaseless regeneration, and he was the painter of sensuality: his painting is sensuality itself. To say that he was an "action" painter, an exponent of "pure painting," would, however, betray the essence of his art. The best description is that he was a "painterly painter," a "painter's painter," an impassioned painter whose lightheartedness, vivacity, and impetuosity were in total harmony with a synthetic and unified vision of composition.

Fragonard was the painter of great passions and of the intensity of life, the painter of health. He depicted the reality of love without the equivocal insinuations of a Baudouin, a Lavreince, and even a Greuze that make us ill at ease, and without false modesty either. There is certainly in his art an appeal to the senses, and an invitation to pleasure "like a promise or a reminder" (Jacques Thuillier). Who, today, would take offense at this?

VIII

People nowadays prefer artists who "pave the way" to those who represent continuity. Fragonard's contemporaries, who were convinced that his name and reputation would not survive, misunderstood him. He did not know how to adapt himself to the "official" world; he was not the painter of commissions, and disregarded the hierarchy of the genres. Mme du Barry rejected the paintings that she had ordered from him because to her they seemed outmoded. Fragonard was considered, even by so perspicacious a critic as Diderot, as the zealous disciple of Boucher, whose artificial and fanciful art had outlived its time. Fragonard had no direct followers (apart from Prud'hon, whose work displayed affinities with Fragonard's late style, and a few sculptors like Clodion, and Joseph-Charles Marin). In short, Fragonard very soon was thought to have been "surpassed."

This is understandable. Many authors, from Walter Friedlaender (1947) to Francis Watson (1971), have noted the "retardataire" aspect of Fragonard's art. At a time when a new aesthetic flourished, whose most perfect representative was David, and Neoclassicism was making its mark in architecture, sculpture, and the decorative arts; when, in England, as well as in Italy, a new type of painting was emerging, and color was giving way to line, the curvilinear to the rectilinear, the sketch to the smooth finish, the frivolous to the exemplary, amorality (or immorality) to virtue, lightness to pomposity, and levity was being replaced by seriousness, Fragonard could only appear as the vestige of a bygone era.

Fragonard. *Portrait of the Abbé de Saint-Non.* Detail of catalogue no. 133

Yet, many consider Fragonard an "anticipator"—a popular figure in today's culture. From Daumier to Renoir, from Bonnard to Dubuffet, the Impressionists, and the "action painters"—all have sometimes been regarded as his emulators. Fragonard is credited with having "liberated" painting, and some have even seen in Fragonard the seed of Jackson Pollock's "gesture." There may be some truth in such a view, but it is also partly exaggeration. Fortunately for him, Fragonard's most successful work is intimately associated with his own time.

IX

According to Renouvier (1863, p. 163), Fragonard is recorded as having said, "I paint with my backside." While there is no reason to doubt this statement's authenticity, perhaps the fact that "Fragonard often spoke of beauty, which he called Nature in perfect health" provides a more telling insight into the artist's genius.

After having been treated with disdain by his illustrious contemporaries, then scorned and forgotten, Fragonard was rediscovered in the nineteenth century, although too often dismissed as the frivolous painter of a frivolous society. His great popularity today does not appear to bode much good, and, to some, even appears suspect: he is presented as no more than the most talented of the minor masters.

Fragonard met Benjamin Franklin in 1778; that same year, he may also have crossed paths with Mozart at the Duchesse de Chabot's. "Cut from the same mold" as Diderot, whose portrait Fragonard painted, in his own way, Fragonard was—like Diderot, Franklin, and Mozart—a free man.

If one must select an artist to symbolize the eighteenth century, we would choose neither Watteau nor David, who are its two extremes; nor Boucher or Carle Vanloo, who represent its official image; nor Chardin, the chaste poet of governesses and dead rabbits—but Fragonard. Fragonard is its fragrant essence—he *is* the eighteenth century.

The Catalogue

I

Fragonard's Early Years (1732–56)

Figure 1. François Boucher. *Venus and Vulcan.* Musée du Louvre

Very little is known of Fragonard's beginnings. The scarcity of facts has led to interpretations that owe more to the imagination of his biographers than to their knowledge of the eighteenth century. For reasons already mentioned, we have decided to rely on contemporary documents and on the reminiscences of Théophile Fragonard, the artist's grandson, set down in a letter of 1847, or as reported by Charles Blanc, the Goncourts, Bellier de la Chavignerie (1865), as well as by Larousse (1872), Jules Renouvier, and Thoré-Bürger himself.

Jean-Honoré was born in 1732, like Beaumarchais and Haydn [and Washington], and one year before Hubert Robert. That same year Boucher triumphed with his *Venus and Vulcan* (figure 1). Fragonard's birthplace was Grasse (figures 2, 3), a Provençal town evoked by the Goncourts at the beginning of their monograph on Fragonard as "a fragrant orchard of oranges, lemons, pomegranates, almonds, citrons, arbutus, myrtle, bergamot, and laurel; a garden of tulips, dazzling carnations . . . a countryside steeped in the scents of thyme, rosemary, sage, spikenard, mint, lavender. . . ." Apart from the fact that the Goncourts never went to Grasse, they forgot that in the eighteenth century it depended less on its perfume and silk production than on its tanneries, and that the narrow, medieval streets of this small industrial town reeked of putrefying animal hides. Nothing is less certain than that its inhabitants "lived the merry life."

Fragonard's family is said to have been of Italian origin. This is not surprising, because it was only one day's journey on foot from Grasse to the border of Savoie, then under Italian rule. His father, François, who named the boy after his own father and godfather, was a glove maker (a specialty of Grasse), described variously as a "glover's assistant" or just as a "glove merchant." Fragonard's family was composed mainly of artisans who seem not to have been entirely without means, even if there were ups and downs in their fortunes.

Grasse had a certain artistic heritage that included, besides the Primitive painters of Provence and Jacques Daret—who worked in the area— Pierre Subleyras, who painted a large *Assumption of the Virgin* for the

Figure 2. View of Grasse

Figure 3. View of Grasse

cathedral in 1741 (figure 4) that Fragonard may have seen, and which is still in place.

The Goncourts, followed by most of Fragonard's biographers, stressed the importance of Provence in the artist's development: "Fragonard was born there, he was of there, and from that land he derived his nature and his temperament.... In all of his works we see a painter who received in his youth the blessing of the Mediterranean skies, of the light of Provence.... In the merest sketch by him there is a warmth, almost a perfume, the fragrance of the land from which he came." According to Fragonard himself, however, he left this region at the age of six: a "certificate of residency" issued in 1794 tells us that Fragonard, born in "Grace," acknowledged having "resided in Paris for fifty-six years." On the other hand, Théophile Fragonard says that his grandfather went to the French capital only at the age of eighteen. However, in a will dated 1743, in which he makes his nephew Jean-Honoré his heir, Pierre Fragonard (died 1752) states that "François Fragonard, his brother, a glover, lives in Paris"; we prefer, therefore, to subscribe to the first version, without excluding the possibility of more or less long and frequent trips between Grasse and Paris by members of his family.

Figure 4. Pierre Subleyras. *The Assumption of the Virgin.* 1741. Cathedral of Grasse

Why, then, did the Fragonards move to Paris? Much effort has already been expended on this subject to rectify an error on the part of the Goncourts, who claimed—doubtless rather brusquely—that Jean-Honoré's father had invested "his small fortune in the speculation of the Périer brothers in the installation of the first fire pump in Paris. When the scheme fell through, his father went to Paris to try to recover some of the funds that he had invested in this sorry venture." In fact, the Périer brothers (or rather, the *Compagnie des Eaux de Paris,* with which Beaumarchais was closely involved), launched their project at the end of the reign of Louis XVI, and so were in no way connected with the financial misfortunes of the Fragonards. However, Théophile's account, according to which Jean-Honoré's "parents" went to Paris because of a "lawsuit that ruined them," does not contradict the version advanced by the Goncourts. We have no information on this lawsuit—nor on any of the others that will come up later—but the Goncourts seem to have confused the Périers with the du Périers. Nor do we know anything about Jean-Honoré's first years in Paris: where his family lived, what were his means of subsistence. We can only repeat what all of his other biographers have written (here, in the words of Théophile): "He was placed as a clerk with a notary, who decided not to keep him because he did nothing else with his pen but draw; his mother interpreted this as a sure sign of a vocation in the arts and took him to see M. Boucher; the latter barely glanced at the sketches and said that he took only pupils who could already paint. Chardin accepted him on the strength of his color sense, and let him paint right away. He told him that with color and effect one could give charm to the most common things and make an interesting painting with just a beer jug and a bunch of onions; yet I do not know—he would say—how one achieves this result; one searches, scrapes, wipes, glazes, repaints, and when one has captured that *je ne sais quoi* that is so pleasing, then the picture is done. The young Honoré, however, had too much imagination to limit himself to portraying vegetables; he invented a way of studying that gave him his facility. On his way to Chardin's, he passed by a church that was full of magnificent pictures, as all churches were then, and he reproduced them from memory one after the other. As for Chardin, he did not bother with his pupil much, being too absorbed in his search for that *je ne sais quoi*! After six months, Honoré returned to Boucher, who was extremely surprised by his rapid progress and took him on immediately...." This passage, besides having escaped the attention of the Chardin specialists, is worth quoting at length because it is our most complete and reliable source. Fragonard's presence in Boucher's studio is an established fact, and yet not until May 18, 1753—one year after Fragonard had been awarded the Grand Prix!—were the names of the two first associated in a contemporary document.

We would certainly like to know more about the notary who saw the signs of Fragonard's beginnings as an artist, to locate the copies of the religious paintings, and to discover exactly when, and for how long, he worked in Chardin's studio (six months?) and with Boucher ("two or three years," according to the Goncourts). There is, however, one fact that cannot be stressed too strongly, and that is that Fragonard never studied at the Academy. As with Chardin, who regretted it all his life, as well as Boucher (who, like his pupil, won the Grand Prix de Rome), Fragonard did not receive the Academy's exemplary instruction. Had he benefited from this instruction, it would no doubt have changed the course of his career—but this is merely supposition.

In 1752, at the age of twenty—David was then four years old, and Goethe three—Fragonard was awarded the Grand Prix of the Académie royale de Peinture. A famous anecdote told by Théophile Fragonard to Thoré-Bürger, who passed it on to the Goncourts (as usual, they probably did not grasp its full meaning, and elaborated on it) relates that when Boucher urged him to "compete for the Prix de Rome," Fragonard replied that he could not enter the competition because he had not studied at the Academy. Boucher supposedly told him: "It doesn't matter, you are my pupil." The following year, Fragonard was admitted to the recently created École royale des élèves protégés, which was directed by another well-known painter of the day, Carle Vanloo. The purpose of the school was to complete the instruction of the future masters of French painting before they left for Rome. These select candidates were pensioners of the king, and they studied history and geography (then taught by Lépicié) and visited the principal monuments of Paris and its environs, among other activities. Each year they had to execute a history painting that was shown to the king in Versailles and submitted to the members of the Academy (if only we knew the opinions of the former and the latter of the two works painted by Fragonard!). Our young artist studied at the school for three years, refusing—along with Monnet and Brenet—to leave in 1754 because he wanted to take advantage of having "such a good master" (Vanloo) to perfect his "color and composition." In October 1756, the year that marked the beginning of the Seven Years' War and the birth of Mozart, Fragonard left for Rome at the age of twenty-four.

"[We are] well informed about Jean-Honoré Fragonard's talents . . . in painting *history subjects* [our emphasis], which he studied for many years with M. Boucher as well as M. Vanloo . . .": it was in these terms that the Marquis de Marigny, the powerful *Surintendant des bâtiments* (he would be known as the Minister of Culture today) and brother of Mme de Pompadour, described the artist when he sent Fragonard his pensioner's certificate for the Académie de France in Rome.

We know for certain of only three works painted by Fragonard before 1756. Two of them are included here: the winner of the Grand Prix of 1752 (cat. no. 8), and the first painting done for admittance to the École in 1753 (cat. no. 9). The third, *Christ Washing the Feet of the Apostles* (figure 5), painted for the Cathedral of Grasse, where it is still to be seen (alas, under poor viewing conditions), was too large to be transported (of the 700 *livres* that the artist was paid for the picture, 572 were spent for the frame!). It has recently been restored and is currently being exhibited in Grasse.

It should be emphasized that these three paintings have no more claim to fame than those by the artist's contemporaries Brenet, Deshays, Doyen,

Figure 5. Fragonard. *Christ Washing the Feet of the Apostles.* Cathedral of Grasse

Lagrenée, or even Monnet, Larue, Traverse, Chardin *fils,* Briard, or Melling —all of whom competed for the Grand Prix de Rome or studied at the École royale des élèves protégés, and have since fallen into oblivion. These works by Fragonard owe as much to Jean-François de Troy, Restout, and Natoire as to his two "official" masters, Boucher and Vanloo. Although we have been able to assemble some sketches and studies of heads related to these paintings, to our knowledge no other authenticated works from before 1756 have come to light.

Also included here is a group of decorative canvases executed in quite a different manner, strongly marked by the influence of Boucher; some of these were later engraved. We know, from Théophile, that Boucher "accepted [Fragonard] immediately [about 1749–50], without asking him for an honorarium, reckoning that he would be useful in more ways than one!" As the entries that follow will show, these paintings and several others (figures 6, 7) are not simply pastiches of Boucher's works. They already reveal Fragonard's personality and certain characteristic features of his art: the colors, the youthful models, the liveliness of the compositions, and the exuberance of nature. Yet, the question remains: when were they painted? Was it before the contest picture for the Grand Prix of 1752—in which case one wonders why the style of the latter differs so much from that of these works, and owes so little to Boucher. Or did Fragonard continue to work for Boucher, and in the master's style, even after 1752, at the École royale—and thus, secretly, because this would not have been allowed?

During this period, Fragonard copied many old masters: the Rembrandts in the Crozat collection, and paintings by Jordaens, van Dyck(?), and, perhaps, by van Ostade. His lost copy of Boucher's *Hercules and Omphale* (figure 8), one of the finest paintings in the recent Boucher exhibition, and one of that artist's most sensual early works, appeared in the Varanchan sale in 1777 and in the Sireul sale in 1781. However, we have no way of knowing if the copies by Fragonard in the Deshays sale in 1765, the Baudouin sale in 1770, and in the sale of the collection of their [Fragonard's and Baudouin's] common father-in-law, Boucher, in 1771, were executed before Fragonard's departure for Italy in 1756. As we will see, our knowledge of Fragonard's career during the three years following his return from Italy in 1761 is among the most obscure. We cannot be certain, either, that all of these copies attributed to Fragonard in the sales catalogues were, indeed, painted by him. Finally, Théophile tells us that Jean-Honoré drew in "pen and ink." Apart from the pen-and-ink drawing in Stockholm, Fragonard's drawings from before 1756 have yet to be found; therefore, how abundant could they have been?

Figure 6. Fragonard, after François Boucher. *Diana and Endymion.* National Gallery of Art, Washington, D.C., Timken Collection, 1959

Figure 7. Fragonard, after François Boucher. *The Awakening of Venus.* Whereabouts unknown

Figure 8. François Boucher. *Hercules and Omphale.*
Pushkin Museum, Moscow

Georges Wildenstein, who published an important monograph on
Fragonard in 1960, could not have ignored Fragonard's early history, and
yet in his catalogue of 545 paintings, eighty-eight of them are dated before
1752! For the period between 1752 and 1761, during which the artist first
traveled to Italy, only thirteen are listed. These figures attest to this
author's difficulties with the problem that has always plagued Fragonard
specialists: the chronology of his work.

Fragonard was an artist of great facility who copied with a passion,
voraciously absorbing all that he saw around him. Nonetheless, he left his
personal stamp on all that he painted. Even before his trip to Italy, the
Fragonard style had already come into being.

CHRONOLOGY

1732

April 5
Baptism in Grasse of "Jean Honoré Fragonard né le jour précédant fils
du sieur françois marchand et de damoiselle françoise Petit son épouse,
le parrein sieur Jean Honoré Fragonard son ayeul et la marraine demoiselle Gabrielle Petit sa tante tous de cette paroisse signé qui a pu
Fragonard Fragonard Martin curé" (Grasse, Arch. Mun. GG 15). His
father was a "garçon gantier," according to the Grasse tax registers
from 1732 to 1734 (Grasse, Arch. Mun. CC 6, 1–2). The following
year, on July 25, 1733, Joseph Fragonard, the brother of Jean-Honoré, is born and dies on May 23, 1734 (Nice, Arch. Dép. 2 E 70/7).

On the occasion of the bicentennial of Fragonard's birth, a commemorative plaque was placed on the house belonging to the de Blic family,
at 23, rue Tracastel (figure 1). However, in its account of this event the
Bulletin de la Société Fragonard (1932, p. 25) mentioned that this
locality was chosen only "dans l'incertitude où l'on se trouve au sujet
de l'emplacement de la maison natale de Fragonard." According to
Barbery (*Le Temps,* July 7, 1938), this site was decided upon by an
archivist from Grasse, Joseph C. Martin, whose presumed research on
Fragonard and his family has not come to light.

June 13
Birth, also in Grasse, of Honoré Fragonard, the artist's first cousin,
who became a famous anatomist and the director of the École Vétérinaire in Alfort. The two cousins, often confused with each other
because of their names, became members of the jury of the temporary
arts commission during the Convention.

1738

Fragonard arrives in Paris, if we are to believe the "certificate of
residency" issued to him in 1794 (Paris, B.A.A.), in which he declares
that he has lived in the city for fifty-six years. This does not exclude the
possibility of trips between Paris and Grasse in the intervening years.
Théophile Fragonard, the artist's grandson, stated in 1847, in a letter
to Thoré-Bürger (Valogne, 1955, p. 9) that his grandfather "vint à
Paris avec ses parents amenés par un procès qui les ruina, il avait alors
dix-huit ans. . . . " We also know that in 1743, Fragonard's father was
already established in Paris (see March 24, 1743, below).

The details of this lawsuit are not known. The Goncourts (1865, p.
247) were the first to mention the fortune lost by the Fragonards in the
speculation involving the Périer brothers, and Portalis (1889, p. 12)
says that he was given the same information by a certain notary in

Grasse, Pérolle, who belonged to the Fragonard family on his wife's
side. Although we have no certainty as to what really brought the
Fragonards to Paris, it would not have involved the Périers, whose
Compagnie des Eaux de Paris was founded only in 1777, but rather, as
Barbery demonstrated (1934, pp. 296–315), the business venture of
François du Périer, an actor and lackey of Molière, and of his son,
Nicolas du Périer-Dumouriez, who introduced the first fire pump into
France at the beginning of the eighteenth century (Caste, 1937, pp.
58–106).

The debate over the Fragonard family's financial situation—were
they poor, or were they sufficiently well-to-do to risk a fortune in a
Parisian business venture? (*Le Temps,* May 24, June 8, July 17, September 1, 14, 1938)—has not helped to shed any additional light on
the reasons for their move to Paris. We are obliged to rely on the
Goncourts, who probably obtained their information from Théophile
Fragonard.

Figure 1. Commemorative plaque on Fragonard's
presumed birthplace

Family Tree

Based, in part, on the genealogy given to the Musée Fragonard, in Grasse, by the Huot family

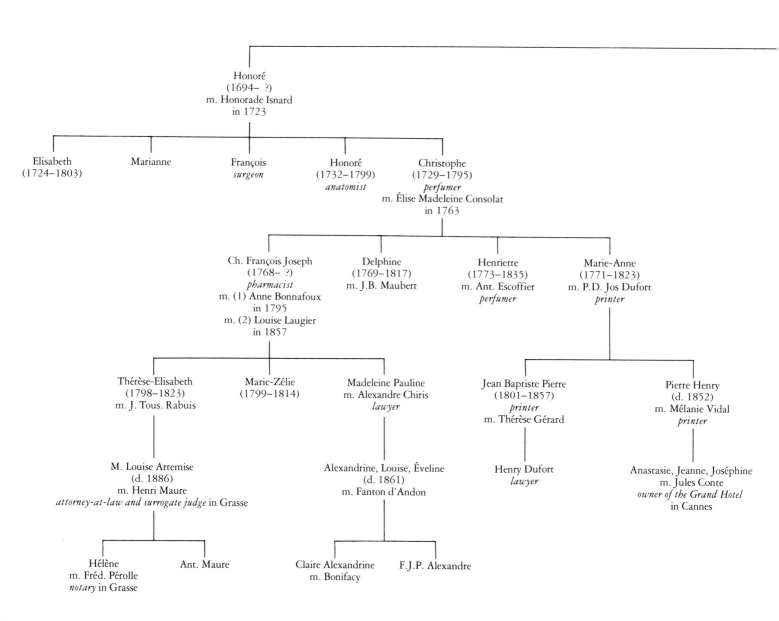

Honoré
(1694– ?)
m. Honorade Isnard
in 1723

Elisabeth
(1724–1803)

Marianne

François
surgeon

Honoré
(1732–1799)
anatomist

Christophe
(1729–1795)
perfumer
m. Élise Madeleine Consolat
in 1763

Ch. François Joseph
(1768– ?)
pharmacist
m. (1) Anne Bonnafoux
in 1795
m. (2) Louise Laugier
in 1857

Delphine
(1769–1817)
m. J.B. Maubert

Henriette
(1773–1835)
m. Ant. Escoffier
perfumer

Marie-Anne
(1771–1823)
m. P.D. Jos Dufort
printer

Thérèse-Elisabeth
(1798–1823)
m. J. Tous. Rabuis

Marie-Zélie
(1799–1814)

Madeleine Pauline
m. Alexandre Chiris
lawyer

Jean Baptiste Pierre
(1801–1857)
printer
m. Thérèse Gérard

Pierre Henry
(d. 1852)
m. Mélanie Vidal
printer

M. Louise Artemise
(d. 1886)
m. Henri Maure
attorney-at-law and surrogate judge in Grasse

Alexandrine, Louise, Éveline
(d. 1861)
m. Fanton d'Andon

Henry Dufort
lawyer

Anastasie, Jeanne, Joséphine
m. Jules Conte
owner of the Grand Hotel
in Cannes

Hélène
m. Fréd. Pérolle
notary in Grasse

Ant. Maure

Claire Alexandrine
m. Bonifacy

F.J.P. Alexandre

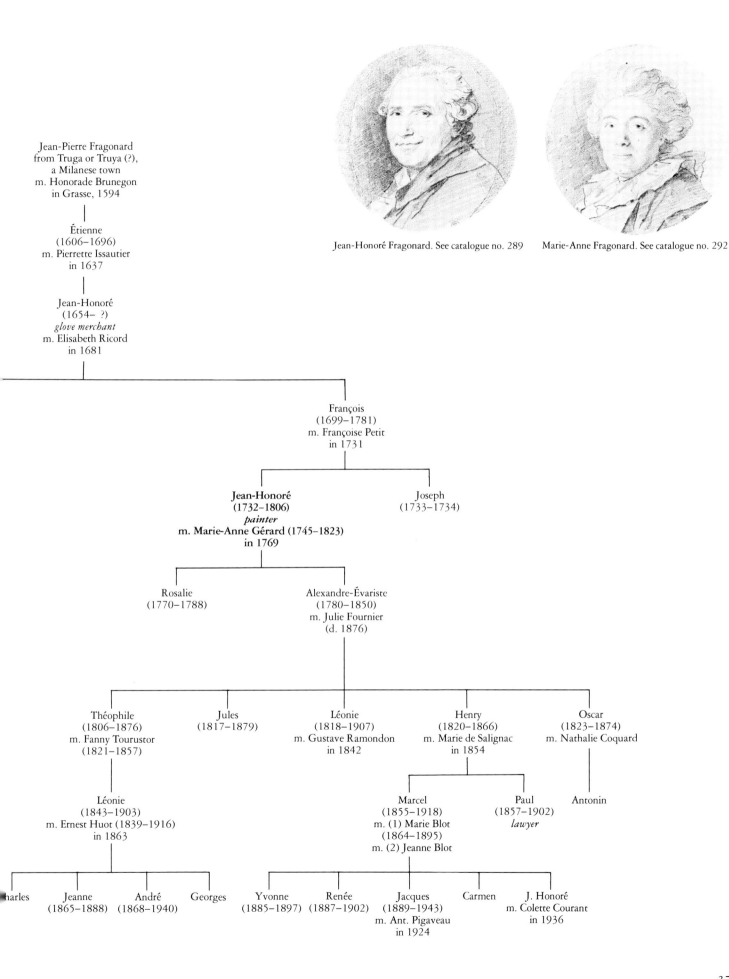

Jean-Pierre Fragonard
from Truga or Truya (?),
a Milanese town
m. Honorade Brunegon
in Grasse, 1594
|
Étienne
(1606–1696)
m. Pierrette Issautier
in 1637
|
Jean-Honoré
(1654– ?)
glove merchant
m. Elisabeth Ricord
in 1681

Jean-Honoré Fragonard. See catalogue no. 289   Marie-Anne Fragonard. See catalogue no. 292

François
(1699–1781)
m. Françoise Petit
in 1731

Jean-Honoré
(1732–1806)
painter
m. Marie-Anne Gérard (1745–1823)
in 1769

Joseph
(1733–1734)

Rosalie
(1770–1788)

Alexandre-Évariste
(1780–1850)
m. Julie Fournier
(d. 1876)

Théophile
(1806–1876)
m. Fanny Tourustor
(1821–1857)

Jules
(1817–1879)

Léonie
(1818–1907)
m. Gustave Ramondon
in 1842

Henry
(1820–1866)
m. Marie de Salignac
in 1854

Oscar
(1823–1874)
m. Nathalie Coquard

Léonie
(1843–1903)
m. Ernest Huot (1839–1916)
in 1863

Marcel
(1855–1918)
m. (1) Marie Blot
(1864–1895)
m. (2) Jeanne Blot

Paul
(1857–1902)
lawyer

Antonin

harles

Jeanne
(1865–1888)

André
(1868–1940)

Georges

Yvonne
(1885–1897)

Renée
(1887–1902)

Jacques
(1889–1943)
m. Ant. Pigaveau
in 1924

Carmen

J. Honoré
m. Colette Courant
in 1936

1743

March 24
Pierre Fragonard, Jean-Honoré's uncle, a Doctor of Theology and a priest in Grasse, designated as "son héritier général et universel le fils ainé qui se trouve actuellement en vie de sieur François Fragonard son frère marchand gantier demeurant à Paris" (Nice, Arch. Dép. 3 E 1/1, minutes of *Maître* Jacques Lambert, notary at Auribeau).

1745

December 23
Baptism of Marie-Anne Gérard, the future wife of Fragonard, "née le jour précédent fille de Claude Gérard marchand parfumeur et de Marie Gilette son épouse" (Nice, Arch. Dép. 2 E 70/9).

1748–1752

Again according to Théophile Fragonard (Valogne, 1955, p. 7), his grandfather began to work as junior clerk to a notary, then with Chardin, on Boucher's recommendation, and then with Boucher, himself; only his presence in the latter's studio is documented (see August 26, 1752, below).

1752

Fragonard submits his application for the Prix de Rome competition, although he is not a student at the Academy: "ça ne fait rien, tu es mon élève, répondait péremptoirement Boucher" (Goncourts, p. 249; probably based on Théophile's account).

April 8
Fragonard is admitted as a contestant for the Grand Prix: "La Compagnie, après avoir vu les épreuves faites par les Étudiants pour concourir aux Grands Prix, a choisi, pour y être admis, les nommés Corrège, St-Aubin, Monnet, Fragonnard et Perronet, pour la Peinture, et les nommés Duhez, Brenet et Dupré pour la Sculpture" (*Procès-Verbaux...*, VI, pp. 312–13).

June 12
Burial of Pierre Fragonard, the painter's uncle, who died the previous day in Grasse (Nice, Arch. Dép. 2 E 70/11).

August 26
"Le Sieur Fragonard qui a fait le tableau marqué D. s'est trouvé mériter le Premier Prix de Peinture" (*Procès-Verbaux...*, VI, p. 331). This was for the painting called *Jeroboam Sacrificing to the Idols* (in the École des Beaux-Arts, Paris; see cat. no. 8).
"Jean Jérôme [*sic*] Fragonard peintre d'histoire élève de M. Boucher attend son tour pour entrer dans l'École" (*Extrait du registre de l'Académie Royale de peinture et de sculpture*, collated on May 18, 1753. It was no doubt on this date that the note: "A remplacé le Sr Briard" was added; Arch. Nat. O¹ 1927, dossier 7).
Fragonard entered the École royale des élèves protégés, founded in 1748 by Lenormant de Tournehem (Courajod, 1874), whose purpose was to complete the instruction of the young artists before their trip to Rome. For three years, the students, six in all, received artistic training, took courses as well in literature and history under the direction of an instructor—in 1752, Carle Vanloo—and had to exhibit one work each year.

1753

May 18
Memorandum submitted to Monsieur de Vandières, Marquis de Marigny, *Directeur et ordonnateur général des bâtiments,* by Carle Vanloo: "Le S. Briard, peintre d'histoire, élève protégé, étant suivant vos ordres breveté pour aller à Rome, j'ai l'honneur de vous proposer pour le remplacer dans l'école le S. Fragonard, élève de m. Boucher qui a remporté le 1° prix de peinture dans le concours qui s'est fait le 26 août 1752" (Arch. Nat. O¹ 1927, dossier 6).

May 19
Memorandum from Vandières: "M. Carle Vanloo gouverneur des élèves protégés par le Roi: recevra à ladite école des élèves protégés le s. Fragonard, peintre d'histoire, élève de m. Boucher, qui a remporté le premier prix de peinture par le jugement qui a été rendu le 26 août 1752" (Arch. Nat. O¹ 1927, dossier 1).
"Fragonard âgé de 22 ans, depuis 8 mois dans l' école: *Psyché fait voir à ses soeurs les présents qu'elle a reçus de l'amour*" (Explication des ouvrages de peintures faits pendant l'année 1753 par les élèves protégés, Arch. Nat. O¹ 1927, dossier 6). This painting is now in the National Gallery, London (see cat. no. 9).

May 20
Record of the "entrée de Jean Baptiste Honoré [*sic*] Fragonard, de Grace, âgé de 20 ans, élève de m. Boucher" (Arch. Nat. O¹ 1927, dossier 1).

September 7
Awarding of the Grands Prix of 1752: "Le 1° Prix de Peinture au Sieur Fragonard" (*Procès-Verbaux...*, VI, p. 363; *Mercure de France,* October 1753, p. 165).

1754

March 4
Vandières presents to Louis XV, at Versailles, the paintings and sculptures executed during 1753 by the students of the Academy, among which was the *Psyche Showing Her Sisters the Gifts She Has Received from Cupid* (Luynes, 1860–65, XIII, p. 209; Arch. Nat. O¹ 1927, dossier 7). Fragonard's painting was listed as number 2.

May 10
Bernard Lépicié proposes to Marigny the names of Fragonard, "depuis un an dans l'École," Charles Monnet, or Nicolas Brenet to fill a vacant sixth place for a painter at the Académie royale de France in Rome. "Cependant, Monsieur, ces trois élèves ressentent si vivement le besoin qu'ils ont encore des leçons et des exemples de M. Vanloo, pour la couleur et pour la composition, qu'ils vous supplient très respectueusement de leur permettre d'achever leur tems sous un si bon maître. En cela j'ose vous assurer qu'ils n'ont d'autre but que de se rendre plus dignes de l'honneur de votre protection, de profiter plus efficacement du voyage d'Italie et de mieux lire dans les productions des Carraches et des Raphaël" (*Corr. des Dir.,* XI, p. 61).

May 18
The Confraternity of the Holy Sacrament of Grasse commissions Fragonard to execute a painting for the Chapel of the Holy Sacrament in the Cathedral (Latil, 1905, p. 66).

1755

April 13
Marigny presents to Louis XV the paintings and sculptures done by the students of the Academy during the previous year; among them, Fragonard's *Christ Washing the Feet of the Apostles* (Luynes, 1860–65, XIV, p. 133). Painted for the Cathedral of Grasse, it still hangs there today, although not in the chapel for which it was intended, but rather, in the right side aisle.

May 3
Teisseire, treasurer of the Confraternity of the Holy Sacrament, receives from Paris "une caisse contenant un tableau peint sur toile sans bordure de la valeur soixante quinze livres" (Grasse, Arch. Mun. GG 39, fig. 2).

May 10
Fragonard sends a receipt to the Confraternity of the Holy Sacrament of Grasse for the sum of 700 *livres,* which he was paid for the painting mentioned above (Latil, 1905, p. 66). On the original (unpublished) document (Grasse, Arch. Mun. GG 39; see figure 2), also cited above, Fragonard wrote down some instructions for varnishing his painting: "on aura attention lorsque ledit tableau qui est celuy dont j'ay fait la quittance cy dessus pour la confrairie du S. Sacrement de la paroisse de la ville de Grasse, sera arrivé de prendre une éponge bien fine humectée

dans de l'eau et de le lavé légèrement et lorsqu'il sera sec avec une brosse on luy donnera une couche de vernis qu'il faut bien étendre le tout avec beaucoup de précaution la ditte brosse sera faitte de crin fin et de cette grosseur'' [followed by a drawing of a circle four centimeters in diameter]. For the walnut frame, commissioned in 1756 from Jean-Baptiste Baillet, Fragonard is paid 500 *livres* plus 72 *livres* "pour augmentation du travail et pour indemnité à raison de la qualité de l'or" (Grasse, Arch. Mun. GG 39; Farnarier, 1981, p. 24).

1756

September 6
Cochin urges Marigny to dispatch the five "élèves protégés, afin de remplir une partie des places vacantes à l'Académie de Rome. Ces cinq élèves sont: Fragonard, peintre, Brenet, sculpteur, Monnet, p., D'Huez, s., et Brenet, p." (*Corr. des Dir.*, XI, p. 122).

September 17
Marigny signs Fragonard's certificate as student painter in Rome (*Corr. des Dir.*, XI, pp. 156–57).

September 23
Fragonard receives the customary 300 *livres* for travel expenses (Arch. Nat. O¹ 2256, fol. 360).

October 20
Fragonard leaves the École des élèves protégés (Courajod, 1874, p. 179).

November 22
Last mention of Fragonard in the register of the École des élèves protégés (Arch. Nat. O¹ 1927, dossier 7).

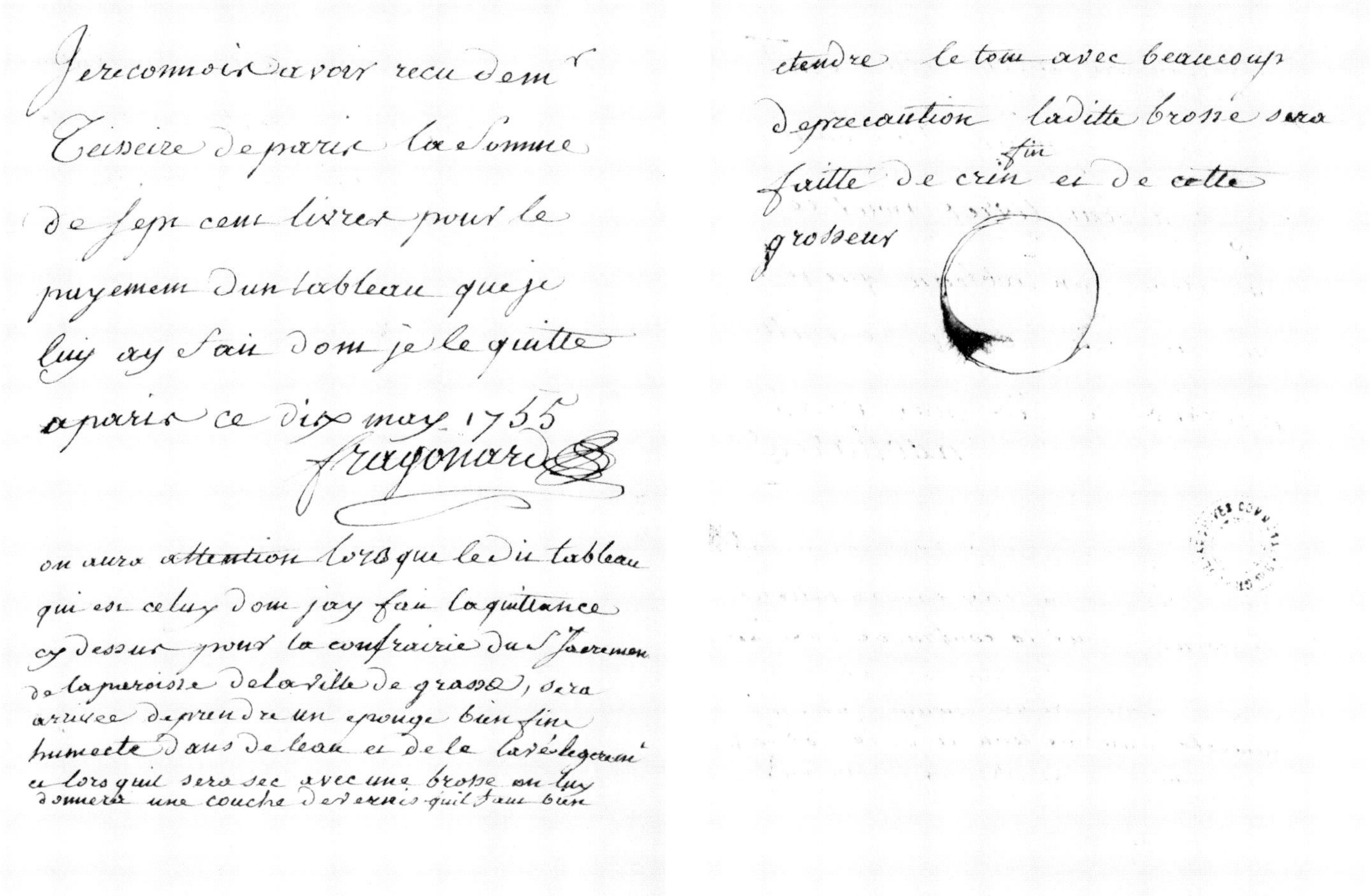

Figure 2. Fragonard's receipt of payment for the *Christ Washing the Feet of the Apostles*

1   The Shepherdess

2   The Harvester

3   Woman Gathering Grapes

4   The Gardener

Oil on canvas (arched tops and bottoms), each, 147.3 x 94 cm., except for *The Harvester*, which is only 85.1 cm. wide

The Detroit Institute of Arts, Founders Society Purchase, Mr. and Mrs. Horace E. Dodge Memorial Fund

Provenance

According to Portalis (1902), these paintings came from the Hôtel de Mortemart-Roche-chouart, today, the École libre de Sciences Politiques, at 27, rue Saint-Guillaume, Paris (Portalis gives the address as the ''rue de l'Université''); Réau (1956) erroneously identifies the house as that of the engraver Demarteau; collection of a ''dame du Nord de la France'' (Apollinaire, 1914); Roger Portalis (sales catalogue, 1971; the renowned scholar died in 1912); sale of the Kraemer collection, Paris, May 5–6, 1913, nos. 32–35, ill.; [Wildenstein and Co., New York]; Judge Elbert H. Gary, the ''Iron King'' (for Gimpel's visit to him on June 15, 1918, see Gimpel, 1963, p. 48); Mr. and Mrs. Horace E. Dodge, Detroit; Anna Thomson Dodge, Rose Terrace, Grosse Pointe Farms, Michigan (sold, Christie's, London, June 25, 1971, nos. 6–9); acquired by The Detroit Institute of Arts, 1971.

Exhibitions

Paris, 1907, nos. 113–116 (not 134)
New York, 1914, nos. 22–25
New York, 1977, no. 36, fig. 44 (*The Gardener*), no. 37, fig. 45 (*The Shepherdess*)

Bibliography

Portalis, 1902 (monograph)
D. and V. 134–137, ill.
Apollinaire, 1914, pp. 16–21, ill.
R. p. 172
W. 36–39, figs. 25–28
W. and M. 34–37, ill.
Sutton, 1980; 1987, p. 104

Related works

Two studies for the *Shepherdess* (figure 1) and for the *Woman Gathering Grapes* (figure 2), the latter transformed into a gardener, are in a private collection in Paris (and not in Switzerland; see W. 35, 34, respectively, who compares them to two paintings of similar dimensions of a gardener and a flower vendor [!], sold on December 28, 1785, no. 79); another study, also smaller in format, for the *Shepherdess* (figure 3), known to us only through a photograph, is in Burlington, Vermont.

Figure 1. Fragonard. *The Shepherdess.*
Private collection, Paris

Figure 2. Fragonard. *The Gardener.*
Private collection, Paris

Figure 3. Fragonard. *The Shepherdess.*
Robert Hull Fleming Museum,
University of Vermont, Burlington

1

Although we know virtually nothing of the early history of these four panels, no one has ever questioned their authenticity, and it is generally agreed that they date from Fragonard's formative period, when he worked in Boucher's studio. Portalis, who first published them in 1902, went so far as to say that Boucher, "having too much work, and wishing to be of service to his best pupil," turned the commission for these paintings over to Fragonard.

The Detroit panels may be compared to three other works included here (see cat. nos. 5–7), and to the *Gardener* and the *Woman Gathering Grapes* (figures 4, 5) formerly in the McCormick collection, Chicago (see Tokyo exhibition catalogue, 1980, nos. 7, 8, ill.), as well as to the *Gardener*, more

appropriately entitled *The Joys of Motherhood* (figure 6), in Indianapolis (see Atlanta exhibition catalogue, 1983–84, no. 49, ill.); the dimensions of the last work are comparable to those of the Detroit pictures.

The subject matter of these decorative works is simply the seasons, rural occupations, and the joys of motherhood; there is no complicated iconography. The paintings are still very close to the works of Boucher, but the colors are less artificial, the handling is freer, and there is a more direct approach to the figures, which have no mythological associations. These early works already display the spontaneity—here, tinged with humor—and the *joie de vivre* that is almost always associated with Fragonard's oeuvre.

Figure 4. Fragonard. *The Gardener.* Whereabouts unknown

Figure 5. Fragonard. *Woman Gathering Grapes.* Whereabouts unknown

Figure 6. Fragonard. *The Joys of Motherhood.* Indianapolis Museum of Art

2

3

4

5 Blindman's Buff

Oil on canvas, 116.8 x 91.4 cm.
Probably cut at the top.

The Toledo Museum of Art, Gift of Edward Drummond Libbey

Provenance
Baron Baillet de Saint-Julien: sold, June 21,
1784, no. 75, "Deux tableaux faisant pendant; l'un représente un jeu de colin-maillard;
composition de quatre figures; l'autre offre
l'amusement de la balançoire avec même
nombre de figures. Ces deux charmants tableaux sont gravés par Bauvarlet [*sic*] Haut.
78 pouce. Larg. 34.T'' (210.5 x 92 cm.);
sold to Le Brun (for 500 *livres*); Morel [or
Morelle] et al.: sold, May 3, 1786, postponed
from April 19, no. 177, very similar description, but the dimensions—42 x 33 *pouces*
[113.5 x 89 cm.]—correspond approximately
to those of the Toledo and Lugano pictures
(to Joubert, for 852 *livres*); Duclos *le jeune*:
sold, posthumously, April 2, 1792, no. 98
(42 x 23 *pouces*!); Comte de Sinéty, Paris,
1889; Baron Nathaniel de Rothschild (before
1902, according to Portalis [1902]); Baron
Alphonse de Rothschild; Baron Maurice de
Rothschild, Vienna, then Pregny, Switzerland; [Rosenberg & Stiebel, New York];
acquired by The Toledo Museum of Art,
1954.

Principal exhibitions
London, 1968, no. 229, pl. VI
Toledo-Chicago-Ottawa, 1975–76, no. 36,
   pl. 82

Bibliography
G. p. 331
P. pp. 15, 62, 273
N. p. 150
Réau, 1927, pp. 147–52, ill. p. 148
R. pp. 39, 158
W. 47, fig. 31
Watson, 1971, p. 80, ill.
W. and M. 53, ill.
Ananoff and Wildenstein, 1976, II, under
   no. 315
Toledo museum catalogue, 1976, pp.
   59–60, colorpl. IX, pl. 203
Posner, 1978, p. 561
Slatkin, 1979, p. 123
Sutton, 1980; 1987, p. 104
Posner, 1982, pp. 81–82, fig. 10, p. 81

Related works
Paintings
Although G. Wildenstein (1960, nos. 45,
46) considers the paintings in the Saint-Julien
collection sale of 1784 and those in the Morel
sale of 1786 as two different sets of works, we
believe that they were one and the same and
that there was a mistake in the height given in
the first catalogue.

   We should mention, however, that there
were two old versions of the Toledo and
Lugano pictures, of respectable quality (figures 1, 2), at the Château de Champ-de-
Bataille (see the undated guide by the Duc
d'Harcourt, ill. p. 24); they were arched at
the top, and their dimensions—210 x 82 centimeters—were the same as those of the Saint-

Figure 1. After Fragonard. *Blindman's Buff*.
Formerly Château de Champ-de-Bataille

Figure 2. After Fragonard. *The Seesaw*.
Formerly Château de Champ-de-Bataille

Figure 3. Attributed to Gabriel
de Saint-Aubin. Sheet of studies.
Whereabouts unknown

Figure 4. Jacques Couché and Jean
Dambrun, after a lost painting by
Fragonard. *La Coquette fixée*.
Musée du Louvre, Paris, Cabinet
des Dessins, Rothschild Collection

Figure 5. Jacques-Firmin Beauvarlet,
"after Boucher." *Blindman's Buff*.
Musée du Louvre, Paris, Cabinet des
Dessins, Rothschild Collection

Figure 6. Jacques-Firmin Beauvarlet,
"after Fragonard." *Blindman's Buff*.
Musée du Louvre, Paris, Cabinet des
Dessins, Rothschild Collection

Julien pictures (the two works were part of a series of six decorative panels).

Many copies of the Toledo picture were made after the engraving in the Musée du Petit Palais, Paris; see also Réau (1927, 1956, fig. 45, p. 158), and the versions—often attributed to Boucher—that have appeared at auction since the beginning of the century. For a watchcase in the Musée du Louvre, whose decoration was inspired by the engraving, see Cardinal (1984, no. 126, ill.); for a Sèvres porcelain vase in the British royal collections, see G. de Bellaigue (London exhibit. cat., 1979–80, no. 46, ill.); for a snuffbox, see the sales catalogue (Christie's, London, October 9, 1962). A Sèvres porcelain flowerpot was sold at Versailles, April 1, 1984; a tapestry (Aubusson?) was sold at Fontainebleau, October 12, 1986.

A reversed version of the Toledo *Blindman's Buff* with a double attribution to Boucher and to Fragonard was sold at Christie's, London, June 28, 1974, no. 119, ill. (A. II, no. 315). Also reproduced in the latter volume are a drawing attributed to Gabriel de Saint-Aubin (figure 3), of this same picture, sold at Christie's, March 28, 1972, no. 123, ill., which copies the painting, as well as a version of *The Seesaw*, with the same composition as the Lugano picture; as well as two other works, *La Coquette fixée*, engraved by Jacques Couché and Jean Dambrun (figure 4); (see A. II, no. 313, and also W. 41), and a painting entitled *Why Not Us?*, sold at

Christie's, London, March 29, 1974 (no. 76, ill.). The drawing bears the following inscription: "Vu chez remy 4 peintures par Mr boucher prffeur" [professeur] "et mr fragonard élève qui ne les aime point. Remy did que l'invention est de deshays 46 p x 70 p." The attributions of the drawing and of the four paintings were questioned by Posner (1978, 1982) and by Slatkin (1979).

Engraving
The engraving by Jacques-Firmin Beauvarlet attributes the composition alternately to Boucher (figure 5) and to Fragonard (figure 6; see Roux, 1933, II, no. 31). It proves that the Toledo painting was, indeed, cut at the top.

6   The Seesaw

Oil on canvas, 120 x 94.5 cm.
Probably cut slightly at the top.

Thyssen-Bornemisza Collection, Lugano

Provenance
See the preceding entry; acquired by Baron Thyssen, 1956.

Principal exhibitions
London, 1968, no. 230 (exhib. cat. has colorpl. on cover)
Paris, 1982, no. 48, pl. 93 (entry by A. Rosenbaum)

Bibliography
G. p. 331
P. pp. 15, 62, 271–72
N. p. 150
R. pp. 39, 158
W. 48, fig. 32
Wentzel, 1964, pp. 211–14, fig. 160
Sterling et al., 1969, no. 98, ill.
W. and M. 54, ill.
Ananoff and Wildenstein, 1976, II, under no. 314
Posner, 1978, p. 561
Slatkin, 1979, p. 123
Sutton, 1980; 1987, p. 104
Posner, 1982, pp. 81–82, fig. 11, p. 81

Related works
Paintings
See preceding entry.

There are many copies, including one in the Musée du Petit Palais, Paris, and one in the Musée des Beaux-Arts, Bordeaux—to mention only those in museums. There is also a version that was the subject of a monograph by Camille Mauclair (undated; probably, 1929).

Regarding designs for a Sèvres porcelain vase and a flowerpot, see the preceding entry.

Engravings
The engraving by Beauvarlet (figure 1), which assigns the composition to Boucher (see Roux, 1933, II, no. 30), preceded the engraving dated 1760 that ascribes it to Fragonard (figure 2).

Figure 1. Jacques-Firmin Beauvarlet, "after Boucher." *The Seesaw*. Musée du Louvre, Paris, Cabinet des Dessins, Rothschild Collection

Figure 2. Jacques-Firmin Beauvarlet, "after Fragonard." *The Seesaw*. Musée du Louvre, Paris, Cabinet des Dessins, Rothschild Collection

Several factors support the attribution to Fragonard of these two companion works, now unfortunately separated: their appearance in eighteenth-century auctions, the engravings after them by Beauvarlet, and their style. The two canvases were sold three times in the eighteenth century. Whether or not there were other autograph versions of these compositions, one thing is certain: they were cut at the top, as shown in Beauvarlet's engravings, from which the paintings get their titles. These engravings have a twofold interest. First of all, *The Seesaw* is dated 1760, by which time Fragonard had been in Italy for four years; thus, the painting must have been done before he left France in 1756. Secondly, before being recognized as after Fragonard, the engravings were

believed to be based upon compositions by his master, Boucher. This seems plausible, for the general spirit of the two works is still close to that of Boucher. The freshness of the colors and the verve of the composition, however, already distinguish the art of Fragonard from that of his master. Furthermore, the youthful couples—no longer children, but not yet adolescents—are of that equivocal age at which Fragonard so often chose to portray his figures: the age at which, to quote from the caption of one of the engravings, "les Amours se mêlent à nos jeux."

The first documented owner of these works, Baron de Saint-Julien, commissioned Fragonard in 1767 to paint his famous picture *The Swing*, now in the Wallace Collection, London. We know exceptionally well the circumstances of this commission. It may be that the present painting—from its style, apparently a first version of the London composition—gave Saint-Julien a taste for Fragonard's work. In any case, themes like "The Swing" and "Blindman's Buff" were among Fragonard's favorites, while Boucher represented them only rarely.

The fact that Beauvarlet's engravings first bore the name of Boucher has additional interest: it lends credence to the supposition that the two works were painted while Fragonard was still working in Boucher's studio, and was not yet a pupil of Carle Vanloo at the École royale des élèves protégés —thus, before 1752.

7   Winter

Oil on canvas, 80 x 163.8 cm.

Los Angeles County Museum of Art, Purchased with funds acquired by Hearst Magazines, Inc.

Provenance
Presumably, part of a series of canvases devoted to the Four Seasons, three of which today decorate the Grand Salon of the Hôtel Matignon at 17, rue de Varenne, Paris (for the history of the Hôtel Matignon, see the exhibition catalogue *La rue de Varenne*, Musée Rodin, Paris, 1981, pp. 27–33): this room was designed by the Duc and Duchesse de Galliéra after 1852; Ferrari de la Renotière (a descendant of the Duc and Duchesse de Galliéra), Paris: sold, June 7, 1922, no. 8; [Wildenstein, 1922–26]; William Randolph

Hearst; Marion Davies, from whose collection it was acquired by the Los Angeles County Museum, 1947.

Exhibitions
Tokyo, 1980, no. 10, colorpl.

Bibliography
G. Wildenstein, 1935, pp. 271–74, fig. 1, p. 271
R. p. 145
W. 56, fig. 40, p. 8 (French edition)
W. and M. 64, ill.

Apollo, 1980, pp. 274–75, fig. 4, p. 273
Sutton, 1980; 1987, p. 104
Musée Rodin, Paris, exhibition catalogue, 1981, p. 35

Related works
The three other paintings of the seasons (figures 1–3) are still in the Hôtel Matignon (see W. 33–35, figs. 37–39).

The Hôtel Matignon has had a very eventful history, but we will limit ourselves to the period during which, it is supposed, Fragonard executed this painting for the Grand Salon on the first floor, along with the three others in the series (still in place). In 1751, at the death of the Duc de Valentinois, the mansion became the property of the count of the same name, who bequeathed it to his son, Honoré-Camille Grimaldi, Prince of Monaco. At the prince's death on May 11, 1795, an inventory was drawn up, and a sale took place on July 4, 1803, which did not include the Fragonards. In fact, the Grand Salon was decorated at the time with copies after Albani (information communicated in a letter from Dr. Bruno Pons). The Hôtel Matignon subsequently changed hands many times (the extravagant Eleonora Franchi, wife of the wealthy Quentin Crawfurd, or Crawford, being not the least colorful of its occupants) before it was acquired in 1852 by Raphaël, Marquis de Ferrari and Duc de Galliéra, a Genoese banker, and his wife, Maria Brignole Sale, who "modernized" most of the *hôtel* before presenting it as a gift to the Emperor of Austria, Franz Josef. As the Austro-Hun-

garian embassy, it was sequestered during World War I, and in 1935 it became an official government residence.

The three paintings of the seasons that are still in place (figures 1–3) represent a mother accompanied by two children picking flowers and distributing grapes. In the Los Angeles picture, a little girl, toppled by a spaniel puppy, has fallen on the ice, to the amusement of two young skaters. The girl's expression of surprise at her sudden fall is depicted with a bemused tenderness. Her elegant muff, long gloves, and cape bear witness to her coquettishness.

Winter was undoubtedly completed before 1756: if certain details are still reminiscent of Boucher's decorations of 1751 for the boudoir of the Château de Crécy (today in the Frick Collection, New York), the two children at the left in the present work recall Carle Vanloo's allegories of painting, sculpture, architecture, and music, of 1752–53, painted for the Château de Bellevue (today in the California Palace of the Legion of Honor, San Francisco). Perhaps *Winter* is contemporary with these celebrated works.

Figure 1. Fragonard. *Spring.* Hôtel Matignon, Paris   Figure 2. Fragonard. *Summer.* Hôtel Matignon, Paris   Figure 3. Fragonard. *Autumn.* Hôtel Matignon, Paris

8 Jeroboam Sacrificing to the Idols

1752
Oil on canvas, 111.5 x 143.5 cm.

École Nationale Supérieure des Beaux-Arts, Paris

Provenance
Awarded the Grand Prix of the Académie royale de peinture et de sculpture, 1752. On April 8 (*Procès-Verbaux . . .*, VI, pp. 312–13), Fragonard was admitted to compete along with "Corrège, St. Aubin, Monnet . . . and Perronet." On Saturday, August 26, his painting "s'est trouvé mériter le Premier Prix de Peinture," the second prize being awarded to Monnet (ibid., pp. 331, 328, 329, respectively), and not to Gabriel de Saint-Aubin, as has been maintained since Duvivier (1857–58, p. 296); Saint-Aubin received second prize in 1753 (see figure 1). The prize, a gold medal (*Mercure de France,* October 1753, p. 165), was presented to Fragonard by "Monsieur de Vandières, *Directeur et ordonnateur général des bâtiments*" (the brother of Madame de Pompadour and the future Marquis de Marigny),

but not until September 7, 1753 (ibid., p. 363). With the collections of the Académie royale, passed to the École des Beaux-Arts during the Revolution.

Exhibitions
Paris, 1921, no. 9, ill.
Tokyo, 1980, no. 22, colorpl.

Bibliography
G. p. 249
P. pp. 14–15
N. p. 11
D. and V. 130, ill.
Jules Guiffrey, 1908, p. 34
Fontaine, 1910, p. 143
Dacier, 1929, I, p. 29
R. p. 141
W. 88, plates 8–10, pp. 8, 10
 (French edition)

A. 1781, no. 1718
Thuillier, 1967, p. 21, colorpl.
W. and M. 96, colorplates V–VII
Goldstein, 1975, p. 107, fig. 10
Sutton, 1980; 1987, pp. 104–5, fig. 1, p. 103

Related works
Réau, and later Ananoff (no. 1718) have compared this painting with a red-chalk drawing (see figure 2: 19.2 x 19.4 cm.; last sold, Paris, Drouot, June 18, 1984, letter H, June 11, 1986, no. 2). There are obvious analogies to Fragonard's composition, but we would hesitate to consider it as an autograph work. Besides, does it represent Jeroboam sacrificing to the Idols or the very closely related subject of the sacrifice of Solomon?

On August 26, 1752, Fragonard, who had turned twenty on April 4, won the Grand Prix de Peinture. This precocious triumph calls for a few comments.

First of all, it rewarded an artist who had not received his training at the Academy. It is true that Fragonard had studied with Boucher—although the earliest mention of his presence in the master's studio dates only from May 18, 1753; nevertheless, in the eighteenth century, rare was the artist who had not studied at the Academy. The quality of its instruction, which was admired and copied throughout Europe, permitted the better students to become history

painters—or, at the very least, to pursue a career. Fragonard lacked this instruction, as well as the basic cultural background that came with it, and this, as we shall see, will explain some of his choices.

What, if anything, does Fragonard's prizewinning work owe to his master's style? As it is, none of the three documented paintings Fragonard completed before his departure for Italy in 1756 (see cat. no. 9, and the *Christ Washing the Feet of the Apostles* in Grasse, illustrated above) attests to the exclusive influence of Boucher, then at the height of his creative powers and reputation. The *Jeroboam* is stylistically

Figure 1. Gabriel de Saint-Aubin. *Nebuchadnezzar and Sedicias.* Musée du Louvre

Figure 2. Attributed to Fragonard. *The Sacrifice.* Art market, Paris

Figure 3. Jean-François de Troy. *The Triumph of Mordecai* (detail). Musée du Louvre

Figure 4. Fragonard. *Jeroboam Sacrificing to the Idols.*
Infrared photograph

closer to Carle Vanloo, whose renown in Europe in 1752 matched Boucher's—and who had been ennobled the previous year—and also to Jean-François de Troy, who had just died in Rome and whose tapestries of the *Story of Esther* were greatly admired (figure 3). It is true that this picture was painted for a contest to be judged essentially by history painters, which meant that Fragonard had to emphasize the poses, the gestures, and the expressions to render the subject as clearly as possible. Yet, all in all, the angular folds of the drapery, the sudden movements of the figures, and even the color scheme owe little to the graceful and curvilinear style of Boucher.

The subject, Jeroboam sacrificing to the Idols (1 Kings: 12–13)—which, it should be remembered, was chosen by the Academicians and not by Fragonard—has not often been represented (unlike the sacrifice of Solomon). Jeroboam, the first king of Israel, was about to make an offering to the

Golden Calf when a prophet came before him; when he gave the order to arrest the prophet, his hand "dried up." Fragonard was faithful to the biblical text, depicting, in particular, the rending of the altar and the ashes pouring out—signs that the sacrifice was a profanation. (An infrared photograph [figure 4] reveals many pentimenti in this part of the picture.)

One last point: this painting is number 88 (out of 545) in Wildenstein's catalogue raisonné (1960) of Fragonard's work. While we are not suggesting that the *Jeroboam* be considered as Fragonard's very first painting, it seems difficult to accept that more than one-sixth of his entire production could have been painted before his twentieth year. As it was, when the young Fragonard entered the École des élèves protégés, he still had much to learn, Boucher's lessons notwithstanding.

9 Psyche Showing Her Sisters the Gifts She Has Received from Cupid

1753
Oil on canvas, 168.3 x 192.4 cm.

The Trustees of the National Gallery, London

Provenance
Presented by Vandières, the future Marquis de Marigny, to Louis XV, March 4, 1754; Comte Denis-Pierre-Jean Papillon de la Ferté (1727–1794) collection, seized during the Revolution (Arch. Nat. F. 17A 1266A 1267 no. 61: "la toilette de psiché composition de 16 figures hauteur 6 pieds largeur 7 pieds sur toile de Fragonard d'ap. Boucher," evaluated at 200 *livres*); returned to the Papillon de la Ferté family: collection sold, Paris, February 20, 1797, no. 100; possibly, Baron Mayer Amschel de Rothschild (died 1874), Ment-

more Towers, Buckinghamshire; fifth Earl of Rosebery (died 1929), Mentmore Towers; seventh Earl of Rosebery, Mentmore Towers: collection sold, Sotheby's, London, May 25, 1977, no. 2422, ill. (as a Carle Vanloo); [Artemis]; acquired by the National Gallery, 1978.

Exhibitions
Versailles, 1754, no. 2
London, 1978, no. 20, colorpl. (entry by David Carritt)
Tokyo, 1980, no. 23, colorpl.

Bibliography
Luynes, 1863, vol. XIII, p. 209
Courajod, 1874, p. 36
P. p. 18
N. p. 14
R. p. 146
W. 89 (lost)
W. and M. 97 (lost)
Pigler, 1974, I, p. 173
Roberts, 1978, p. 409
Massengale, 1979, p. 270
Sutton, 1980; 1987, pp. 105, 103, respectively, fig. 2

On May 30, 1753, several months after having received the Grand Prix de Peinture, Fragonard was admitted to the École royale des élèves protégés. The role of this important school, which was founded in 1749, was to complete the technical and theoretical training of the young painters and to round out their general cultural knowledge before they left for the Academy in Rome (for a history of the school, see Courajod, 1874). In Fragonard's day, the École royale was directed by Carle Vanloo, who displayed great warmth and devotion toward his pupils.

Fragonard began work on the *Psyche Showing Her Sisters the Gifts She Has Received from Cupid* as soon as he entered the École royale. It was exhibited in the apartments of Louis XV at Versailles on March 4, 1754, along with the *Cupid Abducting Cephalus* by Deshays (whose path so often crossed Fragonard's; he won the Grand Prix in 1751, and as a student at the École in 1753 he presented a *Psyche Abandoned by Cupid*, now lost), a *Sacrifice to Bacchus* by Monnet (winner of a second Grand Prix in 1752), and a *Laban Sacrificing to the Idols* by Brenet, as well as sculptures by Guiard and Delarue. The titles of the works are known to us from the Duc de Luynes's account of the event, which, unfortunately, does not include the reactions of the illustrious visitors.

There was no mention of this painting in the eighteenth century. It was seized during the Revolution along with the

rest of the collection of Papillon de la Ferté, the famous director of the *Menus Plaisirs* (the royal divertissements), engraver, art critic, collector, and admirer of the work of Boucher and of Vanloo, who died on the scaffold in 1794. The collection was sold on February 20, 1797, the accompanying catalogue noting that Fragonard's painting measures "72 pouces sur 84 [194.4 x 226.8 cm.] and depicts sixteen figures." The London canvas has, therefore, been considerably mutilated, having lost twenty-seven centimeters at the

Figure 1. Carle Vanloo. *Cupid Taking Leave of Psyche.* Château de Versailles

Figure 2. Charles-Joseph Natoire. *Psyche Receiving the Jewels*. Hôtel de Soubise, Paris, Archives Nationales

Figure 3. François Boucher. *The Toilet of Psyche*. Tapestry. Philadelphia Museum of Art

Figure 4. Paolo Veronese. *The Finding of Moses.*
National Gallery of Art, Washington, D.C.,
Andrew W. Mellon Collection

Figure 5. Alexandre-Évariste Fragonard.
Psyche Showing Her Riches to Her Sisters.
Musée du Louvre, Paris, Cabinet des Dessins

top (which explains why the putti are so oddly cut at mid-section) and almost thirty-five centimeters at the left—resulting in the disappearance of some of the "sixteen figures" in Psyche's company. The glances of Psyche and of her sisters are clearly directed toward what must have been the painting's original focus of attention—the gift of the jewels.

After disappearing during the nineteenth century, the painting resurfaced in 1977 at the Mentmore sale, understandably attributed to Carle Vanloo before it was correctly identified by David Carritt, who sold it to the National Gallery.

Several points are worth discussing. There is nothing surprising about the attribution to Vanloo: Fragonard was his pupil when the *Psyche* was executed. In 1744, Vanloo painted a *Cupid Taking Leave of Psyche* (figure 1) for Versailles that has some features in common with the London picture. Le Brun, who expertized the Papillon de la Ferté collection, no less aptly remarked that the painting was "done" when Fragonard was "in Boucher's school." We will see that the young painter was inspired directly by the compositions of his first master. Certain elements, however, such as the putti; the figure of Envy, at the top; the color scheme, with its acid and saffron yellows; and, especially, the servant braiding Psyche's hair, are typical of Fragonard's work.

This theme was an uncommon one in eighteenth-century French painting and, as Carritt pointed out (1978), it was inspired as much by *The Golden Ass* of Apuleius as by La Fontaine's *The Loves of Cupid and of Psyche*. It was the subject of a painting by Natoire (see figure 2) for the Hôtel de Soubise in 1738, and of one of Boucher's series of tapestries devoted to Psyche. (In 1737, the Beauvais tapestry works had commissioned Boucher to execute six cartoons for

tapestries, illustrating the Story of Psyche. Six sets of five tapestries each were made between 1741 and 1770. [Boucher's cartoon for *The Marriage of Cupid and Psyche*, which was never woven, was recently acquired by the Louvre.] Two complete sets of tapestries are extant—one in Philadelphia and one in Stockholm—as well as three grisaille sketches [on this series, see Hussman, 1977; Standen, 1986; and, especially, Hiesinger, 1976].) Although traces of the style of Natoire—with whom Fragonard would soon study in Rome—are difficult to discern in the present painting, Boucher's influence is evident. However, Fragonard's representation of *Psyche Showing Her Sisters the Gifts She Has Received from Cupid* was based not so much on Boucher's painting of the same subject, but, rather, on the latter's *Toilet of Psyche* (figure 3).

As Howard Couts has pointed out, the central group of Psyche's two sisters was directly inspired by Paolo Veronese's *The Finding of Moses* (figure 4)—either the version (today, in the National Gallery of Art, Washington, D.C.), that belonged to Louis-Michel Vanloo, Carle's nephew, or the engraving of the version (now in Dijon) that was in the royal collections.

One last note: the Cabinet des Dessins at the Louvre owns a drawing of this subject by Fragonard's son, Alexandre-Évariste (figure 5). In 1797, at the age of seventeen (Jean-Honoré was twenty-one when he painted the work in question), and having no doubt seen his father's painting at the Papillon de la Ferté sale, he wanted to show what he could do. The result is an allegory that is closer in style to Prud'hon than to David. The technical perfection, observation of archaeological details, icy purism, and elegant eroticism of this drawing bear witness to the radical change that had taken place in French painting in less than fifty years.

10 The Rest on the Flight into Egypt

Oil on canvas, oval, 190.5 x 221 cm.

The Chrysler Museum, Norfolk, Virginia, on loan from the collection of Walter P. Chrysler, Jr.

Provenance
According to the catalogue of the 1956 exhibition in Portland, Oregon, which quotes the "Vicomte Jacques de Canson, Paris," this picture was in a church in Grasse, for which it may originally have been intended; Baron Franchetti, Venice; acquired from the "Galerie Jamarin," Paris, 1954.

Exhibitions
Portland, Oregon, 1956, no. 67, ill.

Bibliography
Cuzin, 1986, p. 58

Related works
There is an oil sketch, vertical in format (W. 13, fig. 8) and with some variations (figure 1), in the Nationalmuseum, Stockholm, and another, horizontal in format (W. 12, fig. 7), formerly in the collection of Jules Strauss and then of Salavin, that was sold in Paris on December 5, 1973 (see figure 2; Palais Galliéra, no. 34, ill.). There are also two studies for the head of the Virgin, one (figure 3) in the Gösta Serlachiuksen Taidemuseo, Mänttä, Finland, and another (figure 4) that was sold at Sotheby's, London, May 18, 1938, no. 102, ill. Finally, there is a drawing in the Stockholm museum (Bjurström, 1982, no. 950, ill.) that we initially hesitated to accept (Rosenberg, 1984, p. 66), but which we now consider to be one of the earliest drawings that can be attributed with certainty to Fragonard (figure 5).

These works may be compared with a painting (figure 6) of the same subject, also oval but vertical in format, formerly in the Rouart collection (W. 24, fig. 15), and to a drawing (figure 7) sold in 1955 (A. 1775), which we accept with some reservation in spite of its free execution.

We should also mention the canvas in the sale of the Le Prince collection, November 28, 1781, no. 125: "Un repos de Fuite en Égypte de forme ovale en travers: composition grande et d'un effet piquant. Hauteur 33 pouces. Largeur 34 pouces. T."

The Abbé de Saint-Non may have copied Fragonard's painting: "un tableau sur toile de forme ovale, copie par M. de Saint-Non d'après Fragonard et représentant la Vierge considérant l'enfant Jésus endormi dans son berceau" (Wildenstein, 1959, p. 238, nos. 6–7; see also p. 239, nos. 42–49).

Figure 1. Fragonard. *The Holy Family.* Nationalmuseum, Stockholm

Figure 2. Fragonard. *The Holy Family.* Whereabouts unknown

Figure 3. Fragonard. *Study for the Head of the Virgin.* Gösta Serlachiuksen Taidemuseo, Mänttä, Finland

Figure 4. Attributed to Fragonard. *Study for the Head of the Virgin.* Whereabouts unknown

Figure 5. Fragonard. *The Holy Family.* Nationalmuseum, Stockholm

Figure 6. Fragonard. *The Holy Family.* Whereabouts unknown

Figure 7. Attributed to Fragonard.
The Holy Family.
Whereabouts unknown

Figure 8. Fragonard. *The Holy Family.*
Whereabouts unknown

Figure 9. Fragonard. *The Holy Family.*
The Fine Arts Museums of San Francisco

Little has been written about this painting and it has rarely been reproduced, but there is no doubt as to Fragonard's authorship due to the existence of many well-known and unanimously accepted oil sketches (figures 1, 2), detail studies (figures 3, 4), and at least one preparatory sketch (figure 5), all of which prove the importance of this composition for the young artist.

However, nothing is known of the picture's original location: it has been suggested (see *Provenance*, above) that it came from a church in Grasse, but there is no proof of this. It is interesting, though, to compare it with the *Christ Washing the Feet of the Apostles* in the Cathedral of Grasse, commissioned by the city in 1754 and presented to Louis XV on April 13, 1755. The style of the two works is analogous, even if the cool hues and morning light of the Chrysler picture contrast with the warm tones and artificial light of the canvas in Grasse.

Needless to say, Fragonard introduced no innovations in the iconography of this most common of subjects. He directs our attention to the group of the Virgin and Child on the left; Joseph, seated comfortably in the foreground, is shown in three-quarter view, holding a Bible. What is important is that Fragonard took his inspiration directly from the *Holy Family* by Rembrandt (then in the Crozat collection; now in the Hermitage, Leningrad): We know that he copied this painting (see figure 8), and that the copy (W. 7, fig. 2) once belonged to Boucher (posthumous sale, February 18, 1771, no. 111). The date and the present location of the copy are not certain, but Fragonard seems to have repeated the central motif several times. The only version that we have seen is today in San Francisco (figure 9), and it imitates the broad and heavy brushwork so characteristic of Rembrandt. If this work were contemporary with the Chrysler picture, it would prove that in the same period Fragonard was painting in very different manners; for those who know his work, this comes as no surprise.

10

II
Rome
(1756–61)

"You will see over there, my dear Frago, the works of Raphael, Michelangelo, and their imitators; but let me tell you confidentially, and not too loudly, that if you take [these people] seriously, then you will be lost." According to Théophile Fragonard (1847), such were the terms in which Boucher praised Italy to his pupil. Fragonard traveled to Italy in the company of Mme Carle Vanloo, the wife of his master, who was from Turin and was an accomplished singer, and two of his fellow students at the École royale des élèves protégés: the painter Monnet, and the sculptor Dhuez from Arras. He arrived in Rome shortly before December 22, 1756.

We know very little of his four-year stay at the Academy, then located in the Palazzo Mancini on the Corso. Fragonard did not record his experiences, nor did his schoolmates Guiard, Pajou, de Wailly, Louis, Chalgrin, Chardis *fils,* and Amand, among others, leave us any anecdotes. Only Greuze, who met Fragonard in 1757, recalled that Fragonard had nicknamed him the "amorous cherub" because of his blond hair and his love affairs at the time (Montaiglon, 1860, p. 254). As for the director of the Academy, Charles-Joseph Natoire (1700–1777), he played an important role in Fragonard's development, as we will see, but committed to paper only what he felt like writing.

The beginning of Fragonard's stay in Italy was marked by a serious crisis. Naturally, he was not the first artist to be disconcerted by his first encounter with the Italy of antiquity and of the Renaissance, as well as with young Italian and foreign painters such as Anton Raphael Mengs, whose aspirations differed so from those of their French colleagues. Jean-Baptiste Deshays (1729–1765), Boucher's future son-in-law, who had arrived in Rome two years before Fragonard, had experienced the same discouragement (Cochin, 1765). Fragonard's despondency was deep: "I was in awe of Michelangelo's energy. I felt things that I could not express. When I saw the beauty of the Raphaels, I was moved to tears, and I could scarcely hold my pencil. For several months I remained in a state of apathy that I was unable to overcome, until I resolved to study the painters whom I felt I had a chance of rivaling: and so I turned my attention to Barocci, Pietro da Cortona, Solimena, and Tiepolo" (Lenoir, 1816).

Dominique Vivant-Denon (1829) was to experience a similar "languor": "The sight of the works of the great Italian masters discouraged him; he despaired at ever being able to attain their perfection and did not even try to imitate them." This phenomenon has not been fully understood by Fragonard's most recent biographers. He already had his own ideas about painting, as he had shown in Paris, but Italy came as a surprise, and called them into question. In France, he had had no way of imagining what the Raphaels, Michelangelos, or even the frescoes of the Carracci in the Palazzo Farnese—which he would copy in April 1757—were like.

Upon hearing of the crisis that Fragonard and several other pensioners were undergoing, Marigny responded (on July 31, 1758) with comprehension and indulgence: "The sight of the great masterpiece can sometimes cause astonishment. One wants to imitate them, one thinks one needs to change one's style.... The passage from one manner to another necessitates a sort of fumbling that slows one down." How long did this "disheartenment" last, and how did Natoire go about helping Fragonard? The answer may be found in the correspondence exchanged more or less regularly by the directors of the Academy in Rome and Marigny, the *Surintendant des bâtiments*. In 1757, Natoire made absolutely no mention of Fragonard; but on one occasion, he expressed discontent, his reproaches aimed at the pensioners, as a group: "I made them start again what they had already done.... I hope that they will do better" (letter of November 2, 1757). However, on March 15, 1758, came the explosion: explaining why he had not been able to send to Paris any work by the pensioners, Natoire wrote that "the weakness of their talent is the cause of everything.... They do not know how to make choices...." Nonetheless, he added that they "want very much ... to do better than they can. I will do my utmost to make them stronger through these exercises [copies of old master paintings], for they are in great need of learning." According to the Goncourts (who obtained their information from Théophile), Natoire went so far as to accuse Fragonard of "not being the author of the painting that brought him to Rome. He threatened to write to Paris, and Fragonard managed, with great difficulty, to obtain a reprieve of three months." Natoire, however, did not despair: he even negotiated to obtain permission for the three new pensioners—Monnet, Brenet, and Fragonard—to copy works by Caravaggio, Guido Reni, and Pietro da Cortona, as the regulations of the Academy required. He had chosen these works with great care "so that the three different manners of painting would make each [pupil] study what he needed most." In Fragonard's case, the remedy—in the form of Pietro da Cortona's *Saint Paul Restored to Sight* (figure 1)—worked, but his copy has been lost. It was only on May 3, 1758, *almost a year and a half after his arrival* in Rome, that Fragonard was finally mentioned by Natoire, who spelled his name "Flagonart" (and would never get it right): the director sent to Paris a few "studies"—one, of a male nude; some mysterious "drawings"; and a *Head of a Priestess*. The Academicians expressed satisfaction with the "drawings," but found the *Head of a Priestess* "somewhat insipid," and they were disappointed by the study of the male nude: "[Fragonard's] brilliant tendencies" in Paris had led them to expect more from him! In August 1758 and again in October, Natoire still expressed reservations, but he recognized that Fragonard had "tendencies," shrewdly noting that "genius requires a little freedom." Natoire may not have understood him, but he respected him. Besides, Fragonard was working and "advancing" in his studies. The crisis had passed ... so much so that, in August 1759, Natoire agreed with Cochin that it would be good for Fragonard to stay for a fourth year in Rome: "It is more fitting that he enjoy this advantage than the two [Brenet] brothers—all the more so because he strongly wishes it. His talent holds more promise than that of the painter Brenet."

Upon receiving another male figure study in Paris, the Academicians responded in a way that seems surprising today: "We are satisfied.... However, we fear that an excess of care may completely extinguish the fire that we associate with this artist...." There is none of the "easy brushwork," none of the "lively and daring tonalities of the enthusiast" that earned his reputation in Paris. "Everything is blended together, well finished. It is time that M. Fragonard had confidence in his talents and, working with more assurance, regained the spark and the pleasing facility that he had before...." Natoire was able to reassure his Parisian colleagues: "*Flagonard* has much talent" (October 1759); "*Flagonard*'s natural fire is in no danger of dying out. From time to time, I see things by him that give me cause for much hope" (November). Thus had Natoire—

Figure 1. Pietro da Cortona. *Saint Paul Restored to Sight*. Church of the Capuchins, Rome

Figure 2. Gabriel de Saint-Aubin.
Page from the Natoire collection
sales catalogue (1778).
Bibliothèque Nationale, Paris

who owned four of the artist's works (see figure 2), probably all painted in Rome (see cat. no. 33; figures 3–5)—been won over by Fragonard.

In 1760, Fragonard, "working successfully...with much promise," met the Abbé de Saint-Non and spent several months at work in Tivoli (see cat. nos. 24–27). In 1761, he made a short trip to Naples with Ango, and then an arduous return trip to France with Saint-Non (see cat. nos. 43–65). At Colorno, he painted a *Pan and Syrinx* (figure 6) for the powerful minister of Parma, Du Tillot. He was back in Paris on September 26, 1761, with four more years to go before achieving fame.

All of the "official" works that Fragonard was required to execute for the Academy in Rome—including the copy after Pietro da Cortona; the *Head of a Priestess;* the figure studies in oil; and the drawings—have been lost, except for a few life studies of "the model, with drapery and various costumes," such as those in the Louvre and in Montpellier (see cat. nos. 11, 12).

Included here are not only a large number of drawings unquestionably done in Italy, but also a group of paintings that—as we will point out in their respective entries—were also executed in Italy. These paintings may be divided into two categories: the landscapes, such as the *Wagon in the*

Figure 3. Fragonard.
"Two Children in Their Cradle."
Private collection, New York

Figure 4. Fragonard. *War.*
Private collection, Paris

Figure 5. Fragonard. *Peace.*
Private collection, Paris

Figure 6. Fragonard.
Pan and Syrinx.
Private collection, Florence

Mud (in the Louvre), which probably dates to 1759, the *View of Tivoli,* painted one year later, and the *Jeu de la Palette* (in Chambéry); and the scenes of everyday life in Rome: such as female figures at the fountain, laundresses, and washerwomen. To these should be added a major work, *The Stolen Kiss,* which once belonged to the bailiff of Breteuil; it displays the smooth execution and finish that was so little appreciated by the Academicians in 1759, here compensated for by the lively and free brushwork of the oil sketch. Judging from eighteenth-century sales catalogues, Fragonard's output in Rome was abundant. He may have been disheartened during the first two years of his stay, but in the two years that followed he painted a great deal and, as we shall see, drew even more.

Although some of the Roman paintings reflect traces of Boucher's influence (see figure 7), most of them are characterized by an inspiration and an execution that are quite different from those of the works that preceded his departure for Italy; this is evident in a previously unpublished painting (see figure 8), known to have been sold January 30, 1782 (no. 78). *The Stolen Kiss* indicates another direction, but Fragonard was more at ease in works executed rapidly, and in which he did not linger over

Figure 7. Fragonard.
Interior of a Stable, with a Shepherdess.
Private collection, Paris

Figure 8. Fragonard.
Woman with a Child before a Fire.
Whereabouts unknown

details. Why this technique and these subjects? Rapidity of execution reflects accuracy of perception, an evocation of the moment, an "atmosphere" captured with keen penetration. As for the genre scenes, they are in the tradition of the "Bamboccianti" (who originated a style in Rome in the seventeenth century), but nowhere do they express a social consciousness, a search for realism, or even an interest in the picturesque on Fragonard's part. If the subjects chosen are commonplace, "anonymous," it is so that we may better appreciate the virtuosity of his painting and can "savor" it more completely.

The drawings, done in red or in black chalk, are of two main types: landscapes, and copies after old masters. Here again, aside from his virtuosity, the keenness of Fragonard's observation is amazing. If there is anything "photographic" about these works, it is Fragonard's extraordinary ability to choose the right angle; to "frame" the subject from the most surprising, the least recognizable, viewpoint; and to see everything—from the familiar cypress trees, to the masterpieces of Rubens and Raphael—with a fresh eye.

This skill did not come all by itself. Two artists in particular seem to have had something to do with it: Natoire, and Hubert Robert. We know that Natoire was in Tivoli for a few weeks in June (?) 1759, and that he worked there in April 1760 (see cat. no. 36). Natoire liked to draw the Roman countryside (see figure 9), but was not the first—not even the first director of the Academy—to do so, for Nicolas Vleughels had already led the way. Yet, Natoire felt strongly enough about the value of this exercise —at a time when history painting still reigned supreme—to write to his superior: "I consider this part...[drawing] views of the outskirts of Rome... quite necessary for the training of our young pupils. I encourage them not to neglect it by setting an example myself" (January 17, 1759—the date is significant).

Hubert Robert, who had arrived in Rome in 1754, became a pensioner only in 1760, but he soon came to the director's attention (see figure 10). Not more than one month after having sent off his defense of landscape painting, Natoire wrote to Marigny: "I wish that all [who, precisely?]... could make progress as noticeably as Sr. Robert [this is the first mention of his name].... He is a good student, who works with unrelenting ardor, in the manner of Jean Paul [Giovanni Paolo] Panini. Although I keep citing him as an example, there are few who imitate him."

Was Fragonard—Robert's elder by one year—among them? (The question as to who preceded whom is still a subject of heated debate. We will

Figure 9. Charles-Joseph Natoire.
View of Tivoli. 1758. Musée Atger,
Faculté de Médecine, Montpellier

Figure 10. Hubert Robert.
Interior of the Colosseum. 1759.
Musée des Beaux-Arts, Valence

Figure 11. Fragonard.
The Hermit's Court in the Colosseum.
Private collection, United States

Figure 12. Attributed to Hubert Robert.
The Hermit's Court in the Colosseum.
Musée des Beaux-Arts, Besançon

Figure 13. Fragonard.
Roman Landscape.
Private collection, London

Figure 14. Fragonard.
View of the Belvedere.
Museum Boymans-van Beuningen,
Rotterdam

Figure 15. Fragonard.
View of the Porta Maggiore, Rome.
Kupferstichkabinett, Berlin-Dahlem

Figure 16. Fragonard. *View of the Circus
Maximus.* École Nationale Supérieure
des Beaux-Arts, Paris

Figure 17. Attributed to Hubert Robert.
Italian Landscape.
Palais des Beaux-Arts, Lille

Figure 18. Attributed to Hubert Robert.
Italian Landscape ("The Love Nest").
The Art Institute of Chicago

address this issue later, in connection with Saint-Non.) Robert, who was more constant, more professional, but less inspired, had already indicated, in Rome, that he did not have the same ambitions as Fragonard. He preferred ruins to trees.

Fragonard's triumph with the Tivoli series was preceded by much artistic searching, but few drawings have come down to us (from 1757: A. 857. From 1758: A. 1497 a; A. 385, fig. 136; Williams, 1978, no. 2, ill; see figure 11. Can we be certain that the Besançon version—see figure 12—is by Robert? From 1759: A. 2313, 1483, 888—see figure 13—1581, 377. These drawings, and a few others of the same type: A. 313, 317, 368[?], 884, 910[?], 916, 1440—see figure 14—1613, 2310 [in Budapest], 2281, 2283—see figure 15—include only those in museums). A previously unpublished drawing that was recently acquired by the École des Beaux-Arts (see figure 16), along with the collection of the late Paul Mathias, shows how difficult it can be to distinguish between Fragonard and Robert; the characteristic technique—the chalk being pressed heavily against the paper—makes us hesitate to attribute to the former the famous drawings in Lille (see figure 17; A. 960) and in Chicago (see figure 18; A. 959)—all the more so because they are inscribed "Napoli 1760," which would indicate the authorship of Hubert Robert, who was in Naples that year. More surprising is the absence of pen-and-ink drawings, apart from the one in Chicago (see cat. no. 19). Can we accept the drawing sold at Sotheby's, London, October 21, 1963, no. 139, which bears Fragonard's name and the date 1757 (see figure 19)?

What did Italy offer Fragonard? Of the masters of the past, Fragonard himself mentions the names of Barocci and of Pietro da Cortona. In 1758, the Academy reproached him for his dependence on the former: "Barocci is an admirable painter in many respects, but his color is a dangerous example to follow." He copied many of Pietro da Cortona's works, especially for Saint-Non (Fragonard does not mention Castiglione, but there were many of that artist's works in French collections in the eighteenth century). As for contemporary painters, we have little information. The French artists at the Academy in Rome tended to harbor disdain for their foreign colleagues. In 1750, Cochin considered "the French school greatly superior." The only exceptions were Piazzetta, Tiepolo, and Solimena. Fragonard actually encountered the last painter's work only in Naples in March 1761, a few months before the end of his stay in Italy, and he did not discover Tiepolo—interestingly enough, the sole living Italian artist whose work he engraved in Paris, a revealing choice—until he was on his way back to the French capital.

Fragonard, however, returned from Italy with something much more essential: *color*. Not just color for the sake of color—even before Rome, he already liked using a wide range of yellows—but the warmth of color, the cleverness of color. Pierre, who had preceded Fragonard in Rome between 1735 and 1740, and who later succeeded Boucher as First Painter to the King, understood this when he wrote to Marigny in 1770: "All of the artists who return from Italy have a feel for color, often real color; but they lose it little by little because they cater to the prevailing taste for light hues; they must please if they want to find work" (*Corr. des Dir.*, XII, p. 298). Fragonard himself became attracted to light colors, but would he ever lose the *color* that he had learned in Italy?

According to Joseph Farington (1804), the painter Philippe-Jacques de Loutherbourg (1740–1812), who had known Fragonard, said of him that "he had much talent for painting, but soon lost in Paris a great part of the excellence that he had shown in Italy." Cochin wrote as much to Jombert: "Fragonard . . . is a clever man, but by no means should you take him for an example. He spoiled his own work in Rome by a misguided imitation of M. Mengs; before leaving for Italy, he used color like the renowned Lemoine; there, he got his blues, violets, golden yellows, greens, etc." (see Cochin, 1849; Locquin, 1914).

Figure 19. Attributed to Fragonard. *Tancred Baptizing Clorinda.* Whereabouts unknown

CHRONOLOGY

1756

November 24
The Brenet brothers, already in Rome, inform Natoire that Fragonard, Dhuez, and Monnet, who are accompanying Mme Vanloo to Turin, will arrive soon (*Corr. des Dir.*, XI, p. 164).

December 22
Natoire apprises Marigny of the arrival of the last three pensioners at the Académie de France, in the Palazzo Mancini (see figure 1; *Corr. des Dir.*, XI, p. 168).

1757

April 6
The new pensioners make drawings of the Carracci's frescoes at the Palazzo Farnese (letter from Natoire to Marigny, *Corr. des Dir.*, XI, p. 178).

November 2
Natoire suggests to Marigny that the three new pensioners copy Pietro

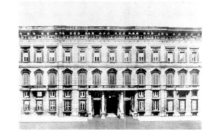

Figure 1. Palazzo Mancini, Rome

da Cortona's *Saint Paul Restored to Sight* and Guido Reni's *Saint Michael* in the Church of the Capuchins, and Caravaggio's *Entombment* in the Chiesa Nuova (today in the Pinacoteca at the Vatican). He adds that he cannot send any of their studies yet because he considers them too weak (*Corr. des Dir.*, XI, pp. 199–200).

November 23
Marigny approves the choice of the three paintings to be copied by the new pensioners (*Corr. des Dir.*, XI, p. 200).

1758

March 15
Natoire still cannot send Marigny any of the studies by the young painters: "la foiblesse de leurs talents et la cause de tout; ils ne sçavent s'arrêtter à aucun party, et, quoyque je puisse dire pour les fixer, je vois à tout moment des changements qui le prouve" (*Corr. des Dir.*, XI, p. 207).

April 12
Natoire writes to Marigny that "les élèves vont commencer leurs copies d'après le Guide, Pietre de Cortone et le Caravage" (*Corr. des Dir.*, XI, p. 209).

May 3
Studies by Dhuez, Fragonard, and Brenet are submitted for the first time (letter from Natoire to Marigny, *Corr. des Dir.*, XI, p. 210).

July 6
Pope Clement XIII succeeds Benedict XIV.

July 31
"La figure académique d'homme, peinte par le sʳ Fragonard, a paru moins satisfaisante que si on n'avoit pas connu les dispositions brillantes qu'il fit paroître à Paris, non qu'il y ait aucune marque de négligence, mais on craint que l'imitation de quelques maîtres ne luy nuise et ne le fasse tomber dans des tons de couleurs maniérés, comme il paroît dans cette figure par plusieurs demies teintes trop bleues et d'autres aurores qui ne sont pas naturelles. On peut croire qu'il les a imitées du sʳ Barrocci, peintre admirable à plusieurs égards, mais dont la couleur peut être dangereuse à imiter. Exortés-le donc à ne regarder dans les grands maîtres que ce qui caractérise en eux une imitation vraye de la nature.
"Il en est de même de sa tête de *Prêtresse*, qu'on trouve peinte d'une manière un peu trop doucereuse; mais on a esté plus satisfait de ses desseins, qu'on trouve dessinés avec finesse et vérité" (letter from Marigny to Natoire, *Corr. des Dir.*, XI, p. 216).

August 30
Natoire replies to Marigny: "*Flagonard*, avec des dispositions, est d'une facilité éthonante à changer de party d'un moment à l'autre, ce qui le fait oppérer d'une manière inégale" (*Corr. des Dir.*, XI, p. 232).

October 18
"Le sʳ *Flagonard* avance celle [the copy] qu'il fait d'après Pietre de Cortone, aux Capucins; ce jeune artiste a un peu de peine à peindre les chairs et à donner le vray caracterre des airs de teste. Je l'exhorte à ne point se lasser pour le retoucher de nouveau, car il s'imagine déjà avoir fait tout ce qu'il faloit et tout ce qu'il pouvoit" (letter from Natoire to Marigny, *Corr. des Dir.*, XI, p. 239).

1759

July 10
Marigny (in a letter to Cochin) agrees to allow Fragonard to prolong his stay in Rome, to fill the fifth place left vacant at the Academy (*Corr. des Dir.*, XI, p. 283).

July 12
"Sur le raport qui m'a été fait des espérances qu'on pourroit concevoir des dispositions du sʳ Fragonard, je serois disposé à luy donner la préférence s'il la désire et s'il est déterminé à en proffiter" (letter from Marigny to Natoire, *Corr. des Dir.*, XI, p. 285).

August 8
Natoire is favorable to prolonging Fragonard's stay: "son talent donne beaucoup plus d'espérances que celuy du sʳ Brenet, peintre" (letter to Marigny, *Corr. des Dir.*, XI, p. 294).

August 22
Natoire sends Marigny "deux accadémies peintes par les sʳˢ *Flagonard* et Monnet" (*Corr. des Dir.*, XI, p. 294).

September 5
"Puisque le sʳ Fragonard mérite la préférence pour lui accorder une quatrième année de résidence à Rome et qu'il la désire, sur les bons témoignages que vous me rendés de lui, je lui donne avec plaisir mon agrément" (letter from Marigny to Natoire, *Corr. des Dir.*, XI, p. 305).

October 11
"On est satisfait de l'exécution soignée et de l'étude qu'on remarque dans la figure académique d'homme, peinte par le sʳ Fragonard; cependant, on craint que l'excès des soins ne refroidisse entièrement le feu que l'on connoissoit dans cet artiste. La peine s'y laisse appercevoir, et l'on n'y découvre point de ces heureux laissés [*sic*], ny de cette facilité de pinceau qu'il portoit peut-être cy-devant à l'excès; mais qu'il ne faut cependant pas perdre entièrement en les rectifiant. Sa couleur ne présente point de ces tons frais, hazardés par l'enthousiasme et qui sont suivis du succès dans un artiste qui a étudié son talent et qui se livre avec connoissance aux mouvements de son génie. Tout est fondu, tout est fini. Il est tems que le sʳ Fragonard prenne confiance en ses talents, et que, travaillant avec plus de hardiesse, il retrouve ce premier feu et cette heureuse facilité qu'il avoit, et qu'il semble qu'une étude trop sérieuse a captivés presqu'au point de les détruire.
"On est très satisfait de ses desseins; ils sont purs, savans et corrects; mais ne sont-ils pas dessinés avec trop peu d'arrondissement et d'effet? Ils seroient infiniment louables s'ils étoient de quelqu'un qui se destinât à la sculpture; mais un peintre doit-il oublier la couleur et l'effet, même quand il dessine?" (letter from Marigny to Natoire, *Corr. des Dir.*, XI, p. 313).

October 24
Natoire sends Marigny the copies after Guido Reni, Caravaggio, and Pietro da Cortona, executed respectively by Monnet, Brenet, and Fragonard: "*Fragonard* a beaucoup de talan; mais le trop de feu et peu de patience l'emporte à ne pas travaillez avec assé d'exatitude ses copies; c'est ce que vous verés dans celle qu'il a fait d'après Pietre de Cortone" (*Corr. des Dir.*, XI, p. 317).

November 7
"Il n'y a point [à] appréhander que le sʳ *Flagonard* rafroidisse le feu qu'il a naturelement pour son talen. Il est vray qu'il arrive quelquefois que, pour vouloir se surpasser, on se trouve au-dessous de soy-même; mais je crois que celuy-cy reprendra aisément ce que la nature luy a donné, et je vois de luy des choses par intervalles qui me donnent de grandes espérances" (letter from Natoire to Marigny, *Corr. des Dir.*, XI, p. 318).

November 21
The Abbé de Saint-Non arrives in Rome with Hugues Taraval, then goes on to Naples (letters from Natoire to Marigny, and from Marigny to Natoire, *Corr. des Dir.*, XI, pp. 319, 322).

November 22
Marigny advises Natoire to take the necessary precautions for the delivery of the copies by Monnet, Fragonard, and Brenet: "j'apprends avec plaisir que vous êtes content de celles [the copies] qu'ils ont faittes pendant les vacances, à dessiner le modèle avec des draperies et différents habillemens. Ils peuvent tirer un grand avantage de cette étude" (*Corr. des Dir.*, XI, p. 321).

1760

March 19
After a second visit to Naples with Hubert Robert, from April to June 1759, Saint-Non makes plans to return to France with Fragonard (letters from Natoire to Marigny, *Corr. des Dir.*, XI, pp. 334, 337, 343).

April 24
Marigny approves this plan: "il voyagera avec un amateur et sera à portée de faire des études des beaux morceaux qui sont à Venise et dans les autres villes sur cette routte" (letter to Natoire, *Corr. des Dir.*, XI, p. 339).

April 30
Cochin informs Marigny that Fragonard will leave the Academy at the beginning of autumn (*Corr. des Dir.*, XI, p. 340).

July
Saint-Non and Fragonard are in Tivoli (letter from Natoire to Marigny, *Corr. des Dir.*, XI, p. 354).

See also the Abbé de Saint-Non's *Journal* (Rosenberg and Brejon, 1986, pp. 159–62): "la Villa d'Est est une des plus agréables habitations que je connoisse, et je me ressouviendrai toujours avec plaisir du séjour que j'y ai fait pendant 2 ou 3 mois de suitte."

August 27
"M. l'abbé de Saint-Nom est depui un moy et demy à Tyvoli avec le pensionnaire *Flagonard*, peintre. Cet amateur s'amuse infiniment et s'occupe beaucoup. Notre jeune artiste fait de très belles études qui ne peuvent que luy aitre très utiles et luy faire beaucoup d'honneur. Il a un goût très piquant pour ce genre de paysage, où il introduit des sujets champestre qui luy réussissent" (letter from Natoire to Marigny, *Corr. des Dir.*, XI, p. 354).

September 26
Marigny expresses to Natoire his satisfaction that Fragonard is working with Saint-Non in Tivoli (*Corr. des Dir.*, XI, p. 359).

November
Fragonard requests authorization to continue lodging at the Academy until after the winter, when he will leave with Saint-Non (letter from Natoire to Marigny, *Corr. des Dir.*, XI, pp. 363–64).

December 17
Natoire thanks Marigny on Fragonard's behalf for his approval of the latter's request (*Corr. des Dir.*, XI, p. 367).

December 24
Marigny informs Natoire that Fragonard must pay for his room and board at the Academy (*Corr. des Dir.*, XI, p. 369).

Beauvarlet makes an engraving of *The Seesaw*, after Fragonard (see cat. no. 6).

1761

January 21
Natoire asks that room and board and the usual prerogatives accorded the pensioners be granted to Fragonard and Monnet, "jusqu'à l'arrivée des deux nouveaux [Gois and Durameau] qui doivent les remplacer" (*Corr. des Dir.*, XI, p. 371).

January 28
Birth in Grasse of Marguerite Gérard, daughter of Claude Gérard, perfume seller, and Marie Gilette (Nice, Arch. Dept.).

February 12
"Je consent, sur les bons témoignages que vous m'avés rendu des sʳˢ Monnet et *Flagonard*, qu'ils jouissent du logement, de la table et des prérogatives de pensionnaires jusqu'à l'arrivée des nouveaux" (letter from Marigny to Natoire, *Corr. des Dir.*, XI, p. 374).

March 18
Fragonard is in Naples: "le sʳ *Flagonard* est bien prest de son départ; M. l'abbé de Saint-Nom, toujour porté à rendre service à ce pensionnaire, puisqu'il l'emmène avec luy, vient de l'envoyer à Naples, pour voir les belles choses que renferme cette ville avant de commancer leur voyage. Cet amateur porte avec luy une quantité de joly morceaux de ce jeune artiste qui, je crois, vous feront plaisir à voir" (letter from Natoire to Marigny, *Corr. des Dir.*, XI, p. 378).

In Naples, Fragonard obtains permission to draw in the Galleria Capodimonte with Ango: "desiderando i professori M. *Flagonard* ed Ango di poter disegnare alcuno dei quadri di celebri autori che si conservano in cod. R. Galleria in Capo di Monte, si è il Ré benignamente servito di concederne loro il permesso che hanno supplicato" (for this document, now lost, see Filangieri di Candida, 1902, p. 224, n. 23; Réau, 1911, pp. 407–8, n. 4).

April 14
"L'abbé de Saint-Non va partir dans le moment pour Florence. Il emmène avec lui le peintre Fragonard, et une bibliothèque de dessins de choses qui ont été copiées mille fois: il a cependant des morceaux de Naples et des environs de Rome, qui n'ont jamais paru et qui seroient bons pour votre ouvrage [*Recueil d'Antiquités*]. Vous les verrez à Paris le mois de septembre, et vous vous arrangerez là-dessus; car il ne m'a rien voulu donner" (*Lettres du père Paciaudi au comte de Caylus*, Serieys, 1802, pp. 228–29).

Saint-Non leaves Rome with Fragonard. Their itinerary is known to us from the abbé's journal, in which, however, his traveling companion is never mentioned (see Rosenberg and Brejon, 1986, p. 163). They

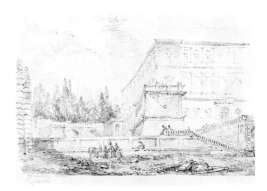

Figure 2. Fragonard. *View of the Palazzo Farnese at Caprarola.* Private collection, Paris

Figure 3. Fragonard. *The Martyrdom of Saint Peter,* after the painting by Titian formerly in Santi Giovanni e Paolo, Venice. Norton Simon Collection, Pasadena

Figure 4. Fragonard. *The Villa Rotonda of Palladio.* Norton Simon Collection, Pasadena

arrived in Ronciglione (see cat. no. 43) at the end of the day and then went on to visit the Palazzo Farnese at Caprarola (see figure 2).

April 15
"M. l'abbé de Saint-Nom vient de partir pour s'en retourner en France et mène avec luy le sr Flagonard, peintre pensionnaire, qui vient de finir son temps. Cet amateur va faire différentes pauses par tout les endroits où il trouvera de belles choses à voir. Ce jeune artiste, qui a fait des progrèst à Rome, profitera avec plaisir de cet avantage et fera encore des études partout où ils s'arrêteront" (letter from Natoire to Marigny, *Corr. des Dir.*, XI, p. 381).

Saint-Non and Fragonard are in Acquapendente (*Journal*, p. 163).

April 16
Siena (*Journal*, pp. 163–67).

April 17–May 5
Florence. From there, they visit Pisa, Livorno, and Lucca (*Journal*, pp. 168–88).

May 6
Bologna (*Journal*, p. 188).

May 7
Ferrara (ibid.).

May 8–June 23
Venice (*Journal*, pp. 189–214); see figure 3.

May 12
In a reply to Natoire, Marigny expresses his pleasure at the prospect of seeing Fragonard again soon (*Corr. des Dir.*, XI, p. 385).

June 3
The sculptor Gois and the painter Durameau arrived in Rome, as of May 28, to replace Monnet and Fragonard at the Academy (letter from Natoire to Marigny, *Corr. des Dir.*, XI, p. 385).

June 23–July 3
Saint-Non and Fragonard visit Padua and Vicenza, making a stop to see the Villa Rotonda built by Palladio: "c'est à coup sûr un de ses plus beaux ouvrages et entierrement terminé. Idée charmante que la forme extérieure de ce petit Edifice, les proportions, la noblesse et la sagesse en même temps de son architecture sont dignes d'être admirés" (*Journal*, pp. 124–224); see figure 4.

July 3–5
Verona (*Journal*, pp. 224–28).

July 5–6
Mantua (*Journal*, pp. 228–30); see figure 5.

July 6
Guastalla (*Journal*, p. 230).

July 7
Reggio (ibid.).

July 8
Modena (ibid.).

July 9–31
Bologna (*Journal*, pp. 230–31); see figure 6.

August 1
Parma (*Journal*, p. 231).

August 2–18
Colorno (*Journal*, p. 231), where they are received by the Minister Du Tillot, Marquis de Felino.

August 4
From Colorno, Saint-Non thanks Du Tillot for his reception in Parma: "... un beau tableau se voit et se laisse sans beaucoup de regrets mais il n'en est pas de même d'un homme aimable. Tout l'art de mon petit camarade [Fragonard] n'y peut rien et je ne voit à celà qu'une chose pour me dédommager, c'est de m'aimer un peu et de me donner quelquefois de vos nouvelles," adding in the postscript: "Frago me charge de ses hommages et je vous prie de présenter mille compliments à Mrs. Pecchetti et Maurini" (B.N., Rés. Est., published in part in Cayeux, 1964, p. 315). (According to A. Cavina [see *Journal*, pp. 314–15], Maurini was the painter Mauro Tesi [1730–1766], and Pecchetti, "should be read as Becchetti, a common name in Bologna.")

August 18
Saint-Non and Fragonard leave Colorno for Piacenza, where they stay until the 21st: "le Dosme est la seule Église qui mérite attention pour les Peintures des Caraches et du Guerchin, dont elle est ornée" (*Journal*, pp. 233–37); see figure 7.

Du Tillot writes to Trombetti, the governor of Piacenza, to announce the visit of Saint-Non, "mon bon ami avec le sieur *Fragonat* sujet de beaucoup de mérite dans la peinture sortant récemment de l'Académie

Figure 5. Fragonard. *The Temptation of Saint Anthony*, after the painting by Veronese, originally in the Cathedral of Mantua, and now in the Musée des Beaux-Arts, Caen. Norton Simon Collection, Pasadena

Figure 6. Fragonard. *Cain and Abel*, after a painting by Niccolò Tornioli in San Paolo, Bologna. Musée des Beaux-Arts, Rouen

Figure 7. Fragonard. *Angels*. Counterproof, after a fresco by Lodovico Carracci in the Cathedral of Piacenza. Private collection, Paris

de Rome; ce dernier désire prendre au vol un croquis des statues équestres de votre ville, et pour celà je le recommande à l'attention de votre seigneurie illustrissime pour qu'il puisse sans aucune difficulté satisfaire sa demande.

"Je sais qu'un autre sujet est actuellement occupé à lever des dessins desdites statues; et comme j'aurais pour infiniment agréable qu'ils fussent parfaits, votre Seigneurie illustrissime pourrait insinuer adroitement à celui qui s'y emploie d'écouter aussi le sentiment du nommé sieur *Fragonat* et de défférer aux conseils que l'habileté et l'expérience de celui-ci sauront suggérer à celui-là. Je suis déjà persuadé qu'il sera content du mérite d'un si excellent sujet et de sa modestie, qui le rend toujours plus aimable" (Parma, Archivio di Stato, carta Moreau de Saint-Méry, Accademia di Belle Arti, 28, Bédarida, 1928, p. 356).

August 21
Saint-Non and Fragonard leave Piacenza for Genoa, where they stay until September 10 (*Journal*, pp. 237–50).

Du Tillot again writes to Trombetti: "j'ai eu plaisir d'apprendre que Gilardo a bien accueilli les suggestions dudit peintre [Fragonard], et que ces étrangers sont partis bien contents des actes de politesses dont ils ont été l'objet et dont je vous reconnais comme le principal auteur" (Parma, Archivio di Stato, ibid.).

September 10
Saint-Non and Fragonard leave Genoa for Alassio (*Journal*, p. 250).

September 11
Antibes (*Journal*, p. 250).

September 12
Le Luc (*Journal*, p. 251).

September 13
Toulon (ibid.).

September 14
Aubagne (ibid.).

September 15
Marseilles (*Journal*, pp. 251–53).

September 16
Aix-en-Provence (*Journal*, pp. 253–54).

September 17
Nîmes (*Journal*, pp. 254–56).

September 18
Pont-Saint-Esprit (*Journal*, p. 257).

September 19
Saint-Vallier (ibid.).

September 20–21
Lyons (ibid.).

September 22
Senecay (ibid.).

September 23
Dijon (ibid.).

September 24
Vermenton (ibid.).

September 25
Moret (ibid.).

September 26
Saint-Non and Fragonard arrive in Paris (ibid.; Wille, 1857, 1, p. 180).

Saint-Non makes an engraving of Fragonard's *Gardens and Walls of the Villa d'Este* (cat. no. 38, figure 3).

70

The Itinerary of Fragonard's Return Trip from Italy, in the Company of the Abbé de Saint-Non

11 Man Seated on the Ground, Clasped Hands Raised to the Sky

Red chalk on paper, 32.5 x 52 cm.
Inscribed in ink on the mount: *fragonard pere fecit*.

Musée Atger, Faculté de Médecine, Montpellier, M. 44

Provenance
Xavier Atger (1758–1833): gift to the
Musée Atger, Faculté de Médecine, Montpellier, about 1828 (at the lower center is the
stamp, Lugt 38).

Exhibitions
Bern, 1954, no. 106

Bibliography
P. p. 300
R. p. 215
A. 244
Bjurström, 1982, under no. 951

Related works
There are three similar red-chalk drawings in
Montpellier (A. 241–243), all vertical in format and lighter in tone. We would attribute
all three to Fragonard (see figures 1–3), and
date them to his first stay in Italy, although
they might have been done slightly earlier.

Figure 1. Fragonard.
*Man Standing, Head Turned
to the Front*. Musée Atger,
Faculté de Médecine, Montpellier

Figure 2. Fragonard.
*Man Standing, Leaning
on His Hands*. Musée Atger,
Faculté de Médecine, Montpellier

Figure 3. Fragonard.
Bald Man, with Bowed Head.
Musée Atger,
Faculté de Médecine, Montpellier

1 2   Man Seated on the Ground, Leaning against a Wall

Red chalk on paper, 41 x 53 cm.
On the verso: counterproof study of a head (see figure 1)

Musée du Louvre, Paris, Cabinet des Dessins, Inv. 32963

Provenance
Comte d'Orsay (1748–1809): his stamp,
Lugt 2239, is at the upper right; entered the
Louvre during the Revolution (the stamp of
the Louvre, Lugt 1886, is at the lower right).

Exhibitions
Paris, 1983 (Orsay), no. 126, ill. (entry by
  J.-F. Méjanès)

Bibliography
Arnaud, 1930, p. 98, no. d. 86

Figure 1. Fragonard. Verso of catalogue no. 12

The Montpellier drawing was attributed to "Fragonard père" by Atger in the early nineteenth century. The Louvre drawing has been ascribed to Pierre Subleyras (1699–1749) by Odette Arnaud, and to André Le Brun (1733–1811) by Jean-François Méjanès, who remarked that "this drawing ... has much in common with the studies of draped figures that were bequeathed by F. X. Atger to the Faculté de Médecine, Montpellier, as by Fragonard: the same vigor, same sureness of line, same feeling for light."

The Louvre and the Montpellier drawings are by the same hand—this is confirmed by the fact that on the verso of the former there is a counterproof of a head of a hooded man that, in several details, is practically identical to the model in the Montpellier drawing—but is it the hand of Fragonard? His studies of draped figures had a certain reputation; engravings of many of them were made after his return from Italy. Three illustrate the chapter on drawing in Diderot's *Encyclopédie* (plates XVII, XVIII, XXVII, engraved by Robert Benard and by A.-J. de Fehrt [1723–1774]. See Roux and Pognon, VIII, 1955, pp. 491–92; Princeton, exhibition

Figure 2. A.-J. de Fehrt.
Kneeling Man with Hands Raised.
Bibliothèque Nationale, Paris

catalogue, 1977, no. 16, and *addenda*; on the *Encyclopédie*, Diderot, and the Beaux-Arts, see Pinault, 1984, 1986. For the third of these studies, which seems to date from before 1763, see figure 2). For works by Gilles Demarteau, see figure 3, and Roux, VI, 1949, no. 365; by Louis-Marin Bonnet, see figure 4, and Hérold, 1935, p. 129, no. 200.

There are a few other drawings that are similar in technique and conception to the ones in the Louvre and in Montpellier: figure 5 (Orléans, A. 770, fig. 213), figure 6 (Stockholm, Bjurström, 1982, no. 951, ill.), and figure 7 (Louvre, new acquisition, 1987, R. F. 41376), as well as others in private collections in Paris; see also Tokyo exhibition catalogue, 1980, no. 159, ill.

Fragonard, of course, was far from the only artist to have drawn academic figures of this type (which, as a group, deserve a comprehensive study). All of the pensioners had to draw some, providing an occasion for them to display their skill. Yet, Fragonard's seem to stand out for their monumentality, their simplified rendering of mass, and, especially, their pictorial unity. These were virtually the same qualities that impressed the Academicians in Paris when they received Fragonard's figure drawings in 1759: "We are very satisfied with his drawings. They are pure, skillful, and correct; but are they not drawn with too much roundness and effect? They would be infinitely praiseworthy if they had been done by one who aspired to be a sculptor. But then, must a painter forget color and effect, even when he draws?" (*Corr. des Dir.*, XI, p. 313).

The question remains: were they done in Rome? We are convinced that Fragonard drew academic figure studies in Paris, before his Italian sojourn, and probably after, but most of the drawings that we have mentioned—the one in the Louvre, and all those in the Orsay collection were unquestionably executed in Rome (an inscription on the Orléans drawing says as much)—date from his stay at the Palazzo Mancini. Natoire, the director of the Academy in Rome, had reintroduced the practice of drawing "during vacation time . . . all sorts of figures, draped in various costumes, especially ecclesiastical ones, which fall in such lovely folds" (letter of October 18, 1758, *Corr. des Dir.*, XI, p. 239). Studies of this kind were considered the best exercises for those who aspired to be history painters. There is no doubt that Fragonard's figure studies fulfilled the expectations of the Academicians in Paris, and convinced Natoire of the talents of his protégé.

Figure 3. Gilles Demarteau.
"Pense-Bien."
Bibliothèque Nationale, Paris

Figure 4. Louis-Marin Bonnet.
Seated Male Nude Pulling on a Rope.
Bibliothèque d'Art et d'Archéologie, Paris

Figure 5. Fragonard.
Standing Man Holding a Book.
Musée des Beaux-Arts, Orléans

Figure 6. Fragonard.
Bishop, with Outstretched Arms.
Nationalmuseum, Stockholm

Figure 7. Fragonard.
Seated Bishop.
Musée du Louvre, Paris, Cabinet des Dessins

13   Le Jeu de la Palette

Oil on canvas, 67.5 x 114.7 cm.
The painting was probably larger originally. A strip of canvas was added at the lower right; restored, 1961 and 1987.

Musées d'Art et d'Histoire, Chambéry

Provenance
[Baron Hector Gariod (or Hector de Garriod; 1803–1883)], an art dealer and native of Savoie, established in Florence; bequeathed to the Chambéry museum, at his death.

Bibliography
Chambéry museum catalogue, 1911, p. 147, no. 328 ("manner of Boucher")
Cuzin, 1986, pp. 58–59, notes 7–10, fig. 2 (color)

Related works
For the paintings in the Bergeret collection (W. 449, 450), see below.
 For the Frankfurt and Valence drawings and others related to this work, see the following entries.

This painting, whose state of preservation is far from perfect (see figures 1, 2), was published by J.-P. Cuzin in 1986; it has recently been restored. Fragonard's authorship is confirmed by the existence of preparatory drawings (see the following entries), but it cannot be confused with the painting representing "a gathering of Shepherds and Shepherdesses playing the game of *la palette*" that, on April 24, 1786, was included in the posthumous sale (no. 107) of the collection of one of Fragonard's principal patrons, Jacques-Onésyme Bergeret de Grancourt. This picture, like its pendant, "Young Boys and Girls swinging on the branch of a Tree; one of them playing a tambourine," measured 79 x 97 centimeters, and thus was squarer in format.

The present painting was executed during Fragonard's first stay in Italy, between 1756 and 1761. The drawings related to it, especially the "vibrant harmonies of the blues offset by the reds and oranges"; the visible brushwork, which is both agitated and supple; the profiles outlined in black—are all characteristic of the style of his Roman works.

Everything argues for a dating (1758?) early in his Italian stay, although it is difficult to establish a chronology for the four long years in which he not only discovered Italian painting, but also experienced a major artistic crisis—one from which he did not recover quickly.

As for how the game of "la palette" was played, the exact details have not come down to us: one of the young men is hitting the palm of a girl's hand with a wooden paddle while she turns her head away; behind him, another girl holds a ring....

As a pendant, Fragonard painted a scene with a seesaw—a subject that he had already represented, in Paris, and that he was to repeat often, although each time in a very different manner (see cat. nos. 6, 15, 162, 170).

Figure 1. Ultraviolet photograph of catalogue no. 13

Figure 2. Catalogue no. 13, with the overpainting removed

14   Le Jeu de la Palette

Red chalk on paper, 33.9 x 46.8 cm.
Folded down the middle.

Städelsches Kunstinstitut, Frankfurt am Main, Graphische Sammlung, Inv. 1234

Provenance
Dr. Johann Georg Grambs (1756–1817); given to the museum at Grambs's death; inventoried, 1862.

Bibliography
A. 820, fig. 222
Cuzin, 1986, p. 58, fig. 3
Stuffmann, 1986, no. 122, ill.

Related works
For the pendant, see the following entry.
A counterproof (figure 1), modified and reworked by Ango (?), was sold by Salamon, Agustoni & Algranti, Milan, November 25, 1985, no. 169, ill.
A bister-wash drawing with a very similar composition (figure 2), bearing "an almost illegible signature and the date 1771," was sold by the Galerie Charpentier, Paris, May 24, 1955, no. 122, ill., as "French school, 18th century."

It is worth mentioning a red-chalk drawing in Valence (figure 3) that is very close in composition and dimensions (32.5 x 43.5 cm.; A. 1439) to the *Jeu de la Palette* in Frankfurt, which came from the collection of Julien-Victor Veyrenc, as did the Frankfurt museum's famous works by Hubert Robert. The drawing was attributed first to Robert, then to Fragonard (Beau, 1968; Cayeux, 1970), and is today rejected as the work of either artist (Cayeux, 1985; Cuzin, 1986). Should this be?

To solve this controversy, we must take into account, on the one hand, Saint-Non's aquatint (see figure 4), dated 1766, after the work by Fragonard (Cayeux, 1964, no. 108), and, on the other hand, the drawing of "une vûe de la Ville d'Estre [*sic*] à Tivoli" that appeared in the Gros sale of April 13, 1778, no. 71, and that is now lost; we have an idea of what it looked like from the quick sketch that Saint-Aubin made in the margin of his copy of the sales catalogue (see figure 5). The composition of the aquatint is oriented like the drawing in Valence; that of the one in the Gros sale is reversed. The latter, therefore, has every chance of being the original drawing by Fragonard, which was later copied in Valence by an amazingly talented imitator. This hypothesis can only be verified once the drawing from the Gros sale resurfaces.

Figure 1. Ango (?), after Fragonard.
Le Jeu de la Palette. Counterproof.
Whereabouts unknown

Figure 2. After Fragonard.
Le Jeu de la Palette.
Whereabouts unknown

Figure 3. Attributed to Fragonard.
Le Jeu de la Palette.
Musée des Beaux-Arts, Valence

Figure 4. Abbé de Saint-Non, after Fragonard.
Le Jeu de la Palette.
Bibliothèque d'Art et d'Archéologie, Paris

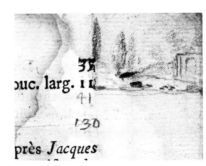

Figure 5. Gabriel de Saint-Aubin.
Detail of a page from the
Gros collection sales catalogue (1778).
Musée du Petit Palais, Paris

15 The Seesaw

Red chalk on paper, 33.9 x 46.2 cm.
Folded down the middle.

Städelsches Kunstinstitut, Frankfurt am Main, Graphische Sammlung, Inv. 1235

Provenance
See previous entry.

Bibliography
See previous entry (A. 821, fig. 223; Stuff-mann, 1986, no. 123, ill.)

Related works
The drawing in the École Polytechnique

(A. 822), which is badly damaged, is a counterproof heightened with a bister wash (figure 1).

The drawing in the Pushkin Museum, Moscow (A. 2112), is by an imitator (see figure 2), as are the ones in Washington (see figure 3; London exhibition catalogue, 1968, no. 613, fig. 269, "H. Robert"; Eisler, 1977, p. 337, dK 279, fig. 301) and in

Turin (see figure 4; Sciolla, 1974, no. 298, ill.).

For the drawing sold on May 24, 1955, no. 123, ill., see the previous entry; figure 5; and also A. 823, figs. 528, 2113.

W. and M. reproduce a painted version of this composition (under no. 595), catalogued among the "paintings attributed" to Fragonard.

The two splendid red-chalk drawings in Frankfurt are among Fragonard's most attractive and successful works from his Roman years. Judging by the crushed appearance of one side of each sheet, counterproofs of them were probably made. The interesting thing about these drawings is that they are very likely related to two paintings in the Bergeret collection that were lost after 1786. In any case, the *Jeu de la Palette* (cat. no. 14) repeats the (fragmentary) composition, viewed from farther away, of the picture in Chambéry (cat. no. 13). If this painting preceded the Frankfurt drawings—which, according to Stuffmann (1986), were done by Fra-

gonard in Paris some time after 1761—it would be impossible to say at what date Fragonard executed the two paintings that were formerly in the Bergeret collection. We date the Frankfurt drawings to 1760.

The fanciful setting for these two drawings is a rustic Rome overgrown with luxuriant vegetation. The games of the adolescents partake of the overabundance of nature. Altogether different is the world depicted by Hubert Robert, which is turned toward a past that he respected, more grandiose but lacking in warmth, more topographical but far less pantheistic.

Figure 1. Fragonard. *The Seesaw.*
École Polytechnique, Massy Palaiseau

Figure 2. After Fragonard.
The Seesaw.
Pushkin Museum, Moscow

Figure 3. After Fragonard.
The Seesaw.
National Gallery of Art, Washington, D.C.

Figure 4. After Fragonard.
The Seesaw.
Biblioteca Reale, Turin

Figure 5. After Fragonard.
The Seesaw.
Whereabouts unknown

15

16　The Stolen Kiss

Oil on canvas, 47 x 60 cm.

The Hermitage, Leningrad

Provenance
The painter Sébastien Leclerc II (1676–
1763): posthumous sale, December 17,
1764, no. 298: ''un jeune homme embras-
sant une jeune fille, pendant que sa camarade
lui tient les mains sur une Table couverte
d'un tapis avec des Cartes dont plusieurs sont
tombées par terre''; the Princes Yussupov,
Arkhangelskoye, from the end of the 18th
century, or from 1839 to 1924 (one of whom
met Greuze and mentioned Fragonard in
1789 and 1790); seized during the Russian
Revolution, and deposited in the Hermitage.

Exhibitions
Paris, 1965–66, no. 17, ill.

Bibliography
Yussupov collection catalogue, 1839,
　no. 369
Ernst, 1924, p. 122, ill.
Réau, 1928, no. 103
R. p. 157
Sterling, 1957, p. 51, pl. 48
Hermitage catalogue, 1958, I, p. 346,
　no. 5646
Zolotov, 1959, pl. 11, color details on cover
W. 118, fig. 75
W. and M. 128, ill.
Nemilova, 1975, pp. 440, 442, fig. 21
Hermitage catalogue, 1976, p. 231, no. 5646
Hermitage catalogue, 1986, no. 46, ill. (with
　detailed bibliography)

Related works
For the pendant, see cat no. 17. For the completed version, see cat. no 18.

16

17   Preparing the Meal

Oil on canvas, 47 x 61 cm.

Pushkin Museum, Moscow

Provenance
See previous entry. Sale of the Leclerc collection, 1764, no. 298: "une femme assise, ayant un enfant entre ses bras; elle découvre un vase qui est sur un fourneau, pour y mettre des herbes qu'un autre enfant apporte."
Deposited in the Hermitage, 1924; in the Pushkin Museum, 1925.

Exhibitions
Paris, 1965–66, no. 18, ill.

Bibliography
Yussupov collection catalogue, 1839, no. 365
Ernst, 1924, p. 124, ill.
Réau, 1928, no. 525
R. p. 168
W. 120, fig. 76
W. and M. 129, ill.
Pushkin catalogue, 1980, no. 66, ill.

Related works
See previous entry.

17

This oil sketch and its pendant were sold in 1764 at the posthumous sale of the collection of Sébastien Leclerc II, a painter of some renown. This is the earliest recorded sale of a painting by Fragonard. Although the two pictures are today divided between Moscow and Leningrad, they were considered—surprisingly enough—as pendants as far back as 1764. The subject of the Leningrad picture is easy to discern. In a rustic interior, two young girls are playing cards in the company of a young man; the one who loses receives a kiss from the young man, as her opponent holds her hands down on the table. Judging from her expression, which shows more curiosity and surprise than fright, she is not defending herself very forcefully.

Does *Preparing the Meal* depict the same young woman, a few years later? In this picture, she holds an infant in her arms and lifts the cover of a steaming kettle placed on a stove, around which three other children are busying themselves. Is there a link between these two subjects; are they two episodes of the same story? This seems unlikely, if only because Fragonard painted a "finished" version of *The Stol-*

en Kiss but, as far as we know, does not seem to have done so for *Preparing the Meal.*

Preparing the Meal has the merit of being a more objective title than those by which the picture was previously known: *The Unhappy Family* (Réau), *A Poor Family* (Wildenstein), and *The Happy Family.*

Mention, in the 1764 Leclerc sales catalogue, of the bold brushwork, which lends a charming freshness and spontaneity to these two oil sketches, indicates that it was already appreciated even then. (Note that in each picture there is a skillfully painted face in profile, with half-open mouth.)

In conclusion, we quote Sterling (1957) on what was then called *The Stolen Kiss:* "[It is] already lighter, executed with fluid strokes. It is a masterpiece of breathtakingly powerful and precise notations; a single line, a single point, suffice to construct a form, make it pulsate with life, render a sudden expression. The anecdotal subject, which is insignificant, has been masterfully sublimated by a pictorial wizardry that seems to be the perfect equivalent of the breath of life itself. It reminds one of the sketches of Rubens."

18 The Stolen Kiss

Oil on canvas, 48.3 x 63.5 cm.

The Metropolitan Museum of Art, New York, Gift of Jessie Woolworth Donahue, 1956, 56.100.1

Bibliography
G. pp. 257, 333
P. pp. 72, 276
N. p. 124 (reproduced between pp. 84 and 85 in the Goldschmidt-Rothschild copy)
R. pp. 65, 157
W. 119, pl. 31
W. and M. 127, ill.
Sutton, 1980; 1987, p. 106, fig. 4, p. 105
Ergmann, 1986, p. 74, ill.

Related works
Paintings
One version was in the Goldschmidt-Rothschild collection in Frankfurt am Main (see figure 1) in 1925 (exhibition catalogue, 1925, no. 73, ill.; 56 x 67 cm.). It had belonged to the Galerie Sedelmeyer in 1900 and in 1903, and may have been sold in Paris March 23, 1874 (no. 22). Another version (see figure 2) was sold in Paris, April 29, 1929 (no. 111, ill.; 45 x 55 cm.).

Drawing
In 1766, François Lonsing (1739–1799) made a drawing of the painting by Fragonard (see figure 3) that belonged to the Bailiff of Breteuil (on Lonsing's stay in Italy, from 1761, see the monograph by Meaudre de Lapouyade). The drawing, which was squared for transfer, was part of an album of copies—most of which were done by Ango—after the principal paintings in the collection of the Bailiff of Breteuil (Breteuil exhibition catalogue, 1986, no. 107).

Engraving
This painting was supposedly engraved in 1766 (Ernst and Réau) by François or Robert Brichet (on Brichet, see Roux, 1934, III, p. 369), who dedicated his engraving to the Marchesa "Gentile Baccupadule" or "Bassopadule" (W. and M.: "Boccapaduli?"). We have not been able to locate this engraving.

According to Le Brun, writing in the sales catalogue of the Bailiff of Breteuil's collection in 1786, "this lovely picture was painted in Italy." The drawing by Lonsing, done twenty years before, proves that Le Brun was alluding to Fragonard's first stay in Italy, between 1756 and 1761. Jacques-Laure Le Tonnelier (1723–1785), Bailiff of Breteuil, Ambassador of the Order of Malta in Rome, moved into the Palace of Malta in June 1758, but made his solemn entrance into Rome only in April 1759. A devoted collector, he had the paintings in his collection copied by Ango, in particular (Breteuil exhibition catalogue, 1986), but also by such other artists as Monnet and Lonsing. It is not known how he became acquainted with Fragonard and commissioned him to paint this scene. He must have gone about it with some discretion, for the pensioners of the Academy were supposed to work only for the king of France.

The precise date of this painting is not known, but it must have been done about 1759. The preceding year, Fragonard had painted a *Study of a Male Nude* (unfortunately lost) so

that the Academicians in Paris could evaluate his progress. Among other things, they noted "some mannered color ... overly bluish halftints and flesh tones that are unnatural. It seems as if they were copied from Barocci." The figure study submitted the following year was not greeted any better: this time, the Academicians criticized Fragonard's "blending" and the "finish" that are so apparent in the New York version of *The Stolen Kiss*.

The "finesse" of its execution has nothing in common with the "boldness" of the Hermitage painting (cat. no. 16), and yet the two works are of similar dimensions, which means that the picture in Leningrad cannot be considered as a preparatory sketch for the work in the Metropolitan Museum.

Although Fragonard did not radically change his colors from one painting to the next, he refined them: the white is silkier, the bright red becomes a lilac pink, and the dark blue, a shade of iris. The scene, which is rustic in one work, becomes pastoral in the other; the peasant tablecloth is

Figure 1. After (?) Fragonard.
The Stolen Kiss.
Whereabouts unknown

Figure 2. After Fragonard.
The Stolen Kiss.
Whereabouts unknown

Figure 3. François Lonsing, after Fragonard.
The Stolen Kiss.
Château de Breteuil

replaced by a "muslin carpet"; the adolescents have been transformed from greedy young people into ribald shepherds. The girl being kissed appears less astonished than curious; the young man less avid, less hurried, and more knowing; and their companion less envious, but more wanton and perverse.

It is interesting to note that in Rome and in Paris Fragonard apparently worked in two entirely different manners and in two opposite directions. Equally interesting is that *The Stolen Kiss*—whose subject we have already discussed in connection with the Hermitage painting—is still close to the world of Boucher: consider the girl on the left, whose head is turned away, all the while anticipating, by its finish and its composition, the works of Fragonard's mature period.

In closing, we quote Max Jacob (*Correspondance*, I, 1876–1921, Paris, 1953, p. 134), who reports that the Goncourts described this painting as "rather overly color-

ful" when they saw it in 1863, while they were working on their book on Fragonard: "It surprised the public by its preciousness—a fluid and highly finished execution that was rare for Fragonard, contrary to his habit and almost to his temperament. The little canvas displayed a refined color scheme of pale violets, straw yellows, moss greens, and soft pinks blending into delightful shades of a tea-colored rose; it seemed to have been painted with the misty palette of the master of *sfumato*, the great painter of the Assumptions and Nativities. Fragonard had tried to reproduce the fluid medium of the Spanish masters, their vaporous light, their hues seemingly wrapped in gauze. The white sleeves and bodice of the dress of the woman being kissed, her yellow skirt and her red petticoats, the faces and flesh tones, all of this gaiety of color softly bathed in a currant-colored light, as in a miniature by Murillo."

19 Wagon in the Mud

Pen and ink, and bister wash, on paper, 21.5 x 39.5 cm.
Signed (?) at the lower left: *fragonard Romae 1759* (the ink of the inscription is different from that of the drawing)

The Art Institute of Chicago, Gift of the Print and Drawing Club, 1936.4

Provenance
H. D[reux]: sold, Paris, February 3–4, 1870, no. 38(?) ("in pen and ink and watercolor. Signed," but no dimensions given); acquired by "Mayor" (for 160 francs); Princess Mathilde; Louis Gauderax, according to the Fauchier-Magnan sales catalogue; anonymous sale, June 12, 1917, no. 6; Viscomte Jacques de La xxx: sold, Brussels, July 3–4, 1919, no. 180, ill.; Adrien Fauchier-Magnan, Paris: sold, Sotheby's, London, December 4, 1935, no. 14, ill.; [Agnew & Son]; acquired by The Art Institute of Chicago, 1936.

Exhibitions
Washington, D.C., 1978, no. 3, ill.
Richmond, 1981, no. 1, ill.

Bibliography
P. p. 296 (the drawing in the Dreux sale)
Stanton, 1936, pp. 77–79, ill.
R. p. 221
W., p. 10 (French edition)
A. 825, ill.
Massengale, 1979, pp. 270–71, fig. 97
Cuzin, 1986, p. 66

Related works
For the painting in the Louvre, see the following entry.

Since Stanton's study (1936), this drawing has been linked with the one in Budapest (see figure 1) inscribed "fragonart" at the lower right (A. 827). The compositions of these two drawings are similarly oriented (and the reverse of the Louvre picture), but the Budapest drawing is much closer to the painting. The latter drawing was attributed to Fragonard by Eunice Williams (Washington, D.C., exhibition catalogue, 1978) and to Hubert Robert by Massengale (1979) and Cuzin (1986).

See also A. 824 (supposedly signed); figure 2 (A. 826, perhaps confused with the red-chalk drawing in the sale of the Maurice Lange collection, December 12, 1936, no. 55, ill.; this drawing, which faithfully copies the Louvre painting, seems to be by Ango); A. 828 (which, like the preceding drawing, comes from the Walferdin collection).

Perhaps even less is known of Fragonard's first drawings than of his early paintings. We have already presented a list—woefully short—of the drawings done before 1759, which is the date of the Chicago sketch, and have also tried to define the artist's style, or, rather, his different styles, before the pivotal date of 1760.

The drawing in Chicago, which has the tremendous advantage of bearing a date, 1759, that is beyond question, has recently been the subject of a study by Eunice Williams (1978). It is not exactly a preparatory sketch for the painting in the Louvre (see the following entry), but more of a first idea. The technique is a masterful combination of red chalk, pen and ink, and wash; the execution is brisk, more nervous and less stiff than that of the painting. In both works, Fragonard contrasted the movement of the heavily laden wagon with that of the herd of sheep arriving from the opposite direction to drink. Yet, the frieze-like composition of the drawing is more summary and less complex than that of the painting. There Fragonard kept the canopy that is flapping in the wind, but left out the shepherd driving his ox.

Figure 1. Attributed to Fragonard.
Wagon in the Mud.
Szépmüvészeti Múzeum, Budapest

Figure 2. Attributed to Ango.
Wagon in the Mud.
Whereabouts unknown

20   Wagon in the Mud

Oil on canvas, 73 x 97 cm.

Musée du Louvre, Paris

Provenance
Dr. Louis La Caze, by 1860; entered the Louvre with his collection, 1869.

Exhibitions
Paris, 1860, no. 157
Paris, 1974, no. 1, ill.

Bibliography
Bürger [Thoré], 1860, p. 349
Gautier, 1860, p. 2
Saint-Victor, 1860, unpaginated
Horsin-Déon, 1861, p. 119
Blanc, 1862, p. 16
G. pp. 281, 339
Mantz, 1870, p. 16
P. pp. 128, 273
R. p. 185
W. 103, pl. 12, p. 10 (French edition)
Thuillier, 1967, p. 70, colorpl.
W. and M. 111, ill., colorplates VIII, IX
Cuzin, 1986, pp. 59–61, 66

Related works
See previous entry.

The *Wagon in the Mud* caused a sensation in 1860 at an exhibition on the Boulevard des Italiens that was among the first to assemble a large number of French eighteenth-century paintings from private collections; it was also one of the first in which the Parisian public was able to rediscover the works of Watteau, Chardin, and Fragonard. Paul de Saint-Victor (1860) wrote appreciatively of "this rustic tragedy.... There is the poetry of a shipwreck in this wagon in distress, this stampeding herd. In this simple work, Fragonard equals the finest storms of Castiglione and of Guaspre [Gaspard Dughet]."

As for the Goncourts, ever lyrical and attentive to their

descriptions, they waxed ecstatic over "the smoky, gloomy, electric sky, shot with cracks of pale daylight, the heavy air, the warm breath of the churning earth, the tremulous agitation, the panic of Nature...."

This painting no doubt played an important part in reestablishing Fragonard's reputation in the mid-nineteenth century. However, it is far from being in perfect condition. Its restoration for this exhibition has rendered it more legible, but the worn areas, which show the coarse weave of the poorly primed Italian canvas, have been left as they were.

The composition is charged with a double, almost cinematographic movement: it is dominated by the covered wagon pulled by a large ox and pushed by two barelegged boys, as the sheep being driven by a young shepherd dressed in red and by a fearsome bulldog rush toward the pond in the foreground, raising a reddish cloud of dust. We can almost hear the grinding of the axles, the stomping of the herd, the dog's bell, and the sound of the rising wind.

Fragonard established a contrast between the greenish-gray sky with its white clouds and the reddish-brown earth. He sought to depict the frenetic activity on a country road, the encounter of two groups both trying to flee before the storm. The agitation of this scene is matched by its bold execution.

20: Detail

21　The Laundresses

Oil on canvas, 61.5 x 73 cm.

The Saint Louis Art Museum, 76.1937

Provenance
Private collection, Moscow (Rogers, 1938);
[Benedict Cathabard (1869?–1917), Lyons],
an antiques dealer, according to Wildenstein;
[Bachstitz Gallery, The Hague, 1921]; Pri-
vate collection, New York; [Arnold Seligmann
and Rey, New York]; acquired by the Saint
Louis Art Museum, 1938.

Exhibitions
New York, 1922, no. 6 (unverified)
Cleveland, 1956, no. 18, ill.
New York, 1958, no. 30, ill. p. 48
Baltimore, 1959, no. 11
London, 1968, no. 232
University of Notre Dame, 1972, no. 29, ill.
Atlanta, 1983–84, no. 51, colorpl.

Bibliography
Bachstitz Gallery catalogue [1921], I,
　no. 68, ill.
Rogers, 1938, pp. 30–31, ill.
Sterling, 1955, p. 152
R. p. 172
W. 361, fig. 153, p. 25 (French edition)
Thuillier, 1967, p. 64, colorpl.
W. and M. 383, ill.
Sutton, 1980; 1987, p. 105
Stockho, 1981, pp. 22–23, ill.

Related works

A smaller copy (42 x 48 cm.; see figure 1), known only from a photograph, has been sold a number of times, most recently at Fischer, Lucerne, June 12–16, 1956, no. 1551, ill. Catalogued by N. (pp. 40, 139), and W. and M. (no. 384), its execution seems more labored than that of the present painting.

For a drawing of the same subject (figure 2), but with an obviously different composition and date, see A. 95, fig. 42; Williams, 1978, no. 26, ill.

Figure 1. Attributed to Fragonard.
The Laundresses.
Whereabouts unknown

Figure 2. Fragonard. *The Laundresses.*
Private collection

Figure 3. Luca Giordano.
Christ Driving the Money-lenders from the Temple.
Chiesa dei Girolamini, Naples

Figure 4. Hubert Robert.
Christ Driving the Money-lenders from the Temple.
Gemäldegalerie, Berlin-Dahlem

Although nothing is known of the provenance of the Saint Louis picture, it is generally agreed that its subject is laundresses (*blanchisseuses*) and not washerwomen (*lavandières*), and that it was executed during Fragonard's years in Rome, between 1756 and 1761. During his first stay in Italy, Fragonard painted scenes of everyday life in the tradition of the seventeenth-century "Bamboccianti."

Here, under a vault that leads to a cellar, two young women surrounded by children tend a fire beneath a large cauldron, while a third carries a heavy basket of laundry on her head. At the right, another woman, leaning against a column on which hangs a gourd of the kind that Fragonard so often represented (see cat. no. 20), watches a child teasing a black dog with sparkling eyes. In the foreground, a shepherd plays with a small child.

A ray of light falls on the two young laundresses in the middle of the picture and on the shepherd and his dog. The flames from the fire cast a red glow on the bodice of one of the laundresses, on the arms of another, and on the face of the little girl at the right.

Fragonard described everyday scenes with great simplicity and without any social commentary. What interested him were the passages of light and shadow, the contrasts between sunlight and fire, and the effects of the steam; with a rapid execution, he tried to capture the scene as if it had been merely glimpsed. He composed with great care, placing the main subject in the middle ground, set off by the arch of the vault, the angle of the terrace, the roundness of the column, and the straight lines of the steps. The laundress who descends the stairs—relieving what would otherwise have been too geometric a composition—recalls a figure in Luca Giordano's fresco *Christ Driving the Money-lenders from the Temple* (figure 3) in the Chiesa dei Girolamini, Naples. Although Fragonard was not in Naples before March 1761, this was a famous fresco, and he could have seen the copy painted by Hubert Robert (figure 4), who had visited Naples with Saint-Non in April 1760.

22 The Laundresses

Oil on canvas, 59.5 x 73.3 cm.

Musée des Beaux-Arts, Rouen

Provenance
Hippolyte Walferdin (1795–1880); acquired by the Rouen museum at the sale of the Walferdin collection, Paris, April 12–16, 1880, no. 22 (for 1,400 francs).

Exhibitions
Paris, Musée de l'Orangerie, 1931, no. 18
Paris, 1934, no. 151
Munich, 1958, no. 58
Brussels, 1975, no. 105, ill. p. 148
Biot, 1985, p. 74, colorpl.

Bibliography
Portalis, 1880, p. 14
P. p. 272
N. p. 138
Réau, 1931, p. 31, ill. p. 20
R. p. 172
W. 362, pl. 72, p. 39 (French edition)
W. and M. 385, ill.
Munière, 1985, pp. 61–62, colorpl.

This painting was acquired in 1880 for the Musée des Beaux-Arts, Rouen, by the museum's curator, Edmond Lebel, through an intermediary, Adrien Darcel, administrator of the Gobelins, at the sale of the Walferdin collection—the largest group of works by Fragonard ever assembled. On this unique occasion only two French museums—those in Rouen and in Le Havre (see cat. no. 211)—obtained works by the artist!

The subject and format of this composition are so similar to those of the Saint Louis picture that the two were once considered as pendants: the same preoccupation with chiaroscuro, the presentation of the scene as if it were taking place on a platform, the illumination of the main figures and the foreground at the right, the backlighting, the column (there are two, and a pedestal, in this example), and the large black dog (here, with a white muzzle) are all features shared by the two works.

Yet, what they have most in common is their execution. The rapidity of the brushwork evokes the scene, rather than describing it precisely, making certain elements difficult to read. A young laundress wearing a white blouse and a yellow skirt, and with a red ribbon in her hair (three colors that Fragonard favored), tries to hang up a large white sheet. A group of helpers is gathered around the fire for warmth, while a young boy wearing a red hood prepares to climb onto a donkey that is resting on the ground.

The Rouen and Saint Louis pictures have often been compared to the "Fountain . . . in a Picturesque spot" (figure 1) and the "Child in an openwork wicker basket" (figure 2)—to quote their eighteenth-century titles. In the eighteenth century, the two paintings belonged to several famous collectors. Le Brun, who authenticated the works at the sale of the Gros collection (that of the painter Antoine-Jean Gros's father), on April 13, 1778, referred to them as "two sketches painted in Italy," alluding no doubt to Fragonard's first trip. Saint-Aubin sketched these compositions in the margin of his copy of the catalogue.

Fragonard probably painted these works—and others in the same spirit—about 1759–60. To quote Portalis (1880), the Rouen picture presents "one of those rays of light that pierces the dark recesses and turns the most sordid rags into bright notes of color" in a "delectable style," so prized in the eighteenth century, whose "spirited brushwork," taste for chiaroscuro and lighting effects, and freedom both in technique and in inspiration are so different from the works of the past—as well as from those by Hubert Robert (see figure 3), of a comparable date.

Figure 1. Fragonard.
Laundresses at the Fountain.
Private collection, New York

Figure 2. Fragonard.
A Mother Watching over Her Children.
Art market, Japan

Figure 3. Hubert Robert. *The Laundress.*
1761. Sterling and Francine Clark Art Institute, Williamstown, Massachusetts

23　The Happy Mother

Oil on canvas, 62 x 74 cm.

Private collection, Paris

Provenance
Barroilhet: sold, March 12, 1855, no. 36: "l'heureuse mère (belle esquisse) Toile. H 58 c. L. 71 c."; Duchesse de Polignac, née Crillon; Comtesse de Béhague; Marquis de Ganay, according to Wildenstein.

Exhibitions
Paris, 1946, no. 370
Bern, 1954, no. 14
Zurich, 1955, no. 88
London, 1968, no. 231, fig. 288

Bibliography
Blanc, 1857, II, pp. 601, 603
P. p. 289
N. p. 132
W. 364, fig. 155
W. and M. 386, ill. (pendant to cat. no. 22)

Related works
There is a second version of this painting (see figure 1), very close in composition, but smaller in format (44 x 53 cm.), that once belonged to the Walferdin and the Hochon collections (W. 363, fig. 154), and which was exhibited in Tokyo in 1980 (no. 55, ill.). We have not examined it, but the execution seems more labored than that of the Paris work.

The version of this subject (see figure 2; 49 x 59.5 cm.; W. 365, pl. 73) that is today in The Metropolitan Museum of Art, New York (see Sterling, 1955, pp. 152–53, ill.; M. Knoedler & Co. exhibition catalogue, New York, 1967, no. 69, ill.), is unquestionably autograph, but in certain details differs noticeably from the present painting.

A mother surrounded by her children—there are seven, but some may be young servants—leans toward her husband, who holds the neck of a sheep whose feet are bound. One of the youngest children tries to get near a plate of apples set on a white cloth. Fragonard must have been pleased with this composition, for, as noted above, he painted at least this one other version of it (figure 2). What is different about the latter is that, at the right, next to an antique altar, two young girls lean toward a cradle in front of which are a cat and a dog (rather awkwardly painted). Was this version painted before the Paris one, as Carla Lord supposes (*Masters of the Loaded Brush*, New York exhibition catalogue, 1967)? It is true that it is more sketchy, and that its sparkling composition appears (even) more improvised. Unfortunately, the relining of the New York picture has crushed the wonderful impasto that was so dear to Fragonard, so that it is difficult to compare it to the present version, which is in a perfect state

of preservation. One thing is certain, though: this painting, along with several others presented here, including those accompanying the introduction to this chapter, can be dated to the artist's first trip to Italy, about 1760.

Blanc (1857) described this picture as a "scene by Greuze illuminated like a Rembrandt by a sudden ray of light," and, as contemporary experts already remarked, with regard to similar works by Fragonard, it was done "at one go." The point for Fragonard was not the subject, nor to invent a surprising new composition, but just to paint with a freedom that, in effect, makes for the whole charm of the picture (and accounts for its appeal). Apart from the originality of the colors, the quality of the light, and the textural effects, there are the finely observed and quite humorous details of the white dog and black cat contemplating the happy family reunion, and the red crests of the turkeys emerging from the shadowy background of this rather modest interior.

Figure 1. Attributed to Fragonard.
The Happy Mother.
Whereabouts unknown

Figure 2. Fragonard.
The Happy Mother.
The Metropolitan Museum of Art, New York

Tivoli

Fragonard's ten red-chalk drawings (in Besançon) of Tivoli and of the Villa d'Este are among his most famous works, and rank with the best ever done in this medium. Although they have been greatly admired, how much do we know about them—of how they came into being, and of their place in relation to Fragonard's own ambitions and their significance for his career?

Natoire, writing from Rome, informed Marigny of the visit to Tivoli of Fragonard and Saint-Non, in a letter dated August 27, 1760: "Mr l'abbé de St No*m* has been at Tivoli with the painter Pensioner *Flagonard* for a month and a half. This *amateur* is keeping himself greatly amused and much occupied. Our young artist is making some very fine studies that will serve him well and do him much honor. He has a very lively taste for this kind of Landscape in which he introduces rustic subjects with great success." Saint-Non arrived in Rome on November 15, 1759, three years after Fragonard—who, as we know, experienced a major artistic crisis at the beginning of his own stay in Italy that he overcame with considerable difficulty.

Natoire's letter is our *only* source of information on this visit to Tivoli, which, according to Saint-Non (who never mentions Fragonard!), lasted "two or three months" (*Journal*, p. 159). Natoire himself had been in Tivoli the year before: "I spent about two weeks . . . in Tivoli. The air did wonders for my health.

Figure 1. Charles-Joseph Natoire. *Caprarola.* 1758. Kunstbibliothek, Berlin (Charlottenburg)

Figure 2. The Villa d'Este in 1909

I managed during my brief vacation to draw a few of the many views that this region offers" (letter to Marigny dated July 4, 1759). The drawing on page 114 (see cat. no. 35, figure 4) proves that Natoire returned there sometime in April 1760, underscoring the important part that he played in the discovery, or rediscovery, of the Roman landscape (see figure 1). We hasten to point out that, contrary to what has often been asserted, and in the absence of any proof, it is doubtful that Hubert Robert accompanied Saint-Non and Fragonard to Tivoli (see Cayeux, 1985, pp. 86–88).

The Villa d'Este was built in the sixteenth century by Pirro Ligorio (1512/14–1583) for Ippolito d'Este and his son Ludovico. In the eighteenth century, the villa and its famous gardens belonged to the Duke of Modena, Francesco III d'Este (1698–1780), the son-in-law of the Duc d'Orléans. It was an indispensable stop for visitors to Rome: "No painter leaves Rome without having made many drawings of the gardens of the Villa d'Este" (Bergeret, 1895 ed.). As Saint-Non wrote: "The situation and gardens of this Palace are the most delightful things in the world . . . [but] since the Duke never comes and puts very little money into their maintenance . . . today they are in a deplorable state" (*Journal*, p. 159; see figure 2). Saint-Non most likely rented the villa for his stay at Tivoli, but we do not know how he arranged this. In any event, he was very pleased with the spot. As he wrote in his *Journal* in a rare moment of exuberance: "I shall never forget my delightful sojourn there."

Fragonard undoubtedly shared his sentiments, and was no less pleased with the drawings that he executed there, for, as soon as he returned to Paris in 1761, he showed them to Mariette: "The Abbé de Saint-Non brought him [Fragonard] back with a large number of drawings that he had him make, and among which I saw many views of Rome done in a manner and a technique that I liked very much." Four years later, Mariette, who had either bought or been given "two landscapes drawn in Rome and four large landscapes . . . of the environs of Rome . . . done in red chalk" (figure 3), wrote of Fragonard: "Being in Rome, he drew a large number of views, especially, of the . . . d'Este gardens at Tivoli, which were done with much spirit and in which a great intelligence prevails" (Mariette, 1853–54, p. 263).

As was the custom in the eighteenth century, the drawings done by Fragonard at the Villa d'Este became the possession of the patron—the Abbé de Saint-Non. He made an aquatint of one, in 1761 (see cat. no. 38), and of three others in 1764 (see cat. nos. 33, 34; figure 4), and lent at least two to the Salon of 1765 (cat. nos. 31, 32), but there is no proof that they were exhibited again in 1767, as has often been

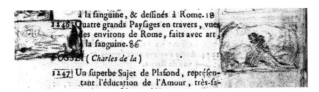

Figure 3. Gabriel de Saint-Aubin. Page from the Mariette collection sales catalogue. Museum of Fine Arts, Boston

Figure 5. Fragonard.
View of the First Cascade at Tivoli.
Musée Atger, Montpellier, Faculté de Médecine

Figure 4. Abbé de Saint-Non, after Fragonard.
View of the Entrance to Tivoli.... 1764.
Bibliothèque Nationale, Paris, Cabinet des Estampes

Figure 6. Fragonard.
Italian Landscape.
Formerly Collection John Nicholas Brown

Figure 7. Fragonard.
The Ruins of Hadrian's Villa, near Tivoli.
Museum Boymans-van Beuningen, Rotterdam

claimed. According to Pierre-Adrien Pâris (1806), he may even have exhibited the entire series in 1765: "This precious collection was presented at the Salon that followed the reception of *flagonard* at the Academy: it was executed for the Abbé de Saint-No*m*." It is not known how these ten drawings found their way into the collection of Pâris, who bequeathed them to his native city, Besançon, in 1819. It may be that, as Brizard reported (1792), in 1765, at the time when Fragonard became an "overnight" celebrity, and his "productions suddenly fetched extraordinary prices," Saint-Non returned to him the drawings that had been in his possession since 1760. Fragonard kept them for a time before selling them—at an undetermined date—to Pâris. This would explain his repetitions (often in bister wash) of such drawings as the *Avenue of Cypress Trees at the Villa d'Este* (cat. no. 31; now in the Graphische Sammlung Albertina, Vienna), as well as the copies by Pâris himself.

While he was at Tivoli, Fragonard executed not just the ten famous red-chalk drawings, but he also made many other sketches (see figures 5–7). While often only vaguely mentioned in eighteenth-century sales catalogues, these sketches were acknowledged as sources of inspiration for his paintings. Of the three that have been published, one is presented here, although there are painted versions of many more of them (see cat. no. 26). When did he paint them? Upon his return to Rome from Tivoli, or back in Paris? An examination of the pictures in the Louvre and the Wallace Collection, and of the one formerly in the Florence Gould collection, has shown that the actual canvas itself is a coarse weave and of a quality that was common in Italy—thus tending to confirm the first hypothesis.

Earlier, we pointed out that in the eighteenth century the Villa d'Este and its gardens were in poor condition and "badly maintained" (de Brosses, 1931 ed., II, p. 304), and Cochin (1758), who visited Tivoli ten years before Fragonard, corroborates this. We have an idea of their true appearance from the rather mediocre but faithful series of engravings made in 1685 by

Figure 8. Hubert Robert.
View of the Temple of Jupiter Serapis.
Private collection, Paris

Figure 9. Attributed to Hubert Robert.
View of the Temple of Jupiter Serapis.
Graphische Sammlung Albertina, Vienna

Giovanni Francesco Venturini. Did Fragonard depict the gardens in their actual state, or did he freely interpret the views that inspired him? The scholarship so far (see Coffin, 1960; Lamb, 1966; Madonna, 1981) has not provided a precise answer to this question. We tend to think that Fragonard approached his subjects more as a poet than as a surveyor, and that he chose views that fired his imagination, that magnified, or "monumentalized" nature to the detriment of buildings and architectural ruins—unlike Hubert Robert, although the three drawings in figures 8–10 (see also figure 11), now ascribed to him, were all attributed to Fragonard at one time or another—and, finally, that he took liberties with what he had before him.

Can we reproach him for this?

His interpretations were so free that, today, it is often very difficult to locate the precise spot at the Villa d'Este where Fragonard sat down to draw. This was not so with Hubert Robert (Beau, 1968), but the differences between the two artists do not end there. Fragonard—as Saint-Non, Natoire, and Mariette soon discovered—did not describe; he idealized, transformed, re-created, imagined. In so doing, he became the most faithful poet of an Italy, which, in the eighteenth century, already had many admirers.

We have already mentioned Natoire's role in this discovery of nature. Later on, we will discuss Robert's contribution, and Fragonard's influence on an entire generation of pensioners—Vincent, Berthélemy, and Suvée, to cite only the most famous names—who imitated him with a facility that, even today, is often misleading.

In 1843, the ten red-chalk drawings in question, which Pâris had bequeathed to his native city, were deposited in the Besançon museum. (The drawings are of similar dimensions, three vertical, and the rest horizontal in format; almost all have a lightly sketched black-chalk underdrawing; see Williams, 1978, p. 42.) Regrettably, the Pâris collection has since been divided between the museum and the library, and A. Estignard's book about Pâris (1902) is as obsolete as it is unreliable. Thus, a new study of the Pâris collection, as a whole, is in order, for it would throw light on an entire generation of artists, only a few of whose names have emerged from oblivion. Not until their respective places have been established will the overriding importance of Fragonard become even more evident.

Fragonard returned to Tivoli on April 2, 1774, in the company of Bergeret (who would prove to be less generous with his drawings than was Saint-Non). They visited the Villa d'Este, and Bergeret noted in his journal (1895 ed., p. 281): "The gardens have their beauty, taken as a whole, and nothing to copy for us!" Fragonard's ten drawings in Besançon strongly contradict this judgment (they have been catalogued here in order of Cochin's description of Tivoli and the Villa d'Este [1756, I, pp. 104–14]).

These red-chalk drawings are works of art in their own right: rarely, before Fragonard, had drawing been taken so seriously, and had it occupied such an important place. Beyond the careful observation of the foliage, the shimmering light, the rippling water, the rustling wind, and the sultry air, they are a hymn to vegetation—a luxurious vegetation—and to trees. The grandiose Nature that Fragonard represents does not deny the existence of Man. It is not meant to be disquieting, but to enchant, and to those who contemplate it, it offers the promise of escape.

Figure 10. Hubert Robert. *View of the Temple of Jupiter Serapis*. Private collection, New York

Figure 11. Carl-Gottlieb Guttenberg, after Hubert Robert. *View of the Temple of Jupiter Serapis* (for the *Voyage pittoresque*). Bibliothèque du Louvre

24   The Ancient Theater at Hadrian's Villa, near Tivoli

Red chalk on paper, over a light underdrawing in black chalk, 35.7 x 49.4 cm.

Musée des Beaux-Arts, Besançon, Inv. D. 2848

Provenance
Abbé de Saint-Non (1727–1791), from 1760 to 1765, at about which date he returned it to Fragonard, who sold it (?) to Pierre-Adrien Pâris (1745–1819); the handwritten inventory of the Pâris collection (1806), p. 59, no. 113, mentions: "neuf beaux dessins de fragonard à la sanguine de 19 à 20 [pouces] sur 14 repr... la vue... d'une Ruine d'un théâtre à Baye connu sous le nom de tombeau d'Agrippine." Pâris bequeathed his collection to Besançon in 1819; Bibliothèque Municipale, Besançon, until 1843; Musée des Beaux-Arts, Besançon (at the lower left is the stamp of the Besançon museum, Lugt 238 c).

Exhibitions
(For a list, see Cornillot, 1957)

Bibliography
G. p. 340
P. p. 314
Martine, 1927, no. 25, ill.
Cornillot, 1957, no. 41, ill. (with a detailed bibliography)
A. 879, fig. 234

Related works
Engraved by Adélaïde Allou, 1771 (figure 1; Roux, 1931, p. 160, no. 4) and entitled *Vuë des restes d'un Theatre que l'on retrouve parmi les débris de la Ville Adriene près Tivoli à 18 milles de Rome.*

    A copy of this drawing (figure 2) was sold in Paris on July 17, 1941, no. 14, colorpl. (A. 880). There is a copy of the right part of the drawing (figure 3) in the Musée des Beaux-Arts, Rouen. Another version, in bister wash and reversed (figure 4), was reproduced in *Le Gaulois artistique*, November 20, 1928, p. 47 (A. 882).

    See also a drawing in a private collection in Paris (A. 883, fig. 526; Rosenberg and Brejon, 1986, no. 120, ill.).

Figure 1. Adélaïde Allou. *The Ancient Theater at Hadrian's Villa*. Bibliothèque Nationale, Paris, Cabinet des Estampes

Figure 2. After Fragonard. *The Ancient Theater at Hadrian's Villa*. Whereabouts unknown

In spite of the title given to the work in 1806 by P.-A. Pâris, "Théâtre antique en ruines à Baïes connu sous le nom de tombeau d'Agrippine," and by which it was known until 1957, this drawing depicts the ancient theater at Hadrian's Villa, as Marie-Lucie Cornillot has shown. This is confirmed by Adélaïde Allou's engraving and by contemporary documents, even though the site was considerably modified in the nineteenth and twentieth centuries.

In the eighteenth century, all that remained of this impos-

ing imperial villa built by Hadrian between the years 121 and 137 were, as Cochin described in 1750, "shapeless piles of bricks: yet, one can still distinguish the theater, which was small" (1756, I, p. 104). In depicting the site ten years later in this drawing (and in the one at the Institut Néerlandais, Paris; see figure 5), Fragonard concentrated on the overgrown trees and on the vegetation that had engulfed the ruins.

Figure 3. After Fragonard.
The Ancient Theater at Hadrian's Villa (copy of the right side of the composition). Musée des Beaux-Arts, Rouen

Figure 4. After Fragonard.
The Ancient Theater at Hadrian's Villa.
Whereabouts unknown

Figure 5. Fragonard.
The Ruins of Hadrian's Villa.
Institut Néerlandais, Paris,
Frits Lugt Collection

25 The Grand Cascade at Tivoli

Red chalk on paper, 48.8 x 36.1 cm.
Inscribed at the lower right, on a cartouche meant to look like a stone block: FRAGO

Musée des Beaux-Arts, Besançon, Inv. D. 2843

Provenance
See previous entry. The handwritten inventory of the Pâris collection (1806) mentions: "la vue ... du dessous du pont d'où l'on voit la grande Cascade du même lieu [Tivoli]." At the lower left is the stamp of the Besançon museum, Lugt 238 c.

Exhibitions
(For a list, see Cornillot, 1957)
Charleroi, 1957, no. 30, ill.
Rome-Turin, 1961, no. 140, pl. 31

Bibliography
G. p. 340
P. p. 302
Martine, 1927, p. 23, ill.
R. p. 222, colorpl. 1, p. 6
Cornillot, 1957, no. 39, ill. (with a detailed bibliography)
A. 1534, fig. 412

Related works
A drawing of the same site, seen from a different angle, is in a private collection in London (see figure 1; A. 1535, fig. 414).
For the painting of this subject in the Louvre, see the next entry.

Figure 1. Fragonard.
The Grand Cascade at Tivoli.
Private collection, London

"The cascade at Tivoli is formed by a small river that drops from a height of 40 to 50 feet and produces a very picturesque effect.... At the bottom of the falls, there is a public washhouse ..." (Cochin, 1756, I, pp. 105–6). In the drawing, Fragonard emphasized the wildness of nature, representing only the gushing water and the rocks, the austere façades of the houses, and the covered bridge that connects them, while, in the painting, he presents a less gloomy, more picturesque view of the site, including the figures of several washerwomen, to lend the scene a human touch.

26 The Grand Cascade at Tivoli

Oil on canvas, 72.5 x 60.5 cm.

Musée du Louvre, Paris, M.I. 1110

Provenance
The posthumous inventory of the collection of the Abbé de Saint-Non, of January 12–February 15, 1792, mentions "un tableau sur toile, étude de paysage par Fragonard avec cascade et figures, vue de Tyvoli" (G. Wildenstein, 1959, p. 239, no. 11). Dr. Louis La Caze; entered the Louvre, 1869.

Exhibitions
Paris, 1933, no. 31
Paris, 1934, no. 295
Bern, 1954, no. 24
Charleroi, 1957, no. 3
Rome-Turin, 1961, no. 128, pl. 30
Paris, 1974, no. 2, ill.
Toledo-Chicago-Ottawa, 1975–76, no. 37, pl. 93
Tokyo, 1980, no. 27, colorpl.

Bibliography
Sentenac, 1919, pl. 20
Wildenstein, 1959, p. 244, no. 11
W. 108, fig. 72, p. 12 (French edition)
W. and M. 116, colorplates XI–XII
Sutton, 1980; 1987, p. 105

Related works
A copy of some quality (judging from a photograph) is in a private collection in Lausanne (see figure 1); it was formerly in the Reininghaus collection (at Rabenstein Castle, Austria), and was sold in Lucerne, May 29, 1979 (no. 119, pl. 15; oil on canvas, 72 x 61 cm.).

Two views of Tivoli by Fragonard, both horizontal in format, were sold in the eighteenth century—one, on April 22, 1776 (no. 92): "la Cascade de Tivoli, faite d'après nature le peintre s'est placé lui-même dans ce tableau plein de goût. Il est à son chevalet, entouré de plusieurs enfans, d'autres s'amusent auprès en tirant à eux un âne sur lequel est monté un jeune garçon"; the other, on December 15, 1777 (no. 324): "une vue des cascades de Thivoly ... sur le devant l'on voit une femme et plus loin un homme et un âne ..." (the Wallace Collection's famous *Le Petit Parc* appeared at this same sale).

A painting by Hubert Robert (figure 2), signed and dated 1776, which features a very similar composition, was sold with the Florence Gould collection in New York, April 25, 1985 (no. 87, ill.); for a smaller version, see the Paris sales catalogue of May 22–23, 1924, no. 35, ill.

For the Besançon drawing and others related to this work, see the previous entry.

This painting was long considered as the work of Hubert Robert (1733–1808). It was reassigned to Fragonard by Charles Sterling on the occasion of the "Hubert Robert" exhibition in Paris in 1933, and today this attribution is unanimously accepted. Georges Wildenstein (1959, 1960), however, does not exclude the possibility of the "collaboration" of Saint-Non (who may have owned this work, as he most certainly owned the drawing of this subject discussed in the previous entry).

It is interesting to compare the Louvre picture with the Besançon drawing, as well as with Fragonard's other Roman "Bambocciante" pictures (cat. nos. 21–23). Although the handling of the figures in the foreground—the washerwomen, and the "tourists" watching them or leaning over the precipice—and of the sunlight that falls on them still displays the qualities of the genre scenes that Fragonard painted in

Rome during this period, the shrubs that cover the face of the rocky cliff down to the bridge are executed in small, nervous brushstrokes that anticipate the style of the *Petit Parc* in the Wallace Collection. Did Fragonard paint this work at the site, in Rome, before his return to Paris, or back in Paris in 1761? We favor the second hypothesis. (Notice on the right, among the many details that do not immediately catch one's attention, the fire for boiling the water used to rinse the wash.)

This famous spot in Tivoli was partially destroyed by the severe flooding of the Aniene River in 1826. Work undertaken to divert the waters was completed in 1834, and the bridge painted by Fragonard—and a host of other artists—was replaced by a new one that changed the appearance of the site. The painting by Gaspare Vanvitelli (1654–1736) shows it in its former state (see figure 3).

Figure 1. Attributed to Fragonard.
The Grand Cascade at Tivoli.
Private collection, Lausanne

Figure 2. Hubert Robert.
The Grand Cascade at Tivoli.
Whereabouts unknown

Figure 3. Gaspare Vanvitelli.
View of Tivoli with the Temple of Vesta.
Private collection, Viterbo

27 The Temple of Vesta and the Temple of the Sibyl at Tivoli

Red chalk on paper, over a light underdrawing in black chalk, 37 x 50 cm.

Musée des Beaux-Arts, Besançon, Inv. D. 2839

Provenance
See entry no. 24. The handwritten inventory of the Pâris collection (1806) mentions: "la vue . . . du temple de la sibylle du même lieu [Tivoli]." At the lower left is the stamp of the Besançon museum, Lugt 238 c.

Exhibitions
(For a list, see Cornillot, 1957)
Rome-Turin, 1961, no. 138, pl. 34
Brussels, 1975, no. 118, ill. p. 162

Bibliography
G. p. 340
P. p. 313
Martine, 1927, no. 26, ill.
R. p. 222
Cornillot, 1957, no. 34, ill. (with a detailed bibliography)
Beau, 1968, ill. under no. 41
A. 867, fig. 228
Jullian, 1978, p. 265, fig. 4

Related works
A counterproof in red chalk is reproduced by P. (between pp. 34 and 35; A. 867 a); another, heightened with a bister wash, is in the Indiana University Art Museum, Bloomington (see figure 1; A.868, fig. 229; Massengale, 1979, fig. 107).

For other views of the Temple of the Sibyl at Tivoli by Fragonard or attributed to him, see figure 3 (A. 870, fig. 527; sales catalogue, Christie's, London, July 7, 1981, no. 195, ill.; A. 871, fig. 707) and figure 2 (A. 869, 2298).

Figure 1. Fragonard. *The Temple of Vesta and the Temple of the Sibyl.* Counterproof. Indiana University Art Museum, Bloomington

Figure 2. After Fragonard. *The Temple of Vesta and the Temple of the Sibyl.* Musée des Beaux-Arts, Lyons

Figure 3. Attributed to Fragonard. *The Temple of Vesta, mistakenly called the Temple of the Sibyl.* Whereabouts unknown

Figure 5. François-André Vincent. *The Temple of Vesta and the Temple of the Sibyl.* Musée des Beaux-Arts, Marseilles

Figure 4. Hubert Robert. *The Temple of Vesta, mistakenly called the Temple of the Sibyl.* Musée des Beaux-Arts, Valence

Figure 6. Jean-Simon Berthélemy. *The Temple of Vesta, mistakenly called the Temple of the Sibyl.* Musée des Beaux-Arts, Besançon

"In the same place there is a small round temple called the Temple of the Sybil [*sic*]: there are few vestiges from antiquity as elegant as this edifice. About half of it remains. It is built of hard stone from Tivoli. The plan is a perfect circle, surrounded by a colonnade; the capitals are squat and the entablature is light. There is little molding on the cornice, but it has a fine profile. The ornamentation of the frieze is very tastefully worked; the columns are light, and elegant in proportion; they are fluted.... Behind this little circular temple [actually, the Temple of Vesta] there is another very small one, an extended square [actually, the Temple of the Sibyl]. The columns that adorn the sides are almost buried in the wall" (Cochin, 1756, I, pp. 106–7).

This famous site, "admired by painters and by architects alike" (Bergeret), was depicted by many artists, including Robert (see figure 4; today in Valence; Cayeux, 1985, no. 6, ill.), Vincent (see figure 5; in Marseilles; Cuzin, 1983), and Berthélemy (see figure 6; in Besançon; Volle, 1979), to mention only French painters of the second half of the eighteenth century.

Fragonard, who was less attentive to topographical exactitude, and more lyrical and sensitive to the exuberance of nature than his successors, portrayed the ruins brought to life by the vegetation.

28 The Small Cascades at Tivoli

Red chalk on paper, with a light underdrawing in black chalk, 36.3 x 48.3 cm.
Signed at the lower right, on the stone block: **FRAGO**

Musée des Beaux-Arts, Besançon, Inv. D. 2838

Provenance
See entry no. 24. The handwritten inventory of the Pâris collection (1806) lists: "... la vue du fond des précipices qui sont au dessous du temple de la sybille à Tivoli." At the lower left is the stamp of the Besançon museum, Lugt 238 c.

Exhibitions
(For a list, see Cornillot, 1957)

Bibliography
G. p. 340
P. p. 302
Martine, 1927, no. 24, ill.
R. p. 222
Cornillot, 1957, no. 33, ill. (with a detailed bibliography)
A. 1532, fig. 403

28

"Opposite, and on the other side of the stream, we see the first and largest of the small cascades, spilling in two or three falls from a very high mountain full of boulders and overgrown with trees and greenery, which makes for a very lovely effect.... This mountain is topped by all sorts of buildings, the largest of which are the ruins of the country house or of the baths of Maecenas" (Cochin, 1756, I, p. 108; on the site itself, see Ducros exhibition catalogue, Lausanne, 1986, no. 52, ill.).

Hubert Robert often represented this site before it was modified in the early nineteenth century: in addition to his paintings in the Musée du Petit Palais, Paris, and in Pau (1768; see figure 1), there are various drawings inspired by the one in Valence (Cayeux, 1985, no. 7, ill.) that represents only the villa of Maecenas with its tiered arcades (for a drawing from 1769 that belonged to Mariette, and is today in the Louvre, see figure 2; for a painting that was sold as the work of Fragonard, April 6, 1954 [no. 76, ill.], see figure 3). The viewpoint selected by Fragonard gives the drawing a breadth, scope, and a power to inspire that surpassed the works of Robert. The whirling water animates the composition and gives it an extraordinary energy.

Figure 1. Hubert Robert.
The Small Cascades at Tivoli.
Musée des Beaux-Arts, Pau

Figure 2. Hubert Robert.
The Small Cascades at Tivoli.
Musée du Louvre, Paris,
Cabinet des Dessins

Figure 3. Attributed to Hubert Robert.
The Small Cascades at Tivoli.
Private collection, Paris

29 The Interior of the Stables of Maecenas at Tivoli

Red chalk on paper, 35.7 x 49.4 cm.

Musée des Beaux-Arts, Besançon, Inv. D. 2846

Figure 1. Louis Chaix.
*The Interior of the Stables
of Maecenas at Tivoli.*
The Metropolitan Museum of Art,
New York

Provenance
See entry no. 24. The handwritten inventory of the Pâris collection (1806) lists: "la vue ... de l'intérieur des Ruines nommé Les Écuries de Mécène aussi à Tivoli." At the lower left is the stamp of the Besançon museum, Lugt 238 c.

Exhibitions
(For a list, see Cornillot, 1957)
Charleroi, 1957, no. 29
Rome-Turin, 1961, no. 139

Bibliography
Besançon museum catalogue, 1844, no. 309 (Hubert Robert)

Besançon museum catalogue, 1879, no. 626 (Hubert Robert)
Besançon museum catalogue, 1886, no. 592 (Fragonard)
R. p. 222
Cornillot, 1957, no. 40, ill. (with a detailed bibliography)
A. 1423, fig. 395
Cayeux, 1985, p. 326

Related works
Another version of this drawing (see figure 2) was exhibited in 1965 at the Galerie Aymonnier; for another view of the Stables of Maecenas, of 1773, by Louis Chaix, see figure 1.

"Afterwards we arrive at the Villa or vacation home of Maecenas. There is a grand vaulted gallery, under which runs a small, fast-moving stream.... These ruins provide some very picturesque views" (Cochin, 1756, I, p. 109).

This drawing was attributed to Hubert Robert between 1844 and 1879, and, more recently, by Cayeux. This attribution is not very surprising, for the emphasis on architecture and the overly vigorous execution certainly recall the manner of Fragonard's friend. However, the vegetation that covers part of the vault, and the plants on the ladder placed across the composition display the lively handling so charac-teristic of Fragonard. On the other hand, a comparison with a drawing undoubtedly by Fragonard (of the same site?), in the Musée Bonnat, Bayonne (see figure 3; A. 1613, fig. 425; probably from the de Boynes collection: sold, March 15, 1785, no. 221), tends to support the old attribution. It would be interesting to know which artist is represented drawing on the right.

Let us hope that a comparison of the Besançon drawing with the others in the series will permit us to settle the attribution question once and for all.

Figure 2. French school, 18th century.
*The Interior of the Stables of Maecenas
at Tivoli.* Whereabouts unknown

Figure 3. Fragonard.
*The Interior of the Stables of Maecenas
at Tivoli.* Musée Bonnat, Bayonne

Red chalk on paper, with a light underdrawing in black chalk, 49.5 x 36.5 cm.

Musée des Beaux-Arts, Besançon, Inv. D. 2842

Provenance

See entry no. 24. The handwritten inventory of the Pâris collection (1806) mentions: "la vue ... de dessous les grands ciprès de la Villa d'Este." At the lower left is the stamp of the Besançon museum, Lugt 238 c.

Exhibitions

(For a list, see Cornillot, 1957)
Salon of 1765, no. 178: "deux Desseins: vûes de la villa d'Este à Tivoli. Ils appartiennent à M. l'Abbé de Saint-Non."
Rome-Turin, 1961, no. 136, pl. 33
Brussels, 1975, no. 117, ill. p. 161

Bibliography

G. p. 340
P. pp. 302, 316
Martine, 1927, no. 19, ill.
R. pp. 222–23
Cornillot, 1957, no. 32, ill. (with a detailed bibliography)
Ananoff, 1959, pp. 61–63, ill.
Coffin, 1960, fig. 136
Ananoff, 1961, p. 9
A. 894, fig. 236
Lamb, 1966, fig. 149
Levey and Kalnein, 1972, pl. 175
Seznec, 1979, p. 43, pl. 68
Bukdahl, 1980, I, p. 174

Related works

For the drawing in the Albertina, see the following entry.

An identical drawing, although not as vigorous, and more flat, with a few variations in the foreground (which contains the possible signature *frago*), is in the Print collection of the library at the University of Warsaw (see figure 1; Heim, London exhibition catalogue, 1974, no. 30, pl. 42; Brunswick-Cobourg, 1982, no. 33, ill.: red chalk, 42.5 x 31.1 cm.). This may well be a copy by Pierre-Adrien Pâris. A fine counterproof in red chalk and bister wash is in the collection of Ian Woodner in New York (see figure 2; sold in Paris, November 29, 1985, no. 61: 45.6 x 34 cm.). There is a copy in the Musée des Beaux-Arts, Rouen (see figure 3; 964.4.55), and one in a private collection in Lyons.

"The Villa d'Este: the garden is very beautiful, although almost abandoned; there are some very handsome cypress and pine trees." Visible in the background of the Besançon drawing, at the end of the central avenue, is the garden façade of the villa, much as it appears today (see figure 4). A few cypress trees from the original cypress rotunda, depicted in a 1685 engraving by Venturini (figure 5), still stand.

According to Pâris (see Introduction), the ten red-chalk drawings that he owned in 1806 were exhibited at the Salon of 1765 while they still belonged to Saint-Non. Only two are mentioned in the Salon catalogue, and they may be identified on the basis of a drawing by Saint-Aubin (see figure 6; Ananoff, 1959). They did not elicit much critical notice. Fréron, on this occasion, called Fragonard the "painter of harmony" (*L'année littéraire*, October 4, 1765, p. 157), and Mathon de la Cour commented on them in his *Troisième lettre à Monsieur XXX* (1765, p. 21), but Diderot, who, generally speaking, was not particularly sensitive to drawing, said nothing.

This drawing rightly deserves its fame: Fragonard focused

Figure 1. Attributed to Pierre-Adrien Pâris. *The Avenue of Cypress Trees at the Villa d'Este.* Library, University of Warsaw, Print collection

Figure 2. Fragonard. *The Avenue of Cypress Trees at the Villa d'Este.* Counterproof. Collection Ian Woodner, New York

Figure 3. After Fragonard. *The Avenue of Cypress Trees at the Villa d'Este.* Musée des Beaux-Arts, Rouen

Figure 4. The Villa d'Este at Tivoli today

on the cypress trees, accentuating their size; they are the true subject of the scene, more than the villa and the famous fountains. Fragonard chose his viewpoint and held to a very classical composition. The giant scale of the trees does not have the dizzying effect of Piranesi's creations.

Yet, there is all the calm of an Italian garden, the heat of the sun, the coolness of the shade, the foliage of the trees, the shimmering light. In the absence of man, there are just the trees and, above all, the sensual essence of nature—and of life.

Figure 5. Giovanni Francesco Venturini. *The Rotunda of Cypresses,* 1685. Engraving

31   The Avenue of Cypress Trees at the Villa d'Este

Bister wash on paper, with an underdrawing in black chalk, 46.5 x 34.3 cm.
Signed at the lower right, in bister wash: *fragonard*
Inscribed at the lower left, in lead pencil: *Vue de la Ville d'Este à Tivoli*

Graphische Sammlung Albertina, Vienna, Inv. 12.735

Provenance
Compared by A. to a drawing in the Sireul sale, December 3, 1781, no. 242: "un superbe Dessin de ce Maître [Fragonard] lavé au bistre sur papier blanc. Il représente une longue avenue en perspective. Le Dessin est d'un effet piquant et orné de figures ana-logues" (16 p. sur 13=43.2 x 35.1 cm.). We would also mention a drawing in the sale of the de Boynes collection, March 15, 1785, no. 217: "la vue de l'entrée de la villa d'Este à *Trivoli* l'on distingue les différents paliers qui conduisent au cazin.... Hauteur 20 pouces, largeur 15 pouces 3 lignes." Listed in the 1822 inventory of the collection of Duke Albert of Saxe-Teschen (p. 914: "cinq pay-sages et vues"); the stamp of the Albertina, Lugt 174, appears at the lower left.

Exhibitions
Paris, 1931, no. 82
London, 1932, no. 1015 (no. 676, pl. CLXXV of the commemorative catalogue)
Paris, 1937, no. 532
Paris, 1950, no. 150, ill.
Vienna, 1950, no. 122
Bern, 1954, no. 53, pl. XIII
Vienna, 1969, no. 384
Washington, D.C., 1984–85, no. 73, ill.

Bibliography
Hempel, 1924, p. 10, fig. 1, p. 22
Fosca, 1954, pp. 52–53, pl. 8
R. p. 222
A. 1434, fig. 392

Related works
See previous entry.

Figure 6. Gabriel de Saint-Aubin, after Fragonard. *The Salon of 1765.* Drawing. Musée du Louvre, Paris, Cabinet des Dessins

31

Although the attribution to Fragonard of this splendid drawing is unquestioned, its dating is still a subject of debate. While many consider it contemporary with the version in Besançon, Christine Ekelhart recently suggested (Washington exhibition catalogue, 1984–85) that it be dated to Fragonard's second trip to Tivoli (he was accompanied by Bergeret) on April 2, 1774. The reasons for her dating are easy to understand: in 1760, Fragonard used bister washes very rarely and completely differently—both in a less descriptive and less monumental way. Apart from the fact that, according to Bergeret, Fragonard did not have time to draw during that visit (see Introduction), we may infer

from the differences between the Vienna and the Besançon drawings that he had the latter in front of him when he repeated it. For him to have drawn the Vienna version from life would mean that he placed himself in exactly the same spot where he had drawn fourteen years before, which seems no more likely than that the cypress trees had not changed in the intervening years. Fragonard must therefore have copied his original drawing, adding the tiny figures in the foreground in Paris sometime after 1765, when Saint-Non gave him back the Besançon drawings, and before he sold them to Pierre-Adrien Pâris.

32 The Fountain of Pomona and the Avenue of the Hundred Fountains at the Villa d'Este

Red chalk on paper, 48.8 x 36.1 cm.

Musée des Beaux-Arts, Besançon, Inv. D. 2845

Provenance
See entry no. 24. The handwritten inventory of the Pâris collection (1806), p. 59, no. 112, lists a "beau dessin à la sanguine de fragonard représent. la vue de l'Entrée du fontanone de la Villa d'Este de Tivoli" (in this inventory, a sheet by Berthélemy is given as the "pendant" to Fragonard's drawing; see Cornillot, 1957, no. 4, ill.). At the lower left is the stamp of the Besançon museum, Lugt 238 c.

Exhibitions
(For a list, see Cornillot, 1957)
Salon of 1765, no. 178 (figure 1; see cat. no. 30)
Rome-Turin, 1961, no. 135
London, 1979–80, no. 80

Bibliography
G. p. 340

P. pp. 304, 316
Martine, 1927, no. 22, ill.
R. p. 222
Cornillot, 1957, no. 38, ill. (with a detailed bibliography)
Ananoff, 1959, pp. 61–63, ill.
A. 908, fig. 716
Lamb, 1966, fig. 148
Bukdahl, 1980, I, p. 174, fig. 84

Related works
There is a counterproof of this drawing, which is attributed to Hubert Robert by A. (IV, p. 383, no. 908), in a private collection in Montreal (see figure 2; Ottawa, exhibition catalogue, 1976, no. 23, ill.). A. catalogues another counterproof (no. 2159 a; see also A. 1561). There is also a copy in a private collection in Lyons.

Figure 1. Gabriel de Saint-Aubin, after Fragonard. *The Salon of 1765.* Musée du Louvre, Paris, Cabinet des Dessins

Figure 2. Hubert Robert. *The Fountain of Pomona and the Avenue of the Hundred Fountains.* Counterproof. Private collection, Montreal

Figure 3. Giovanni Francesco Venturini. *The Avenue of the Hundred Fountains.* Engraving

This drawing depicts the Fountain of Pomona with, on the left, the path that leads to the Fontana dell'Ovato, and, on the right, the so-called Avenue of the Hundred Fountains. The right side of the composition is recognizable in an engraving by Giovanni Francesco Venturini from 1685 (figure 3).

For this famous drawing, Fragonard chose as his subject an abandoned part of the gardens. The fountains are barely recognizable. Several large trees grow wild in the midst of what was once one of the most beautifully designed gardens in the Western world.

33　Villa d'Este: L'Escalier de la Gerbe

Red chalk on paper, 35 x 48.7 cm.

Musée des Beaux-Arts, Besançon, Inv. D. 2844

Provenance
See entry no. 24. The handwritten inventory
of the Pâris collection (1806) mentions: "la
vue . . . d'un même jardin [Villa d'Este] de
devant l'Escalier de la gerbe." At the lower
left is the stamp of the Besançon museum,
Lugt 238 c.

Exhibitions
(For a list, see Cornillot, 1957)
Rome-Turin, 1961, no. 134
London, 1979–80, no. 79, ill.

Bibliography
G. p. 340
P. p. 304
Martine, 1927, no. 21, ill.
R. p. 222
Cornillot, 1957, no. 37, ill. (with a detailed
　bibliography)
A. 891, fig. 235
Lamb, 1966, fig. 146
Williams, 1978, p. 175, fig. 11

Related works
A painting, which was once in Natoire's collection and was sold in 1778, is directly
related to this drawing; it was recently sold
again with the Florence Gould collection (W.
105; Sotheby's, New York, April 25, 1985,

no. 86, colorpl.). A strip about thirty centimeters wide was cut off at the left (see figure
1).
　For other paintings of Tivoli by Fragonard,
see catalogue no. 26. A counterproof heightened with bister wash was sold November

Figure 1. Fragonard. *L'Escalier de la gerbe.*
Whereabouts unknown

Figure 2. Fragonard. *L'Escalier de la gerbe.*
Counterproof. Whereabouts unknown

21, 1941, no. 9, ill. (see figure 2; A. 892, fig. 711).

See also A. 893, 1542 (published in the Los Angeles exhibition catalogue, 1976, no. 161), 1543a (see figure 3), 2661, fig. 588.

The Abbé de Saint-Non, who owned this drawing, made an engraving of it, in reverse, in 1764 (Cayeux, 1964, no. 40) entitled *View of the Gardens of the Villa d'Este at Tivoli* (see figure 4).

See also the painting "signed, and dated 1769" by Saint-Non, which was directly inspired by compositions by Hubert Robert; it was sold June 14, 1983 (no. 11, ill.).

Figure 3. Fragonard. *L'Escalier de la gerbe.* Counterproof. Private collection, Paris

Figure 4. Abbé de Saint-Non. *View of the Gardens of the Villa d'Este at Tivoli.* Bibliothèque Nationale, Paris

In this drawing, Fragonard depicted the staircase that dominates the celebrated Fountain of the Dragon. He later painted a picture directly inspired by this drawing, and Saint-Non made an engraving after it, in 1764. Fragonard chose once again to depict the great cypress trees pointing skyward like torches in full sunlight, leaving the steps in the shade. A little girl, in silhouette, walks carefully along the parapet. Fragonard played on the contrasts of strong sunlight and shade to animate the composition, accentuating its complex design. He succeeded admirably in conveying the sensation of the stifling heat of summer.

34 The Fine Group of Cypresses at the Villa d'Este, with a View of the Fountain of the Organ

Red chalk on paper, 35.6 x 48 cm.
Signed in the center, on a stone: FRAGO

Musée des Beaux-Arts, Besançon, Inv. D. 2841

Provenance
See entry no. 24. The handwritten inventory of the Pâris collection (1806) mentions: "la vue du beau groupe de ciprès des jardins de Villa d'Este à Tivoli." At the lower left is the stamp of the Besançon museum, Lugt 238c.

Exhibitions
(For a list, see Cornillot, 1957)
Rome-Turin, 1961, no. 137
Brussels, 1975, no. 119, ill. p. 162

Bibliography
G. p. 340
P. p. 302
Martine, 1927, no. 20, ill.
R. p. 222
Cornillot, 1957, no. 36, ill. (with a detailed bibliography)

A. 1435, fig. 396
Lamb, 1966, fig. 150

Related works
An engraving after this drawing, made in 1764 by the Abbé de Saint-Non, is entitled *View of the Gardens of the Villa d'Este at Tivoli* (see figure 1; Cayeux, 1964, no. 38).

This drawing may be compared to one attributed to P.-A. Pâris, sold in Monte Carlo February 15, 1983, no. 822, ill.; to A. 904 (see figure 2; Williams, 1978, no. 7, ill.), of which there is a copy (a counterproof of a counterproof?) in the Musée Borély, Marseilles (see figure 3; A. 905); to a drawing today in the United States, formerly owned by Cailleux (Galerie Cailleux, Paris, exhibi-

Figure 1. Abbé de Saint-Non. *View of the Gardens of the Villa d'Este at Tivoli.* Bibliothèque Nationale, Paris

Figure 2. Attributed to Pierre-Adrien Pâris. *Roman Landscape.* Formerly Collection John Nicholas Brown

Figure 3. After Pierre-Adrien Pâris. *Roman Landscape.* Counterproof. Musée Borély, Marseilles

tion catalogue, 1978, no. 13, colorpl.); and
finally to A. 858, fig. 723 (formerly in the
Dormeuil collection; a counterproof of the
red-chalk drawing sold at Boerner, Leipzig,
November 28, 1912, no. 122, ill.).

The beautiful drawing in Orléans (A. 909,
fig. 237) is attributed today to Berthélemy
(see figure 4; Volle, 1979, no. 131, fig. 99;
there is a copy—not a very old one—in
Detroit).

The counterproof of this drawing (A. 1507;
Bourgarel sale, June 15–16, 1922, no. 90,
ill.) is inscribed: "A Tivoli 1774."

Figure 4. Attributed to Jean-Simon Berthélemy.
The Cypress Trees at the Villa d'Este.
Musée des Beaux-Arts, Orléans

Figure 5. Cypress trees at the Villa
d'Este, 1909

Here again, Fragonard selected a view that emphasized
nature: waterfalls and figures, steps and balustrades are
almost entirely covered by vegetation. A man converses with
two seated young women as a shepherd leads his donkey
beneath the great cypress trees (see figure 5). There is nothing melancholic about the park: it vibrates with life in full
sunlight. What is extraordinary is the seriousness with which
Fragonard rendered it, and that he chose to transpose into
red the symphony of greens that was before him.

35 The Gardens and Terraces of the Villa d'Este at the Foot of the Fountain of the Organ

Red chalk on paper, 35.6 x 49 cm.

Musée des Beaux-Arts, Besançon, Inv. D. 2840

Provenance
See entry no. 24. The handwritten inventory of the Pâris collection (1806) mentions: ''la vue ... du même jardin [of the Villa d'Este] du pied d'une cascade.'' At the lower left is the stamp of the Besançon museum, Lugt 238 c.

Exhibitions
(For a list, see Cornillot, 1957)

Bibliography
G. p. 340
P. p. 304
R. p. 222
Cornillot, 1957, no. 35, ill. (with a detailed bibliography)
A. 919
Lamb, 1966, fig. 159

Related works
A counterproof (figure 1), heightened with wash, is in a private collection in Paris (A. 920, fig. 244). There is a bister wash drawing, signed and dated on the verso 1788, that once belonged to the Goncourts (figure 2; A. 917, fig. 243; Tokyo exhibition catalogue, 1980, no. 160, ill.).
 See also: A. 918, fig. 245, recently sold in Munich; A. 914, fig. 240, which entered the Musée Borély, Marseilles, with the Feuillet de Borsat collection; A. 2207, sold in Paris, March 7, 1961, no. 4, ill.; and a drawing attributed to Robert (figure 3) that copies the present drawing and is said to have belonged to the Deglatigny collection (at Herbert H. Feist, 1972, reprod. in an advertisement in *The Burlington Magazine*, September 1972).

Figure 1. Fragonard.
The Gardens and Terraces of the Villa d'Este at the Foot of the Fountain of the Organ. Counterproof. Private collection, Paris

Figure 2. Fragonard.
The Gardens and Terraces of the Villa d'Este at the Foot of the Fountain of the Organ. Drawing. Private collection, New York

Figure 3. Attributed to Hubert Robert, after Fragonard. *The Gardens and Terraces of the Villa d'Este at the Foot of the Fountain of the Organ.* Whereabouts unknown

Figure 4. Charles-Joseph Natoire.
The Fountain of the Organ and the Apse of the Chiesa della Carità at Tivoli. The Metropolitan Museum of Art, New York

Figure 5. Attributed to Pierre-Adrien Pâris.
The Gardens of the Villa d'Este and the Apse of the Chiesa della Carità at Tivoli. Institut Néerlandais, Paris, Frits Lugt Collection

Figure 6. Giovanni Francesco Venturini.
The Fountain of the Organ. 1685. Engraving

This drawing details the right side of the preceding work: the hydraulic organ (or Fountain of the Organ) as it was in 1760, the balustrade, the waterfall, and, on the right, the apse of the Chiesa della Carità, at Tivoli. However, it is not as faithful to its subject as is Natoire's drawing (figure 4), executed several months earlier, or the one attributed to Pâris (figure 5). A 1685 engraving by Venturini (figure 6) shows that the site was completely different then.

Inspired by the abandoned state of this garden, Fragonard, here again, preferred to render the effects of the wind and the sun on the foliage, and the mist over the water, rather than precisely depicting the scene.

36 The Small Cascades at Tivoli

Red chalk on paper, 36.3 x 50.3 cm.
Folded down the middle.

Musée Borély, Marseilles

Provenance
Anonymous sale, April 30, 1855, no. 2978: "vue des cascatelles, à Tivoli. Belle étude d'après nature, largement exécutée à la sanguine"; Pierre Decourcelle: sold, Paris, May 29–30, 1911, no. 90, ill. (for 1,020 francs); sold, January 29, 1927, no. 133 (for 12,550 francs); Maurice Feuillet; Feuillet de Borsat (stamp of the collection, Lugt 1864a, appears at the lower left); gift to the Musée Borély, 1969.

Exhibitions
Paris, 1907, no. 169, *3* (?)
Paris, 1950, no. 108
Marseilles, 1971, no. 58, ill.

Bibliography
Le Gaulois artistique, February 22, 1927, p. 66, ill.
A. 915, fig. 241
Marseilles exhibition catalogue [1969], no. 95, ill.

36

This work is a fine example of the red-chalk drawings that Fragonard made at Tivoli in the summer months of 1760. It is similar in format and subject to a drawing in Besançon (see cat. no. 28) and to one in Montpellier (A. 916, fig. 242; see page 95, figure 5). The vantage point chosen by Fragonard here allowed him to depict the small cascades without the Villa of Maecenas and the so-called Temple of the Sibyl.

The only human presence in this grandiose setting is some travelers who have stopped to contemplate the falls. This view of the small cascades at Tivoli, more tranquil than the Besançon drawing and reminiscent of the paintings by Dughet of similar subjects, is a meditation on Man's fragility and insignificance before Nature. Fragonard, however, did not dwell on the moralistic aspect of the theme, but concentrated his attention on the rush of the water and the clouds of spray in the shimmering light.

37   Italian Landscape, with Two Figures

Red chalk on paper, 36 x 45 cm.
On the verso: counterproof study of a young man.

Musées d'Angers

Provenance
Blondel d'Azincourt: sold, April 18, 1770, no. 67, according to A.: "deux beaux Paysages avec architectures et figures, à la sanguine . . . 13 pouces de haut [= 35.1] sur 18 pouces de large [= 48.6]"; Lancelot Théodore, Comte Turpin de Crissé (1772–1859); gift to the Angers museum, 1859; stolen about 1965 and recently recovered.

Bibliography
Jouin, 1885, p. 229, no. 42
Recouvreur, 1932, pp. 14–15
Angers museum catalogue, 1933, p. 153, no. 245
A. 2360, fig. 595

Related works
The pendant (figure 1; A. 2361, fig. 596) disappeared about 1965. The counterproof in the Besançon museum (figure 2) was formerly in the Gigoux collection (D. 929).

37

Figure 1. Fragonard.
Landscape with Cascade.
Formerly Musées d'Angers

Figure 2. Fragonard.
Landscape with Cascade.
Counterproof.
Musée des Beaux-Arts, Besançon

This splendid red-chalk drawing can be dated with certainty to Fragonard's first trip to Rome—probably, to 1760. Its pendant is so close to one of the Besançon drawings (see cat. no. 35) that it may very well have been done in Tivoli also.

Two young women seated alongside a stream contemplate a cascade. In this hymn to nature, Fragonard, concentrating on the foliage, rendered the plants—indicated by sharp, nervous touches—the disposition of the trees and shrubs, and the sunlight that bathes the scene with his usual small zigzagged strokes. The interest of the drawing lies in its simplicity, its poetry—which is devoid of any artifice—and in the originality of its composition, which draws us into this sun-drenched landscape.

38   View of a Park

Gray and bister wash on paper, over an underdrawing in black chalk, 27.8 x 39.7 cm.

The Metropolitan Museum of Art, New York, Harris Brisbane Dick Fund, 52.14

Provenance
Comte de Montesquiou (according to the vendor); [Wertheimer], 1951; [M. Knoedler & Co., New York]; acquired by the Metropolitan Museum, 1952.

Exhibitions
Washington, D.C., 1978, no. 6, ill.
Richmond, 1981, no. 8, ill.

Bibliography
A. 2215
Massengale, 1979, pp. 271–72
Bean and Turčić, 1986, no. 115, ill.
Cuzin, 1986, p. 61

Figure 1. Fragonard.
View of a Park with a Temple.
Allen Memorial Art Museum,
Oberlin College, Oberlin, Ohio

Figure 2. Fragonard.
View of a Park with a Fountain.
Private collection, Paris

38

This drawing is part of a group, executed in the same medium and technique, and in a similar spirit, that includes the *View of a Park with a Temple* (figure 1; A. 948, fig. 257; Williams, 1978, no. 20, ill.) and the *View of a Park with a Fountain* (figure 2; A. 944, fig. 256). These drawings present motifs directly inspired by the compositions of Boucher—here, the elegant figure of the woman pushing her wheelbarrow—some architectural elements, and a vision of nature that is typically Italian.

According to Williams (1978), the present drawing dates from about 1760, and the one in figure 2 was done four or five years later; for J.-M. Massengale (1979), the two are contemporary (autumn–winter 1761). Massengale rightly compares the former drawing with an aquatint by Saint-Non, the *Gardens and Walls of the Villa d'Este*, from 1761 (figure 3), and to the *Appian Way* (?) in a private collection in Paris (Rosenberg and Brejon, 1986, no. 120, ill.).

If these works postdate the red-chalk drawings of Tivoli, but predate the copies of old masters that were also made for the Abbé de Saint-Non, then they would be proof of Fragonard's versatility and talent, and of his ability to change styles rapidly.

Figure 3. Abbé de Saint-Non.
The Gardens and Walls of the Villa d'Este.
Bibliothèque Nationale, Paris,
Cabinet des Estampes

The Return to France of Fragonard and the Abbé de Saint-Non

Fragonard, who had arrived in Rome in December 1756, should have stayed at the Palazzo Mancini for only three years, but he was granted an extension of one year (see introduction to this chapter), and afterward, thanks to the Abbé de Saint-Non, he was permitted to continue lodging there until April 1761.

A comprehensive study of the work and career of the Abbé Jean-Baptiste-Claude-Richard de Saint-Non (1727–1791), one of the many *abbés commendataires* of the eighteenth century, may be found in the journal of his travels in Italy that was recently edited and published for the first time (Rosenberg and Brejon, 1986).

The Abbé de Saint-Non left Paris on October 1, 1759, passed through Geneva, where he visited Voltaire, and arrived in Rome on November 15. He was a guest of the Bailiff of Breteuil (see cat. no. 18), and traveled in the company of the pensioner-painter Hugues Taraval (whom Diderot associated with Fragonard in his comments on the Salon of 1767, judging both artists equally severely). After spending some time in Naples, he returned to Rome in December 1759, revisiting Naples and Paestum on April 17, 1760, this time in the company of Hubert Robert (see figure 1). By June 4, he was back in Rome, remaining there until he began his trip back to Paris on April 14, 1761, except for "two or three months" spent in Tivoli (see cat. nos. 24–35).

The abbé, or the "petit abbé" as Caylus called him, was a cultivated man, related to the Boullongne family on his mother's side, a friend of the arts and of artists; he frequented the best circles, and was a friend of Mme Geoffrin, the Abbé Delille, and Chamfort. Paciaudi described him as "very polite, full of erudition, very pleasant and eager to learn," and in Rome, "he exhausted himself drawing, engraving, painting, and

playing the violin." The two great areas of accomplishment in his life were aquatint engraving, which imitates wash drawing, and which he indulged in abundantly, and the publication of a book, the *Voyage pittoresque ... de Naples et de Sicile* (1781–86), which, although it ruined him, was undoubtedly one of the most luxurious and richly illustrated "guides" of the eighteenth century (figures 2, 3). His travels in Italy were related to both of these enterprises.

As early as March 1760, Saint-Non was already thinking of returning to France, but a "tender commitment"—to use his own expression—kept him from doing so for another year; understandably enough, the abbé remained discreet as to the nature of this "commitment." The important thing for us is that he asked Fragonard to accompany him on the return trip. Their names are mentioned together for the first time in a letter written by Natoire on March 19, 1760. They went to Tivoli together, and then in March 1761 (according to Natoire), "always willing to be of service to this pensioner," Saint-Non sent Fragonard (see figure 4) and Ango (see figure 5) to Naples. For what purpose? Ostensibly, "to see the fine things that this city contains" (*idem*); but the abbé had a more ambitious project in mind. In Naples and in Rome, he asked Fragonard—as he had asked Hubert Robert—to copy the most important works of art, both antiquities (in Robert's case) and paintings. On the trip back to Paris, he had Fragonard work for him again, copying the things that he considered interesting to record. Thus, from Ronciglione to Nîmes, passing through Siena, Florence, Pisa, Venice, Padua, Vicenza (figures 6, 7), Verona, Mantua, Reggio, Modena, Bologna, Parma and Colorno, Piacenza, Genoa, and Saint-Rémy-de-Provence, the artist executed no less than

Figure 1. Hubert Robert. *Paestum*. Musée des Beaux-Arts, Rouen

Figure 2. After Fragonard. Dedicatory illustration in the first volume of the *Voyage pittoresque ...*

Figure 3. Preparatory drawing for figure 2. Whereabouts unknown

three hundred copies after old masters, as well as a number of views of famous sites. The journey lasted more than five months. Fragonard and Saint-Non had the opportunity not only to see the finest paintings and to visit the most famous monuments in each of these cities, but also to attend the Carnival in Venice and the opera in Padua. They also met many renowned people of the day, including the art critic Algarotti (see figure 8) (who owned a drawing by G. B. Tiepolo upon which Saint-Non later based an aquatint; see figure 9) and Du Tillot, the powerful minister of Parma, for whom Fragonard painted a *Pan and Syrinx* (figure 6, p. 63).

What were Saint-Non's intentions in writing his *Journal* and in having Fragonard accompany him? Some of them are easy enough to guess. Upon his

Figure 4. Fragonard, after Nicolas Poussin (?). *The Holy Family.* Norton Simon Collection, Pasadena

Figure 5. Ango, after Nicolas Poussin (?). *The Holy Family.* Musée des Beaux-Arts, Besançon

Figure 6. Fragonard, after Giovanni Battista Tiepolo. *Antony and Cleopatra.* Norton Simon Collection, Pasadena

Figure 7. Giovanni Battista Tiepolo. *Antony and Cleopatra.* Private collection, New York

Figure 8. Letter from the Abbé de Saint-Non to Francesco Algarotti, dated August 4, 1761. Bibliothèque Nationale, Paris, Cabinet des Estampes

Figure 9. Abbé de Saint-Non, after Giovanni Battista Tiepolo. *Pulcinella.* Bibliothèque Nationale, Paris, Cabinet des Estampes

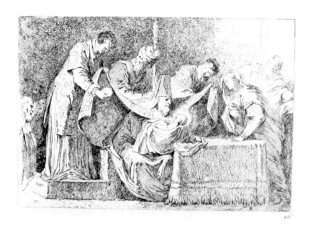

Figure 10. Fragonard, after Tintoretto. *The Circumcision.*
Musée du Louvre, Paris, Cabinet des Dessins, Rothschild Collection

Figure 11. Fragonard, after Lodovico (not Annibale) Carracci.
Angel Holding a Crown. Musée du Louvre, Paris, Cabinet des Dessins,
Rothschild Collection

return to Paris, the abbé made many aquatints after
Fragonard's drawings, and Fragonard produced sixteen etchings (two in 1764) after works by Lanfranco,
Preti, Mehus, Liss, Tintoretto (figure 10), Ricci, Tiepolo, Castiglione, Liberi, and Lodovico Carracci (figure 11). Saint-Non probably intended to publish his
journal and to illustrate it with his aquatints. This
project was never fully realized as such, but with the
Voyage pittoresque he came close.

Several points should be clarified. Fragonard and
Saint-Non held each other in mutual esteem; the trips
to Tivoli and to Naples are evidence of this. In addition, the abbé had his portrait painted by Fragonard
(cat. no. 133), and owned a large number of works by
the artist—many of which he copied in pastel (cat. no.
157). The abbé's (unpublished) will indicates that the
two men remained friends throughout their lives
(Saint-Non asked his brother, M. de La Bretèche, to
select from among his drawings, prints, and "those
many paintings that were done by me," works to be

given as "souvenirs and tokens of friendship" to Fragonard, Hubert Robert, Pierre-Adrien Pâris, Seroux
d'Agincourt, and the abbés Tersan and Brizard,
among others). One wonders, however, why there is no
mention of Fragonard in Saint-Non's journal, especially since his admiration for the painter is beyond
doubt. As Saint-Non wrote to his brother (see Guimbaud, p. 98): "M. Fragonard is all fire; he draws constantly, one after the other; I find them charming.
There is magic in them."

Most of Fragonard's copies after old masters were
done in black chalk (a dozen in red chalk have come
down to us). There are a large number of counterproofs of them, the finest of which are in the British
Museum and in the Norton Simon Collection in Pasadena, California. (A close examination of the Simon
counterproofs, which are not included here, would
undoubtedly have yielded more exhaustive information about Fragonard's and Saint-Non's five-month
journey through Italy.)

In a letter to Marigny written on April 14, 1761,
the day that Saint-Non and Fragonard left Rome,
Natoire comments that "this *amateur* has with him a
number of fine pieces ["morceaux"] by this young
artist [Fragonard] that I think will please you very
much." The "morceaux" executed in various Italian
cities stand out not only for the artistic ability that they
reveal but also for their compositions and for the intelligence in the artist's choice of details. Of course, Fragonard respected the integrity of the original, and its
artistic personality, and, therefore, did not distort its
style. Although he copied with precision, and sometimes took liberties with the originals, he endowed
everything that he did with the same natural elegance
and irrepressible energy that characterizes all his works.

In return, it was to the likes of Rubens, Raphael,
Pietro da Cortona, Castiglione, van Dyck, the Carracci, Tiepolo, and Piazzetta that Fragonard owed his
phenomenal education. As Caylus (Nisard, 1877, I, p.
142) predicted to the Abbé de Saint-Non: "he [has]
amassed a storehouse that will nourish him for a
lifetime."

39 Saint Luke

(after Giovanni Lanfranco)

Etching, in two states: first state, 11 x 8 cm.; copperplate, 12.4 x 9.2 cm.
Inscribed: *Lanfranco a naple aux St Apotre*

Musée du Louvre, Paris, Cabinet des Dessins, Rothschild Collection

Bibliography
G. Wildenstein, 1956, no. XVII, ill. (with
   bibliography and lists of past exhibitions,
   sales, and collections with an example of the
   etching)
Pognon and Bruand, 1962, IX, p. 288,
   no.16
Rosenberg and Brejon, 1986, under no. 12

Related works
Lanfranco's *Saint Luke* decorates one of the
pendentives of the dome of the Chiesa dei
Santi Apostoli, in Naples (see figure 1). Fragonard's drawing after this fresco (accompanied by drawings of two Prophets, after
Ribera), with the figure facing in the same
direction as in the present etching, is in the
Norton Simon Collection, Pasadena (see figure 2).
   An aquatint of the etching was made by
Saint-Non, in 1773, for his *Fragments* (no.
24) and his *Griffonis* (no. 223; see figure 3,
for the aquatint from the copy of the *Griffonis* that belonged to the abbé, in the Bibliothèque Nationale, containing unique
counterproofs inscribed by him), and by
Charles E. Gaucher, in 1778, for the *Voyage
pittoresque* (see figure 4).
   For a discussion of Saint-Non's *Fragments*
and *Griffonis*, see our edition of his *Journal*
(Rosenberg and Brejon, 1986; see also the
Chronology).

Figure 1. Giovanni Lanfranco.
Saint Luke. Detail of a fresco in the
Chiesa dei Santi Apostoli, Naples

Figure 2. Fragonard.
Saint Luke (after the fresco by
Giovanni Lanfranco) and *Two Prophets*
(after Jusepe de Ribera). Drawing.
Norton Simon Collection, Pasadena

Figure 3. Abbé de Saint-Non,
after Fragonard. *Saint Luke*.
Counterproof of an aquatint.
Bibliothèque Nationale, Paris,
Cabinet des Estampes

Figure 4. Charles E. Gaucher.
Saint Luke.
Bibliothèque du Louvre

40 Saint Mark

(after Giovanni Lanfranco)

Etching, in two states: second state, with shaded background, 11 x 8 cm.; copperplate, 11.5 x 9 cm.
Inscribed: *Lanfranc aux Sts Apotres à Naples; frago*

Musée du Louvre, Paris, Cabinet des Dessins, Rothschild Collection

Bibliography
G. Wildenstein, 1956, no. VII, ill. (see previous entry)
Pognon and Bruand, 1962, IX, p. 286, no. 6
Rosenberg and Brejon, 1986, under no. 27

Related works
Lanfranco's fresco of *Saint Mark* fills one of the pendentives of the dome of the Chiesa dei Santi Apostoli in Naples. Fragonard's drawing of this fresco (figure 1) is in the Norton Simon Collection (a counterproof is in a private collection in Paris; see figure 2).

Saint-Non made an engraving of it in 1773 (*Fragments,* no. 24; *Griffonis,* no. 234, a counterproof of the aquatint in the Bibliothèque Nationale; see figure 3 and previous entry), as did Gaucher in 1778 for the *Voyage pittoresque* (see figure 4).

Figure 1. Fragonard, after the fresco by Giovanni Lanfranco in the Chiesa dei Santi Apostoli, Naples. *Saint Mark.* Drawing. Norton Simon Collection, Pasadena

Figure 2. Fragonard. *Saint Mark.* Counterproof. Private collection, Paris

Figure 3. Abbé de Saint-Non, after Fragonard. *Saint Mark.* Counterproof of the aquatint. Bibliothèque Nationale, Paris, Cabinet des Estampes

Figure 4. Charles E. Gaucher. *Saint Mark.* Bibliothèque du Louvre

Fragonard did not make many prints; Wildenstein (1956) attributed only twenty-five etchings to him, sixteen of which are copies after works by the Italian masters Lanfranco, the Carracci, Castiglione, Liberi, Liss, Mehus, Preti, Ricci, Tiepolo, and Tintoretto, and a seventeenth reproduces a work by Boucher. *All* of Fragonard's original etchings are presented here, as well as a few of his engravings after old masters, to evoke the highlights of his journey from Italy back to France. During his stay in Italy, he of course executed his drawings from life (no less than four hundred have

come down to us!), but this was not so for the engravings. Two of these are dated 1764, and all indications are that the entire series was executed at roughly the same time. By then Fragonard had been back in France for more than two years and wanted to make a name for himself. He thus tried his hand at different genres.

The Abbé de Saint-Non's journal (Rosenberg and Brejon, 1986) records his impressions of his two visits to Naples, but no such document exists for Fragonard. All that is certain is that he went there in March 1761 at Saint-Non's expense

Figure 5. Fragonard.
The Madonna of the Rosary.
Norton Simon Collection, Pasadena

Figure 6. Ango.
The Madonna of the Rosary.
Art market, Paris

and in the company of Ango, an artist who is still confused with Fragonard (see figures 5, 6). Had Saint-Non prepared a list of the works that he wanted them to copy? Did Fragonard and Ango have any freedom of choice? We do not know. What we do know is that today some forty drawings

by Fragonard exist, after compositions by the foremost Neapolitan masters—especially, Preti, Giordano, and Solimena —but also after works by Ribera, Pontormo, Ricci, Reni, Domenichino, Schedoni, and Poussin that he saw at the Galleria Capodimonte or in the principal private collections in the city.

While his stay in Naples was short, it had a lasting influence on him: he was impressed by the works of Solimena, in particular, but also by the art of Giordano, whose pictures he saw again in Florence, and of Schedoni (see cat. no. 268). He never forgot the paintings of Lanfranco (1582–1647) either, especially the putti in his *Saint Luke* and *Saint Mark* frescoes, which became the models for the graceful and curly headed Cupids that Fragonard included in a good many of his works, although they were rather more profane in spirit.

Saint-Non (*Journal,* p. 117) admired the "boldness and astonishing energy" as well as the "beautiful color" of Lanfranco's frescoes in the Chiesa dei Santi Apostoli— qualities that describe perfectly many of the works of his artist friend.

41 God Creating the Heavens and The Prophet Joel

(after Michelangelo)

Black chalk on paper, 29.5 x 20.5 cm.
Inscribed in black chalk, at center right, by Saint-Non: *Michelange/Chapelle Sistine*

Harvard University Art Museums (Fogg Art Museum), Cambridge, Massachusetts, Gift of René Gimpel, 1928.152

Provenance
René Gimpel; gift to the Fogg museum, 1928.

Exhibitions
Washington, D.C., 1978, no. 10, ill.

Bibliography
Fogg Art Museum catalogue, 1940, no. 606
A. 1085, fig. 293
Rosenberg and Brejon, 1986, no. 59, ill.

Related works
In 1770, Saint-Non made an aquatint (see figure 1; *Fragments,* no. 11; *Griffonis,* no. 157) of this drawing by Fragonard after the frescoes by Michelangelo (figure 2).

Figure 1. Abbé de Saint-Non, after Fragonard.
God Creating the Heavens and *The Prophet Joel.* Aquatint.
Bibliothèque d'Art et d'Archéologie, Paris

Figure 2. Michelangelo.
God Creating the Heavens and *The Prophet Joel.*
Sistine Chapel, Vatican

42 The Erythrean Sibyl and The Prophet Daniel
(after Michelangelo)

Black chalk on paper, 21.4 x 29.5 cm.
Inscribed in black chalk, at lower center, by Saint-Non: *Michelange chappelle Sistine*

Rijksmuseum, Amsterdam, Rijksprentenkabinet, 49:538

Provenance
Acquired from Colnaghi, London, 1949.

Exhibitions
London, Colnaghi, 1949, no. 46

Bibliography
A. 1827, fig. 457
Rosenberg and Brejon, 1986, no. 60, ill.

Related works
The Louvre has a counterproof of the right side of the drawing (see figure 1; A. 1828).
  This drawing is the subject of an aquatint by Saint-Non (see figure 2; *Fragments,* no. 55; *Griffonis,* no. 154).

Of the many copies after what were then famous paintings in Rome, which Fragonard executed for Saint-Non, some eighty drawings are known to exist today; those after Raphael and Michelangelo predominate, but there are also works by the great masters of the Baroque, such as the Carracci, Caravaggio, Rosa, Serodine, Rubens, and Poussin. The two Fragonard drawings included here—engravings of both were made by Saint-Non for the *Fragments* and the *Griffonis*—copy Michelangelo's famous frescoes in the Sistine Chapel (see figures 3, 4, and also 5). Saint-Non (pp. 140–41) did not comment on the ceiling of the chapel, and was scarcely appreciative of the *Last Judgment*: it certainly held "a lesson for all painters," but it was also "the most extravagant and the most poorly composed of works," with, however, some "admirable . . . details . . . by a proud and awesome genius."

Boucher had advised his pupil (see Introduction to this chapter) not to take Raphael or Michelangelo too seriously when in Rome. Fragonard, however, did not follow his advice. He was "moved" by the former and "in awe" of the latter; so impressed was he that he almost renounced painting. It took all of his energy and Natoire's and then Saint-Non's attentive support for him to overcome his discouragement.

Fragonard's copies are interesting in that they retain the form of Michelangelo's figures, but not their force. He dispensed with their "terribilità," disguised the baldness of the prophets, revitalized the putti, and emphasized elegance instead of power.

Figure 1. Fragonard, after Michelangelo. *The Prophet Daniel.* Counterproof. Musée du Louvre, Paris, Cabinet des Dessins

Figure 2. Abbé de Saint-Non, after Fragonard. *The Erythrean Sibyl* and *The Prophet Daniel.* Aquatint. Bibliothèque d'Art et d'Archéologie, Paris

Figure 3. Michelangelo.
The Erythrean Sibyl.
Sistine Chapel, Vatican

Figure 4. Michelangelo.
The Prophet Daniel.
Sistine Chapel, Vatican

Figure 5. Ango. *God Creating the Heavens.*
Whereabouts unknown

43   View of Ronciglione

Black chalk on paper, 20.6 x 29.1 cm.
Inscribed at the lower left, by Saint-Non: *Vüe de Ronciglione 14 avril 1761*

Trustees of the British Museum, London, 1936.5.9.1

Provenance
The "antiquarian" Sir Samuel Rush Meyrick
(1783–1848), ancestor of Mrs. Spencer
Whatley, who gave the drawing to the British
Museum in 1936, along with 70 other copies
of old masters and a few views of sites and
monuments by Fragonard.

Exhibitions
Tokyo, 1980, no. 92, ill.

Bibliography
Senior, 1936, pp. 5–9, ill. pl. V a
A. 2126, fig. 568
Cayeux, 1985, p. 98
Rosenberg and Brejon, 1986, no. 123, fig. V

"Left Rome at noon on April 14, 1761, to spend the night
in Ronciglione, a small town 5 posts outside of Rome [54
km.], which is situated in an unusual setting; Remarkable
rocks, very picturesque forges and foundries" (*Journal,* p.
163). Thus began Saint-Non's five-month journey back to
Paris in the company of Fragonard. This drawing, one of the
few that is dated, is the earliest from that trip, and is
interesting in that it depicts a site instead of a monument or a
work of art.

The exceptionally detailed and careful technique is explained by the fact that Saint-Non wanted to assemble a set
of drawings that would be both precise and faithful to the

Figure 1. Hubert Robert. *View of Ronciglione.*
Musée des Beaux-Arts, Valence

original—in this case, the topography of a site. This exactitude does not prevent us from admiring the lightness of the handling and the fineness of the details—especially, in the passages of light and shadow. A comparison of Fragonard's sketch with a famous red-chalk drawing by Hubert Robert (figure 1), most likely executed at the same time (Robert may have accompanied Saint-Non and Fragonard as far as Caprarola), shows the differences between the two artists. Robert's drawing is more powerful and more monumental, but it has neither the depth, the delicacy, nor—especially in such details as the laundresses grouped around the washhouse—the charm of Fragonard's work.

44 The Courtyard of the Palazzo Pitti, Florence

Black chalk on paper, 20.2 x 29.5 cm.
Inscribed at the lower left, by Saint-Non: *Palais Pitti, florence 25 avril 1761*

Trustees of the British Museum, London, 1936.5.9.19

Provenance
See entry 43.

Exhibitions
Tokyo, 1980, no. 93, ill.

Bibliography
Senior, 1936, pp. 5–9
A. 2292, fig. 593
Rosenberg and Brejon, 1986, no. 126, fig. VIII

Figure 1. The courtyard of the Palazzo Pitti today

After leaving Rome, the two travelers made their first major stop in Florence, where they arrived on April 18 or 19, 1761, and stayed for two weeks. The abbé wrote in his *Journal* (pp. 168–69): "It is one of the best-built cities in Italy and the one in which the architecture is, in general, in the best taste, but the dark brown color of the stone they use gives the streets a somewhat sad and gloomy aspect," adding, with regard to the Palazzo Pitti: "The architecture of this palace is very closely related to that of the Luxembourg in Paris [*sic*], but it is even more massive and more fitting for a fortress than for a Palace."

On April 25, from the gallery on the first floor, Fragonard drew Ammanati's interior courtyard (see figure 1), which is much the same today, and part of the gardens. Hubert Robert (figure 2) also drew this courtyard (in an unusual departure for him, in three different colored chalks), probably during his stay in Florence between December 1762 and March 1763—to judge from the detail of the guards warming themselves around a fire.

Figure 2. Hubert Robert.
The Courtyard of the Palazzo Pitti.
Musée des Beaux-Arts, Lille

45 Giambologna's Fountain of Venus

Black chalk on paper, 28.6 x 20.7 cm.
Inscribed in black chalk, at the lower left, by Saint-Non: *Jardins de Boboli/florence 19. avril 1761*

Trustees of the British Museum, London, 1936.5.9.17

Provenance
See entry no. 43.

Exhibitions
Tokyo, 1980, no. 94

Bibliography
Senior, 1936, pp. 5–9
A. 1048, fig. 727
Rosenberg and Brejon, 1986, no. 164, ill.,
 fig. XXIII

Related works
There is a counterproof in a private collection
in Paris (see figure 1; A. 1049). In 1776,
Pigache owned a counterproof of this drawing; it was sketched by Saint-Aubin in the
margin of the sales catalogue (see figure 2;
also, cat. nos. 47, 49).

Figure 1. Fragonard.
The Fountain of Venus.
Counterproof.
Private collection, Paris

In his *Journal,* Saint-Non makes no allusion to Giambologna's famous fountain representing Venus emerging from
her bath, watched by four satyrs, which occupies one of the
grottoes in the Boboli Gardens (see figure 3).

This drawing is one of only three made in Florence that
bears a date (see the previous entry, and no. 127 in Rosenberg and Brejon), and it is very faithful to the original (which
he placed in an outdoor setting, against a cloudy sky).
Fragonard could not have remained indifferent to the sensual elegance of this work.

Figure 2. Gabriel de Saint-Aubin.
Detail of a page from the Pigache
collection sales catalogue (1776).
Bibliothèque Nationale, Paris,
Cabinet des Estampes

Figure 3. Giambologna.
The Fountain of Venus.
Boboli Gardens, Florence

46 The Horrors of War

(after Peter Paul Rubens)

Black chalk on paper, 19.7 x 29.4 cm.
Inscribed in black chalk, at the lower left: *Rubens. Palais Pitti. florence*

Trustees of the British Museum, London, 1936.5.9.22

Provenance
See entry no. 43.

Bibliography
Senior, 1936, pp. 5–9, pl. IV b
A. 1099, fig. 313
Watson, 1971, p. 81, ill.
Rosenberg and Brejon, 1986, no. 129, ill.,
   fig. IX

Related works
A very faded version in black chalk heightened with gray wash is in the Musée des
Beaux-Arts, Grenoble (Inv. M.G.D. 1317;
figure 1). There is a counterproof in the Norton Simon Collection (figure 2; A. 1100,
fig. 314).

Figure 1. Fragonard. *The Horrors of War.*
Musée des Beaux-Arts, Grenoble

Figure 2. Fragonard.
The Horrors of War. Counterproof.
Norton Simon Collection, Pasadena

Figure 3. Peter Paul Rubens.
The Horrors of War.
Palazzo Pitti, Florence

"Rubens seemed to be as much a Poet as a great Painter in
a Capital Picture by him, whose allegorical subject represents
the furor of War or the destruction of the arts. It is a work
full of fire and of Enthusiasm" (Saint-Non, *Journal,* p.
170).

Fragonard, an unconditional admirer of Rubens, may
have softened some of the brutality, emotion, and pathos of
his masterpiece—which is still preserved in the Palazzo Pitti
(figure 3)—but he succeeded in capturing its vitality and
élan.

47 Minerva Wresting Adolescence from the Arms of Venus

(after Pietro da Cortona)

Black chalk on paper, 20.4 x 28.4 cm.
Inscribed at the lower left, by Saint-Non: *du Cortone Palais Pitti. florence*

Trustees of the British Museum, London, 1936.5.9.20

Provenance
See entry 43.

Bibliography
Senior, 1936, pp. 5–9
A. 1852, fig. 466
Rosenberg and Brejon, 1986, no. 137, ill.,
  fig. XII

Related works
Among the known counterproofs are: one, in
the Norton Simon Collection (see figure 1; A.
1853, fig. 467), whose inscription, "Luca
Giordano Gallerie Ricardi a florence," contains an error; a second, in Besançon, red
chalk on a black-chalk counterproof, formerly in the Pierre-Adrien Pâris collection
(see figure 2; A. 1854; Cornillot, 1957, no.
51, ill.), without an inscription; another paler
example in a private collection, Paris (see figure 3; ibid.); and a fourth, which was in the
Darmstadt museum before World War II (see
figure 4; counterproof of a counterproof),
also without an inscription.

A counterproof inscribed at the top "gior-
dane ricardi florence" was drawn by Saint-
Aubin in the margin of his copy of the
Pigache sales catalogue of October 21, 1776,
lots 493–499 (see figure 5; also, cat. nos.
45, 49).

Figure 1. Fragonard.
*Minerva Wresting Adolescence from the
Arms of Venus*. Counterproof.
Norton Simon Collection, Pasadena

Figure 2. Fragonard.
*Minerva Wresting Adolescence from the
Arms of Venus*. Counterproof.
Musée des Beaux-Arts, Besançon

Figure 3. Fragonard.
*Minerva Wresting Adolescence from the
Arms of Venus*. Counterproof.
Private collection, Paris

Figure 4. Fragonard.
*Minerva Wresting Adolescence from the
Arms of Venus*. Counterproof of a counterproof.
Formerly in Darmstadt

Figure 5. Gabriel de Saint-Aubin. Detail
of a page of the Pigache collection sales
catalogue (1776). Bibliothèque Nationale,
Paris, Cabinet des Estampes

Figure 6. Pietro da Cortona.
*Minerva Wresting Adolescence from the
Arms of Venus*. Palazzo Pitti, Florence

"But one of the principal adornments of the Palais Pitti is a series of ceilings decorated by Cortona, in which this great painter combined the richest and most pleasing composition with the most harmonious color" (Saint-Non, *Journal,* p. 170).

In Rome, the pensioner Fragonard had copied Pietro da Cortona's *Saint Paul Restored to Sight.* The subject here is more appealing (see figure 6). As usual, Fragonard's figures are more youthful: the young girl holding a crown of flowers at the right center inspired a figure in the *Venus and Cupid* (figure 7)—one of the overdoors from the old Château de Louveciennes (today in Dublin).

Figure 7. Fragonard. *Venus and Cupid.* National Gallery of Ireland, Dublin

48   Night and Day

(after Michelangelo)

Black chalk on paper, 18.9 x 29.8 cm.
Inscribed at the lower left, by Saint-Non: *Michelange/florence Sacristie de St Laurent.*
    Tombeau de Laurent de Medicis duc de Nemours

Trustees of the British Museum, London, 1936.5.9.15

Provenance
See entry no. 43.

Exhibitions
Tokyo, 1980, no. 101, ill.

Bibliography
Senior, 1936, pp. 5–9
A. 1830, fig. 756
Rosenberg and Brejon, 1986, no. 149,
    fig. XV

Related works
A counterproof was sold at Sotheby's,
London, June 10, 1959, part of lot 19.

Figure 1. Michelangelo.
Night, from the tomb of Giuliano de' Medici.
San Lorenzo, Florence, Medici Chapel

Figure 2. Michelangelo.
Day, from the tomb of Giuliano de' Medici.
San Lorenzo, Florence, Medici Chapel

Fragonard copied not only the figures of *Night* and *Day* (figures 1, 2) on the tomb of Giuliano de' Medici, but also those of *Dusk* and *Dawn* from the tomb of Lorenzo de' Medici (Saint-Non reversed the captions), in the New Sacristy of San Lorenzo, in Florence. Both drawings are in the British Museum (see Rosenberg and Brejon, 1986, no. 150, ill., for the second one, and no. 151, ill., for the portrait of Lorenzo de' Medici).

"These two tombs are remarkable for the admirable statues carved by Michelangelo, although one might object to their exaggerated poses [which Fragonard, as usual, toned down] . . . they are so dignified and so clever in form that they may be recognized as the work of the greatest of sculptors" (Saint-Non, *Journal,* p. 175).

49 Allegory of Temperance
(after Luca Giordano)

Black chalk on paper, 27.6 x 20.6 cm.
Inscribed at the lower left, by Saint-Non: *Luca Giordano / Palais Riccardi. florence*

Trustees of the British Museum, London, 1936.5.9.29

Provenance
See entry no. 43.

Exhibitions
Tokyo, 1980, no. 106, ill.

Bibliography
Senior, 1936, pp. 5–9
A. 1840
Rosenberg and Brejon, 1986, no. 159, ill.,
fig. XX

Related works
There is a counterproof in the Norton Simon
Collection (see figure 1; A. 1841).
A drawing by Saint-Aubin in the margin of
his copy of the Pigache sales catalogue of
October 21, 1776, lots 493–499 (see figure
2), today in the Bibliothèque Nationale,
indicates that Pigache owned a counterproof
of the present drawing (see also cat. nos. 45,
47).

Figure 1. Fragonard, after Luca
Giordano. *Allegory of Temperance.*
Counterproof. Norton Simon
Collection, Pasadena

Figure 2. Gabriel de Saint-Aubin.
Detail of a page from the Pigache
collection sales catalogue (1776).
Bibliothèque Nationale, Paris,
Cabinet des Estampes

Figure 3. Luca Giordano.
Allegory of Temperance (detail).
Fresco. Palazzo Medici-Riccardi, Florence

"The Palace ... of the marquis Riccardi ... contains a gallery whose entire ceiling was decorated by Luca Giordano, and it is certainly one of the most beautiful and most pleasing works by this great master; the composition may be a bit too overloaded with allegories, but they were painted so tastefully and delightfully that one never tires of admiring them; all of the figures are imbued with a charming form and a color harmony that is enchanting. For me, it was one of the most pleasing things in Italy" (Saint-Non, *Journal,* p. 179).

Fragonard executed for Saint-Non at least seven drawings of Giordano's frescoes in the Palazzo Medici-Riccardi, in Florence (most of them are in the British Museum; see figure 3; Rosenberg and Brejon, 1986, nos. 156–162, ill.). There is no doubt that the inventiveness of Giordano, the genius of *fa presto,* the freedom of his brushwork, and his taste for improvisation held great importance for Fragonard, who had already admired Giordano's paintings in Naples; later, he would copy other works by Giordano in Venice, Padua, Vicenza, and Genoa.

50 Pisa: the Baptistery, the Campo Santo, the Duomo, and the Leaning Tower

Black chalk on paper, 18.3 x 28.9 cm.
Inscribed at the lower left, by Saint-Non: *Vüe de l'Église du Dosme de Pise—1ᵉʳ may 1761*

Trustees of the British Museum, London, 1936.5.9.35

Provenance
See entry 43.

Bibliography
Senior, 1936, pp. 5–9
A. 1495, fig. 405
Rosenberg and Brejon, 1986, no. 166, ill.,
    fig. XXV

Saint-Non and Fragonard made a "little side trip to Pisa and Livorno" at the end of April and during the first days of May 1761. They admired the "[well-]cultivated ... countryside" (not to mention the "beautiful girls"!).

Pisa "has nothing interesting to see apart from three or four very Gothic monuments, *but* [italics added] they have a beautiful form, and being close together, are a very fine sight to behold" (Saint-Non, *Journal,* pp. 179, 182, 186). Saint-Non did not forget to mention the Duomo, the Baptistery, the Campo Santo, and the leaning tower (an "odd thing"). He also gives us a very long description of the Jeu du Pont, the games that were held on "a very beautiful marble bridge" every three years. How unfortunate that Fragonard did not leave us a few sketches of this event!

51 The Feast of Antony and Cleopatra
(after Giovanni Battista Tiepolo)

Etching, in two states: first state, 15 x 10.7 cm.; copperplate, 16.5 x 11.5 cm.

Musée du Louvre, Paris, Cabinet des Dessins, Rothschild Collection

Bibliography
G. Wildenstein, 1956, no. XII, ill. (with
    bibliography and lists of exhibitions, sales,
    and collections containing an example of
    this etching)
Pognon and Bruand, 1962, IX, p. 287,
    no. 11
Rosenberg and Brejon, 1986, under no. 212

Related works
Fragonard's drawing for this etching is in the Norton Simon Collection, Pasadena (see figure 1; A. 1108, fig. 311; Williams, 1978, no. 12, ill.; Rosenberg and Brejon, 1986, no. 212, ill., pl. XXXVII).
    The counterproof is in the Bibliothèque Nationale (see figure 2; A. 1109, fig. 312). Saint-Non's aquatint dates from 1775 (figure 3; *Fragments,* no. 40; *Griffonis,* no. 267).

Figure 1. Fragonard,
after Giovanni Battista Tiepolo.
The Feast of Antony and Cleopatra.
Drawing. Norton Simon
Collection, Pasadena

Figure 2. Fragonard. *The Feast
of Antony and Cleopatra.*
Counterproof. Bibliothèque
Nationale, Paris, Cabinet
des Estampes

Figure 3. Abbé de Saint-Non,
after Fragonard.
The Feast of Antony and Cleopatra.
Aquatint. Bibliothèque d'Art
et d'Archéologie, Paris

Figure 4. Giovanni Battista
Tiepolo. *The Feast of Antony
and Cleopatra.* Palazzo Labia,
Venice

Fragonard and Saint-Non arrived in Venice May 8, 1761, and stayed until June 23, leaving this city "without any regret!" Apart from the works of art and the Carnival, what they appreciated most were the conservatories of young girls and the regattas (*Journal,* pp. 189–214). Some sixty drawings by Fragonard after works by the Venetian masters Titian, Veronese, Tintoretto, S. Ricci, and Tiepolo, and by Giordano and Castiglione, have come down to us.

Most of these drawings are in the Norton Simon Collection, and are not included here; instead, we must rely on three original etchings by Fragonard to evoke—however incompletely—this sojourn in Venice.

"A large number of palaces and churches are filled with the works of Tiepolo, all of which have a distinctive character and a manner that are easy to recognize, but always by a man of taste rather than by a great master." Did Fragonard share these reservations? Judging by the influence exerted on him by Tiepolo (1696–1770) and by the copies of Tiepolo's works that he executed in Venice (about ten) and in Vicenza, Fragonard would have been among his admirers. In any

event, Tiepolo was the only living artist after whose works he made engravings.

The date of the visit of the two companions to the Palazzo Labia is not known, but it is interesting to compare Saint-Non's impressions with those set down by Bergeret thirteen years later (1895 ed., p. 388). Of the *Feast of Antony and Cleopatra* (figure 4) in this palace, Bergeret wrote that "everything is grand and noble, supremely rich in composition," adding, "I would have liked more nobility in the figures of Cleopatra and Mark Antony, but the details are wonderful. All manner of accessories, dogs, and dwarves are admirable, and well placed."

To quote a writer of our own time: "—It looks a lot like Tiepolo, Sigrid said—Indeed, he copied him in Venice in 1761, the year that Casanova fought a duel in Paris. It was summer. He was there with an abbé with the prophetic name of Saint-Non—No?—Yes. The picture by Tiepolo that interested him was a banquet with Antony and Cleopatra!" (Philippe Sollers, *Le Coeur absolu,* 1987, p. 324).

52 The Virgin in Glory with Saint Catherine, Saint Rose Holding the Christ Child, and Saint Agnes

(after Giovanni Battista Tiepolo)

Etching, in only one state, 21.3 x 13 cm.; copperplate, 23 x 16 cm.

Bibliothèque Nationale, Paris, Cabinet des Estampes

Bibliography
G. Wildenstein, 1956, no. IX, ill. (with detailed discussion)
Pognon and Bruand, 1962, IX, p. 286, no. 8
Rosenberg and Brejon, 1986, under no. 215

Related works
Fragonard's drawing has not come down to us, but Saint-Non made an aquatint of it in 1775 (figure 1; *Fragments,* no. 37; *Griffonis,* no. 295; see figure 2 for the abbé's unique counterproof of this aquatint, in the Bibliothèque Nationale).

Figure 1. Abbé de Saint-Non, after Fragonard. *The Virgin in Glory, with Three Saints.* Bibliothèque Nationale, Paris, Cabinet des Estampes

Figure 2. Abbé de Saint-Non, after Fragonard. *The Virgin in Glory, with Three Saints.* Annotated counterproof of the aquatint. Bibliothèque Nationale, Paris, Cabinet des Estampes

Figure 3. Giovanni Battista Tiepolo. *The Virgin in Glory, with Three Saints.* Santa Maria della Fava, Venice

Tiepolo's painting of this subject is still preserved in Santa Maria della Fava, Venice. In this same church, Fragonard copied the more famous *Education of the Virgin,* which had a lasting influence on him (see cat. no. 233; Rosenberg and Brejon, 1986, no. 214, ill.).

In the present work, Fragonard took certain liberties with Tiepolo's painting (figure 3), leaving out the nimbi and adding more putti in the sky. When the etching is compared with Saint-Non's aquatint (figure 1) and with the unique counterproof of it that the abbé made for his own use (figure 2), the result needs no comment.

53 Saint Jerome and the Angel

(after Johann Liss)

Etching, in three states: first state, 15.2 x 10.5 cm.; copperplate, 16.3 x 11.3 cm.

Musée du Louvre, Paris, Cabinet des Dessins, Rothschild Collection

Bibliography
G. Wildenstein, 1956, no. XIV, ill. (with details on the states, extant examples, list of sales, and complete bibliography)
Pognon and Bruand, 1962, IX, p. 287, no. 13
Rosenberg and Brejon, 1986, under no. 216

Related works
The original drawing has been lost, but a counterproof (figure 1) is in the collection of Ian Woodner, New York.
Saint-Non made an engraving of Fragonard's drawing in 1772 (figure 2; *Fragments*, no. 15; *Griffonis*, no. 273).

Figure 1. Fragonard.
Saint Jerome and the Angel.
Counterproof. Collection
Ian Woodner, New York

Figure 2. Abbé de Saint-Non, after the drawing by Fragonard.
Saint Jerome and the Angel.
Aquatint. Bibliothèque d'Art et d'Archéologie, Paris

Figure 3. Johann Liss.
Saint Jerome and the Angel.
San Nicolò da Tolentino, Venice

The influence of the work of Johann Liss on Fragonard has already been noted (Sterling, 1964, and Liss exhibition catalogue, Augsburg-Cleveland, 1975–76, among others), and yet neither Saint-Non nor Bergeret made any mention of his masterpiece, *Saint Jerome and the Angel* (figure 3), which is still preserved in San Nicolò da Tolentino, Venice.

The light colors, the pastel pinks, the free brushwork, and the sensuality of the handling in Liss's painting surely appealed to Fragonard, who was sensitive to the blend in this Northern artist of a Baroque, Rubenesque energy and warm, Venetian coloring. Fragonard copied the work faithfully, but not without endowing the composition with his stamp: the angel in the sky, holding a book, has a dreamy and engaging smile that is Fragonard's personal touch.

54 The Massacre of the Innocents

(after Guido Reni)

Black chalk on paper, 29.4 x 20.8 cm.
Inscribed in black chalk, at the lower right, by Saint-Non: *Du Guide Eglise de San Domenico/Bologne*

Private collection

Bibliography
A. 2596, fig. 651
Rosenberg and Brejon, 1986, no. 278, ill.

Related works
A counterproof was formerly in the museum in Darmstadt (figure 1).
  An aquatint was made by Saint-Non in 1772 for the *Fragments* (no. 30) and for the *Griffonis* (no. 179; see figure 2, a counterproof of the aquatint, with inscription by Saint-Non, in the Bibliothèque Nationale).

Figure 1. Fragonard.
The Massacre of the Innocents.
Counterproof.
Formerly in Darmstadt (destroyed)

Figure 2. Abbé de Saint-Non,
after Fragonard.
The Massacre of the Innocents.
Counterproof of the aquatint.
Bibliothèque Nationale,
Paris, Cabinet des Estampes

Figure 3. Guido Reni.
The Massacre of the Innocents.
Pinacoteca Nazionale,
Bologna

Fragonard and Saint-Non stayed in Bologna during July 1761. "The Massacre of the Innocents by Guido [then in San Domenico, today in the Pinacoteca]... is one of the most beautiful pictures by this famous master and one of the most appealing, for the liveliness of the expressions" (Saint-Non, *Journal,* p. 83). This judgment is no more surprising than the choice of works copied by Fragonard: examples by the Carracci, Guercino, Albani, and a few less-well-known seventeenth-century Bolognese masters.

  The copy of Guido Reni's *Massacre of the Innocents* (figure 3) is extremely accurate. Fragonard, however, softened the expressions, and seemed more sensitive to the rhythm of the composition than to its tension. He ignored the pulse and the terrible violence of Reni's work, retaining only its elegance. Did he have in mind the admirable figure of the woman kneeling in the foreground and clasping her hands when he drew *S'il m'était aussi fidèle!* (cat. no. 119)?

55 The Entry to Genoa from the Fort of San Tommaso

Black chalk on paper, 20.3 x 28.9 cm.
Inscribed at the lower left, by Saint-Non: *Vüe de L'entrée de Gesnes du Coté du Bastion San Tomasi. 7.7.bre 1761*

Trustees of the British Museum, London, 1936.5.9.36

Provenance
See entry no. 43.

Exhibitions
Tokyo, 1980, no. 95, ill.

Bibliography
Senior, 1936, pp. 5–9
A. 930, fig. 247
Cailleux, Paris exhibition catalogue, 1983,
   under no. 25
Rosenberg and Brejon, 1986, no. 343, ill.,
   fig. LV

After passing through Parma, Colorno (see Introduction to this chapter), and Piacenza, Fragonard and Saint-Non arrived in Genoa, their last stop in Italy. There, Fragonard copied many paintings for the abbé, and drew the principal palaces and certain picturesque spots. Depicted here, according to E. Gavazza, is the Fort of San Tommaso, which was near the Palazzo Doria and which has since been destroyed. Another drawing by Fragonard, a "Second View of the entry to Genoa," shows the same fort from a different angle (see figure 1; Rosenberg and Brejon, 1986, no. 342, ill.).

This view is dated September 7, 1761. Three days later, "at six o'clock in the morning, we left the port of Genoa by boat..." (Saint-Non, *Journal,* p. 250). The drawings of Genoa, most of which are in the British Museum, are among the most beautiful made by Fragonard during his trip back to France.

Figure 1. Fragonard. *The Entry to Genoa from the Terrace of the Palazzo Doria.* Whereabouts unknown

56 The Palazzo Balbi, Genoa

Black chalk on paper, 20.2 x 29.2 cm.
Inscribed at the lower left, by Saint-Non: *Palais Balby donné aux Jesuites. à Gesnes*

Trustees of the British Museum, London, 1936.5.9.43

Provenance
See entry no. 43.

Exhibitions
Tokyo, 1980, no. 97, ill.

Bibliography
Senior, 1936, pp. 5–9, pl. V b
A. 927, fig. 248
Rosenberg and Brejon, 1986, no. 330, ill.

Saint-Non and Fragonard admired the riches of Genoa, the painting collections as well as the palaces, whose "interiors ... perfectly matched [the] magnificence of the exteriors" (Saint-Non, *Journal,* p. 244).

Fragonard drew many of these palaces, including the Palazzo Filippo Durazzo—called the Durazzo-Pallavicini—and the Palazzo Marcellino Durazzo, called the Palazzo Reale (Rosenberg and Brejon, 1986, nos. 319, 323). The Palazzo Balbi, today the Palazzo dell'Università, was built by Bianco, beginning in 1634, as a Jesuit college (which Saint-Non did not forget to point out). The staircase that connects the atrium and the courtyard was designed by Parodi, and the lions by F. Biggi.

57 Christ in the House of Simon

(after Paolo Veronese)

Black chalk on paper, 20.1 x 28.3 cm.
Inscribed at the lower left, by Saint-Non: *Paul Veronese, Palais de M.ⁿᵒ Durazzo. Gesnes*

Trustees of the British Museum, London, 1936.5.9.61

Provenance
See entry no. 43.

Exhibitions
Tokyo, 1980, no. 110, ill.

Bibliography
Senior, 1936, pp. 5–9
A. 1801, fig. 758
Rosenberg and Brejon, 1986, no. 329, ill.

Related works
A counterproof of a counterproof, with an inscription, is in a private collection in Paris (figure 1).

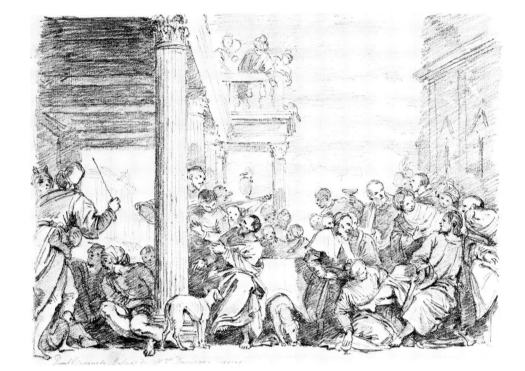

Figure 1. Fragonard, after Paolo Veronese.
Christ in the House of Simon.
Counterproof of a counterproof.
Private collection, Paris

"The Palazzo Marcellino Durazzo owns in particular a famous picture by Paul Veronese that may certainly be considered as his best work and the most [*sic*] preserved one anywhere" (Saint-Non, *Journal,* p. 245). This famous picture, which represents Mary Magdalene washing the feet of Christ during the supper at the house of Simon the Pharisee, is today in the Galleria Sabauda, Turin (figure 2).

Although seemingly executed with great rapidity, Fragonard's rendition is extremely accurate. Understandably, these copies would prove valuable as exercises, for the painter, in his later work.

Figure 2. Paolo Veronese. *Christ in the House of Simon.* Galleria Sabauda, Turin

58 Birds of Every Species

(after Giovanni Benedetto Castiglione)

Black chalk on paper, 22.2 x 26.6 cm.
Inscribed at the lower left, by Saint-Non: *Benedette. Palais de Philippo Durazzo, Gesnes*

Trustees of the British Museum, London, 1936.5.9.66

Provenance
See entry no. 43.

Bibliography
Senior, 1936, pp. 5–9
A. 1823, fig. 754
Rosenberg and Brejon, 1986, no. 320, ill.,
  fig. L

The original painting by Castiglione (1609–1663/65; see figure 1), which was formerly in the Palazzo Durazzo, is today in the Palazzo Durazzo-Pallavicini, Genoa. Fragonard copied the part of the painting with the exotic and domestic species of birds, leaving out the left side (which may post-date Fragonard) and the top (the figure has been variously identified as God and as Jupiter).

"A master whose works are extremely rare elsewhere, but abundant here, is Benedetto, or rather Greghetto, as he is called in Genoa, his birthplace. He is a painter who is full of fire, genius, and taste, especially in the pictures of bacchanalia and animals that he liked to paint and in which he excelled" (Saint-Non, *Journal,* pp. 245, 247).

Figure 1. Giovanni Benedetto Castiglione.
Jupiter Surrounded by Birds of Every Species.
Palazzo Durazzo-Pallavicini, Genoa

59   The Nativity

(after Giovanni Benedetto Castiglione)

Black chalk on paper, 28.8 x 19.2 cm.
Inscribed in black chalk, at the lower left, by Saint-Non: *Benedette-Eglise di St Luc. Gesnes.*

Trustees of the British Museum, London, 1936.5.9.42

Provenance
See entry no. 43.

Bibliography
Senior, 1936, pp. 5–9
A. 1817, fig. 755
Rosenberg and Brejon, 1986, no. 350, ill.

Related works
A counterproof of a counterproof, without
any inscription, is in a Paris private collection
(see figure 1; A. 1818, fig. 757; see also A.
1821: probably the same drawing as the
present one, but with the inscription missing).

Figure 1. Fragonard, after
Giovanni Benedetto Castiglione.
The Nativity.
Counterproof of a counterproof.
Private collection, Paris

Figure 2. Giovanni
Benedetto Castiglione.
The Nativity.
San Luca, Genoa

The *Nativity* of 1645 by Castiglione (figure 2)—one of the
artist's "most beautiful" paintings (Saint-Non)—is still in
San Luca, Genoa. Saint-Non's admiration for Castiglione,
which we have already mentioned, was shared by Fragonard
and by most of his contemporaries. Boucher was often
inspired by the work of this Genoese master.

For Fragonard, the work of Castiglione, who had made
many copies of the pictures in the collection of Consul Smith
in Venice, captured the outdoor, pastoral life with contin-
uously fresh imagination and inspiration.

60 Saint Alexander Sauli

(after the sculpture by Pierre Puget)

Black chalk on paper, 27.3 x 16.9 cm.
Inscribed in black chalk, below, by Saint-Non: *Du Puget. Eglise de Carrignano. Gesnes.*

Trustees of the British Museum, London, 1936.5.9.38

Provenance
See entry no. 43.

Exhibitions
Tokyo, 1980, no. 108, ill.

Bibliography
Senior, 1936, pp. 5–9
A. 2590, fig. 654
Rosenberg and Brejon, 1986, no. 352, ill.

See the following entry.

Figure 1. Pierre Puget.
Saint Alexander Sauli.
Santa Maria di Carignano,
Genoa

Figure 2. Edme Bouchardon,
after Pierre Puget.
Saint Alexander Sauli.
Musée du Louvre, Paris,
Cabinet des Dessins

61 Saint Sebastian

(after the sculpture by Pierre Puget)

Black chalk on paper, 28.6 x 17.9 cm.
Inscribed at the bottom left, by Saint-Non: *Du Puget/Eglise de Carignano à Gesnes.*

Trustees of the British Museum, London, 1936.5.9.37

Provenance
See entry no. 43.

Bibliography
Senior, 1936, pp. 5–9
A. 2589, fig. 653
Rosenberg and Brejon, 1986, no. 351, ill.

"In this church [Santa Maria di Carignano] are Puget's two famous statues, one of which represents Saint Sebastian bound to a tree, and the other, a Bishop saint wearing a miter and pontifical vestments [see figure 1, cat. no. 60], works of great beauty, especially the Bishop" (Saint-Non, *Journal*, p. 247). The abbé distinguished himself from his contemporaries, almost all of whom preferred the *Saint Sebastian* (figure 1). The list of the artists who copied this work is a long one (Florence exhibition catalogue, 1968, no. 39). Fragonard's drawings may be compared to those of Edme Bouchardon (1698–1762), who, in his lifetime, was considered one of the greatest, if not the greatest, draftsmen of his day (see figure 2; cat. no. 60, figure 2). The figure in Bouchardon's copy is unquestionably more solid and more vigorous, but it lacks the inspired elegance that characterizes Puget's two admirable creations.

Figure 1. Pierre Puget.
Saint Sebastian.
Santa Maria di
Carignano, Genoa

Figure 2. Edme Bouchardon,
after Pierre Puget.
Saint Sebastian.
Musée du Louvre, Paris,
Cabinet des Dessins

60   61

62 The Villa Lomellini Rostan at Multedo, near Genoa

Black chalk on paper, 19.9 x 28.4 cm.
Inscribed in black chalk, at the lower left, by Saint-Non: *Chateau de Multado appartenant au Serenissime Aug. de Lomellini
Doge de Gesnes 1761*

Trustees of the British Museum, London, 1936.5.9.69

Provenance
See entry no. 43.

Exhibitions
Tokyo, 1980, no. 96, ill.

Bibliography
Senior, 1936, pp. 5–9
A. 1489, fig. 404
Sutton, 1980; 1987, p. 106, fig. 11, p. 112
Rosenberg and Brejon, 1986, no. 357, ill.,
fig. LVII

"Before arriving [at the gardens of Prince Doria], there is Multado [*sic*], which belongs to the Lomellini and whose chief curiosity, for that part of the country, is a small field of about two and a half acres, surrounded by trees in a semicircle, which is very pleasant to stroll in; this little esplanade of sorts is framed by the treetops, which correspond in height to the first story of the house" (Saint-Non, *Journal,* p. 250). Fragonard placed the villa in the background, framed by the arching branches of the trees. In the foreground, children play, and a couple is embracing; the artist here superseded the copyist!

63 The Triumphal Arch at Saint-Rémy-de-Provence

Black chalk on paper, 19.3 x 27.4 cm.
Inscribed at the lower left, by Saint-Non: *Arc de triomphe près S^t. Remy petite Ville de provence à 3 Lieux de Tarascon*

Trustees of the British Museum, London, 1936.5.9.70

Provenance
See entry no. 43.

Exhibitions
Tokyo, 1980, no. 99, ill.

Bibliography
Senior, 1936, pp. 5–9
A. 864, fig. 525
Rosenberg and Brejon, 1986, no. 358, ill.,
  fig. LVIII

Figure 1. Hubert Robert.
The Triumphal Arch at Orange
(detail, showing the triumphal
arch at Saint-Rémy). Musée du Louvre

Fragonard's last three drawings from his return trip to Paris—the only three done in France—are all of monuments from antiquity: the triumphal arch at Saint-Rémy-de-Provence (Glanum) was built at the entrance to the city about 40 B.C. On either side of the central arch, between the fluted columns, two groups of male and female captives may be distinguished.

While Saint-Non had enlisted the services of Hubert Robert to draw the Greek and Roman monuments in Italy—especially at Paestum—to our knowledge he did not have Fragonard copy any on the journey back to France. Saint-Rémy is not even mentioned in his journal.

Did Fragonard, far from Rome—and from Hubert Robert—want to prove that he was as good as his friend at depicting the monuments of antiquity? His drawing of this arch does not have the power of Robert's examples, but it is not a banal copy either. He chose an interesting vantage point and animated his composition with silhouetted figures in the style of Panini.

In the middle ground of his famous *Triumphal Arch at Orange* (figure 1), which he painted for the Palais de Fontainebleau in 1787, Robert also depicted the triumphal arch at Saint-Rémy.

145

64 The Mausoleum at Saint-Rémy-de-Provence

Black chalk on paper, 26 x 19.4 cm.
Inscribed at the bottom, by Saint-Non: *Tombeau antique à S'. Remy en provence./au dessous de La frise du P'. ordre est Cette inscription.* SEX. L. M. JULI. AE J.C.F. PARENTIBUS SUIS

Trustees of the British Museum, London, 1936.5.9.71

Provenance
See entry no. 43.

Bibliography
Senior, 1936, pp. 5–9
A. 885, fig. 712
Rosenberg and Brejon, 1986, no. 359, ill.,
fig. LIX

Related works
A counterproof, with an inscription, is in a
private collection in Paris (A. 885 a).

Figure 1. The Mausoleum at
Saint-Rémy-de-Provence as it
appears today

The Mausoleum at Saint-Rémy-de-Provence (Glanum) is one of the most famous monuments of Roman Gaul, and dates from about the first century A.D.; according to Henri Roland, it was built as a cenotaph commemorating the grandsons of Augustus (see figure 1). Fragonard copied very precisely two of the bas-reliefs of the lower story, the arcades of the middle section, and the columns and entablature that support the dome. In the eighteenth century, it was already one of the best-known antique monuments in France. Hubert Robert represented it in the middle ground of his *Triumphal Arch at Orange* (see figure 2), which he painted in 1787 for the Palais de Fontainebleau. In his drawing, Fragonard depicted some tourists contemplating the ruins.

In the background, there is a cypress that recalls the ones in Tivoli; 128 years later, during his internment in Saint-Rémy, van Gogh indefatigably drew and painted these same trees, giving us an altogether different but equally moving impression of them.

Figure 2. Hubert Robert.
The Triumphal Arch at Orange (detail,
showing the Mausoleum at Saint-Rémy).
Musée du Louvre

65 The Maison Carrée, Nîmes

Black chalk on paper, 19.4 x 28.9 cm.
Inscribed at the lower left, by Saint-Non: *Vüe de La Maison Quarrée à Nismes*

Staatliche Kunsthalle, Karlsruhe, Kupferstichkabinett, 1980.21

Provenance
Henri Lacroix, 1889; Camille Groult: sold, Paris, Palais d'Orsay, December 14, 1979, no. 7, ill.; [Adolphe Stein]; acquired by the Karlsruhe museum, 1980.

Exhibitions
Karlsruhe, 1983, no. 33, ill. p. 75 (entry by Eckart von Borries)

Bibliography
P. p. 316, ill. p. 156
R. p. 224
A. 877
Jahrbuch der Staatlichen Kunstsammlungen in Baden Württemberg, 1981, p. 138, fig. 11
Rosenberg and Brejon, 1986, no. 360, ill., fig. LX

Related works
A counterproof, with an inscription, is in a private collection in Paris (A. 877 a).

The Maison Carrée, "unique for its beauty and condition," dates from the Augustan period, and was one of the most admired Gallo-Roman monuments in the eighteenth century. Saint-Non and Fragonard visited it on September 17, 1761 (*Journal,* p. 254); Hubert Robert's exceptionally fine painting of the temple dates from a quarter of a century later (figure 1).

Fragonard faithfully depicted the Maison Carrée, but also added such details as the surrounding buildings, visitors, passersby, and some workers who seem to be loading blocks of stone. Unlike Hubert Robert, who isolated the temple in a timeless setting, Fragonard represented it in the context of its actual surroundings, and even with a certain familiarity. He was just as interested in rendering the time of day and the picturesqueness of the site as in evoking the grandeurs of the past.

Figure 1. Hubert Robert. *The Maison Carrée.* Musée du Louvre

III

(1761–65)

Figure 2. Fragonard, after Pietro Liberi. *Female Figures in the Clouds.* Musée du Louvre, Paris, Cabinet des Dessins, Rothschild Collection

Figure 1. Fragonard, after Sebastiano Ricci. *The Supper at Emmaus.* Musée du Louvre, Paris, Cabinet des Dessins, Rothschild Collection

Figure 3. Abbé de Saint-Non, after Fragonard. *The Dancing Bear.* Musée du Louvre, Paris, Cabinet des Dessins, Rothschild Collection

On September 26, 1761, Fragonard arrived in Paris, and on March 30, 1765, he was accepted into the Academy. The details of his activity in the intervening three and a half years remain a matter of much speculation.

At first, he made engravings of a few drawings after works by old masters that he had copied in 1761 (figures 1, 2; see cat. nos. 39–40, 51–53). In 1763, he engraved four bacchic scenes inspired by antique models (cat. nos. 67–70). These are as much appreciated today as they were when they served as inspiration for sculptors from Sergel to Clodion. He adapted a drawing of the Villa d'Este that he had made in Italy for the etching entitled *Le Petit Parc* (cat. no. 66). However, it was Saint-Non who made aquatints of most of the works executed by his traveling companion in Italy (one, as early as 1761). Caylus had predicted as much when he said that "he [the abbé] amassed a storehouse that would supply him for the rest of his life." One of the first of these aquatints, *The Dancing Bear* (figure 3), deserves mention because the preparatory drawing (A. 2115; Tokyo, 1980, no. 114, ill.) has been identified, and, like the etching, might date from 1762. Yet, precise points of reference for Fragonard's artistic activity, not to mention the events of his personal life, are few and far between; all that we have are hypotheses (and these are many).

Then, all of a sudden, in March 1765, Fragonard presented to the Academy not only a very large composition, the *Coresus and Callirhoë* (cat. no. 104), but also "several nicely colored and executed landscapes [see cat. nos. 30–32], as well as some drawings in various manners" (Wille), and, according to an old source, a painting called *The Parents' Absence Turned to Account* (cat. no. 108). It is important to recognize that Fragonard produced not only history paintings, but also genre scenes, landscapes, and drawings, and that he worked in very different styles. Unbelievably enough, the Annecy landscape (cat. no. 86), which is so Dutch in feeling; the Hermitage picture *The Parents' Absence Turned to Account,* which owes much to Greuze; and the Louvre's *Coresus* are all contemporary.

The sheer number of these works and the ambition they reveal represent an immense effort that must have kept Fragonard considerably occupied during most of this period—which may be a partial answer to our questions concerning his activity. This is confirmed by the works exhibited a few months later at the Salon; the "drawings" that Fragonard submitted to his future colleagues at the Academy may well have been done in Italy, but the *Coresus and Callirhoë* was executed in Paris. The "well-informed sources" of the day were aware that something "big" was underway. The group of works submitted to the Academy was the result of a long effort. A close reading of the correspondence exchanged between Cochin, the secretary of the Academy, and Marigny, the *Surintendant des bâtiments,* gives the impression that both had been able to follow the progress of the *Coresus and Callirhoë* before it was presented in March 1765.

A few months later, this same work created a sensation at the Salon (the entry below quotes some of the most laudatory critics, as well as those expressing reservations). Diderot's long text, one of the most thorough that he devoted to a painting, was not published in the eighteenth century, but it was known, and it drew the public's attention to the author of the *Coresus*. This triumph, however, was not due to Fragonard's talents alone. Carle Vanloo, then the most famous painter in France, who was respected both for his humanity as well as for the quality of his teaching, and admired for his seriousness and skill as an artist, had just died—as had Deshays (Boucher's talented brother-in-law, and the owner of Fragonard's copies after Rembrandt), the prime painter upon whom rested the hope of the French school. It was absolutely essential that a replacement be found to become the official painter of France. The *Coresus and Callirhoë* herald-ed an artist of this stature; as Grimm remarked to Diderot, "You did well in singling out the picture by Fragonard that captured the public's atten-tion, not so much for its particular merits, but because of our need to find a successor to Carle Van Loo and Deshays."

For Fragonard, acceptance by the Academy meant the purchase of the *Coresus and Callirhoë* by the king (for 2,400 *livres,* paid, however, with the usual administrative delays), a commission for a pendant (cat. no. 107), and lodgings at the Louvre. The artist happened to be in great need of this income and support. In light of Marigny's procrastination (could he do otherwise?), Cochin pleaded for an advance on the payment for the *Coresus*—otherwise, "he [Fragonard] will find himself in such want that he will be obliged to produce works that are unworthy of his genius, and this will delay the success that legitimately may be expected of him."

Thus, with these interesting remarks we conclude our brief evocation of Fragonard's beginnings as an artist in Paris and the importance to his career of the Salon of 1765.

We have already mentioned the friendship between Fragonard and Saint-Non that lasted from 1760 until the abbé's death in 1791. Howev-er, insufficient attention has thus far been paid to a disclosure made by Saint-Non's biographer, the abbé Brizard, like him an "abbé commenda-taire": "A famous painter of our day had received from him, in Italy and in France, many signs of the great interest that he showed those who dis-played distinguished talent as well as amiability. Due to a particular event, the productions of this artist [most certainly, Fragonard] suddenly began to fetch extraordinary prices. The Abbé de Saint-Non, who owned a large number of them, gave them back, saying: 'My friend, I have greatly appreciated these works, but I have been unaware of the value that others attached to them; I return them to you so that you may benefit from their favor with the public, and derive from them the profit that you are entitled to expect.'"

Clearly, not only did Saint-Non return Fragonard's drawings to him (especially, those from the trip to Tivoli and the sojourn at the Villa d'Este) after the "particular event" that "suddenly" catapulted the artist to fame in 1765, but he also gave him financial assistance during the difficult years between 1762 and 1764.

Fragonard is traditionally considered a frivolous artist who painted with great spontaneity, creating with as much facility as speed. Yet, all of the contemporary accounts of his early years, without exception, give an entirely different impression. "The timidity that prevails in this artist's character holds him back; he is never satisfied with his work, but keeps erasing and starting again; this kind of method is a hindrance to talent, and may do much harm to this young artist," Mariette wrote in 1765, adding: "This would make me angry, for his efforts to do well deserve a better fate." Cochin, on April 1, 1765, was no less explicit: "I would add that one of the merits of this artist is a modesty that borders on an extreme self-distrust." We will have occasion to quote other accounts of this

Figure 4. Gabriel de Saint-Aubin.
Page from the Verrier collection sales catalogue
(1776). Bibliothèque Nationale, Paris,
Cabinet des Estampes

"timidity" and lack of self-confidence. Surely, Fragonard had other qualities, but, as we shall see, these had their consequences.

To quote from Grimm again: "When one thinks of all those young
people back from Rome and accepted by the Academy, but who do not
offer the least hope, it does not augur well for the glory of the French
school, which is already decried enough as it is. We have only one
Fragonard able to stand above the crowd of Briards, Brenets, Lépiciés,
Amands, and Taravals, who will certainly never do much of anything. I do
not think that Fragonard's painting is without merit, far from it, but we
must wait until the next Salon to see what this artist will become. This will
not have been the first time that we have seen a painter freshly returned
from Rome, his head full of the riches of Italy, begin brilliantly enough,
only to weaken and fade away from Salon to Salon...."

As for the "works that were unworthy of his genius," one sees only too
clearly what kind of pictures Cochin had in mind. Fragonard had surely
painted some of these before 1765, and they were to become one of his
specialties. The problem is not so much that of establishing a list of them,
as of trying to identify which he painted first during those obscure years.
Some are very risqué (see cat. nos. 72, 73; figure 4), while others are not at
all. The dates for all of them are uncertain. They confirm the variety of
Fragonard's talents, the diversity of his styles, and his facility, which is all
the more apparent when combined with a rapid execution. Fréron may not
have been entirely wrong when he wrote in the *Année littéraire* of 1765:
"M. Fragonard has the particular advantage of not appearing to be the
imitator of any great Painter."

CHRONOLOGY

1762

Saint-Non engraves *The Dancing Bear,* after Fragonard (see figure 3,
p. 149).

1763

Fragonard makes a series of four etchings variously titled *Les Moeurs
des Nymphes et des Satyres* or *Bacchanals* (see cat. nos. 67–70).

February 7
First sale of drawings by Fragonard (subjects not specified).

April 1
"Vu 1° avril 1763," is handwritten in the margin of de Fehrt's engraving after Fragonard, *Draperie jetée sur le Mannequin* (B.N., Kc.
14, petit in-fol.; see cat. no. 12, figure 2).

1764

Fragonard makes two engravings, the *Moses and a Prophet* after Annibale [actually, Lodovico] Carracci (figure 1) and the *Saint Roch in
Prison Comforted by the Angel* after Tintoretto (the print in the museum
in Grasse bears the handwritten inscription "fragonard sculp."; see
figure 2).

Figure 1. Fragonard, after Annibale (actually,
Lodovico) Carracci. *Moses and a Prophet.*
Musée du Louvre, Paris, Cabinet des Dessins,
Rothschild Collection

Figure 2. Fragonard, after Tintoretto.
*Saint Roch in Prison Comforted by
the Angel.* Musée Fragonard, Grasse

151

Saint-Non makes an engraving of Fragonard's *View of the Entrance to Tivoli and of the Walls of the Villa d'Este* and of two other drawings, each entitled *View of the Gardens of the Villa d'Este at Tivoli* (see figure 4, p. 95; cat. no. 33, figure 4; cat. no. 34, figure 1).

December 17
The Leclerc collection sales catalogue mentions two paintings by Fragonard (cat. nos. 16, 17).

1765

March 30
Fragonard is accepted into the Academy after submitting the *Coresus and Callirhoë* (cat. no. 104; *Liste de messieurs les agréés à l'Académie Royale de peinture et de sculpture*, Bibliothèque de l'École des Beaux-Arts, ms. 45; *Procès-Verbaux...*, VII, p. 295; Wille, 1857, I, p. 284; Mariette, 1853–54, II, p. 263, gives the date as March 31).

April 1
Cochin writes of Fragonard's acceptance to Marigny: "La satisfaction que vous avés bien voulu marquer des ouvrages de M. Fragonard me donne lieu de croire qu'il ne peut que vous être agréable que j'aye l'honneur de vous proposer des moyens de l'encourager et de développer ses talens; j'ajouteray qu'un des mérites de cet artiste est une modestie qui va jusqu'à une défiance outrée de soy-même. C'est pourquoy je croy qu'il a besoin plus que personne des encouragemens qu'il mérite d'ailleurs si bien."

He proposes to have a tapestry executed at the Gobelins after the *Coresus and Callirhoë,* and commissions the artist to paint a pendant in replacement of the two commissions given to Deshays, who had just died. Fragonard would thus be able to succeed Deshays in his studio at the Louvre: "M. Fragonard paroist dans la carrière des Arts avec un éclat si supérieur au leur [Brenet and Lépicié] qu'il n'est plus question de droits d'ancienneté: c'est pourquoy j'ay l'honneur de vous demander pour lui cet atelier. Ces bienfaits encourageans le mettront à portée de suivre des talens qui paroissent destinés à soutenir la gloire de notre école" (Furcy-Raynaud, 1904, XX, pp. 10–11).

April 3
"J'adopte d'autant plus volontiers, Monsieur, tout ce que vous me proposés pour M. Fragonard que vous ne faites que me confirmer dans les dispositions où j'étois en sa faveur.

"Vous pouvés donc luy annoncer que je retiens pour les Gobelins son tableau de *Callirhoé,* que je le charge d'en faire un autre de la même grandeur pour servir de pendant, et que je lui accorde l'atelier dont feu M. Deshays jouissoit au Louvre" (Furcy-Raynaud, 1904, XX, pp. 11–12).

April 16
Marigny informs Natoire of Fragonard's acceptance by the Academy: "Le sr Fragonard vient d'être reçu à l'Académie avec une unanimité et un applaudissement dont il y a peu d'exemple. On espère qu'il contribuera beaucoup à nous consoler de la perte de M. Deshays, voilà un beau sujet d'émulation pour vos élèves" (*Corr. des Dir.*, XII, p. 77).

May 15
"Je suis bien charmé que le sr *Flagonard* ce soit fait honneur dans sa réception à l'Académie, et encore, de plus, que vous ayés la bonté de me le confirmer; c'est flateur pour luy et pour moy, attendu l'intérest que je dois prendre à tout ceux qui s'élèvent sous ma direction, et un bel exemple d'émulation pour les autres qui viendrons après luy" (letter from Natoire to Marigny, *Corr. des Dir.*, XII, p. 80).

August 5
"J'ay remis longtemps à vous faire une prière en faveur de Mr Fragonard, mais son besoin m'y détermine. Il se trouveroit obligé par ce besoin de se livrer à des ouvrages peu conformes à son génie et qui retarderoient les succès que l'on a droit d'en attendre. Je vous supplie donc de vouloir bien lui accorder un acompte sur le tableau de *Corésus se sacrifiant pour Callirhoé* que vous avés bien voulu retenir pour la manufacture des Gobelins; cet à-compte, si vous voulés bien l'en favoriser, peut être de 1.200 liv., et ce secours le mettroit en état de travailler, tant au tableau qui y fera pendant qu'à celui qu'il doit faire pour sa réception à l'Académie" (letter from Cochin to Marigny, Furcy-Raynaud, 1904, XX, p. 27).

August 8
Cochin writes Marigny to insist that Fragonard be paid: "Maintenant, la grâce que je vous demande pour lui, c'est de l'aider de quelques secours d'argent.

"Ce tableau de *Callirhoé* est un morceau d'environ 13 pieds de large sur 10. Les figures sont de proportion moyenne; il est fort riche et très fini: s'il étoit de quelqu'un de nos anciens, je ne pourrois l'estimer moins de 3.600 liv., prix auquel ont été estimés les tableaux qui ont servi aux tapisseries de votre salon, qui sont moins chargées d'ouvrage et n'ont que 10 pieds de large. J'use un peu de la jeunesse de M. Fragonard, et quoiqu'il soit aisé de prévoir qu'il prendra bientost un vol aussi élevé que ces Mrs, néanmoins je n'estime son tableau que 2.400 liv." (Furcy-Raynaud, 1904, XX, p. 28).

August 17
Fragonard receives 1,200 *livres* as partial payment for the *Coresus and Callirhoë* (Registre du Louvre, *Paiements,* recorded on August 16, Bibliothèque du Louvre, Réserve, 8², fol. 49).

August 25
Fragonard exhibits three paintings at the Salon, the *Coresus and Callirhoë,* a *Landscape,* and *The Parents' Absence Turned to Account* (cat. nos. 104, 86, 108), and at least two drawings of views of the Villa d'Este at Tivoli (see cat. nos. 30, 32) (*Livret* of the Salon of 1765).

Campion engraves an indoor scene and inscribes it: "Frago. Delin. Romae-c. Campion Sc. antipoli 1765" (see figure 3).

September 15
Fragonard gives a drawing to Aignan-Thomas Desfriches (1715–1800). The following description appeared in the Calando sales catalogue of December 11–12, 1899, no. 54: "habitation devant un cours d'eau, dans le fond, une vieille tour. Contrépreuve d'un beau dessin à la sanguine. Au verso, on lit: 'dessin d'après nature de Monsieur Fragonard, dont il m'a fait présent le 15 septembre 1765. Desfriches' (H. O, 32; L. O, 43)."

Figure 3. Campion, after Fragonard.
Indoor Scene. Musée du Louvre,
Paris, Cabinet des Dessins,
Rothschild Collection

66   Le Petit Parc

Etching, 10.3 x 14 cm.; copperplate, 11.2 x 16.5 cm.
Signed at the center, on the pedestal of the statue: *fragonard*

Bibliothèque Nationale, Paris, Cabinet des Estampes

Bibliography
G. Wildenstein, 1956, no. II, ill. (with complete bibliography and lists of sales and of collections with an example of this etching)
Pognon and Bruand, 1962, IX, p. 289, no. 22

Related works
Engraving
There exists a narrower variant of this etching, which is considered by some to be a second state; G. Wildenstein (1956, after P. p. 329, no. 129) attributes it to Saint-Non (see figure 1).

There is a copy by Franz Edmund Weirotter of the lower part of this etching (see figure 2).

Painting
In the Wallace Collection there is a famous painting fairly similar in its overall composition (figure 3; W. 106, pl. 13).

Drawings
There are several drawings related both to the painting and to the etching (A. 351, fig. 125, today on the art market in New York: see figure 4; A. 352, fig. 126, formerly in the Beurdeley collection, probably the engraved drawing: see figure 5; see also A. 2148, fig. 578, a strengthened counterproof, formerly in the Crocker collection).

A gouache on vellum (A. 1575), formerly on loan to the museum in Portland (Oregon), was sold at Sotheby's, New York, January 14, 1987, no. 181, colorpl., and is today in a private collection in New York (see figure 6).

Le Petit Parc is among Fragonard's most famous compositions: the existence of the Wallace Collection painting, and of two drawings, a gouache (recently rediscovered), and an engraving that was already copied twice in the eighteenth century raises the question of the order in which these works were executed. A date of 1763 is now generally agreed upon for the etching (see the excellent entry by Victor Carlson, Baltimore exhibition catalogue, 1984–85, no. 46, ill.), even though it was long thought to have been done while Fragonard was still in Rome. The painting is generally considered to date from after the Roman period, but as the coarse fiber suggests that the canvas is Italian (as Richard Beresford has noted), we would hesitate to accept this hypothesis.

Be that as it may, Fragonard's work, which derives directly from the drawings and paintings done at Tivoli and at the Villa d'Este in the summer of 1760, is one of the most vibrant homages to nature—a nature certainly tamed by man, but which holds its own and flourishes exuberantly.

The etching perfectly renders the vitality of the trees and shrubs that thrive in the park, covering the balustrades and statues. Fragonard did not set out to exclude all human presence—but the strollers in the park seem to have been "absorbed" by the vegetation.

Figure 1. Abbé de Saint-Non. *Le Petit Parc.*
Musée Fragonard, Grasse

Figure 2. Franz Edmund Weirotter. *Le Petit Parc.* Private collection, Paris

Figure 3. Fragonard. *Le Petit Parc.*
Wallace Collection, London

Figure 4. Fragonard. *Le Petit Parc.*
Art market, New York

Figure 5. Fragonard. *Le Petit Parc.*
Whereabouts unknown

Figure 6. Fragonard. *Le Petit Parc.*
Private collection, New York

67–70 Bacchanal or Satyrs' Games

Etchings: height, from 13.4 to 13.6 cm., width, from 20.3 to 20.4 cm.;
copperplate: height, from 14.3 to 14.7 cm., width, from 21 to 21.3 cm.
Two states exist for each of the etchings (the first state is reproduced here).

Bibliothèque Nationale, Paris, Cabinet des Estampes

67 Nymph Stepping over the Hands of Two Satyrs

Signature scratched at the lower center: *frago 17* [inverted 6] *3*

68 The Satyr's Family

Signed at the bottom left, in capital letters: FRAGO

69 Young Girl Astride a Satyr

Signed at the lower left: *Frago*

70 Satyrs' Dance

Signed at the center, below the medallion: FRAG 90

Bibliography
G. Wildenstein, 1956, nos. III–VI, ill. (the second states, with detailed bibliography, and lists of exhibitions, sales, and collections in which there are examples of the entire series)
Pognon and Bruand, 1962, IX, pp. 284–86, nos. 2–5

Related works
No drawings by Fragonard for these etchings have yet been identified with any certainty (however, see A. 2142, 1660, 1667, 2413, 982, 1662, 1663, and also the article by P. Culot, 1974). For the drawings formerly in the Destailleur collection, which entered the Fogg Art Museum with the Philip Hofer collection, see, most recently, E. W[illiams]., Cambridge, Mass., exhibition catalogue, 1984, no. 31. They cannot be attributed to Fragonard, but perhaps were done by Saint-Non himself (figures 1–4). In any event, the abbé did make engravings of some, as well as of the central medallion of cat. no. 67 (figure 5; Cayeux, 1964, no. 86, and also 61)—most likely after one of his drawings (figure 6)—and the drawings accompanying cat. nos. 69, 70 (figures 7, 8).

67

68

These four bacchic scenes by Fragonard are undoubtedly among the most delightful etchings of the entire eighteenth century. One of them is dated 1763, and there are good reasons to believe that the others were executed at about the same time.

It has often been said that "Fragonard executed the drawings for these etchings in Italy after the bas-reliefs at Herculaneum" (G. Wildenstein, 1956), but only Vermeule (1964, pp. 129–30) has tried to identify them. The *Nymph Stepping over the Hands of Two Satyrs* could be a parody of a

relief on a sarcophagus, which is, today, partially destroyed but was then in the famous Mattei collection in Rome, and was reproduced in the *Monumenta Matheiana* (of 1779; see Reinach, 1912, III, p. 303, no. 4; see also figure 9). In fact, the subject was probably the birth of Aphrodite! As for the *Satyrs' Dance,* Vermeule suggested that it was not based on any particular bacchic sarcophagus relief, but was, instead, "the perfect expression of what Fragonard thought should be represented in this type of bas-relief."

Like Vermeule, we do not regard Fragonard as an "anti-

quarian,'' or as a meticulous archaeologist devoted to histor-ical verisimilitude, but, rather, as an artist who gave free rein to his imagination, to fantasy (especially in the importance that he gave to luxuriant vegetation—inspired by certain etchings by Castiglione), as well as to humor (for example, in *The Satyr's Family*) tinged with an amusing note of licentiousness.

Perhaps not enough attention has been given in the past to the counterproof inscription on the first state of the etching (noted by Wildenstein), whose legibility depends on the quality of the print: ''Bergeret invenit et fecit.'' This inscrip-tion is evidence that, by 1763, Fragonard was already ac-quainted with one of the members of the family of the

fermier général Jacques-Onésyme Bergeret (1715–1785) that was to prove so important to him. Jacques-Onésyme seems to have been elected ''associate-at-large'' of the Acad-emy in 1754 (he planned to visit Italy in 1762, but it appears that he never made the trip). This same first state (or, perhaps, Saint-Non's aquatint of it), representing the nude figure of a nymph, stepping over the hands of two satyrs, was copied by Johan Tobias Sergel (see figure 10; Göthe, 1919, p. 60, ill.; Antonsson, 1942, p. 145, ill.); it is not surprising that the celebrated Swedish sculptor, who lived in Rome from 1767 to 1778 (did he meet Fragonard there?), was inspired by Fragonard's most risqué subject.

Figure 1. Abbé de Saint-Non. *Satyr Embracing a Little Girl.* Fogg Art Museum, Harvard University, Cambridge, Massachusetts

Figure 2. Abbé de Saint-Non. *Satyr Embracing a Little Girl.* Bibliothèque d'Art et d'Archéologie, Paris

Figure 3. Abbé de Saint-Non. *Nymph Astride a Satyr.* Fogg Art Museum, Harvard University, Cambridge, Massachusetts

Figure 4. Abbé de Saint-Non. *Nymph Astride a Satyr.* Bibliothèque d'Art et d'Archéologie, Paris

70

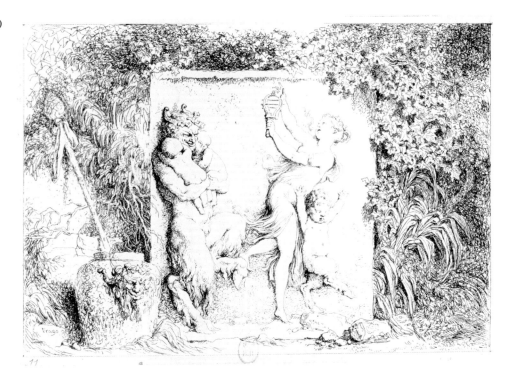

Figure 5. Abbé de Saint-Non. *Nymph Stepping over the Hands of Two Satyrs.* Bibliothèque d'Art et d'Archéologie, Paris

Figure 6. Attributed to the Abbé de Saint-Non. *Nymph Stepping over the Hands of Two Satyrs.* Fogg Art Museum, Harvard University, Cambridge, Massachusetts

Figure 7. Abbé de Saint-Non. *Young Girl Astride a Satyr.* Bibliothèque d'Art et d'Archéologie, Paris

Figure 8. Abbé de Saint-Non. *Satyrs' Dance.* Bibliothèque d'Art et d'Archéologie, Paris

Figure 9. Abbé de Saint-Non. *The Birth of Aphrodite.* After a sarcophagus formerly in the Palazzo Mattei, Rome (from Reinach, 1912)

Figure 10. Johan Tobias Sergel. *Nymph Stepping over the Hands of Two Satyrs.* Fogg Art Museum, Harvard University, Cambridge, Massachusetts

71 "The Master of the World"

Oil on canvas, 52 x 44 cm.
Inscribed at the upper left: *Fragonard/après son/retour d'Italie.* ; at the lower right: *Le Maître du Monde.*

Private collection, Paris

Provenance
Marcille collection, according to W. and M.;
Hippolyte Walferdin (1795–1880): sold
posthumously, April 12–16, 1880, no. 53
(for 810 francs); Malinet; Comte Mniszech,
1889; Landau-Finaly, Paris and Florence;
private collection, Paris.

Bibliography
P. p. 282
N. p. 155
W. and M. 239, ill.

Figure 1. Nicolas de Largillière.
Geneviève Houzé de la Boulaye as Eros.
Private collection, France

This painting, which is very little known in spite of its well-documented history, was brought to our attention by Jacques Wilhelm. According to the uppermost inscription, it was painted upon Fragonard's return from Italy—which is confirmed by the style.

The other inscription tells us the subject: "the master of the world," who is none other than Love, personified as a handsome winged youth. There is nothing original about the iconography; Nicolas de Largillière, among others, had treated it in a similar fashion as early as 1726 (figure 1).

This picture is, in fact, a quick study for a much more ambitious composition, which, for reasons unknown to us, the artist never finished. The preparation of the canvas is still visible around the edges, which were left unpainted. However, the movement displayed by the figure floating toward heaven, and the briskness of the execution anticipate such works as the *Rinaldo in the Enchanted Forest* and the *Rinaldo in the Gardens of Armida* in the Veil-Picard collection.

71 A   Rinaldo in the Enchanted Forest

Bister wash on paper, over a very light underdrawing in black chalk, 33.5 x 46.2 cm.

Private collection, Paris

Provenance
F. de Villars: sold, March 13, 1868, no. 33; Demidoff, Prince of San Donato: sold, April 27–28, 1874, no. 75; the expert Féral: sold, February 27, 1877, no. 64; according to A., "coll. de la Rochefoucault, chez Guiraud frères, Paris; coll. Jacques Guerlain"; private collection, Paris.

Exhibitions
Paris, 1951, no. 35

Bibliography
P. p. 303
Ananoff, 1960, p. 8, ill.
A. 1703, fig. 404
Ananoff, 1968, pp. 12–16, p. 13, fig. 3

Related works
The pendant to this drawing, *Rinaldo in the Gardens of Armida* (figure 1; A. 1702, fig. 435), whose whereabouts are unknown, was sold with the collection of Natoire, December 14, 1778, no. 102 (see figure 2), and of the Comte de Vaudreuil, November 26, 1787, no. 163. The two drawings appear to be studies for the two famous paintings in the Veil-Picard collection, *Rinaldo in the Enchanted Forest* (figure 3; W. 214, pl. 25) and *Rinaldo in the Gardens of Armida* (figure 4; W. 213, pl. 24). These two paintings are illustrated in color in the Tokyo exhibition catalogue, 1980, nos. 38, 37, respectively.

This drawing, along with the celebrated painting in the Veil-Picard collection (figure 3), has always been mentioned in connection with another drawing (figure 1) and with the painting representing *Rinaldo in the Gardens of Armida* (figure 4). However, eighteenth-century sales catalogues do not associate the works with these two subjects, and mention only one composition, which is always titled, "Renaud dans la forêt enchantée" (Mercier collection sale, October 1, 1778, no. 16). Thanks, once again, to Gabriel de Saint-Aubin, we know that at least one of these compositions (and very likely all three), in fact, depicts *Rinaldo in the Gardens of Armida*.

Torquato Tasso's great epic poem *Gerusalemme liberata,* and especially the sequence concerning Rinaldo and Armida, inspired many artists of the seventeenth and eighteenth centuries, not the least of whom were Poussin, Tiepolo, Vouet, and the Carracci (see Rensselaer Lee's famous essay, first published in 1940).

The enchantress Armida discovers Rinaldo, her worst enemy, asleep, and falls in love with him. She tries to keep the hero, a sort of Christian Hercules, in her enchanted gardens, and to prevent him from resuming the struggle to liberate Jerusalem from the infidels. Fragonard seems to have taken his inspiration not from Tasso's work—where, in chapter XVI, the gardens of Armida and the languorous passion of the two lovers are described—but from the popular 1686 opera by Lully and Quinault: Rinaldo fights against the harpies guarding the enchantress's realm, before she reveals herself to him in all her radiant beauty. In both of Fragonard's compositions, it is this scene that seems to be the underlying inspiration.

There are significant differences between the drawing and the painting, especially in the central part of the composition. What is extraordinary is that the wealth of detail, the sphinxes, and the serpents do not detract from the legibility of the work or from its great evocative power.

The opera by Lully and Quinault, superseded by Gluck's version in 1777, was performed in Paris in 1761 and 1764; Fragonard probably executed the drawings and paintings between these years.

Figure 1. Fragonard.
Rinaldo in the Gardens of Armida.
Drawing. Whereabouts unknown

Figure 2. Gabriel de Saint-Aubin.
Page from the Natoire collection sales catalogue (1778).
Bibliothèque Nationale, Paris, Cabinet des Estampes

Figure 3. Fragonard.
Rinaldo in the Enchanted Forest.
Oil on canvas.
Collection Veil-Picard, Paris

Figure 4. Fragonard.
Rinaldo in the Gardens of Armida.
Oil on canvas.
Collection Veil-Picard, Paris

72 La Chemise enlevée

Oil on canvas, oval, 35 x 42.5 cm.
Slightly enlarged at the bottom.

Musée du Louvre, Paris, M.I. 1057

Provenance
Possibly included in the sale of the Gros collection, April 13, 1778, no. 57: "deux tableaux faisant pendant. L'un et l'autre représentent une femme couchée sur un lit et jouant avec des amours. Esquisses ovales en travers. H. 13 pouc. [=35.1 cm.], larg. 16 pouc. [=43.2 cm.] T."; sold for 180 (or 250) *livres* to "Vautrier" (Dacier), or "Vauthier" (W.), or Vautrin; sketched by Saint-Aubin in the margin of his copy of the sales catalogue, today in the Musée du Petit Palais, Paris (see cat. no. 73, figure 2); Dr. Louis La Caze, from 1860 (according to G., p. 276): "M. La Caze m'a dit l'avoir trouvée exposée sur un trottoir et l'avoir payée un louis," "en 1835," according to W.; see also the file on this painting in the Service d'études et de documentation du Louvre; bequeathed to the Louvre, along with the rest of the La Caze collection, in 1869.

Exhibitions
Paris, 1860, no. 150
Paris, 1974, no. 15, ill.

Bibliography
Bürger [Thoré], 1860, p. 349
Gautier, 1860, p. 1
Saint-Victor, 1860, n.p.
Horsin-Déon, 1861, p. 119 (and 244)
G. pp. 275–77, 327
Mantz, 1870, p. 16
P. pp. 69, 132, 273
N. p. 59 [and 120?]
Dacier, 1909, p. 41; 1913, pp. 17–18, 25
Gillet, 1929, p. 85, ill. p. 86
R. p. 158
W. 230, pl. 29, pp. 15, 40 (French edition)
Thuillier, 1967, colorpl. p. 108
W. and M. 242, colorpl. XXI

Related works
The often-mentioned version, formerly in the Paul de Saint-Victor collection (sold, Paris, January 23–24, 1882, no. 26) and in the Récipon collection (P. p. 273; N. p. 120; R. p. 158), does not seem to be an autograph work.
See also the sales in Bièvres, February 16, 1964, no. 28, ill., and in Paris, Drouot, March 28, 1979, no. 165, ill.
The miniature in the Panhard collection, exhibited in 1921 (no. 108), was sold in Paris (Galliéra, December 5, 1975, no. 61, ill.; see figure 1).
A vertical version of the painting, with, at the bottom, the Torch of Love "tombée et brûlante encore," was engraved by E. Guersant at Massard's (see figure 2), as a pendant to the *Cupid Punished by His Mother* (*Journal de Paris*, May 19, 1787, p. 603; *Mercure de France*, July 7, 1787, p. 47; see also P. p. 323, no. 40; Bruand and Hébert, 1970, XI, p. 92, no. 2). For an engraving by Louis-Marin Bonnet, see Hérold, 1935, no. 301.

73 Le Feu aux poudres

Oil on canvas, oval, 37 x 45 cm.

Musée du Louvre, Paris, R. F. 1942.21

Provenance
Sold with the Gros collection, and drawn by Saint-Aubin (see figure 2): see previous entry; F. de Villars: sold, Paris, March 13, 1868, no. 29 (43 x 36 cm.; for 1,520 francs) (?); Merton: sold, Paris, March 24, 1874, no. 14 (for 2,550 francs) (?); Bécherel: sold, November 26–28, 1883, no. 21 (for 2,000 francs); Jacques Doucet: sold, June 6, 1912, no. 148, ill. (for 111,000 francs); Pardinel; François Coty, from 1921; Carlos de Beistegui (acquired from Cailleux, 1935); given to the Louvre with life interest, 1942; entered the Louvre, 1953.

Exhibitions
Paris, 1921, no 80 (ill. in error as no. 82)
Paris, 1974, no. 16, ill.

Bibliography
G. pp. 277–78, 330
P. p. 277
N. pp. 59, 120
Dacier, 1909, I, p. 41; 1913, IV, pp. 17–18, 25
R. pp. 70, 158–59
W. 229, pl. 28, p. 15 (French edition)
Galerie Cailleux, 1962, ill.
Thuillier, 1967, colorpl. p. 109
W. and M. 241, ill.
Bernier, 1977, pp. 62–63

Related works
Although it is certain that the Louvre's *Feu aux poudres* appeared in the sales of the Bécherel and Doucet collections, Nolhac and then Réau suggested that it was not the same picture as the one in the Villars and Merton sales. The Villars picture measured 43 by 36 centimeters; the dimensions may have been reversed by mistake, but the catalogue does not mention the oval format, and its description does not correspond exactly to the subject of the painting in the Louvre ("*des* amours jettent le trouble dans son sommeil en l'embrasant avec *des* torches...").
No old engravings of the work are known, but there are many nineteenth-century copies (one is in the Louvre: M.N.R. 983; see figure 1).

Although the two paintings in the Louvre are very well known and figure among the works by Fragonard that are reproduced most often, a number of points have yet to be elucidated.

The two paintings included in the sale of the Gros collection in 1778, which were sketched by Gabriel de Saint-Aubin in the margin of his copy of the sales catalogue (see figure 2), are very close in composition to the paintings in the Louvre—but were they, in fact, the same? A comparison of these two works—the *Chemise enlevée* entered the Louvre with the La Caze collection in 1869, and the *Feu aux poudres,* almost a century later, with the Beistegui collection, which, according to the conditions of the gift, must be displayed as a unit, and, thus, at a distance from the galleries devoted to eighteenth-century French painting—leaves one with the impression that they were not originally intended as

72

companion pictures. Their color schemes, their execution, and even their spirit are different. In our opinion, the two pictures in the Louvre are the same as the ones in the Gros sale, but they may have been spuriously paired to interest a particular collector—perhaps Jean du Barry, the brother-in-law of Mme du Barry (see W. 290).

The title *La Chemise enlevée* comes from the engraving by E. Guersant (which presents the same composition, but vertically). According to the Goncourts, it was M. de Villars, its owner, who "baptized" the second picture *Le Feu aux poudres*. However, is the Louvre's *Feu aux poudres* the same one that was in the Villars and Merton collections? The entry in the Villars collection sales catalogue (1868; see *Related works*) and the Goncourts' description of the painting—

which, let us not forget, follows that of *La Chemise enlevée*—as "a bunch of torches . . . ," would tend to make us doubt it.

As for the dates: until now, Wildenstein was the only one to venture an opinion; he placed the two paintings between 1765 and 1772. However, we would date them closer to Fragonard's return from Italy, before 1765. During this period, the artist had to earn his living by painting *"polisson-neries"* (or "dirty jokes"), as Lempereur described them in 1778, in the margin of his catalogue of the Gros sale (preserved in the Bibliothèque Nationale). Lempereur, evidently critical, commented that they were "sold for more than they were worth."

Yet, even if we accept the fact that the subjects are complementary—*La Chemise enlevée* is a morning scene of gentle

Figure 1. After Fragonard.
La Chemise enlevée. Miniature.
Whereabouts unknown

Figure 2. E. Guersant.
La Chemise enlevée.
Bibliothèque Nationale, Paris,
Cabinet des Estampes

73

awakening, bathed in sunlight, while *Le Feu aux poudres* is a nocturnal scene of restless sleep, artificially lit by torchlight —we still find it difficult to assign them the same date. The lightness of the execution of *La Chemise enlevée,* the delicacy of its grays and yellows, and the modesty with which this audacious subject was treated argue in favor of a date several years after *Le Feu aux poudres,* which is painted more vigorously, in browns and dark earth colors, and is more overtly suggestive.

La Chemise enlevée created a sensation when it was presented to the public for the first time in 1860: "The flesh tones against this mat white are of a tonality that few painters ... Velázquez, Rembrandt, Titian ... have dared use. Above, set apart from the pink bed-curtains, a clever

Cupid flies off with his plunder, turning his head back to admire again one of the most attractive women in Fragonard's seraglio" (Bürger [Thoré], 1860). "The scene is a lively one, but it is veiled by the dream-like coloring that envelops it" (Paul de Saint-Victor, 1860). "The[se] medallions of nudity, these lively little pictures, these poems, so free, how does Fragonard preserve them? ... He only half shows them. His lightness is his decency." Apropos of *Le Feu aux poudres* the Goncourts added: "In impurity ... there is neither dirt, nor disgust, nor shame.... This picture remains a shining inspiration."

Let us content ourselves with admiring the closed eyes of the two sleeping young women, smiling at their dreams.

Figure 1. After Fragonard.
Le Feu aux poudres.
Musée du Louvre

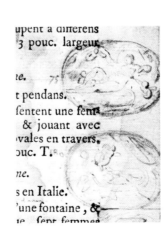

Figure 2. Gabriel de Saint-Aubin.
Page from the Gros collection sales
catalogue (1778).
Musée du Petit Palais, Paris

74 The Bathers

Oil on canvas, 64 x 80 cm.

Musée du Louvre, Paris, M.I. 1055

Provenance
Du Barry [possibly Mme du Barry; see Dacier, 1910, II, p. 12]: sold, March 11, 1776, no. 77 (for 550 *livres*, to Jo[m]bert?), and sketched by Saint-Aubin in the margin of his copy of the sales catalogue, now in the Philadelphia Museum of Art (see figure 1; the illustration, published here for the first time, enables us to identify two other compositions by Fragonard); [Varanchan] de Saint-Geniès, *fermier général* of the Tobacco Administration: sold, December 29–31, 1777, no. 12 (for 542 *livres*); Abbé de Gevigney: sold, December 1–29, 1779, no. 594; probably acquired by La Caze from the expert Féral for 3,000 francs in 1854, according to Rochefort (1905, p. 4; he added: "on serait heureux, en 1905, de les acquérir au centuple"); bequeathed by Dr. Louis La Caze to the Louvre, 1869.

Exhibitions
Paris, 1860, no. 151
London, 1932, no. 196 (no. 171, pl. LXIX of the commemorative catalogue)
Copenhagen, 1935, no. 68
Vienna, 1966, no. 30, pl. 43 (not exhibited)
Paris, 1974, no. 14, ill.

Bibliography
Bürger [Thoré], 1860, p. 349
Gautier, 1860, p. 2
Saint-Victor, 1860, n.p.
Horsin-Déon, 1861, p. 119 (and 244)
Blanc, 1862, p. 16
G. pp. 280, 330
Mantz, 1870, p. 16
P. pp. 66, 69, 271 (engraved ill. between pp. 64 and 65)
N. pp. 59, 118, colorpl. between pp. 120 and 121
D. and V. pl. 93
Gillet, 1929, p. 86, ill. p. 87
Boudet, 1936, p. 99
Rudrauf, 1947, pp. 10–14, ill.
R. p. 152
W. 233, plates 32–33, colorpl. facing p. 16
Seznec and Adhémar, 1963, p. 7
Thuillier, 1967, ill. p. 90, color detail p. 93
W. and M. 245, ill., colorpl. XVIII

Related works
A version painted on cardboard, formerly in the collection of Jules Strauss and exhibited in 1921, no. 79, has often come up for sale in London in recent years (see figure 2), the last time at Christie's, March 7, 1980, no. 36; W. and M. 246; see also W. and M. 247, 248 (on wood, formerly in the Walferdin collection, sold April 12–16, 1880, no. 79, April 27, 1928, no. 69), 249 (Walferdin collection sale, April 3, 1880, no. 13; Salomon collection sale, New York, April 4–7, 1923, no. 387, ill.). Many copies were made in the nineteenth and twentieth centuries (one recently decorated the set of Zeffirelli's production of *La Traviata* at the Paris Opera).

For the "pendant" (?) to the Louvre picture, see W. 234, fig. 115; Tokyo exhibition catalogue, 1980, no. 41, colorpl.

P. (p. 322, nos. 21, 22) mentions two nineteenth-century engravings after the Louvre picture.

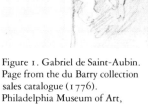

e.
ivertiffant entr'elles baignent. Plufieurs e verdure y répan eur. Ce Tableau touché avec éner brillante. Larg. 30 s. T. 550 *debur*

e.
à mi-corps. Elle , & tient une guir derriere elle , eft le le feu facré. Ce ovale. Haut. 26 . T. 321 *pavllete*

Amours grouppés t deux qui paroif 3 pouces, larg. 18
C ij

Figure 1. Gabriel de Saint-Aubin. Page from the du Barry collection sales catalogue (1776). Philadelphia Museum of Art, John G. Johnson Collection

Figure 2. After Fragonard. *The Bathers.* Whereabouts unknown

Figure 3. Fragonard. *The Bathers* (detail of figure 2)

Figure 4. Peter Paul Rubens. *Maria de' Medici Arriving in the Port of Marseilles* (detail). Musée du Louvre (formerly in the Palais du Luxembourg, Paris)

74

Since its first presentation to the Parisian public in 1860, Fragonard's *Bathers* has inspired many critics, but few have concerned themselves with its date. Bazin situates it before 1756 (1957, p. 228); Wildenstein, in the period between 1765 and 1772; while Seznec and Adhémar (III, 1963, p. 7) suggest that it may have been one of the two paintings "ready to be put in place" at the Salon of 1767, which Fragonard withdrew, out of "overscrupulous delicacy" (*Mercure de France,* October 1767, p. 171), because of their subject matter. Mantz (1870) contradicts himself when he says that it could be a work "in Fragonard's first manner, from the period when . . . he was still very close to Boucher," and then dates it to just before 1777. We will not venture to settle the matter, for we think that the juxtaposition here of Fragonard's principal paintings will enable the essential problems of chronology to be resolved quite naturally.

Gautier in 1860 and others after him have rightly called attention to the influence of Rubens (see figure 3)—in particular, of the "Life of Maria de' Medici" series, which was in the Palais du Luxembourg at the time (figure 4). Fragonard finally managed to obtain permission to work there in October 1767 (see p. 227); 1767 is also the date of *The Swing* in the Wallace Collection—a painting whose execution, coloring, and spirit are diametrically opposed to those of the *Bathers.*

The influence of Boucher's compositions was strong. Fragonard most certainly wished to succeed him, following his death in 1770, but even before then he tried to entice Boucher's clientele away from him—especially since in the years following his return from Italy in 1761 Fragonard was beset by severe financial difficulties. We would date the *Bathers* to this period.

The experts at the three sales in which this painting appeared in the eighteenth century praised such qualities as its "freshness," the "energy" of the brushwork, its "brilliant color," and the "playfulness" of its composition. Bürger mentioned the "Heaps of flowers, in which the rose predominates" (1860). Saint-Victor described "Laughter, smiles, and play, expressions wild and wanton enough to make the Fauns return. The flesh gleams like a wet flower" (1860).

"The *Bathers* presents the female complexion in a full range of colors, a bouquet of living flowers framed by the reeds of a pond," wrote Gautier in 1860. The troubling eroticism of this collective bath soon wore off, and the voluptuousness of the eight female nudes did not stifle the admiration of a critic (who signed his name as "Hix") who wrote, in 1870 (p. 331): "These whipped-cream nymphs show all they can; but when the naughtiness is so impalpable, it could be approved by the Archbishop of Tours." Jacques Thuillier's analysis (1967) remains the most thorough: "First one should just enjoy this confusion of colors, deep pinks, amber, ash green, this indistinct blending of nudes, foam, and foliage. And then, return to one's senses. A few moments are necessary to perceive the logic of the scene. At first we had not noticed the tree fallen across the river and across the painting, which is both its pretext and its key. Little by little we make out the two banks, the foliage becomes distinguishable from the sky, the reeds from the roots and the drapery. Two masses of greenery take shape, mixed with blues and earth colors, separated by a broad diagonal along which all of the warm tones are arranged: the golden or milky-white bodies of the bathers, the rosy-pink drapery heightened by a few dabs of vermillion. How not to realize that the picture is first of all just that: a bouquet of colors? A charming subject, to be sure, and one that wants to please, that obviously tries to please. But it is not a representation. What does verisimilitude matter here? The fallen tree, the arching reeds, the sliding and tumbling bodies: all elude not only rest but also that other burdensome inertia that is reality. The reeds are not reeds, but streaks of pigment; the draperies being swept away by the slightest gust of wind are actually just a few slashes of pink and white. The rapid brush has borrowed from the sky the shadow on a leg or a breast, and has drawn from the background the very transparency of the modeling. The painter's hand seems to be racing, forms take shape before our eyes, the whole canvas is shot through with rhythms: and there you have the painting, no longer the translation of a spectacle, but a picture woven from edge to edge with the same silky strands.

"We too readily believe that all 'pure' painting is necessarily 'flat' painting.... Yet it is important to feel (as certain contemporary abstract painting prepares us to do) that the play of forms can be organized within a dynamic space. We could even distinguish between two different spiritual families, which equally like to exalt the brushwork or combine the patches of color: one prefers the surface of the canvas, and the other, the inner space of the painting.... Tintoretto and Tiepolo, the Neapolitan decorative painters, or even Rubens, were the masters of this last approach. Fragonard joined their ranks, and a work like the *Bathers* is the perfect example of this painterly concern reconciled with the search for space."

75   The White Bull in the Shed

Oil on canvas, 72.5 x 91 cm.

Musée du Louvre, Paris, R.F. 1975.10

Provenance
Sigismond Bardac, before 1913 (mentioned in the catalogue of the Heseltine collection, no. 30); [Wildenstein]; acquired from Nathan Wildenstein by David David-Weill; gift to the Louvre from Éliane and Michel David-Weill, 1975.

Exhibitions
Paris, 1921, no. 21, ill.
London, 1932, no. 238 (no. 163, pl. LXX of the commemorative catalogue)
Paris, 1934, no. 146
Paris, 1980–81, no. 50, ill.
Lille, 1985, no. 50, ill.

Bibliography
Henriot, 1926, I, pp. 145–46, pl. p. 147
R. p. 173
W. 115, pl. 15, p. 12 (French edition)
W. and M. 124

Related works
For the drawings, see the following entries.
For a *Bull* formerly attributed to Fragonard, sold at Christie's, London, June 29, 1982, no. 50, see W. and M. 124 A.
The Louvre picture may be compared to the *Bull in the Shed* (see figure 1; formerly in the Veil-Picard collection; W. 114, pl. 14) and to *The Cow Shed,* of a later date (figure 2; formerly in the Rothschild collection; A. 849).

Figure 1. Fragonard. *The Bull in the Shed.* Private collection, Paris

Figure 2. Fragonard. *The Cow Shed.* Whereabouts unknown

Figure 3. Paulus Potter. *The Bull.* Mauritshuis, The Hague

Fragonard painted and drew many pictures of bulls—if, indeed, they are *all* bulls—during his career (see cat. nos. 77, 79); we have grouped them here arbitrarily. The present picture is definitely the finest as well as the most impressive one. The animal, the focus of the composition, is the only subject: there is no anecdotal detail. The only signs of a human presence—and humorous signs, at that—are the shepherd's large curved staff and his old flattened straw (or felt) hat—one of Fragonard's "signature motifs."

The bull, whose white, "slightly amber" hide illuminates the picture, stands in front of his trough, and feeds from a sheaf of hay (or is it corn?). The warm color scheme—all yellows, dark reds, and browns—accentuates the chiaroscuro effect. The vigorous and bold execution, and the broad brushstrokes recall *The Bathers* (cat. no. 74) and the *Mercury*

and Argus (cat. no. 121), both of which were painted after the artist's return from Italy.

H. Oursel (Lille exhibition catalogue, 1985) established a list of seventeenth-century Dutch paintings representing bulls, with the famous one by Potter in the museum in The Hague (see figure 3) in first place. Fragonard's picture certainly owes much to Northern painting, although perhaps more to the aesthetic of Rembrandt than to that of the painters who specialized in animal subjects. Yet, in emphasizing the creature's power, in rendering its presence and its force, and in sacrificing the anecdotal detail—contrary to his usual custom—Fragonard was innovative. He was concerned less with depicting the animal's physical appearance than with portraying its character (as did the naturalist Buffon, in his own field); this is the real subject of the picture.

76 The Escaped Heifer

Bister and watercolor wash on paper, over an underdrawing in black chalk, 31.8 x 42.5 cm.

Private collection, New York

Provenance
[Verrier]: sold, November 14 [in fact, 18],
1776, no. 133 (not sketched by Saint-Aubin
in the margin of his catalogue); [Leroy de
Senneville]: sold, April 5–11, 1780, no. 144
(for 200 *livres*, to Paillet; bought back);
[Leroy de Senneville]: sold posthumously,
April 26, 1784, no. 105 (for 144 *livres*, to
Paillet); de La Mure ["M. de Namur"]: sold,
April 19, 1791, no. 59 (for 1,200 *livres*,
according to the Cronier collection sales catalogue, 1905); Le Brun: sold, September 26,
1806, no. 231 (for 910 *livres*, to Constantin); A. Miron: sold, March 17–19, 1823,
no. 122; Jacques de Bryas: sold, April 4–6,
1898, no. 51, ill. (for 11,100 *livres*, to
Chappey); Ernest Cronier: sold posthumously, December 4–5, 1905, no. 29, ill.
(for 35,500 francs); Duc Decazes, who still
owned it in 1910; Mrs. Reginald Fellowes,
1931; Lucien Guiraud: sold posthumously,
June 14–15, 1956, no. 55, pl. X (for
1,850,000 francs); [Wildenstein]; private
collection, New York.

Exhibitions
Berlin, 1910, no. 176 (limited edition)
Paris, 1931, no. 50
Paris, 1951, no. 55

Bibliography
P. p. 309
R. p. 209
A. 301, fig. 116
Huisman, 1969, p. 40, pl. p. 41

Related works
For bulls and oxen painted or drawn by
Fragonard, see cat. nos. 75, 77, 79, 80.

This drawing very certainly appeared in the sales of the Leroy de Senneville collection in 1780 and 1784 (in which it was associated with an "ox at his food rack" that some have confused with the *Bull* in the Albertina: cat. no. 77). The old description—"A watercolor Drawing representing a land-scape in the middle of which there is a fine white cow, a herd of sheep and a young boy behind them who raises his stick to hit them, being accompanied by a dog"—precludes identifi-cation of the subject of the work as a "bull," as many have claimed up to now. The catalogue of the Verrier sale in 1776 is even more precise, for it mentions a "lovely heifer, daz-zlingly white," and goes on to describe: "A very spirited drawing in watercolor, amazingly executed ... this piece is admirable for the magic of its color and the great brilliance of its composition."

This drawing was sold again on September 26, 1806, with the Le Brun collection, its catalogue written by the famous art connoisseur himself, who was a friend of Frago-nard. The text is interesting, for it was written a few weeks after Fragonard's death on August 22, at a time when his fame had declined: "If then [at the Senneville sale] the love of a picturesque composition and passages of light and shadow, balanced with a rare and delicate taste, put a con-siderable price on this drawing, we can only applaud the justice that was rendered Fragonard, and the pleasure that we have had in appreciating him; for this ever new and creative genius will often and for a long time be consulted by the masters of art." One hundred years later, Gide (*Journal*, December 2, 1905; 1955 ed., pp. 187–88) attended the exhibition before the sale of the Cronier collection, where Fragonard's *Love Letter* (now in The Metropolitan Museum of Art, New York; W. 388, colorpl. between pp. 24 and 25) caused a sensation: "Delicious, marvelous, or whatever you like, but not to the point of paying three hundred thousand [francs] for it, as they are urging the Museum [Louvre] to do!" The picture sold for 420,000 francs, in the midst of general acclaim; Le Brun had been proven right.

77 The Bull and the Dog

Bister wash on paper, over an underdrawing in black chalk, 31.8 x 43.7 cm.

Graphische Sammlung Albertina, Vienna, Inv. 12734

Provenance
[Leroy de Senneville]: sold, April 5–11, 1780, no. 145 (for 59 *livres* 19 *sols,* to Paillet; bought back) (?): "l'intérieur d'une étable où l'on voit un boeuf à son ratelier"; [Leroy de Senneville]: sold, April 26, 1784, no. 106 (for 20 *livres* 2 *sols,* to Basan) (?); Chabot and Duc de La Mure or Desmarets: sold, December 17–22, 1787, no. 161 (for 272 *livres* 19 *sols,* to Paillet); Albert, Duke of Saxe-Teschen (1738–1822), Vienna (at the lower left is the stamp, Lugt 174).

Exhibitions
(For a more complete list, see Fosca, 1954; Benesch, 1964)
Paris, 1931, no. 49
Paris, 1950, no. 151, ill.
Bern, 1954, no. 119

Bibliography
Meder, 1923, p. 521, pl. 58 (detail)
Leporini, 1925, pl. 6
Fosca, 1954, pp. 57–58, pl. 18
R. p. 210
A. 285, fig. 101
Benesch, 1964, no. 222, ill.

Related works
A drawing of the same bull, but with a young woman sleeping at the right and holding a dog, is in a private collection in New York (see figure 1; A. 281, fig. 102; see also A. 282, sales, Paris, March 25, 1953, no. 89, ill., December 8, 1964, no. 65, ill.). An eighteenth-century sales catalogue (Vassal de Saint-Hubert collection, March 29, 1779, no. 182) mentions a drawing of this subject, most likely the one exhibited at the Salon de la Correspondance in August 1782, no. 13.

A drawing of the same bull, but eating hay and with a dog at the right (in the drawing in the Aubert collection sale, March 2, 1786, the dog was said to be on the left), whose back is turned, was sold in Monte Carlo, November 11, 1984, no. 2, ill. (see figure 2; A. 283, fig. 103; A. 284; see also, sale, Versailles, June 8, 1974, no. 12, ill.).

See also the sales of the Basan collection, December 1–19, 1798, part of no. 94, and the Bruun-Neergaard collection, August 30, 1814, no. 129, and the drawings in the museum in Saint-Quentin (see figure 3; A. 287) and in the Cottin collection (A. 288), which we have not examined.

For the painting in the Louvre, see cat. no. 75.

Figure 1. Fragonard.
The Bull and the Sleeping Young Woman.
Private collection, New York

Figure 2. Fragonard. *The Bull and the Dog.*
Private collection, Paris

Figure 3. Attributed to Fragonard.
The Bull in the Shed. Musée Antoine Lécuyer, Saint-Quentin

77

We hesitate to identify this very well-preserved drawing as the one that appeared in the sales of the Leroy de Senneville collection in 1780 and 1784. The catalogues of both of these sales mention an "ox at his food rack," which is obviously not the case here. On the other hand, it is certain that this drawing was in the collection of the Duc de La Mure before 1787, in which a "Bull" was paired with a "Lion" (see the following entry). "They are, respectively, inside a stable and a cage, which are picturesquely rendered. These two Drawings, admirably confident in execution, have contours drawn as perfectly as they are in life." The young bull, and the dog who seems to be guarding his master's clothes turn to look at us, and seem to be posing for the painter. Like the Louvre picture discussed above (cat. no. 75), which must date from several years earlier (five?), this drawing was intended more as a portrait than as a simple exercise in technical virtuosity.

Also, Fragonard did not content himself here with just drawing a study from life, as did most of the great artists of his time; he wanted to create a work that was as finished as a painting.

78   Lion

Bister wash on paper, over an underdrawing in black chalk, 33.4 x 44.5 cm.

Graphische Sammlung Albertina, Vienna, Inv. 12733

Provenance
"Cabinet Puisegur," according to an inscription penciled at the lower center, above the half-erased inscription *fragonard* (on Puisegur, see Sandoz, 1983, p. 405); Chabot and Duc de La Mure or Desmarets: sold, December 17–22, 1787, no. 161 (for 272 *livres* 19 *sols*, to Paillet, with the pendant, cat. no. 77, most likely bought back); sold posthumously with the de La Mure collection, April 19, 1791, no. 57; Albert, Duke of Saxe-Teschen (at the lower left is the stamp, Lugt 174): mentioned in the inventory of his estate, 1822, p. 914: "un vieux lion."

Exhibitions
Paris, 1931, no. 48
Paris, 1950, no. 152
Bern, 1954, no. 120, pl. XXIV
Munich, 1958, no. 269
Vienna, 1969, no. 383

Bibliography
Fosca, 1954, p. 58, pl. 19
Wilhelm, 1955, p. 373, fig. 7
R. p. 210
A. 291, fig. 106

Related works

For the "pendant," see the previous entry.

There is a study for this *Lion* (figure 1; A. 289, fig. 505) in the Kupferstichkabinett, Berlin-Dahlem, which presents very few differences when compared with the Vienna drawing. Also in Berlin is a sheet of studies of a sleeping lion (figure 2; A. 290, fig. 506).

Several "lions" by Fragonard are mentioned in eighteenth-century sales catalogues (those of the Varanchan collection, December 29, 1777, no. 14; the Hall collection, 1778; and the Denon collection, May 1, 1826, no. 154; see W. 116, 117).

Figure 1. Fragonard. *Lions.*
Kupferstichkabinett, Berlin-Dahlem

Figure 2. Fragonard. *Studies of a Lion.*
Kupferstichkabinett, Berlin-Dahlem

The *Lion* and the *Bull* in the Albertina do not seem always to have been associated; that was the case in 1787, and again when they entered the collection of Duke Albert of Saxe-Teschen in the early nineteenth century, but it was not so in 1791. They are not identical in format.

Entitled *The Lion in His Cage,* this drawing was described thus, in the catalogue of the 1791 sale: "This skillful study admirably renders the pride and force of the King of Beasts," but there is no mention of the young woman (?) at the left, who is teasing the animal and imprudently passing her hand through the bars.

Where could Fragonard have drawn this lion? At the *ménagerie* in Versailles, as Wilhelm (1955) suggests, or at the Jardin des Plantes in Paris? Other such drawings and paintings by Fragonard (see *Related works*) prove that the Vienna drawing is not an isolated work.

The extraordinary freshness of the drawing and the artist's perfect technical mastery are still a wonder to behold; unlike Rembrandt, whose famous drawing in the Louvre is of the animal and nothing else, Fragonard drew everything—the trough, the straw, the brick walls—but the lion, masterfully indicating it by utilizing the ground of the paper, accented with a few strokes of the point of his brush.

79 The Bull in the Shed

Bister wash on paper, over a light underdrawing in black chalk, 36.3 x 49.3 cm.

The Art Institute of Chicago, Helen Regenstein Collection, 1962.116

Provenance
Calonne Angelot: sold, May 11, 1789, no. 271: "un dessin au bistre sur papier blanc représentant l'étable d'un taureau. Ce dessin savamment fait est piquant d'effet. H. 14 p. L. 21 p. [37.8 x 56.7 cm.]" (?); Hippolyte Walferdin (1795–1880): sold posthumously, April 12–16, 1880, no. 195 (for 305 francs); Baronne de Ruble, Paris, 1889; Alfred Beurdeley (1847–1919): sold, Paris, March 13–15, 1905, no. 78 (for 11,000 francs; the stamp of his collection, Lugt 421, is at the lower left); Comte de Moltke; William K. Vanderbilt, about 1920; Princess Charles Murat, née Vanderbilt, New York: sold, Sotheby's, London, November 29, 1961, no. 29, ill. (for 7,000 pounds); [R. Munns]; acquired by Chicago, 1962.

Exhibitions
(For a more complete list, see Washington, D.C., 1978)
Paris, 1879, no. 584

Toronto . . . , 1972–73, no. 49, ill.
Paris, 1976–77, no. 17, ill.
Washington, D.C., 1978, no. 37, ill.

Bibliography
Ph. de Chennevières, 1880, p. 110
P. pp. 200, 313, ill. between pp. 170 and 171
R. pp. 209, 210 (confusion over the different drawings of bulls)
A. 280, fig. 105
Joachim, 1962–63, p. 69, ill. p. 70

Related works
A second, almost identical work, formerly in the Decourcelle and David-Weill collections, is today in a private collection in New York (see figure 1; A. 279, fig. 104; Tokyo exhibition catalogue, 1980, no. 135, ill.). A. (IV, p. 352) mentions a copy in a private collection in Paris.

For the study in Grasse, see the following entry.

For other drawings or paintings of bulls (or oxen), see cat. nos. 75, 77.

Figure 1. Fragonard. *The Bull in the Shed.*
Private collection, New York

79

The Chicago drawing is rightly famous, but it cannot be identified with any of the ones mentioned in eighteenth-century sales catalogues (with the exception of the drawing referred to above and the—rather dubious—one of a "white bull" that was in the Basan collection sale, December 1, 1798, part of lot no. 94). Eunice Williams dates it to Fragonard's second trip to Italy, about 1773–74, which seems rather late.

The Chicago drawing is a complex work that blends refinement and humor, and should not be considered as a mere animal study. The hay in the food rack is rendered with a few strokes of the brush, and there is a great intelligence at play in the distribution of the spots of brown and bister color. The strong presence with which Fragonard endowed this bull, who turns his head furiously in our direction, is in marked contrast to the amusingly conceived light-colored cow (?), sketched in the middle ground.

80   Two Oxen in a Shed

Black chalk and bister wash on paper, 25 x 38.5 cm.

Musée Fragonard, Grasse

Provenance
Walferdin collection (according to the catalogue of the Beurdeley sale?); Alfred Beurdeley (like cat. no. 79): sold, Paris, March 13–15, 1905, no. 79 (for 1,100 francs, to Danlos; the Beurdeley collection stamp, Lugt 421, is at the lower left); Baron J. Vitta; gift to the Musée Fragonard.

Exhibitions
Paris, 1921, no. 288

Bibliography
Fajol, 1937, p. 8, ill.
A. 278, fig. 100

Related works
See the previous entry.

This drawing, like the one in Chicago for which it was a preparatory study (cat. no. 79), is particularly fascinating because it permits us to see Fragonard's special way of working. The artist began by blocking in the large forms of the composition very rapidly in black chalk. He then covered the sheet with very lightly sketched long and supple chalk lines, in a brisk back-and-forth motion, repeatedly accenting this muscle or that curve in a seemingly haphazard and casual manner. Then, using a softer piece of black chalk, he indicated certain details: the muzzle of the ox, its horns, or

its chest. . . . Next came the first bister wash, which enabled him to vary the planes and to give volume to the forms. A second wash—this would be the last step, as in the Chicago drawing—served to accentuate the masses, enliven the drawing, and give a feeling of color. . . .

Although Fragonard drew many bulls, the subject here seems to be oxen. As noted, we have chosen to group Fragonard's representations of bulls (and oxen) after the painting in the Louvre (cat. no. 75), irrespective of the chronology.

81   The Cow Shed

Bister wash on paper, over an underdrawing in black chalk, 14.6 x 18.3 cm.

Musée Cognacq-Jay, Paris, Inv. 139

Provenance
Baron Louis-Auguste de Schwiter (at the lower left is his stamp, Lugt 1768): sold, Paris, April 20–21, 1883, no. 39 (for 500 francs; was it the drawing sold February 24, 1883, no. 17: "L'Étable," no dimensions given?, or "Le Berger entreprenant," sold June 20–21, 1833, no. 22, no dimensions?); Hochon, 1889; Marquis de Biron: sold, Paris, June 9–11, 1914, no. 20, ill. (for 13,500 francs): [Stettiner]; Gabriel Cognacq et Louise Jay.

Exhibitions
Washington, D.C., 1952–53, no. 86
Bern, 1954, no. 96

Bibliography
P. p. 300
R. pp. 197, 209, fig. 124, p. 250
A. 97, fig. 34
Thuillier, 1967, p. 110, colorpl.
Burollet, 1980, no. 130, ill. (with a detailed bibliography)

Related works
There is a copy in San Francisco (A. 1232; see Hattis, 1977, no. 55, who reproduced a second copy, no. 55 b).

"Well, here, in the Musée Cognacq-Jay, is [the drawing entitled] *The Cow Shed*. A simple peasant scene: but who would think of Boucher's *La Cage,* or of his *Berger galant?* A young man tumbles in the hay a suddenly frightened young girl. It is done with neither brutality nor reticence. The story is that of the song, 'Il pleut, il pleut, bergère...,' but without the trite compliments or the white sheep" (Thuillier, 1967, p. 114).

A bull (?) contemplates the scene with an "evil eye," a cow (?) is feeding from a trough, and a little dog yelps with amusement. The shepherd's hat and staff and the shepherdess's pitcher have rolled to the foreground. Fragonard handled the subject with the directness and the tension that mark even his most modest works.

We regret not being able to exhibit *The Indiscreet Bull,* a famous drawing in a similar vein that once belonged to the Goncourts (Jules de Goncourt made an engraving of it; see figure 1) and is today in New York (figure 2; A. 99, fig. 47). In this work, a shepherd upsets a shepherdess who cries out slightly, while a bull (if, indeed, it is one) watches them. Fragonard moved the scene to the right side of the composition, against the edge of the water trough, but in both pictures the significance of the bull is obvious enough—no psychoanalytic references are necessary.

Figure 1. Jules de Goncourt, after Fragonard. *The Indiscreet Bull.* Engraving. Bibliothèque Nationale, Paris, Cabinet des Estampes

Figure 2. Fragonard. *The Indiscreet Bull.* Private collection, New York

82 Taking Out the Flock

Bister wash on paper, over an underdrawing in black chalk, 28.2 x 37.5 cm.
Inscribed at the lower left: FRAGO

Musée Fabre, Montpellier

Provenance
Louis-Antoine-Auguste [de] Rohan Chabot:
sold posthumously, December 8, 1807, no.
44: "un autre dessin au bistre sur papier
blanc, offrant le sujet d'un jeune pâtre faisant
sortir son troupeau de l'étable" (for 21 *livres*
95); Bonnet Mel, of Pézenas, about 1841;
gift to the Musée Fabre, 1864 (at the lower
right is the stamp, Lugt 919).

Exhibitions
Paris, 1939, no. 145
Bern, 1954, no. 97
Montpellier, 1980, no. 60, ill.

Bibliography
Lafenestre and Michel, 1878, no. 191
Fosca, 1954, p. 69, pl. 45
R. pp. 209, 225, fig. 86, p. 170
A. 840, fig. 226

Related works
A preparatory study (figure 1) acquired at a
sale in Paris, December 5, 1984, no. 68
("Casanova") was exhibited at Cailleux,
Paris, 1985, no. 15, ill.
 The drawing in the museum in Romorantin
(A. 2135) seems to have disappeared (!), and
we know nothing about A. 2134.
 A painting by Hubert Robert (figure 2)
that was inspired by Fragonard's drawings

and by Saint-Non's aquatint was once in the
Decourcelle collection (sold, May 29–30,
1911, no. 38, ill.).
 The Montpellier drawing may be compared
to *The Frightened Flock* (figure 3; A. 300,
fig. 100), which, like its pendant *The Broken
Strap* (figure 4; A. 98, fig. 44), appeared in
the de Bièvres collection sale, March 10, 1790,
no. 29.
 For Saint-Non's engraving of the drawing,
dated 1776 (which reverses the composition;
see figure 5), which was intended for his
Griffonis, see G. p. 338; Guimbaud, 1928,
p. 200, no. 71 (ill. between pp. 32 and 33),
and Cayeux, 1964, no. 298.

Figure 1. Fragonard. *Taking Out the Flock.* Art market, Paris

Figure 2. Hubert Robert. *Taking Out the Flock.* Art market, Paris

Figure 3. Fragonard. *The Frightened Flock.* Whereabouts unknown

Figure 4. Fragonard. *The Broken Strap.* Whereabouts unknown

Figure 5. Abbé de Saint-Non, after Fragonard. *Taking Out the Flock.* Engraving. Bibliothèque Nationale, Paris, Cabinet des Estampes

The Montpellier drawing directly inspired a painting by Hubert Robert, which proves that the two artists were still on friendly terms after their respective returns from Italy. The drawing has suffered from prolonged exposure to light, and so has lost some of its sharpness, unlike the preparatory study. The focus of the composition is the well-observed gesture of the cowherd opening the stable door. Fragonard succeeded perfectly in rendering the bleating of the sheep, the stamping of their feet as they rush out of the stable, and the sound of the ram's bell. Two large chained dogs stand watch.

The date of the drawing is a problem: according to Roland Michel (Cailleux, Paris exhibition catalogue, 1985), the study dates from about 1761–65. Is the Montpellier drawing contemporary, or much later in date?

Fragonard's Travels in Holland

While no one would think of questioning Fragonard's sojourns in Italy from 1756 to 1761 (pp. 94–97) and from 1773 to 1774 (pp. 361–64), whether or not he went to Holland was long a subject of debate, especially for scholars at the beginning of this century. Some, like the Goncourts and then Fourcaud in 1907, contended that Fragonard had no reason to go to the Netherlands to discover Dutch and Flemish painting. There was enough of it in Paris, and artists did not have to leave France to see the masterpieces of the Northern European schools. Others, like Thoré, Portalis, and especially Nolhac (1907, 1918), considered that there were too many references to the North in eighteenth-century documents to discount the possibility of a trip that would surely have enriched an artist with such an appetite for painting as Fragonard.

The question has since been settled; the sale of the Gros collection in 1778 (see figures 1, 2; cat. nos. 83, 84) featured drawings by Fragonard after works by Rembrandt, van Dyck, and Jordaens that he could only have copied *in situ*. Other drawings mentioned in eighteenth-century sales or that have appeared since provide irrefutable evidence of such a trip.

The remaining question is: when could Fragonard have made such a trip? To summarize the different opinions on this matter: Nolhac (1907) suggests a date between 1761 and 1769; Réau (1932), either 1766, with Boucher and Randon de Boisset, or between 1775 and 1778, after the second trip to Italy; Wilhelm (1948), between 1762 and 1773; Ananoff (1959), like Tornézy in 1895 (p. 34), situates it shortly before 1773, and in the company of Bergeret; Massengale (1979), who has the largest consensus, proposes 1769.

Figure 2. Gabriel de Saint-Aubin. Page from the Gros collection sales catalogue (1778). Musée du Petit Palais, Paris

Figure 1. Jean-Antoine Gros. *Portrait of Drouais*. Musée du Louvre, Paris, Cabinet des Dessins

Before taking sides, a few remarks about Fragonard's possible traveling companions are in order. We know that Randon de Boisset went to Holland in 1766; Sireul said as much in the preface to the sales catalogue of the Randon de Boisset collection, and there are documents proving this in the archives of the Ministère des Affaires Étrangères (*Franchises, exemptions de droits—1738–1783,* vol. 2033, April 1766, F°81 r°). Randon de Boisset traveled with Boucher (who accompanied him for only part of the trip), but not with Fragonard. Ananoff believes that Fragonard made the trip with Bergeret, basing his hypothesis on a close reading of the *Journal* of Bergeret's travels in

Figure 3. Fragonard, after van Dyck. *Christ and the Paralytic.*
Private collection, Paris

Figure 4. Anthony van Dyck. *Christ and the Paralytic.*
Alte Pinakothek, Munich

Italy (1773–74), which we will discuss later (pp. 361–64). In it we find certain allusions—which should not be read to imply more than they do—to the effect that when Bergeret left for Italy not only "was he not yet worn out from stopping at inns in Holland and Germany," but also that he considered Fragonard "easy to travel with." The two men had known each other for a long time—since at least 1763 (see cat. nos. 67–70). Bergeret had lent his collection of Fragonards to the Salons of 1765 and 1767. A drawing by Fragonard (figure 3) after van Dyck's *Christ and the Paralytic* (figure 4) supports Ananoff's hypothesis. The painting that Fragonard copied was most certainly in Düsseldorf in 1766 when Bergeret—as we know from his Italian journal—traveled there.

As for the date of 1769 advanced by Massengale, it is based upon a drawing, after Rubens, representing Decius Mus, entitled *The Dismissal of the Lictors* (figure 5), which bears this date inscribed in a very old hand; the painting itself was surely in the collection of the Princes of Liechtenstein in Vienna, but Massengale points out that in 1773 four paintings from this series, from Brussels—probably copies—came up for sale in London. In support of Massengale's argument, it should be noted that the baptismal certificate of Fragonard's daughter, Henriette-Rosalie, dated December 17, 1769, mentions him as "absent."

Let us examine the two dates more closely. They are both surprising for the same reasons. In 1769 and in 1773, Fragonard was extremely busy with commissions, among them, the ceiling of the Hôtel Voyer d'Argenson and the "figures de fantaisie," as well as works for Mme du Barry and Mme Guimard....
Besides, as a member of the Academy since 1765, Fragonard would have had to have asked for permission for a leave of absence during those years—which Pierre reproached him for failing to do in 1773, when he left for his second trip to Italy!

It would be convenient to settle the question based on the style of these copies, but such is not possible. The copies drawn in black chalk (cat. no. 84) still seem to be too close to the copies after the Italian masters done in 1761; others, like the *Blessed Herman Joseph* (cat. no. 85), anticipate the vertical compositions with many figures, from about 1775, such as *La Rêveuse* or *La Lecture* (cat. nos. 271, 270). On the other hand, the use of wash in the *Apotheosis of Prince Frederick Henry* (cat. no. 83) or in the *Education of the Virgin,* after Rubens (figure 6), is still rather awkward.

Our conclusion will be prudent, if disappointing. We would say that Fragonard made several trips to the North: the first time was perhaps in 1763 or 1764, in the company of Bergeret (who, on July 17, 1762, had been recommended by Marigny to Natoire at the Academy in Rome, but we know that he cancelled that trip), when he enjoyed a great deal of freedom; the second time was for a shorter period, around 1772, when he was possibly with Le Brun, for whom he seems to have worked throughout his career.

Figure 5. Fragonard, after Rubens. *The Dismissal of the Lictors.*
Whereabouts unknown

Yet, finally, is the date of Fragonard's trip to Flanders and Holland so important? We have already observed that the artist had a great avidity for painting and that he absorbed all that he saw. He put to good use what he learned from the masters of the past, indicating his preferences through his selectivity. Although there is no doubt that the art of painters like Rembrandt and Ruisdael, and Jordaens and van Dyck counted a great deal in his development, we do not think that the trip to Holland brought any radical changes to his way of seeing, or of painting.

Figure 6. Fragonard, after Rubens. *The Education of the Virgin.* Musée du Louvre, Paris, Cabinet des Dessins

83 The Apotheosis of Prince Frederick Henry

Bister wash on paper, over an underdrawing in black chalk, 35.5 x 43.5 cm.
Inscribed in pen and ink, at the lower right: f

Musée du Louvre, Paris, Cabinet des Dessins, R. F. 36.737

Provenance

The miniaturist Jean-Antoine Gros (1725–1784/86), of Toulouse, father of Baron Gros, the painter: sold, Monday, April 13, 1778, no. 72: "Un sujet allégorique d'après Jacques Jordaens, executé dans la maison du Prince d'Orange dans le bois de la Haye ... sous verre"; a long inscription on the verso (see figure 1) notes that Abraham Fontanel acquired the drawing in Paris for 500 *livres* (it "made" only 130 *livres,* according to the copy of the sales catalogue in the Bibliothèque Doucet) for the Viscomte de Saint-Priest, Administrator of the Languedoc (who owned it, for certain, in 1779), and it passed to his son-in-law M. de Masclary, who exchanged it with Fontanel; A. Carrier: sold, March 9–10, 1846, no. 165 (for 23 francs; catalogue written by Thoré); Camille Groult, before 1907 (acquired "pour mille francs": Gimpel, 1963, p. 160, under the entry for April 23, 1920); Pierre Bordeaux Groult: gift to the Louvre, 1978 (at the lower left is the stamp of the Louvre, Lugt 1886).

Exhibitions

Montpellier, 1779, no. 61
Paris, 1984, no. 92, ill.
Lille, 1985, no. 55, ill.

Bibliography

Nolhac, 1907, pp. 20–21, ill.
Dacier, 1913, IV, pp. 18–19, 26–27
Stein, 1913, pp. 376, 394
Nolhac, 1918, pp. 211–12
Nolhac, 1931, pp. 220–21
Réau, 1932, pp. 99, 103
Mathey, 1933, p. 185

Mesuret, Toulouse exhibition catalogue, 1954, pp. 19–21
R. pp. 55, 234
Ananoff, 1959, p. 16, fig. 1
A. 480, fig. 165
Massengale, 1979, p. 271
Slive, 1981, pp. 272–73, 275, n. 12

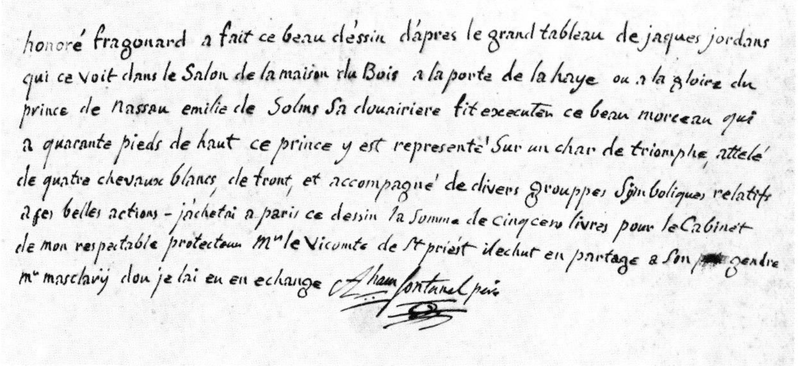

honoré Fragonard a fait ce beau dessin d'apres le grand tableau de jacques jordans qui ce voit dans le Salon de la maison du Bois a la porte de la haye ou a la gloire du prince de nassau emilie de Solms Sa douniriere fit executer ce beau morceau qui a quarante pieds de haut ce prince y est representé Sur un char de triomphe attelé de quatre chevaux blancs, de front, et accompagné de divers grouppes Symboliques, relatifs a ses belles actions - jachetai a paris ce dessin la Somma de cinqcens livres pour le Cabinet de mon respectable protecteur Mr le Vicomte de St priest ilechut en partage a Son gendre mr masclary don je lai eu en echange / Abam fontanel peir

Figure 1. Verso of catalogue no. 83

83

Pierre de Nolhac deserves the credit for having been the first to realize the full significance of this drawing when he published it in 1907. This was the "definitive document" that he had been looking for, the "proof of the visit that Fragonard made to his dear Dutch masters." Here, the artist

Figure 2. Jacob Jordaens.
*The Apotheosis of Prince Frederick
Henry of Orange.*
Huis ten Bosch, The Hague

Figure 3. Gabriel de Saint-Aubin.
Page from the Gros collection sales catalogue
(1778). Musée du Petit Palais, Paris

copied Jordaens's huge composition *The Apotheosis of Prince Frederick Henry of Orange* (of 1652), which is still in the Huis ten Bosch in The Hague (see figure 2). How, indeed, could Fragonard have copied it without going to the Netherlands, since there were no engravings of it, and the sketches that we know are all very different from the picture in The Hague?

Réau, in 1932, discovered that Fragonard's drawing had appeared in the sale of the Gros collection in 1778 and that Saint-Aubin had sketched it precisely, in the margin of his catalogue (now in the Musée du Petit Palais, Paris; see figure 3). We do not know under what conditions Jean-Antoine Gros, the father of the famous painter and himself a painter and miniaturist, came to assemble his valuable collection, which included no less than seven copies by Fragonard after Northern masters, nor why he had to sell it—for a tidy sum, at that. In any case, Le Brun, who expertized the sale, confirmed Fragonard's trip to Holland by mentioning that the artist "executed" his drawing "*in* [italics added] the house of the Prince of Orange." On the dates of his copy and his trip, see the discussion above (p. 179).

While Fragonard, indeed, took some liberties with Jordaens's composition, especially in the top part, he enlivened his version by using different washes, and succeeded in capturing the vitality of the original.

84　The Coronation of Saint Catherine

Black chalk on paper, 20.9 x 18.5 cm.

Musée du Louvre, Paris, Cabinet des Dessins, Inv. 26643

Provenance

Gros collection: sold, April 13, 1778, no. 79 (for 60 *livres*, to Langlier; see previous entry); [de Ghendt]: sold, November 15–22, 1779, no. 272; Chevalier de Saint-Morys; entered the Louvre during the Revolution with the collections seized from emigrés (at the lower right and in the center are the stamps, Lugt 1886 and 2207).

Exhibitions

Paris, 1921, no. 226
Bern, 1954, no. 126
Lille, 1985, no. 57, ill.

Bibliography

Guiffrey and Marcel, 1910, V, no. 4051, ill. (under no. 4050)
Dacier, 1913, IV, pp. 18–19, 27
Martine, 1927, no. 2, ill.
Réau, 1932, pp. 99, 103
Mathey, 1933, pp. 185–86
R. pp. 55, 233, 272
Ananoff, 1959, p. 16
A. 2618, fig. 660

Figure 1. Peter Paul Rubens.
The Coronation of Saint Catherine.
Toledo Museum of Art

Figure 2. Gabriel de Saint-Aubin. Page from the Gros collection sales catalogue (1778). Musée du Petit Palais, Paris

Fragonard copied without any modifications the *Coronation of Saint Catherine* painted by Rubens (figure 1) in 1633 for the altar of Saint Barbara in the Augustinian church at Malines, where it remained until 1765. Between 1765 and 1779, it was in the collection of Gabriel-François-Joseph de Verhulst in Brussels. It was acquired by the Toledo Museum of Art in 1950 (Toledo museum catalogue, 1976, pp. 146–47, pl. 102).

This drawing, like the one after Jordaens discussed in the previous entry, was part of the Gros sale in 1778 (the sketch by Saint-Aubin—see figure 2—is very pale). At this date, Le Brun, who expertized the sale, knew that the original painting was "in Brussels"; he undoubtedly had seen it there.

Of the seven drawings after Rembrandt (one, in fact, was a copy after van der Helst), van Dyck, and Rubens in the Gros collection, only the ones after Jordaens (see previous entry) and Rubens have been found. Of the copies after Rubens (see figure 2, p. 228) two—after the *Adoration of the Shepherds* in Antwerp and the *Christ Giving the Keys to Saint Peter* (the version today in East Berlin, in the Bodemuseum?; see Freedberg, 1984, p. 94)—are lost.

For the very problematic date of Fragonard's trip to Holland, see pp. 178–80. It should be noted, however, that this copy in black chalk is close to the many copies that Fragonard executed in 1761, after his return from Italy.

85 The Blessed Herman Joseph Kneeling before the Virgin

Bister wash on paper, over an underdrawing in black chalk, 24.6 x 21.7 cm.
The stamp of the owner of the drawing appears at the lower right.

Private collection

Provenance
[Vassal de Saint-Hubert]: sold, March 29,
1779, no. 186: "Saint Herman composition
de quatre figures dans le goût de Van Dyck
..." (for 64 *livres*); acquired by its present
owner, 1985.

Bibliography
A. 458 (lost)

This drawing is a faithful copy of a picture by van Dyck
(figure 1) that represents the Blessed Herman, a Premon-
stratensian of the thirteenth century who was greatly devoted
to the Virgin. The painting, which is today in the Kunsthistorisches Museum, Vienna, was executed in 1629 for the
Confraternity of Bachelors of Antwerp, and was sold by the
Jesuits of that city in 1776. Fragonard, therefore, made the
drawing in Antwerp (or perhaps in the cathedral of Saint-
Aubin in Namur, where there is a copy of the painting), and
not in Vienna, where he stopped on his way back from his
second trip to Italy in 1774.

Along with Rembrandt and Rubens, whose works he also
liked to copy, van Dyck was the Northern painter that
inspired him the most. He stayed very close to the original,
but not to the point of completely effacing his own talent.
Thus, the young man at the left who witnesses the scene
directly inspired the figure in Fragonard's *Rêveuse* (cat. no.
271).

Figure 1. Anthony van Dyck.
The Blessed Herman.
Kunsthistorisches Museum, Vienna

Fragonard and the Dutch Landscape

"Jacques Ruysdael, *A Path in the Woods*...This rare and admirable Picture in the best and most brilliant manner of this master once belonged to us. We turned it over to M. Fragonard, to whom it served as inspiration for his charming landscapes...." This passage, published here for the first time, is from the catalogue of a sale organized by Le Brun (April 16, 1811, no. 93), whose friendship with Fragonard is well documented. The preface to this catalogue tells us that the painting by Ruisdael belonged to Le Brun in 1773—and to Fragonard not long after.

Fragonard's admiration for Ruisdael is well known. All who have studied the influences of Northern art on the master from Grasse—from L. Réau (1932) to the team that prepared the catalogue of the recent exhibition in Lille (1985), A. Schnapper, J. Foucart, and H. Oursel, who followed the irreplaceable H. Gerson (1942), J. Wilhelm (1948), and Carpenter (1955)—have noted it. One should not forget to cite Le Carpentier (1821): "Fragonard's facile genius lent itself to all the different genres of painting. We have often seen him imitate Ruisdael and other painters of this school deceptively well." All mention the numerous sales catalogues (Wildenstein established a first list; see also Slive, 1981, and, for example, that of March 5, 1789, no. 17) in which, beginning in 1780, the names of these two artists were regularly associated: "Two landscapes...with brushwork as spirited as in the best works by Ruisdael" (Leroy de Senneville collection sale, April 5, 1780, no. 53); or: "This lovely picture is as vigorous and as delightful as one of Ruysdael's best paintings" (La Ferté sales catalogue,

February 20, 1797, no. 101; for an example of the drawings that were sold in the eighteenth century, we would mention one in the sale of May 31, 1790, no. 181: "A picturesque landscape in the style of Ruisdael"; see also no. 308).

Seymour Slive has recently shown that Fragonard's debt to Ruisdael did not involve just his influence. The catalogue of the Leroy de Senneville sale of April 5, 1780, no. 49, mentions: "A landscape full of trees... two young women are doing the wash in a pond and on the right a dog is chasing ducks. This piece was rapidly dashed off to capture the effect of M. Lempereur's picture by Ruisdael...." The work, which was long considered to be lost (W. 185), has recently been acquired by the Fort Worth museum (see figure 1), but Ruisdael's painting is lost, and is known to us only through a photograph (figure 2). Fragonard, of course, copied Ruisdael's painting, although he modified the composition slightly by adding to the landscape—which must have seemed too empty for him—some washerwomen and a dog, but Paillet, who expertized the Leroy de Senneville sale, rightly noted that "because of [the painting's] spirited and easy brushwork, it becomes original."

Another example bears witness to certain practices of the eighteenth century: the Chevalier de Clesle collection sale, December 4, 1786 (no. 16), included a "landscape" by "J. Ruisdael." The catalogue gives a long description of the work, adding: "M. *Fragonnard,* whom we consulted to add some figures to this skillful work, has taken advantage—clever Artist that he is—of this patch of daylight to compose a group of

Figure 1. Fragonard, after Jacob van Ruisdael. *The Pond.* Kimbell Art Museum, Fort Worth, Texas

Figure 2. Jacob van Ruisdael. *The Pond.* Whereabouts unknown

Figure 3. Fragonard. *Flock of Sheep Descending a Hill.*
Art market, Paris

Figure 4. Fragonard. *Shepherd Running after His Sheep.*
Private collection, New York

three figures and a cow, whose disposition and handling are in perfect harmony with the general effect!" (Ruisdael's picture was no doubt considered too sparse for eighteenth-century taste.)

The eighteenth-century critics who commented on Fragonard's landscapes did not only mention Ruisdael; sometimes they also evoked the names of Castiglione and Claude Lorrain. In one case (the de Boynes collection sales catalogue of March 15, 1785, no. 92), "a landscape . . . in which countrywomen are doing their wash . . ." by Fragonard was the pendant to a picture by Jan Wynants "from the same collection." Yet, Ruisdael was the main rival, the one to emulate. In the nineteenth century, the critic Thoré and then Portalis mentioned, besides Ruisdael and Wynants, the names of Berchem and Hobbema, among others.

We know today that the greatest French collectors of the second half of the eighteenth century had a passion for Dutch landscapes of the preceding century, and that some of the finest works in this genre were sold at the time in Paris. Fragonard—as is generally recognized today—did not necessarily have to go to Holland to study or to seek inspiration from them. This is why the issue of the date of his trip (see pp. 178–80) has little bearing on the present discussion.

Is it possible to date these Dutch landscapes by Fragonard? We cannot say definitely, but it seems to us that, fairly soon after Fragonard's return from Italy in 1761, very likely in 1775, too (see cat. no. 91), and perhaps again through the 1780s, Fragonard continued to paint these works that are so different in spirit from his Italian landscapes.

Figure 5. Fragonard. *Landscape with a Downpour.*
The Detroit Institute of Arts

Figure 6. Fragonard. *Landscape, with a Boy at the Edge of a Pond.*
Private collection, Paris

Figure 7. Fragonard. *The Hillock.*
Private collection, Great Britain

Figure 8. Fragonard. *Hillock, with an Amorous Couple.*
Whereabouts unknown

Figure 9. Fragonard. *The Stream.*
Museu Calouste Gulbenkian, Lisbon

While it is true that Fragonard liked and admired Northern painting (and not just landscapes; see cat. nos. 83, 85), that his own paintings sold well, that he was less concerned with producing precise (or deceptive) copies than with creating "inspired pastiches" that collectors could recognize as such and distinguish from the Dutch models, there is still the question of his personal involvement.

In his effort to rival the Dutch painters, did Fragonard want to show that he could do *the same thing,* or, like many of his colleagues who were proud to have asserted the independence of the French school, did he want to prove that he could do *as well?*

86 Shepherd Playing the Flute, while a Peasant Girl Listens

Oil on canvas, oval, 40 x 30 cm.

Musée-Château d'Annecy (on loan from the Louvre)

Provenance
Jacques-Onésyme Bergeret, 1765 (?);
[Nogaret]: sold, February 23, 1778, no. 51:
"un agréable paysage de forme ovale, où se
voit sur le devant un troupeau de moutons et
deux figures avec un chien sur une élévation
de terrain 15 pouc. sur 11 de larg. [40.5 x 29.7
cm.]" (?); Vassal de Saint-Hubert: sold,
April 24, 1783, no. 66: "... on y voit sur un
plan élevé une jeune fille ayant le bras droit
posé sur l'épaule d'un jeune homme qui joue
du flageolet en gardant des moutons ...
ovale ... 14 pouces 3 lignes de haut sur 10
pouces de large"; Henri Rouart: sold, Paris,
December 9–11, 1912, no. 38, ill. (for 70,000
francs); B.: offered for sale in Paris,
December 10, 1935, no. 36, ill., but unsold;
Fabiani (according to W.); assigned to the
Louvre by the Office des Biens Privées
M.N.R. 870; lent to Annecy, 1954 (our
thanks to Jacques Foucart for drawing our
attention to this important work).

Exhibitions
Salon of 1765, no. 177: "un Paysage" (?)
Salon de la Correspondance, 1782 (*Nouvelles
de la République des Lettres et des Arts,* June
12, 1782, p. 171, no. 8; June 19, p. 180, no. 6
[identical descriptions]: "un paysage dans
lequel on voit sur un terrain élevé un jeune
homme jouant du flageolet et une jeune
fille qui garde des moutons ..." [?])

Bibliography
Bellier de la Chavignerie, 1865, p. 84
G. pp. 317–18
P. pp. 272, 284
N. pp. 134–35
G. Wildenstein, 1926, pp. 11, 19
Wilhelm, 1948, p. 302, fig. 6
R. p. 186
Seznec and Adhémar, 1960, II, pp. 43,
    198–99
W. 153, 153 a, fig. 85; pp. 7, 12–13 (French
    edition)
W. and M. 169, 170
Bukdahl, 1980, I, pp. 174, 278

Related works
Wildenstein catalogued under three different numbers three different versions of the same composition.

Diderot's description of the painting exhibited at the Salon of 1765 corresponds to the picture in Annecy; however, according to the booklet, it measured 60 x 48.5 centimeters ("22 pouces sur 18"). The expert at the Nogaret sale does not say if the landscape mentioned was oval. As for the painting at the Salon de la Correspondance of 1782, neither its format nor its dimensions are known. Nothing excludes the possibility that these various references all involve the same painting.

W. (fig. 85 a; see figure 1) published a second version of the Annecy picture, with the same dimensions, which is supposed to have come from the Beurnonville collection (sold, Paris, May 9–16, 1881, no. 75—not 65). It differs from the present painting in the absence of the long-stemmed reed set against the sky, behind the shepherd. W. associates it with a *Shepherd at Rest* (figure 2; W. fig. 85 b; no. 76 in the Beurnonville sale), today on the art market in Paris; it features the monogram "L 1769," probably for Loutherbourg (P. p. 272).

The present painting may be compared to a rectangular drawing with a similar subject (figure 3; A. 847, fig. 227), of which there is a version without figures (A. 970) that was sold at Christie's, London, March 28, 1972, no. 109.

Figure 3. Fragonard.
Shepherd Playing the Flute.
Whereabouts unknown

Figure 1. Fragonard.
Shepherd Playing the Flute.
Whereabouts unknown

Figure 2. Attributed to Philippe-
Jacques de Loutherbourg.
Shepherd at Rest. Art market, Paris

"In it we see a shepherd standing on a low hill. He is playing the flute, with his dog next to him, while a peasant girl listens. On the same side are fields; on the other side, rocks and trees. The rocks are beautiful. The shepherd is well lit and impressive; the woman is weak and indistinct. The sky, poor." From this description by Diderot we know that the picture in Annecy (or perhaps an identical but larger version; see above) was presented at the Salon of 1765. The other critics of this Salon limited themselves to laconic comments such as "a fairly good landscape." Diderot, true to form, thought it was "vigorously colored, but the handling is not sure, two very different things; the setting is not varied enough; the little figures, though done with humor and wit, are weak, and the foreground is far from being as good as the mountains."

The ray of sunlight that strikes the rocks behind the shepherd and his companion is the most original feature of this traditionally composed landscape, with its very distinct planes. It is interesting to note that, four years after his return from Italy, Fragonard painted a landscape so Northern in feeling. How could he have done so without going to Holland?

The broken tree, which stands out against the clouds and looks as if it had been struck by lightning, is the leitmotif of the painting.

87 "Annette at the Age of Twenty"

Oil on canvas, 37 x 46 cm.

Galleria Nazionale d'Arte Antica, Rome

Provenance
Vassal de Saint-Hubert, from 1772: sold, January 17, 1774, no. 107 (for 2,000 *livres,* with its pendant, acquired by Quesnet); Vicomte Adolphe du Barry (son of Jean "le Roué," brother-in-law of the countess): sold, November 21, 1774, no. 104 (for 1,400 *livres,* with its pendant, to Boileau); Prince de Conti: sold, April 9, 1777, no. 757 (for 1,597 *livres,* with its pendant, to Quesnet, which confirms the du Barry provenance);

Boulogne: sold, November 22, 1787, no. 71 (for 1,611 *livres,* with its pendant; mentions the Conti provenance); according to G. (p. 338), who perhaps confuses this work with our cat. no. 91, the picture "a repassé à la vente Robert de Saint-Victor où il s'est vendu 150 francs"; [Wildenstein]; Duc de Cervinara (died 1960), London; bequeathed to the museums of Rome.

Exhibitions
London, 1968, no. 233
Tokyo, 1980, no. 31, colorpl.

Bibliography
G. p. 338
P. pp. 116, 270–71, 284, 321–22
N. p. 142
Dacier, 1910, II, pp. 12, 28

Figure 1. After Fragonard.
"Annette at the Age of Fifteen."
Private collection, Italy

Figure 2. Gabriel de Saint-Aubin. Page from the du Barry collection sales catalogue (1774). Musée du Petit Palais, Paris

87

Wilhelm, 1948, p. 302
Wilhelm, 1955, p. 374
R. p. 160
W. 129, pl. 16, pp. 13–15 (French edition)
Carpenter, 1962, p. 361
Cervinara collection catalogue,
    Rome, 1962, no. 15, ill.
W. and M. 161, ill.
Sutton, 1980; 1987, p. 107
Paris exhibition catalogue 1984, *La
    Nouvelle Athènes,* p. 20, under no. 20
Boerlin-Brodbeck, 1987, p. 168, n. 46

Related works
The pendant, *"Annette at the Age of Fifteen"*
(W. 128, fig. 82: the engraving), was associated with *"Annette at the Age of Twenty"*
between 1772 and 1787, but it has not come
down to us (see figure 1 for a copy). The two
pictures were sketched by Gabriel de Saint-
Aubin (see figure 2) in his copy of the catalogue of the du Barry sale (1774). Engravings
of them were made by François Godefroy (see
figures 3, 4) in 1772 (*Mercure de France,*
November 1772, p. 173; *Avant-coureur,*
October 19, 1772, p. 659; *Affiches,
Annonces, Avis divers,* 1772, p. 882; Hébert,
Pognon, and Bruand, 1968, X, pp. 369–70,
nos. 32–33).
    The two prints were dedicated to "Mr. Vas-

sal de S^t· hubert, Ecuyer, Conseiller, Fermier
G^l· du Roy.... " The Boulogne sales catalogue
(1787) says that they were "gravés par
Marchand."
    The pendant may be seen in the *Salon de
Mme Geoffrin* by Anicet-Charles-Gabriel
Lemonnier (of 1810; see figure 5 for the
smaller version in the Musée des Beaux-Arts,
Rouen). Lemonnier seems to have copied the

original, which he probably knew—not the
engraving. He met Fragonard in Rome on his
second trip to Italy (see also cat. no. 149);
Jean-François Marmontel, the author of the
novel that inspired these works, is, of course,
represented in his painting.
    For a related drawing, see A. 2144 (sold,
Paris, Palais Galliéra, December 7, 1973, no.
8, ill.; see also no. 9).

Figure 3. François Godefroy, after
Fragonard. *"Annette at the Age of Fifteen."*
Engraving. Bibliothèque Nationale,
Paris, Cabinet des Estampes

Figure 4. François Godefroy, after
Fragonard. *"Annette at the Age of Twenty."*
Engraving. Bibliothèque Nationale,
Paris, Cabinet des Estampes

Figure 5. Anicet-Charles-Gabriel
Lemonnier. *Le Salon de Mme Geoffrin*. Detail.
Musée des Beaux-Arts, Rouen

In 1761, Marmontel published his novel *Annette et Lubin,* which was adapted by Charles-Simon Favart for light opera the following year. That Fragonard's painting and its pendant (now lost) illustrated the—then popular but now forgotten—tale of innocent love between a brother and his half-sister is confirmed by the captions of the 1772 engravings of these works and by a passage from the entry in the catalogue of the 1787 sale in which both paintings appeared: "Two very fine landscapes, pendants, graced with subjects drawn from Annette and Lubin."

There is nothing surprising in the fact that Fragonard wanted to please Marmontel, who became *Secrétaire des bâtiments* in 1758; a man of letters, he was a powerful figure at the *Mercure de France,* for which he had obtained the royal privilege, and was also a familiar figure in literary and artistic circles during the second half of the eighteenth century. Fragonard seems to have known him well, judging from an

entry in the catalogue of the Collet sale of May 14, 1787 (no. 414): "Two drawings subjects from the moral tales of M. de Marmontel."

Fragonard boldly placed the scene in the shadows: on a little hill, in a thicket, Annette, holding her baby tightly against her, tenderly gazes at the shepherd, who grasps her hand; in front of her are her basket and wheelbarrow. At the right, some sheep doze under the watchful eye of the sheepdog. The painting succeeds primarily because of the effect of backlighting and the grayish-green and blue-gray color scheme of the woods and hills in the distance.

This is unquestionably one of Fragonard's most delicate pastoral scenes. Its date, which has been much discussed, cannot be before 1762, or after 1772. A comparison with the *Shepherd . . .* in Annecy (see cat. no. 86) would argue for a date closer to 1765.

88   Tending the Herds

Gouache and oil on paper, 31.4 x 43.6 cm.

Musée des Arts Décoratifs, Lyons, Inv. 534

Provenance
Acquired by the Chamber of Commerce of Lyons in the latter half of the nineteenth century (stamped at the lower left, Lugt 1699 a).

Bibliography
Cuzin, 1986, pp. 64–65, no. 25, colorpl. 9

Figure 1. Fragonard. *Girl Tending Geese.*
Musée des Beaux-Arts, Rouen

Formerly attributed to Loutherbourg, this rough sketch is undoubtedly the work of Fragonard. Cuzin rightly dates it to the years following the artist's return to Paris, about 1762. The kinship between this work and one like the *Wagon in the Mud* (cat. no. 20) is obvious.

A shepherdess, seated on top of a rise, watches over her oxen and cows, while, with the help of his black dog, a young shepherd is herding some sheep. "The pistol shot of a peas-ant's red skirt" (Goncourts, *Journal,* 1894, IV, p. 689), the turquoise blues of the sky, the "reddening browns" of the ground enliven this unpretentious work, which recalls the *Girl Tending Geese* in Rouen (see figure 1; formerly in the Baderou collection), *Leaving the Farm,* and the *Watering Place* in a private collection in New York (W. 130, 131, figs. 79, 81).

89   Shepherd Seated on a Rock

Gouache and pastel, 24.8 x 39.5 cm.

Private collection, Paris

Provenance
A. Carrier: sold, May 4, 1875, no. 15 (for 95 francs); Philippe Burty: sold, March 2–3, 1891, no. 91 (for 585 francs); Léon Michel-Lévy: sold, June 17–18, 1925, no. 57; M. D.: sold, December 9, 1952, no. 14, pl. VI; sold, Orléans, June 7, 1975, letter A., ill.

Bibliography
P. p. 309
La Chronique des arts et la curiosité,
   March 14, 1891, p. 1
A. 297

The variety of Fragonard's subjects is as great as that of his techniques. He tried his hand at all kinds of themes, at all of the genres (except, perhaps, still life), and worked in black or red chalk and bister, as well as in pen and ink (although more rarely). Some of his watercolors and pastels (too fragile to be lent for exhibition) have come down to us, and even a few gouaches. This one, combining gouache and pastel, is little known. It is reminiscent of the painting in the Roy Chalk collection in New York, *A Shepherd Seated on a Rock* (figure 1; W. 148, fig. 84), and should be dated similarly— that is, to the mid-1760s. In the foreground, a shepherd in the company of his dog, who is lying on the ground, turns his back to his flock, while a herdsman sitting on a large rock on higher ground watches over his herd.

Figure 1. Fragonard.
A Shepherd Seated on a Rock.
Collection Roy Chalk, New York

90   The Return of the Herd

Oil on canvas, 64.1 x 80 cm.
Signed at the lower right: *fragonard* (see figure 1)

Worcester Art Museum, Worcester, Massachusetts, Theodore T. and Mary G. Ellis Collection, 1940.62

Provenance
Hippolyte Walferdin (1795–1880): sold
posthumously, April 16–18, 1880, no. 55
(for 3,850 francs, to the expert Féral) (?);
Marquise d'Harcourt, 1907, 1921; Marquis
d'Harcourt, 1925; [Germain Seligmann],
1929; T. T. Ellis, Worcester; given to the
Worcester museum by Mary G. Ellis, 1940.

Exhibitions
(For a complete list, see Worcester museum
      catalogue, 1974)
Paris, 1907, no. 106
Paris, 1921, no. 17, ill.
Paris, 1923, no. 20
Paris, 1925–26, no. 109, ill.
Baltimore, 1959, no. 12, ill. p. 51
Tokyo, 1980, no. 35, colorpl.
Richmond, 1981, no. 19, ill.

Bibliography
G. p. 339(?)
Portalis, 1880, p. 13(?)
P. p. 287(?)
N. p. 133(?)
R. pp. 184, 225, 270
W. 152, pl. 18
W. and M. 168, ill.
Worcester museum catalogue,
      1974, pp. 244–46, ill. p. 588
Conisbee, 1981, p. 195, fig. 164

Related works
An engraving of the painting, in reverse, was
made by Vivant-Denon (1747–1825; see
figure 2; G. p. 338; Roux, 1949, VI, p. 554,
no. 190) before 1791.

A preparatory drawing (A. 309) once
belonged to Le Brun (sold, April 11, 1791,
no. 312), who mentions that "l'on en connaît
l'estampe gravée ... par Denon." Is it the
same as the Cailleux drawing (figure 3; A.
310; Richmond exhibition catalogue, 1981,
no. 13); or as the one formerly in the collection of Marius Paulme, which was "détruit
par le feu," according to R., and which seems
to have been signed (figure 4; A. 311); or
maybe as the one that was in the Zarine collection (A. 312)?

Another drawing—not the one in the Le
Brun collection sale—was owned by Collet
(sold, May 14, 1787, no. 371).

Figure 1. Signature, catalogue no. 90

Figure 2. Dominique Vivant-Denon,
after Fragonard. *The Return of the Herd.*
Engraving. Bibliothèque Nationale, Paris,
Cabinet des Estampes

Figure 3. Fragonard.
The Return of the Herd. Drawing.
Art market, Paris

Figure 4. Fragonard.
The Return of the Herd (destroyed). Drawing.
Formerly Collection Marius Paulme

Figure 5. Fragonard.
The Windmill.
Musée Fragonard, Grasse

Figure 6. Jacques Couché, after Louis
Carmontelle. *The Windmill in the
Parc Monceau.* Bibliothèque Nationale, Paris,
Cabinet des Estampes

90

This painting must have been famous in the eighteenth century, for an engraving of it was made by Vivant-Denon before 1791, and two preparatory drawings are described in sales catalogues of 1787 and 1791. However, it is not mentioned before 1880, nor is it at all certain that it can be identified with the picture in the Walferdin collection.

The windmill (see also figure 5) at the right has been a subject of much discussion. To paint one in such detail, must not Fragonard have gone to Holland? We know today that Fragonard, indeed, traveled to the Netherlands (see pp. 178–80), but the artist could have seen similar windmills in Paris—for example, at the Parc Monceau (see figure 6, the engraving by Jacques Couché, after Louis Carmontelle: "View [of the] water Mill and of the Bridge leading to it," which illustrates Carmontelle's book *Le Jardin de Monceau*).

The date of the present work has, of course, been the subject of debate: Wildenstein suggests a date of about 1765; D. Catton Rich dates it to 1770 in the catalogue of the Worcester Art Museum. We favor the first suggestion, as

does Philip Conisbee (1981), who compares *The Return of the Herd* to the *Pastoral Landscape* painted by Loutherbourg in 1763 (in the Liverpool museum)—an exemplary artist and painting, for Fragonard.

The subject is a commonplace one for the period: a herdsman (or is he a miller?) tries to persuade or otherwise win over a somewhat reluctant shepherdess. A dog, two "oxen" (that Le Brun called bulls), and some sheep enliven this landscape graced with "many trees of picturesque form." The creamy coloring of the animals and the red skirt of the shepherdess brighten the composition. Fragonard's skill lies in the placement of the dallying couple on the downward slope of a hill.

The picture contains no precise moralistic message, true to Fragonard's spirit at this point in his career. The young couple, who seem to be going through the motions of a dance, give this scene a liveliness and a gaiety that distinguish it from the works of his contemporaries.

91 The Two Windmills

Oil on canvas, 32 x 40.9 cm.
Signed at the lower center: *Frag . . .*

Private collection

Provenance
Président Robert de Saint-Victor (1738–1822), Rouen: sold, November 26, 1822–January 7, 1823, no. 621 (for 79 francs); possibly Huot-Fragonard: sold, May 19–20, 1876, no. 6: "le Moulin. Il est auprès de deux chaumières construites au bord d'une rivière; ciel nuageux. Paysage inspiré des oeuvres de J. Ruysdaël" [Oil on canvas, 30 x 38 cm.]; Beurnonville: sold, June 3, 1884, no. 383: "le moulin à vent. Un moulin de bois est construit sur une éminence baignée par un cours d'eau, a[u]près de deux cabines entourées de palissades. Ciel gris" [Oil on canvas, 31 x 40 cm.]; Félix (1842–1891) and then Hippolyte-Adrien Panhard.

Exhibitions
Paris, 1921, no. 85

Bibliography
Blanc, 1862, p. 15
P. pp. 283, 284
N. p. 143
Ratouis de Limay, 1913, p. 439
R. p. 185
W. 180, fig. 97
Carpenter, 1962, p. 360
W. and M. 152, ill.

Related works
For the pendant, see below.

Figure 1. Fragonard. *The Herd.* Whereabouts unknown

This painting is unquestionably one of Fragonard's finest landscapes in the Dutch style. Centered on a large windmill in the middle ground, the composition—with its trees and bushes, its vast cloudy sky, and its shafts of sunlight—has the simplicity and the "naturalness" that were so valued by eighteenth-century art lovers and collectors.

In this riverside landscape, the otherwise muted color scheme of pale grayish greens and russets is enlivened by the touches of white on the cows, and of bright red on the peasants' cap, skirt, and vest.

At the same time, this work has an added interest: in the Fragonard exhibition of 1921, it was associated with a *Herd* (figure 1; W. 179, fig. 96), which has unfortunately disappeared, and, according to the catalogue (no. 86; see also Wilhelm, 1948, p. 302, fig. 2), this picture was not only signed, like the *Two Windmills,* but also dated 1775. Dated paintings by Fragonard are rare, and the dating of his "Dutch" landscapes is particularly problematical; hence, the importance of this date.

If, however, the *Two Windmills* is, in fact, the pendant to the *Herd,* then why were they not both in the collection of Robert de Saint-Victor when it was assembled in Rouen in the late eighteenth century? Not until its companion is found can the present work be dated positively to 1775.

92 The Watering Place

Oil on canvas, 51.5 x 63 cm.

Private collection, Switzerland

Provenance
Mme [de Saint-Sauveur]: sold, February 12, 1776, no. 53; Randon de Boisset: sold, February 27, 1777, no. 230 (for 1,650 *livres,* to Mercier); anonymous sale, May 23, 1780, no. 40 (for 800 *livres*); Comte de Choiseul Gouffier, 1783 (?); Duc de Choiseul (or Chabot): sold, December 10, 1787, no. 67 (for 610 *livres,* to Dulac); anonymous sale, July 8, 1793, no. 14: "un autre tableau offrant un point de vue de paysage avec diverses figures et des animaux. Ce beau morceau est digne d'être comparé à la belle touche de Ruisdael" (?); [not in the anonymous sale, December 28–29, 1846, no. 50: "paysage. Des boeufs s'abreuvent dans une rivière. Plus loin des ruines et des arbres. sur bois"]; Laperlier: sold, April 11–13, 1867, no. 33 (for 790 francs, to Féral); H. Walferdin: sold, April 3, 1880, no. 14 (for 1,230 francs); Mme Charles Kestner; G. de Lauverjat; Arthur Veil-Picard; private collection: sold, Sotheby's, Monte Carlo, June 20–21, 1987, no. 289, colorpl.; private collection, Switzerland.

Exhibitions
Paris, Salon de la Correspondance, August 1783, no. 156 (or 157)
Paris, 1860, no. 158: "le troupeau qui s'abreuve. Sous la garde d'un berger à cheval, un troupeau de vaches et de moutons vient boire à une fontaine placée au bas d'un coteau boisé"; the description coincides fairly well, but not the dimensions—35 x 45 cm.—and, also, the painting is said to belong to Walferdin (?)
London, 1954–55, no. 210
Zurich, 1955, no. 92
Tokyo, 1980, no. 29, colorpl.

Bibliography
Journal de Paris, March 25, 1777, no. 84, p. 2, no. 230 (the text is incomplete)
Blanc, 1862, p. 15
G. p. 339
Le Hir, 1867, p. 128
P. pp. 127, 269, 289
N. p. 140
G. Wildenstein, 1921, p. 20
Wilhelm, 1948, p. 302
R. pp. 183, 186
W. 126, fig. 78
W. and M. 158, ill.

Related works
For the watercolor and the preparatory drawing(s), see the following entry.
For the actual pendant, see cat. no. 94.
For the picture regarded as the pendant in the eighteenth century, see cat. no. 93.

Figure 1. Jean Mathieu, after Fragonard. *Stormy Weather.* Engraving. Bibliothèque Nationale, Paris, Cabinet des Estampes

A connection has been established today between the *Watering Place* and *The Rock* (cat. no. 94), but when these two works were in the Walferdin collection they were considered unrelated, and were sold at separate times.

The *Watering Place* appeared, alone, in five (or four) sales between 1776 and 1793 (or 1787). It may at one point have been associated with a picture entitled *Stormy Weather,* of which Jean Mathieu made an engraving (figure 1), after 1784, when it belonged to the Comte de Choiseul Gouffier. The latter lent to the Salon de la Correspondance in 1783 two "landscapes with figures of men and animals," which, in our opinion, were the present picture and *Stormy Weather*

—but to what extent may these two works be considered as pendants? The existence of two splendid watercolors in the Lagoy collection (see the following entry), which were kept together until recently, argues in favor of their association.

The experts at the sales in the eighteenth century were, of course, unanimous in their praise of the author of this painting, "whose varied and indefatigable talent always gives us so much pleasure in whatever genre he undertakes" (1787 sales catalogue). Only one (in 1776; see also 1793) linked this work with Dutch landscapes: "This picture compares favorably with those of the reputed masters of the Netherlandish school."

A white cow drinks from a water trough protected by a jutting rock, as a shepherd on horseback watches over some reddish-brown cows and some sheep. On the hill, a young couple tends a flock of sheep. The eye-catching red of the shepherdess's skirt is a characteristic motif. The sun illuminates only part of the painting: the young couple, the rocks, and the back of the white cow.

Although he was obviously acquainted with Northern examples, Fragonard did not content himself with an imitation or a pastiche. The brushwork—composed of free and varied strokes that allowed him to accentuate details that he wanted noticed—is his own, as is the color scheme of maroons and muted greens, of warm and cool tones, which he skillfully combined.

As for the date of the work, it is again not easy to be definite, but we would tentatively suggest the 1770s.

93   The Watering Place

Watercolor, over an underdrawing in black chalk, 34 x 45.6 cm.

Private collection, Paris

Provenance
[W. A. Lestevenon, a Dutch art dealer and collector established in Rome and Paris, one of the founders of the Teylers Museum, in Haarlem, according to the Lagoy inventory]; Marquis de Lagoy (1746–1829; his stamp, Lugt 1710, appears at the lower right; mentioned in the handwritten inventory drawn up between 1800 and 1820, which was brought to our attention by Mme A. de Moustier); Camille Groult; private collection.

Exhibitions
Paris, 1921, no. 115

Bibliography
A. 832, fig. 170
Ananoff, 1968, p. 99, colorpl.
Williams, 1978, p. 126

Related works
A very close version in bister wash, which formerly belonged to the Goncourts, is in the British Museum (figure 1; A. 306, fig. 360; see also A. 829).

For the painting, see cat. no. 92.

For the pendant, also in watercolor (figure 2), see A. 842, fig. 722 (see also A. 828, sold, Paris, Galerie Charpentier, March 18, 1959, no. 95, ill., today in New York).

For the painting *Stormy Weather* (figure 3), after which Jean Mathieu (1749–1815) made an engraving (see cat. no. 92, figure 1), and which corresponds to this pendant, see W. 167, fig. 89; sold, Paris, Palais Galliéra, December 7, 1971, no. 13, colorpl.; see also the previous entry.

Watercolors are rare in Fragonard's work: *The Watering Place* is among the most luminous. The watercolor and the oil painting of the same subject (see previous entry) are identical, except for their color schemes. The oil depicts a sultry autumn evening, while the light and fresh tones of the watercolor evoke, instead, a vibrant summer morning. Fragonard proceeded in the same way with the pendant, the *Stormy Weather*: the painting features warm and reddish tones, while the watercolor is all cool tones of grayish greens and steely blues.

It seems certain that the two watercolors, first brought together about 1800, were executed as companion pieces. It is equally obvious that they were done after, and from, the paintings. We do not know if Fragonard made these watercolor copies at the same time as the paintings or at a much later date—such as about 1780.

With regard to the study in bister wash for the *Watering Place,* owned by the Goncourt brothers (today, in the British Museum), Watson (1971, p. 84, ill.) published it as "after Ruysdael." Without going that far, Chennevières (1880, p. 111) considered it as a "sort of composition à la Ruysdael, a chic Ruysdael...." The latter term applies equally well to the present version of the *Watering Place,* which is so like English watercolors and yet still very French in feeling.

Figure 1. Fragonard. *The Watering Place.*
British Museum, London

Figure 2. Fragonard. *Stormy Weather.*
Whereabouts unknown

Figure 3. Fragonard. *Stormy Weather.*
Whereabouts unknown

94 The Rock

Oil on canvas, 55 x 64 cm.
Signed at the lower left: *fragonard*

Private collection, Paris

Provenance
Hippolyte Walferdin (as early as 1860 ?):
sold, April 12–16, 1880, no. 54 (for 5,900
francs, to Malinet); Auguste C[ourtin]: sold,
March 29, 1886, no. 7 (for 2,550 francs);
anonymous sale, March 4, 1897, no. 16;
anonymous sale, April 8, 1908, no. 9 (for
11,000 francs); G. de Lauverjat; Arthur
Veil-Picard; private collection.

Exhibitions
Paris, 1860, no. 135: "des chevaux viennent
à un abreuvoir taillé à droite dans le pro-
longement d'un rocher qui occupe le milieu
de la composition. Signé Fragonard" (this
description is partially in error, as are those
of the three other landscapes by Fragonard
in the Walferdin collection lent in 1860)
London, 1954–55, no. 204
Zurich, 1955, no. 93
Tokyo, 1980, no. 30, colorpl.

Bibliography
Bürger [Thoré], 1860, p. 347 ("le *Rocher*,
signé en toutes lettres, ce qui est rare")
Saint-Victor, 1860, n.p.
G. pp. 338–39
Portalis, 1880, pp. 11–12
P. pp. 126–27, 287
N. p. 141
R. p. 186
W. 127, fig. 80
W. and M. 159, ill.

Related works
For the "pendant," see cat. no. 92.
An autograph replica (figure 1), executed
more freely but the same in format, was sold
in Paris, at the Palais Galliéra, June 9, 1964,
no. 65, colorpl.

Figure 1. Fragonard. *The Rock.*
Whereabouts unknown

This painting, which was much admired when it was in the
Walferdin collection, was not associated with the *Watering
Place* (cat. no. 92) until the turn of the century. They are
both very close in composition, inspiration, and date.

Already in 1860, Thoré had pointed out the rarity for
Fragonard of a full signature. According to Thoré, this
picture evoked the work of Berchem, but recent critics have
argued that it is more like Ruisdael's paintings of fleeting
clouds.

95 Shepherd and Sheep on a Sunny Hillside

Bister wash on paper, over an underdrawing in black chalk, 34.4 x 46.6 cm.

The Pierpont Morgan Library, New York, III, 114

Provenance
Sir James Knowles (1831–1908; the drawing, however, does not appear to bear his
stamp, Lugt 1546): sold posthumously,
Christie's, London, May 27–29, 1908, no.
238; Charles Fairfax Murray; J. Pierpont
Morgan.

Exhibitions
Washington, D.C., 1978, no. 49
New York, 1981, no. 105, ill. (lists previous
  exhibitions)

Bibliography
P. p. 309(?)
A. 1380, fig. 389
Massengale, 1979, p. 271, fig. 104
Sutton, 1980; 1987, p. 106

Related works
See A. 303, fig. 111, for a drawing that
unconvincingly repeats one of the motifs in
the present work.

This exceptionally large and fresh drawing is of the highest
quality. It is a perfect demonstration of the principles of
Fragonard's technique. The artist began by faintly sketching
the composition in black chalk. Then, with his brush, he
indicated the dark masses of the foliage, the trees, and the
rocks in the foreground, indicating more lightly the thatched
cottage and the fence in the middle ground, and the trees in
the distance. He did not cover the sheet entirely, but,
instead, skillfully played with the white of the paper, applying a light wash to render the sunlit hills and the clearings.
Through his brisk and meticulous brushwork, in little nervous strokes, Fragonard was able to capture, like no other
painter of his time, the shimmering quality of the light and
practically even the movement of the air.

Massengale dates this drawing before 1765; Eunice Williams, in our opinion more accurately, dates it ten years later.

96 Landscape with Washerwomen by a Pond, and a Donkey

Oil on canvas, 73 x 91.5 cm.

Musée Fragonard, Grasse

Provenance
"Coll. de M. Belizar," according to Le Brun (who expertized the Vaudreuil sale); Comte de Vaudreuil: sold, November 26, 1787, no. 110 (for 1,235 *livres*, to Beryten); Louis XVIII, 1822, acquired for the Château de Saint-Cloud ("compris dans les 20,000 francs de tableaux, acquis de M. de Langeac," September 25, 1822, Inv. Louis XVIII, 2 DD 1); Galerie d'Apollon, Musée du Louvre (Inv. 4544), 1837: on loan to Compiègne, 1887–1959; to Grasse, from 1959.

Exhibitions
London, 1949–50, no. 94
Bern, 1954, no. 3
Bordeaux, 1956, no. 74
Charleroi, 1957, no. 2
Tokyo, 1978, no. 34, colorpl.

Bibliography
Thiéry, 1787, II, p. 547
Saint-Cloud catalogue, 1831, no. 196
Louvre catalogue, 1855, no. 209
  (with reversed dimensions)
Blanc, 1862, p. 16
Lejeune, 1863, p. 294
Gautier, 1882, p. 184
P. p. 284
N. p. 139
R. p. 185
W. 183, fig. 99
Thuillier, 1967, p. 71, colorpl.
W. and M. 194, ill.
Rosenberg and Compin, 1974, p. 192

This painting, which was so admired in the eighteenth century—by Le Brun, as well as by Thiéry, in his *Guide des Amateurs* of 1787 ("a grand and delightful landscape by Fragonard")—as a "magnificent landscape," "one of the most considerable and the most finished by this artist," is no longer what it used to be.

Purchased by Louis XVIII, it was the second Fragonard to enter the Louvre—the first was the *Coresus,* bought by Louis XV. By the middle of the nineteenth century, however, it was already in a sorry state: this "poor landscape full of cracks" (Blanc) "had suffered greatly from the passage of time and the unintelligent restorations to which it had been subjected" (Lejeune). The presence of bitumen now makes it difficult to read.

It is obvious that Fragonard tried to rival the seventeenth-century Dutch landscape painters: he included even more picturesque details, such as "rustic steps," tree trunks, a ladder, and a thatched cottage. The washerwomen at the edge of the pond, the donkey waiting for its load (there is a similar one in a landscape in the Virginia Museum of Fine Arts, in Richmond; see figure 1; W. 160, pl. 19), and a couple "sitting at the foot of a haystack" also attract our

Figure 1. Fragonard.
Landscape with Washerwomen.
Virginia Museum of Fine Arts, Richmond

attention. The work is unified by the shaft of sunlight that strikes the top of a rock, and by the large pasture that extends for the width of the composition.

Dated by Wildenstein between 1761 and 1765, the painting appears to us to have been done much later.

97   The Ford

Oil on paper, mounted on wood, 28.5 x 38 cm.

Musée des Beaux-Arts, Chartres

Provenance
Justin Courtois; gift to the Chartres museum, 1889.

Exhibitions
Paris, 1925–26, no. 110
London, 1949–50, no. 95
Bern, 1954, unnumbered (between nos. 6 and 7)
Charleroi, 1957, no. 27
Lille, 1960, no. 70, pl. XIX

Bibliography
Wilhelm, 1948, p. 301
W. 164, fig. 87
W. and M. 183, ill.

This splendid rough sketch, painted on paper, owes much to Dutch art, while, at the same time, its execution and spirit anticipate the landscape studies of the Barbizon painters.

One can imagine Fragonard sitting down one summer evening to paint these riders fording a stream under a sky full of clouds, while the cows and oxen blend into the darkening shadows under the sheltering trees. The artist sacrificed detail to capture the impression of the moment.

It is not easy to give a precise date for this work: we would suggest about 1765–70.

"A Head of an Old Man, Painted in the Manner of Rembrandt"

At the Salon of 1767, Fragonard exhibited a "Head of an Old Man. A round painting." The only other detailed information we have is from Diderot, who says that "this old man is looking into the distance." This does not permit us to identify this work, with any certainty, with the painting that is today in the Ball State University Art Gallery, in Muncie, Indiana (see figures 1, and also 2; W. 207, fig. 105). None of the critics who reviewed this Salon mentioned the name of Rembrandt any longer in connection with this work, and yet, beginning in 1770, a large number of "Heads of old men painted [by Fragonard] in the manner of Rembrandt" began to appear on the art market.

The work of Rembrandt, which was very much admired in France in the second half of the eighteenth century (see, most recently, Cayeux, 1975), was for Fragonard (and for many of his contemporaries; see figure 3) both an example and a pretext. Indeed, Fragonard adapted Rembrandt's compositions to the prevailing taste (and even copied them; see the Choiseul-Stainville sales catalogue, May 21–24, 1784, no. 8), but he rendered only their external aspect—the brushwork, the chiaroscuro, the warm brown color scheme, and the golden-toned shadows. Yet, he does not seem to have been sensitive to the Rembrandt who probed the human soul and sought to move the spectator. Fragonard was concerned with showing—not without pride—what he was capable of. He wanted his technique to be admired; he liked to paint, and he wished to communicate this pleasure. How can one fail to be enchanted by the fine impasto that he handled with so much assurance, by the skill with which his brush made the model serve his own demands, and by the way that he gave life to the pictorial material.

It is evident that Fragonard was not trying to paint portraits, and that he was not concerned with likenesses. Today, we evoke the names of Rubens (see cat. no. 102), Hals, or Tiepolo (see cat. no. 98) in connection with these pictures, while his contemporaries referred to Guido Reni (apropos of the *Head* in the Salon of 1767), van Dyck, or Jean Grimou (see cat. no. 103).

When did Fragonard paint these old men? In the same year, or at least in the same period? Wildenstein considered the possibility of a commission from the engraver and art dealer Emmanuel de Ghendt (1738–1815). Like the author of the entry for the Cincinnati painting in the 1967 exhibition catalogue (E. V., New York; see cat. no. 100, figure 1), we believe that these heads were not part of a series, but are variations on a theme, representing a personal aspect of Fragonard's work.

Were these heads painted before the *Coresus and Callirhoë* (1765), in which there are many figures of old men, at the same time as the Muncie *Head* (if, indeed, it dates from 1767), or closer to the "Figures de fantaisie," which are arbitrarily assigned to 1769? The first mention of these heads is in the catalogue of the Baudouin sale in 1770 (Baudouin was Boucher's son-in-law). Some of them seem closer in date to Fragonard's return from Italy—as, for instance, the one in the Musée Jacquemart-André (cat. no. 98); others appear to be much later, like the *Old Man* in Nice (cat. no. 99), which recalls the portrait of Mlle Gui-

Figure 1. Fragonard. *Head of an Old Man.*
Ball State University Art Gallery, Muncie, Indiana

Figure 2. Fragonard. *Head of an Old Man.*
Private collection, Paris

Figure 3. Louis-Jean-Jacques Durameau.
Head of an Old Man. Signed and dated 1773.
Art market, Paris

Figure 4. Fragonard. *Head of an Old Man.*
Private collection

mard (cat. no. 125) or the *Philosopher* in Hamburg (cat. no. 101; reminiscent of the portrait of Naigeon, cat. no. 134), or the *Old Man* in Amiens (cat. no. 102). The latest one, the *Head of an Old Man* (figure 4; formerly in the André Meyer collection, Paris; W. 208, pl. 23), seems to date from just before 1770; the subordination of subject to technique was pushed to the limit here.

98   Bust of an Old Man Wearing a Cap

Oil on canvas, 54 x 43.5 cm.
Originally, an oval.

Musée Jacquemart-André, Paris

Provenance
Acquired in 1867 for 1,500 francs by Édouard André, from F. de Villars (one year before the famous sale of this *amateur*'s collection).

Exhibitions
Paris, 1878, no. 104
Tokyo, 1980, no. 36, colorpl.

Bibliography
P. p. 290
R. pp. 183, 268, fig. 109, p. 230
W. 205, fig. 104, p. 14 (French edition)
Zolotov, 1968, p. 154, ill.
W. and M. 216, ill.
Cayeux, 1975, p. 299
[Gétreau-Abondance, 1976, no. 21]

Related works
A copy in pastel by the Comte de Brehan, supposedly signed and dated 1778 (figure 1), appeared in the sale of the Georges Bourgarel collection, November 13–15, 1922, no. 69, ill. (on Brehan, who copied the works of Fragonard, see cat. no. 138).

Figure 1. Comte de Brehan, after Fragonard. *Bust of an Old Man Wearing a Cap.* Pastel. Whereabouts unknown

Figure 2. Radiograph of catalogue no. 98

This painting was framed as an oval in 1878, and, in fact, X-ray photography (figure 2) has shown that originally the canvas, too, was oval, before it was enlarged to form a rectangle in the nineteenth century. Before 1867 it belonged to F. de Villars, who also owned *Le Feu aux poudres* (today in the Louvre; see cat. no. 73).

Of all Fragonard's portraits of old men, the one in the Musée Jacquemart-André is the most "Venetian." This had

been noticed by Portalis, who described it as being "in the manner of Tiepolo." Fragonard had studied and copied works by G. B. Tiepolo in Venice and in Vicenza on his way back to Paris in 1761 (see Rosenberg and Brejon, 1986). He was able to admire firsthand Tiepolo's frescoes in the Villa Contarini, at Mira (today, in the Musée Jacquemart-André), but not those in the Villa Pisani, at Strà, "which were not yet finished."

Figure 3. Giovanni Battista Tiepolo. *Head of an Old Man*. Whereabouts unknown

Figure 4. Giovanni Domenico Tiepolo, after Giovanni Battista Tiepolo. *Head of an Old Man*. Private collection, Paris

98

Figure 5. Rembrandt. *Self-Portrait*. 1633. Musée du Louvre

Did he ever meet Tiepolo? There is no answer to this question in the travel journal kept by the Abbé de Saint-Non. In any case, these works no doubt dazzled and made an indelible impression on him. The present picture was influenced by the Oriental heads that Tiepolo painted about 1755 (see figures 3, 4), but, as with the works inspired by those of Rembrandt (see figure 5), Fragonard retained only the physiognomic type and the presentation; he did not try to imitate the Venetian artist, or to make copies of his paintings.

Fragonard played up the contrast between the warm coloring of the face and the golden yellow of the collar, chain, and beard, and the lilac grays of the toque and the mantle. The bravura of the execution is positively amazing: Frago-

nard "built up" the beard, the forehead, and the nose in order to give maximum solidity to the face. The model's tightly closed mouth, and his severe and distant gaze accentuate the work's expressive power.

There is an *F* inscribed on the pendant, which hangs from the chain worn by the sitter; could this initial be the artist's signature?

99 Old Man with White Hair

Oil on canvas, oval, 60 x 49 cm.

Musée des Beaux-Arts Jules Chéret, Nice

Provenance

B[ellanger ?]: sold, March 17, 1788, no. 30;
perhaps the painting sold with the painter
Sauvage's collection, December 6, 1808, no.
38: "une étude de tête de vieillard, d'une
touche heurtée et de goût, au premier coup
. . . ," which measured 20 *pouces* by 18 [54 x
48.6 cm]? (the catalogue does not mention an
oval format); the painter Fernand Sabatté, of
the Institute (born, 1874; pupil of Gustave
Moreau): sold posthumously, November 18,
1945, at Chamigny, near La Ferté-sous-
Jouarre (to benefit the Sisters of Saint-
Vincent-de-Paul, who inherited Sabatté's
estate); acquired by the Louvre (R. F.
1945–27) and lent to Nice, 1946.

Exhibitions

Geneva, 1949, no. 76
Paris, 1953, no. 49, ill.
Bern, 1954, no. 18
Bordeaux, 1956, no. 76
Grasse, 1957, no. 14
Brussels, 1975, no. 26, ill.
Lille, 1985, no. 51, colorpl.

Bibliography

Arts, December 14, 1945
Gazette de l'Hôtel Drouot, November 9,
  1945, p. 1, ill.; November 16, 1945, p. 1
Bernard, 1946, pp. 40–41, ill.
R. p. 183
W. 206, fig. 106
W. and M. 217, ill.
Nice museum catalogue, 1986, no. 12,
  colorpl.

Related works

Jacques Wilhelm, in his unpublished monograph on Fragonard, mentions that there was
"dans la coll. de Mme Meunié . . . un pastel
ovale identique," which he attributes to the
Comte de Brehan.
  The posthumous inventory of the collection
of the Abbé de Saint-Non lists an oval "figure de St Pierre, copie de Fragonard par M.
de St Non." Was it a copy of the present
painting (see G. Wildenstein, 1959, p. 239,
no. 8; W., p. 244, n. 8, mentions that there
was in the church of "Pothières . . . une tête
d'expression qui pourrait être celle-ci ou une
autre copie de Saint-Non")?

Wilhelm identified this figure as a representation of Saint
Peter (he holds a key in his right hand). This hypothesis is
not to be dismissed, although Fragonard does not seem to
have been overly concerned with the subject of the work.
However, if he did attach some importance to it, perhaps he
did so with humorous intent, for he gave the saint the red
nose of a drunkard (as he did all of his representations of
"Saint Jerome" and of "philosophers").
  One is struck by the wonderful technique and by the
virtuosity of the execution and the brushwork. The painting
is in perfect condition; the impasto has not been "crushed,"
as so often happens when paintings are relined. It has thus
kept the spontaneity, the vigor, and the vitality that are the
hallmarks of Fragonard's work. A marvelous detail is the
ruby cabochon pendant that sparkles on the sitter's chest.
  This painting seems to be very close in date to the *Portrait
of Mlle Guimard* in the Louvre (cat. no. 125).

100 Head of an Old Man

Red chalk on paper, circular, diameter, 21.2 cm.
On the verso is an old inscription attributing the drawing to Jean-Baptiste Jouvenet.

Bibliothèque Municipale, Rouen

Provenance
Bequest of Jules Hédou (1833–1905): at the
lower center is his stamp, Lugt 1253.

Exhibitions
Rouen, 1970, no. 16, ill.
Washington, D.C., and other cities, 1981,
  no. 39, pl. 76

Related works
For the painting formerly in the collection of
George A. Reutschler in Cincinnati (figure 1;
W. 192, pl. 22), see below (see also A. 707,
fig. 201).

The *Head of an Old Man* in Rouen seems to be the study for the small oil painting on paper, signed *frago,* formerly in a Cincinnati private collection (figure 1). This painting, which may have been in the Baudouin collection sale in 1770 (February 15, no. 37: "the head of an old man seen full face," measuring 39 x 32.4 cm.), is very close to the present drawing: the only differences are in the format, the amount of the sitter's hair (more abundant in the drawing), and the eyes (raised upward slightly more in the painting than in the drawing). The two works seem to be contemporary (from about 1767 ?).

Figure 1. Fragonard.
Head of an Old Man.
Private collection, United States

Figure 2. Rembrandt.
Study of an Old Man.
Musée du Louvre

Oil on canvas, oval, 59 x 72.2 cm.

Kunsthalle, Hamburg

Provenance
De Ghendt (1737–1815): sold, November 15, 1779, no. 28: "un philosophe à tête chauve et barbe blanche; il est assis et a les yeux fixés sur un grand livre; on reconnaît dans ce morceau la main habile et savante de son auteur. Ce tableau de forme ovale porte 2 pieds sur 18 pouces de haut [48.6 x 64.8 cm.] . T." (Was this the same work as the "Saint Jérôme lisant, plein d'enthousiasme" that belonged, before 1778, to the miniaturist Peter Adolf Hall [Villot, 1867, p. 75], who paid "144 livres" for his painting?; the one in the de Ghendt collection sold for 120 *livres* according to W.); anonymous sale, May 23, 1903 (to Michel-Lévy); Léon Michel-Lévy: sold, June 17–18, 1925, no. 138, ill. (for 415,000 francs); [Wildenstein]; David, then Pierre David-Weill: sold, Sotheby's, London, June 10, 1959, no. 86, ill. (for 13,000 pounds); [Hallsborough]; acquired by the Hamburg museum, 1960.

Bibliography
G. p. 333
Le Figaro artistique, July 16, 1925, p. 633, ill.
Henriot, 1926, I, p. 129, ill.
R. p. 182
W. 202, fig. 102, p. 14 (French edition)
Mathey, 1961, p. 304, fig. 4
Roskamp, 1961, pp. 72–78, ill.
Francis, 1966, p. 68, fig. 4
Kunsthalle catalogue, 1966, p. 63, no. 777, ill.
Watson, 1971, p. 85, ill.
W. and M. 213, ill.

Fragonard painted a great many figures of bearded old men: "philosophers," "Saint Jeromes," and "Saint Peters." Judging from the eighteenth-century sales catalogues in which they are mentioned, unfortunately often very imprecisely, they have not all come down to us. The present work was certainly in the sale of the de Ghendt collection in 1779, in which there were a number of "Heads of old men." Did it once belong to the Swedish miniaturist Hall, who also owned a "Study for the head of an old man"? It is even less certain that Hall regarded the painting that he owned as a "Saint Jerome"; in the catalogue, the expert described the picture in the de Ghendt sale as a "philosopher."

Could these heads have been part of a series commissioned by Emmanuel de Ghendt, a Flemish engraver established in Paris, as Wildenstein prudently suggests? Our hypothesis is that they were, rather, variations on a theme, inspired by the work and the example of Rembrandt. As we have already seen, Rembrandt's oeuvre exercised a considerable influence on Fragonard, but this did not keep the young artist from adhering to his own very characteristic manner.

Fragonard placed the head of the old scholar, who is absorbed in his reading, in shadow, while his large book is fully illuminated. The light falls on a few wisps of white hair, and on the old man's shoulder, collar, the reddish tip of his nose, and on his left forearm. The color scheme, which ranges from acid yellow to olive green, along with some more or less warm earth colors, is deliberately restrained in favor of the artist's style: the very prominent brushwork is the true subject of the painting.

102 Head of a Bald Old Man

Oil on canvas, oval, 54 x 45 cm.

Musée de Picardie, Amiens

Provenance
Anonymous sale, April 29, 1782, no. 35 (not
82): "une tête peinte à l'huile très savamment. Hauteur 20 pouces, largeur 17 pouces
[54 x 46 cm.]"; the brothers Olympe and
Ernest Lavalard, of Roye, since at least 1862
(Horsin-Déon: "tête d'homme dans la manière de Rubens" [!]); bequeathed, 1890, and
entered the Amiens museum, 1894.

Exhibitions
Paris, 1921, no. 26, ill.
Besançon, 1956, no. 17
Bordeaux, 1956, no. 75, pl. 29
Charleroi, 1957, no. 17, ill.

Bibliography
Horsin-Déon, 1862, p. 144
R. pp. 182–83, fig. 110, p. 235
W. 204, fig. 103
W. and M. 215, ill.

This work (along with those discussed in cat. nos. 99, 101) used to be identified as a representation of Saint Peter. There is nothing to either prove or disprove this interpretation, nor is there any proof that the Amiens *Head* was that mentioned as being in the Hall collection in 1778 (Villot, 1867, p. 74), in the sale of the de Ghendt collection (November 15, 1779, no. 32: "a head of an old man, seen full face with white hair and beard, very skillfully executed [49.6 x 40.5 cm.]"), or of the Gevigney collection (December 1, 1779, no. 596: "a head of an old man, painted in the manner of Rembrandt [no dimensions given]"), to mention only three examples.

The figure is only a pretext for the brushwork, which we can see—as Fragonard wanted us to—at play: the face, the hair, and the beard are rendered in broad and thick undulating brushstrokes, while the collar is indicated by an even more rapid motion of the brush. Rarely has the subject of a painting been so completely dominated by the pictorial medium.

Notice the incongruous spot of steel-blue paint on the figure's right shoulder.

103 Young Girl

Oil on canvas, 62.9 x 52.7 cm.
Inscribed at the lower right: *Grimou*

Governors of Dulwich Picture Gallery, London

Provenance
[Possibly, the art dealer Noël-Joseph Desenfans, born in Douai, 1745]; Sir Francis Bourgeois; bequeathed to Dulwich College, 1811.

Bibliography
Dulwich catalogue, 1816, no. 123
Réau, 1930, p. 210, no. 40
Rosenberg and Compin, 1974, pp. 191–92, fig. 9
Murray, 1980, p. 65, no. 74, ill.
Pupil, 1985, p. 299

Figure 1. Attributed to Fragonard.
Head of a Young Girl.
The Hermitage, Leningrad

On the strength of its "signature," this painting was long considered to be the work of Jean-Alexis Grimou (1678–1733), who in his day was called the "French Rembrandt," because, like Fragonard half a century later, he liked to imitate this master's work. Along with Jean Raoux and Jean-Baptiste Santerre, he is also known for having introduced into France and made fashionable the "Spanish" costume: large lace collars, slit sleeves, and the fancy dress of the stage. However, in execution, none of his works is anything like the Dulwich picture: The bold and direct manner, the freedom and briskness of the handling, and the nervous yet assured brushwork anticipate the style of Fragonard's "figures de fantaisie."

This painting is not the only one ascribed to Grimou that may be reassigned to Fragonard. The oval *Head of a Young Girl* (figure 1), in the Hermitage, is now attributed to

Fragonard (Nemilova, 1978, pp. 12–13, ill; Hermitage catalogue, 1985, p. 139, colorpl.). In the B[ellanger ?] sale, March 17, 1788, no. 30, there was "a head of an old man [by Fragonard] and, as its pendant, a copy by Grimou...."

There is nothing surprising in the fact that the artist painted this very young girl more delicately and elegantly than he did his more usual old men. He was not indifferent to the small, fine-featured face of his model, her hazel eyes, and the pearl on her right ear, but when he applied broad brown streaks of paint to her "Spanish" dress, or rendered her billowing white collar as if it were "whipped," he reverted to his very personal style.

This imitation by an imitator, as François Pupil called the Dulwich picture is, however, not devoid of the note of humor that one frequently discerns in Fragonard's work.

104 "The High Priest Coresus Sacrifices Himself to Save Callirhoë": Coresus and Callirhoë

Oil on canvas, 311 x 400 cm.

Musée du Louvre, Paris

Provenance
Presented by Fragonard to the Académie as his "morceau d'agrément," March 30, 1765 (*Procès-Verbaux...*, VII, p. 295). On April 1, Cochin "propose 'à Marigny, le surinten-dant,' de prendre pour les Gobelins ce tab-leau qui se trouve exécuté avec tant de succès et de vouloir bien lui en ordonner un autre pour y faire pendant" (Furcy-Raynaud, 1904, pp. 10–11).

On August 8, 1765, a few days before the opening of the Salon, the picture was pur-chased by the king for 2,400 *livres*, with the intention of having it adapted to a tapestry (Cochin remarked, ibid., p. 28, "s'il était de quelqu'un de nos anciens, je ne pourrais l'estimer moins de 3,600 livres").

By August 5, Cochin had asked for an advance of 1,200 *livres* for Fragonard (ibid., p. 27), and on August 17 Fragonard signed the receipt. He received an additional 600 *livres* on May 24, 1766 (order dated the 13th); but the "parfait payement" was not forthcoming until January 1, 1773! (Enger-and, 1901, pp. 194–95; see also *N.A.A.F.,* 1888, p. 120).

The tapestry, however, was never woven: in September 1794, the commissioners of the *Jury des Arts* discovered the painting still waiting at the Gobelins, and decided to reject it, finding "le sujet ... ne rappelant que des idées superstitieuses" (Guiffrey, 1897, p. 366; see also p. 383).

At the Musée spécial de l'École française, at Versailles (cat. 1801, no. 99); in the collec-tions of the Louvre since 1824 (at the latest).

Exhibitions
Salon, 1765, no. 176 (we have retained the title assigned to the picture in the Salon brochure)
Paris, 1974, no. 3, ill.
Paris, 1984–85, no. 55, ill.

Bibliography
Launay, 1859, n.p.
Houssaye, 1860, p. 325
Blanc, 1862, pp. 5–6
Lejeune, 1863, p. 294
Renouvier, 1863, p. 166
Bellier de la Chavignerie, 1865, p. 83
G. pp. 258–61, 292, 317, 324
Lachaise, 1866, p. 335
P. pp. 48–54, 274 (ill. engraving)
Engerand, 1901, pp. 194–95
N. pp. 51–53, ill.
D. and V. p. XIII, pl. 103
Fenaille, 1907, IV, p. 198
Locquin, 1912, pp. 26, 28, 233, 235–37, 241, pl. XIII
Gillet, 1929, pp. 80–81, pl. 86
Pigler, 1931, pp. 192–97
R. pp. 26–27, 38, 64–65, 123–24, 148, 239, ill.
Seznec and Adhémar, 1960, pp. 6–8, 11, 43, 188–200
W. 225, pl. 27, p. 15, n. 3 (French edition)
Levey, 1972, p. 180, pl. 177
W. and M. 232, ill.
Bukdahl, 1980–82, I, pp. 133–35, 250, 317–20, 326, 352, 455, 491, 501, fig. 52; II, pp. 109, 173, 185–86, 229–30, 233, 282, 330, 338
Fried, 1980, pp. 142, 145, 234–35, fig. 62, p. 144
Sutton, 1980; 1987, pp. 102, 107–8
Bryson, 1981, p. 196, fig. 76
Crow, 1985, pp. 168–69, fig. 78
Wright, 1986, pp. 54–59, ill.

Related works
Paintings
For a sketch, see cat. no. 105.

In the Museo de la Real Academia de Bellas Artes de San Fernando, Madrid, there is a sketch with few notable differences (see fig-ure 1; 30 x 55 cm.; W. 224, fig. 111; W. and M. 234, colorpl. XVI). It is reputed to have come from the collection of Godoy, Prince de la Paix (London exhibition cata-logue, 1968, no. 236). Another sketch (fig-ure 2; 69.2 x 92 cm.; W. 222, fig. 112; W. and M. 235 reproduced the Angers sketch by mistake) was included in the 1980 Frago-nard exhibition in Tokyo (no. 39, colorpl.). Could it have been the Bergeret sketch, sold posthumously, April 24–29, 1786, no. 104, 65 x 92 cm.?; according to the *Diderot* exhi-bition catalogue, Paris, 1984–85, p. 212, "S'agit-il vraiment d'une oeuvre authentique?"

The sketch in the [Trouard] sale, February 22–27, 1779, no. 78 (62 x 78.5 cm.) and in the [d'Espagnac and Tricot] sale, May 22, 1793, no. 122 (59 x 78 cm.) has yet to be discovered; perhaps it was the one, "à un anonyme," exhibited at the Salon de la Cor-respondance in 1783, no. 155 (not no. 1555, as indicated in the catalogue).

The sketch in the Quimper museum (figure 3; 873.1.669) was in a sale on November 25–December 15, 1927, no. 120, ill., and was sold again in Marseilles November 28, 1986, and in Bourg-en-Bresse April 12, 1987, no. 13, ill., but cannot be attributed to Fragonard (we have no information about the *Sacrifice* that was sold in Paris June 21–22, 1920, no. 69).

For the *Sacrifice to the Minotaur,* see cat. no. 107.

Drawings
For a related drawing, see cat. no. 105. A drawing in the Louvre (figure 4) and an oil

Figure 1. Fragonard. *Coresus and Callirhoë.*
Museo de la Real Academia de Bellas Artes de San Fernando, Madrid

Figure 2. Attributed to Fragonard. *Coresus and Callirhoë.*
Private collection, New York

Figure 3. French school, 18th century. *Coresus and Callirhoë.*
Musée des Beaux-Arts, Quimper

Figure 4. Attributed to Fragonard. *Head of an Old Man*. Musée du Louvre, Paris, Cabinet des Dessins

Figure 5. Attributed to Fragonard. *Head of an Old Man*. Private collection, Paris

Figure 6. Jacques-Claude Danzel. *Coresus and Callirhoë*. Bibliothèque Nationale, Paris, Cabinet des Estampes

sketch on paper (figure 5) may have been studies for this work.

Saint-Aubin drew this painting twice: in the famous watercolor (figure 7) in the Louvre that depicts the Salon of 1765, and on page 34 of an album of his drawings, also in the Louvre (see figure 8; on this album, see the two studies by Dacier, 1944; the drawing by Saint-Aubin was previously unpublished).

Engravings

In 1773, an engraving of this painting was made by Jacques-Claude Danzel (1737–1809), "très connu par sa belle Estampe de Callirhoé d'après Fragonard" (figure 6; Roux, VI, 1949, p. 13, no. 11); Joullain (1786, p. 42) added: "il faut l'avoir avant les rouleaux." Saint-Non owned an example of this engraving (G. Wildenstein, 1959, p. 241, no. 232), as did Berthélemy (Volle, 1979, pp. 24, 142).

Charles-Pierre-Joseph Normand made another engraving of it for the second edition of Landon (1832, I, pl. 43, pp. 91–94; the text, "emprunté à Taillasson," is one of our most valuable sources of information on Fragonard).

Figure 7. Gabriel de Saint-Aubin. *The Salon of 1765* (detail). Musée du Louvre, Paris, Cabinet des Dessins

Figure 8. Gabriel de Saint-Aubin. Page from an album of drawings. Musée du Louvre, Paris, Cabinet des Dessins

The *Coresus and Callirhoë* is far from being Fragonard's most popular work, but it is certainly the one that has received the most comment. There are two reasons for this: it was acclaimed as an event when it was exhibited at the Salon of 1765, as we will see, and for a long time (until the gift of the La Caze collection in 1869), it was the only work by Fragonard of any importance that could be seen at the Louvre. It is true that Louis XVIII acquired a *Landscape* for the Château de Saint-Cloud in 1822 (see cat. no. 96; today in Grasse) that was exhibited in the Galerie d'Apollon from 1837, and that Hippolyte Walferdin and Charles Sauvageot (see cat. no. 218) each gave a painting by the artist to the Louvre, in 1849 and in 1856, respectively; but none of these works could rival the *Coresus and Callirhoë*.

On March 30, 1765, Fragonard's acceptance by the Academy was greeted with "applause." The entry for that day in Wille's *Journal* (1857, I, pp. 284–85) tells us that the artist "presented a very large and beautiful history paint-

ing, a number of well-executed and well-colored landscapes, and also some drawings in various manners, which had much merit." Marigny, the *Surintendant des bâtiments*, "had seen" the *Coresus and Callirhoë* before. On April 1, Cochin, the powerful secretary of the Academy (Furcy-Raynaud, 1905, pp. 10–11), suggested that the work be acquired for the royal collections in order to have a tapestry woven after it at the Gobelins. He also wanted to commission a pendant from Fragonard, and to offer the artist the studio in the Louvre that had been left vacant by the death of Deshays. Cochin had considered assigning it to Brenet or Lépicié, but "Fragonard appears to be so much more brilliant a candidate for a career in the Arts than they, that seniority is beside the point." By April 3, Marigny writes that he "adopt[s] all the more willingly everything that you [Cochin] suggest for M. Fragonard ... you only confirm the arrangements that I myself favored for him." On April 16, he announced to Natoire, the director of the Académie de

France in Rome, not without some pride, that "Fragonard has just been unanimously received [in fact, accredited] at the Academy with an acclaim that has rarely been seen" (*Corr. des Dir.,* XII, p. 77). Natoire, his former master, replied, "It is flattering for him and for me" (ibid., p. 80).

On August 25 of that same year, the *Coresus and Callirhoë* was presented at the Salon: as we can see in Saint-Aubin's watercolor (figure 7), it was hung in a good place, next to the stairway, although "the top of the painting was not well lit" (*Journal encyclopédique,* 1765, p. 84). The critics of the Salon were very generous with their praise (see the excellent study by Seznec and Adhémar, 1960; also Bukdahl, 1980–82; Sahut, 1984–85): "M. Fragonard ... appears in this Exhibition with an uncommon brilliance" (Fréron, *L'Année littéraire,* 1765, p. 155, adding on p. 157 that he was a "Painter of harmony"). "This painting ... catches everyone's eye" (*L'Avant Coureur,* p. 556). "This piece does much honor to its author" (Mathon de la Cour, 1765, p. 21). "With a little more boldness in his brushwork, this young Artist will be able to aspire to the glory of the greatest masters" (*Journal encyclopédique*). "This painter deserves great praise" (Le P[aon], 1765, p. 31).

Diderot's long, almost cinematographic analysis (Fried, 1980) contrasts with these platitudes. "Imagining, like Plato, a shadow play viewed by spectators whose backs are turned to the light source, Diderot begins by describing to Grimm a sequence of four compositions that culminates in a fifth, the final outcome, the moment chosen by the painter" (Volle, in Paris exhibition catalogue, 1984–85). Diderot concluded that "Fragonard [has made] a beautiful picture. It has all of the magic, all of the intelligence, the whole picturesque works. The visionary aspect is sublime in this artist...."

This work was purchased for 2,400 *livres,* but the last payment was not made until January 1, 1773. This delay must doubtless have been a factor in Fragonard's subsequent lack of interest in official commissions. Although the picture generally received high praise, some reservations were expressed: on the day that it was presented to the Academicians, Mariette, who showed less enthusiasm than his colleagues, found it "pleasantly composed, but laboriously executed." Certain critics at the Salon, while admiring its chiaroscuro (which Diderot discussed again in 1766 in his *Essais sur la peinture,* 1968 ed., pp. 681–82), did not like its overly yellow color. More specifically, the figure of Coresus was criticized for not being adequately "characterized, either as a man, or as a high priest; besides, there is too much monotony [in] the poses..."(Bachaumont, 1784, II, p. 227).

The public's admiration took on a particular significance in the context of this Salon. Deshays, the most promising painter of the next generation, had died in 1765, the same year as Carle Vanloo, First Painter to the King and "first painter of Europe." Their places had to be filled at all costs.

Turning, at last, to the painting itself, one notes that the subject is obscure. To quote Armand Dayot's summary (unpaginated, undated [1907]): "A plague, sent by the gods, was decimating the Athenian population. A propitiatory victim had to be found, and the lot fell to a young girl, Callirhoë. Coresus, the high priest of Dionysus, had to perform the sacrifice, but he was in love with Callirhoë, and, instead of immolating her, he took his own life." This dramatic legend, recorded by Pausanias, inspired the libretto

Figure 9. Charles-Joseph Natoire.
Coresus and Callirhoë.
Musée Jules Chéret, Nice

Figure 10. Carle Vanloo.
The Sacrifice of Iphigenia.
The Metropolitan Museum of Art, New York

Figure 11. Gabriel-François Doyen. *La Mort de Virginie.*
Galleria Nazionale, Parma

Figure 12. Joseph-Théodore Richomme.
Coresus and Callirhoë. École Nationale
Supérieure des Beaux-Arts, Paris

by Roy for an opera by André-Cardinal Destouches that was performed several times in the eighteenth century. Few artists had been tempted by the subject before Fragonard: the Louvre owns one such drawing attributed to Luca Giordano (Pigler, 1931), and there is a drawing by Natoire in the Musée Jules Chéret, in Nice (see figure 9; Vilain, 1975, 1977). A drawing by Boucher, the *Death of Callirhoë,* appeared in the Randon de Boisset sale (1777) and in the Sireul sale (1781; Ananoff, 1966, no. 749). The main influence, however, was Carle Vanloo's *Sacrifice of Iphigenia*—doubtless more so the large drawing in The Metropolitan Museum of Art (figure 10) than the picture in Potsdam completed in 1757, when Fragonard was already in Italy. It would not be surprising if, after the young artist returned from Italy, Carle Vanloo suggested that he paint this subject, in order to make a name for himself in Paris. It will be remembered that Gabriel-François Doyen created a sensation at the Salon of 1759 with his large composition *La Mort de Virginie,* which Fragonard could have studied in Paris in August 1761 (figure 11). Another influence was theater, as Beth S. Wright (1986) aptly pointed out.

Fragonard's painting was never forgotten, and it inspired many artists (limiting ourselves to the subject of Coresus and Callirhoë, we cite only the above-mentioned sketch in Quimper, and the one by Joseph-Théodore Richomme, which dates from 1840; see figure 12, and also Grunchec, 1986, p. 90, no. 43, colorpl.). The critics of the Salon of 1767 regretted that Fragonard did not present anything comparable. In 1785, the author of the *Discours sur l'état actuel de la peinture* reproached Fragonard with having "not

taken a loftier flight." At the beginning of the nineteenth century, while there was a general condemnation of the eighteenth century and of Fragonard, the *Coresus* escaped this disaffection. The work "suffices to rank its author among the leading painters of his century" (Gault de Saint-Germain, 1808, p. 232). Landon wrote regretfully in 1808: "But he abandons his noble compositions and serious studies to devote himself to inferior subjects . . ." (p. 8). However, with the rediscovery of Fragonard's art, this painting became an embarrassment: his illustrious critics expressed their admiration, but their reservations show through: "a praiseworthy but unique effort" (Portalis, 1885, p. 482), "Rembrandt chez Ruggieri" (G. p. 261). Its theatrical and melodramatic qualities were no longer appreciated. Sam Francis summed up the opinion in our own time: "ludicrous, insensitive. No emotion" (Schneider, 1971, p. 181). That the "divine" Fragonard was able to paint a history painting, a great "construction" full of highly artificial pathos, would be evidence of the injuriousness and perversity of "official" taste in his day. The work remained unique in Fragonard's oeuvre, distinguished from other contemporary history paintings. Locquin's splendid analysis (1921) tells us how: "the subject . . . is not only new, but it is a great drama of love . . . the sacrificer, instead of immolating the one that he loves, designated by the oracle, plunges the knife into his own breast. The composition is designed so as to produce the strongest impression. Each detail has its function. The tragic group is gathered between two columns. A great poetic strain pervades the scene and attenuates its horror." The terror "becomes sublime." Less than ten years after the *Coresus and Callirhoë,* Fragonard again tried to paint subjects involving the passions of the heart, but he preferred allegory to history.

This description by Diderot provides an apt conclusion: "Through the darkness, I saw an infernal demon hovering, I saw it: its haggard eyes bulging out of their sockets; in one hand he held a dagger, in another he wielded a fiery torch; he was crying out. It was Despair, and Love, fearsome Love, was being carried on its back.

"Fragonard is back from Rome: the *Coresus and Callirhoë* is his reception [in fact, accreditation] piece: he presented it a few months ago to the Academy, which received him with acclaim. It is, indeed, a beautiful thing, and I do not think that there is another painter in Europe capable of conceiving anything better."

We will leave the last word to Fréron (*L'Année littéraire,* 1765, p. 155): "M. Fragonard has above all the advantage of not appearing to be the imitator of any great painter."

105 Coresus and Callirhoë

Oil on canvas, 129 x 188 cm.

Musée des Beaux-Arts, Angers

Provenance
Marquis de Lassay (?): sold ("dont la majeure partie provient du célèbre Cabinet de M. le Marquis de Lassay"), May 22, 1775, no. 102; Mercier: sold, October 1, 1778, no. 15: "Le Sacrifice de Callirhoé, grande et superbe composition et première pensée du tableau du roi qui fait tant honneur à ce célèbre artiste...."; Pierre-Louis Éveillard, Marquis de Livois (1736–1790), Angers (catalogue of the collection issued posthumously by Pierre Sen-

tout, 1791, no. 243); believed to have been among the property of the heirs of the Livois estate—who were either away or had emigrated—which was seized during the Revolution for the Angers museum.

Exhibitions
Paris, 1921, no. 23, ill.
Geneva, 1949, no. 75
Besançon, 1956, no. 18
Vienna, 1966, no. 27

Bibliography
G. p. 324
Jouin, 1885, p. 21
P. pp. 49, 274
N. p. 154
Locquin, 1912, p. 237, n. 1
Recouvreur, 1932, pp. 247–57
W. 221, fig. 110
Thuillier, 1967, p. 26, colorpl.
W. and M. 233 (reproduced by mistake as pl. XVII, no. 235)

Related works
See the previous and the following entries.

The differences between the sketch in the Museo de la Real Academia de Bellas Artes de San Fernando and the *Coresus and Callirhoë* in the Louvre are very slight, unlike the variations between the large sketch in Angers and the two finished paintings. The unfortunate Callirhoë, wrists bound with a garland of roses, lowers her eyes. Coresus is not yet the androgynous adolescent that Bachaumont criticized in the

painting, but the traditional high priest with beard and moustache, and Callirhoë is not swooning against the sacrificial tripod. True, the same moment is depicted, but the Angers sketch lacks the clarity of the Louvre's finished work. The shaft of sunlight that, like a beam from a projector, falls on the heroes of the drama; the terror-stricken expressions of those officiating and of those witnessing the scene; the allegorical figures of Despair (borrowed from the figure of Envy in the *Psyche* in London; see cat. no. 9) and of Love—none of these wonderful inventions is present as yet.

The Angers oil sketch has suffered: Fragonard probably reworked the composition many times. It is only distantly related to the Louvre picture, a first conception that is not without some awkwardness. The two young women in the foreground, at the left, and the child playing, recall the "Bambocciante" works that Fragonard painted in Rome between 1758 and 1760, while the style of the excessively repeated folds of the drapery is close to that of the studies he made at the École royale des élèves protégés and at the Académie de France, in Rome (cat. nos. 11, 12).

To quote Mariette (1853–54 ed., II, p. 263): "The timidity that dominates in this artist's character holds him back, and, never satisfied with his productions, he keeps erasing and correcting himself...."

106 Coresus and Callirhoë

Brown and bister wash on paper, over an underdrawing in black chalk, 34.7 x 46.5 cm.

The Pierpont Morgan Library, New York

Exhibitions
Baltimore, 1959, no. 47, fig. p. 47
New York, 1977, no. 87, fig. 89
Washington, D.C., 1978, no. 18, ill. (with a complete list of exhibitions)

Bibliography
G. p. 324
P. p. 297
N. p. 51, ill. between pp. 50 and 51
R. pp. 148, 192
A. 1714, fig. 433
Massengale, 1979, p. 271

Related works
For paintings, see the two previous entries. See also cat. no. 107.

A. 1716 (Musée Borély, Marseilles) is not by Fragonard (see also A. 1715).

At the Le Breton collection sale (December 6–8, 1921, no. 62, ill.), there was a drawing entitled *Coresus et Callirhoë* (A. 667) that, in fact, showed a wedding scene: a young man leading a young girl before a priest.

The drawing in the Turpin de Crissé collection in Angers is not the work of Fragonard (Recouvreur, 1932, p. 257, ill.; Musée Turpin de Crissé, catalogue, 1933, p. 56, no. 19, ill.), nor is the one that was sold on May 3, 1913, no. 84c, ill.

Provenance
Varanchan de Saint-Geniès: sold, December 29–31, 1777, no. 58: "s'il y a plusieurs répétitions de cette belle composition qui a été gravée, on peut assurer que celle-ci est la mieux rendue; hauteur 13 pouces; largeur 17 pouces [35.1 x 47.4 cm.]"; [Morel]: sold, April 19, 1786, no. 375: "le dessin réunit l'avantage d'être le véritable parmi ceux que l'on connaît. Hauteur 16 pouces et demi, largeur 20 pouces et demi [44.5 x 55.1 cm.]" (?); Maherault: sold, May 27–29, 1880, no. 58: "dessin pour le tableau qui est au Musée du Louvre. Estompe et crayon noir [33 x 42 cm.]" (?); C. Fairfax Murray; J. Pierpont Morgan, 1910.

Sometimes associated, without any proof, with a drawing in a sale [Huser], December 10 [13], 1765, no. 269: "un Grand-Prêtre à l'Autel, belle composition de plus de douze Figures dessiné avec esprit à la plume et au bistre par Fragonard, jeune Artiste nouvellement agréé sur un Tableau exposé au dernier Salon qui a eu tout le suffrage des connoisseurs."

We agree with Eunice Williams, who does not believe that this drawing from the Pierpont Morgan Library was a preparatory study for the *Coresus and Callirhoë,* but, rather, a finished autograph replica—a "record," after the painting. Massengale goes even further, dating this drawing to about 1769 for stylistic reasons. One thing is certain: there are no notable differences between this drawing and the painting. It is equally certain—and not surprising—that, in the eighteenth century, there were other studies by Fragonard for (or after) the *Coresus and Callirhoë:* "several repetitions" are mentioned in the sales catalogues (see *Related works*).

Fragonard did not always—perhaps it was even the exception—make preparatory drawings for his paintings: he preferred to do oil studies of the composition, the grouping of the figures, and the colors. This drawing, like the oil sketch in Angers (cat. no. 105), is an example of his very personal working methods.

The melodramatic drawing in the Pierpont Morgan Library is a unique document of Fragonard's technical ability and of his taste for theatrical scenes.

107   The Sacrifice to the Minotaur

Watercolor, and bister and gray wash on paper, over an underdrawing in black chalk, 33.6 x 44.2 cm.

Private collection

Provenance
Godefroy: sold, November 15 (instead of April 25), 1785, no. 98: "un sujet d'histoire représentant une jeune fille ôtant d'un vase des billets comme pour savoir son sort; dessin lavé de bistre" (?; A. 1645); Bruun-Neergaard: sold, August 30, 1814, no. 127: "jeunes hommes et jeunes Filles tirant au sort pour être livrés au minotaure. Morceau colorié et d'un bel effet. Haut. 10 p.; larg. 16 p. [27 x 43.2 cm.]" (?); [Guyard, "marchand de tableaux à Tours"]: sold, November 26–28, 1824: "les Athéniennes tirant au sort" (?); Jacques Doucet: sold, Paris, June 5, 1912, no. 16, ill. (for 48,500 francs); E. M. Hodgkins: sold, Paris, April 30, 1914, no. 25, ill.; Seymour de Ricci; Mortimer Schiff, New York; private collection.

Exhibitions
Washington, D.C., 1978, no. 19, ill.

Bibliography
G. p. 325
R. p. 192
A. 418, fig. 150 (see also A. 416, 417,
    figs. 149, 1645)
Rosenberg and van de Sandt, 1983, p. 81,
    fig. 23

Related works
A. catalogues four drawings of this subject
(A. 416–418, 1645). Apart from the work
included here, he illustrates only one other,
which we have never seen.

We know of two oil studies of this subject.
One, which is very close to the present drawing, was in the Walferdin and the Doucet
collections (figure 1; W. 217, pl. 26), and is
today in a private collection in Paris; the
other, which we have not been able to locate,
was previously in the collection of Mme
Jacques Doucet (figure 2; W. 218, fig. 109),
and is very different in composition (it has
even been interpreted as a *Sacrifice of Iphigenia*). The two works are of similar dimensions: it is difficult to say if they (and which)
can be identified with the paintings in the
Varanchan sale, December 29–31, 1777, no.
15, and in an anonymous sale, July 8, 1777,
no. 31 ("Le Sacrifice d'Iphigénie"; "Un
Sacrifice").

Figure 1. Fragonard.
The Sacrifice to the Minotaur.
Private collection, Paris

Figure 2. Fragonard.
The Sacrifice of Iphigenia (?).
Whereabouts unknown

Figure 3. François-Guillaume Ménageot.
Polyxena's Farewell to Hecuba.
Musée des Beaux-Arts, Chartres

The present drawing and the superb oil sketch that
belonged to Jacques Doucet are very close. Eunice Williams
(1978) is probably right in considering the drawing not as a
finished study for the painting, but, rather, as a faithful and
masterful copy of it. There is no reason not to interpret the
scene as a Sacrifice to the Minotaur, in spite of the liberties
taken with the ancient legend (not just young women, but
young men, as well, were sacrificed). Fragonard made a
habit of such inexactitudes, and the very fact of choosing to
paint and to draw this subject was original in itself.

The principal source of the theme is Plutarch. To avenge
the death of his son, King Minos of Crete captured Athens,
and he granted peace to the city on the condition that each
year a certain number of young men and young women
would be sacrificed to the Minotaur. The scene depicted here
shows the designated victims drawing lots.

Why did Fragonard choose to paint this subject? We have
already discussed his triumph with the *Coresus and Callirhoë*
(cat. no. 104), noting that Cochin advised Marigny to
acquire the picture for the king in order to have a tapestry
woven after it. On April 3, 1765, Marigny commissioned a
pendant from Fragonard (it was mentioned again in the
Correspondance on August 5 and 8, after which there is no
further allusion to it). No eighteenth-century document
affirms with any certainty that Fragonard chose the *Sacrifice
to the Minotaur* as his subject. Yet, the compositions of the
oil sketches and of the drawing, as well as a comparison with
the different versions of the *Coresus and Callirhoë* included
here, argue convincingly in favor of this possibility.

Although we do not know why Fragonard never painted
the finished work, one may suppose that the slowness with
which he was paid for the *Coresus* surely did not encourage
him to complete the pendant. In any event, by 1777, he had
given up the project: at this date, d'Angiviller, Marigny's
successor, wrote to Pierre, the new First Painter, about François-Guillaume Ménageot's *Polyxena's Farewell to Hecuba*
(figure 3), today in Chartres: "This very beautiful painting,
it seems to me, would make an appropriate pendant to the
one by M. Fragonard and would be useful for the Royal
Manufactory of the Gobelins, which has a great need for new
subjects and paintings" (Furcy-Raynaud, 1905, XXI, p.
162; Willk-Brocard, 1978, p. 62).

The present drawing is exceptionally fresh and skillfully
executed: the light falls on the unfortunate victim of the
lottery, who drops the fateful piece of paper and falls into a
swoon. The particularly effective detail of the grieving
mother appears in the foreground. As in the *Coresus*, attention is focused on the moment that decides the young girl's
fate. Fragonard wanted to describe the emotions at the peak
of the tension in the drama.

108 The Parents' Absence Turned to Account (also called The Farmer's Family)

Oil on canvas, 50 x 60.5 cm.

The Hermitage, Leningrad

Provenance
"L'un des morceaux d'agrément à l'Académie" (noted Le Brun, in the Lambert and Porail sales catalogue of 1787); Jacques-Onésyme Bergeret de Grancourt (1715–1785), 1770, according to the inscription on Beauvarlet's engraving; Lambert and [Porail]: sold, March 27, 1787, no. 222 (for 1,830 *livres*); Dr. Cochu: sold, February 21, 1799, no. 17 (for 395 *livres*); Queen Hortense de Beauharnais (1783–1837), daughter of Josephine, wife of Louis, King of Holland, Duchesse de Saint-Leu, and mother of Napoleon III; acquired by Nicholas I of Russia, 1829; The Hermitage.

Exhibitions
(For a complete list, see the Hermitage catalogue, 1986)
Salon, 1765, *hors concours*
Tokyo, 1980, no. 40, ill.
Paris, 1984, no. 56, ill. (in the catalogue, but not exhibited)

Bibliography
(For a complete list of the reviews of the Salon of 1765, see Volle, in Paris exhibition catalogue, 1984–85, p. 214)
Landon, 1808, p. 9
Blanc, 1862, p. 7
G. p. 331
P. pp. 54, 115, 122, 269, 279
N. pp. 54, 82, 132, ill. between pp. 132 and 133

Réau, 1928, no. 101
R. p. 152
Sterling, 1957, p. 218
Seznec and Adhémar, 1960, II, p. 43, pl. 72
W. 226, pl. 30, p. 25 (French edition)
W. and M. 237, ill.
Seznec, 1979, p. 43, fig. 62
Bukdahl, 1980, I, pp. 203, 387
Paris exhibition catalogue, 1984, no. 56, ill.
Hermitage catalogue, 1986, no. 47, ill.
   (with detailed bibliography)

Related works

A study by Fragonard for the young girl defending herself, in the background of the Hermitage painting, is in the museum in Amiens (figure 1; oval format, oak panel, 56 x 46 cm.; W. 227, fig. 113).

An engraving of the painting, in reverse, was made by Jacques-Firmin Beauvarlet in 1770, and entitled *The Farmer's Family* (Roux, 1933, II, p. 24, no. 74; figure 2 shows the engraving in the state before the inscription was added). Engravings were also made by Clément-Pierre Marillier, Antoine-Louis Romanet (P. p. 326, nos. 83, 82), and Michal Podolinski, and there is a lithograph after the picture by Hippolyte Robillard.

Figure 1. Fragonard. *La Résistance.* Musée de Picardie, Amiens

Figure 2. Jacques-Firmin Beauvarlet, after Fragonard. *The Farmer's Family.* Bibliothèque Nationale, Paris, Cabinet des Estampes

Le Brun, a friend of Fragonard who expertized the 1787 sale, confirms that this painting, entitled by Diderot "L'Absence des pères et mères mise à profit," was among the paintings submitted by Fragonard in March 1765 for accreditation by the Academy. We will recall that he was admitted "as with a single voice" (see cat. no. 104). The picture was not included in the catalogue of the Salon; Diderot tells us that "it was exhibited . . . only later," but not why.

The critics of the Salon greeted this painting "in the rustic genre" with mixed reviews; not surprisingly, there was not the same unanimity accorded the *Coresus.* They appreciated its "very realistic color," the only "progress" that the artist had yet to make, but Mathon de la Cour criticized the "figures . . . of an olive-green color. The artist has sought for effect; but it would have been better had he not sacrificed the truth." Diderot's remarks were, of course, the most interesting: "It is a nice little painting. . . . The subject has been cleverly imagined."

Three young children in a peasant interior play with two farm dogs. The youngest child tries to give one of them an apple. In the background, we "can barely make out," Diderot writes—and the thick yellow varnish does not help much—"the most interesting part of the picture, the little boy who is taking advantage of the little girl," which explains the title of the work.

This picture is similar in dimensions to *The Stolen Kiss* (cat. no. 18), and is directly descended from it, but we do not think that it was painted before 1761 in Italy. When Diderot mentions Greuze and Loutherbourg to prove that their representations of dogs, unlike Fragonard's, "are the real ones," he recognizes Fragonard's debt to these two artists, the others who triumphed at the Salon of 1765. In this painting, Fragonard not only tried to imitate the subject matter of Greuze, in particular, but also his way of combining tender and picturesque themes. The only detail that betrays Fragonard is that of the boy trying to kiss the young girl, while her little brothers are not watching. Throughout his career, Fragonard liked to paint young people at the age when their senses are awakening. Henceforth, he would place the scene in the full light of day.

IV

Fragonard, between Vice and Virtue (1766–70)

When Fragonard triumphed at the Salon in 1765, his future seemed secure. Yet, in just a few years, this artist, who had such a promising official career ahead of him, "was content to distinguish himself... in the boudoirs and the dressing rooms" (Bachaumont, 1769). What were the reasons for this sudden change of course?

Fragonard's private life during this period remains a mystery. We know that he lived at the Louvre. A critic, once again, mentioned his modesty (1767). Another, Bachaumont (1769), noted his "thirst for profit"—a reproach that would be leveled at the artist by others, as well. As for his love life, many writers and critics since 1850 have credited him with seducing all of the dancing girls of his day, and all of the mistresses of the king, but there is not a single contemporary account to support this. On September 6, 1767, Bachaumont, however, well informed and with a wicked tongue, wrote: "Why has M. Fragonard, for whom we had such great expectations after the last Salon, whose talents were publicly proclaimed, which was very flattering to his self-esteem, why has he stopped all of a sudden? Has he been softened by the delights of Capua?" A few years earlier, these same "delights" had stifled the creativity of Gabriel-François Doyen, who became passionately enamored of a famous actress, Mlle Hus. Would Fragonard, Bachaumont asks, make a dazzling comeback—as Doyen had with his *Miracle des ardents* (figure 1), the painting most admired at the Salon of 1767?

During this same period, Fragonard took on several students: Jean-François Martin from Cahors in 1767, and, the following year, a sixteen-year-old Parisian, Louis-André Dalbeau. A young woman from Grasse appealed to him for some advice. Marie-Anne Gérard, born in 1745, "the eldest of twelve children of a family of distillers [in fact, perfumers] from Grasse"—according to the Goncourts, who obtained their information from Fragonard's grandson Théophile—had been sent to Paris to earn a living. She had found work with a colleague of her father's named Isnard, but seemed to be more inclined toward miniatures, and painted decorated fans. This is how she met Fragonard. Their marriage contract (now lost) was signed on September 21, 1768, hardly a year after Bachaumont's insinuations. The banns were posted on May 21, 1769, at the church of Saint-Germain-l'Auxerrois, near the Louvre, and the wedding was celebrated on September 2, 1769, oddly enough at Saint-Lambert, in the Vaugirard quarter, far from the artist's parish. It may be that Marie-Anne, who was six-months pregnant, did not want to be seen thus near the Louvre where she was to live, and where so many of Jean-Honoré's friends and colleagues already resided. In any case, on the 16th (not the 9th) of December, their daughter Henriette-Rosalie was born, and the following day she was baptized at the nearby church of Saint-Eustache.

Two interesting points to note: The (unpublished) birth certificate tells us that, at his daughter's baptism, the "father was declared absent." What reasons were important enough to account for this strange absence? In 1806, at the death of her husband, Marie-Anne declared—in the deed of October 10 (see figure 2) that divided the property between herself and

Figure 1. Gabriel-François Doyen.
Le Miracle des ardents. Saint-Roch, Paris

223

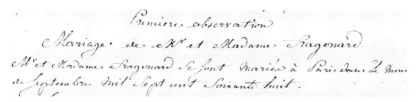

Figure 2. Deed dividing Fragonard's property between his widow and his son, Alexandre-Évariste. Minutier central, Paris

her son—that she married Jean-Honoré in 1768. It would seem that Mme Fragonard did not want to draw attention to her precipitous wedding.

We will have other occasions to encounter Mme Fragonard, who, judging from the two portraits of her included here (cat. nos. 291, 292), was not especially beautiful. Yet, nothing suggests that the marriage was not compatible. According to the Goncourts (whose information, as usual, came from Théophile), Fragonard spoke of her as being his "treasurer." A more severe description of her from the first years of the *Empire* appears in a biography that seems to have been written by Camille Vernet, the older sister of Horace Vernet and the future wife of Hippolyte Lecomte, who was born in 1788 (P. p. 242; H. Delaroche-Vernet, 1923, p. 224): "Mme Fragonard was rather tall, heavyset, and quite common. And what taste. She spoiled the few charms that had survived her youth by the most extravagant incongruities in her attire.... From Grasse she had kept ... a terribly strong accent...."

By "virtue," we mean the official commissions that began to increase, after 1765: first, there was the one from Cochin and Marigny for a pendant to the *Coresus and Callirhoë*; followed by the "reception piece" (*morceau de réception*); one of the ceilings in the Galerie d'Apollon at the Louvre; two overdoors for the Salon des Jeux at the Château de Bellevue— "*Day*, represented by Apollo in his chariot, preceded by Dawn, who is scattering flowers, and followed by the Hours," and "*Night*, represented by Diana in her chariot, drawn by does, preceded by Dusk spreading its star-studded veil, and followed by Dreams"; and lastly, four paintings, in collaboration with the young Jean-Baptiste Huet, for the king's dining room at Versailles.

None of these projects was completed. One reason is that the State was slow to provide payment, and its coffers were often empty; the last installment for the *Coresus* was not paid until January 1, 1773. Fragonard liked money, and earned a lot of it. The State may have brought him prestige, but did not pay him enough to cover his everyday expenses. There was also the commission from Louveciennes: on more than one occasion, as we will see, Fragonard used the decorations for Mme du Barry as an excuse for his delays in finishing other work. Then there was the death of Louis XV in 1774, and Marigny's replacement by d'Angiviller, who released Fragonard from his obligations. However, these explanations do not seem adequate to us. Were these official commissions, these overdoors, ceilings, and decorative programs, suited to Fragonard's genius? Indeed, he gave them a try—as attested by the references in various sales catalogues, such as that of July 8, 1793, no. 17, which mentions an "allegorical subject of Night spreading its veil," the *Triumph of Venus* in Besançon (figure 3). Perhaps he always stopped along the way, and these projects never came to fruition, either because he quickly realized that he was not the man for the job, or that his artistic education was insufficient, or else, that his impatient temperament, which favored small-format rapidly executed works, was not suited to longer endeavors that required reflection and deliberation. In support of this interpretation we would mention two examples *a contrario*: at the Salon of 1767 (from which he had two large paintings removed, for

Figure 3. Fragonard. *The Triumph of Venus*. Musée des Beaux-Arts, Besançon

Figure 4. Louis-Jean-Jacques Durameau. *Summer (Cérès et Ses Compagnes implorant le soleil).* Musée du Louvre, Paris, Galerie d'Apollon

reasons of "overscrupulous delicacy"), Fragonard exhibited his *"Groupes d'enfants dans le ciel"* (cat. no. 109), which Diderot called an "omelette of children," comparing it to the work of Taraval, also a traveling companion of Saint-Non. Other critics were no less severe than Diderot. Temporarily misunderstood, Fragonard learned his lesson from this failed effort: he would not be a history painter. Another commission, previously unpublished and brought to our attention by Monique Mosser (see also the *De Wailly* exhibition catalogue, Paris, 1979, p. 44), was equally unsuccessful: on April 4, 1767, the architect de Wailly wrote that "next Monday, Fragonard will begin to paint" a ceiling for the dining room of the Chancellerie d'Orléans, in the rue des Bons-Enfants, commissioned by Marc-René, Marquis de Voyer (1722–1782), and the son of the famous Comte d'Argenson, *Chancelier d'Orléans* and *Secrétaire d'État à la Guerre.* Fragonard was not the only artist to work in this residence. Louis-Jean-Jacques Durameau was also asked to decorate a ceiling (figures 5, 6), and, like Fragonard, had been commissioned to paint as his "reception piece" a ceiling in the Galerie d'Apollon; he finished it in 1774 (see figure 4), whereas Fragonard was released, in 1776, from completing his part. On June 5, 1769, "the ceilings were done": "You will perhaps not be as happy with the ceiling by Fragonard as with Durameau's, which has received unanimous praise." Unfortunately, the Hôtel d'Argenson was destroyed in 1916 to make room for the Banque de France. The painted decorations were put in storage in Asnières: the *Lever de l'Aurore* has been preserved, but Fragonard's work has not been found. We would guess that de Wailly's judgment was not wrong.

As for the "vice," we would not apply this term to such pictures as the *Head of an Old Man* (see p. 202, figure 1), exhibited at the Salon of 1767, which met with little success. Along with other works of this type, it attested to Fragonard's admiration for Rembrandt, whom he regarded as an exemplar. Nor would it apply to the request that Fragonard addressed to Marigny on October 20, 1767, for permission to "make studies in the *Gallerie* du Luxembourg." The authority of the *surintendant* was necessary in order for the "key" to be "entrusted" to him. Yet Fragonard was not alone in asking for this favor: Boucher's son-in-law, Baudouin, who specialized in elegant yet risqué gouaches, accompanied him.

Fragonard would follow another course...

The commission for *The Swing* (figures 7, 8), one of the most widely reproduced eighteenth-century paintings, illustrates Fragonard's new di-

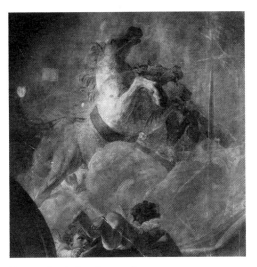

Figure 5. Louis-Jean-Jacques Durameau. *Le Lever de l'Aurore* (detail). Banque de France

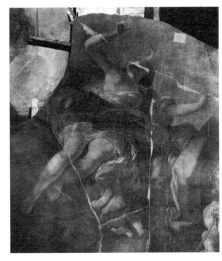

Figure 6. Louis-Jean-Jacques Durameau. *Le Lever de l'Aurore* (detail). Banque de France

225

Figure 7. Fragonard. *The Swing*. Wallace Collection, London

Figure 8. Nicolas Delaunay. *The Swing*.
Bibliothèque Nationale, Paris, Cabinet des Estampes

rection. The circumstances are known from Collé's account in his *Mémoires* (Paris, 1868, III, pp. 165 ff.): "I returned to Paris on the first of this month [October]. The following day, I met the painter Doyen, who had just won a prize at the Salon in August for a painting in the *grand genre* [see figure 1].... Would you believe it—this painter told me—just a few days after the exhibition of my picture at the Salon, someone from the Court summoned me to commission a work in the genre that I am about to describe? ... He asked me to paint madame (pointing out to me his mistress) on a swing being pushed by a bishop. I was to place him in such a way that he could see the legs of this beautiful child, and even more...." Doyen was "petrified"! "Since I was in no way inclined to paint such a subject, so far removed from the genre in which I work, I referred this personage to M. *Fagonat*, who accepted, and who is presently executing this singular work."

We do not know the names of the "bishop" or of the "mistress" in question, but the patron was the Baron de Saint-Julien, the official *Receveur du clergé* in France. He liked Fragonard, and had, in his collection, several important paintings by him (see cat. nos. 5, 6), and by Chardin (about whom he wrote). What counts most of all, however, is that we know the painting, itself—a green-and-blue triumph of forest, accented with the pink of a dress and a slipper. How unlike the bawdy boudoirs of Baudouin! *The Swing*, a unique work, combines a pantheistic vision of nature with the love of life of the period.

Such are the facts: Was the reference to the "delights of Capua" in 1767 an allusion to Fragonard's coming betrothal? Was he absent at the baptism of his daughter, Henriette-Rosalie, in 1769 because he was in Holland at the time?

In 1765, the *Coresus*; in 1767, *The Swing*; in 1769, the "figures de fantaisie": the ground that he covered and his ambition were immense. When Boucher died on May 30, 1770, would Fragonard be able to take his place, and would he want to?

1766

May 24
Fragonard receives a second payment—of 600 *livres*—for the *Coresus*; the order was issued on the 13th (recorded, May 21, *Registres du Louvre, Paiements*, 1762–85, Bibliothèque du Louvre, Réserve, 8, fol. 61).

May 31
Fragonard and Durameau "seront chargés, pour leur réception [to the Academy] de peindre chacun un des plafonds qui restent à faire pour achever la décoration de la Galerie d'Apollon qui a été accordée à l'Académie" (*Procès-Verbaux...*, VII, p. 331).

July 15
Cochin submits to Marigny a project for the commissioning of paintings for the Château de Bellevue: "dans le salon des Jeux, il y a deux dessus de porte, que j'ay l'honneur de vous proposer de donner à M. Fragonard. Les sujets proposés du *Jour* et de la *Nuit* avec leurs emblêmes poëtiques, fournissent à son génie pittoresque..." (Furcy-Raynaud, 1904, XX, p. 51; Engerand, 1901, pp. 246–47, n. 1).
We know the decorative program from the list of the *Tableaux pour les appartements du château de Bellevue* (Furcy-Raynaud, 1904, XX, p. 53): "SALON DES JEUX, Deux dessus de porte: M. Fragonard. Il promet d'y travailler tout à l'heure. *Le Jour*, représenté par *Apollon sur son char précédé par l'Aurore qui répand des fleurs et suivy par les Heures. La Nuit*, représentée par *Diane sur son char traîné par des biches, précédée de la Nuit qui étend son voile parsemé d'étoiles et suivie par des Songes.*"
These works do not seem to have been executed (see December 23, 1771, and March 29, 1773).

September 15
Announcement in *L'Avant-coureur* (no. 37, pp. 577–78) of Charpentier's engraving *The Somersault* (figure 1), after Fragonard: "composition piquante et pittoresque."

December 20
In a letter to Marigny, Cochin discusses the project for a contest conducted as a lottery in which: "ni les Boucher, ni les Pierre, ni les Vien, etc... ne seroient tentés de hazarder leur réputation à de pareils essais. Ce ne seroit cependant pas une raison pour rejetter entièrement le projet, puisque les jeunes artistes, les Fragonard, les Durameau, Taraval et autres, en pourroient profiter; mais il se rencontre une autre petite difficulté: quel usage feront de leur tableau ceux qui n'auront pas de prix? C'est de quoy en arrêter beaucoup" (Furcy-Raynaud, 1904, XX, p. 97).
In Rome, Lonsing copies Fragonard's *L'Enjeu perdu* (cat. no. 18, figure 3), which belonged to the Marquis de Breteuil.

Figure 1. Charpentier, after Fragonard. *The Somersault.*
Bibliothèque Nationale, Paris, Cabinet des Estampes

Saint-Non makes two engravings entitled *Couronne d'amours* (cat. no. 109, figures 2, 4), and one after Fragonard's *Gardens of the Villa d'Este* (cat. no. 14).

1767

April 4
The architect de Wailly reports to Marc-René d'Argenson, Marquis de Voyer (1722–1782), on the progress of the work in his Hôtel in the rue des Bons-Enfants (formerly, the Chancellerie d'Orléans; today, the seat of the Banque de France): "... 1° La corniche et les guirlandes de la salle à manger qui restaient à dorer le sont, les fonds des arabesques du plafond ont été essayés de toute manière et nous avons reconnu qu'ils devoient rester comme ils étoient en obscurcissant insensiblement les parties qui entourent le tableau de Fragonard afin de le fair valoir; Mr Fragonard commencera lundy prochain à peindre" (Poitiers, Bibliothèque Universitaire, Archives du Marquis Voyer d'Argenson, presently being catalogued; kindly communicated by Monique Mosser).

June
Jean-François Martin, from Cahors, "protégé par M. Boucher, élève de M. Fragonard," and residing with him in the Cour du Louvre, is admitted to attend courses at the Académie (Bibliothèque de l'École des Beaux-Arts, *Liste de Messieurs les élèves*, ms. 45, fol. 124).

August 23
At Marigny's request, Cochin confirms that Fragonard's painting the *Coresus and Callirhoë*, intended to be executed as a tapestry, was, indeed, made in the service of the king (Gerspach, 1888, p. 120).

August 25
Fragonard exhibits at the Salon: "N° 137. Tableau ovale, représentant des grouppes d'Enfans dans le Ciel. Tiré du Cabinet de M. Bergeret [see cat. no. 109]. N° 138. Une Tête de Vieillard. Tableau de forme ronde [see p. 202]. N° 139. Plusieurs dessins, sous le même N°" (*Livret* of the Salon of 1767).
From Diderot (Seznec and Adhémar, 1963, III, p. 280), we know that among these drawings there was a *Paysage, Un Homme appuyé sur sa bêche*, and an "espèce de brocanteur, assis devant sa table dans un fauteuil à bras."
According to the *Mercure de France* (October 1767, p. 171), Fragonard had considered exhibiting two other pictures: "On nous assure que sa délicatesse trop scrupuleuse lui a fait enlever du *sallon* deux grands tableaux prêts à être mis en place."

October 2
This is the date of the famous story of *The Swing* (figure 7, p. 226). Doyen informed Collé of the commission proposed to him by the Baron de Saint-Julien, *Receveur du clergé de France*: "ce seigneur [the Baron de Saint-Julien] étoit à sa petite maison avec sa maîtresse lorsque je me présentai à lui pour savoir ce qu'il me vouloit. Il m'accabla d'abord de politesses et d'éloges, et finit par m'avouer qu'il se mouroit d'envie d'avoir, de ma façon, le tableau dont il alloit me tracer l'idée.
"'Je désirerois,' continua-t-il, 'que vous peignissiez madame (en me montrant sa maîtresse) sur une escarpolette qu'un évêque mettrait en branle. Vous me placerez de façon, moi, que je sois à portée de voir les jambes de cette belle enfant, et mieux même si vous voulez égayer davantage votre tableau, etc.'—'J'avoue,' me dit M. Doyen, 'que cette proposition, à laquelle je n'aurois jamais dû m'attendre [Doyen had just triumphed at the Salon with his *Miracle des ardents*], vu la nature du tableau d'où il partoit pour me la faire, me confondit et me pétrifia d'abord.' Je me remis pourtant assez pour lui dire presque sur-le-champ: 'Ah! monsieur, il faut ajouter au fond de l'idée de votre tableau, en faisant voler en l'air les pantoufles de madame, et que des amours les retiennent'" (Collé, 1868 ed., III, pp. 165–67).

October 20
Fragonard and Baudouin request permission from Cochin "de pouvoir faire des études dans la *Gallerie* du Luxembourg" where the "Life of Maria de' Medici" cycle by Rubens was exhibited (Paris, Arch. Nat., O¹ 1911).

October 26
Cochin, in support of the request of Fragonard and Baudouin, appeals to Marigny (Furcy-Raynaud, 1904, XX, p. 128).

Figure 2. Attributed to Fragonard, after Rubens. *Head of a Satyr*. Musée du Louvre, Paris, Cabinet des Dessins

November 7
Permission is granted for Fragonard and Baudouin to copy pictures in the Galerie du Luxembourg (Paris, Arch. Nat., o¹ 1911). None of the copies that Fragonard made there has survived. In the Cabinet des Dessins at the Louvre, there is a gouache and watercolor (Inv. 20033; with a handwritten inscription on the back, "4 VIII 1956," as noted by E. Starcky), catalogued as by Jordaens, that Michael Jaffé has attributed to Fragonard (see figure 2); it is a copy, after Rubens, of the satyr's head in the *Félicités de la Régence*.

1768

May
Louis-André Dalbeau, "protégé par M. Boucher élève de M. Fragonard," is admitted to the Académie (Bibliothèque de l'École des Beaux-Arts, *Liste de Messieurs les élèves*, ms. 45, fol. 46).

September 21
A marriage contract is established between Fragonard and Marie-Anne Gérard (the contract is no longer in the minutes of the Étude Marchand, répertoire C9, but there is a copy [?] in the Archives de la Seine [DC⁶ 187], registered May 24, 1780, which gives the date of the contract as September 21, 1778 [*sic*]). According to the terms of this contract, Catherine-Henriette La Fond donated 6,000 *livres* to the future couple in exchange for room and board. François Fragonard, the artist's father, made him a gift of 600 *livres* "de rente et succession viagière pour par les dits donateurs en jouir pendant la vie dudit."

Saint-Non makes an engraving after Fragonard's drawing *Vénus Endormie avec l'Amour, épiés par un satyre* (see figure 3), a copy after a

seventeenth-century Caravaggesque work in the Palazzo Durazzo (see Rosenberg and Brejon, 1986, no. 322).

1769

June 5
De Wailly again reports to the Marquis de Voyer on the progress of the work on his Hôtel: " ... vous ne serez peut estre pas aussy content du planfons de Fragonard que de celui de Durameau qui réuni tous les sufrages" (Poitiers, Bibliothèque Universitaire, Archives du Marquis Voyer d'Argenson, presently being catalogued).

Fragonard's work has not come down to us, but Durameau's, *Le Lever de l'Aurore*, is in storage at the warehouse of the Banque de France in Asnières (see figures 5, 6, p. 225). According to Anne Leclair, the painting *Hébé Versant le nectar à Jupiter* (figure 4), by Jean-Jacques Lagrenée (1739–1821), probably replaced Fragonard's work, which was poorly received.

June 17
Fragonard and Marie-Anne Gérard are married at the church of Saint-Lambert, in the Vaugirard quarter; the certificate, which is lost, was published by the Goncourts (1910, pp. 286–87); a copy exists, "collationné à l'original par nous pretre bachelier en théologie, curé de la ditte paroisse de Vaugirard ce deux septembre mil sept cent soicente neuf" (Bibliothèque du Musée de Grasse, MF 16, fol. 1). The banns were posted in Grasse and at Saint-Germain-l'Auxerrois in Paris, and the couple was engaged on May 27. The matrimonial benediction was given by Granchier, a priest at Saint-Germain-l'Auxerrois. Present at the wedding were Jean-Honoré's father, François "bourgeois de Paris demeurant au Louvre," and Jean-Gérard, Marie-Anne's brother.

August 25
Fragonard was criticized by Bachaumont for not having exhibited at the Salon that year: "M. Fragonard, ce jeune Artiste, qui avoit donné, il y a quatre ans, les plus grandes espérances pour le genre de l'histoire, dont les talens s'étoient peu développés au *Sallon* dernier, ne figure d'aucune façon à celui-ci. On prétend que l'appas du gain l'a détourné de la belle carrière où il étoit entré et pour la posterité, il se contente de briller aujourd'hui dans les boudoirs et dans les gardes-robes" (*Mémoires secrets*, XIII, pp. 32–33).

Nolhac (1907, p. 21) dates the trip to Holland to this time (see pp. 178–80).

Fragonard signs and dates a "figure de fantaisie" (cat. no. 132); this date seems to be confirmed by a label found on the back of the painting: "Portrait de La Bretèche, peint par Fragonard en 1769, en une heure de temps." A similar label was affixed to the back of the portrait of Saint-Non (cat. no. 133).

December 16
Birth, in Paris, of Henriette-Rosalie Fragonard, the daughter of Jean-Honoré and Marie-Anne, baptized the next day in Saint-Eustache; the father is mentioned as being absent (see the excerpt from the birth certificate, collated May 30, 1794, Minutier central, XCVI-568).

Figure 3. Abbé de Saint-Non, after Fragonard. *Vénus Endormie avec l'Amour*. Whereabouts unknown (according to Guimbaud)

Figure 4. Jean-Jacques Lagrenée. *Hébé Versant le nectar à Jupiter*. Banque de France, Paris

"Groupes d'Enfants dans le ciel"

Oil on canvas, oval, 65 x 56 cm.

Musée du Louvre, Paris, R.F. 1949-2

Provenance

Probably, Jacques-Onésyme Bergeret de Grancourt (1715–1785), 1767; very likely, Comte [du Barry]: sold, March 11, 1776, no. 75 (in fact, no. 76; the catalogue mistakenly lists two works as no. 75): "un Tableau de forme ovale. Il représente une foule de petits Amours groupés sur des nuages, les uns avec les autres. Ce morceau, composé avec beaucoup de goût, est fait avec une intelligence de couleurs ordinaire à ce Maître . . ." (for 2,090 *livres*, to [H]"amon"; according to Dacier, 1910, II, p. 12, certain paintings in this sale belonged to the Comtesse du Barry); should not be confused with no. 94 in the sale, April 22, 1776 (actually, no. 78 *bis* in the du Barry sale, 1776); [Masso and Benoît]: sold, April 10, 1786, no. 42 (for 999 *livres* 19 *sols*, to Hutin?); this painting was in another sale (see figure 1), the details of which are not known; Baron de Beurnonville: sold, May 9–16, 1881, no. 58 (for 13,500 francs); Henri, then André Péreire; given to the Louvre, with life interest, in 1949; received in 1974.

Exhibitions

Paris, Salon of 1767, no. 137: "tableau ovale représentant des grouppes d'Enfans dans le Ciel"
Paris, 1921, no. 29
London, 1933, no. 14, ill.
Paris, 1974, no. 4, ill.
Paris, 1984–85, no. 57, ill. (N. V[olle] mentions the exhibitions in which this painting appeared, as well as all the reviews of the Salon)

Bibliography

Blanc, 1862, pp. 7–8
G. pp. 262–63, 317
P. pp. 54, 81, 270, 276, 278
N. pp. 54–55, 158
G. Wildenstein, 1926, pp. 12–13
R. pp. 38, 145
W. 78, fig. 54, pp. 15–16 (French edition)
G. Wildenstein, 1961, pp. 50, 59, n. 27
Carpenter, 1962, p. 360
Seznec and Adhémar, 1963, III, pp. 37, 279–80, 283, 296, 318
Thuillier, 1967, colorpl. p. 44

W. and M. 86, ill.
Rosenberg and Compin, 1974, p. 187, n. 12
Rosenberg, 1975, pp. 262–64, ill.
Bukdahl, 1980, I, pp. 135, 272, 337, 340
Sutton, 1980; 1987, p. 108

Related works

This painting has sometimes been confused with no. 78 *bis* in the du Barry sale, March 11, 1776. The sketch by Saint-Aubin (figure 7) gives a precise idea of the composition of this work (it probably cannot be identified with the picture that belonged to M. Rémy, which was exhibited at the Salon de la Correspondance, January 25, 1786, no. 25: the *Nouvelles de la République des Lettres et des Arts*, p. 45, notes that there exists an "engraving" of this painting). In 1766, Saint-Non made two engravings of the *Couronne d'amours* (figures 2, 4), after drawings by Fragonard (figure 3; Albertina, Vienna, Inv. 12722, A. 2449; see also A. 1634, fig. 428, 2452, fig. 613); they display an obvious kinship with the painting in the Louvre. (See also figures 5, 6.)

Figure 1. Old label on the verso of catalogue no. 109

Figure 2. Abbé de Saint-Non, after Fragonard. *Couronne d'amours*. 1766. Engraving. Musée du Louvre, Paris, Cabinet des Dessins, Rothschild Collection

Figure 3. Fragonard. *Couronne d'amours*. Graphische Sammlung Albertina, Vienna

Figure 4. Abbé de Saint-Non, after Fragonard. *Couronne d'amours*. 1766. Engraving. Musée du Louvre, Paris, Cabinet des Dessins, Rothschild Collection

Figure 5. Comte de Paroy. *Couronne d'amours*. Bibliothèque Nationale, Paris, Cabinet des Estampes

Figure 6. Attributed to Fragonard. *Guirlande d'amours*. Musée des Beaux-Arts, Besançon

Figure 7. Gabriel de Saint-Aubin.
Page from the du Barry sales catalogue
(1776). Philadelphia Museum of Art,
John G. Johnson Collection

This famous painting raises a certain number of problems. The previously unpublished sketch by Gabriel de Saint-Aubin (figure 7) confirms that the picture was in the sale of the Comte du Barry's collection in 1776 (and seems to have kept the same frame ever since!), but there is no proof that it was the same work as that in the Salon of 1767. The doubts of Wildenstein (1926) and of Thuillier (1967) are justified, even if the indications in favor of the 1767 hypothesis are quite strong. The Salon picture belonged to "M. Bergeret." Was this the famous Jacques-Onésyme Bergeret, whom we have often mentioned, or, as Wildenstein claimed in 1961, the uncle, Bergeret de Grancourt, who died in 1777 and most certainly owned a *Landscape* by Fragonard at that date?

More important and more controversial is the painting's date: Wildenstein, and Seznec and Adhémar hold that it was painted in 1750, while Fragonard worked in Boucher's studio, and, thus, well before his trip to Italy; Carpenter, in his review of Wildenstein's monograph, suggests a date of about 1765. That Fragonard could have painted this work two years after the *Coresus and Callirhoë* (cat. no. 104) is less surprising when one recalls that, during this period, Fragonard received many commissions for ceiling decorations; the "groupe d'enfants dans le ciel," to cite the title of the painting in the Salon catalogue, could very well have been a study for one of them.

In addition to this work, Fragonard exhibited at the Salon of 1767 "A Head of an Old Man. A round picture," and several drawings. We have already discussed this painting above (p. 202). Diderot recorded the titles of the drawings (most of which have yet to be identified): a *Landscape,* which he judged "poor," a "Man leaning on his hoe," and a "sort of second-hand dealer in an armchair, at his table," as well as "other" drawings "in red chalk on blue paper"(!), which he called "lovely and well drawn."

The critics of the Salon were disappointed by Fragonard's contributions: "The public was expecting something more considerable from the author of *Callirhoë*" (*Mercure de France*). Diderot's comments are as notorious as they are severe: "It is a nice big omelette of children in the sky.... It is flat, yellowish, dull, and monotonous in tonality, and painted like cotton wool. The word is perhaps not yet out [it became famous], but he renders it well, so well that one could mistake this composition for the fleece of a sheep ... Mr Fragonard, this is incredibly insipid. A nice omelette, very fluffy, all yellow and all burnt." How to explain Diderot's reservations? "Fragonard's fricassee of angels is an imitation of Boucher.... From Rome, he came back with the same taste, carelessness, and the style of Boucher that he took with him." With such barbs aimed at Boucher, then the First Painter to the King, Diderot—who, incidentally, seems to date this work to after Fragonard's return from Italy—was unable to appreciate this "Essaim d'amours" (as it was titled in the catalogue of the Beurnonville sale of 1881), which seemed to copy Boucher. Yet, this composition marks a radical break with Boucher's mythological subjects. True, it has none of the didacticism of the *Coresus,* but the artist's aim was totally different.

As we have mentioned above, in these years Fragonard received many important commissions for painted decorations. This work, therefore, seems to be more than just an illusionistic tour de force or an exercise in pure virtuosity, but, rather, an attempt—misunderstood by his contemporaries—at what, in his day, was considered to be the summit of art: the ornamentation of a vault or the decoration of a ceiling. Fragonard had been able to admire the most famous examples of this genre in Italy; he knew that since François Lemoine's Salon d'Hercule at Versailles no vast project of this kind had been successfully realized in France. There was a vacuum. Did he try to fill it? Had he for once shown some signs of ambition?

109

110

"Young Girl in Her Bed, Making Her Dog Dance"
(erroneously called La Gimblette)

Oil on canvas, 89 x 70 cm.

Alte Pinakothek, Munich, Collection Bayerische Hypotheken- und Wechsel-Bank, HuW 35

Provenance

The widow of Lebas de Courmont: sold, May 26, 1795, no. 40: "une légère ébauche du sujet d'une jeune fille sur son lit qui fait danser son chien. Haut. 33 p. larg. 26 p. T. [90.5 x 71 cm.]"; Demidoff *père:* sold, April 8–13, 1839, no. 88: "très belle esquisse avancée de la gimblette; connue par la gravure" (?); anonymous sale, December 10–11, 1847, no. 38: "la Gimblette. Jeune fille couchée et jouant avec un petit chien. Il existe trois ou quatre compositions de la Gimblette. Celle-ci, qui est d'une adorable couleur, provient de M. Théophile Fragonard" (?); anonymous sale, March 14, 1868, no. 8: "esquisse du tableau intitulé la *Gimbelette* [no dimensions given]" (?); Hippolyte Walferdin (1795–1880): sold posthumously, April 12–16, 1880, no. 61 (for 7,000 francs, to Haro); Poidatz, 1889 (P.); Arthur Veil-Picard, before 1906 (purchased for 25,000 francs; Gimpel, 1963, p. 173); Jeannette Veil-Picard; acquired by the Bayerische Hypotheken- und Wechsel-Bank, for the Alte Pinakothek, 1977.

Exhibitions

Geneva, 1951, no. 27, pl. IV
Paris, 1953, no. 81, ill.
Paris, *Bernheim,* 1954, no. 21
Besançon, 1956, no. 1
Paris, 1956, no. 39, ill.
Grasse, 1957, no. 13
Munich, 1958, no. 59

Bibliography

Blanc, 1862, p. 11
Renouvier, 1863, p. 168
G. p. 329
Lachaise, 1866, p. 335
Portalis, 1880, pp. 15–16
P. pp. 68, 226, 278, pl. between pp. 60 and 61
N. pp. 59, 60, 119
R. pp. 70, 159
W. 280, pl. 49, pp. 18–19, 35, 37 (French edition)
Connaissance des arts, November 1965, p. 29, ill.
W. and M. 299, ill.
Hohenzollern, 1977, p. 393, ill.
Münchner Jahrbuch der bildenden Kunst, 1978, pp. 242–44, ill.
Sutton, 1980; 1987, p. 110

Related works

Three versions of the *"Young Girl in Her Bed, Making Her Dog Dance,"* or, more simply, of *La Gimblette* (the title is discussed below), are mentioned in eighteenth-century sales catalogues: that of July 8, 1793, no. 21, "une jeune fille dans son lit et accompagnée de son chien [Oil on canvas, 35 x 40.5 cm.]"; the present picture, which was sold, May 26, 1795 (see above), and August 10, 1795 ("23 thermidor, an III"), no. 77: "une

jeune fille couchée sur le dos et dans un lit voluptueux, s'amusant avec un joli épagneul auquel elle présente une gimblette … [Oil on canvas, 70 x 86.5 cm.]"; W. 281 mistakenly mentions another *Gimblette* in the Varanchan collection, sold, December 29–31, 1777, no. 32.

The first painting may perhaps be identical with one in the Walferdin collection (sold, April 12–16, 1880, no. 62) that was acquired by Cedron (W. 282), but has since been lost. The Goncourts described it with great warmth (p. 275), yet it was sold for only 1,010 francs, while, in the same sale, the Munich painting, which was the preceding lot number, sold for 7,000!

The third picture, which once belonged to the Baron de Bézenval, is also lost, but records of the composition are furnished by the engravings by Charles Bertony (figures 1, 2), announced in the *Journal de Paris* on April 19, 1783; a larger version than the original, which was sold in Paris at the Palais Galliéra, December 11, 1961, no. 39, ill. (see figure 3); and also by a preparatory study for the head of the young girl (A. 107, fig. 690, sold at the Palais d'Orsay, Paris, December 14, 1979, no. 5, ill. [figure 4]). For another drawing of *La Gimblette,* its title

rightly rejected by A. 691, see the sales catalogue of November 20, 1941, no. 7, ill.).

There is a fourth picture, known in three versions, all variants of very uneven quality: the painting from the Mühlbacher collection (figure 5), sold, May 13–15, 1907, no. 23, ill. (Oil on canvas, 72 x 90 cm.; sold, Versailles, February 23, 1969, no. 25, color cover); the Kraemer painting (figure 6), sold, May 3, 1913, no. 36, ill. (63 x 80 cm.; sold, Paris, June 4, 1970, no. 164, ill.); and the Cailleux painting (figure 7; Oil on canvas,

Figure 1. Charles Bertony, after Fragonard. *La Gimblette* ("clothed" version). Engraving. Bibliothèque Nationale, Paris, Cabinet des Estampes

Figure 2. Charles Bertony, after Fragonard. *La Gimblette* ("nude" version). Engraving. Musée du Louvre, Paris, Cabinet des Dessins, Rothschild Collection

Figure 3. Attributed to Fragonard. *La Gimblette.* Private collection, Geneva

Figure 4. Fragonard. *Head of a Young Girl.* Whereabouts unknown

Figure 5. Attributed to Fragonard. *La Gimblette.* Whereabouts unknown

Figure 6. Attributed to Fragonard.
La Gimblette. Whereabouts unknown

Figure 7. Attributed to Fragonard.
La Gimblette. Art market, Paris

NEW THOUGHT.

London Pub.ᵈ May 8 ʲ 1785. by V.M.Picot, Nᵒ 62 St Martins Lane.

Figure 8. Victor-Marie Picot.
"New Thought." Bibliothèque Nationale,
Paris, Cabinet des Estampes

61 x 77.5 cm.; New York exhibition catalogue, 1967, no. 70, color cover; but see D.
Posner, 1967, p. 363, and also Steinberg,
1967, p. 44, ill.).

Many versions of the *Gimblette* were sold in
the nineteenth and the twentieth centuries
(see M. Clay, 1959, pp. 82, 102), but it is
very difficult to tell them apart as the old
descriptions were vague and the dimensions
were not always given. We would add to the
examples cited by N., R., and W., the
"jeune femme à son reveil [qui] joue avec un
jeune chien auquel elle donne des *gimbe-
lettes*," which was sold December 16, 1833,
and measured 65 x 81 centimeters.

The history of the Munich picture between
1795 and 1880, as given above, is uncertain,
but we have adopted the provenance established by W. In any event, if, as noted in an
1847 sales catalogue, it belonged to Théophile Fragonard, the painter's grandson, it
hardly seems likely that it was the same
painting that was sold in 1795. Engravings
of the composition were made by François-
Antoine Hémery (untitled), and by Victor-
Marie Picot (1744–1802) in London, May
18, 1783 (circular format, with an error in
Fragonard's first name, "Ra."), entitled
"New Thought" (figure 8; see also Bourcard,
1885, p. 188, who mentions an engraving by
"L. Guyot en couleurs, in 4°, ovale et publiée
à Londres"; see also Portalis and Béraldi,
1881, II, pp. 366–67).

The copy in the Cabinet des Dessins at the
Louvre, a miniature (figure 9; R. F. 4999),
may be the same as the one that was sold
November 19, 1783, no. 359, "Fragonard.
Une miniature en rond connue sous le nom
de la Gimblette" (?). There is also a copy—a
drawing—in the Fogg Art Museum (figure
10; 1957.179).

The composition was imitated by many
artists, including the engraver Augustin-
Claude-Simon Legrand (figure 11), and
Nicolas Lavreince.

Figure 9. After Fragonard. *La Gimblette*.
Musée du Louvre, Paris, Cabinet
des Dessins

Figure 10. After Fragonard. *La Gimblette*.
Fogg Art Museum, Harvard University,
Cambridge, Massachusetts

LE JOLI CHIEN

Figure 11. Augustin-Claude-
Simon Legrand. *"Le Joli Chien."*
Bibliothèque Nationale, Paris,
Cabinet des Estampes

Figure 12. Clodion. *La Gimblette*.
Musée des Arts Décoratifs, Paris

Misunderstanding surrounds the usual title of this picture,
La Gimblette. A "gimblette" is a type of pastry that is dry
and ring-shaped (and Provençal in origin, according to *Larousse*). In certain versions of this painting the young girl,
indeed, offers such a pastry to the little dog—but not in the
Munich painting. The August 10, 1875, issue of *L'Intermé-
diaire* (W. 473) mentions that the engraving by Bertony
"was also known by the title *La Caroline*, which was an

allusion to women suspected of a certain vice and to the
pug-dog that plays an important role in the painting" (on
this subject, see Rochefort, 1905, p. 10, who accuses Mme
du Barry of this "strange distraction,"! and Le Coat, 1987,
p. 182).

The engravings by Bertony—whose work, otherwise, did
not make much of an impact (Roux, 1933, II, p. 463)—
must have created a scandal. Certain versions, in which the

figure is less clothed (see Réau), bore an inscription addressed to the print dealers of the eighteenth century: "This subject should not be displayed." The picture made a strong impression on the Goncourts (G. p. 275): "Her nightcap has fallen off, her eyes are gay and full of youth, she has a broad smile on her lips, and does not care what her raised nightshirt reveals; with her feet, this adolescent girl lifts up into the air a little poodle that has the face of a bewigged barrister.... This is *La Gimblette*, a flower of eroticism, very fresh, and very French...." Walferdin owned two examples of this composition. From the Goncourts again, we know that the (now lost) version, "a rather lifeless horizontal painting," was far inferior to the first, the picture that is today in Munich, which was "more freely painted, lighter, more *fragonardisante,* the girl's nudity

resplendent against the golden yellow of the bed-curtains"; the respective prices paid for these two works, 7,000 and 1,010 francs, confirm the Goncourts' judgment.

This painting, which is generally dated to about 1768, while not really erotic, is one of the most risqué images in French eighteenth-century art. Once again, the painter glorified the bed; the "young girl surrounded by her russet-tinted curtains does not have a *gimblette* to give to the little white puppy that she holds up with her pink feet, but the coloring of her skin is marvelously youthful and of a rosy pink, the rosy pink color of the dawn of life!" (Portalis, 1889).

Several terracottas (figure 12) by Clodion—who also was in the employ of the Baron de Bézenval—or attributed to him, were more or less directly inspired by Fragonard's composition.

I I I A Metamorphosis of Jupiter

Bister wash on paper, over an underdrawing in black chalk, 24.2 x 37.3 cm.

Musée "Ile de France," Saint-Jean-Cap Ferrat, Fondation Ephrussi de Rothschild

Provenance
Three drawings with similar subjects appeared in eighteenth-century sales: that of the Caffieri collection, October 10, 1775, no. 62: "Jupiter et Danae, dessin à la plume et au bistre, d'une composition neuve et d'un

effet piquant," the Vassal de Saint-Hubert collection, March 29 [April 13], 1779, no. 180: "Danaé et ses courtisanes" (sold for 360 *livres*), and the Chabot and Duc de La Mure (or Desmarets) collection, December 17–22, 1785, no. 165: "Io recevant Jupiter

transformé en nuage ... " (sold for 120 *livres* 2 *sols,* to Quesnet); Saint: sold, May 4 [30], 1846, no. 13 b: "Danaé, dessin lavé à la sépia" (for 32 francs); Walferdin: sold posthumously, April 12–16, 1880, no. 211 (for 950 francs, to Goupil); Henri Meilhac, 1889

(P.); Émile Straus, by 1907: sold, June 3–4, 1929, no. 70, ill. (for 500,000 francs, to Stettiner); Mme Maurice Ephrussi: given, in memory of her father, Baron Alphonse de Rothschild, to the Institut de France (Musée "Ile de France"), 1933.

Exhibitions
Paris, 1907, no. 208
Paris, 1921, no. 164

Bibliography
G. p. 325
Portalis, 1880, p. 26
P. p. 298 (see also pp. 198–99)
R. p. 191
Réau, 1960–61, pp. 78–79, pl. 1
A. 395, fig. 143

Related works
For a similar composition, see cat. no. 112.
See also A. 393, 397, and a drawing in the Eugène Tondu collection sale, May 10–13, 1865, no. 219: "Danaë. Charmant petit dessin lavé à l'encre de Chine."

Figure 1. Jean-Baptiste Deshays. *Danaë*. Musée du Louvre, Paris, Cabinet des Dessins

Figure 2. Jean-Baptiste Greuze. *Aegina Visited by Jupiter*. The Metropolitan Museum of Art, New York

Figure 3. Jean-Baptiste Greuze. *Aegina Visited by Jupiter*. Musée du Louvre, Paris

The subject of this drawing, and of the very similar version of it discussed in catalogue no. 112, is not easy to decipher. The sales catalogues of the eighteenth century seem to hesitate between identifying the heroine as Io or Danaë, with more recent writers tending to favor Danaë. Jennifer Montagu, in a written communication, sees the work as an "inexplicable combination" of Jupiter's different amorous conquests. He is unmistakably personified as an eagle—but what is the identity of the heroine? Is it Io, whom the god Jupiter visited in the form of a cloud; Danaë, to whom he appeared as a shower of gold, often represented being gathered by an eager servant; or Semele, who wanted to see Jupiter in all his splendor, but was consumed by the blaze that enveloped him? A possible origin for this "new composition" may have been a specific commission to illustrate some more or less erotic "tale" than has since fallen into oblivion.

On the back of the related drawing (see cat. no. 112) there is an old inscription, perhaps written by Fragonard himself (D. Carritt, quoted by Richardson), which merits attention: "jupiter chez la Mde de Modes . . ." ["Jupiter at the Dressmaker's"] (see cat. no. 112, figure 1). As mentioned earlier, Fragonard copied the "*Danaë*" (actually Lia) by Rembrandt when it was in the Crozat collection (today it is in the Hermitage); this copy belonged to Deshays, and was sold after the artist's death in 1765. Deshays himself drew and painted many versions of the *Danaë* (one of which was exhibited at the Salon of 1763; see figure 1), and, shortly before 1767, Greuze (according to E. Munhall, Dijon exhibition catalogue, 1977, no. 65, ill.) painted a large picture representing Danaë—unless it is the related subject of Aegina visited by Jupiter (the painting is in The Metropolitan Museum of Art, New York: see figure 2; the preparatory sketch is in the Louvre: see figure 3).

The drawing in the Musée "Ile de France," probably executed between 1765 and 1770, is rich in picturesque details: an incense burner resting on a tripod, a large basin of precious metal, and a mirror decorating a regal apartment. The glances of the heroine's five companions "en négligé" are turned toward her, as she swoons with pleasure. A servant in the foreground gathers up the gold pieces. Two of the young women sprinkle water on the "burning vapors." The surprise and astonishment of her companions, the delight of the heroine, who closes her eyes in rapturous enjoyment, the rapaciousness of the servant—all contribute to the strangeness of this particularly animated and ambitious composition.

112 A Metamorphosis of Jupiter

Bister wash on paper, over an underdrawing in black chalk, 33.5 x 45.4 cm.
Inscribed on the verso: *jupiter chez la M^{de} de Modes / Bambochade / h fragonard, N° 422* (see figure 1)

Private collection

Provenance
See the previous entry.
  The mount bears the dry mark (Lugt 1042) of François Renaud, a mounter of drawings in the second half of the eighteenth century; the architect Pierre-François-Léonard Fontaine (1762–1853) (?); Foulon de Vaux, 1921; [Wildenstein]; Albert L. Meyer, Paris; [Germain Seligmann, by 1931]: his stamp, not inventoried by Lugt, is at the lower right, on the mount; acquired by the Kimbell Art Museum, 1979: sold, Sotheby's, London, July 6, 1987.

Exhibitions
Paris, 1921, no. 290

Paris, 1931, no. 5
Paris, 1937, no. 537

Bibliography
Seligmann, 1952, pp. 88–89, fig. 36
R. p. 191
A. 396
Richardson, 1979, no. 22, ill.

Related works
For a similar composition, see cat. no. 111.
  There is another, more finished version of this drawing (A. 394, fig. 144), whose provenance is known only as far back as 1883 (figure 2).

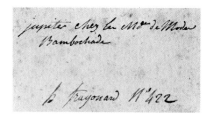

Figure 1. Verso of catalogue no. 112

Figure 2. Attributed to Fragonard.
A Metamorphosis of Jupiter.
Whereabouts unknown

Of the few differences between the present drawing and the one in Saint-Jean-Cap Ferrat (cat. no. 111), the principal one concerns the heroine: here, she raises her head toward the eagle, while in the other drawing she turns her head away.

113 The Girls' Dormitory

Bister wash on paper, over an underdrawing in black chalk, 23.9 x 36.7 cm.

Harvard University Art Museums (Fogg Art Museum), Cambridge, Massachusetts, Gift of Charles E. Dunlap, 1954.106

Provenance

The engraver Gabriel Huquier (his stamp, Lugt 1285, is at the lower right): but not mentioned in the posthumous sale of his collection, November 9, 1772 (on Huquier, see Bruand, 1950). Was it the same drawing as the one in the [Varanchan de Saint-Geniès] sale, December 29–31, 1777, no. 63: "l'intérieur d'une chambre à coucher où l'on voit beaucoup de jeunes filles paraissant éveillées par la chaleur dans une nuit d'été," purchased by the miniaturist Peter Adolf Hall for 240 *livres* ("le Dortoir vente Varaujean"; Villot, 1867, p. 77)? Or the drawing in the [de Ghendt] sale, November 15–22, 1779, no. 261 (sold for 550 *livres,* with its pendant):"le dortoir d'une pension de jeunes filles dans lequel on voit trois lits et sept jeunes fillettes en chemises occupées à plusieurs ouvrages du matin"? Or the one in the [Boyer de Fons-Colombes] collection: sold, December 13, 1790, no. 116: "composition de sept figures au bistre sur papier blanc"? Or the one in the Destaisniche sale, November 16, 1806, no. 29 (sold for 170 francs): "le dortoir des marchandes de mode" ? (For a drawing, possibly of the same

subject, in the H. Robert collection sale in 1809, see cat. no. 114.) Saint: sold, May 4 [actually 30], 1846, no. 15: "le coucher des ouvrières" (?; at no. 16: "le Maître de danse enlevant son élève"); Brunet-Denon: sold, February 2, 1846, no. 245: "le coucher des ouvrières" (?); Norblin: sold, March 16–17, 1860, no. 56: "le lever des ouvrières modistes composition de sept figures . . . "(?). Also worth mentioning is the drawing in the Chevalier de C[lesle] collection: sold, December 4, 1786, no. 114: "un dortoir de jeunes filles dans lequel on compte sept figures variées entre elles par différentes attitudes intéressantes," which, perhaps, could be identified with the one in the Walferdin collection: sold, April 12–16, 1880, no. 213 (for 1,100 francs, to Haro; but see Williams, 1978, no. 25, and cat. no. 117, figure 1), and in the Groult collection (see Portalis, 1880, p. 27; P. p. 297; and *Related works,* cat. no. 117). Lastly, we cite the drawing at Bélizard's, "an II" [1794]: "le réveil des ouvrières, dessin au bistre . . . 14 p. sur 18 . . . *flagonard*" (Arch. Nat. F¹⁷ 372, p. 154, no. 23), attributed by the *Commissaires de la saisie révolutionnaire* to "Denon": was it

the drawing in the Brunet-Denon collection sale in 1846? [Wildenstein, 1928]; David David-Weill; [Wildenstein, 1938]; given to the Fogg museum by Charles E. Dunlap.

Exhibitions

Paris, 1928, no. 167
Paris, and other cities,1958–59, no. 46, pl. 66
Washington, D.C., 1978, no. 22, ill. (with complete list of exhibitions)

Bibliography

G. pp. 298, 330
P. pp. 66, 194, 297
R. p. 197
A. 1988, fig. 540
Starobinski, 1964, pp. 120, 125, ill. p. 121
Massengale, 1979, fig. 99

Related works

For the pendant, see cat. no. 114.

For the version exhibited in Grasse in 1957 (no. 59, pl. XVI), see A. 1989 (also A. 1990).

For the provenance of A. 1991, fig. 541, see above. See also Geraldine Norman, *The London Times,* March 9, 1978.

Figure 1. Fragonard. *The Raising of Lazarus.*
Whereabouts unknown

Figure 2. François-Nicolas-Barthélemy
Dequevauviller, after Nicolas Lavreince.
Le Coucher des ouvrières. Bibliothèque
Nationale, Paris, Cabinet des Estampes

"It is, as we can guess, a nest full of young girls disrobing unconcernedly, or stretching themselves out on their beds, and, an amusing detail, two of them are peering into their nightshirts as if looking for . . . a flea!" (Portalis).

As noted above, this drawing once belonged to Gabriel Huquier. In the margin of his copy of the catalogue of the posthumous sale of Huquier's collection, Mariette noted the following about a drawing by Jean-Baptiste Leprince (1734–1781) and Fragonard's *Raising of Lazarus* (the drawing shown in figure 1 is believed to be this one), which were sold under the same number: "They did them as a joke, at the same table at Huquier's" (P. p. 201). This remark, apart from attesting to Fragonard's virtuosity, associates the names of two artists who occasionally imitated one another's styles, to the extent that, even today, their works are sometimes difficult to tell apart.

This drawing (or a second version of it) was mentioned as having been in several important eighteenth-century collections, including those of Varanchan (a knowledgeable connoisseur, who was very partial to Fragonard's works), the miniaturist Hall, and, quite possibly, Hubert Robert. Most interesting is that an approximate date of before 1772—probably about 1770, at the latest—may be assigned to it with some certainty.

As usual, Fragonard began with a line drawing in black chalk. Then, using the tip of his brush, he outlined the bodies, indicated the eyes and the folds of the garments, and rendered volume by delicately applying a more or less dark bister wash to the passages that he wanted to leave in the shadow.

The present drawing, often referred to as either "the dormitory of the dress-shop assistants," "the bedtime of the dressmakers"—probably, an allusion to a famous work by Nicolas Lavreince (see figure 2)—or, in 1779, as "the dormitory of a girl's boarding school," reaches the limits of licentiousness (or of voyeurism?). Whether they are looking for fleas or trying to keep cool by disrobing during a hot summer night, the two young girls, whose charms are revealed by the clever lighting effects—by the "complicity of the backlighting" (Starobinski, 1964)—are definitely there for our delectation. The girl playfully spanking one of her lightly clad companions is a further delight to the beholder.

114   The Dancing Lesson

Bister wash on paper, over an underdrawing in black chalk, 25 x 36.5 cm.

Museu Calouste Gulbenkian, Lisbon

Provenance
Like the previous drawing, perhaps [Varanchan de Saint-Geniès]: sold, December 29–31, 1777, no. 62: " . . . l'intérieur d'une chambre où l'on voit plusieurs dames assises devant une cheminée et s'amusant à faire tenir droit un petit chien; derrière elles, un jeune homme fait sauter une jeune demoiselle, et plus loin est une autre personne s'occupant à lire" (for 385 *livres,* according to the catalogue; 416 *livres,* according to the Swedish miniaturist Peter Adolf Hall); Hall ("vente Varaujean," Villot, 1867, p. 77). May be identified with the drawings in the following sales: [de Ghendt]: sold, November 15–22, 1779, no. 262 (for 550 *livres,* with its pendant): " . . . derrière elles un jeune homme qui s'amuse à faire sauter devant un miroir une demoiselle"; Chevalier de C[lesle]: sold, December 4, 1786, no. 113; Hubert Robert: sold, April 5, 1809, no. 172: "trois dessins légèrement lavés de bistre par Fragonard, dont la Leçon de danse" (for 40 francs, to Constantin); Amédée Constantin: sold, March 29, 1830, no. 91 (for 71 francs): " . . . réunion de jeunes femmes, dont une occupée à lire" (?); Saint: sold, May 4 [actually, 30], 1846, no. 16 (?; for 120 francs; see cat. no. 113, and *Related works* below); Émile Norblin: sold, March 16–17, 1860, no. 5 of the supplement (for 250 francs); Camille Marcille, by 1862 (Burty, 1876, p. 15): sold, March 6–7, 1876, p. VII, no. 78 (for 2,020 francs); Josse, by 1889: sold posthumously, May 28–29, 1894, no. 11, ill. (for 10,900 francs; the catalogue erroneously states that it came from the Dreux collection); Marquis de Biron, Paris, by 1899; Mme de Polès; David David-Weill, 1921; [Wildenstein, 1937]; acquired by C. S. Gulbenkian, 1937; Calouste Gulbenkian Foundation.

114

Exhibitions
Paris, 1884, no. 275
Paris, 1921, no. 157
Porto, 1964, no. 62, ill.

Bibliography
G. pp. 297–98, 329, 330
P. pp. 194, 196, 307, reproduced between
    pp. 192 and 193
Martine, 1927, no. 40, ill.
Henriot, 1928, III, pp. 173–74, ill. p. 175
R. p. 197
A. 1992, fig. 544

Related works
Another version, in the Donadieu Dreux collection, was sold, February 3–4, 1870, no.
40 (for 430 francs); anonymous sale, March
23–25, 1874, no. 30 ("collection Saint [see
Provenance above], Donadieu et Dreux");
Horace de Choiseul, by 1889 (P. p. 311):
sold, May 7, 1897, no. 10 (see figure 1; R.
ill. p. 36; A. 1993, fig. 545: this last catalogue is the only one that gives a date,
1784); see also A. 1994, 1995 (Grappe,
1913, II, ill. between pp. 18 and 19).
    Jules de Goncourt made an engraving of
part of the composition (figure 2) in 1862
(to illustrate the 1865 edition of the Goncourts' monograph; Burty, 1876, p. 15,
no. 68).

Figure 1. Fragonard. *The Dancing Lesson.*
Whereabouts unknown

Figure 2. Jules de Goncourt.
"*Le Maître à danser.*" Bibliothèque Nationale,
Paris, Cabinet des Estampes

Figure 3. Nicolas Delaunay, after
Nicolas Lavreince. *Qu'en dit l'abbé?*
Bibliothèque Nationale, Paris,
Cabinet des Estampes

The present drawing has often been referred to as "Qu'en dit l'abbé?" ("What does the abbé think of it?"), after the title of a famous composition by Lavreince (figure 3). The Lisbon drawing, or a second version of it, was associated with the *Dormitory* (cat. no. 113) in the collections of Varanchan de Saint-Geniès, Peter Adolf Hall, Emmanuel de Ghendt, the Chevalier de Clesle, and Hubert Robert (and Saint in 1846!). It should be noted that it does not bear the stamp of the engraver Huquier (see previous entry).

The subject is a pleasing one, the description of which we leave to Edmond de Goncourt (whose brother, Jules, as noted, made a fine engraving after Fragonard's composition): "While some ladies are amusing themselves in front of a fireplace with a little dog, who is begging, next to the stool on which rests his small violin the charming little dancing master lifts and whirls about in his arms his beautiful pupil, unwittingly revealing part of her lovely legs to the sly looking abbé reading his breviary over in the window seat." On the floor, the flounce of the girl's dress, a landscape painting,

and a mirror reflecting a portion of the scene, complete the composition.

"Fragonard, dipping his pen into a drop of bister, has never dashed off a more witty and gay, a more brilliant and lively *billet doux* than this little sketch of château life with the title: *Qu'en dit l'abbé?*" (Paul de Saint-Victor, preface to the Marcille collection sales catalogue, 1876, p. VII).

In spite of the many interesting motifs—the little dog; the young girl's raised dress; the abbé, who looks up at just the right moment—Fragonard managed to create a very unified composition, which the expert at the 1786 sale qualified as being particularly "mirthful."

115   Les Pétards

Bister wash on paper, over an underdrawing in black chalk, 26.2 x 38 cm.

Museum of Fine Arts, Boston, Otis Norcross and Seth K. Sweetser Funds, 44.815

Provenance
Paignon Dijonval (catalogued by Bénard, 1810, p. 154, no. 3652): sold by his grandson, Vicomte Morel de Vindé, December 17, 1821, and the days following: "trois femmes couchées sur un lit et effrayées par des fusées que l'on tire dans leur chambre par une trappe"; "Jacob de la Cottière, Directeur de la Librairie Hachette," who gave it to Émile

Templier, "de la Société des Gens de Lettres" (this inscription is said to have been on the back of the drawing); Templier's son-in-law, M. Desclosières, director of the Librairie Hachette: acquired from him by David David-Weill, 1913; [Wildenstein, 1938]; acquired by the Museum of Fine Arts, Boston, 1944.

Exhibitions
Paris, *Beaux-Arts,* 1935, no. 310
Paris, 1958–59, no. 45, pl. 65
London, 1968, no. 259, fig. 299
Washington, D.C., 1978, no. 23, ill. (with a list of exhibitions and complete bibliography)

Bibliography
G. pp. 273–74, 329
Portalis and Béraldi, 1880, I, p. 54
P. p. 194
Martine, 1927, no. 43, ill.
Henriot, 1928, III, pp. 165–66, pl. p. 167
Wilhelm, 1951, p. 25
R. pp. 70, 196–97
A. 2009, fig. 552

Related works
The engraving of this drawing, by Pierre-Laurent Auvray (1736– ?), was entitled "Les Pétards" (figure 1), and bore the following lines: "De ces feux apprêtés ne craignez point les *flames* / Punissez plutôt l'indiscret: / Les feux que vos appas allument dans nos ames / Font moins d'éclat mais plus d'effet" (P. p.

328, ill. p. 193; Roux, 1930–31, I, p. 270, no. 6). See also A. 2010, 2011.

A copy in gouache by Nicolas-Louis Barbier is mentioned in the Barbier sales catalogue of July 19, 1779, no. 18: "le jeu des Seringues et celui des Pétards, à gouache d'après H. Fragonard, par le même [L. Barbier]. Hauteur 6 pouces 6 lignes, largeur 9 pouces 3 lignes." (See also the following entry.)

For no apparent reason, this drawing is sometimes linked with the painting "Fragonard et la Citoyenne Gérard" that was in the Villers sale, December 2, 1795, no. 5: ". . . deux jeunes filles auxquelles un Amant invisible présente un bouquet et une lettre, à travers une trape pratiquée dans le plafond. . . ."

Figure 1. Pierre-Laurent Auvray. *Les Pétards*. Bibliothèque Nationale, Paris, Cabinet des Estampes

The *Pétards* and the *Jets d'eau* (cat. no. 116) were unquestionably associated, between 1810 and 1938. The two drawings included here are probably those after which engravings were made, at some unknown date, by Pierre-Laurent Auvray, who collaborated with Saint-Non on the *Voyage pittoresque,* and are also very likely the ones copied in gouache by Barbier some time before 1779. It is generally agreed that they date from about 1770.

A hand extends from a trapdoor in the ceiling to throw firecrackers (the source of the title). Their explosions frighten three sleeping young girls and their cat, and illuminate the room, revealing the not very well hidden charms of the surprised victims. The mock fright of the young girls is, of course, only a pretext. Fragonard addressed himself to the latent voyeur present in all spectators: "Levity is his decency."

116   Les Jets d'eau

Bister wash on paper, over an underdrawing in black chalk, 26.5 x 38.4 cm.

Sterling and Francine Clark Art Institute, Williamstown, Massachusetts

Provenance
Three drawings of this subject are mentioned in the sales catalogues of eighteenth-century collections: [Varanchan de Saint-Geniès]: sold, December 29–31, 1777, no. 64 (for 480 *livres*); [Dulac] and Lachaise: sold, November 30, 1778, no. 77 (for 140 *livres*);

[de Boynes]: sold, March 15, 1785, no. 218 (for 200 *livres*); Paignon Dijonval (catalogue by Bénard, 1810, p. 154, no. 3652): sold by his grandson, Vicomte Morel de Vindé, December 17, 1821, and the following days: "trois femmes couchées sur un lit, on leur jette de l'eau avec des pompes par une trappe

qui est ouverte au pied de leur lit," and inscribed on the verso: "ce dessin a été donné à M. Émile Templier, Directeur de la Librairie Hachette par M. Jacob de la Cottière, de la Société des Gens de Lettres"; acquired by David David-Weill from M. Desclosières, Émile Templier's son-in-law,

Figure 1. Pierre-Laurent Auvray.
Les Jets d'eau. Bibliothèque Nationale, Paris, Cabinet des Estampes

Figure 2. Fragonard. *Les Jets d'eau*. Whereabouts unknown

Figure 3. Fragonard. *Les Jets d'eau*. Whereabouts unknown

116

and the director of the Librairie Hachette, 1913; [Wildenstein, 1938]; purchased by R. S. Clark, 1941.

Exhibitions
Paris, *Beaux-Arts,* 1935, no. 311
Washington, D.C., 1978, no. 24, ill.

Bibliography
G. pp. 274, 329
Portalis and Béraldi, 1880, I, p. 54
P. pp. 66, 194, 304
Martine, 1927, no. 42, ill.
Henriot, 1928, III, pp. 145–46, pl. p. 147
R. pp. 70, 124, 196

A. 2012, fig. 547
Haverkamp-Begemann, 1964, no. 36, pl. 36

Related works
The engraving of this drawing by Pierre-Laurent Auvray (1736–?), entitled "Les jets d'eau" (figure 1), bears the following lines: "Cessés jeunes Beautés d'opposer un rideau / À cette invention gentille; / Pour éteindre le feu qui dans vos yeux petille / Il faudroit bien d'autres jets d'Eau" (P. p. 328; Roux, 1930–31, I, pp. 269–70, no. 5). We know of at least two autograph versions of this drawing (A. 2013, fig. 548; A. 2014: sold, Paris, October 13, 1983, no. 9, ill.; A.

2015, fig. 546; A. 2016, Paris exhibition catalogue, 1931, no. 18, ill.). The smaller version (now lost), formerly in the collection of Marius Paulme (sold, May 13, 1929, no. 80, ill., for 295,000 francs), and then in the collection of Franz Koenig, in Haarlem (Paris exhibition catalogue, 1937, no. 542), was quite different in composition (figure 2). The drawing formerly in the Veil-Picard collection was exhibited in Tokyo in 1980 (no. 120, ill.; see figure 3).

For the copy in gouache by Barbier, see previous entry.

The compositions alternately titled *Les Jets d'eau* and *Le Jeu des seringues,* like the *Pétards* (see previous entry), were copied and engravings were made after them in the eighteenth century. Yet, the three versions of the *Jets d'eau* that were sold in the eighteenth century were never accompanied by *Les Pétards.* Thus, there is no proof that any of the drawings in the sales of the Varanchan, Dulac, and de Boynes collections can be identified with the one in Williamstown.

From a trapdoor in the floor, two spurts of water douse three young girls who have just gotten out of bed—not very successfully hiding their charms—and do not seem to be defending themselves with much conviction. A young companion, framed in an oval window, holds a lamp with a shade that illuminates the scene. "Fragonard loved those mischievous frolics, in which the body of a woman, who is surprised in the unconsciousness of her first impulse, is bathed in light" (Goncourt). A "very playful" scene (Varanchan sales catalogue, 1777), "rendered with the utmost grace and delight" (1785 sales catalogue), the Williamstown drawing is a perfect example of the freer vein in Fragonard's oeuvre.

243

117 The Awakening

Bister wash on paper, over an underdrawing in black chalk, 24 x 36.8 cm.
Signed (?) at the lower right, below the niche (kennel), in a different color ink: *frago*.
At the lower left is a blue star (possibly a collector's mark).

National Gallery of Art, Washington, D.C., Samuel H. Kress Collection, 1963.15.10

Figure 1. Fragonard. *Le Coucher des ouvrières*. Art market, New York

Figure 2. François-Nicolas-Barthélemy Dequevauviller, after Nicolas Lavreince. *Le Lever des ouvrières en modes*. Bibliothèque Nationale, Paris, Cabinet des Estampes

Figure 3. Nicolas Lavreince. *Le Lever des ouvrières en modes*. Musée des Arts Décoratifs, Paris

Provenance

Adrien Fauchier-Magnan: sold, Sotheby's, London, December 4, 1935, no. 13, ill. (for 440 pounds); [Richard Owen, Paris]; Samuel H. Kress, from 1936; gift to the National Gallery of Art, 1963.

Eunice Williams (1978) suggested that this drawing could be identified with no. 213 in the Walferdin sale (April 12–16, 1880): "le lever des ouvrières en modes. Première pensée très supérieure à la composition gravée." She observed that there were no engravings after the Washington drawing, but that its composition was close to that of

the drawing in the Louvre *Ma Chemise brûle* (cat. no. 118), of which a mediocre engraving exists. This hypothesis is very intriguing.

The Goncourts (G. p. 330), however, who had seen the Walferdin drawing, compared it to one described in the catalogue of the de Ghendt sale (1779), in which "*sept* [not four] fillettes sont occupées à leur toilette," and Portalis mentions the Walferdin drawing twice. In 1880 (p. 27), he notes that, "le lever des ouvrières, dans son aimable abandon, rappelle avec plus de gaieté et d'esprit la composition bien connue de Lavreince"; then, in 1889 (p. 297), he gives it the title

"Le coucher des ouvrières" in the catalogue. More importantly, he mentions the name of its new owner, Camille Groult, and reproduces it (between pp. 200 and 201); the drawing remained in the Groult collection until very recently (see figure 1).

Exhibitions

Washington, D.C., 1978, no. 25, ill.

Bibliography

R. p. 198
A. 87, fig. 339
Eisler, 1977, p. 337, no. dK 451, ill.

Since 1935, this drawing has been known by three different titles: "*Ma Chemise brûle*," *Le Coucher,* and, more prudently, *La Chambre à coucher.* The first title is more understandable in connection with the drawing discussed in the next entry, which is very similar in composition—but it is not justified. The second title is no more convincing: the girl in the foreground, leaning forward and showing her breasts, appears to be dressing. The comparison with Nicolas Lavreince's famous gouache *Le Lever des ouvrières en modes* seems to be perfectly conclusive (figures 2, 3; this 1783 work belongs to the Institut Tessin, Paris).

The scene, indeed, takes place in a lovely bedchamber—but what are the young women up to? And what has the visitor, greeted by a yelping dog, come to announce? Fragonard has described with great vivacity and without any pretension a scene from everyday life.

Did the artist himself inscribe his name on the dog's kennel? This touch of humor on Fragonard's part would not be at all surprising.

118   "Ma Chemise brûle"

Bister wash on paper, over an underdrawing in black chalk, 24.6 x 37.2 cm.

Musée du Louvre, Paris, Cabinet des Dessins, R. F. 4059

Provenance

[Chabot and the Duc de la Mure (or Desmarets)]: sold, December 17–22, 1787, no. 160: "l'intérieur d'une Chambre à coucher où l'on voit quatre jeunes femmes agréablement ajustées, dont une est encore dans son lit" (for 68 *livres* 19 *sols,* to Constantin); Jean Marc (also called John Dupan), Geneva: sold, March 26–28, 1840, no. 1392 (the stamp of this collection, Lugt 1440, is at the lower left); Marquis de Chennevières-Pointel (1820–1899): "acheté en 1862 d'un restaurateur de curiosités, demeurant dans la Cité, près Notre-Dame de Paris" (Chennevières, 1897, p. 176; his stamp, Lugt 2073, is at the lower left): sold, May 5–6, 1898, no. 50, ill. (for 16,500 francs, to Lunel, for Camondo); Comte Isaac de Camondo; gift to the Louvre, 1911 (the Louvre's stamp, Lugt 1886, is at the lower right).

Exhibitions

Paris, 1921, no. 160
Copenhagen, 1935, no. 363
Paris, 1946, no. 373
Vienna, 1950, no. 118

Bibliography

G. pp. 274, 329
P. p. 307
Chennevières, 1897, p. 175 (Prat, p. 204)
Martine, 1927, no. 11, ill.
Lavallée, 1938, no. 10, ill.
R. pp. 198, 254, fig. 128
A. 86, fig. 338

Related works

Augustin-Claude-Simon Legrand, also called Legrand-Furcy (1766–1815), made an engraving of this drawing—or, rather, a noticeably different version of this work—in 1788 (*Gazette de France,* Tuesday, December 23, 1788, p. 456; Sjöberg and Gardey, XIII, 1974, p. 568, no. 37). The engraving was dedicated to "Mlle/Amable/Irene/Des F/S/ et H...." See figure 1 for a first state (Hérold, 1935, p. 399, no. 1085, in catalogue four).

A. (171, fig. 345) curiously compares this drawing with one representing a "Jeune fille nue s'enfuyant," which is, in fact, closer to *La Fuite à dessein* (W. 308, fig. 59).

Figure 1. Augustin-Claude-Simon Legrand. "*Ma chemise brûle.*" Musée du Louvre, Paris, Cabinet des Dessins, Rothschild Collection

118

This drawing is very close in composition and in certain details to the *Awakening* in Washington (see cat. no. 117): the birdcage hanging from the ceiling, the pier glass above the fireplace, the bed, the half-opened door at the right, the delectable figures, and the composition are all the same . . . but here a different episode unfolds.

While a young girl in a large canopied bed parts the bed-curtains, her companion, whose nightshirt is on fire,

hastily grabs a jug of water to extinguish the flames. On the floor is the cause of the incident—a portable heater. "This charming composition has been treated with all of the spirit and all of the charm that this skillful and pleasing Artist puts into his productions."

Fragonard liked scenes in which a young girl, running, fleeing, or crying out in mock terror, in her fright and her haste inadvertently reveals one of her breasts.

119   S'il m'était aussi fidèle!

Bister wash on paper, over an underdrawing in black chalk, 24.8 x 38.3 cm.

The J. Paul Getty Museum, Malibu, Inv. 82 GB 165

Provenance
Comte Jacques de Bryas: sold, Paris, April 4–6, 1898, no. 58 (for 1,705 francs); Pierre Decourcelle, 1907: sold, May 29–30, 1911, no. 87, ill. (acquired by Danlos); James Edmond de Rothschild (1845–1934); Mme Albert-Max de Goldschmidt-Rothschild (1879–1941): sold, Basel, January 24, 1970, no. 28, ill.; acquired by the Getty museum, 1982.

Exhibitions
Paris, 1907, no. 169
Washington, D.C., 1978, no. 27, ill. (extensive discussion of the provenance)
Tokyo, 1980, no. 122, ill.

Bibliography
D. and V. 158, ill.

R. p. 198
A. 636, fig. 198
Cailleux, 1962, p. iii, fig. 3
Sutton, 1980; 1987, p. 112
Launay, 1983–84, under no. 8108

Related works
There is a second version of this drawing in the Musée "Ile de France" in Saint-Jean-Cap Ferrat (Fondation Ephrussi de Rothschild) (figure 1; A. 637; catalogue 1969, ill. p. 35), which is supposed to have been in the Goncourt collection, and which bears the stamp of François Renaud, Lugt 1042, at the lower *left*. We believe that this drawing is a fake—rather than a copy by Saint-Non. It was probably substituted for the original at some unknown date, but, in our opinion, after 1931.

See also A. 638 (a drawing that we have not seen), and a copy in Orléans (Inv. no. 7294).

An engraving of this drawing "en bistre" was made by the Abbé de Saint-Non in 1776 (figure 2). Guimbaud (1928, p. 201, no. 72) points out that this aquatint is "rare." We have not come across it, but its existence cannot be questioned: Portalis also mentions it (pp. 313, 331, no. 157) and reproduces it (p. 228).

Antoine-François Dennel made an engraving of a vertical version of this drawing, entitled "*S'il m'étoit aussi fidel* [*sic*]." His engraving is dedicated to "Madame Yon de St Pierre" (Roux, 1949, VI, p. 509, no. 12). See figure 3 for the state before the inscription was added.

119

The subject of this picture is obvious: a young girl *en déshabillé* kneels on her unmade bed, looking sadly at her little dog; the title of the engraving (see *Related works,* and figure 3) explains the reason for her chagrin. Like a repentant Magdalene, the forsaken young girl is absorbed in her reverie (Fragonard must surely have taken his inspiration from famous compositions by Titian or by Rubens, for example, and, in a dubious display of humor, replaced the

skull with a puppy!). A bed that is much too big, a mirror, and a shelf occupy the otherwise bare room.

As this drawing must have been made before 1776, the date of the aquatint by Saint-Non, and doubtless before the second trip to Italy in 1773, it probably is from about 1770. Fragonard skillfully combined black chalk and a bister wash. The quality of the work lies in the simplicity of the composition, which unfolds like a frieze.

Figure 1. After Fragonard. *S'il m'était aussi fidèle!* Musée "Ile de France," Saint-Jean-Cap Ferrat, Fondation Ephrussi de Rothschild

Figure 2. Abbé de Saint-Non, after Fragonard. *S'il m'était aussi fidèle!* Whereabouts unknown (according to Portalis)

Figure 3. Antoine-François Dennel, after Fragonard. *"S'il m'étoit aussi fidel!"* Musée du Louvre, Paris, Cabinet des Dessins, Rothschild Collection

120 The Aggressor Is Punished

Bister wash on paper, over an underdrawing in black chalk, 25 x 38.4 cm.

Museum Boymans-van Beuningen, Rotterdam, F-I-102

Provenance
Baron Roger: sold, December 23–24, 1841, part of no. 112; Émile Norblin: sold, March 16–17, 1860, no. 55 (for 185 francs, to Marmontel); Marmontel: sold, May 11–14, 1868, no. 234: "scène d'ivresse" (for 400 francs); Gustave Mühlbacher: sold, May 15–18, 1899, no. 122; Marquis de Biron: sold, June 9–11, 1914, no. 19, ill. (for 29,500 francs); [N. Beets]; acquired by Franz Koenigs (Lugt 1023 a), 1927; given to the Rotterdam museum by C. D. van Beuningen, 1940.

Exhibitions
Paris, 1952, no. 92
Washington, D.C., . . . , 1952–53, no. 85, pl. 27
Bern, 1954, no. 135
Rotterdam, 1957, no. 64, ill.
London, 1968, no. 277 (with a complete list of exhibitions in which this drawing was included)
Amsterdam, 1974, no. 46, ill.

Bibliography
G. p. 335
P. pp. 306, 312, 313
Boucher and Jaccottet, 1952, pl. 88
Fosca, 1954, pp. 59–60, no. 23, ill.
R. p. 197
A. 671, fig. 199

Related works
There is a copy in a New York private collection.

This drawing has been known by various titles since the nineteenth century—among them, "les suites de l'orgie," "la débauche," "scène d'ivresse," "une fête galante"—which attests to the perplexity of the specialists. Yet, the subject is not very difficult to interpret: a bold young man tumbles a young girl who, in falling, grabs onto his hair. A young woman tries to hold back the aggressor, while the other banqueters look on with glee; at the left, a couple is embracing; under a stool, a large dog chews on a bone.

The scene is certainly a lively one. Fragonard did nothing to hide the disarray of the young woman's dress, but the tone is one of humor, more than of ribaldry, for it is the young rake's painful surprise at having his hair pulled that causes the banqueters much amusement. Fragonard put equal stress on the young man's audacious assault and on his involuntary punishment.

The Rotterdam drawing is devoid of vulgarity, and, rather, recalls the Flemish kermesses and tavern scenes painted by such artists as Teniers, van Ostade, and Steen, as well as Rubens, who was admired by Fragonard and his contemporaries, alike. Fragonard gave to each of the participants just the right gesture and expression. He captured the animation of the scene, depicting the rapid activity with an equal rapidity of execution.

Like Roland Michel (Cailleux exhibition catalogue, Paris, 1983, under no. 26), we would date this drawing to about 1765, or slightly later.

121   Mercury and Argus

Oil on canvas, 59 x 73 cm.

Musée du Louvre, Paris, R. F. 1981-17

Provenance
Hippolyte Walferdin (1795–1880): sold
posthumously, Paris, April 12–16, 1880,
no. 47 (for 700 francs, to Lazard); anonymous sale, Paris, Hôtel Drouot, March 25,
1981, no. B in the catalogue: "école française

du XVIIIe siècle . . . Le Berger endormi"
(acquired by the Louvre).

Exhibitions
Paris, 1983, pp. 49–50
Lille, 1985, no. 53, ill., pp. 13, 15–16

Bibliography
G. p. 325
P. p. 283
N. p. 162
R. p. 186
C. Brown, 1986, p. 799, fig. 19

This painting, which, like so many of the Louvre's finest
Fragonards, belonged to Hippolyte Walferdin, was lost sight
of between his death in 1880 and its acquisition by the
Louvre in 1981. Its story concerns Argus, who was given the
task by Juno of watching over the nymph Io, who had been
transformed into a cow by Jupiter. Here, Mercury, disguised
as a shepherd, has just put Argus to sleep with the sound of
his flute, and prepares to kill him and to steal his flock.

Fragonard faithfully copied a signed picture by Carel
Fabritius (1622–1654; see figure 1; Brown, 1986;
Duparc, 1986). Recently sold in Monte Carlo (June 22,
1985, no. 147, colorpl.), the painting is today on the art

Figure 1. Carel Fabritius. *Mercury and Argus.*
Richard L. Feigen & Company, New York

market in New York. Could it be the same as the "Argus endormi par Mercure," attributed to a certain "Rimbrandt Vanrin," which was sold in Paris June 19, 1764, no. 20, the difference in dimensions notwithstanding (113.8 x 97.2 cm., instead of 104 x 73.5)? The former dimensions could have included the frame ("avec bordure"), and may have been inverted. This would be all the more interesting because the signature of Fabritius was only discovered after a recent restoration.

Be that as it may, Fragonard copied both faithfully and freely the work of his Dutch predecessor (who died an untimely death in the explosion of the Delft arsenal). Fabritius's work was very vigorously executed, and must surely have appealed to Fragonard. As usual, he eliminated the extraneous details, simplified the forms, and accentuated the warm and reddish tones, but he did not noticeably alter the composition or the color scheme. Fragonard applied the paint with broad, thick, and violent strokes: his brushwork is rapid and flowing, and as brutal as the figure of Mercury leaning over his victim to see if he is asleep, so that he can commit the crime. Fragonard copied (but he did not imitate), in the same way that Delacroix copied Rubens: as much to learn as to show what he himself was capable of doing.

The picture is worked in such a way that the bluish ground of the canvas may be seen.

As for the date of the copy: the original by Fabritius seems to have been sold in Paris in 1764—at which time Fragonard could have copied it, for the sale was organized by his friend, Le Brun. In any event, this *Mercury and Argus* anticipates Fragonard's *figures de fantaisie*.

122   The Return of the Soldier (?)

Oil on canvas, 74.5 x 99.5 cm.

Private collection, Paris

Provenance
Trouard ("contrôleur des bâtiments du roi"): sold, February 22, 1779, no. 80: "sur la droite un homme, une jeune femme et un enfant assis devant un feu; à gauche est un vieillard endormi"; anonymous sale, Paris, June 9, 1903 (only item in the sale), ill. (for 43,000 francs); Jacques Doucet: sold, June 6, 1912, no. 147, ill. (for 125,000 francs, to E. M. Hodgkins); Eduardo Guinle, Rio de Janeiro; Arthur Weisweiller: sold, Paris, May 25, 1976, no. 35, colorpl. (for 2,300,000 francs); private collection, Paris: sold, Monte Carlo, November 11, 1984, no. 8, colorpl. ("succession d'un grand amateur" [Rossignol]: unsold at 8,500,000 francs).

Exhibitions
Paris, 1921, no. 44
Paris, 1934, no. 148
Paris, 1937, no. 161

Bibliography
G. p. 333
N. p. 133
R. pp. 151–52
W. 358, pl. 71, p. 25 (French edition)
W. and M. 378, ill.

Related works
For the drawings, see the following entry.

This painting is famous for having belonged to a great architect, Louis-François Trouard, to a great couturier, Jacques Doucet, and to a great collector, Arthur Weisweiller. Yet, it remains a very curious and, in certain respects, a mysterious work.

Wisely, the eighteenth-century expert Paillet did not give the picture a title, but referred to it as "a fervently done sketch, with a strong effect." When the painting resurfaced in 1903, Marius Paulme wove a tale around the episode depicted, which he titled "Souviens-toi"! The young couple, reunited next to the fire, are evoking their recent loves. At the Doucet sale in 1912, Marcel Nicolle, doubtless influenced by the title by which the drawing in the Walferdin collection was known, from 1880 on (see the following entry), decided to call the painting *The Beggar's Dream,* and this title has remained ever since.

As is so often true of Fragonard's work, the subject of this nocturnal scene is puzzling: At the left, a bearded old man wearing a cap leans on a stone post as he sleeps by a fire, while, at the right, a young woman seated on a bundle of cloth warms herself and the blond baby on her knees, who stretches out his bare feet toward the fire. A young man with a plumed hat and a sword has arrived. With his left hand, he tenderly holds the young woman around the neck, as she makes a sign to him to keep quiet so as not to wake the old man. Fragonard may simply have wished to represent the nighttime return of a soldier to his humble home.

The scene, in a rundown peasant interior, is as much an out-of-doors as an indoor one. A few tiles, a kettle suspended over a glowing log, a column with—for some reason —a basket placed upon it, and the dog fascinated by the embers all underscore the poverty of the surroundings.

The most appealing features of this painting are the brushwork and the color. The rough and forceful execution, and the broken, nervous, and very visible brushstrokes, enabled Fragonard to convey gesture, pose, and movement with great economy. As for the color, rarely has Fragonard so successfully rendered the white of a sleeve, the obscurity of a smoky night sky, the coal black of a cauldron, the mossy green of stone, the turquoise blue and the cinnabar red of the plumed hat, and a whole range of yellows, from buttercup to saffron.

The date of the picture remains problematical: the briskness of the brushwork recalls that of the paintings from Fragonard's first Italian sojourn, the reddish coloring is like that of the *Mercury and Argus,* and the broad strokes anticipate the technique of the *figures de fantaisie,* which were done shortly afterward.

251

123   The Beggar's Dream (or The Old Man Asleep)

Black chalk on paper, over an underdrawing in black chalk, 33.5 x 50.5 cm.
Inscribed at an angle, at the lower left: *frago*

Private collection, Paris

Provenance
Vassal de Saint-Hubert: sold, March 29, 1779, no. 178 (for 421 *livres*); anonymous sale, July 8, 1793, no. 67: "un beau dessin lavé au bistre représentant un intérieur de cuisine dans laquelle des femmes et des enfants sont autour du feu; aussi un vieillard endormi"; anonymous sale, April 9–10, 1827, no. 101: "un des dessins les plus capitaux de cet artiste"; anonymous sales, May 6–7, 1859, no. 64, and February 2, 1860, no. 48 ("signé Frago"); Hippolyte Walferdin, by 1860: sold posthumously, April 12–16, 1880, no. 202 (for 1,025 francs, to Fournier, according to P.); Mme Ernesta Stern; Jacques Doucet: sold, June 5, 1912, no. 20, ill.; Maurice de Rothschild, Sigismond Bardac, and then Adrien Fauchier-Magnan, Paris: sold, Sotheby's, London, December 4, 1935, no. 11, ill.; M. de L.: sold, Paris, June 22, 1938, no. 4, pl. 1; [Wildenstein]; sold, Paris, March 30, 1981, no. 6, colorpl.; Monte Carlo, November 11,

1984, no. 3 (not sold; private collection, Paris).

Exhibitions
Paris, 1860, no. 11

Bibliography
G. pp. 242, 336
P. p. 313
N. p. 49, ill.
R. p. 195
A. 75, fig. 683

Related works
In the Cabinet des Dessins at the Louvre there is a small-format version of this drawing (figure 1), dated 1786 at the lower left (R. F. 6759; A. 76), whose attribution to Fragonard has been rightly rejected by Ananoff (see also A. 1186). The drawing in the Adolphe Thibaudeau collection, sold, April 20–25, 1857, no. 726, measured 29 x 35 centimeters.

Figure 1. After Fragonard. *The Beggar's Dream*. 1786. Musée du Louvre, Paris, Cabinet des Dessins

The relationship between this work and *The Return of the Soldier* (cat. no. 122) is tenuous: the only common feature is the old man asleep at the left in each. The old man in the drawing, it should be noted, has bare feet and arms, and seems to be reclining more. We have chosen not to adopt the painting's traditional title, *The Beggar's Dream*, but accept it for the drawing—in which a sleepy old man, accompanied by his dog, warms himself by a fire. He dreams of the food that will bring him comfort. In the vaulted kitchen, "a flurry of young fairies" (G.) busy themselves with various tasks.

The drawing doubtless postdates the painting; both works are mentioned for the first time in 1779 in the catalogues of two famous sales that were both rich in "admirable" works by Fragonard. In our opinion, it can be dated to about 1772–73.

124   The Cradle

Oil on canvas, 46 x 55 cm.

Musée de Picardie, Amiens

Provenance
Sometimes identified (groundlessly) with a painting in a July 8, 1793, sale (no. 15); presumed to have been in the Dubois sale, 1860, but the catalogue has not come to light. Ernest and Olympe Lavalard, Roye, by 1862; bequeathed to the Amiens museum, and entered the collections, 1894.

Exhibitions
Paris, 1883–84, no. 52
Paris, 1921, no. 67
Paris, 1931, no. 16
Besançon, 1956, no. 21
Bordeaux, 1956, no. 77
Brussels, 1975, no. 106, pl. p. 148
Tokyo, 1980, no. 72, colorpl.
Lille, 1985, no. 52, ill.

Bibliography
Horsin-Déon, 1862, p. 144
P. p. 272 (?)
N. p. 128
Brière, 1931, p. 199
Réau, 1932, p. 102
R. pp. 164–66
W. 457, pl. 100
Thuillier, 1967, p. 69, colorpl.
W. and M. 481, ill., colorplates LVII–LVIII
Cayeux, 1975, p. 299, n. 64

Figure 1. Rembrandt.
The Holy Family.
The Hermitage, Leningrad

Throughout his career, Fragonard enjoyed painting cradles. He copied them from the work of Rembrandt, and there is a cradle in one of his first paintings, *The Rest on the Flight into Egypt* (cat. no. 10). They also figure importantly in the *Retour au logis* and in the *Visite à la nourrice*; while there are many versions of both compositions, none is included here (however, see cat. no. 211). There is one in *Le Premier Pas de l'enfance* (cat. no. 303), which was probably painted by Marguerite Gérard. The rustic cradle in the present work owes much to the famous *Holy Family* by Rembrandt (figure 1; now in The Hermitage), which was in the Crozat collection in the eighteenth century and which Fragonard very likely copied before 1770.

When did Fragonard paint the present picture? In its vigorous execution, brisk and fluid brushwork, and impasto it recalls the works that he executed after his return from Italy, at a time when the effects of chiaroscuro prevailed in his work. Yet, the picture is not far from the *figures de fantaisie,* or, at any rate, from *The Return of the Soldier* (cat. no. 122). The light, which enters from the left, illuminates the oval of a face, a white coif, the cheek and the bare arms of the sleeping child, as well as the fat rusty colored cat observing the scene. The touches of red and yellow stand out amidst the shadows in the room. All those present—boys, girls, a young mother, and an older sister—contemplate the newborn child with astonished admiration.

In spite of the example of Rembrandt, there is nothing sacred about Fragonard's family scene, which was not a very common subject in French painting of the eighteenth century. However, he rendered his subject with great sensitivity and an evident joy.

To quote the critic Horsin-Déon (1862), one of the least well known of Fragonard's nineteenth-century "rediscoverers": "Fragonard endowed this painting with all of the poetic qualities that characterize his best works. There is nothing more heartwarming than the sight of these envious little girls contemplating the lovely infant sleeping calmly despite the agitation all around him...."

The Figures de fantaisie

We are very fortunate in having been able to assemble for the exhibition accompanying this catalogue *all* the known *figures de fantaisie* ("imaginary portraits") by Fragonard. This series of paintings, undoubtedly among the finest in all of eighteenth-century art, is also one of the most mysterious. For whom were these exceptional works painted? When? And whom or what do they represent?

Under the category of *figures de fantaisie,* we have grouped a certain number of works of identical dimensions (80 x 65 centimeters), representing richly costumed half-length figures of men and women, seen behind stone balustrades. The ruffs, high stiff collars, large white collars, gold chains, plumed hats, swords, and gauntlets that they wear are typical accessories that help to identify the paintings in the series. The scale of the figures in relation to the pictorial space is always the same. Fifteen works correspond to this description—there must have been many more—six of them representing men and nine, women. The *Portrait of Jérôme de Lalande* in the Musée du Petit Palais (cat. no. 126) should be counted among the *figures de fantaisie,* although it is distinctly smaller in format. The splendid *Cavalier Seated by a Fountain* (cat. no. 129), also called *Portrait of the Abbé de Saint-Non* (now in Barcelona)—which is larger in format and completely different in composition—was mentioned in sales catalogues in 1777 and in 1779, and has been associated with this series ever since it was rediscovered after World War II. (It seemed to us ill-advised not to include it, especially since we relate it chronologically to the *figures de fantaisie,* but it cannot be classified among them.)

There was no mention of the *figures de fantaisie* in the eighteenth century; no allusions in the literature, no archival document enabling us to determine their original provenances. Of course, a few are mentioned in eighteenth-century sales catalogues, but they are the least characteristic works. An example is the *Liseuse* (cat. no. 136), now in Washington, which was sold with the Comte du Barry's collection in 1776 (confirmed by a sketch by Saint-Aubin)—but can it really be considered a *figure de fantaisie?* The same is true of the *Portrait of a Man,* in Chicago (cat. no. 128), from the Mauperin sale of 1780.

The absence of any information on the precise origins of these works has naturally given rise to much conjecture, which falls into two categories. Were the paintings part of a single series (see W. pp. 16–17)? If not, how are they to be divided up and grouped? For whom was the series painted? There have been many hypotheses, few of which are very convincing. Although it is generally agreed that the two portraits until recently in the Harcourt collection (cat. nos. 140, 141) were painted for the sitters (in the respective

entries we will discuss the supporting evidence), two names keep coming up—again, groundlessly: those of the Abbé de Saint-Non and Jacques-Onésyme Bergeret de Grancourt. One thing is certain: at their deaths in 1791 and 1785, respectively, neither owned any *figures de fantaisie.* Fragonard's relations with Bergeret were not always good, and there is no indication that Bergeret commissioned the series or even part of it. As for Saint-Non, it is true that at the time of his death he owned "five pictures in pastel representing different *têtes de fantaisie* after Boucher, Fragonard, and Greuze; two other busts in pastel, one representing a woman writing, the other a woman reading a letter; two other busts, also in pastel, a portrait of a man in Spanish costume" (this is the first encounter with the term "à l'espagnole," which we will discuss subsequently), "and an old man" (according to the posthumous inventory of the collection of the Abbé de Saint-Non, study by Maître Giard, XVIII, 899; see also G. Wildenstein, 1959, p. 239, nos. 21–29). While it is possible that some of these pastels were copies—very likely executed by Saint-Non—of certain *figures de fantaisie,* nothing indicates that he owned any himself. It has been suggested (Vilain, Sydney exhibition catalogue, 1980–81) that Saint-Non may have given the *figures de fantaisie* back to Fragonard when "the productions of this Artist suddenly began fetching extraordinary prices" (Brizard, 1792), but this cannot have been the case. As we have already noted, this "particular event" occurred very precisely in 1765, at which date the *figures de fantaisie* had not yet been painted.

Our own hypothesis is, admittedly, a delicate one, but nevertheless merits discussion. From 1765 on, Fragonard lived and worked at the Louvre, where he welcomed many visitors (for example, in 1782, the Comte du Nord, the future Emperor Paul I of Russia). We also know from Fragonard's grandson Théophile (1847) that "he received many distinguished foreigners, who had not seen everything if they had not seen the gallery of paintings that Honoré had made for himself.... This gallery of paintings *entirely by his own hand* [our emphasis] was acquired from him by the Duc de Luynes, who payed him a considerable sum of gold, those were the conditions for the deal." The duke in question was probably Louis-Joseph (1748–1807), and the sale must have taken place shortly before the Revolution. In his residence at Dampierre, the Duc de Luynes kept one of the most famous contemporary portraits "à l'espagnole," that of the Comtesse d'Egmont, painted by Alexander Roslin in 1763 (figure 1).

Théophile's text was written before the reappearance of the *figures de fantaisie* in the nineteenth century (see also Blanc, 1862, p. 12, whose biography of

Fragonard precedes this date, and who obtained his information from the same source; Launay, 1859, n.p.; Renouvier, 1863, p. 168, whose text was also written well before this date; and the entry on Fragonard in the Louvre catalogue by Frédéric Villot, 1855, p. 127). La Caze lent two *figures de fantaisie* to the famous exhibition in 1860, where they caused a sensation; François Marcille *père*, Barroilhet, and Cypierre owned examples that were sold in 1857, 1856, and 1845, respectively, but in the midst of general indifference toward the artist.

We do not know today how many pictures were in this "gallery," but it is not unlikely that Fragonard painted the likenesses of his visiting friends and patrons "in one hour's time," in order to decorate his apartment with their portraits (see cat. nos. 132, 134, 138). Moreover, long familiarity with Théophile Fragonard's letters, and with the texts based directly on his reminiscences, has proven that his information is most often trustworthy.

As for the dating of the *figures de fantaisie*: while two are signed (cat. nos. 132, 133), only one (cat. no. 132) bears a date—1769, the year of Fragonard's marriage. This same date also appears on two old labels on the backs of two of the paintings, and is the date generally assigned to the series as a whole. Two of the original *figures* (cat. nos. 133, 138), which were copied by the Comte de Brehan in pastel in 1773, are thus earlier in date; the *Liseuse* (cat. no. 136) was sold in 1776; and two years later, the Swedish miniaturist Hall mentioned that he owned "a head, after myself, from the time when he [Frago-

nard] painted portraits in a single sitting for one *louis* [which Hall estimated at 36 *livres*]" (Villot, 1867, p. 74; see figure 2).

Fragonard may have painted some of his finest *figures de fantaisie* in 1769, but the creation of his gallery undoubtedly must have taken several years —perhaps beginning with his move to the Louvre in 1765, and ending shortly before his second trip to Italy in 1773.

Fragonard did not necessarily paint the seventeen works included here for his gallery, and he must have painted others that have since been lost; the Williamstown picture (cat. no. 135) was unknown before 1964! Some of the works, as we have already said, were sold between 1776 and 1780. We have tried to date each, individually, realizing, of course, the tentativeness of our proposals.

Whom do they represent? What do they represent? Once again, no answer is provided by eighteenth-century documents. Are they portraits, character studies, or personifications of professions?

Saint-Non and his brother La Bretèche are identified from the old labels mentioned above. The present Duc d'Harcourt recognizes his ancestors in the two paintings that were formerly in his collection. Although refuted by Maurice Tourneux, the leading Diderot specialist, the identification of Diderot's portrait by Fragonard is now universally accepted; curiously enough, however, the expansive Diderot himself made no mention in his writings of this portrait. After much hesitation, the paintings in the Musée du Petit Palais and in the Louvre (cat. nos.

Figure 1. Alexander Roslin. *Portrait of the Comtesse d'Egmont in a Spanish Costume.* 1763. Musée du Château de Versailles

Figure 2. Peter Adolf Hall. *Self-Portrait.* Nationalmuseum, Stockholm

126, 125) are now recognized as portraits of the astronomer Lalande and of the dancer Mlle Guimard. Other, more or less recent, identifications have proved less certain—which is not surprising, considering the lack of comparative material—but it seems clear that Fragonard, *in his own way*, wanted to be a portraitist.

He was not trained as a portraitist, however, and he never really aimed at capturing a likeness, or tried to depict in detail the features of a face (even if he did make more effort with women than with men, although often with less success), nor did he try to reveal the psychology of the sitter. Fragonard was a portraitist after his own fashion; but was he also concerned with representing the *position,* and the profession of his sitters? Certain attributes relate to the occupations of writer, singer, and soldier, while, in other cases, the subject matter is more abstract: inspiration, or music. However, we do not think that there was a precisely considered program involved; this would have been contrary to the very nature of Fragonard's genius and to his concept of art. The *figures de fantaisie* are, thus, neither portraits—as defined in the eighteenth century—nor studied and deliberate representations of the liberal arts or of the Muses, and, therefore, they elude all attempts at classification.

We have already mentioned that, in the eighteenth century, Fragonard's *figures de fantaisie* met with virtual silence, but we do know that although his free brushwork and "rapid-fire" execution were admired, these works were considered only *sketches* ("esquisses"), and not finished efforts. The term *esquisse,* often used in the nineteenth century, did not yet have the favorable associations that it has gained since the days of the Impressionists. It was used particularly in connection with the sitters' costumes, the only thing "Spanish" about them being their name. The term *espagnol* is used in the sales catalogues of the Varanchan (1777), Dulac (1778), and Mauperin (1780) collections, and when, in 1791, Le Brun described a certain drawing in his collection (cat. no. 266; now in Chicago), he pointed out with a hint of humor that the young people were "dressed in picturesque costume that was somewhat Spanish."

We will not discuss the history of this fashion here —it has recently been studied in detail by François Pupil (1985)—but it must be said that the vogue for Spanish costumes was an old one in France, revived by one of Fragonard's masters, Carle Vanloo, in the *Concert espagnol* (figure 3; signed and dated 1754, and exhibited at the Salon of 1755) and the *Lecture espagnole* (figure 4; shown at the Salon of 1761); the two paintings, commissioned by Mme Geoffrin, have been in Russia since 1772. Finally, in 1769—significantly enough—Louis-Michel Vanloo, Carle's nephew, and the author of a more recognizable portrait of Diderot (seen at the Salon of 1767), exhibited as a pendant to his *Allemande jouant de la harpe* an *Espagnole jouant de la guitare* (see figure 5; see also figure 6). Fragonard's paintings are definitely quite different from these works, but there is no doubt that he wanted to rival these artists—*without in the least imitating them.*

Of all the old masters, the work of Rubens, in particular, influenced Fragonard; it was from the Flemish painter that he borrowed the high, stiff collars à la

Figure 3. Carle Vanloo. *Le Concert espagnol.*
The Hermitage, Leningrad

Figure 4. Carle Vanloo. *La Lecture espagnole.*
The Hermitage, Leningrad

Maria de' Medici (Fragonard, it should be recalled, made copies in the Galerie du Luxembourg in 1769), and, as Charles Sterling so brilliantly demonstrated in 1964, the Venetians Tintoretto and also Domenico Feti (see cat. no. 127).

Regarding the term "portrait de fantaisie" (see also cat. no. 140), the *Encyclopédie,* as Mary D. Sheriff recently pointed out in an excellent article, gives the following definition: "a painter makes a *portrait de fantaisie* when it is not from life." The "tête de fantaisie, peinte en miniature," of Mme Fragonard (sold, June 3, 1793, no. 109), certainly must have corresponded to this definition. Fragonard probably painted—off on his own—what he remembered of an image (which would explain certain "errors," such as the color of Diderot's eyes; see cat. no. 127). It would not be surprising if Fragonard, like Watteau, kept a stock of theatrical costumes in his studio. Yet, most

impressive of all are still the fury of his execution, the blaze of color. Fragonard ruthlessly dominated his models with his brush (and his imagination), but it was to make them come alive before our eyes—to make them move, if only for an instant.

Some, like Jacques Thuillier (1967), have reflected on the limits of this art: "The brush races along: its play is what really counts, its very speed becomes an end in itself.... Speed, no matter how great its virtuosity, oftentimes leaves only hollow outlines ... the hand sets down with confidence...." This, however, misses the point: Fragonard never let himself be dominated by the model; on the contrary, the model served only as the pretext for the painting. This was a very modern attitude, but it was not until the end of the nineteenth century that it became the essential in a work of art, understood and practiced by all.

Figure 5. Gabriel de Saint-Aubin, after Louis-Michel Vanloo. *Espagnole jouant de la guitare.* Detail of a page from the catalogue of the Salon of 1769. Bibliothèque Nationale, Paris, Cabinet des Estampes

Figure 6. Louis-Michel Vanloo. *Le Concert.* 1768. The Hermitage, Leningrad

125 Portrait of Mlle Guimard

Oil on canvas, 81.5 x 65 cm.

Musée du Louvre, Paris, R. F. 1974.1

Provenance
François Marcille (1790–1856): sold post-humously, January 12–13, 1857, no. 64: "portrait d'une actrice" [no dimensions given] (?); Hippolyte Walferdin (1795–1880), by 1860 (see Godard): sold, April 12–16, 1880, no. 35 (for 9,100 francs, to Fichel); Mme Watel, by 1885; Watel-Dehaynin, Paris; entered the Louvre, 1974.

Exhibitions
Paris, 1885, no. 81
Paris, 1974, no. 13, ill.
Paris, 1974–75, no. 106
Toledo-Chicago-Ottawa, 1975–76, no. 38, ill., colorpl. XIII
Paris, 1978, no. 5, colorpl.
Bordeaux, 1980–81, no. 19, colorpl. p. 23
Paris, 1980–81, no. 51, colorpl.

Bibliography
Godard, 1860, p. 297
G. p. 322
Portalis, 1880, pp. 18–19
P. pp. 92–93, 134, 278, ill. between pp. 84 and 85
E. Goncourt, 1893, pp. 310–11
N. p. 111, pl. between pp. 110 and 111
R. p. 178
W. 342, colorpl. facing pl. 66 and p. 22 (French edition)
Sterling, 1964, n.p., fig. 10
W. and M. 362, ill.
Gazette des Beaux-Arts, La Chronique des Arts, 1974, p. 7, fig. 2
Rosenberg and Compin, 1974, pp. 188–91, colorpl. p. 189
Sheriff, 1987, p. 85, fig. 6

Related works
The iconography of the portrait of "la Guimard" is as voluminous as it is dubious. See the monograph by Goncourt, 1893; Rosenberg and Compin, 1974, p. 188, n. 21.
    There was a *Portrait de Mlle Guimard* in the Barroilhet collection sale, March 10, 1856, no. 28.

This justly famous work is the best preserved, although not the most characteristic, of the *figures de fantaisie.* The below-waist-length portrait of the dancer was painted not with broad, visible brushstrokes that blocked in the forms, but with a more careful technique that rendered detail, like that of the *Old Man,* in Nice (cat. no. 99), which must date from about the same time.

Is the subject really Mlle Guimard (1743–1816)? Since Godard (1860), most specialists informed about Fragonard (and about the dancer) agree on this point. Sterling (1964), however, sees the figure as a painter of miniatures, who is holding in her right hand "a paint-stained rag, placed next to two shells containing colors, like those used by miniaturists." While it is true that the objects on the stone parapet are very difficult to decipher (the Goncourts identified them as crumpled letters, and a medallion; more recently, it has been suggested that they are part of the artist's makeup kit!), the identity of the dancer cannot be doubted. One might hesitate to recognize the likeness of Mlle Guimard in other portraits by Fragonard (or attributed to him) that are generally believed to represent her, but a comparison with her portrait bust in marble by Gaetano Merchi (1747–1823), signed and dated 1779, provides conclusive evidence (figure 1).

The story of Mlle Guimard's life is not relevant here, but is the subject of Goncourt's very charming book (1893), which recounted her long series of love affairs. Much has been said—both good and bad—about her extraordinary slimness (or skinniness, as her enemies would say, and she had many of them). Sophie Arnould, alluding to the "feuille des bénéfices" (profit sheet, or, literally, "leaf") from which Monseigneur de Jarente, one of her lovers, drew his finances, quipped: "I can't understand why this little silkworm is not fatter; it lives on such a fine leaf!"; and seeing Mlle Guimard dance with Vestris and Dauberval, who were looking at her lovingly, Mme Arnould compared "the trio to two dogs fighting over a bone!" It is often forgotten, however, that she was a dancer of great talent: "Her dancing was only a sketch [*esquisse*], she took only tiny steps, but with such graceful movements that the public preferred her to all other dancers; she was small, slim, very well put together, although somewhat homely, but her face was so fine-featured that, at the age of forty-five [she would have been barely twenty-five when Fragonard painted her], on the stage she did not seem to be more than fifteen," Mme Vigée Le Brun admiringly wrote (1835, I, p. 133).

There is no doubt that Fragonard knew Mlle Guimard; some authors even linked them romantically, but this is not alluded to in any contemporary sources. Their contemporaries, however, were severe and indiscreet enough concerning the artist and his patroness. As we will see, if there was no love story between them, money was certainly an issue. We know today that in 1769 or 1770, Fragonard was commissioned by Mlle Guimard to decorate her *hôtel* in the rue d'Antin built by Ledoux. Fragonard's decorations have since been lost, but certain drawings in Besançon, and some very precise descriptions provide an idea of his work.

In the Louvre painting, Mlle Guimard wears a dress with a tight-fitting bodice that pinches in her waist, and she leans her head gracefully to her left. Her powdered hair is gathered under "the black ruching of a small cap, topped with white plumes" (Goncourt, 1893). The large ruff and the blue ribbon frame her long neck and the face that could not fail to charm. The precise and delicate way in which the head is painted contrasts with the free handling of the green and ruby-colored velvet dress. Her pensive expression is quite moving, and not easily forgotten.

Figure 1. Gaetano Merchi.
La Guimard.
Musée des Arts Décoratifs, Paris

260

126 Portrait of Jérôme de Lalande

Oil on canvas, 72 x 59.5 cm.

Musée du Petit Palais, Paris

Provenance
Edouard Larcade, 1921; Alec Weisweiller;
acquired by the city of Paris, 1978 (for
1,726,500 francs).

Exhibitions
Paris, 1921, no. 32, ill.
Tokyo, 1980, no. 44, colorpl.
Bourg-en-Bresse, 1982, I.2, color cover

Bibliography
R. pp. 90–91, 174
W. 253, fig. 121
Sterling, 1964, n.p., n. 3
W. and M. 271, ill.
Laffon, 1981, pp. 297–98, ill.

Figure 1. Jean-Antoine
Houdon. *Lalande*. Musée
de l'Observatoire, Paris

Figure 2. Joseph Ducreux.
Lalande. Musée du
Château de Versailles

The history of this painting before 1921 remains a mystery. At the time, it was thought to represent "Naudin, astronomer and painter." The sitter was correctly identified as the astronomer Jérôme de Lalande (1732–1807), Fragonard's exact contemporary, by Louis Réau, and this was confirmed by comparison with the portraits assembled for the 250th anniversary of his birth in his hometown of Bourg-en-Bresse: a late bust by Jean-Antoine Houdon (figure 1), a pastel by Joseph Ducreux (figure 2), and a number of caricatures by François-André Vincent (figures 3–6). The astronomer's characteristically shaped head—in particular, his prominent forehead—is easily recognizable, even if Fragonard somewhat "erased" his ugliness, which was attested by his contemporaries. Lalande gained fame at an early age for his

work with comets and also, as Jean-Claude Pecker recalled in the preface to the Bourg-en-Bresse catalogue, for "organizing, on a world-wide scale, the observations made in 1761 and in 1769 of the passage of Venus in front of the sun." These are the same dates as those of his portrait by Fragonard. Lalande traveled to Italy in 1765 and 1766, and published his *Voyage d'un français en Italie* in 1769–70, which, along with the books by Richard and Cochin, was a popular guide for eighteenth-century tourists (it was used by Bergeret, who quotes from it on many occasions). While it is well known that Lalande was an art lover, there is no evidence that he was also a painter, and perhaps the brushes at the left, in the present painting, can be attributed to Fragonard's habitual artistic license.

Figure 3. François-André Vincent.
Lalande. Musée des Beaux-Arts,
Rouen

Figure 4. François-André
Vincent. *Lalande*. Musée des
Beaux-Arts, Rouen

Figure 5. François-André Vincent. *Lalande*. Musée
des Beaux-Arts, Rouen

Figure 6. François-André
Vincent. *Lalande*.
Private collection, Paris

126

This portrait, which does not seem to have been cut down at the sides, is noticeably smaller in format than the *figures de fantaisie,* although it corresponds, in part, to the type: a half-length figure behind a stone parapet; head turned vigorously to the right; commanding pose; brisk execution, with an evident penchant for yellows—only the usual collars, cuffs, and gold chains are missing. The portrait must date to after Lalande's return from Italy, and shortly before Frago-

nard painted the portrait of Diderot (whom Lalande would meet in Holland in 1774).

Typical of Fragonard is one humorous detail: the terrestrial globe, on which Lalande rests his arm, is conspicuously placed at the left side of the composition, while, in the center of the picture, is the no less smooth "globe" of the astronomer's head.

127 Portrait of Diderot

Oil on canvas, 81.5 x 65 cm.

Musée du Louvre, Paris, R. F. 1972.14

Provenance
Hippolyte Walferdin (1795–1880), by 1877 (the painting was in Nice): sold posthumously, Paris, April 3, 1880, no. 10 (for 6,000 francs); Baron de Beurnonville: sold, May 9–16, 1881, no. 61 (for 6,900 francs, to Lannoy); Count Daupias, Lisbon: sold, May 16–17, 1892, no. 17 (for 16,000 francs); Léopold Goldschmidt, Paris; Comte André Pastré, 1902–31; Comtesse Charles de Vogüé, Paris, 1934; entered the Louvre, 1972.

Exhibitions
Paris, 1878, no. 537
Paris, 1894, no. 119
Paris, 1907, no. 130
Paris, 1921, no. 92, ill.
Paris, 1934, no. 158, ill.
Paris, 1974, no. 12, ill.

Paris, 1974–75, no. 105, ill. p. 131
Paris, 1977–78, no. 4, ill.
Paris, 1984–85 , no. 1, ill. (with a complete list of exhibitions)
Paris, 1986–87, no. 105, ill.

Bibliography
G. p. 322
Assézat and Tourneux, 1877, XX, pp. 115–16
Tourneux, 1878, p. 126
Eudel, 1881, p. 151
P. pp. 135, 275
Nevill, 1903, p. 291, ill.
N. p. 110
Tourneux, 1907, p. 100
Nicolle, 1931, p. 49, fig. 3
R. pp. 88, 90, 130, 173
W. 250, colorpl. p. 275 and p. 17 (French edition)

Sterling, 1964, n.p.
Zolotov, 1968, p. 161, ill.
W. and M. 268, ill.
Rosenberg and Compin, 1974, pp. 186–88, fig. 5
Bukdahl, 1980, I, p. 2 (ill.)
Fried, 1980, p. 139, fig. 58
Rubin, 1980, p. 78, fig. 5
Sutton, 1980; 1987, p. 82, fig. 1
[Fride, 1984–85, pp. 90–93, pl. 8]
Sheriff, 1987, p. 82, fig. 1

Related works
Walferdin also owned a "copie moderne" that was in Paris in 1877 (Assézat and Tourneux, 1877).

For the iconography of Diderot, see Tourneux, 1878; the article by Wilhelm (1969); [Fride]; and the *Diderot* exhibition catalogue, Paris, 1984–85.

Although this painting did not enter the Louvre until 1972, it has often been exhibited and published over the last century. However, as far as we know, there was no mention of it before 1877. At that date, it belonged to Hippolyte Walferdin, along with many other fine Fragonards. A native of Langres, like Diderot, and a staunch *républicain,* Walferdin worshiped both the philosopher and Fragonard, his favorite painter; he was the first to give the Louvre a work by Fragonard (in 1849), but he did not say where he had acquired this particular painting. Maurice Tourneux, the first author to mention it, at first hesitated to recognize this rough draft as a "sketch of the philosopher."

Tourneux's doubts are understandable: a picture that was as perfunctorily painted, with such summary brushwork, could not, in his eyes, be considered a *portrait* in the sense in which the term was understood then—and in the eighteenth century. He might also have noticed that Fragonard had

given his subject blue eyes, while Diderot's were brown!

Strangely enough, Diderot himself never mentioned this portrait. In 1765, we will remember, he shared the same hopes as the other critics, who saw Fragonard as the artist who would be a source of consolation after the deaths of Deshays and Vanloo, and would eventually take their place, but, after the Salon of 1767, Diderot expressed his disappointment. Afterwards he said nothing, except for an allusion in his *Essais sur la peinture* and a witty remark in *Jacques le Fataliste* (Assézat ed., VI, 1875, p. 194) that has often been overlooked but would deserve comment. The reasons for this silence are not clear. If Diderot did sit for Fragonard, the chances are that it was a brief session. In any case, the artist does not seem to have made much of an impression on him. If, as we suppose, this painting, along with the other *figures de fantaisie,* was part of the "gallery" that Fragonard assembled in his lodgings at the Louvre (see

127

127: Detail

the Introduction to this chapter), it would scarcely have been noticed—especially by Diderot, who, as far as we know, did not frequent Fragonard's studio.

The date of the work has been much debated, but we agree on shortly before 1769—the opinion of the majority of specialists. Louis-Michel Vanloo exhibited his portrait of Diderot (figure 1)—which has the same dimensions as the present painting—at the Salon of 1767. It seems certain that Fragonard, who surely did not know of Diderot's reservations about Vanloo's portrait, tried to rival and even to challenge this work. Instead of a faithful, prudent, and stiff image, he strove for an original work that would reveal not just the man, but the writer, as well. What better way to represent him than in costume, wearing—no doubt, this was intentional—a heavy gold chain like the philosophers of

Rembrandt (see figure 2), or by the Venetian artist Domenico Feti (one recalls, in particular, his *Poet,* today in the Nationalmuseum, Stockholm; figure 3).

The following comment by Diderot expresses the artist's difficulty in capturing in paint the fleeting expressions and thoughts of the model: "I think of the Abbé Le Blanc; and I yawn with boredom. I think of the Abbé Trublet; and my face takes on an ironic expression. I think of my friend Grimm or of my Sophie [Volland]; and my heart flutters . . ." (*Oeuvres esthétiques,* 1968 ed., p. 680). As Edmond de Goncourt noted in his *Journal* (November 15, 1859, I, pp. 226–27): "Sometimes I imagine Fragonard having come out of the same mold as Diderot. In both there is the same verve, the same effervescence. Is not a painting by Fragonard just like a page of Diderot?"

Figure 1. Louis-Michel Vanloo. *Diderot.* Musée du Louvre

Figure 2. Rembrandt. *Self-Portrait.* Musée du Louvre

Figure 3. Domenico Feti. *The Poet.* Nationalmuseum, Stockholm

128   Portrait of a Man (formerly entitled Don Quixote)

Oil on canvas, 80.5 x 64.7 cm.

The Art Institute of Chicago, Gift of Mr. and Mrs. Leigh B. Block in honor of John Maxon, 1977.123

Provenance
Said to have been in the Mauperin collection sale, December 4, 1780, no. 38: "un portrait d'homme ajusté selon le costume espagnol. Ce morceau Étude et d'une touche savante est d'un grand effet. Hauteur 30 pouces, largeur 24 T. [81 x 64.8 cm., Oil on canvas]''; anonymous sale, April 20, 1885, no. 14: "portrait d'homme vu jusqu'à la ceinture, tourné à droite, la main appuyée sur la poignée de son épée [not visible in the Chicago painting], le front chauve, moustaches

épaisses et barbiche; il porte un costume espagnol rayé. Superbe esquisse exécutée avec une fougue et un brio étonnants" (for 2,900 francs); Camille Groult (1890–1953); [Wildenstein, 1954]; Mr. and Mrs. Leigh B. Block, Chicago; given to The Art Institute of Chicago, 1977.

Exhibitions
Chicago, 1978, no. 9, ill. (with list of previous exhibitions)
Houston, 1986–87, no. 15, ill., colorpl. p. 23

Bibliography
P. pp. 277, 286
W. 247, colorpl. facing pl. 42, p. 17 (French edition)
Sterling, 1964, n.p., fig. 17
W. and M. 264, ill.
Washington, D.C., Detroit, Los Angeles exhibition catalogue, 1975–76, p. 30
Sutton, 1980; 1987, p. 110
Wise, forthcoming (with complete bibliography)

Figure 1. Domenico Feti. *Portrait of an Actor.* The Hermitage, Leningrad

Figure 2. Fragonard, after (?) Domenico Feti. *Portrait of an Actor.* Manchester City Art Gallery

and "very impressive" prove that the Mauperin painting was, indeed, a *figure de fantaisie.*

Although Fragonard executed such works to decorate his "gallery," he must also—as some eighteenth-century sales catalogues show—have painted them for enlightened connoisseurs. The allusion to the "Spanish costume" is interesting (and may explain the portrait's recent—unjustified—title, *Don Quixote*). There was a considerable vogue for such costumes—which, however, were not in the least Spanish—in the latter half of the eighteenth century, inspired as much by the theater as by fashions during the reign of Louis XIII. Such accoutrements satisfied the prevailing taste for sumptuous disguises evocative of the past.

Fragonard, once again, took his inspiration directly from a Venetian work, the famous *Portrait of an Actor* by Domenico Feti (1588/89–1623) that is today in the Hermitage but was in the collection of Pierre Crozat until 1772 (figure 1). It has been suggested that Fragonard copied part of this work in pastel (Yves Le Moyne sales catalogue, February 5, 1912, no. 47, ill; A. 2063) and in oil (figure 2; Manchester City Art Gallery catalogue, 1980, p. 36, ill.). These hypotheses seem less convincing, but Feti's influence on Fragonard is undeniable.

The sitter's long, drooping moustache and beard blend into his brown costume, and the bright yellows and the vermilions of his blotchy face stand out against the greenish background. As with all the *figures de fantaisie,* what really holds our attention is the rapidity, the intensity, and the spontaneity of the execution, which, for the time, was unusually free.

Is this the same painting that was in the Mauperin sale, in 1780 (we do not even know Mauperin's first name, only that he was a painter at the Académie de Saint-Luc)? The description in the sales catalogue is too vague to offer any affirmation. Yet, this description: "a portrait of a man dressed in a Spanish costume"; the dimensions: 81 x 64.8 centimeters; and the designations: "masterful execution"

129   Cavalier Seated by a Fountain

Oil on canvas, 94 x 74 cm.

Museu d'Art de Catalunya, Barcelona, Cambo Collection

Provenance
Varanchan de Saint-Geniès (*fermier général de la Régie du tabac*): sold, December 29–31, 1777, no. 16: "un cavalier vêtu à l'Espagnol [*sic*]: il est assis près d'une fontaine, et tient la bride de son cheval qui se désaltère; ébauche librement touchée, hauteur 37 pouces, largeur 27 pouces 6 lignes [100 x 74 cm.]" (for 61 *livres,* according to W.); [de Ghendt]: sold, November 15, 1779, no. 599: "un guerrier très pittoresquement vêtu, assis sur une pierre faisant abreuver son cheval qui se voit derrière lui T. 3 pieds sur 2 pieds 4 pouc. de large"; [Paul Cailleux, 1932]; Don Francisco Cambo, Montreux; bequeathed to the Barcelona museum, 1941.

Exhibitions
London, 1932, no. 219 (no. 165 in the commemorative catalogue)

Paris, 1934, no. 880
Paris, 1934 (*Portraits*), no. 33, ill.
Copenhagen, 1935, no. 71
Paris, 1937, no. 158, pl. 59 of the album
Bern, 1954, no. 21, ill.

Bibliography
P. p. 273
N. p. 112
Nolhac, 1932, pp. 35–38, ill.
Florisoone, 1934, p. 4, ill.
Sánchez Cantón, 1955, pp. 105–7, pl. LVII
R. p. 174
Réau, 1956, pp. 20–21
G. Wildenstein, 1959, pp. 239, 244
W. 251, pl. 41, pp. 17, 34 (French edition)
Cailleux, 1962, n.p., ill.
Châtelet and Thuillier, 1964, p. 246, cover detail
Sterling, 1964, n.p., fig. 12, notes 3, 8, 16

Thuillier, 1967, p. 78, colorpl.
Zolotov, 1968, pp. 158, ill., 159 (detail)
Watson, 1971, p. 78, ill.
W. and M. 269, ill., colorpl. XXIX
Bjurström, 1976, p. 26, fig. 10
Sutton, 1980; 1987, p. 110
Pupil, 1985, p. 301, ill. p. 300

Related works
According to Wildenstein (1959), the "portrait d'homme vêtu à l'espagnole," a pastel mentioned in the posthumous inventory of Saint-Non's collection, was by the abbé himself—which seems likely—and is thought to be a copy of the Barcelona picture, which is less likely since the pastel "portrait" is only a "buste."

The *Cavalier Seated by a Fountain* is not a *figure de fantaisie* in the strict sense of the term. Its dimensions and its composition—it is a full-length portrait—are radically different. However, in its conception—it is a costumed portrait—execution, and coloring it displays a kinship with this group of works, and it would be an arbitrary decision to exclude it.

This painting appeared in two sales in the eighteenth century: first, in 1777, with the collection of a rich *fermier général* and great admirer of Fragonard, and then two years later, with the collection of Emmanuel de Ghendt, a necessitous engraver who was a friend of the Abbé de Saint-Non, and who owned several representations of heads of old men by Fragonard inspired by those of Rembrandt (see cat. no. 101).

Subsequently, this painting was lost sight of for a century and a half. In 1932, it was published by Nolhac, who recognized it as a portrait of the Abbé de Saint-Non—an identification that has not been seriously questioned since then. (This point will be discussed in more detail in connection with the *Portrait of the Abbé de Saint-Non* in the Louvre [cat. no. 133].) The first catalogue, prepared by Paillet, described the figure as a "cavalier dressed in the Spanish style" (and the work as "a freely painted rough sketch"!), and the second catalogue, as a "very picturesquely dressed

warrior." If the picture does, indeed, portray the Abbé de Saint-Non, then either Fragonard did not paint it for him, or else the abbé gave away the portrait before 1777.

The "horseman" is sitting by the edge of the fountain, resting one hand on the pommel of his saber; with the other hand, he holds the bridle of his horse, while it "slakes its thirst." He wears a vermilion doublet with a white collar and cuffs, high, fawn-colored leather riding boots, and a brown plumed hat with a red bow. He wears a long chain, and across his chest, a wide golden-yellow sash.

"This canvas is a synthesis ... of all of Fragonard's qualities: the brilliance, the vitality, and the virtuosity of his brush, which seeks out difficulties for the pleasure of resolving them and for the greater joy of the connoisseurs. In spite of its abundant caprices, the composition is an amazing balance in which the figure, by the placement of the sword, the bridle, the arms, and the legs, is inscribed in an exact lozenge.... Naturally, one may detect the diverse influences that shaped him, including that of Tiepolo, Boucher, and Hals, for this work belongs precisely to that period in his career when these various affinities succeeded one another, and the resulting originality appears in full bloom" (Nolhac, 1932).

130 Portrait of a Man (called The Writer)

Oil on canvas, 80.5 x 64.5 cm.

Musée du Louvre, Paris, M.I. 1060

Provenance
Dr. La Caze (1798–1869); bequeathed to the Louvre, 1869.

Exhibitions
Brussels, 1935, no. 943
Rennes..., 1964–65, no. 16, ill.
Paris, 1974, no. 8, ill.
Atlanta, 1983–84, no. 34, colorpl.

Bibliography
G. pp. 281–82, 322, n. 1
P. pp. 132, 279
Grappe, *Figaro (supplément artistique)*, May 2, 1929, cover ill. (mistaken for the *Portrait of the Abbé de Saint-Non*, cat. no. 133)
R. pp. 88, 181–82
W. 241, fig. 117, pp. 16–17 (French edition)
Sterling, 1964, n.p., fig. 3

Zolotov, 1968, p. 157, ill.
W. and M. 257, ill., colorpl. XXII
Rubin, 1980, p. 79, fig. 6

Related works
There are engravings by Eugène Wallet, reproduced by P. between pp. 144 and 145 (see also p. 323, no. 38) and by Mlle Jacob in the *Catalogue illustré de l'Exposition Internationale de Blanc et Noir*, Paris, 1888, p. 17.

In 1869, Dr. Louis La Caze bequeathed to the Louvre a collection that included, among other marvels, four *figures de fantaisie*. In 1860, he had lent two of them to an exhibition organized by Philippe Burty that led to a rediscovery of eighteenth-century French painting. It is not known where and when Dr. La Caze came by these works, but it would seem—and this is confirmed by the Goncourts—that he acquired them in a single lot.

Their attribution has never been challenged, but there is still some question as to whether the four paintings were part of a unified series, and whether they were painted for the Abbé de Saint-Non, who is represented in one of them. The problem would appear to be resolved in light of our discussion (see page 256) of the "gallery" of *figures de fantaisie* that Fragonard created in his lodgings at the Louvre.

As for the identity of the model (see figure 1), a number of specialists, including Réau, have noted a certain resemblance

Figure 1. Detail of catalogue no. 130 (X-ray photograph)

to the sitter in what is known as the *Portrait of the Abbé de Saint-Non* in the Louvre (cat. no. 133), but we reserve judgment on this point. Fragonard was not a professional portraitist; he was not concerned with likenesses, and he often gave a similar expression to each head that he painted. Could this picture be a generalized representation of a writer, with the "attributes" of his profession, the quill and notebook? Or is it perhaps a simple allegory of Inspiration, according to the iconography set down by Ripa? We do not doubt that Fragonard wanted to paint portraits, and especially portraits that alluded to the profession of the sitter, but that was not his only ambition. His portraits were pretexts. He sought to capture motion and the changing expressions of a face through his rapid execution.

Of the four *figures de fantaisie* from the La Caze collection, this one seems to be the earliest.

131   Portrait of a Singer, with a Music Book

Oil on canvas, 81.5 x 65.5 cm.

Musée du Louvre, Paris, M.I. 1059

Provenance
Randon de Boisset (1708–1776), *Receveur général des Finances de Lyon,* according to Philippe Burty, the author of the 1860 exhibition catalogue, but there is no proof; Dr. Louis La Caze (1798–1869), by 1860; bequeathed to the Louvre, 1869.

Principal exhibitions
Paris, 1860, no. 148
London, 1933, no. 470, ill.
Rome, 1962, no. 92
Vienna, 1966, no. 29, pl. 41
London, 1968, no. 239, fig. 298
Paris, 1974, no. 9, ill.
Frankfurt, 1986–87, no. 20, ill.

Selected bibliography
Bürger [Thoré], 1860, p. 349
Godard, 1860, p. 297
Saint-Victor, 1860, n.p.
G. pp. 281–82, 322, n. 1
P. pp. 93, 132, 276
N. ill. between pp. 90 and 91
Gillet, 1929, p. 87, pl. 92, p. 88
Pouthas, 1938, p. 226, figs. 6, 7
R. pp. 88, 182
W. 244, fig. 118, p. 16 (French edition)
Sterling, 1964, n.p., fig. 9
Thuillier, 1967, p. 83, colorpl.
W. and M. 260, ill., colorpl. XXIII
Rosenberg and Compin, 1974, p. 191

Related works
Réau reproduces (1949, p. 71) a replica of this painting, which was once in the Stroganoff collection in Saint Petersburg and which he considers as an autograph work. There was a copy in the J.W. Church collection in London in 1926, and another, oval in format

and showing only the head, was sold with the Verrier collection in Brussels, December 8–9, 1924 (it may be the same work as the one reproduced by D. and V. 131, then in the collection of Waldemar von Rehling-Quistgaard; see figure 1). This painting is visible in Vuillard's *La Salle La Caze* (figure 2; Vuillard exhibition catalogue, Roussel, Munich-Paris, 1968, no. 156).

For nineteenth-century engravings, see P. (between pp. 4 and 5, reproduction of the engraving by Eugène Wallet) and W. There is an engraving by Albert Bellenger in the supplement to the June 22, 1907, issue of *L'Illustration.* Figure 3 shows a page of engravings after Fragonard, from a set that was recently acquired by the Musée des Beaux-Arts, Valenciennes. This picture was also reproduced on a one-franc stamp in 1972.

Figure 1. After Fragonard. *L'Étude* (detail). Whereabouts unknown

Figure 2. Édouard Vuillard. *La Salle La Caze.* Whereabouts unknown

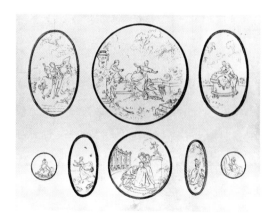

Figure 3. After Fragonard. Nineteenth-century engravings. Musée des Beaux-Arts, Valenciennes

Of the four *figures de fantaisie* in the La Caze collection (see previous entry), this is the only female subject. Contrary to Philippe Burty's claim that it belonged to Randon de Boisset, we believe that the picture was part of Fragonard's "gallery" at the Louvre (see Introduction to this chapter). This painting has often been interpreted as an allegory of Study, Poetry, or even of Music. The young woman seems to be leafing through a music book, and the double-keyboard harpsichord (see figure 4) in the background at the left (which reappears in the Louvre's much later *Music Lesson;*

see figure 5) confirms the interest in music. Could this be the portrait of a singer whose name has since been forgotten? Her identity should not be impossible to discover, for her facial features are very individualized.

The overall harmony of the golden yellow and brown color scheme is enlivened by a few touches of vermilion. The large white ruff, in the style of Maria de' Medici, is a reminder that in 1769 Fragonard copied Rubens's works in the Galerie du Luxembourg. Thus, this work should be dated slightly afterward.

Figure 4. Harpsichord with
a double keyboard.
Musée Instrumental du Conservatoire
National Supérieur de Musique, Paris

Figure 5. Fragonard. *The Music Lesson*.
Musée du Louvre

132   Portrait of M. de La Bretèche

Oil on canvas, 80 x 65 cm.
Signed and dated at the lower right: *frago 1769* (see figure 1)
A label on the verso is inscribed: *Portrait de M^r. de La Bretêche,/peint par fragonard,/
en 1769, en une heure de temps.* (see figure 2)

Musée du Louvre, Paris, M.I. 1058

Provenance
See the previous entry; La Caze collection.

Exhibitions
Paris, 1860, no. 147
Charleroi, 1957, no. 5, pl. 1 (reversed)
Grasse, 1957, no. 16
Paris, 1957–58, no. 29
Munich, 1958, no. 55, fig. 17
Paris, 1974, no. 7, ill.
Tokyo, 1980, no. 43, colorpl.

Bibliography
Bürger [Thoré], 1860, p. 349
Gautier, 1860, p. 2
Saint-Victor, 1860, n.p.
Blanc, 1862, p. 16
G. pp. 281–82, 322
Mantz, 1870, p. 16
P. pp. 132, 283

Guimbaud, 1928, ill. between pp. 126
  and 127
R. pp. 89, 129, 173
W. 242, pl. 38
Sterling, 1964, n.p., fig. 1
Mirimonde, 1966, p. 156, fig. 28
Thuillier, 1967, p. 82
Watson, 1971, p. 78, ill.
W. and M. 258, ill., colorpl. XXV
Mirimonde, 1977, p. 38
Sutton, 1980; 1987, p. 110, fig. 9,
  p. 109
Conisbee, 1981, p. 142, fig. 119
Sheriff, 1987, p. 83, fig. 3

Related works
R. (p. 173) catalogues a second portrait of M. de La Bretèche (figure 3), in the Fogg Art Museum, which seems to be a nineteenth-century work.

Figure 1. Signature, catalogue no. 132

Figure 2. Old label on the verso of the painting

Figure 3. French school, nineteenth century (?). *Portrait of a Man.* Fogg Art Museum, Harvard University, Cambridge, Massachusetts

Nom la-Bretèche, near Versailles), which reverted to his younger brother, the abbé. The two were inseparable, and La Bretèche supported the abbé both morally and financially—especially, the costly publication of the *Voyage pittoresque de Naples et de Sicile.* "Never did the slightest cloud mar the purity of their union," wrote Brizard (1792), Saint-Non's biographer. In 1791, La Bretèche was designated in the abbé's will as his "sole heir and executor" (Minutier central: XX, 752; communicated by Françoise Arquié-Bruley). We do not know, however, if La Bretèche shared his brother's enthusiasm for Fragonard's work.

Wearing a curious cap, decorated with red bows and plumes, La Bretèche "turns his mocking face toward the spectator.... With a few chalk lines, a few strokes of the brush, the painter sculpted the mask, colored the flesh, fashioned the costume, and cast onto this lively image a warm ray of sunlight," Paul de Saint-Victor wrote admiringly, in 1860, although not without some reservations about the "improvisation" of the work: "time has nothing to do with it." Even the Goncourts' appreciation was somewhat reticent: "It took him only one hour to pose, dash off, and wrap up these large portraits that show off all this Spanish-style whimsy with which the painters of the time liked to adorn and ennoble their contemporaries."

The "rediscoverers" of Fragonard in the nineteenth century did not appreciate any more than had the critics of the century before the sketchy aspect of these works, which they considered unfinished, and simply "rough drafts." With the triumph of Impressionism and of "pure painting," in which the subject serves only as a pretext, a complete change in taste was brought about.

We leave the last word to Théophile Gautier (1860): "Speed, no matter what has been said about it, has its merits, when the work itself is not sacrificed to it. Certainly, M. de La Bretèche would not have come out any better after twenty sittings with a less skilled and less confident artist."

This is the best documented of all Fragonard's *figures de fantaisie*—the only one *both* signed and dated (1769). Furthermore, not only does the old, anonymous label on the back of the canvas provide the name of the sitter, the Abbé de Saint-Non's older brother, but it also notes that the artist painted the portrait in "one hour's time."

We see no reason to question these facts, and yet no other portraits of Louis de La Bretèche exist, and we know nothing of his musical tastes—and, in particular, whether he favored the guitar. The eldest son of Jean-Pierre Richard, "Receveur général des Finances pour la généralité de Tours," and of Marie-Anne Boullongne, a descendant of the family of famous painters, Louis-Richard, in 1747, took the name of one of the estates acquired by his father, La Bretèche, which was close to the estate of Saint-Non (the present-day Saint-

133   Portrait of the Abbé de Saint-Non

Oil on canvas, 80 x 65 cm.
Inscribed on the verso: *Portrait de M.ʳ l'abbé de Sᵗ Non, /peint par fragonard,/ en 1769. en une heure de temps* (see figure 1)

Musée du Louvre, Paris, M.I. 1061

Provenance
See catalogue no. 131; La Caze collection.

Exhibitions
Paris, 1953, no. 48
Besançon, 1956, no. 27
Grasse, 1957, no. 15
Paris, 1957–58, no. 28, pl. XX
Bordeaux, 1958, no. 168
Copenhagen, 1960, no. 17, ill.
Vienna, 1966, no. 28, pl. 40
Saint-Paul-de-Vence, 1973, no. 774, colorpl.
Paris, 1974, no. 6, ill.
Sydney, 1980, no. 38, ill., colorpl. 1
Shanghai, 1982, no. 52

Bibliography
G. pp. 281–82, 322, n. 1
P. pp. 132–33, 281
Guimbaud, 1928, pl. between pp. 132 and 133
R. pp. 89, 174
G. Wildenstein, 1959, pp. 226–44
W. 243, pl. 40, pp. 16–17 (French edition)
Sterling, 1964, n.p., fig. 2
Thuillier, 1967, p. 78, colorpl.
W. and M. 259, ill., colorpl. XXIV
Haskell, 1976, fig. 181
Harris, 1979, p. 60, fig. 7
Rosenberg and Brejon de Lavergnée, 1986, color frontispiece
Sheriff, 1987, p. 84, fig. 5

Figure 1. Old label on the verso of the painting

Related works

Réau (1935, p. 4) and Ratouis de Limay (1946, p. 164) mention that this work was copied in pastel by the Comte de Brehan (on this *amateur*, see cat. no. 138). This copy, unlike the *Singer* (cat. no. 138), does not seem to be dated. P. and W. believe that Brehan copied *The Actor* (cat. no. 137; E. M. Hodgkins collection sale, Christie's, London, June 29, 1934, part of no. 1).

An engraving was made in the nineteenth century by Eugène Wallet, according to W.

For the painting in Barcelona and two other pictures in the Louvre that have sometimes been identified as portraits of Saint-Non, see cat. nos. 129, 130, 134.

For the drawing in the Musée Atger, Montpellier, see cat. no. 199.

Figure 2. Abbé Charles-Philippe de Tersan. *Self-Portrait.* 1766. Bibliothèque Nationale, Paris, Cabinet des Estampes

Figure 3. Georges Séroux d'Agincourt. *Portrait of Saint-Non* (?). 1782. Engraving. Bibliothèque Nationale, Paris, Cabinet des Estampes

Figure 4. Remi-Henri-Joseph Delvaux, after Augustin de Saint-Aubin. *Portrait of Saint-Non.* 1774. Engraving. Private collection, Paris

Figure 5. Infrared photograph of catalogue no. 133

From the old label formerly affixed to the back of the canvas, it may be supposed that this is, indeed, a likeness of the Abbé de Saint-Non. There is, however, very little basis for comparison: the engraved "self-portrait" reproduced as the frontispiece of Louis Guimbaud's book on Saint-Non and Fragonard (1928), in fact, represents another "antiquarian," the Abbé Charles-Philippe de Tersan (figure 2). Like Charles Sterling (1964, n. 4), we cannot positively identify the 1782 engraving by Georges Séroux d'Agincourt (figure 3; reproduced in Wildenstein, 1959, fig. 1) as a portrait of Saint-Non. There was a miniature by Hall exhibited at the Salon of 1775 (see Seznec and Adhémar, 1967, IV, p. 291), which seems to be lost, and an engraving by Remi-Henri-Joseph Delvaux (figure 4), after a pastel by Augustin de Saint-Aubin, dated 1774 (copied by Legénisel in the nineteenth century; see Rosenberg and Brejon, 1986, p. 11, fig. a).

The Abbé de Saint-Non (1727–1791), whom we have often had occasion to evoke in these pages (see also our edition of the journal of his travels in Italy), was one of the few unconditional admirers of Fragonard in the eighteenth century. The two men met in Rome in 1760 and remained lifelong friends. Fragonard was one of the artists—along with Hubert Robert and Pierre-Adrien Pâris—mentioned in the abbé's will. Saint-Non collected Fragonard's drawings and paintings, made aquatints after them, and even copied some in pastel, but there is no evidence that he ever owned this portrait of himself.

Of the four *figures de fantaisie* from the La Caze collection, the *Portrait of the Abbé de Saint-Non* is the most accomplished: the keys to its success are its execution and its vibrant color harmonies—the Prussian blue doublet, the deep saffron hue of the sash, the spot of lemon yellow, the white collar and cuffs, the gray plumes of the hat set atop the stone parapet, and the fawn-colored gloves. While the close association between the brushwork and the play of colors detracts from both the realism of the details and the psychological penetration of the sitter, all that matters is the artist's stunning technical mastery and his evident pleasure in painting.

There is a visible pentimento: originally, the abbé's glove was depicted sliding off the edge of the parapet (see figure 5).

134 Portrait of Jacques-André Naigeon (?)

Oil on canvas, 81.5 x 65 cm.
Signed at the lower center: *frago* (see figure 1)

Musée du Louvre, Paris, R. F. 1942.20

Provenance
"M. Naigeon," 1885; [Cailleux, 1933];
Carlos de Beistegui, by 1934; given to the
Louvre, with life interest, 1942; entered the
Louvre, 1953.

Exhibitions
Paris, 1885, no. 82 ("Inconnu")
Paris, 1974, no. 10, ill.

Bibliography
P. p. 286
Réau, 1956, p. 20
R. pp. 89, 91, 174, color detail on cover
W. 254 (see also English edition), fig. 122,
    p. 17 (French edition)
Cailleux, 1962, n.p., ill.

Sterling, 1964, n.p., fig. 4
W. and M. 272, ill.
Coulon and Cornoy, 1976, p. 190
Coulon, 1977, n.p.
Dijon exhibition catalogue, 1982–83,
    p. 126, fig. 199, p. 127

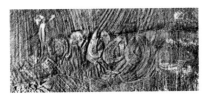

Figure 1. Signature, catalogue no. 134

Figure 2. François-André Vincent.
Portrait of Jacques-André Naigeon.
Musée des Beaux-Arts, Rouen

The identity of the sitter has been the subject of much debate; he has been variously identified as the painter Jean Naigeon (1757–1832), who, like Fragonard, played an important role in the administration of the Beaux-Arts at the Louvre during the Revolution; the Abbé de Saint-Non (Cailleux, 1962); and Pierre-Jacques Bergeret (1742–1807), the son of Jacques-Onésyme Bergeret (Coulon, 1976; 1977). The first hypothesis rests on the fact that when this painting first reappeared in 1885, it belonged to a "M. Naigeon"; the second, on the "resemblance" between the sitter and the portrait of Saint-Non in the La Caze collection (cat. no. 133); and the third, on its kinship with a celebrated drawing in the Louvre (cat. no. 175) that is presumed to represent the younger Bergeret.

None of these identifications is fully convincing. If we agree with Daniel Wildenstein and Gabriel Mandel (1972), who identified the sitter as Jacques-André Naigeon (1738–1810), it is because this supposition has the merit of associating the name of the man who owned the work in 1885 with that of a painter who was converted to the philosophy of Materialism, and was a friend of Diderot (he was even nicknamed "the ape of Diderot"!). There is also an undeniable resemblance to Vincent's caricature of the painter Naigeon (figure 2)—but, again, this is only one hypothesis, among others.

Fragonard employed a limited color scheme: a bright oxblood, a golden yellow, and a pure white. A shaft of light falls on the handsome face of the young man, who turns his head with such a sudden motion that it seems about to pop out of the canvas. The dynamism of the execution matches the vitality of the subject of this *figure de fantaisie*—one of the most perfect and the most inspired of the series.

135 Portrait of a Man (called The Warrior)

Oil on canvas, 81.5 x 64.5 cm.

Sterling and Francine Clark Art Institute, Williamstown, Massachusetts

Provenance
Sabatier d'Espeyran, Montpellier (the same collection "depuis près de trois générations": Ananoff, 1965; Sterling, 1964); [Wildenstein, 1963]; acquired by the Clark Art Institute, 1964.

Exhibitions
Williamstown, 1964 (see Sterling, 1964)
New York, 1967, no. 14
London, 1968, no. 238, fig. 280

Bibliography
Sterling, 1964, n.p., fig. 6, color cover,
    details of the head and arm, plates 2, 3
Ananoff, 1965, p. 113, ill.
Thuillier, 1967, p. 80, colorpl.
Watson, 1971, p. 79, ill.
W. and M. 261, ill., pl. XXVI

134

135

On the occasion of the rediscovery and purchase of the *Portrait of a Man (The Warrior)* by the Sterling and Francine Clark Art Institute, in 1964, Charles Sterling published his brilliant study of this painting, whose subject has yet to be identified.

Unlike most of the other *figures de fantaisie,* Fragonard took pains to render the features of the model—"a spare and austere older man." He lingered over the arrogant and "unsettled" face, with its tight-lipped and authoritarian expression, but the pose is as contrived and unnatural as the gaze is falsely assured: we are closer to the world of the theater than to the art of war. Not without humor, Fragonard painted a portrait of an "armchair" warrior.

The sparkling whites of the collar, the slit sleeve, and the cuff, the bright yellow of the costume, and the deep red of the mantle stand out against the scumbled slate-gray background. The vigorous and choppy brushwork both builds up and condenses forms—for instance, the hand at the right, the fingers and thumbnail of which are indicated by broad strokes of ocher highlighted with dabs of black and white to convey their roundness and volume.

136   La Liseuse

Oil on canvas, 81.3 x 64.8 cm.

National Gallery of Art, Washington, D.C., Gift of Mrs. Mellon Bruce, in memory of her father, Andrew W. Mellon, 1961.16.1

Provenance

Comte du Barry: sold, March 11, 1776, no. 80 (for 190 *livres;* sketched by Gabriel de Saint-Aubin in his copy of the sales catalogue, now in the Philadelphia Museum of Art; see figure 1); anonymous sale, February 7, 1777, no. 15; [Leroy de Senneville]: sold, April 5, 1780, no. 59 (for 121 *livres* 1 *sol,* to Duquesnoy, according to W.); Duquesnoy: sold, March 10, 1803, no. 19: "une jeune fille assise tenant un livre de la main droite, l'autre appuyée sur une table. Esquisse de 28 pouces 6 lignes de haut sur 22 pouces de large" (for 24 *livres,* according to W.); anonymous sale, April 26, 1844, no. 14 (no dimensions given); Marquis de Cypierre, by 1844: sold, March 10, 1845, no. 55 (for 300 francs; no dimensions given); Comte de Kergolay, 1889; [Wildenstein]; Ernest Cronier: sold, December 4–5, 1905, no. 8, ill. (for 182,000 francs, to Ducrey); Dr. Tuffier, by 1910–until at least 1921; [Wildenstein]; Mrs. Alfred W. Erickson, New York, 1932: sold, Parke-Bernet, New York, November 15, 1961, no. 16, ill. (for $875,000 old francs); given to the National Gallery of Art in 1961.

Exhibitions

Paris, 1909, no. 64

Berlin, 1910, no. 138 (small edition), no. 51 (large edition)
Paris, 1921, no. 56, ill.
London, 1933, no. 517
Tokyo, 1980, no. 61, colorpl. and color cover

Bibliography

Bürger [Thoré], 1844, p. 3
P. pp. 202, 282
N. pp. 146, 147 (ill. between pp. 146 and 147)
Brière, 1909, p. 129
Meier-Graefe, 1910, pp. 269–70, ill. p. 262
Siple, 1932, p. 115, pl. II B
R. p. 171
W. 391, pl. 80
Gimpel, 1963, pp. 310, 415, ill. p. 303
W. and M. 416, ill., colorpl. XLI
Sutton, 1980; 1987, p. 111, color cover
Cuzin in *La France et la Russie,* exhibition catalogue, Paris, 1986–87, p. 75

Related works

For a *Lettre* comparable to the *Liseuse,* see cat. no. 142.

For a drawing (figure 2) of the same sitter reading, see A. 640 (see also A. 64, fig. 29; Williams, 1978, no. 59, ill.; Tokyo, 1980, no. 125, ill.).

Figure 1. Gabriel de Saint-Aubin. Page from the du Barry collection sales catalogue (1776). Philadelphia Museum of Art, John G. Johnson Collection

Figure 2. Fragonard. *La Liseuse.* Whereabouts unknown

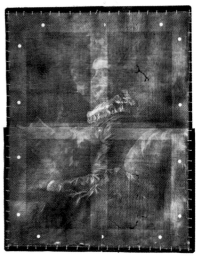

Figure 3. Radiograph of catalogue no. 136

While the treatment of the model's face distinguishes this picture from the *figures de fantaisie,* the dimensions and the sitter's costume relate the work to the others in the series. The recent restoration of this painting has provided some indication of Fragonard's working methods. Laboratory examinations (figure 3) have shown that the head was painted over a previous one—whether a man's or a woman's is unclear—that was turned ironically toward the spectator. For reasons presently unknown, Fragonard thus transformed a *figure de fantaisie* into this image of a young girl reading.

The painting was sold three times between 1776 and 1780, and the entries in the sales catalogues make for instructive reading. The first, that of the du Barry sale (some of the paintings came from the collection of the countess; Dacier, 1910, II, p. 12), gives only a description, but the third one tells us that the picture was painted "from life," and, like the second catalogue, mentions that it was done "in a single sitting," adding that it "has a finished effect due to the sureness of the brushwork and the harmony of the colors."

What sources there are make it seem as if Fragonard's contemporaries considered the *figures de fantaisie* as intended for the artist's own use; they were not destined for the art market, and could only have interested a few connoisseurs, like Varanchan. In keeping with the aesthetics of the period, art collectors preferred more "finished" works.

Note that the handle of the brush was used to render the ruff of the young girl, who is absorbed in her reading. As early as 1844, Thoré wrote the following about the *Liseuse*: "her fresh-looking face is as soft as the skin of a peach; the paint was scored with the tip of the brush handle to indicate the fluting of the white ruff: she wears a pale lemon-yellow dress, large areas of which catch the light. She leans on a lilac-colored cushion with deep-purple highlights. It would be difficult to imagine a more direct and more lively execution."

137   Portrait of a Man (called The Actor)

Oil on canvas, 80 x 65 cm.

Private collection

Provenance
Possibly, G[odefroy]: sold, 1794 (see catalogue no. 138); Émile Vallet (curator at the Musée des Beaux-Arts, Bordeaux), by 1882: sold, Paris, January 25, 1884, no. 15: "signé et daté" (ill. of an engraving by Eugène-André Champollion); acquired for 16,500 francs, by Gaucher, for the Baron Alphonse de Rothschild; Édouard de Rothschild; the Rothschild family.

Exhibitions
Bordeaux, 1882, no. 2460
Paris, 1946, no. 19

Bibliography
P. pp. 113, 285
N. p. 111
R. p. 182
W. 245, fig. 119
Sterling, 1964, n.p., fig. 5

Thuillier, 1967, p. 84, colorpl. and color detail, p. 86
W. and M. 262, ill.

Related works
For the engraving by Eugène-André Champollion, see *Provenance*.

    According to P. and W., the Comte de Brehan copied this work in pastel, but, in fact, it was the *Portrait of the Abbé de Saint-Non* (cat. no. 133; see Ratouis de Limay, 1946, p. 164).

After undergoing a recent restoration, this painting has proved to be in an excellent state of preservation. It was sold in 1884 along with the *Portrait of a Singer Holding a Sheet of Music* (cat. no. 138), which many consider to be its pendant. The title, *The Actor,* or *The Comedian,* is recent, and unjustified—no doubt explained by the figure's very showy pose.

The execution is particularly rich. Fragonard painted the head and the hair of the sitter, the costume, and the hands and gloves with the same broad and fluid strokes. "His paintbrush applies the colors in lashes. . . . Under his brush, feverishly darting back and forth, the collars billow and stiffen, the folds writhe, the mantles twist, the vests arch, the fabrics puff up and hum . . . " (Goncourt, p. 282). A few spots of blue and red resonate against the fluid browns of the costume. Light animates the face, the shoulder, and the hand resting on the sword, and illuminates a pale blue cuff. Rarely has Fragonard so successfully subordinated his subject to his brush.

Oil on canvas, 81 x 65 cm.
Signed at the bottom right: *fragao 17..*

Private collection

Provenance
May be identified with the "jeune dame, vue à mi-corps et galamment ajustée; elle tient un papier à musique et semble sourire. Ce morceau est bien touché et d'une bonne couleur … hauteur 29 pouces, largeur 24 pouces [78.3 x 64.8 cm.]" in the R[oettiers] sale, January 13, 1778, no. 20 (sold for 161 *livres*); possibly the painting in the [Dulac] and Lachaise sale, November 30, 1778, no. 218: "le Portrait d'une jeune Demoiselle vue à mi-corps, et ajustée à l'Espagnole; elle tient d'une main un papier à musique. Ce morceau gracieux et librement touché est d'un ton de couleur transparent … 17 pouces sur 14 p. [46 x 38 cm. !]"; W. supposes that the painting (and its present pendant; see catalogue no. 137) may have been identified with the "deux tableaux. Portraits d'homme et de femme" in the G[odefroy] sale, April 2, 1794, no. 24; Émile Vallet (curator of the Musée des Beaux-Arts, Bordeaux), by 1882: sold, Paris, January 25, 1884, no. 14, ill. with an engraving by Eugène-André Cham-

pollion (acquired for 25,000 francs by Gaucher, for the Baron Alphonse de Rothschild); Baron Édouard de Rothschild; the Rothschild family.

Exhibitions
Bordeaux, 1882, no. 2461

Bibliography
P. pp. 133, 285–86, ill. of the engraving between pp. 280 and 281
N. p. 112
Wilhelm, 1951, p. 26
R. pp. 119, 182
W. 246, pl. 42, p. 16 (French edition)
Sterling, 1964, n.p., fig. 11
W. and M. 263, ill.

Related works
This work, recorded as signed and dated 1773 at the bottom right, was copied in full size, in pastel, by Comte Jean-René-François Almaric de Brehan (1734–after 1813; see figure 1); Hodgkins sale, Christie's, London,

June 29, 1934, part of no. 1 (on Brehan, see Réau, 1935, p. 4, fig. 7; W. p. 14; vol. IX of the *Procès-Verbaux* … of the Académie, pp. 59–64, 307; *Biographie Michaud*, vol. 59, pp. 211–12).

For a copy in oil, after Noël Hallé de Brehan, signed and dated 1782, see the following sales catalogues: Sotheby's, Monte Carlo, December 9, 1984, no. 616, ill., and Troyes, June 2, 1985, ill.

An engraving by Eugène-André Champollion illustrates the sales catalogue of the Vallet collection, of 1884, and the book by Portalis.

A pastel that presents some analogies with this portrait was in the Vassal de Saint-Hubert collection sale, April 24, 1783, no. 102: "le buste d'une jeune femme ornée d'une fraise," which W. (p. 16, French edition) compares with a pastel in the Félix Doisteau collection (see figure 2), sold: June 9, 1909, no. 91, ill.; Sotheby's, London, October 16, 1963, no. 535 (A. 1256).

Figure 1. Comte de Brehan, after Fragonard. *Portrait of a Singer Holding a Sheet of Music.* 1773. Whereabouts unknown

Figure 2. Attributed to Fragonard. *Head of a Young Girl.* Whereabouts unknown

Figure 3. Peter Paul Rubens. *Portrait of Helena Fourment.* Alte Pinakothek, Munich

This portrait, recently restored and in fine state, has been associated since at least 1884 with the *Portrait of a Man (The Actor)* (cat. no. 137), but there is no evidence that this connection existed in the eighteenth century. In any case, the picture, which has been identified with the painting(s) in the Roettiers and Dulac sales in 1778, was sold by itself. In addition, it was copied in pastel by an amateur artist, the Comte de Brehan, as a pendant not to the above-mentioned *Actor,* but to the *Portrait of the Abbé de Saint-Non* (cat. no. 133).

The present painting, which bears the curious inscription "fragao," is one of the three *figures de fantaisie* to be signed. It was probably also dated, but only the first two numerals are clear (the last two were already illegible in 1884, the date of the Vallet sale). In any case, this work cannot have been

done after 1773—the date that can be read on the pastel copy by Brehan; it seems to have been painted about 1770.

This *Singer* is the most Rubenesque of the *figures de fantaisie* (see figure 3); the high starched collar, the sitter's plumpness, her full red-cheeked face, and even her coiffure recall the portraits of young women by the Flemish master. The necklace of large pearls, the pearls in the figure's hair, and the heavy pendant are like those worn on the stage. The individualization of the features—the youthful and somewhat awkward face, with its turned-up nose—indicates that the artist, indeed, wished this to be a portrait.

Note the technique of scoring the paint with the handle of the brush to render the collar, and the masterful foreshortening of the singer's gloved left hand, which holds the sheet of music.

139 Portrait of a Lady with a Dog

Oil on canvas, 81.3 x 65.4 cm.

The Metropolitan Museum of Art, New York, Fletcher Fund, 1937.118

Provenance
Possibly, anonymous sale, June 25, 1779, no. 265: "une femme jouant avec un petit chien [no dimensions given]"; "Mme Jager-schmid," 1897; according to D. and V. (1907, p. XI): "ce tableau provient de la col-lection de M. Féral qui le tenait de deux familles De Cambise ou Des Isnards"; Mme Louis Burat (by 1907 until at least 1921): sold posthumously, June 17, 1937, no. 3 (for 1,450,000 francs; in fact, this work belonged to J. Besnier, by 1932); acquired by the Metropolitan Museum, 1937.

Exhibitions
Paris, 1897, no. 59
Paris, 1907, no. 91
Paris, 1921, no. 31, ill.
London, 1932, no. 264 (no. 164 of the commemorative catalogue)
Paris, 1934, *Louis XV*, no. 150
Leningrad-Moscow, 1975, no. 52, ill.

Bibliography
D. and V. 77
Williams, 1938, pp. 14–16, colorpl.
Sterling, 1955, pp. 154–55, ill.
R. pp. 182, 252
W. 256, fig. 123, p. 17 (French edition)
Sterling, 1964, n.p.
W. and M. 273, ill.
Providence exhibition catalogue, 1975, p. 155, fig. 18, p. 154

Figure 1. Peter Paul Rubens. *Henri IV Entrusts the Rule of His Kingdom to the Queen* (detail). Musée du Louvre

Figure 2. Fragonard. *Jeune Fille aux chiots*. Private collection, Paris

This representation of a woman of rather ample proportions is not devoid of humor. Some have identified the sitter (without justification) as "Rosalie Fragonard, the artist's aunt." Her impressive ruff, her pearls "fit for a queen of the stage," her costume jewelry—all evoke the theater, and the eighteenth-century taste for disguises. This painting is, in fact, an homage to Rubens (figure 1). The woman (who reminds us irresistibly of Mme Castafiore in *Tintin*) holds a lap dog (to which this painting owes much of its fame), with a blue-ribbon collar and a somewhat ravenous look.

Fragonard sought to elicit a smile from us by contrasting the gracile animal with such an imposing person-age, but he did not succeed nearly as well as with his portraits of equally corpulent men, for there is a certain garishness here, in both the color scheme and the execution.

A few years before painting this work, Fragonard explored a similar theme: a very young girl holding two puppies against her bare breasts (figure 2)—but in the latter work the erotic element predominated above all other considerations.

Oil on canvas, 81.5 x 65 cm.

Private collection, Switzerland

Provenance
Duc d'Harcourt: sold, Sotheby's, London, December 8, 1971, no. 21, ill. (for 340,000 pounds, to the present owner).

Exhibitions
Paris, 1921, no. 90
Paris, 1929, no. 31
Paris, 1934, no. 133

Bern, 1954, no. 22
Paris, 1957, no. 33

Bibliography
G. Wildenstein, 1921, p. 360
R. pp. 88, 174, pl. 93, p. 181
W. 239, pl. 37 (not 36), pp. 16–17 (French edition)
Sterling, 1964, n.p.

Zolotov, 1968, p. 160, ill.
W. and M. 256, ill. (identification of the sitter confused with 255)
Rosenberg and Compin, 1974, pp. 184–86, fig. 4
Art de Basse-Normandie, 1979, no. 78, p. 34
Sutton, 1980; 1987, p. 110

Figure 1. Anicet-Charles-Gabriel Lemonnier. *François-Henri, Duc d'Harcourt.* Musée des Beaux-Arts, Rouen

Figure 2. French school, eighteenth century. *Portrait of a Man with a Sword.* Southside House (near London)

Figure 3. Jean-Baptiste Pigalle. *The Mausoleum of the Comte d'Harcourt.* Notre-Dame, Paris

This painting and its pendant (cat. no. 141) were mentioned for the first time in 1921. They were kept together until 1971, and have been reunited here.

By 1921, they were identified as portraits of François-Henri, Duc d'Harcourt and governor of Normandy (1726–1802) and of his younger brother, Anne-François d'Harcourt, Duc de Beuvron (1727–1797). They have often been exhibited and published—and confused with one another. We endeavored to put an end to this confusion (Rosenberg and Compin, 1974) by comparisons with other eighteenth-century portraits of the two dukes; a drawing by Anicet-Charles-Gabriel Lemonnier in the Musée des Beaux-Arts, Rouen (figure 1), confirms the identification of the duc d'Harcourt.

Not only is there no record of the two portraits before 1921; the Château d'Harcourt at Thury-Harcourt was not always in the Harcourt family. It was plundered during the Revolution, changed hands in the first half of the nineteenth century, and was largely destroyed in 1944; hence, the legitimate doubt as to the identity of the sitters represented in these paintings.

A letter from the present duc d'Harcourt in 1964 (or 1969, preserved in the archives of the Service d'Études et de documentation du département des Peintures du Louvre), often cited in recent years, offers evidence for the presence of the paintings at Harcourt in the eighteenth century: "It may interest you to know that the late Count Potocki owned in

Poland a painting by Fragonard that was inscribed on the reverse 'painted at Harcourt.' A family tradition has it that Fragonard painted at Harcourt (Calvados) six portraits, or rather six figures disguised for one of the many costume balls that were given there. Some were held in the 'Pavillon de Fantaisie' that was built on the castle grounds, and still stands." Unfortunately, the *Portrait of a Man with a Sword* (figure 2), sold March 26, 1952, with the collection of Alfred Potocki de Làncut (Sotheby's, London, no. 37, ill.; Royal Academy exhibition catalogue, London, 1954–55, no. 203; W. and M. 261 A, ill.), today at Southside House, near London, cannot be assigned to Fragonard.

Nevertheless, there was a relationship between the Harcourt family and Fragonard, if only a professional one: on November 16 (actually 11), 1784, a drawing (no. 157) was sold that represented the "Tomb of the Comte d'Harcourt" ("Hymen and Love plunging their torches into the ashes of the count to re-create him; his Wife throws herself into his arms, while Hymen and Love repell Death ... [!]"). Henri-Claude, Comte d'Harcourt, lieutenant general in the king's army, died in 1769; in 1771, his widow commissioned Jean-Baptiste Pigalle to execute a splendid mausoleum (figure 3) that may still be seen in the Cathedral of Notre-Dame, in Paris. Fragonard probably painted the two portraits of the two dukes, the late count's nephews, between these two dates.

In the portrait, François-Henri displays a very proud bear-

ing; his sword at his side, he turns his head to the right and his smile betrays a certain self-satisfaction. He seems to be holding a hat with white plumes in his left hand, and a fine gold chain in his right. Fragonard painted him wearing an aquamarine doublet and a short red-and-black cape—but, above all, the artist succeeded in capturing the sitter's unmistakable vitality.

141   Portrait of Anne-François d'Harcourt, Duc de Beuvron

Oil on canvas, 81.5 x 65 cm.

Musée du Louvre, Paris, R. F. 1970.32

Provenance
Mentioned for the first time—to our knowledge—in 1921, when it was at the Château d'Harcourt, Thury-Harcourt; at the Château de Champ-de-Bataille, after World War II; given to the Louvre, with life interest, by the Duc d'Harcourt, 1970.

Exhibitions
Paris, 1921, no. 89
Paris, 1929, no. 30
Paris, 1934, *Louis XV,* no. 134
Bern, 1954, no. 23
Paris, 1974, no. 11, ill.

Bibliography
G. Wildenstein, 1921, p. 360
R. pp. 88, 174
W. 240, pl. 36 (not 37), pp. 16–17 (French
   edition)
Sterling, 1964, n.p.
W. and M. 255, ill. (identification of the
   sitter confused with 256)
Rosenberg and Compin, 1974, pp.
   184–86, fig. 1
Art de Basse-Normandie, 1979, no. 78,
   pp. 34, 36, colorpl. and color cover
Sutton, 1980; 1987, p. 110

Figure 1. (?) Vanloo. *Anne-François d'Harcourt, Duc de Beuvron.* Private collection, France

The identification of the sitter as Anne-François d'Harcourt (1727–1797), the duc de Beuvron, and the younger brother of the duc d'Harcourt (see previous entry), seems to be confirmed by a portrait of him attributed to one of the Vanloos (see figure 1), which is still in the Harcourt collection.

Anne-François rests his two hands on the pommel of his sword. His bright sunflower-yellow costume casts a golden light on his cuffs, his cape, and his large ruff. The streak of red on the slit sleeve further enlivens the composition. The head of the sitter, the details of which are rather hastily painted, is turned abruptly to the left.

With his usual speed, Fragonard, indeed, painted a portrait, but one that captures the intangible—a fleeting expression, a gesture, a pose—not so much the psychology of the sitter, but, rather, his mood at the moment.

V

Mme du Barry and Mlle Guimard (1770–73)

Figure 1. Charles de La Fosse.
Le Temps, Apollon et les quatre saisons.
Manchester City Art Gallery

François Boucher died in 1770 (two months after Tiepolo), and was replaced as *Premier peintre* by Jean-Baptiste-Marie Pierre, who soon took Cochin's place as adviser to Marigny, the *Surintendant des bâtiments.* Boucher had been an art collector, and at the sale of his collection on February 18, 1771, Fragonard acquired some paintings, drawings, and engravings. His choices are revealing, apart from the fact that they confirm that he had become financially successful. He purchased a "Burgomeister" (formerly ascribed to van Dyck) then attributed to "Jean Van Kalcker," and four paintings by Charles de La Fosse (possibly, the "Temps, Apollon et les quatre saisons," today in the Manchester City Art Gallery: see figure 1; and an *Assumption,* either the one in the Musée Magnin, Dijon: see figure 2, or the one in the Musée des Beaux-Arts, Caen: see figure 3); drawings by La Fosse, Bramer, Roos, Verdier, Stella, and, of course, by Boucher; some anonymous studies, oil sketches of flowers, plants, and fruit; and, finally, a number of engravings by Cornelis Schut, Wenzel Hollar, Rembrandt, and Luyken, among others.

The fate of Fragonard's patiently assembled collection of "prints from his time" is a sad story, indeed: "One day ... he saw smoke coming from behind a door; inside the room, he found his son in front of a bonfire of burning paper, and when he asked him, 'what are you doing, you wretch,' his son replied, very seriously, 'I am making a sacrifice to good taste.' He was burning his father's print collection!" (Goncourt, pp. 306–7, n. 2).

Charles de La Fosse (1636–1716) had participated in the debate that caused a split among French artists of the early eighteenth century into two opposing factions, the *rubénistes* and the *poussinistes*—the partisans of color versus the defenders of line—Rubens against Raphael, and Venice

Figure 2. Charles de La Fosse. *The Assumption.* Musée Magnin, Dijon

Figure 3. Charles de La Fosse. *The Assumption.* Musée des Beaux-Arts, Caen

against Bologna. Fragonard's choice is, therefore, significant. We are fortunate in having a record of a statement that he made about La Fosse to Michel Nitot (1759–1828), an opera singer during the Revolutionary period, who called himself Dufresne (P. Ratouis de Limay, 1950, p. 76, published certain passages from Nitot's notes). We quote here from the original manuscript preserved in the Bibliothèque des Arts Décoratifs, Paris: "M. Fragonard *père*, who had the same understanding of coloristic effects as Rembrandt, showed me a sketch of a ceiling by La Fosse, one of our best colorists; he especially admired the sensibility of the artist, who treated colors as large masses, or groups, such that each group of clouds, figures, or ground had a general tonality; the effect of the picture was determined first, and then each mass was diversified by light, shadow, and the variety of more or less bright related hues with which he enriched it."

There is nothing surprising in Fragonard's appreciation of La Fosse, and the analysis of the "ceiling sketch" in Fragonard's possession—an *Assumption*, one of those mentioned above—tells us much about his artistic concepts. As far as we know, nowhere else are they formulated as clearly. What he admired in his predecessor were the great masses of color that were variously treated, according to the lighting, the shadows, and the "variety of related hues." It was not only a La Fosse, but also a Fragonard that Fragonard had described!

Between 1770 and 1773, to the chagrin of the critics, Fragonard stopped exhibiting his works. Thus, a certain "Raphaël le Jeune" (actually Daudet de Jossan) wrote a mock letter, in 1771, to one of his friends in Rome: "He [Fragonard] has abandoned the *grand genre*; he has renounced glory; he paints little Portraits, which do not go for very much, but little streams make big rivers, and then, one always enjoys a little bit of vainglory." "Vainglory never lasts," his friend replied. "It is a waste of time and of his fine youth, we should pity him that the Arts lost him so soon after such fine hopes." Mme d'Épinay, in a letter to the Abbé Galiani (see Diderot, XI, 1964, p. 204), expressed the same opinions as this pamphleteer: "M. Fragonard? He is wasting his time and his talent; he is making money."

The most interesting document, which has often been cited, since the time of Portalis, but rarely studied in its entirety, comes from the painter Antoine Renou, the presumed author of the *Dialogues sur la peinture*, "imprimé chez Tartouillis, aux dépens de l'Académie" ["printed by Tartouillis at the Academy's expense"], in 1773. This pamphlet, whose vehemence is matched only by the mediocrity of its style, and which is full of now-obscure allusions, is supposed to record a conversation between "Milord Littelton," "Monseigneur Fabretti, Roman Prelate," and "Monsieur Remi, Art Dealer" (Rémy was a famous art expert; the identity of the others remains unknown) on the Salon of that year, the state of the Arts in Paris as compared to England and Rome, and, in particular, of "Painting, considering the extreme peril in which it is in France." The three art lovers approved of the sculptors of the day, but they spared neither Pierre, the *Premier peintre,* Vien and the first advocates of the Classical revival, nor Doyen, whose free execution to them seemed contrived.

"Just imagine some virtuous Roman in our midst ... and all the filth of the likes of le Pr[ince]., Frago ... and la Gre[née] ... " (p. 164). So much for the tone. (We will refer again to this part of the text in connection with Louveciennes.) One of the strongest criticisms aimed at Fragonard, as well as at "Bri[ard]" and "Caza[nova]," was that he did not exhibit at the Salon: "I begin to see why many painters persist in not exhibiting anything here. Frago ... is one of the more prudent ones, he has not risked himself at the Salon since his accreditation. Their reasons are plain to see; they prefer taking refuge in their studios instead of venturing out in public." "A few art lovers, friends, acquaintances, are the only ones to see them, to praise them, whether in good faith or to court the master of the house, but not the public, which is never admitted into the *Sallon des Turcarets* decorated by these gentlemen...." "If they but once came out into the open, the public would be quick to let them know what's what" (pp. 30–31).

That Fragonard did not exhibit, nor complete any of his official commissions, was, he said, because of his "work for Mme la comtesse du Barry." (His decorations for her at Louveciennes will be discussed in detail below; see pp. 320–25.) What is interesting is Renou's reaction, which has often been quoted, and which proves that Fragonard's oeuvre was not as unnoticed as has been claimed: "There is also at Lussienne the *nec plus ultra, pour le heurté, le roullé, le bien fouetté, le tartouillis* ["bruised, rolled, whipped, smeared"]. He's the one, he's the real *Tartouillis*," Remi exclaims. Msgr Fabretti asks: "*Le roullé, le bien fouetté, le Tartouillis,* are these insults?" "What! You must be joking, I am speaking of the divine Fragr., the number one brush according to our leaders of painting," Remi replies. Neither Msgr Fabretti nor Milord Littelton seems to share the enthusiasm of Remi (which, as we shall see, was tainted by commercial considerations), who offers a final argument: "He has, nevertheless, made a reputation for himself among the financiers, and for a Painter that is as good as any other." To which Milord Littelton replies disdainfully, "Midas, the good Midas, can make him his First Painter, then."

Could this have been an allusion to the duc de Chartres, one of the wealthiest men in France? On July 30, 1772, the future Philippe-Égalité wrote to his mistress, Mme de Genlis, that he wanted to have painted "two pictures after the tale that you know" (here, she was more fortunate than we are), a "charming tale" that had made him "cry." "I commissioned them from Fragonard, who found the idea quite lovely and assured me that I would be very happy with them" (Maugras, 1904, pp. 36–38). At this point in his career, Fragonard must often have been called upon by various high officials (the *Fermiers généraux,* or tax collectors, were among Fragonard's favorite clients) to execute a drawing or a painting.

Fragonard had painted the portrait of Mlle Guimard about 1769 (cat. no. 125). Entrusted to Fragonard was the decoration of the grand Salon of her house in Paris built by Ledoux, the architect of Louveciennes, and dedicated to Terpsichore. The following text by Grimm (*Correspondance littéraire,* March 1773, X, 1879, p. 210)—in fact by Meister, who began writing for this journal in 1773—has been quoted by all of Fragonard's biographers since 1806: "The *hôtel* of Mlle Guimard is almost finished; if it was paid for by Amor, it was designed by Volupté, and this divinity never had a temple in Greece more worthy of her cult. The salon is full of paintings; Mlle Guimard is represented as Terpsichore, with all of the attributes that could characterize her in the most appealing way. These paintings were not yet finished when, for some reason, she had a quarrel with her painter, M. Fragonard; the quarrel was so considerable that he was dismissed and another painter had to be called upon. Later, M. Fragonard, curious to see what was becoming of his work in the hands of another artist, found a way of getting into the house. He made his way to the salon without encountering anyone. Noticing a palette and colors in a corner, he immediately saw the means for his revenge. With four strokes of the brush, he wiped the smile off Terpsichore's face and gave it an angry and furious expression, without altering the likeness. Having committed his mischief, he quickly stole away, and, as fate would have it, Mlle Guimard arrived shortly thereafter with a group of friends who had come to evaluate the new painter's talent. Imagine her indignation at seeing herself so disfigured! Yet, the angrier she became, the more she resembled her portrait."

The "other painter" in question was the young David. A letter from

Figure 4. Fragonard.
The Muse Calliope
(actually, *Terpsichore*).
Musée des Beaux-Arts,
Besançon

Figure 5. Fragonard.
The Muse Terpsichore.
Musée des Beaux-Arts,
Besançon

Figure 6. Fragonard. *A Muse*.
Bibliothèque Municipale, Besançon

Figure 7. Fragonard. *A Muse*.
Musée des Beaux-Arts, Besançon

Pierre to Ledoux, dated November 15, 1773 (first published by Régis Michel, 1981–82), gives this version of the facts: "I was able to see M. David only this morning, Sir . . . He claims that M. Fragonard had agreed to do the work for 6,000 *livres,* and that after having finished the underpainting, he demanded 20,000 *livres* [he was paid 18,000 for the decorations at Louveciennes] and four years' time, and that, frightened by this last sum, Mlle Guimard renounced her project, relieved to have had to pay only what *louis* she had already disbursed to M. Fragonard, who, for his part, either out of negligence or design, left the salon unfinished.

"M. Fragonard then left [for Italy] and was too outspoken about not caring that he had left the work unfinished, such that S[ieur]. David did not write him, having been assured by many people of M. Fragonard's disgust.

"The first mistake was in asking six thousand *livres* for a work that was worth twenty or more, even by a beginner; hence, the problems and complaints all around.

"If Mlle Guimard does not want M. Fragonard any more, and if M. Fragonard has tacitly renounced his work, nothing can be done. Surely Mlle Guimard has the right to choose, and David does not seem to be the kind of man who has anything to reproach himself for. Far from it; he firmly believes that he is obliging M. Fragonard in ridding him of a chore that revolts and repels his highly spirited temperament."

This version of the story is less colorful than the first, yet does not appreciably contradict it (see the version recounted by the Goncourts, p. 283 [note], who learned of it from Théophile). It does provide an idea of Fragonard's character, and of his capricious and unreliable nature.

David finished the decorations (and also painted a portrait of Mlle Guimard). The "four large paintings, the most attractive we know [3.09 x 2.60—or 2.45 meters, for the two smallest]," were sold December 21–22, 1846 (no. 16), and have been lost. Perhaps they were in some way related to the four drawings from the Musée des Beaux-Arts, Besançon, reproduced here (figures 4–7).

Fragonard's fiascoes with Mme du Barry and Mlle Guimard probably cut more deeply than Pierre's letter indicates, and they must have been in

Figure 8. Abbé de Saint-Non, after Fragonard. *Hercules and Antaeus,* after Guercino. Bibliothèque Nationale, Paris, Cabinet des Estampes

large part responsible for his departure for Italy on October 5, 1773. However, he still had his devotees, and had not completely fallen out of favor.

In *Jacques le Fataliste,* Diderot alludes to the painter. Jacques has just given a lively description of an incident in the street:

> The Master: "Good heavens! Jacques, your composition is well arranged, rich, pleasant, varied, full of movement. When we get back to Paris, take this subject to Fragonard, and you will see what he will be able to do with it."
>
> Jacques: "After what you have told me of your knowledge of painting, I can accept your praise without blushing" (Assézat ed., VI, 1875, p. 194).

The Abbé de Saint-Non did not forget Fragonard either. He made aquatints of the drawings that his young friend had done during his first trip in Italy. For his personal collection, from each of these aquatints he printed a first example, in counterproof, which does not reverse the original composition. Saint-Non inscribed one of these aquatints (figure 8): "Ceiling of the palais Sampieri painted by/Guercino/in Bologna. *Il divo fragonard,* del[ineavit]!"

CHRONOLOGY

1770

May 30
Death of François Boucher.

June 5
Claude-Nicolas Ledoux is granted permission to construct a new *hôtel* for Mlle Guimard in the Chaussée-d'Antin (see Gallet, 1980, pp. 84, 252). It was probably at about this date that the dancer commissioned Fragonard to undertake the decorations. The date coincides with the time limit of four years requested by the painter to complete the work—as indicated in a letter from Pierre to Ledoux dated November 15, 1773 (see below).

June 24
The Comtesse du Barry buys from François-Hubert Drouais (1727–1775): "quatre dessus de portes, pour l'ancien pavillon de Louveciennes, l'un représentant les Grâces, l'autre l'amour qui embrase l'univers, l'autre Vénus & l'amour & l'autre la nuit. Ces quatres dessus de portes, peints par Mr Fragonard, peintre du Roy. Ils ont été achetés par madame la comtesse au Sr Drouais, à qui ils appartenoient, 1.200.

"Selon l'ordre de madame la comtesse, avoir fait remettre sur toille, trois des dessus de portes cy-dessus, les avoir r'agrandis, fait repeindre & accorder les agrandissages, argent déboursé 420" (*Mémoire* that belonged to Baron Pichon, which he published in 1856, pp. 288–89).

The four paintings in question were identified by Jacques Wilhelm (1956) as: *The Three Graces* (cat. no. 153), *L'Amour embrasant l'Univers* (cat. no. 152), *Venus and Cupid* (National Gallery of Ireland, Dublin), and *Night* (Edmond de Rothschild collection, Switzerland).

September 20
Ange-Jacques Gabriel, *Premier architecte du Roi,* receives at the Gobelins, in the presence of Marigny, the *Coresus and Callirhoë* (cat. no. 104), its design to be adapted for a tapestry. "Lequel tableau nous avons trouvé d'une belle composition et exécution" (Gerspach, 1888, p. 120).

Its price of 2,400 *livres* is documented (see January 31, 1773).

December 3
Pierre suggests to Marigny that Fragonard and Huet execute four paintings for the king's dining room at Versailles: "...on les leur partageroit; quoyque l'idée des sujets que j'ay eu l'honneur de vous

proposer paroisse pouvoir réussir par la nouveauté, je vous supplie cependant, Monsieur, d'agréer que je ne la présente à ces deux artistes que comme un canevas, qui ne doit point donner d'entraves à leur génie" (Furcy-Raynaud, 1904, XX, p. 220).

December 10
Marigny accepts Pierre's proposition, but leaves the choice of subjects to the artists: "j'agrée aussi Mrs Fragonard et Huet pour l'exécution des quatre tableaux de la salle à manger du même appartement. Vous pouvez les leur distribuer, deux à chacun, sans leur imposer néanmoins absolument la loi des sujets que vous m'avez proposés. Je sçais combien ces sortes d'entraves sont gênantes pour un artiste et nuisent à l'exécution de son ouvrage" (Furcy-Raynaud, 1904, XX, p. 221).

Fragonard's and Huet's pictures, which were estimated at 1,600 *livres* (see 1774), seem never to have been finished (see 1771).

An 1841 lithograph by Barathier (figure 1), after Fragonard's *La Toilette* (W. 314, fig. 140), dates this work to 1770.

Saint-Non engraves *The Donkey's Stable* (figure 2). A drawing entitled *The Stable* (A.1),which belonged to the Goncourts, was signed and dated 1770; its whereabouts are now unknown (see Launay, 1983–84, no. 99), but it was described at length by Edmond de Goncourt, and seems to correspond to the engraving reproduced here. The same scene is depicted in a wash drawing (figure 3) preserved in the Musée "Ile de France," Saint-Jean-Cap Ferrat.

Publication of the first series (Rome) of *Fragments choisis dans les Peintures et les Tableaux les plus intéressants des Palais et des Églises de L'Italie,* with engravings by Saint-Non after Fragonard, Robert, and Ango. The other series—on Bologna, Naples, and Venice—were published in 1771, 1772, 1773, and 1774.

1771

Probably at the beginning of the year, the Comtesse du Barry (1743–1793) commissioned Fragonard to paint four panels (today in the Frick Collection, New York; see cat. nos. 154, 155) for her new residence at Louveciennes, built by Ledoux; construction began in late December 1770 (see Gallet, 1980, p. 252). In a report of the "ouvrages faits dans le courant des six premiers mois de l'année 1771, sous l'ordre et conduitte de monsieur Le Doux architecte; par Carbilliet, mtre menuiser," dated September 30, 1772, there is the following passage: "Plus fait et fourny 4 grand chassis pour les tableaux de mr

299

Figure 1. Barathier, after Fragonard. *La Toilette*. Bibliothèque Nationale, Paris, Cabinet des Estampes

Figure 2. Abbé de Saint-Non. *The Donkey's Stable*. Bibliothèque Nationale, Paris, Cabinet des Estampes

Figure 3. Fragonard. *The Donkey's Stable*. Musée "Ile de France," Saint-Jean-Cap Ferrat, Fondation Ephrussi de Rothschild

Flagonard, les d[its] de 9 pied 10 po[uces] sur 6 pied 8 po[uces], dont deux de cintré en pland, valent pour les droits 12 livres piesse, et les cintré 20 livres piesse, font les 4 ensemble 64 livres." This sum was reduced by Ledoux to 46 *livres* (Bibliothèque Nationale, ms. fr. 8160, "compte de Me du Barry," fol. 155 *v.*, published by Cayeux, 1935, p. 45, n. 1).

February 18
Fragonard purchases a number of works at the posthumous sale of Boucher's collection (see the annotated catalogue in the Bibliothèque d'Art et d'Archéologie, Paris), including "Un bourguemestre, figure en pied," attributed to van Dyck, but catalogued as by Jean van Kalcker (van Calraet ?), no. 11; several paintings by La Fosse (nos. 58, 61, 65), and numerous drawings by Bramer, Roos, Verdier, Stella, and Boucher (nos. 253, 263, 336, 488), and some prints, mostly Flemish and Dutch (nos. 548, 586, 604). In addition to his well-established taste for Northern art, one notices an interest in studies for ceiling decorations (no. 343).

July 13
In Mme du Barry's account books, a sum of 1,200 *livres* was paid "A Fragonard, sur un mandat de madame la comtesse." In the margin is the note: "le mandat n'est pas acquitté" (Bibliothèque Nationale, ms. fr. 8158, fol. 83, "Paiements faits sur les 300.000 du mois de juin," published by Vatel, 1883, p. 325).

October
Fragonard's absence at the Salon is remarked upon by a critic: the author, "Raphaël le Jeune" (pseudonym of Daudet de Jossan), a painter at the Académie de Saint-Luc, imagines a dialogue between the paintings, overheard by a guard at the Louvre: "M. Fragonard... — M. Fragonard! M. Fragonard! Il n'y sera pas... —Pourquoi?—Oh! c'est qu'il a abandonné le grand genre" (*Lettre... sur les peintures, sculptures et gravures qui sont exposées cette année au Louvre*, from which we have already quoted, p. 296).

October 4
Mme d'Épinay (1725–1783), in a letter to the Abbé Galiani (1728–1787; *Correspondance de Diderot*, Roth ed., 1964, p. 204), summarizes Raphaël le Jeune's *Lettre* in these terms: "M. Fragonard? Il perd son temps et son talent: il gagne de l'argent."

November 25
Another 1,200 *livres* is disbursed to Fragonard, with no other mention (Bibliothèque Nationale, ms. fr. 8158, fol. 86, "État des paiements faits sur les 300.000 du mois de septembre"; Vatel, 1883, p. 528).

Munhall and Davidson (1968, p. 102) have linked these payments to the series of paintings executed for Louveciennes (see p. 323).

December 23
Marigny orders Pierre to see to the acceleration of the work undertaken at Versailles: "... il faudroit savoir de MM. Briard et Fragonard quand ils comptent pouvoir y travailler, et les presser de s'y mettre le plus tôt possible, sans préjudice néanmoins des ouvrages de Mme la comtesse du Barry" (Furcy-Raynaud, 1904, XX, p. 247).

A report on the paintings for Bellevue and for the new Trianon mentions the slowness of Fragonard's progress: "Bellevue, ordonnés en 1766: le jour, la nuit par m. Fragonard qui promet d'y travailler en diligence en décembre 1772.

"Petits appartements du Roi à Versailles, ordonnés en décembre 1770: deux tableaux pour la salle à manger, par m. Fragonard qui y travaille en ayant été empéché par ses ouvrages pour madame la comtesse du Barry" (Archives Nationales, O¹ 1912).

Diderot writes *Jacques le Fataliste*, published in installments in Grimm's *Correspondance littéraire* from 1778 to 1780. The following quotation is from one of the "additions" that were sent to subscribers to the *Correspondance littéraire* in 1780. Jacques relates an intriguing incident, which provokes a most interesting response from his Master:

Jacques: "Voyez au milieu de la rue un fiacre, la soupente cassée, et renversé sur le côté."
Le Maître: "Je le vois."
Jacques: "Un moine et deux filles en sont sortis. Le moine s'enfuit à toutes jambes. Le cocher se hâte de descendre de son siège. Un caniche du fiacre s'est mis à la poursuite du moine, et l'a saisi par sa jaquette; le moine fait tous ses efforts pour se débarrasser du chien. Une des filles, débraillée, la gorge découverte, se tient les côtés à force de rire. L'autre fille, qui s'est fait une bosse au front, est appuyée contre la portière, et se presse la tête à deux mains. Cependant la populace s'est attroupée, les polissons accourent et poussent des cris, les marchands et les marchandes ont bordé le seuil de leurs boutiques, et d'autres spectateurs sont à leurs fenêtres."
Le Maître: "Comment diable! Jacques, la composition est bien ordonnée, riche, plaisante, variée et pleine de mouvement. A notre retour à Paris, porte ce sujet à Fragonard; et tu verras ce qu'il en saura faire" (Assézat ed., 1875, VI, pp. 193–94).

Adélaïde Allou makes an engraving entitled *Vuë des restes d'un Theatre que l'on retrouve parmi les débris de la Ville Adriene près Tivoli à 18 milles de Rome* (see cat. no. 24, *Related works*, and figure 1).

1772

July 20
Bachaumont describes the *pavillon* at Louveciennes in his *Mémoires*

Figure 4. Johann Christian von Mannlich. *Silvio and Dorinda.*
Alte Pinakothek, Munich

Figure 5. Johann Christian von Mannlich. *Satyr and Coriska.*
Alte Pinakothek, Munich

secrets (XXIV, p. 161): "les artistes les plus renommés se sont efforcés d'enrichir de leurs productions un séjour aussi délicieux. Le plafond d'un des salons de côté est du Sieur Briard; la devise en est ruris amor et représente les plaisirs de campagne. De l'autre côté, c'est un ciel vague, et quatre grands tableaux du Sieur Fragonard, qui roulent sur les amours des bergers et semblent allégoriques aux aventures de la maîtresse du lieu; ils ne sont pas encore finis."

July 30
Letter from the Duc de Chartres, the future Philippe-Égalité (1747–1793), to Mme de Genlis (1746–1830): "j'ai commandé ce matin deux tableaux d'après le conte que vous connaissez. Je l'ai relu encore deux fois, ce charmant conte. Rien ne me fait ce plaisir et cet effet-là. J'ai encore pleuré en le relisant la dernière fois. Oh! mon amour, mon cher enfant, il n'y a rien de tendre et d'aimable comme vous. J'ai bien trouvé l'adresse de Pérignon {most likely Nicolas Pérignon (1726–1782), the landscape painter}, mais il est en Hollande, ce qui fait que je les ai commandés à Fragonard, qui a trouvé l'idée fort jolie et qui m'a assuré que j'en serais content. Je n'avais pas besoin de son assurance, car de quelque manière qu'il la rende, cela me rappellera toujours ... et me rendra bien content" (Maugras, 1904, pp. 36–38).

October 19
Announcement in *L'Avant coureur* (p. 659) for two engravings by François Godefroy after Fragonard's paintings, "*Annette at the Age of Fifteen*" and "*Annette at the Age of Twenty*" (see cat. no. 87, figures 3, 4).

November
Announcement for the same engravings in the *Mercure de France* (p. 177).

November 9
Portalis (1889, p. 201) quoted from the copy of the Huquier collection sales catalogue that Mariette annotated (and which once belonged to Baron Pichon): "à propos de deux dessins de Leprince et de Fragonard, représentant l'un des soldats russes, et le second, celui de Frago, la *Résurrection de Lazare* ... Mariette a mis en note de sa main: Ils les firent en badinant et sur la même table chez Huquier" (figure 1, p. 239).

That same year, Henri Gérard, Marguerite's brother, arrives in Paris (*Registre des cartes de sureté,* June 13, 1793, Archives Nationales, F⁷ 4806).

Saint-Non makes an engraving of *The Dancing Bear* after Fragonard (figure 3, p. 149).

The German painter Johann Christian von Mannlich (1740–1822), then in Paris, finishes two pictures inspired by Giovanni Battista Guarini's *Pastor Fido,* and shows them to several painters: "Da ich jeden Morgen sech eifrig an einem Bilde arbeitete, das ich unvollendet von Zweibrücken mitgebracht hatte, führte ich es trotz meines bewegten Lebens in Paris bald zu Ende. Es stellte die von Silvio verwundete Dorinda dar, ein Vorwurf, zu dem mich ebenfalls Guarinis 'Pastor Fido' angeregt hatte. Ich zeigte dieses Gemälde sowie meinen 'Satyr und Koriska' den Künstlern, mit denen ich immer verkehrte, Vernet, Vien, Greuze, Doyen, Fragonard und meinen alten Kamaraden von Rom" ("I worked ardently every morning on a painting that I had brought unfinished from Deux-Ponts, which, in spite of my active life in Paris, I soon finished. It represented Dorinda wounded by Sylvio [see figure 4], my sketch for which was inspired by Guarini's *Pastor Fido.* I showed this painting, as well as my *Satyr and Coriska* {figure 5], to artists that I knew: Vernet, Vien, Greuze, Doyen, Fragonard, and my old comrades from Rome").

1773

January
The *Mercure de France* (pp. 183–84) announces the publication of two engravings by Marchand "représentant deux baisers d'après les pastels de M. Fragonard, qui sont dans le cabinet de M. Jallier, architecte" (figures 6, 7). They are dedicated "à Monseigneur le Duc de la Vallière."

January 31
Fragonard receives 600 *livres* owed to him since 1769, the last payment for the *Coresus and Callirhoë* (Archives Nationales, O¹ 1934 B, published by Engerand, 1901, pp. 194–95; see also *Registre des paiements,* Bibliothèque du Louvre, fol. 151 a, signed by Fragonard, February 18).

March
Meister, Grimm's successor at the *Correspondance littéraire* (Grimm, 1879, X, pp. 210–11), recounts the famous anecdote about Fragonard's problems with Mlle Guimard, quoted above (pp. 297–98).

Figure 6. Jacques Marchand, after Fragonard.
The Kiss. Musée du Louvre, Paris,
Cabinet des Dessins, Rothschild Collection

Figure 7. Jacques Marchand, after Fragonard.
The Kiss. Musée du Louvre, Paris,
Cabinet des Dessins, Rothschild Collection

Alexandre Lenoir, in an unpublished manuscript that belonged to Georges Wildenstein (W. [French edition], p. 41), gives practically the same version, claiming to have heard it from Fragonard himself: "en 1773, chargé de peindre le Salon de Melle Guimard, elle fut représentée en Terpsichore avec les attributs qui caractérisent la Muse de la danse. On raconte que les tableaux n'étaient pas encore terminés, lorsqu'on ne sait pourquoi elle se brouille avec son peintre et en choisit un autre. Fragonard curieux de savoir ce que devenait son ouvrage entre les mains de son successeur, trouva le moyen de s'introduire dans la maison. Il pénètre jusque dans le salon sans y rencontrer personne; apercevant dans un coin une palette et des couleurs, il imagina sur le champ le moyen de se venger. En quatre coups de pinceaux il efface le sourire, sans nuire à la ressemblance du portrait. Cela fait il se sauve au plus vite, et le hazard veut que Melle Guimard arriva quelques moments après avec plusieurs de ses amis qui venaient juger les talents du nouveau peintre. Quelle fut son indignation en se voyant défigurée de la sorte! mais plus sa colère éclate plus la métamorphose devient ressemblante.... Comme je l'ai déjà remarqué, les peintres se sont souvent servis du pinceau pour consacrer publiquement un juste ressentiment. J'ai consacré cette anecdote que le peintre m'a raconté lui-même, dans un article imprimé dans la *Biographie* des frères Michaud" (vol. 15, p. 421).

(See November 15, for another version of this story.)

March 29
A report on the "état des tableaux commandés pour le château de Bellevue" also mentions Fragonard's lateness in completing his commissions: "M. Fragonard a eu l'honneur de passer chez M. de Montucla pour l'assurer de ses civilités et lui rendre réponse à la lettre qu'il a reçu [sic] touchant les tableaux qu'il a à faire pour le Roi; jusqu'à présent, il n'a pu y travailler ayant été occupé des tableaux dont il était chargé pour Madame du Barry. Présentement, il assure qu'il va y travaillé avec tout le zèle et l'assiduité" (Archives Nationales, O¹ 1531, published by Bapst, 1892, with the reference O¹ 1514, and by Engerand, 1901, p. 196).

August
Fragonard again does not exhibit at the Salon, but Vien shows two paintings (nos. 5, 6): "deux jeunes Grecques font serment de ne jamais aimer et se jurent un attachement éternel sur l'autel de l'Amitié; le Temps endormi et sa faux brisée, dont les débris servent à entretenir le feu qui brûle sur l'autel, indiquent que leur union sera durable; mais l'Amour qui se rit de pareils sermens et qui favorise les voeux du jeune homme qu'on aperçoit dans le fond du Tableau, profite du sommeil du Temps pour allumer son flambeau à l'autel même de l'Amitié... [et] de jeunes Grecques rencontrent l'Amour endormi dans un jardin; elles s'en approchent sans le connoître, et s'amusent à le parer de guirlandes de fleurs. Ces deux Tableaux, l'un de 10 pieds de long, sur 6 pieds 9 pouces de large, appartiennent à Madame la Comtesse du Barry, et sont destinés pour Lucienne [Louveciennes]. Le dernier ne pourra être exposé que dans le courant du Salon."

Little is recorded abut Vien's paintings for Mme du Barry, and even less about Fragonard's. However, the *Dialogues sur la peinture,* a pamphlet published that year *"chez Tartouillis"* and probably written by the painter Antoine Renou (1731–1806), contains some ironic comments aimed at Fragonard and other artists of his generation; the pretext is an imaginary argument about them among the famous art expert Rémy ("Remi"), a mysterious Monseigneur Fabretti, and an unidentified "Englishman" called Milord Littelton (pp. 20–21, 24, 30, 31, 83, 84, 164):

"—M. Remi: Vous avez vu à Lussienne encore le *nec plus ultra,* pour le heurté, le roullé, le bien fouetté, le tartouillis. Le voilà, le voilà le véritable Tartouillis.
—M. Fabretti: Le roullé, le bien fouetté, le Tartouillis, sont-ce des injures, Monsieur Remi, ou des éloges?
—M. Remi: Comment, vous vous moquez, je crois, c'est du divin Fragr. dont je vous parle, le pinceau le plus capable selon les chefs de notre peinture. Pour celui-là rien ne lui manque. Il va paroître sous peu une dissertation de l'ami Foliot [another art expert] dans laquelle il déduit fort au long que le divin Fragr. est un Michel-Ange et un Titien, les deux à lui tout seul.
—M. Fabretti: M. Fragr. n'en déplaise au dissertateur, les amis de Michel-Ange et de Titien ne seront jamais les vôtres. J'imagine que la dissertation essuiera une réponse.
—Milord: Il y a plus de trente ans que Rousseau l'a faite.

'Griffon, rimailleur subalterne,
Vante Siphon le barbouilleur,
Et Siphon, Peintre de taverne,
Prône Griphon le rimailleur,
Or en cela certain railleur,
Trouve qu'ils sont tous deux fort sages.
Car sans Griphon et ses ouvrages,
Qui jamais eut vanté Siphon,
Et sans Siphon et ses suffrages,
Qui jamais eut prôné Griphon.'

—M. Remi: Il s'est fait cependant une réputation chez les financiers, et pour un Peintre elle vaut bien un[e] autre. Pour l'un c'est un Raphaël, pour l'autre un Guerchin. Tous leurs cabinets sont ornés de ses oeuvres.
—Milord: De pareils châlans ne m'étonnent pas, et Midas le bon Midas peut bien en faire son Premier Peintre.
(...)
—M. Remi: En 1755, on imprima à Paris chez les libraires associés un livre intitulé, l'art de devenir Peintre en trois heures, et d'exécuter au pinceau les ouvrages des grands maîtres sans avoir appris le dessein. Cette recette eut, comme vous l'imaginez, un succès prodigieux, et cette seule année valut à notre Académie plus de sujets que tout le siècle n'en avait fourni: les Frago[nard]., les Casa[nova]., les Ha[llé]., les Tar[aval]. et une foule d'autres.
(...)
—M. Fabretti: (...)On entend dire que les Bri[ard]., Frago[nard]., Caza[nova]. ont rempli quelques cabinets de leurs précieux ouvrages, on le répète sans en avoir rien vu. Quelques amateurs, des amis, des connoissances, sont les seuls à les voir, à les vanter, de bonne foi ou pour faire leur cour au maître du logis, et jamais le public, qui n'est point admis dans le *sallon* des Turcarets que ces messieurs décorent.
(...)
—Milord: Leurs tableaux sont comme les lectures de société qui enthousiasment tous les auditeurs. Ainsi la *Pucelle* de Chapelain fut pendant vingt ans une chose sublime, pour être à sa juste place, il faut paroître sur la scène. Que les auteurs se fassent imprimer, que les Peintres peignent des coupoles à St. Roch [Le Moyne], qu'ils se montrent au *sallon;* et vous verrez alors ces messieurs, qui dans leurs cercles sont toujours les premiers hommes du siècle, une fois en raze campagne, le public sera prompt à leur sillier [*siffler* or *signifier ?*] le contraire.
—M. Remi: Je commence à concevoir pourquoi, plusieurs s'obstinent à ne rien exposer ici. Frago[nard]. ... est un des plus prudents, il ne s'est point hazardé au *sallon* depuis son agrément. Je vois bien leurs raisons; ils aiment mieux rester retranchés dans quelques cabinets que de s'avanturer dans la place publique.
(...)
—M. Remi: Je sçai si ce salon fait bien à l'art, mais il fait grand mal à la plûpart des Artistes. La critique les désole; et c'est pourquoi Gre[uze]., Pie[rre]., Frago[nard]., Bri[ard]., Caza[nova]. n'y ont pas paru cette année.
—Milord: Mais ils n'y gagnent rien, et à propos de Peinture, c'est comme à propos de botte, il est aisé de parler du grand Turc si l'on veut.
—M. Remi: Il est vrai que vous ne vous êtes pas mal égayés sur leurs comptes, et les absents ont été souvent interloqués.
(...)
—Milord: (...) Selon un ancien sage, les Artistes forment les moeurs plus sûrement et brièvement que les philosophes. Les statues des héros, la représentation d'une belle action, d'un acte de vertu enflammoient le grand Scipion."

October 4
Pierre, *Premier peintre du Roi,* addresses a note to Fragonard (previously unpublished; brought to our attention by Udo van de Sandt), which shows how little respect the artist had for the Academy: "Monsieur Fragonard, J'apprends monsieur par une lettre de m. Bergeret que vous este déterminé à refaire le voyage d'Italie. Je vous en fais mon sincere complimen mais vous ne pouvez pas partir sans un congé parce que vous êtes attaché à une académie Royale. Peut être avez vous peu de tems: le moyen d'abréger serois de m'écrire un mot sur lequel je vous obtiendroi la permission de partir et vous *santez* bien qu'il m'est impossible de ne l'en pas informer" (Archives Nationales, AP², folios 246–247).

142 La Lettre

Oil on canvas, 38 x 30 cm.
According to an 1873 sales catalogue, the verso of the stretcher reads: La plume sera inhabile à décrire le charme et la grâce répandu [*sic*] sur cette délicieuse figure de Fragonard

Private collection

Provenance
[Bachet, Brilliant, de Cossé, Quenet]: sold, April 22, 1776, no. 91: "une jeune et belle Italienne vue à mi-corps, accoudée contre un pupitre et s'appuyant la joue contre sa main: elle tient une lettre décachetée et semble la lire avec émotion.... Hauteur 12 pouces longueur 8 pouces [32.4 x 21.6 cm.]" (?); Comte de Merle: sold, March 1, 1784, no. 31: "une jeune fille, vue à mi-corps, assise et appuyée devant une table, lisant une lettre.... 11 pouces 6 lignes, 8 pouces 6 lignes" (for 200 *livres*) (?); Volpeto and Morghen: sold, November 6, 1822, no. 20: "deux petits tableaux faits avec facilité et avec goût, représentant deux jeunes filles dont l'une a la tête appuyée sur sa main, et est occupée à lire une lettre"; Marquis de Roche Bousseau: sold, May 5–8, 1873, no. 122: "appartenait, sous le premier Empire, à Mme Récamier" (3,800 francs); Comte de La Béraudière, by 1874: sold, May 18–30, 1885, no. 25 (for 6,000 francs, to Féral); Mühlbacher, by 1889: sold, May 15–18, 1899, no. 16 (for 44,500 francs, to Stettiner); Marquis de Chaponay, by 1906–until 1918 (Gimpel, 1963, p. 38); [Wildenstein]; David David-Weill, by 1921; Fritz Mannheimer (first husband of the present owner), 1936.

Exhibitions
Paris, 1874, no. 150
Paris, 1883–84, no. 47
Paris, 1921, no. 55, ill.
Paris, 1946, no. 15
London, 1968, no. 240, fig. 290
New York, 1977, no. 39, fig. 46
Tokyo, 1980, no. 60, colorpl.

Bibliography
G. p. 335
P. pp. 65, 202, 282
N. p. 147, ill. between pp. 158 and 159
Henriot, 1926, I, pp. 123–25, ill. p. 126
R. pp. 168, 171
W. 386, fig. 164, pp. 26–27 (French edition)
Thuillier, 1967, p. 37, colorpl.
W. and M. 410, ill., colorpl. XL

Related works
An etching after the painting was made by Paul-Edme Le Rat (1849–1892) before 1873 (P. p. 329, no. 121; Naquet, 1890, ill. p. 72; Sjöberg and Gardey, 1977, XIV, pp. 89–90, no. 18).

A sketchier version, but of good quality (figure 1) although slightly smaller in size (33 x 27 cm.), was in the Hahnloser collection: sold, Sotheby's, London, June 30, 1965, no. 27, ill.).

Fragonard's most recent biographers believe that *La Lettre* was sold with the de Ghendt collection, November 15, 1779 (no. 30). Several facts contradict this: the de Ghendt picture measured only 32.5 x 24.5 centimeters, and the sitter was holding the letter "*de la main droite*" [our emphasis]. We believe that this picture was the pendant to the "vieillard portant chapeau sur sa tête ... sa main droite est appuyée sur un livre, et de la gauche il tient une bourse," which was in the same sale. The two works seem to have belonged to Hall in 1778 (Villot, 1867, p. 74): "une petite fille tenant une lettre 144 [*livres*]" and "un avare tenant un sac d'argent, de M. Telusen 401 [*livres*]." Could this "Telusen" have been the Thélusson who sold a "buste de vieillard" on December 1, 1777? The two pictures were sold again November 28, 1783, no. 29: "vieillard tenant un sac de la main gauche et la droite appuyée sur un livre, ayant un chapeau sur sa tête ...," and "une tête de jeune fille coeffée en cheveux, le bras droit appuyé sur une table, tenant un *livre* [our emphasis] à la main."

This *Old Man* does not seem to be identifiable with W. 385, pl. 78 (see figure 2; a replica [?] of which was sold in Chartres December 5, 1971, no. 59, colorpl.). Among the gouaches and miniatures in the Vassal de Saint-Hubert collection, sold April 24, 1783, no. 87, were a: "femme à mi-corps tenant un miroir par M. Hall et une autre femme tenant une lettre par Honoré Fragonard [10.8 x 21.6 cm.!]."

Also related to this *Lettre* is a painting in the Cincinnati Art Museum (figure 3), which was in the collection of Paul de Saint-Victor and then of Wildenstein (P. 280; N. p. 147), and which shows a woman not reading, but about to write a letter. The picture has the same dimensions as *La Lettre* and, judging as much by the freedom of the handling as by the style of the sitter's décolletage, may be included among the *figures de fantaisie*.

Figure 1. Fragonard. *La Lettre.* Whereabouts unknown

Figure 2. Fragonard. *Old Man.* Private collection, New York

Figure 3. Fragonard. *Woman about to Write a Letter.* Cincinnati Art Museum

A very young girl with a tender but somewhat mischievous smile is reading a letter whose seal is broken, leaning her elbow on an open drawer full of letters. Light falls on her hair, her white bodice, and on the hand holding the letter, while her face, with its rounded chin, is in half-light.

This canvas, probably painted shortly before the artist's second trip to Italy (1773–74), was admired in the eighteenth century (1776) for the "transparency of the colors" and for its "charm." The simplicity of the composition, the limited yet contrasting color scheme of browns and vermilions, the freedom in the handling of certain passages, as compared with the delicate nuances in the shadows on the youthful face, make this one of Fragonard's most graceful and poetic works.

143   Perrette et le pot au lait

Oil on canvas, oval, 53 x 63 cm.

Musée Cognacq-Jay, Paris

Provenance
Prault (*imprimeur du Roi*): sold, November 27, 1780, no. 26 (for 110 *livres*); Nicolas Ponce, by 1787: sold posthumously, Paris, December 12–16, 1831, no. 1: "esquisse ovale [for] 1 fr. 55 cent. . . . devant l'enchère ridicule, on serait tenté de douter de l'originalité, si ce n'était pas à la vente de Ponce le graveur de la composition" (G. p. 329); anonymous sale (often mentioned, but the catalogue has not come to light), February 9, 1848, no. 65; sold, November 26, 1849, no. 58: "la cruche renversée" (?; a picture with the same title was in the Barroilhet collection sale, March 1, 1856, no. 22). This picture cannot be identified either with the painting in the collection of the Duc de La Rochefoucault-Liancourt: sold, March 20–23, 1827, no. 24: " . . . une jeune fille désolée d'avoir cassé sa cruche; un jeune garçon, appuyé sur la fontaine, se moque d'elle; l'Amour placé en haut de cette fontaine semble observer," or with "La cruche renversée" in the other sales of the Barroilhet collection, April 2–3, 1860, no. 104, and May 3, 1876; Mme Bl[anc]: no. 5 (100 x 81 cm.); [acquired for 300,000 francs (?), by Jonas, 1923, according to Gimpel, 1963, p. 248]; François: sold to Ernest Cognacq, December 15, 1913 (for 525,000 francs, according to an inventory of the collection written about 1924–25); Ernest Cognacq and Louise Jay, 1928; in the Musée Cognacq-Jay, since its founding, 1929.

Exhibitions
(For a complete list, see Burollet, 1980, p. 80)

Bibliography
G. pp. 328–29

P. p. 286
N. p. 123
R. p. 161
W. 283, fig. 134
Zick, 1969, pp. 178–79, 184–85, fig. 126
W. and M. 301, ill.
Burollet, 1980, no. 27, colorpl. (cover detail)

Related works
A modest replica (figure 1) on parchment (?), known to us only from a photograph, was formerly in the Doistau collection, and was sold March 5–6, 1937, no. 30, ill.

For a drawing of the same subject, see A. 1922.

Nicolas Ponce (1746–1831) made an engraving of the painting—not in reverse, and in an oval frame (see figure 2)—in 1787 (*Journal de Paris*, June 17, 1787, p. 745; *Journal général de France*, June 28, 1787,

p. 307; P. p. 330, no. 136, ill. p. 229; Clermont-Ferrand exhibition catalogue, 1977,
no. 58), adding a few details, particularly in
the upper part of the composition. As a pendant, Ponce made an engraving of *Le Verre
d'eau* (figure 3) after a lost painting by
Fragonard (see W. 284, 285; G. p. 276,
most likely the painting sold June 23, 1926,
no. 31, ill.).

Figure 1. After Fragonard. *Perrette et le pot
au lait*. Whereabouts unknown

Figure 2. Nicolas Ponce, after Fragonard.
Le Pot au lait. Bibliothèque Nationale, Paris,
Cabinet des Estampes

Figure 3. Nicolas Ponce, after Fragonard.
Le Verre d'eau. Bibliothèque Nationale, Paris,
Cabinet des Estampes

There were six paintings by Fragonard in the Prault collection sale in 1780, all oval in format. Concerning two of these works, Le Brun, the expert at the sale, wrote: "For each of the paintings by M. Fragonard that we have just described, we could have added specific praise, but we prefer to save our homage to his talents for a separate article. In them, we recognize the new and delightful handling that characterizes his oeuvre." We have not been able to locate the article that he promised, but these lines prove that in Le Brun, the husband of Mme Vigée Le Brun, and the most respected art expert in Paris, Fragonard, indeed, had a champion.

This painting, inspired by one of La Fontaine's most popular fables, *La laitière et le pot au lait* (see Zick, 1969),

was the subject of a 1787 engraving by Ponce. What is interesting about the latter, apart from the many details that Ponce added, is its more precise description of what was merely suggested by Fragonard. Perrette's dream, in Fragonard's work, was rendered only by a swirling, blue-tinged cloud of smoke issuing from the glazed terracotta jug. A few spots of brown and yellow sufficed to evoke a herd of animals, and a few white "commas," the birds; in the engraving, these become sheep, cows, and birds, all painstakingly depicted. Also noteworthy is that, as a pendant to the *Perrette,* Ponce made an engraving called *Le Verre d'eau,* in which the main figure is in an even more advanced state of undress.

In both works, a spectator of each sex observes the amusing scene (which, in one case, was provoked), and care has been taken to make this not-so-innocent event as accessible as possible. The spilt milk, on which Perrette based her daydreams of prosperity, is only a pretext to draw our glance to the shapely calves of the peasant girl, as the scarlet skirt directs our attention to her "flyaway" petticoat. Her hands crossed over the jug hide her tears from her two laughing companions.

Fragonard only used La Fontaine's fable as a pretext, without taking into account its moral: "Quel esprit ne bat la campagne? / Qui ne fait châteaux en Espagne . . . / Chacun songe en veillant, il n'est rien de plus doux. . . . "

Wildenstein dates the picture between 1765 and 1772; Thérèse Burollet believes it to have been painted in 1770, closer to the *figures de fantaisie*—which seems most likely.

Fragonard, it so happens, was the most famous illustrator of La Fontaine's *Contes* (not the *Fables*). This well-known, but complex, aspect of Fragonard's oeuvre is unfortunately not represented here.

144   L'Amour de l'or

Black chalk on yellow paper, with pastel highlights, oval (horizontal), 18.6 x 23.4 cm.

Private collection, Paris

Provenance
Laurent Laperlier: sold, December 22–23, 1856, no. 30 (for 38 francs); Frédéric Villot: sold, May 16–18, 1859, no. 115 (for 24 francs, to the Goncourts); Edmond and Jules de Goncourt (their stamp, Lugt 1089, is at the lower center): sold posthumously, February 15, 1897, no. 91 (for 1,600 francs, to the Marquis de Biron); Marquis de Biron: sold, March 29, 1900, no. 38 (for 290 francs; bought back), and June 9–11, 1914, no. 22, ill. (for 5,350 francs, to Seymour de Ricci, for Robert Boas); anonymous sale,

October 28–29, 1919, no. 61 (for 6,900 francs); Bourgarel, by 1921: sold, June 15–16, 1922, no. 84, ill. (for 3,000 francs, to Jules Straus); Jules Straus (sometimes Strauss), until 1933; M. Nast, Nice: sold, Paris, March 7, 1967, no. 3, ill. (for 29,000 francs).

Exhibitions
Paris, 1921, no. 148
Paris, 1931, no. 8
Paris, 1933, no. 193
Paris, *Pastel français,* 1933, no. 9

Bibliography
Goncourt, 1881, p. 80
P. p. 294
R. pp. 192, 228
Mathey, 1961, pp. 304, 305, fig. 6
A. 49, fig. 336
[Launay, 1983–84, no. 97]

Related works
For the "avare tenant un sac d'argent" in the Hall collection, in 1778 (Villot, 1867, p. 74), see catalogue no. 142.

This drawing was owned by the Goncourts as early as 1859, and was thus described in *Maison d'un artiste* (1881): "an old man bent over sacks of money, which his hands seem to be defending from the envious gaze of a young woman looking at them over his shoulder." Its title is more evocative than precise, and dates back to the Laperlier sale in 1856. This drawing is, in fact, a variation on the themes of venal love and the mismatched couple, which were in vogue in the sixteenth century.

The present drawing, with its vigorous pastel accents—blues and pinks—on the old man's mantle, is not unrelated to the heads of old men painted by Fragonard about 1765–69 (but whether it dates from the same period is not certain). As with the latter works, he intensified his "nervous" technique, applying chalk accents here and there to emphasize movement and the liveliness of a gaze. He placed his figures in the foreground, eliminating all superfluous detail (while adding incongruous ones, like the sixth finger on the old man's hand!). Above all, he wanted the swiftness of the execution and the pleasure that it offers to be conspicuous, as an integral part of the work.

145 The Kiss

Oil on canvas, oval (horizontal), 54 x 65 cm.

Private collection, Paris

Provenance
Anonymous sale, November 26, 1834, no. 41: "le baiser, tableau de forme ovale représentant deux personnages à mi corps" (?; the sales catalogue has not come to light); the 1860 Amiens exhibition catalogue mentions a "baiser amoureux. Provient de la coll. du marquis Desandrouin; a été gravé et lithographié (appartient à M. Boca à Amiens)," which may not have been the same as the present picture; Laperlier: sold, February 17–21, 1879, no. 12 (for 1,750 francs, to Lenoir; no. 19 in this sale was the painting now in Stockholm [see cat. no. 146, figure 1]); Deglise, 1889: sold, December 2, 1896,

no. 17; Charvet; [Wildenstein, 1919, 1921]; Robert de Rothschild; Alain de Rothschild, 1954–55; private collection, Paris.

Exhibitions
Amiens, 1860, no. 23(?)
Paris, 1921, no. 34, ill.
London, 1954–55, no. 224

Bibliography
Mantz, 1860, p. 6 (?)
G. p. 270 (?)
L'Art, 1879, p. 22
Burty, 1879, p. 150
P. pp. 72, 196, 198, 271

N. p. 118
G. Wildenstein, 1921, p. 356, ill.
R. p. 157
W. 272, pl. 43
G. Wildenstein, 1961, p. 249
du Colombier, 1962, p. 68
Gimpel, 1963, p. 99
W. and M. 290, ill.

Related works
An engraving was made by Adolphe Lalauze for the Laperlier collection sales catalogue, in 1879 (P. p. 322, no. 23, reproduced between pp. 196 and 197).

The January 1773 issue of the *Mercure de France* announced the publication of "two prints representing two *Baisers* after the pastels by M. Fragonard that are in the collection of M. Jallier, architect" (see ill. p. 301). Three years before, Claude-Joseph Dorat had published his *Baisers* to good reviews (see Wildenstein, 1961)—which, perhaps, inspired Fragonard to paint "seven small Pictures of different shapes, assembled in the same frame, with different compositions, and the subject of 'Baisers'" (sold, July 8, 1793, no. 20).

Judging from the present painting, it is unfortunate that these works have been lost (for a fairly similar drawing in the Ronald Lauder collection, New York, see Williams, 1978, no. 42, ill.).

A couple embracing is depicted close up. The young man has his arms around his companion, and buries his head in her shoulder. She presses him tightly against her, and kisses him on the cheek while closing her eyes. The scene is inscribed in a perfect oval. We can admire the curvilinear rhythms, the vitality, and the motion that are so typical of Fragonard's work. A few notes of color—the pinks of the cheeks, the blacks in the eyebrows and eyelashes, the young woman's blond hair, the whites of the cushions and the garments, the green curtains, the curious grays of the young man's curly hair—enliven the otherwise muted tonality of the composition.

The couple are absorbed in their reverie, removed from worldly concerns. We, too, are far from the risqué genre scenes that were so in vogue during the eighteenth century. Fragonard has portrayed the lovers with seriousness and respect, as well as—paradoxically, considering the artist's general reputation—with gravity, but, above all, with great sensitivity and poetry.

146   The Happy Moment

Bister wash on paper, heightened with watercolor, over an underdrawing in black chalk, 23 x 34.7 cm.
Inscribed at the bottom right, in pen and ink, and bister wash: *frago*; at the upper right, in pencil, upside down: *frago*

Collection Mr. and Mrs. George M. Cheston

Provenance
[de Bièvres]: sold, March 10, 1790, no. 30: "deux autres, dont un colorié, représentant un jeune homme et une jeune femme sur un lit...." (?); Brunet Denon: sold, February 2, 1846, no. 331: "la résistance: sujet de deux figures" (?; see also no. 273); Frédéric Villot: sold, May 16–18, 1859, no. 120: "femme couchée sur un lit tenant un jeune homme dans ses bras. Aquarelle très vigoureuse. Au verso, différents croquis pour la même com-position"(?); Henri Michel-Lévy, by 1907: sold, May 12–13, 1919, no. 79, ill. (for 33,100 francs); David David-Weill, by 1921: sold, Sotheby's, London, June 10, 1959, no. 79 (for 4,500 pounds); Jean Davray, Paris, 1963; [Knoedler & Co.]; Cheston collection.

Exhibitions
Paris, 1907, no. 179 ("Le baiser") (?)
Paris, 1921, no. 161
London, 1968, no. 276, fig. 301
Washington, D.C., 1978, no. 28, ill. (with complete list of exhibitions)
Tokyo, 1980, no. 127, ill.

Bibliography
D. and V. 174, ill.
Martine, 1927, no. 41, ill.
Henriot, 1928, III, p. 177, ill.
R. p. 198 (and 227?)
A. 88, fig. 36 (and A. 89?)

Leymarie, in Cooper, 1963, p. 254, ill.
Sollers, 1987, pp. 323–24

Related works
According to Réau (p. 298) "un dessin analogue a passé dans une vente anonyme le 14 mai 1936." This drawing (no. 28) is unrelated to the present one.
   There is a replica in a private collection in Caluire-et-Cuire.
   A drawing entitled *Le Baiser* was sold in London, April 21, 1926, no. 31 D, ill.; it repeats the composition of the present drawing, combined with that of the well-known but not very convincing drawing in Besançon known as *Le Lit aux amours* (A. 2431, fig. 614).

Figure 1. Fragonard. *La Feinte Résistance.* Nationalmuseum, Stockholm

Figure 2. Fragonard. *Jeune Femme frappant un garçonnet avec un oreiller.* The Fine Arts Museums of San Francisco

Like the present drawing, two paintings by Fragonard—more or less rightly—have also often been known by the traditional title of *La Résistance inutile.* The painting in Stockholm (figure 1; W. 276, pl. 46) shows a young woman who is offering no resistance to her lover's advances; in the San Francisco picture (figure 2), a young woman pommels a young boy, hidden in the sheets, with her pillow. However, a contemporary engraving by Géraud Vidal considerably modified the composition and altered its meaning; hence, the title, *La Résistance inutile* (see figure 3—the better-known engraving by Regnault). In the present drawing there is little sign of resistance: the young woman leans over her lover as if to give him a kiss; with her right hand she unconvincingly tries to push him away, while embracing him with her left arm. In the large, unmade curtain-framed bed, the young couple abandon themselves to their happiness.
   The scene whirls like a kermess by Rubens. It may be sensual, but it is honest and direct, and, while there is no

Figure 3. Nicolas-François Regnault. *"La Résistance inutile."* Bibliothèque Nationale, Paris, Cabinet des Estampes

prudery, it is not improper. Far from the outside world, the lovers embrace, absorbed in their mutual discovery. Rarely did Fragonard succeed in portraying so delicately the tenderness of a young couple.

147   The Happy Lovers (L'Instant désiré)

Oil on canvas, 49.6 x 60.3 cm.

Private collection

Provenance
Hoentschel (according to Wilhelm, unpublished monograph); J. Pierpont Morgan, 1907; "M.T.B.," 1921; Comtesse de La Béraudière, 1928 (not the same *Instant désiré* as that in the La Béraudière collection: sold, New York, December 11–13, 1930, no. 10, ill.); private collection.

Exhibitions
Paris, 1907, no. 127
Paris, 1921, no. 33, ill.
Paris, 1946, no. 368
London, 1954–55, no. 193, ill.

Bibliography
D. and V. 111, ill.
Mayer, 1928, p. 281, pl. between pp. 282 and 283

Brookner, 1955, p. 43
R. p. 159
W. 288, fig. 135, p. 18 (French edition)
Vermeule, 1964, p. 129
W. and M. 306, ill.

Related works
There is another (autograph) version, slightly larger in format (figure 1; W. 287, pl. 48).
A copy in pastel (figure 2) is in a private collection in Avignon.
   G. (p. 328) and P. (p. 322, no. 27) mention an engraving whose pendant was a *Baiser amoureux* (W. 289): "très petites pièces," "sans nom de graveur," "édités chez Esnault et Rapilly."

Figure 1. Fragonard. *The Happy Lovers.* Veil-Picard collection, Paris

There are two very similar versions of this deservedly famous composition: the first, in the Veil-Picard collection, has been known since the Walferdin sale in 1880; the present one was first exhibited in Paris in 1907, and is slightly smaller. (It was recently restored by Mario Modestini.)

Figure 2. After Fragonard. *The Happy Lovers.* Private collection, France

The two paintings have similar color schemes (for the one in Paris, see the colorplate in Thuillier, 1967, p. 106): the more or less unmodulated browns and beiges, the pinks of the bodies and the cheeks, and the sky blue of the cushion are identical. However, they differ markedly in their execution. The Veil-Picard picture was more heavily painted, and is more sketchy yet more precise than the second, more delicate version. While the brushwork in the first painting is vigorous and visible—or legible—here, the strokes blend together for a more vaporous effect.

It is difficult to determine which of the two was executed first, for we still do not know much about Fragonard's procedures. Wildenstein (Paris exhibition catalogue, 1921) dates the Paris picture between 1767 and 1771, and we believe that it predates the present work, which is more finished, and a more idealized conception.

The subject was influenced by the mythological iconography favored by Rubens, or perhaps Titian in the *Venus and Adonis* (National Gallery, London; see Vermeule, 1964). Fragonard, however, softened these references, concentrating on the simple reality of the scene, and on its sensual aspects, presenting them directly, without equivocation or sentimentality. In the embrace and mutual abandon of the young lovers there are none of the innuendos found in a work by Baudouin or Lavreince; in this unabashed scene of lovemaking there is none of the cynicism or perversity of Laclos (see Sutton, 1987, p. 86). "The accessories fade away and the pretexts vanish," leaving the way open for love.

"For some, this charming female body . . . will seem only a sketch, a simple preparation; but for those who are initiated into the master's secret, the unfinished aspect is . . . a further grace. We do not think it possible to show, in a painting burning with the fire of improvisation, warmer skin tones, more subtle blue halftones, more exquisitely pale pinks, a more delectable and life-like delicacy in the flesh tints" (Paul Mantz, on the Veil-Picard picture, in his preface to the Courtin collection sales catalogue, 1886).

148 The Little Mischief-maker

Oil on canvas, 90 x 76 cm.

Private collection, Paris

Provenance
Laurent Laperlier (1805–1878), by 1860: sold, April 11–13, 1867, no. 31 (for 1,120 francs, to Moreau); Baron Édouard de Rothschild; Rothschild collection.

Exhibitions
Paris, 1860, no. 154
Paris, 1946, no. 18

Bibliography
Gautier, 1860, p. 2
Saint-Victor, 1860, n.p.
G. p. 331
Burty, *La Liberté*, March 1867 (introduction from the sales catalogue of the Laperlier collection)
Le Hir, 1867, p. 128
Burty, 1879, p. 148

P. p. 276
N. p. 131
R. p. 162
W. 480, colorpl. facing pl. 106
W. and M. 509, ill.

"A little girl sitting on a stool laughs, as she pulls the hair of a Chinese figurine placed on a table." Such was the description of this painting at the exhibition on the Boulevard des Italiens in 1860. This exhibition made history by permitting the art public in Paris and elsewhere to discover the forgotten painters of the eighteenth century—and their originality.

The little girl is about ten years old. The stool on which she is seated is Neoclassical in style (and, according to Stéphane Loire, possibly dates to about 1765–70). She pulls on the stringy hair of the figurine with malicious concentration, and is not really laughing. According to Amina Okada and Jacques Giès, the costume (especially the emblem on the robe) and the conical hat identify the statuette as a Chinese mandarin. (The specialists at the Musée Guimet regard it as Western in origin—something of a pastiche of Chinese figurines—but there is also the possibility that Fragonard took liberties in representing the object. This is the case with the small round table on which it stands—it is a free "invention" by the artist, based on models from about 1755–60.)

While the figurine attests to the vogue for chinoiserie, the puppet lying face down on the floor—its strings held by the young girl—recalls the prevailing fashion for such toys in Paris in 1746. (Barbier [1856, IV, pp. 211–12] relates that Boucher decorated puppets and also made drawings of them, after which engravings were later made.) Wildenstein dates this work about 1777–79; Wilhelm, about 1771–72. The little girl's dress and the technique argue for the second dating.

Burty (1867) waxed enthusiastic about this painting: "It is a resounding work, spontaneous like the laughter of a naughty child." The color harmonies are particularly enchanting: the Nile green of the dress; the reds of the puppet, skirt, shoes, and of the lacquer of the figurine; the pink ribbons that work so well with the green of the dress and with the grayish green of the wide-brimmed hat; the royal-blue string around the little girl's neck.

The elegance, budding coquetry, and dance-like motion of the sitter suggest that she is conscious of being observed. What Fragonard wanted to depict, above all, was the world of childhood, and children's games—a world far removed from ours, which was being discovered, with delight, by such eighteenth-century figures as Rousseau.

149 The Battle of Minerva and Mars

Oil on canvas, 45 x 37 cm.

Musée des Beaux-Arts, Quimper, Inv. 873-1-387

Provenance
"Feu L. [Anicet-Charles-Gabriel Lemonnier, 1743–1824]": sold, April 8, 1843: "combat de Mars et de Minerve. Sujet tiré de l'Iliade. Quatre figures. Esquisse d'une charmante couleur" (?); bequest of Jean-Marie-François-Xavier, Comte de Silguy (1785–1864), 1864.

Exhibitions
Paris, 1931, no. 19 (another painting from Quimper was sent by mistake; see entry below)
Geneva, 1949, no. 80
Besançon, 1956, no. 19

Bibliography
Quimper museum catalogue, 1873, no. 614
P. p. 289
Vergnet-Ruiz and Laclotte, 1962, p. 236
Cariou, 1985, p. 24, colorpl.
Cuzin, 1986, p. 62, fig. 6, p. 65, notes 20–21

Figure 1. Jacques-Louis David. *The Battle of Minerva and Mars*. Musée du Louvre

Figure 2. Joseph-Benoît Suvée. *The Battle of Minerva and Mars*. Musée des Beaux-Arts, Lille

Figure 3. Joseph-Benoît Suvée. *The Battle of Minerva and Mars*. Musée des Beaux-Arts, Rouen

Figure 4. Fragonard. *Niobe and Her Children*. Whereabouts unknown

Figure 5. Fragonard. *"Trois Enfants dont un représente la Folie."* Whereabouts unknown

One of the most delicate oil sketches by Fragonard in a French museum, this work was the victim of an unfortunate mix-up: intended to be lent to the important exhibition of masterpieces from provincial museums, in 1931, another sketch attributed to Fragonard was sent by mistake to Paris, in its place, to the great disappointment of the art historians (Réau, for example). Nicolle (p. 23), among others, considered it "insignificant." "It is the trivial work of a skillful, late-eighteenth-century decorator," wrote Gaston Brière (1931, p. 191; see also p. 217). The painting actually exhibited, a *Sunrise,* was, in fact, by Berthélemy (Volle, 1979, no. 25, fig. 22).

Jacques Wilhelm (unpublished monograph) is responsible for having rediscovered this work and for correctly attributing it to Fragonard. Interpreting the subject proved to be

more of a problem, but it has since been positively identified as the *Battle of Minerva and Mars*—an episode from the *Iliad*—as confirmed by comparison with the compositions by Jacques-Louis David (figure 1; in the Louvre) and, especially, by Suvée (figure 2; in Lille), winners, respectively, of the second and the first Prix de Rome in 1771. The sketch for the painting by Suvée (figure 3; in Rouen) was attributed to Fragonard until 1967 (Rosenberg, 1967, pp. 33–34, ill.).

Wilhelm dates this sketch between 1762 and 1765, while Cuzin opts for a much later date—1783, or shortly before. However, a comparison with the contemporary sketches (cat. nos. 154, 155) for the panels in the Frick Collection argues convincingly for 1771. Fragonard may have wanted to show his capabilities as a history painter, the most valued

genre at the time, in order to attract a pupil preparing for the Prix de Rome. The Quimper sketch seems to postdate by at least five years the *Niobe and Her Children* (figure 4), formerly in the Heijne collection, in Sweden (D. and V. 99, ill.; sold, Christie's, London, July 7, 1972, no. 79, ill.; see Rosenberg, 1968, p. 137), but to be just a few years later than the *"Trois Enfants dont un représente la Folie,"* which was in the Dulac collection sale, November 30, 1778, no. 7 (W. 316, lost; sold at Sotheby's, Monaco, October 26, 1981, no. 529, ill.; see figure 5).

Fragonard depicted the moment when Venus intervenes to prevent Minerva from again striking the wounded Mars with the javelin given to her by Diomedes. With just a few strokes of the brush, the artist recounted the story. Accents of blue, white, and lacquer red, set down with an astonishing assurance, stand out against the browns and the milky blues of the sky. A few drops of paint applied with the tip of the brush indicate Venus's eyes, nose, and mouth; her breasts are rendered in the same technique—with precision as well as humor.

Oil on canvas, oval (horizontal), 50 x 63 cm.

Musée Jacquemart-André, Paris

Provenance
J. Folliot: sold, April 15–16, 1793, no. 49: "Un peintre dans son atelier, occupé à poser le modèle, esquisse sur toile... hauteur 19 pouces largeur 23 pouces [51.3 x 62.1 cm.]" (on Folliot, see Renou, 1773, p. 20); Barroilhet: sold, March 10, 1856, no. 27: "le peintre et son modèle" (for 75 francs; no dimensions given); anonymous sale, March 18, 1857, no. 16: "le Modèle" (no dimensions given); Hippolyte Walferdin (1795–1880) by 1860: sold posthumously, April 12–16, 1880, no. 31 (for 15,000 francs, to Mme Édouard André); Jacquemart-André.

Exhibitions
Paris, 1860, no. 141
Paris, 1883–84, no. 58
Bordeaux, 1958, no. 169, pl. 29
Paris, 1974–75, no. 107, ill.
Tokyo..., 1983–84, no. 15, colorpl.

Bibliography
Bürger [Thoré], 1860, pp. 348–49
Gautier, 1860, pp. 1–2
Saint-Victor, 1860, n.p.
G. p. 334
Portalis, 1880, pp. 16, 18
P. pp. 69–70, 275, ill. between pp. 66–67
N. p. 145
D. and V. 118, ill.
R. pp. 73–74, 89, 160, pl. 56, p. 109
W. 293, colorpl. facing p. 50, p. 39 (French edition)
Brookner, 1961, p. 112
Sterling, 1964, n.p.
W. and M. 403, ill.
Getreau-Abondance, 1976, no. 22
Georgel and Lecoq, 1982–83, p. 197, fig. 345
Sheriff, 1986, p. 346, n. 44, fig. 1, p. 347

Related works
The rectangular-format copy in the G. Soulier collection (R. p. 160) is reproduced in Algoud, 1941, pl. 57; for the copy in the Alexis Andréieff collection, see G. Grappe, 1913, II, p. 62. Florence Getreau-Abondance (1976) mentions a copy in a private collection in Béziers.

W. and M. compare the sitter in the *Tête de femme* (no. 404, ill.) with the one in the Jacquemart-André painting.

Figure 1. Pierre-Antoine Baudouin. *Le Modèle honnête*. National Gallery of Art, Washington, D.C.

A young artist is lifting the skirt of his new blond model with his maulstick. Her obliging mother—who looks young enough to be her older sister—bares the young girl's breasts. This painting has been much admired ever since it was first presented to the Parisian public in 1860. However, in 1961, Anita Brookner aired her criticisms of the model's anatomy: "a wax doll with Kapok legs," observing, like Thoré ("un berger de Watteau"), that the pose and gesture of the young artist, and even his pink suit, owe much to Watteau.

By 1860, the name of another artist, Pierre-Antoine Baudouin (1723–1769), was associated with that of Fragonard. Baudouin, according to Saint-Victor, would have made a "priapic scene out of this studio subject." At the Salon of 1769, this artist had exhibited a gouache entitled *Le Modèle honnête* (figure 1), which became very popular through the engraving that was made after it. This gouache—recently given by Ian Woodner to the National Gallery of Art, Washington, D.C. (Paris exhibition catalogue, 1984–85, no. 34, ill.)—was the subject of caustic comment at the Salon because of the subject's overt ambiguity.

Diderot's reaction, as usual, is interesting: Greuze had told him, in 1767, "I would like very much to paint a female nude, but without offending modesty..." [to which Diderot replied]: "paint the model honestly." Diderot then described the picture as he saw it: "... her expression would be one of innocence, shyness, and modesty, her mother

should be at her side... she should hide her face in her hands... her mother's clothing should indicate extreme poverty... and the artist, witnessing this scene, should be touched and moved to the point of dropping his palette...." Two years later, writing about Baudouin's gouache, Diderot provided a new description of his ideal painting: "a young girl completely naked, seated on the artist's stool, leans her head on one of her hands as two tears fall from her lowered eyes, and rests her other arm on her mother's shoulders, her ragged clothing scattered beside her; this honest, impoverished mother hides her face in her apron. The painter, stopping his work, looks upon the two figures with a compassionate gaze, and thus the whole story is told."

Fragonard did not follow Diderot's virtuous program any more exactly than did Baudouin. As this painting and these lengthy expositions attest, the artistic concepts of the writer and the painter were very different, and they apparently agreed on very little.

Fragonard could not have had much in common with Baudouin, either. Although the two artists copied the works at the Galerie du Luxembourg in 1767—and, together, had requested permission to do so—Baudouin's hypocritical scene is the antithesis of Fragonard's marvelous invention.

There is every chance that Fragonard was acquainted with Baudouin's *Modèle honnête,* and that, two years later, he wanted to create his own version of it. The works are diamet-

rically opposed, as exemplified by each artist's approach: Baudouin began by making a sketch of Diana on the canvas, à la Boucher, while Fragonard fit his composition into an oval that denied the original rectangular shape of the canvas.

It has often been observed (Gautier, 1860) that in the *Débuts du modèle*, the lightness of the brushwork is what makes the subject a light one: the brush seems to have slid over the surface, with hardly any pressure; it suggests, but does not describe form. The directness with which Fragonard treated the theme has also been noted. The quality of the execution, the delicacy of the color, and the subtlety of the light have been appreciated as well, but less has been said about the slight irony in Fragonard's rendition: the model's false modesty, the questioning gaze of the affable mother, the painter's evident satisfaction. There is already an understanding among the three protagonists, but, in keeping with the mores of the time, each of them continues to play his or her role for a bit longer.

151 Le Dessinateur

Black chalk on paper, 34.6 x 24.2 cm.
Inscribed in pen and ink on the mount, at the lower right: Fragonard

The Metropolitan Museum of Art, New York, Robert Lehman Collection, 1975.1.626

Provenance
The engraver Gabriel Huquier (1695–1772;
his stamp, Lugt 1285, is at the lower left);
Emmanuel de Ghendt: sold, November
15–22, 1779, no. 266: "la vue d'un joli
Bosquet, dans le fond duquel est la statue de
l'Amour: on voit sur le devant un Dessina-
teur assis; ce dessin est à la pierre noire 14 sur
10 de l. [37.8 x 27 cm.]" (for 12 *livres* 1 *sol*,
to Desmarest); Camille Groult; anonymous
sale, March 26, 1953, no. 90, ill.; Robert
Lehman; given to the Metropolitan Museum,
1975.

Exhibitions
Washington, D.C., 1978, no. 21, ill. (with
list of previous exhibitions)
New York, 1980, no. 12, ill.
Tokyo, 1980, no. 140, ill.

Bibliography
A. 650, fig. 702
Munhall, 1971, pp. 406–7, 404, fig. 9
Massengale, 1979, p. 271, fig. 102
Apollo, November 1980, p. 349, fig. 2

This drawing is noteworthy, as it bears the stamp of Gabriel Huquier (see cat. no. 113), which has led Eunice Williams (1978) to date it slightly before the engraver's death in 1772. However, J.-M. Massengale (1979) believes that it may have been stamped (posthumously) by the collector's son. The presence of the drawing in the de Ghendt sale of 1779 affirms that it is earlier than that date.

Munhall (1971) tried to show that the drawing was related to one of the compositions for Louveciennes, *The Lover Crowned* (p. 319, figure 1), but failed to convince

Eunice Williams. In both works, the artist, who is sketching in the right foreground, is seen from the back. The relationship between these two works, as Williams believes, is fortuitous. The Lehman Collection drawing is an independent and complete work—whose dating remains a particularly delicate problem.

Seated in a sort of vast winter garden, an artist is copying a statue that appears to be a personification of Love. The vigorous black-chalk accents scattered throughout endow the work with an enchanting vivacity and movement.

The Louveciennes Paintings

Figure 1. Fragonard. *The Meeting.* The Frick Collection, New York

Figure 2. Fragonard. *The Pursuit.* The Frick Collection, New York

Figure 3. Fragonard. *The Lover Crowned.* The Frick Collection, New York

Figure 4. Fragonard. *Love Letters.* The Frick Collection, New York

Fragonard's masterpiece, an ensemble of fourteen canvases, has been in the Frick Collection in New York since 1915. There are four large major compositions, over three meters high (see figures 1–4), all of which are signed; two other large but narrower canvases, *Love Triumphant* (figure 5) and *Reverie* (figure 6); four overdoors, of almost square format, representing Cupids (figures 7–10); and four narrow vertical panels depicting hollyhocks (figures 11–14).

The Comtesse du Barry (1743–1793) (see figure 15) was the mistress of Louis XV, and was given the Château de Louveciennes in 1769 by the king. She first decorated the old château, and then commissioned the architect Claude-Nicolas Ledoux (1736–1806) to build a country house that became a milestone in architectural history, by virtue of its modernity (see Cayeux, 1935; Gallet, 1980). The *Pavillon neuf* was finished after nine months of work, and was inaugurated, with great pomp, in the presence of the king, on September 2, 1771 (see figure 16).

For the château, Mme du Barry purchased four overdoors (see cat. nos. 152, 153) by Fragonard, through the painter Drouais, and then commissioned Fragonard to paint the present decorations for the new house. Before describing this decoration in detail, we will summarize the story of its rediscovery. It was mentioned in 1858 in a short, anonymous note in the *Revue universelle des Arts* that went unnoticed: "Today in Grasse, in the Département of the Var, there are fourteen paintings by Fragonard executed for Madame Dubarry [*sic*]. They are pastoral subjects.

Figure 7. Fragonard. *Love the Sentinel.* The Frick Collection, New York

The story goes that after the work was finished, the artist and the countess disagreed on the price. Fragonard therefore went back to Grasse, taking the paintings with him, and they have been in the same house ever since." Léon Lagrange was the next to mention them, in 1867: "[At Grasse, in] the house of M. Malvillars [actually Malvilan]," there are "fourteen paintings" that Fragonard painted for Mme du Barry. The Goncourts spoke of them, but knew them only through Lagrange's article, and from two letters: one from Malvilan, dated January 26, 1865, and the other, written by Ernest Chesneau on April 17, 1865, which states that du Sommerard had "seen" the paintings (Bibliothèque Nationale, ms. fr. 22468 folios 342–343; ms. fr. 22457 folios 98–99). However, it was Roger Portalis (1885) who first drew attention to the great importance of these works.

To visit the Malvilan house was not an easy matter, however, and the caretaker obliged those requesting to do so to buy (for 500 francs!) engravings after the paintings by Marcellin-Gilbert Desboutin (one of the victims of this scheme was Camille Groult, the celebrated collector of Fragonard's work). The entire set of canvases was sold by Malvilan in 1898 for 1,250,000 francs through Charles Wertheimer to Thomas Agnew and Sons, who sold them to J. Pierpont Morgan. The originals, which were replaced in Grasse by copies painted by Auguste de La Brély (at a cost of 25,000 francs), were first kept in London; at J. P. Morgan's death in 1914, they were acquired by Duveen, who sold them to Henry Clay Frick (according to an erroneous report in *The New York Times*, for the sum of $1,425,000). The paintings were recently restored by John Brealey to their original, delightful freshness.

Figure 5. Fragonard. *Love Triumphant.* The Frick Collection, New York

Figure 6. Fragonard. *Reverie.* The Frick Collection, New York

Figure 8. Fragonard. *Love the Jester.*
The Frick Collection, New York

Figure 9. Fragonard. *Love Pursuing a Dove.*
The Frick Collection, New York

Figure 10. Fragonard. *Love the Avenger.*
The Frick Collection, New York

What is of interest is how the panels got to Grasse —for it seemed that Fragonard had not kept any ties with his native city. According to Malvilan (1865), the paintings were returned to the artist, and he kept them rolled up in his studio until 1790. If Fragonard, accompanied by his wife, his sister-in-law Marguerite Gérard, and his son Évariste, left Paris at this date, it was not for political reasons, but because of his deter-

Figures 11–14. Fragonard. *Hollyhocks.*
The Frick Collection, New York

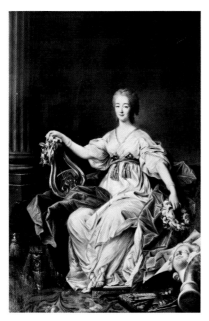

Figure 15. François-Hubert Drouais. *Portrait of Mme du Barry.* Chamber of Commerce, Versailles

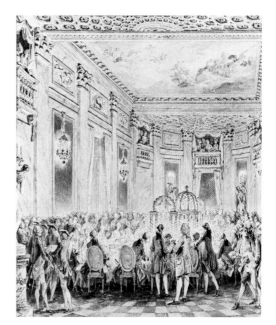

Figure 16. Moreau le Jeune. *The Inauguration of the Pavillon neuf at Louveciennes.* Musée du Louvre, Paris, Cabinet des Dessins

iorating health. He moved in with his cousin Alexandre Maubert, bringing with him the Louveciennes panels, which he completed in Grasse: a receipt dated March 10, 1791 (the last numeral of the date looks like a zero, but the verso of the receipt confirms our reading of 1791; see figures 17, 18) informs us that Fragonard was paid 3,600 *livres* by Maubert for "Painted works." The artist was back in Paris in August 1792. Although Malvilan's letter of January 26, 1865, may contain some errors, it is worth quoting: "During his stay, which lasted about three years, he decided to arrange some rooms for his canvases, which are still there. He came to an agreement with my grandfather, and returned to Paris to bring back, some time later, the four paintings intended for Mme Dubarry [*sic*], as well as some period furniture. To harmonize everything, he painted two new canvases and some overdoors. . . . " Malvilan then went on to elaborate on the painter's "indefatigable activity" and "great facility," as well as on the trompe-l'oeil and grisaille decorations that still may be seen (though they have scarcely been studied) above the staircase of the house that has since become the Musée Fragonard (figure 19).

The presentation of these decorations—first at Louveciennes, then in Grasse, London, and New York—was changed at each step of the way. Their current arrangement in the Frick Collection owes nothing to history. Of the ten paintings supposedly executed by Fragonard in Grasse, some—primarily the overdoors representing *Love the Sentinel, Love the Avenger,* and, especially, *Love the Jester* and *Love Pursuing a Dove—*

jay Reçu de Mon cher cousin
Maubert pour ouvrages de Peinture
la somme trois mille six cent livres
dont quittance jusqua ce jour pour
solde de tout compte a grasse ce
dix mars 1790 fragonard peintre
du roy

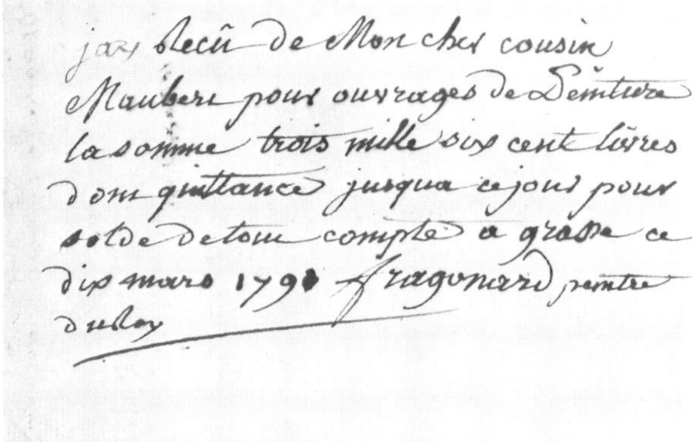

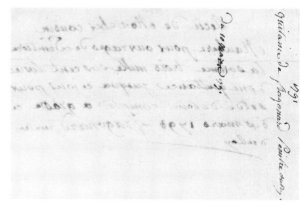

Figure 17. Fragonard's receipt for "Painted works." The Frick Collection, New York

Figure 18. Verso of the receipt in figure 17

appear to have been executed long before 1790, probably at the same time as the four principal compositions for Louveciennes; this appears to be so for documentary as well as for stylistic reasons.

The question as to who recommended Fragonard to Mme du Barry has yet to be resolved, although the names of Drouais and of Ledoux have been proposed. There is a good chance that an important part was played by the countess's "brother-in-law," Jean du Barry (1723–1794), known as "Le Roué" ("the Rogue"), a great collector of Fragonard's work, as indicated by the du Barry sales of 1774 (actually, the collection of his son, Vicomte Alphonse du Barry) and 1776.

The precise dates of the commission are not known either, but Fragonard was at work as early as 1771. On December 23 of that year, Marigny wrote to the recently appointed *Premier peintre* Pierre, informing him that the king knew that the reason for Fragonard's delay in the execution of the "paintings ordered for the small apartments" at Versailles was that he was working "for Mme la comtesse du Barry." Marigny added that Fragonard should "hurry and get to work as soon as possible, although without jeopardizing the works for Mme la comtesse du Barry." In an oft-quoted text dated July 20, 1772, Bachaumont mentions that the paintings "are not yet finished.... They deal with the romances of shepherds and seem to involve allegories of the affairs of the mistress of the house." Finally, on March 19, 1773, Fragonard again used the Louveciennes project as an excuse for his delay in executing the royal commissions. By this time, it is very likely that the countess had already rejected Fragonard's paintings and commissioned Joseph-Marie Vien (1716–1809) to paint four compositions (see figures 20–23) to replace them (he exhibited two of them at the Salon of 1773; these paintings are today divided between the Louvre and the Préfecture de Chambéry; see Gaehtgens's and Lugand's forthcoming publication). Mme du Barry paid 16,000 *livres* for them, while Fragonard, according to his grandson Théophile (see Portalis), was paid 18,000 *livres* (the difference may be explained by the overdoors).

The apse-shaped room for which Fragonard's four paintings were designed is well known (see figure 24), and it seems that at one point the paintings were in place there. The evidence for this is a passage in the intriguing pamphlet, published in 1773, containing the conversation between "M. Fabretti" and the expert Rémy (see the Introduction to this chapter, and also two excellent articles by Cayeux, 1935): "you have seen at Lussienne the *nec plus ultra* of the *heurté,* the *roullé,* the *bien fouetté,* the *tartouillis...*" ["the bruised, the rolled, the whipped, the smeared"]. However, the paintings probably did not remain there for long.

Figure 19. Jean-Honoré and Alexandre-Évariste Fragonard. Staircase in the Musée Fragonard, Grasse

The question that has divided art scholars most, for the last century, is the sequence of the decorative program: Lagrange, Portalis (1885), Brière (1949), Réau (1956), Biebel (1960), Sauerländer (1968), and Posner (1972), with whom we agree, have all debated this issue: does *The Meeting* precede *The Pursuit*? Does *The Lover Crowned* follow the *Love Letters* (this last painting has been closely analyzed by Sauerländer, especially in relation to the sculpture group that is depicted in it)? As Marianne Roland Michel noted (1980), too much time has been spent on this point. For those who recognize Fragonard's taste for improvisation, his lack of concern for narrative exposition and exactitude, the idea of a *progression* in the series does not appear very convincing. On the other hand, Vien, "homme d'un programme," was the painter of the "Progress of Love in the Hearts of Young Girls." Fragonard's only aim was to represent "four different avatars of romantic love." Curiously enough, for all the continuity in the story, there is no movement to speak of in the intentionally stiff works in Vien's series, while Fragonard's four canvases are virtually bursting with dynamic energy.

We will not linger over the scarcity of sketches and preparatory drawings (see cat. nos. 154–156), the order in which Fragonard painted these pictures, or even the artist's intentions. In recent years, these issues have been the object of many "over interpretations" by the younger generation of art historians (for example, Lynne Kirby, 1982), and are usually beside the point, where Fragonard's art is concerned. The most important question is why Mme du Barry rejected Fragonard's paintings. While numerous hypotheses have been advanced, it is generally agreed, since Franklin Biebel's proposal (1960), that the countess preferred the then-emerging and fashionable Neoclassical style—as represented by Vien—to the more spontaneous, freer, and seemingly less deliberate art of

Figure 20. Joseph-Marie Vien. *Deux Jeunes Grecques font serment de ne jamais aimer.* Préfecture de Chambéry

Figure 21. Joseph-Marie Vien. *Deux Jeunes Grecques parant de fleurs l'amour endormi.* Musée du Louvre

Figure 22. Joseph-Marie Vien. *Amant couronnant sa maîtresse.* Musée du Louvre

Figure 23. Joseph-Marie Vien. *Le Temps de l'Hymen.* Préfecture de Chambéry

Fragonard, which she considered outmoded. Having built a house that was in the vanguard of the new style (as Michel Gallet humorously put it, in connection with the inauguration of the *Pavillon neuf* September 2, 1771: "Louis XV was seated, in Mme du Barry's house, on a Louis XVI chair"), she naturally wanted the decoration to match. For the avant-garde of 1773, Fragonard was a thing of the past: a century would pass before he would be avenged! Unfortunate as it may have been, Fragonard's plight is thought-provoking for us today—and not unique.

What is most surprising about the Louveciennes decorations in the Frick Collection (especially, following their recent restoration) is the amazing explosion of color—the deep marine blues, the wide range of greens, the pinks—and the luxuriant, almost tropical vegetation that is depicted. The paintings are an ode to life *en plein air.*

Then there is the obvious pleasure that Fragonard took in painting these pictures, so that we can almost see him at work—a delight bordering on true happiness. Painting itself is triumphant.

Never before—or since—has a decorative work of art so completely filled its role, or found more noble justification.

Yet, the Louveciennes panels have not surrendered all of their secrets. Nothing is known of the terms of the commission; the iconographic program is still a subject of controversy; and there is the problem of the inevitable modifications that were made each time that the series changed hands.

The evidence seems to point to a dating before 1790 for the fourteen compositions (not just for the four main compositions), but Fragonard's intentions—and his ambitions—remain a mystery. Even if the influence of the paintings—kept rolled-up and in storage in Grasse for a century—is negligible, it is time that these masterpieces of French art were studied with the depth and thoroughness that they deserve.

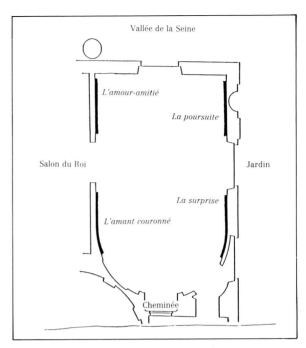

Figure 24. Plan of the apse-shaped Salon in the *Pavillon neuf* at Louveciennes, showing the placement of the paintings (according to Posner, 1972)

152 L'Amour embrasant l'Univers

Oil on canvas, enlarged on all sides, 116 x 145 cm. (the original measurements were 79 x 139 cm.; see the following entry)
Inscribed on a label on the back of the stretcher: n° 694; in pen and ink: Lagrenée. L'Amour

Musée de Toulon, Inv. 5572 a

Provenance
Acquired by the Comtesse du Barry from the painter François-Hubert Drouais (1727–1775), with three other overdoor panels, June 21, 1770. Dulaure (1786) mentions four overdoor panels in the salon of the *Pavillon neuf:* they were seized during the Revolution, but contemporary reports, not all of which we consulted firsthand, are contradictory—Boizot (see L. Tuetey, 1902), on "29 frimaire an II," mentions only one "tableau du citoyen Fragonard, représentant la Nuit," in the dining room of the old château; Beaumont (1872) published another inventory, dated "2 pluviose an II" (or "22 pluviose," according to Molinier, c. 1896, p. 177), the original of which has been lost, but there is a copy in the Bibliothèque du Louvre: the "quatre dessus-de-porte par fragonard rep. la nuit et les trois parties du

jour," estimated at 800 *livres,* were then in the Château de Louveciennes. The four panels were transferred to Versailles; reclaimed (unsuccessfully) by the heirs of Mme du Barry, 1830 (Bibliothèque de Versailles, ms. fr. 272 fol. 2, 46° pièce); no. 694 of Inv. B of the Louvre; under Napoleon III, transferred to the Cercle d'Artillerie de la Garde Impériale, Versailles; on permanent loan to Toulon, since April 18, 1895.

Exhibitions
Grasse, 1957, no. 2

Bibliography
Dulaure, 1786, p. 19
P. Villiers, 1802, I, pp. 516, 518–19
Pichon, 1856, pp. 288–89
G. p. 147
Beaumont, 1872, p. 132

Portalis, 1885, pp. 484, 486
P. pp. 93–94, 275
Molinier, n.d. (between 1896 and 1911), p. 177
L. Tuetey, 1902, I, p. 242
N. pp. 62–63
Cayeux, 1935, pp. 41–42
R. p. 145
Wilhelm, 1956, pp. 215–22, fig. 4, p. 220
Andia, 1960, p. 24, ill.
W. 298, fig. 137, p. 19 (French edition)
W. and M. 312, ill.
Rosenberg and Compin, 1974, p. 192, note in appendix
Toulon exhibition catalogue, M. A. D[upuy].–P. R[osenberg]., 1985, no. 12, ill. (with complete bibliography)
Thuillier, 1987, p. 9, fig. 2

153 The Three Graces

Oil on canvas, 89 x 134 cm.

The panel was enlarged (originally, it was 80.5 cm. high). Laboratory examinations at the Louvre have determined that the additions, visible to the naked eye, were made in the eighteenth century, and that the canvas was folded under (by as much as 7cm. at the top, and 10 cm. at the bottom; this is hidden by the frame). This overdoor (and no doubt the three others) was removed during the Revolution and given a rectangular format to resemble an easel painting.

Musée Fragonard, Grasse, Inv. 5572.

Provenance
See previous entry.
   No. 695 of Inv. B of the Louvre; on permanent loan from the Louvre, since 1958.

Exhibitions
Grasse, 1957, no. 1

Bibliography
See previous entry.
Louvre catalogue (Brière), 1924, no. 451
Wilhelm, 1956, pp. 215–22, fig. 3, p. 218

Cailleux, 1960, pp. i–ix, figs. 10–18
W. 297, fig. 136, pp. 19–20 (French edition)
Cailleux, 1961, pp. i–iii
Carpenter, 1962, p. 359
W. and M. 311, ill.

Related works
Wilhelm (1956, p. 221, fig. 5) reproduces an autograph version, with variants, in a private collection in Paris (figure 1; 62.5 x 138 cm.).

Figure 1. Fragonard. *The Three Graces.* Private collection, Paris

The series called "The Progress of Love," painted by Fragonard for Louveciennes (and today in the Frick Collection in New York), is famous and is rightly considered his masterpiece, but the four overdoor panels painted by the artist for the same place are much less well known. As a result of the recent studies by Cayeux, Wildenstein, and, especially, Wilhelm (1956), our knowledge of these works is more complete.

Very soon after Louis XV gave the Château de Louveciennes to his mistress, the Comtesse du Barry, on July 24, 1769, she decided to restore the old château and to entrust the building of a separate house to Ledoux, and its decoration to Fragonard (see cat. nos. 154, 155). On Sunday, June 24, 1770, to decorate the château, she purchased for 1,200 *livres,* from the painter François-Hubert Drouais, four "overdoors by M. Fragonard painter to the King...one representing the Graces; another, Cupid setting the Universe ablaze; another, Venus and Cupid; and another, Night." On the same day, the countess disbursed 420 *livres* to "have three of the above-mentioned overdoors applied to another canvas, to have them enlarged, repainted, and to have the additions matched."

In the eighteenth century, only Dulaure mentions them as being in the *Pavillon neuf:* "The salon, very richly decorated, has Overdoors painted by M. Fragonard." The documents relating to their seizure during the Revolution contain contradictory information as to their arrangement and number (see *Provenance*). After much research, it is now possible to identify the "Graces" with the painting that was attributed for a century and a half to Jean-Jacques Lagrenée (1740–1821), on loan from the Louvre to the Musée Fragonard

Figure 2. Fragonard. *Venus and Cupid.*
National Gallery of Ireland, Dublin

Figure 3. Fragonard. *Night.* Private collection, Switzerland

since 1958; "Cupid setting the Universe ablaze" with the Toulon picture rediscovered by Jacques Wilhelm in 1956 (cat. no. 152); "Venus and Cupid" with the painting acquired by the National Gallery of Ireland, Dublin, in 1978 (114 x 133 cm.; W. 299, fig. 138; see figure 2); and, finally, "Night" with the canvas in Switzerland in the Edmond de Rothschild collection in Pregny (W. 300, pl. 51; see figure 3).

These four works do not seem to have been intended to form a coherent iconographic program—for example, showing the three Graces accompanied by the Hours—but, rather, to have been associated arbitrarily, enlarged, and repainted (by whom?; see figure 4) to satisfy the countess's request as quickly as possible.

Their date is still the subject of greatest controversy: were they painted by Fragonard for the countess shortly before 1770, or, as Jacques Wilhelm (1956) suggested, and as we discussed in connection with the Toulon painting, in 1985, might they have been done before the artist's first trip to Rome in 1756?

Boucher's influence is still very apparent, but the putti in the *Night* present analogies with those in the "Groupes d'Enfants dans le ciel," exhibited at the Salon of 1767 (cat. no. 109). Perhaps once the Toulon panel is restored, it may be compared, along with the recently restored painting in Grasse, with those works whose dates are known, thus helping to resolve the question.

The two paintings were, above all, meant to be decorative; Fragonard was certainly tempted by a genre to which Boucher owed his fame and fortune. Beginning in 1765, he received many commissions—both official and private—for decorations. Of all of these projects, only one was finished. The four overdoor panels from Louveciennes, hastily delivered to the countess, who was anxious to decorate her château, might well be the remnants—diverted, completed, and artificially assembled—of some of these projects.

If all four decorative panels could be exhibited together, perhaps their importance, as well as their coherence, might be better appreciated.

Figure 4. Radiograph of catalogue no. 153

154 L'Escalade

Oil on canvas, 69 x 38 cm.

Private collection, Paris

Provenance
The miniaturist Auguste-Joseph Carrier (1800–1875): sold, March 9–10, 1846, no. 100, with its pendant (catalogue by Thoré): "les indiscrets . . . ; dans l'un, quelques jeunes filles cachées dans un bosquet, s'enfuient tout à coup à l'approche d'un garçon comme une volée d'oiseaux, dans l'autre, une jeune fille assise toute seule, sur le gazon, au dessous d'une statue, écoute avec inquiétude, tandis qu'un jeune garçon grimpe une échelle pour arriver sur cette petite éminence" (for 180 francs, according to P.); Hippolyte Walferdin (1795–1880), by 1860: sold posthumously, Paris, April 12–16, 1880, no. 33 (for 15,000 francs, to Fichel); Mme Watel, from 1885.

Exhibitions
Paris, 1860, no. 143
Paris, 1880, no. 98
Paris, 1887, no. 46

Bibliography
Bürger [Thoré], 1860, p. 348
Gautier, 1860, p. 2
G. p. 334
Portalis, 1885, p. 490, ill. p. 485
P. pp. 276, 279
N. pp. 121, 122
W. 302, pl. 53, p. 21 (French edition)
Sauerländer, 1968, p. 136, fig. 5
Munhall, 1971, p. 402, fig. 5
W. and M. 320, ill.

Related works
For the painting in the Frick Art Museum, Pittsburgh, see the following entry.
For a drawing by or after Fragonard (no published illustrations are known), see A. 675.

155 The Pursuit

Oil on canvas, 70 x 38 cm.

Private collection, Paris

Provenance
See previous entry.
Hippolyte Walferdin: sold posthumously, Paris, April 12–16, 1880, no. 32 (for 15,000 francs).

Exhibitions
Paris, 1860, no. 143 a
Paris, 1880, no. 98 a
Paris, 1887, no. 47

Bibliography
Bürger [Thoré], 1860, p. 348
Gautier, 1860, p. 2
G. p. 334
Portalis, 1885, p. 490, ill. p. 489
P. pp. 279, 286
N. p. 122
W. 301, pl. 52, p. 21 (French edition)
Munhall, 1971, p. 401, fig. 3
W. and M. 322, ill.

Related works
There is a rather weak study in the Frick Art Museum, Pittsburgh (see figure 1; 28 x 36 cm.; W. 303, fig. 139; probably from the J. D. sale, May 16–17, 1906, no. 71).
For the painting in the Frick Art Museum, see entry.

For a discussion of the four great panels in the Frick Collection in New York, including their turbulent history, the vicissitudes of the commission, their date, the order of their execution, the interpretation of their subjects, and the progression of the narrative in the four scenes, see the Introduction to this section.

These two oil sketches have been known since 1846. In 1860, Théophile Gautier wrote about them enthusiastically. By 1880, they had become associated with the celebrated Frick panels, then still in Grasse.

There are considerable differences between the study for *L'Escalade* and the final composition (figure 2). In the

Figure 1. Fragonard. *The Pursuit.* The Frick Art Museum, Pittsburgh

Figure 2. Fragonard. *L'Escalade.* The Frick Collection, New York

Figure 3. Radiograph (detail) of catalogue no. 155

Figure 4. Fragonard. *The Pursuit.* The Frick Collection, New York

sketch, only the head of the young rogue appears at the top of the ladder. The finished painting features architectural elements—a stone parapet, the shaft of a column, a large pedestal for the statue of Venus, an urn with flowers—which are not present in the sketch. Interestingly enough, however, the recent restoration of the painting and a radiograph (figure 3) show that Fragonard started by faithfully transposing the composition of the sketch onto the canvas. A further discrepancy is that the heroine of the scene, dressed all in white in the final work, wears a yellow and raspberry-colored dress in the sketch.

The variations between the oil sketch for *The Pursuit* and the finished painting (figure 4) are not as great: in the latter, the young suitor offers the heroine a rose, and Fragonard dispensed with one of her companions. The color of the clothing and the hairstyles was also modified.

These sketches are most remarkable for their execution, which is so different from that of the finished works: the luminosity of the brushwork, the sureness of each stroke, the freedom and the vitality—all attest to the artist's technical mastery; Fragonard composed them directly with his brush, as if he were drawing.

154   155

156 L'Abandonnée

Bister wash on paper, over an underdrawing in black chalk, 33.8 x 25 cm.

Harvard University Art Museums (Fogg Art Museum), Cambridge, Massachusetts, Gift of Charles E. Dunlap, 1955.186

Provenance
Hippolyte Walferdin: sold posthumously, Paris, April 12–16, 1880, no. 209 (for 545 francs, to Albert Meyer); Camille Groult, by 1889; [Wildenstein]; Charles E. Dunlap: given to the Fogg museum, 1955.

Exhibitions
Paris, 1921, no. 205
Washington, D.C., 1978, no. 61, ill.

Bibliography
G. p. 336
P. pp. 100, 294 (ill. between pp. 100 and 101)
R. p. 196
A. 723, fig. 520
Munhall, 1971, p. 406, fig. 14

Related works
For the painting of the same subject (figure 1) in the Frick Collection, New York, see the entry.

Figure 1. Fragonard. *Reverie.*
The Frick Collection, New York

As noted, *L'Abandonnée* was not among the paintings commissioned in 1771 for Louveciennes by Mme du Barry. Fragonard took back these works and brought them to Grasse in 1790–91, placing them in the salon of his cousin Alexandre Maubert; probably that same year, it is presumed that he completed the original decorative program.

It is not certain whether the Cambridge drawing preceded or followed (as Eunice Williams [1978] believes) the paint-

ing. There are also some differences in details between the two works: in the drawing, the figure of Love, perched on the sundial, points toward the abandoned woman instead of toward the spectator. It is a late work, and has some features in common with drawings done by Fragonard after 1780: the underdrawing is more prominent; the line, less vigorous; the strokes, less nervous. The work has become more narrative, more anecdotal.

157 The Two Sisters

Oil on canvas, 71.3 x 55.9 cm.

The Metropolitan Museum of Art, New York, Gift of Julia A. Berwind, 53.61.5

Provenance
Louis-Gabriel de Veri Raionard, Marquis de Veri: sold posthumously, December 12, 1785, no. 35 (for 350 *livres*, to the Marquis de Saint-Marc): " ... deux jeunes filles occupées à des jeux de leur âge; la plus petite est montée sur un cheval de carton porté par des roulettes et sa soeur est auprès d'elle qui la soutient et pousse l'équipage. Elles sont toutes deux coëffées en cheveux et vêtues d'ajustements gracieux ... Hauteur 37 pouces largeur 30 pouces T. [100 x 81 cm.; Oil on canvas]"; Marquis de Saint-Marc (1728–1818); A. Zarine, Consul General of Russia, Paris, 1916 (he "found it in Sweden," according to Vauxcelles); [Wildenstein]; sold by Gimpel, June 10, 1918, for $194,000, to Edgar J. Berwind, the "King of Coal" (according to Gimpel, 1963, p. 46); given to the Metropolitan Museum, with life interest, by his daughter, Miss Julia A. Berwind, 1953; entered the museum, 1961.

Exhibitions
Tokyo, 1980, no. 77, colorpl.

Bibliography
G. p. 331

P. pp. 63, 275
N. p. 131
New York Herald Tribune, December 2, 1916, p. 4 (French edition)
Damécourt, 1916, pp. 141–42; 1917, p. 182
Davenport, 1917, p. 5, ill.
V[auxcelles], 1917, pp. 9–11, ill.
R. p. 167
G. Wildenstein, 1959, p. 228
W. 476, pl. 106, p. 29 (French edition)
W. and M. 501, ill.
Williams, 1978, p. 136
Harris, 1979, pp. 57–61, ill.

Related works
For the sketch in Lisbon (there is a copy, on panel, in a private collection in northern France), see the following entry.

An engraving after the painting was made by Géraud Vidal, of Toulouse (1742–1801), and entitled *"Les Jeunes Soeurs"* (figure 1; P. p. 329, no. 116, reproduced between pp. 114 and 115; Toulouse exhibition catalogue, 1951, no. 428). A copy in pastel (figure 2), signed and dated 1779 (rather than 1770) by the Abbé de Saint-Non (1727–1791), and measuring 80.3 x 63.5 cm., was given to

the Metropolitan Museum in 1977 by Daniel Wildenstein; it had been sold in Nice on November 2 (7 ?), 1951 (the pastel was published in the November 16, 1951, issue of *Arts* magazine).

Figure 1. Géraud Vidal, after Fragonard. *Les Jeunes Soeurs.* The Metropolitan Museum of Art, New York

Figure 2. Abbé de Saint-Non, after Fragonard. *The Two Sisters.* The Metropolitan Museum of Art, New York

Figure 3. Fragonard. *The Visit to the Nursery.* National Gallery of Art, Washington, D.C.

Figure 4. Attributed to Fragonard. *Fillette debout de profil.* Private collection, London

This work is only a fragment; in 1785, it measured 100 x 81 centimeters. Between the latter date and 1916, 25 centimeters were cut from the sides, and about 30 from the top and bottom. The engraving by Vidal (figure 1), however, gives us a good idea of the original composition. At the bottom, between the wheels of the cardboard hobbyhorse, there was a puppet; at the top, decorative columns and an oculus (?) completed the composition. The pastel by Saint-Non (figure 2) is closer to the original painting, but it only depicts the central part of the composition, either because it,

too, was already cut down, or because Saint-Non chose to copy only this section.

The pastel is of considerable interest because it is dated, although the last two numerals have been read variously as 70 (Mary Ann Wurth Harris, 1979), 90, or 99 (Tokyo exhibition catalogue, 1980)—yet Saint-Non died in 1791! Today, 1779 is the date generally agreed on.

Several famous names are associated with *The Two Sisters.* One of its owners, the Marquis de Veri (1722–1785), was an avid collector, highly appreciated Fragonard's work (see

cat. no. 236), and knew the artist personally. The marquis's biographer, Colin Bailey (1985, p. 70), tells us that he assembled the body of his collection between 1775 and 1779. The Abbé de Saint-Non copied many works in pastel by Fragonard with whom he remained on intimate terms (G. Wildenstein, 1959).

The exact circumstances of the commission, and the identity of the models are not known. There is little chance that they are Rosalie Fragonard and her aunt Marguerite Gérard, born respectively in 1769 and 1761. Not only do the engraving by Vidal and the catalogue of the Veri sale both identify the models as "sisters," but there does not seem to be an age difference of almost nine years between them. Furthermore, Marguerite Gérard had blue—not gray or black—eyes. Lastly, for stylistic reasons this work cannot have been done later than 1770.

In Saint-Non's pastel copy, and even more so in the engraving, the features of the little girls (who are not very pretty as it is) are banal and insipid. Contrary to his usual practice, like a portraitist Fragonard made an effort at rendering likenesses. Yet, the picture owes its success to the harmony of pinks, greens, and yellows (which are absent in the pastel), the quality of the lighting on the faces, and the complicity of the two little girls pausing momentarily in their game.

The older sister reappears at the far right in the *Visit to the Nursery*, of which several versions exist (figures 3, 4).

158 The Two Sisters

Oil on panel, 31.7 x 24 cm.

Museu Nacional de Arte Antiga, Lisbon

Provenance
Acquired by the museum from Mr. Ribeiro da Cunha, through the Valmor Bequest, 1915.

Exhibitions
Lisbon, 1966, no. 309

Bibliography
R. p. 183
Lisbon museum catalogue, 1959, no. 299
Watson, 1961, p. 39, fig. 1, p. 38
Lisbon museum catalogue, 1966, no. 309
Harris, 1979, p. 58, fig. 4

Related works
See the previous entry.

This is the first sketch for the *Two Sisters* in The Metropolitan Museum of Art (cat. no. 157). Fragonard executed few painted studies. This one, hardly known, must have been done very rapidly, possibly directly from the models; their poses and hairstyles were modified in the later work. With just a few quick strokes of the brush, Fragonard created an image and endowed it with life.

Oil on canvas, oval (vertical), 48.9 x 39.2 cm.

Private collection

Provenance
Marie-François Ménage de Pressigny (*Fermier général*), 1779; the painting is mentioned in the register of works of art received, "trouvés chez les émigrés et condamnés" (Archives Nationales, F¹⁷ 372 fol. 116), "26 brumaire an III" [November 16, 1794] and following days: "Ménage de Presigni, condamné, rue des Jeuneurs, nº 8 La Bonne Mère, gravé par Delaunay hauteur 17 pouces ½, de largeur 13 pouces ½ forme ovale (de fragonard)" (value estimated at 600 *livres*); "Prisé 300 livres par Le Brun dans l'inventaire dressé par lui le 17 brumaire an III [November 7, 1794] et remis le 20 à la Commission temporaire des Arts" (Archives Nationales, F¹⁷ 1268, no. 175; see W. 452).

Several works whose subject was the "bonne mère," generally associated with the painting sold in Boston (see *Related works*), were sold in the nineteenth century, but the catalogues rarely give the dimensions. It is difficult to determine if any of these corresponds to the present painting.

According to Alvin-Beaumont (1913), the painting belonged to Baron d'Aubigny ("descendant direct de Ménage de Pressigny": Apollinaire, 1914) and Charrette; Arthur Veil-Picard, by 1907; Mme Jeannette Veil-Picard, 1958; private collection.

Exhibitions
Paris, 1907, no. 142
Berlin, 1910, no. 65 (small-format publication)
Bern, 1954, no. 10 (confusion as to the provenance)
London, 1954–55, no. 218
Zurich, 1955, no. 89
Besançon, 1956, no. 3
Munich, 1958, no. 57

Bibliography
G. pp. 306, 331 (engraving)
Tourneux, 1907, p. 100
Alvin-Beaumont, 1913, pp. 25–31
Alvin-Beaumont, *Le Temps*, December 1, 1913, p. 5
Thiébault-Sisson, *Le Temps*, November 9, 1913, p. 3; November 27, p. 3
Apollinaire, 1914, pp. 8, 11–14
Wilhelm, 1954, p. 2
R. p. 171
W. under no. 452 ("semble avoir été exécuté d'après la gravure"), p. 36 (French edition); see also W. 451
W. and M., under no. 476 ("copie")
Saint Petersburg, Florida, exhibition catalogue, 1982–83, under no. 11

Related works
Paintings
In the Boston Museum of Fine Arts there is a larger version (figure 1; 65 x 54 cm.) that is somewhat different from the present painting (W. 451, pl. 98; Tokyo exhibition catalogue, 1980, no. 71, colorpl.); it has been known since 1883, and probably was in a sale [La Fontaine or Cochu], February 22, 1798, no. 146: "ce morceau gracieux a longtemps jouit d'une réputation que justifioit le talent de cet artiste." It is difficult to study because of its poor state of preservation, but, at best, it seems to be no more than a mediocre replica.

Engravings
This work was popularized through the engraving by Nicolas Delaunay (1739–1792), which is cited by all of the past Fragonard scholars. The most famous version of this engraving "est dédiée à M. Ménage de Pressigny, Conseiller, Fermier général de S. M. . . ." (*Journal de Paris*, December 3, 1779, no. 337, p. 1373; see also November 28, 1779, no. 332, p. 1353; *Mercure de France*, January 1, 1780, p. 45), and was exhibited at the Salon of 1779 (no. 288). According to Delteil (1910, pp. 141–42), Delaunay sold it for 6 *livres*. The version reproduced here (see figures 2, 3) is rare, and does not contain the usual dedicatory inscription. For the other versions of this engraving, see P. p. 323, nos. 34–36; Delteil; W.; and Hébert and Sjöberg, XII, 1973, no. 196.

The Goncourts (p. 306), often quoted, state that, during the Revolution, "Fragonard . . . dédie la *Bonne Mère* à la Patrie." The source for this information is Launay (1859): "Il a peint aussi l'*Heureuse mère* qu'il dédia à la patrie, lorsque la révolution eut éclaté."

For the gouache, see the following entry.

Figure 1. Attributed to Fragonard.
The Good Mother.
Museum of Fine Arts, Boston

Figure 2. Nicolas Delaunay.
The Good Mother. Musée du Louvre, Paris, Cabinet des Dessins, Rothschild Collection

Figure 3. Nicolas Delaunay.
The Good Mother. Musée du Louvre, Paris, Cabinet des Dessins, Rothschild Collection

This painting is not very well known; in 1913–14, it was the object of a heated debate between Thiébault-Sisson, who defended the Boston version (see *Related works*), and Alvin-Beaumont and Guillaume Apollinaire—"paid by Jacques Seligmann [to] publish . . . a brochure in which he attacked the original [*sic*] of *La Bonne Mère* by Fragonard" (Gimpel, 1963, p. 258)—both of whom argued in favor of the picture then in the Veil-Picard collection.

Since that time, it has not been seen much, nor studied very closely. Jacques Wilhelm (unpublished monograph) and David Carritt (see Saint Petersburg exhibition catalogue, 1982–83) have been the only ones to argue that the

159

painting after which Delaunay made his engraving in 1779 could be identified with the present one. Delaunay had dedicated the engraving to the powerful *Fermier général* (tax collector) Marie-François Ménage de Pressigny. During the Revolution, a *"Bonne Mère"* very similar in dimensions to the present work was seized along with Ménage de Pressigny's property.

Fragonard probably painted this picture first, and then, a few years later, executed the gouache (cat. no. 160) that was exhibited at the Salon de la Correspondance in 1781. Wilhelm (1954) believes that this picture was painted "shortly after [Fragonard's] return from his first trip to Italy," and Wildenstein dates it 1777–79, but it more likely dates from shortly before the second trip to Italy in 1773–74.

This work, which has very recently been restored, is a perfect example of the kind of family scene that forms an important aspect of Fragonard's oeuvre. A mother wearing a stylish white bonnet is about to wash the face of her little

girl. A little boy, hiding modestly behind his large hat, is pouring water into a dish. At the right, a baby sleeps in a large cradle. A big white cat rubs itself affectionately against the mother's neck.

For Sutton (1987, p. 112), this painting evokes the art of Greuze. According to Grayson (1980, pp. 20–26), it was directly inspired by Rousseau's *Émile* (1762), which is dedicated to a "good mother," Mme de Chenonceaux.

In keeping with contemporary taste, Fragonard depicted many "picturesque details" (the cat, the pot curiously placed in the tree, abundant vegetation). Especially successful in enlivening the composition is the bright light that illuminates the happy face of the young mother (and her breasts), the sleeping baby, and the hollyhocks—flowers that the artist particularly favored.

A familiar subject, the *Good Mother* is also a classically composed, delicately colored outdoor scene, full of calm, simplicity, and happiness.

160 The Good Mother

Bister wash and watercolor on paper, heightened with gouache, oval (vertical), 42 x 34.2 cm.

Museum of Fine Arts, Saint Petersburg, Florida, Gift of Mrs. Acheson Stuart, 79.7

Provenance
The architect Trouard: sold, February 22,
1779, no. 192: "un morceau peint à gouache
et de forme ovale en hauteur; sur le devant,
on voit une mère qui va débarbouiller son
enfant qui est auprès d'elle; plus loin un berceau, et dedans un petit enfant endormi. Le
fond de ce morceau piquant et agréable est
terminé par un Paysage"; Vassal de Saint-
Hubert: sold posthumously, April 24, 1783,
no. 465: "... une femme et trois enfants,
dont un dans son berceau; le fond est du paysage avec des rosiers et autres fleurs"; E.
Norblin: sold, March 16–17, 1860, no. 59;
David David-Weill, 1913 (see Thiébault-
Sisson, 1913); Édouard Jonas, 1931; [Wil-
denstein]; A. E. Ball, New York: sold
Sotheby's, London, July 9, 1968, no. 50, ill.;
given to the Museum of Fine Arts, 1979.

Exhibitions
Salon de la Correspondance, 1781, no. 5:
"deux tableaux peints à l'aquarelle représentant l'un, une jeune mère de famille
vaquant aux soins de ses enfants, sujet très
connu par la belle estampe de M. de
Launay ... un pied et demi de haut sur un
pied trois pouces de large [48.6 x 40.5
cm.]" (for "the other work" mentioned,
see cat. no. 229)
New York, 1926, no. 4
Paris, 1931, no. 20 (dimensions incorrect)
Saint Petersburg exhibition catalogue,
1982–83, no. 10, ill. (colorpl. and cover)

Bibliography
Bellier de la Chavignerie, 1865, p. 84
P. p. 306
Apollinaire, 1914, pp. 12–13
R. p. 227, fig. 76, p. 153
A. 632, fig. 195 (see also 631, 633)
Grayson, 1980, pp. 20–26, fig. 2, p. 23

Related works
See previous entry (*Paintings* and
Engravings).
  See also A. 630. Bellier de la Chavignerie
(1865) owned a "copie contemporaine au
pastel."

It would be difficult to prove that this version of the *Good Mother* is, in fact, the same as that in the Trouard (1779) and Vassal de Saint-Hubert (1783) sales, or in the Salon de la Correspondance of 1781. We do know that, in 1781, Pahin de la Blancherie (or Fragonard) paired a *Good Mother* with a *Rest on the Flight into Egypt* (cat. no. 229), which was also an oval-format watercolor, and that the two works were very likely sold together in 1783. This gouache-and-watercolor version, which seems to postdate the oil painting, is probably close in time to Delaunay's 1779 engraving (see previous entry).

As was his wont, Fragonard contrasted an everyday scene with a subject of great religious significance, as if to empha- size the similarity of the themes: the happiness—however precarious—of motherhood.

161 The Fête at Saint-Cloud

Oil on canvas, 216 x 335 cm.

Banque de France, Paris

Provenance
See entry.
   Mentioned for the first time on February 7, 1862, the occasion of an "Estimation des tableaux et des boiseries de la Galerie Dorée en vue de l'assurance contre l'incendie ... Un Fragonard ... 3,000 francs" (the note itself is known only from a copy; the appraiser for the Banque de France was a "M. Petit"; see also Cayeux, 1948).

Exhibitions
Paris, 1907, no. 87
Paris, 1921, no. 51, ill.
Paris, 1937, no. 159, pl. 75 of the album
Paris, 1943, no. 29, ill.
Paris, 1948, no. 10, pp. 7–8 (Adam Saulnier), 11–14 (Jean de Cayeux), ill.
Amsterdam, 1951, no. 9, ill. and cover
Paris, 1951, no. 86
London, 1954–55, no. 200, ill.
Paris, 1974, no. 108, colorpl. p. 112
Bordeaux, 1980–81, no. 20, colorplates pp. 20–21
Berlin, 1983, n.p., colorpl.

Bibliography
Portalis, 1885, p. 483
Gonse, 1889, p. 77
P. pp. 82, 83, 202, 277, ill. of an etching by de Mare between pp. 78 and 79
Naquet, 1890, p. 36
Champeaux, 1893, p. 241
N. pp. 69–70
Tourneux, 1907, pp. 90, 100, ill. p. 99
Rudrauf, 1947, p. 16
R. p. 144
Plaisirs de France, January 1960, p. 32 (detail)
W. 436, pp. 84–85, 87, 89, colorpl. opposite p. 40, and pp. 26, 35 (French edition)
G. Wildenstein, 1960, pp. 45–50, fig. 3, p. 47
Thuillier, 1967, ill. pp. 120–21, 123
Levey, 1972, p. 180, fig. 176
W. and M. 458, colorplates XLVIII–L
Sutton, 1980; 1987, pp. 111–12
Conisbee, 1981, p. 194, fig. 163
Gaehtgens, 1983, pp. 26–35, 78, colorpl.
Wakefield, 1984, p. 144, fig. 173

Related works

There are three existing sketches for the composition, all with variants: one, formerly in the Arthur Veil-Picard collection, is today in an important private collection in Paris (figure 1; W. 435, fig. 185); the other two, formerly in the E. G. Bührle Collection, Zurich, are today in a private collection, New York (figure 2: W. 434, pl. 88; figure 3: W. 433, pl. 86, and Rotterdam-Brunswick exhibition catalogue, 1983–84, no. 64, ill.).

All three were exhibited in London in 1968: no. 243, fig. 281; no. 244, fig. 283; and no. 245, fig. 279.

For a small "vue de Saint-Cloud" on panel, which was seized during the Revolution, and has not yet come to light, see W. 437 (the document in the archives mentions "un tableau de paisage"!).

For the drawing in the Lehman Collection, see cat. no. 274 (see also A. 1452, fig. 402, which should be compared with the sketch by Saint-Aubin reproduced here).

Figure 1. Fragonard. *Les Marionettes.* Private collection, Paris

Figure 2. Fragonard. *The Toy Seller.* Private collection

Figure 3. Fragonard. *Les Charlatans.* Private collection

Figure 4. Nicolas Delaunay, after Moreau le Jeune. *The Fête at Saint-Cloud.* Bibliothèque Nationale, Paris, Cabinet des Estampes

Figure 5. Gabriel de Saint-Aubin. *The Cascades at Saint-Cloud.* National Gallery of Scotland, Edinburgh

Figure 6. Charles-Nicolas Cochin, after François Boucher. *Country Fair.* Musée du Louvre, Paris, Cabinet des Dessins, Rothschild Collection

Figure 7. After a model by Étienne-Maurice Falconet. *Les Marchands de plaisirs au tourniquet.* Bisque. Musée National de Céramique, Sèvres

Figure 8. Detail of catalogue no. 161

This work is as beautiful as it is mysterious (and this, in spite of all our research): its early history is not known, its dating is unsure, and there is nothing certain about its title.

The *Fête at Saint-Cloud* is believed to have been painted for the Duc de Penthièvre, or at least for his Hôtel de Toulouse, today the seat of the Banque de France; but this has still not been confirmed. The painting is not cited in any eighteenth-century guidebooks to Paris, and it is not listed in the inventories of works seized during the Revolution. The Hôtel de Toulouse was looted, became the "Imprimerie de la République" in 1795, and then the "Imprimerie Impériale," before being sold in 1808 to the Banque de France. In

1862, at the bank's request, the picture was appraised—although not mentioned by title—with a view to securing a fire insurance policy. Roger Portalis (1885) seems to have been the first to publish it.

A dating between 1775 and 1780—after the artist returned from his second trip to Italy—is today unanimously agreed upon. This is supported by our knowledge of Fragonard's manner and his artistic development, as well as by the style of the costumes. This dating, however, does not sufficiently take into account the reasons for Fragonard's trip, and the resulting evolution of his style. For this reason, there is a chance that this work was painted before—though only shortly before—1773.

The title is from 1885, and has been retained since no better one has been found. In the eighteenth century, each year, on the last three Sundays in September, a fair very popular with Parisians was held in the lower park at Saint-Cloud (the upper park was reserved for the royal family). The artists Robert, Carle Vernet (see G. Wildenstein, 1960), Gabriel de Saint-Aubin, and Moreau le Jeune (see figure 4), among many others, attended the fête, and sketched the fountains (figure 5). There is no evidence, however, that this is the event that Fragonard wanted to represent here. On the contrary, his genius led him to invent and to evoke sites,

rather than to faithfully represent them.

(Fragonard did not forget Boucher's example—specifically, a work like his *Country Fair*, after which Cochin made an engraving in 1740 [figure 6].)

Perhaps the *Swing* and the *Blindman's Buff* in Washington were pendants to the present composition. At the sale of the collection of Louis-René Marchal de Saincy, April 29, 1789, there were (no. 41): "five large Pictures" by Fragonard "executed for the decoration of a Salon; they represent diverse Landscape subjects in various elegant settings, peopled with interesting figures" (unfortunately, the catalogue does not give any dimensions). Saincy was the patron of the painter Casanova, and owned many works by him. Michael Clark has discovered that Saincy lived in a house at 6, rue d'Aboukir that was bought by the Banque de France in 1806. Also enlightening is this (rarely quoted) passage by the Goncourts (p. 284, n. 1), once again based on the testimony of Théophile, the artist's grandson: "Fragonard always liked to decorate his houses. He made paintings for his country house in Carrières, and then for the one in Petit-Bourg, on the decoration of which his son collaborated."

Since its discovery a century ago, this work has gradually come to be universally admired. Not easily accessible, it is

161: Detail

considered one of the "secret masterpieces" of Paris. Two of the finest art historians of our time, Francis Haskell—who made the picture the subject of a lecture (alas, unpublished) —and Thomas Gaehtgens (1983) regard it as "one of the most beautiful paintings in the world," equaled in its time only by Watteau's *Enseigne de Gersaint*. How to explain this fascination?

The subject is simple enough: at the center is a grand fountain, behind a stone balustrade; at the sides are enormous trees and little groups of people watching the various sideshows. At the left are some charlatans and a toy seller; at the right is a puppeteer. In each of these passages (three sketches for them have come down to us; see figures 1–3), Fragonard included some amusing details: a little girl tries to escape from her mother; a man sitting on a wooden enclosure waves his hat at the attractive hawker on the stage; near her, a hoop and a monkey evoke the circus and magic tricks. Then there is a tent containing dolls, a wooden horse, a little boy selling fritters, and a woman selling wafers (figures 7, 8) that she distributes by means of a "loterie" (we can discern the dial, with its numerals, and the drum) and, finally, the puppeteer on a stone platform, standing on a low box with drawers; at his feet are a drum and some balls.

The majestic color harmony of greens and golds ("from amber to emerald": Thuillier) is punctuated by the bright red of the pennant and of the parasol held by a little black boy wearing a white turban with red and black feathers. The sunlight composes the scene, defining the different levels of space, and illuminates certain of the figure groups and the statue of Pan at the far right, partly hidden among the trees, that makes one think of Watteau. The overall beauty of this work resides in the fusion of nature and the elements—the foam of the fountain's spray, the wind that has toppled the planter with its orange tree, the "vagabond" rays of sunlight, the great vaporous clouds. It is a totally peaceful and civilized Nature—with nothing disquieting—one hospitable to Man.

Less of a "paysagiste" than Moreau the Elder, whose concept of nature is very reminiscent of that of Rousseau; less "sublime" and heroic in his art than Claude-Joseph Vernet; less sensitive to architecture and to the presence of Man than Hubert Robert—Fragonard was, nonetheless, like them, a man of his time (and of his country, as the great Venetian masters Canaletto, Guardi, Bellotto were of theirs). More so than the budding Romantic Burke, in his vision, as Gaehtgens noted, Fragonard was a contemporary of Diderot: for him Man domesticated Nature the better to admire it and to enjoy it happily, free of care.

162 The Swing

Oil on canvas, 215.9 x 185.4 cm.

National Gallery of Art, Washington, D.C., Samuel H. Kress Collection, 1961.9.17

163 Blindman's Buff

Oil on canvas, 216.2 x 197.8 cm.

National Gallery of Art, Washington, D.C., Samuel H. Kress Collection, 1961.9.16

Provenance
Casimir Perrin, Marquis de Cypierre (1784–1844): sold posthumously (catalogue by Thoré), March 10, 1845, nos. 52 (*La balançoire*, for 751 francs, with the following no.), 53 (for 300 francs, according to Blanc); Montesquiou-Fezensac, according to Wildenstein (W., English ed.; Eisler, 1977, p. 331 indicates that a copy of the Montesquiou-Fezensac collection sales catalogue of 1897, annotated by L. Soulié, mentions that Haro privately purchased two Fragonards and a Chardin from this collection, for Groult); Camille Groult, by 1889 (P.), until 1952; [Wildenstein, 1952]; acquired by Samuel H. Kress, 1954; entered the National Gallery, 1961.

Exhibitions
Previously unexhibited

Bibliography
Thoré [Bürger], *Le Constitutionnel*, October 1, 1844, p. 3
Bulletin de l'alliance des arts, February 10, 1845, p. 243
Blanc, 1862, p. 16
G. p. 334
P. pp. 272 (*La Balançoire*), 273 (*Le Colin-maillard*)
N. pp. 69–71, 150 (ills. of the two paintings between pp. 70 and 71; details between pp. 150 and 151, and pp. 152 and 153)
Réau, 1927, pp. 150–51, details p. 151 (*Le Colin-maillard*)
R. p. 158
M. Clay, 1959, p. 78, ill. (*La Balançoire*)
G. Wildenstein, 1959, p. 244, nos. 1, 2

W. 447, plates 92, 94 (*La Balançoire*), 448, plates 93, 95, and colorpl. facing pl. 94; p. VIII (English edition), p. 25 (French edition)
Wentzel, 1964, pp. 214–16, p. 215, fig. 162 (*La Balançoire*), and p. 217, fig. 163 (*Le Colin-maillard*)
W. and M. 471, colorplates LIII, LV, 472, colorplates LII, LIV
Eisler, 1977, pp. 328–31, figs. 296, 298 (*La Balançoire*), 295, 297 (*Le Colin-maillard*), with complete bibliography
Girod de l'Ain, 1977, pp. 168–69
Fried, 1980, p. 139, fig. 60, p. 141 (*Le Colin-maillard*)
Sutton, 1980; 1987, p. 112
Conisbee, 1981, p. 178, colorpl. 15, p. 189 (*La Balançoire*)
Posner, 1982, p. 80, figs. 8 (*Le Colin-maillard*), 9 (*La Balançoire*)

Like Pierre de Nolhac (1906), we believe that the *Swing* and the *Blindman's Buff* in Washington originally formed a single composition. In the Groult collection, between the two world wars, the two canvases had been joined in a fairly convincing manner (see figure 1), but laboratory examinations conducted at the National Gallery of Art proved that the two works had been separated since the eighteenth century.

The reason that we attach so much importance to this point is that these two works are exactly the same height (216 cm.) as the "*Fête at Saint-Cloud*" in the collection of

the Banque de France (see cat. no. 161). Together, the two paintings in Washington are wider by about fifty centimeters than the so-called "*Fête*." Could they not have been part of the decoration of the same room, even if the *Swing* and the *Blindman's Buff* may have been separate panels? When these three works are exhibited together, it will surely prove that this was the case.

Where were these paintings? G. Wildenstein (1959, pp. 238, 244) identifies the two Washington pictures with the *Swing* and the *Game of Hot Cockles* in the Saint-Non collection, but the 1792 posthumous inventory of the abbé's effects mentions that the pictures were painted "in Italy" (without giving their dimensions). Furthermore, it associates a *Swing*, a very common theme for Fragonard, with a *Game of Hot Cockles*, which was a subject that he rarely represented (see cat. no. 165), and which cannot be confused with the game of blindman's buff.

The two Washington paintings are mentioned for the first time in 1844 as being in the collection of the Marquis de Cypierre, a famous collector who also owned Watteau's *Gilles*, but their previous provenance is not known. Fragonard painted too many such subjects for us to conclude that the *Swing* and the *Blindman's Buff* in the collection of Gérard de Nerval (1808–1855), "bought somewhere for 50 francs" (Simches, 1964, p. 68; see also Tourneux, 1887; Bizet, 1928), may be identified with the two pictures in Washington.

There is a possibility that the two works, along with the "*Fête at Saint-Cloud*," were in the collection of Louis-René de Saincy, sold in 1789 (see the previous entry), or that they

Figure 1. Catalogue nos. 162 and 163, joined together. Formerly in the Groult collection

162

345

Figure 2. Fragonard. *Blindman's Buff.*
Private collection, Switzerland

Figure 3. Pierre-Adrien Pâris.
Trois Femmes tenant des urnes.
Musée des Beaux-Arts, Montreal

decorated one of the country houses near Paris that Fragonard bought when he became successful. A passage from the
Goncourts (see cat. no. 161), based on the memories of
Fragonard's grandson, Théophile, confirms that the artist
liked to decorate his houses. Alphonse de Launay, writing in
1859, described Fragonard's studio in the Louvre, which he
had "decorated himself ... [with] a vegetation of a richness
unknown in these parts ... trees, vines, climbing plants,
flowers, and rocks." More importantly, he added that, "in a
corner" of his studio, Fragonard had "a swing on which he
posed his models."

Three representations of the theme of the *Swing* are
included here (cat. nos. 6, 15, 170), each showing a characteristic aspect of Fragonard's talent (the fourth one, in the
Wallace Collection, is the most famous and the most studied
—see Wentzel, 1964; Posner, 1982—if not the most beautiful of his variations on this theme). The fact that there are as
many versions of the *Blindman's Buff* (including one in the
Rothschild collection in Pregny; W. 313, pl. 60; see figure
2) demonstrates Fragonard's interest (see Réau, 1927) in
these two subjects, which he so liked to pair up.

In the first painting, a young woman, from her swing,
tosses flowers to her companions, who are resting on the
ground beneath her. Between two "Egyptian" stone lions
spouting thin streams of water is a couple—he is standing,
and she is seated—who are holding the guy ropes attached to
the swing; in the foreground, a young woman is bathing a
little white poodle in one of the fountains. Another woman,
seated on a stone bench at the right, points a telescope
toward the sky. The scene takes place on the terrace of a park
overlooking a wooded valley. In the distance are some
mountains "of chalky stone rising above the white plain."

In the *Blindman's Buff,* a young woman who is blindfolded seems about to twirl like a dancer. At the far left,
there is an antique-style fountain (see figure 3). At the
center, in the foreground, a young man is holding the hand

of his ladylove; a little above them is a small cascade. At the
right, on a terrace, also in the foreground—dominated,
above, by a statue of Minerva and by a large fountain—are a
couple, and two mothers and their children are gathered
around a table, about to enjoy a light meal.

These two large pictures in Washington (see the excellent
study by Eisler, 1977)—although each has sustained some
paint damage as a result of relining—are unquestionably
among Fragonard's most perfect and most characteristic
creations: never have his yellows and greens, and the warm
browns punctuated by a few passages of red, been so reso-
nant. Fragonard's vision of Nature is a happy one: fountains
spouting water, great vaporous clouds, majestic trees,
flowers, bushes, and shrubs, and the sunlight that makes
them all vibrate—Nature civilized by man, whose presence is
visible everywhere. Children and adults are at ease, and seem
to have no fear of it; they are not aware of its beauty, much
less in awe of it.

Fragonard's approach was new, and he did not attract any
true successors. He evokes neither the solitude of Watteau
nor the appealing artificiality of Boucher, and does not
prefigure the realism of the Barbizon painters, or the anguish
of the Romantics. While his vision does not lack grandeur, it
is not grandiose, or at all frightening. Fragonard was not a
painter of the outdoors; a painter of landscapes, as the
Impressionists would be; a "visionary," like Turner; or a
"painter of the sun," like Monet. He avoided sentiment,
and all excessive lyricism. He painted a *friendly* Nature, in
all its beauty, and the happiness of those who experienced it.

"All this is fabulous, fantastic, impossible; but it is the
most amusing art to be seen anywhere. It is an airy and
melodious poetry, like the *Island of Cythera* by Watteau,
which is in the Louvre. One would have thought that only
music could express such fleeting effects as the morning
breeze" (Thoré, 1844).

163

164 A Game of Horse and Rider

Oil on canvas, 115.3 x 87.6 cm.

National Gallery of Art, Washington, D.C., Samuel H. Kress Collection, 1946.7.5

165 A Game of Hot Cockles

Oil on canvas, 115.6 x 91.4 cm.

National Gallery of Art, Washington, D.C., Samuel H. Kress Collection, 1946.7.6

Provenance
"Ils proviennent de l'ancienne galerie de M.
Hope qui les avait donnés à la belle Mme
Jenny Colon" (Bürger [Thoré], 1864); Émile
and Isaac Péreire: sold, March 6–9, 1872,
nos. 61, 60 (for 10,400 francs, to Pillet-
Will); Comte Pillet-Will, still in 1910;
[Wildenstein, 1932]; Calouste Gulbenkian;
[Wildenstein]; Samuel H. Kress, 1942;
given to the National Gallery, 1946.

Exhibitions
Paris, 1885, nos. 192 (entitled *Colin-maillard*), 193
Berlin, 1910, nos. 317, 320 (respectively,
nos. 44, 45, in the large catalogue)

London, 1932, nos. 183, 211 (nos. 166,
167, in the commemorative catalogue)

Bibliography
Bürger [Thoré], 1864, p. 201
Portalis, 1885, p. 483
P. pp. 82, 273 (*Le Cheval fondu*), 282
(*La Main chaude*)
Naquet, 1890, p. 36
Champeaux, 1898, p. 318
N. p. 159
G. Wildenstein, 1932, p. 66, figs. 14, 13,
respectively
The Illustrated London News, April 9, 1932,
ills. pp. III, II
R. p. 158

W. 443, pl. 96; 444, pl. 97, color frontis-
piece, and p. 25 (French edition)
Carpenter, 1962, p. 360 (*La Main chaude*)
W. and M. 468, ill., 469, ill.
Haskell, 1976, p. 84, pl. 200 (*La Main
chaude*)
Eisler, 1977, pp. 331–32, figs. 293, 294
(with complete bibliography)
Sutton, 1980; 1987, p. 112

Related works
Engravings of the two paintings were made
by Jules-Jacques Veyrassat to illustrate the
Péreire collection sales catalogue in 1872 (P.
p. 323, no. 41, with a reproduction of *La
Main chaude* between pp. 276 and 277).

The similar dimensions of these two paintings, the scale of the figures in relation to the landscape, their subjects, their history—all attest to the fact that they were obviously intended to form a pair.

The games of "le cheval fondu" and "la main chaude" were very popular in France until the nineteenth century, but today are virtually forgotten. The first was a boys' game, requiring two opposing teams; the players of the first team lined up, bent forward, and held onto the person in front so as to form a sort of many-legged "horse." The person at the

head of the line had to brace himself (here, by leaning against a tree), as the "riders" on the second team, one after the other, jumped astride the backs of each of their adversaries on line; even if the "horse" crumbled under the weight of the "riders"— and, literally, "melted"— the "horses" had to continue their role.

"La main chaude" was played by boys and girls together, both children and adolescents: a player chosen by drawing lots had to kneel, keeping his eyes closed (or, as in Frago-nard's painting, hiding his head in the lap of a person called

Figure 1. Étienne-Maurice
Falconet. *L'Amour menaçant.*
Musée du Louvre

Figure 2. Fragonard.
A Game of Hot Cockles (detail)

Figure 3. Fragonard. *A Game of Horse and Rider*. (detail)

Figure 4. Fragonard. *A Game of Hot Cockles*. (detail)

the "confessor," who did not participate in the game), and placing his open hand on his back. Each of the other players struck the hand in turn. The first player had to identify who hit him. If he guessed right, he was replaced in the "confessional" by the person who let himself be discovered.

Nothing is known of the origin of these paintings. At his death in 1791, Saint-Non owned "a landscape study done by Fragonard in Italy, with figures, its subject la Main chaude," which had as a pendant a "Swing valued together at 100 *livres*" (G. Wildenstein, 1959, p. 238). The Bailiff of Saint-Julien provenance (exhibition catalogue, 1932; Mauclair [1929]) sometimes suggested seems to be based on a confusion with the *Blindman's Buff* and the *Swing* that are today in Toledo and in the Thyssen collection, respectively (cat. nos. 5, 6); the William Hope–Jenny Colon provenance goes back to Bürger [Thoré] (1864). Jenny Colon (1808–1842), the mistress of William Hope, was also at one time the mistress of Gérard de Nerval, who was among Fragonard's first admirers in the nineteenth century, and who owned a version of *The Swing* and of the *Blindman's Buff* "that he had bought for fifty francs at an antique shop" (Bizet, 1928, p. 94; see also Tourneux, 1887; Simches, 1964).

The dating of the present paintings is no longer a subject of debate, so conclusive is the similarity of their style and their coloring to the "*Fête at Saint-Cloud*," but it is not certain whether they were done before or after this last work. Perhaps this will become clear when the three works are exhibited together. At the Salon of 1779, Hubert Robert exhibited a "large Fountain in an Italian garden: in the foreground, some Women are playing *la main chaude*."

The two pictures inspired Thoré's admiration: "I do not know of any that are more direct, more pure, more delightful." They were less appreciated by Portalis, who did not like Fragonard's "approximations" and criticized their "inconsistency," which he attributed to this "art of decoration, which calls for so much lightness and so few shadows."

The *Game of Horse and Rider* seems to take place on an island, which would explain the boat in the background. The *Game of Hot Cockles* is set in an equally imaginary but more domesticated landscape (has anyone tried to identify the trees?). The presence at the right side of the composition of Étienne-Maurice Falconet's *Amour menaçant* (executed for Mme de Pompadour; shown at the Salon of 1757; now in the Louvre; see figures 1, 2), which Fragonard had already made use of, in *The Swing* now in the Wallace Collection, suggests that the games of adults are of a different order than those of children. In each of the paintings there is a couple—seated on the ground in the first painting, and on a long bench, a distance from the players, in the second (figures 3, 4)—who serve as a link between the two works.

Both of the charming Washington paintings are in an excellent state of preservation, and display a remarkable freshness of execution. The sunlight—Fragonard's usual "vagabond" rays—makes them seem to vibrate. The freedom and spontaneity of the technique, and their chromatic richness are pure delights to the eye.

The *joie de vivre* of those participating in the games is quite irresistible.

165

Oil on canvas, 62.5 x 45.1 cm.

Timken Art Gallery, San Diego, The Putnam Collection

Provenance
Hippolyte Walferdin (1795–1880): sold
posthumously, April 3, 1880, no. 12 (for
3,500 francs, to Beurnonville); Camille
Groult, by 1889: probably sold with the
Groult collection, 1952 (see advertisement in
The Burlington Magazine, 1952); [Wilden-
stein, 1954]; acquired by the Putnam Foundation, 1954.

Exhibitions
Paris, 1885, no. 199
Minneapolis and New York, 1954, no. 11

Bibliography
G. p. 335
P. p. 273
N. p. 150
Art News, November 1954, p. 50, ill.
R. p. 158
W. 446, fig. 188, p. 26 (French edition)
du Colombier, 1962, p. 73, ill.
A. and E. Mongan, 1969, no. 37, pp. 98,
   132, ill. p. 99
W. and M. 379, ill.

Figure 1. Catalogue no. 166
before restoration

Figure 2. Fragonard. *Blindman's Buff.*
Whereabouts unknown

This painting is a fragment of a larger composition: at the
left of an old photograph of the picture (figure 1), part of a
male figure is visible; it was probably removed when the
painting was restored, about 1952–54. Many of the figures
turn to the left, observing a scene that no longer exists. The
subject is difficult to identify: according to Daniel Wildenstein and Gabriele Mandel, who cite Réau (without giving
references), on the left side of the composition there was a
"group of figures around a swing."

Fragonard painted many versions of *Blindman's Buff:* one
(cat. no. 5), before his first trip to Italy, and at least four
others after 1761. Three are included here (cat. nos. 5, 163,
167). The only one that cannot be exhibited is the small—
and no doubt latest—version in the Rothschild collection in
Pregny (see cat. no. 163, figure 2; W. 313, pl. 60; Tour-
nézy, 1895, p. 41), which was in the important Trouard
collection sale, February 22, 1779, no. 79, and which we
have not seen (the whereabouts of the fine drawing with a
related composition, which was in the Samson and Meunié
collections, are unknown; see figure 2).

There are some who still criticize Fragonard's works for
their lack of invention, and for being monotonous, but these
pictures attest to his formidable capacity for renewal over a
period of twenty years. Each of them is an original creation

that borrows little from the preceding one. The overall
conception, the color, the scale of the figures in the landscape, and the action itself are handled in a very different
way each time, despite the limitations of the theme.

The *Blindman's Buff* in San Diego is the one closest to the
fine version in Washington. According to Agnes and Elisabeth Mongan (1969), it was painted after 1776, shortly
after the Washington picture, but this seems to be a rather
late date. The light golden-toned coloring, with patches of
pinks and pastel blues; the autumnal foliage of the large
scraggly tree; the architectural elements in the park, such as
the steps and the balustrade; the statue, which seems to be
watching over the scene (practically the same as the one in
the *Coresus and Callirhoë* in Angers, cat. no. 105); the
fountain above the cascade; and even the tree tipped over in
its planter in the foreground all evoke the large compositions
in Washington as well as the *"Fête at Saint-Cloud"* (owned
by the Banque de France).

Fragonard depicted the moment before the game begins:
two young women blindfold a young man who is protected
from the sun by a pink parasol. He lifts the blindfold to try
to see what has caught the attention of his companions. The
composition is awash in sunlight—the true "life of the
party"—which gives the scene its extraordinary spark.

167   Preparing for Blindman's Buff

Oil on canvas, 38 x 45 cm.

Musée du Louvre, Paris, R. F. 2556

Provenance

[Baudouin]: sold posthumously, February 15, 1770, no. 39: "une Récréation, après la collation faite, dans un jardin: ce Tableau agréable et frais de coloris est peint sur toile qui porte treize pouces six lignes de haut, sur seize pouces six lignes de large [36.5 x 44.5 cm.]" (for 50 *livres*, to Basan) (?); the miniaturist Jean-Antoine Gros (father of the painter Baron Gros): sold, April 13 (not 14), 1778, no. 56: "un Paysage d'un stile frais et champêtre, pris des environs de *Meudon.* Sur le devant du tableau, et sur une terrasse, on voit plusieurs groupes de jeunes filles et de garçons, dont les uns se disposent à jouer à *colin-maillard,* et les autres, près d'une table, s'occupent à différens autres jeux . . . [35.1 x 44.5 cm.]" (for 400 *livres,* to Feuillet);

Nicolas Delaunay (1739–1792): sold posthumously, May 7, 1792, no. 6: "vue intérieure d'un jardin: sur le devant des jeunes Filles et des jeunes Garçons jouent au Colin-Mayard; des Masses de Paysages et des Cascades terminent cette agréable production . . . [37.8 x 44.5 cm.]"; "un paysage vue des environs de Meudon hauteur 14 pouces sur 15. de fragonard [37.8 x 40.5 cm.]," seized from Papillon de la Ferté (1727–1794) during the Revolution (Archives Nationales, F 17^A 1266^A 1267 no. 30), valued at 300 *livres* (?); acquired for 250,000 francs by the Louvre, from M. Alexandre Poliakoff, 1926, "grâce à la bienveillante et généreuse intervention de M. David-Weill" (*Beaux-Arts,* November 15, 1926, p. 295, ill.).

Exhibitions
Ipswich, 1927, no. 13
Paris, 1933, no. 91
Paris, 1946, no. 367
San Francisco,1949, no. 13
Amsterdam, 1951, no. 46
Paris, 1974, no. 19, ill.
Tokyo, 1980, no. 70, colorpl.

Bibliography
G. p. 338
P. p. 273 (pp. 16, 287 ?)
N. p. 150
Dacier, 1913, IV, p. 25
Réau, 1927, pp. 148–52, ill.
Gillet, 1929, pp. 87–89, pl. 93
R. pp. 95, 158, pl. 122, p. 249
W. 445, fig. 187, p. 26 (French edition)
W. and M. 470, ill., colorpl. LI

The painting's provenance from the Gros sale, of 1778, is confirmed by the sketch by Gabriel de Saint-Aubin in the margin of his copy of the sales catalogue (figure 1; Musée du Petit Palais, Paris, Collection Dutuit). The subsequent owner, the engraver Delaunay, popularized some of Fragonard's most famous works, including the *Swing* in the Wallace Collection. There is no proof, however, that this painting is the "Récréation après la collation..." sold in 1770 with the collection of the painter Baudouin, Boucher's son-in-law; the dimensions mentioned in the sales catalogue do not coincide perfectly (not unusual in the eighteenth century) with those of the Louvre's *Blindman's Buff,* and the description in the catalogue, which makes no reference to the game, is too imprecise to permit a positive identification of the works. This is an important point insofar as the chronology and the complex evolution and transformation of Fragonard's work are concerned. There is no doubt that this version of the *Blindman's Buff* was painted prior to 1778, and probably closer to Fragonard's second trip to Italy, shortly before his departure in 1773.

Before its recent restoration, the painting had a thick coat of yellow varnish that obscured the original lightness of the gray and blue tints in the sky, as well as the green and gold harmonies.

A specific detail in the 1778 catalogue of the Gros sale, by the expert Le Brun—a close friend of Fragonard and, according to some old sources, perhaps even his pupil—has a certain importance. Le Brun says that the scene takes place "near Meudon." Indeed, all of the places that Fragonard was commissioned to decorate—the châteaux of Bellevue, Louveciennes, and Versailles—and where he worked more or less assiduously between 1766 and 1773 were near Meudon.

The Louvre's *Blindman's Buff* is the smallest of the four versions included here (see also cat. nos. 5, 163, 166, and cat. no. 163, figure 2, a fifth example of this theme). It is also the one in which the actual game occupies the least space: a young girl blindfolds a young man, who takes advantage of the opportunity to hold her around the waist. At the right, a young boy tumbles a girl, while her companions set the table. The scene is merely a pretext to paint a sunlit park with its hedges, trellises, flowerbeds, and dense masses of greenery.

"Fragonard [in this work] reveals himself as Watteau's successor" (*Beaux-Arts,* November 15, 1926), "a certain Watteau, the Watteau of *L'Île heureuse* and of the *Assemblée dans un parc,* the Watteau of small figures in vast landscapes" (Gillet, 1929). This aspect of his work may be less apparent today, but the painting made an impression on Saint-Aubin, who took particular care in his sketch of it at the Gros sale. This was not true of the collector and diamond merchant Jean-Denis Lempereur (1701–1779); alongside the entry in his copy of the Gros sales catalogue (today in the Bibliothèque Nationale), he wrote the word "mediocre!"

Figure 1. Gabriel de Saint-Aubin. Page from the sales catalogue of the Gros collection (1778). Musée du Petit Palais, Paris

168   The Island of Love

Oil on canvas, 71 x 90 cm.

Museu Calouste Gulbenkian, Lisbon

Provenance
[Jean-Benjamin Delaborde (1734–1794)]: sold, June 14, 1784, no. 10; Duclos-Dufresnoy: sold, August 18–21, 1795, no. 29 (for 2,000 *livres "en assignats"* [French paper money, 1789–97] at the rate of 100 *assignats* per 2 *livres,* according to N.); Villeminot: sold, May 25, 1807, no. 22 (for 74.5 *livres,* to "Renout") (?); Guérin: sold, April 30, 1810, no. 30; Marquis de Sayve, Paris; [Wildenstein]; C. S. Gulbenkian, May 1928; on loan to the National Gallery, London, 1936–50 (except during World War II), and to the National Gallery of Art, Washington, D.C., 1950–60.

Exhibitions
Salon de la Correspondance, 1782, no. 24: "un charmant paysage, représentant une grotte ornée d'architecture, avec figures," or no. 6: "un Tableau représentant un Paysage orné d'arbres et d'eaux en cascade" (?)
London, 1937, p. 30
Washington, D.C., 1950, no. 11, ill. (entry by Fern Rusk Shapley)
Paris, 1960, no. 15, ill.
Porto, 1964, no. 3, ill. (with a list of exhibitions in which the painting figured)

Bibliography
Nouvelles de la République des lettres et des arts, August 21, 1782, p. 253 or 271 (?)
G. p. 339
N. pp. 142, 151
Rudrauf, 1947, pp. 14–15, ill.
R. p. 185
W. 439, plates 90–91, p. 26 (French edition)
Vaudoyer, 1961, pp. 22–23, colorpl.
Carpenter, 1962, p. 360
Thuillier, 1967, colorpl. p. 124, details pp. 126–27, and cover
W. and M. 464, ill.
Sutton, 1980; 1987, p. 112

Related works
This canvas may be related to a small painting on panel (now lost), sold, March 22,
1790, no. 344: "la vue d'une Forêt, au bord
de laquelle passe une rivière où l'on voit plusieurs barques, pleines de gens qui s'amusent,
quantité d'autres figures ornent ce charmant
tableau qui est une des plus belles productions de ce Maître" (W. 440).
   For the Straus gouache and Fragonard's
drawings, see the following entry.

Rarely has such a famous work so jealously guarded its
secrets. Its traditional title, *The Fête at Rambouillet,* dates
back only to the nineteenth century: the gouache version in
the Straus collection (see cat. no. 169) was sold in 1868, and
the author of the catalogue, Haro, described it as the "celebration given for the royal family by the Duc de Penthièvre
in the park at Rambouillet." This interpretation, however, is
not supported by any solid evidence. Réau (1956), as well as
the catalogue of the 1937 exhibition in London of the
Gulbenkian collection, interpreted it as "a record of the
celebrations given at Chantilly by the Prince de Condé in
honor of the Grand Duke of Russia (the future Paul I, son of
Catherine II), who traveled in France as the Comte du Nord.
The Duchesse de Chartres and the Princesse de Lamballe
played the role of ferriers to the Island of Love." Here, again,
there is no basis for this "reading," although we know that
during his visit to France in 1782, the "Comte du Nord"
visited Fragonard's studio in the Louvre. According to a
third hypothesis, proposed by Fern Rusk Shapley in 1950,
the picture represents the park at the Château de Cassan,
owned by Bergeret de Grancourt, but, again, this is not
confirmed by any documentary evidence.

This painting was sold four times between 1784 and
1810 (and a drawing in 1787), but in none of the catalogues
was it given a "historical" title. Each time, it was greatly
admired ("[this] painting is admirable as much for its magical effect and the harmony of the color as for the spirited

168

brushwork and the generally pleasant composition"; 1784), and the extremely detailed descriptions prove the importance that was accorded to it, but only one catalogue (1795) attempted to identify the subject, "L'Îsle d'amour..."; hence, we have adopted that title.

At the right, a boat approaches a gondola. Atop a stairway that recalls one in the park at Saint-Cloud (see the drawing by Saint-Aubin in Edinburgh; cat. no. 161, figure 5), some couples are conversing in the shade. At the center, and also at the far left, some men and women leaning on balustrades contemplate the river and the falls. Further back, to the left of center, is a leafless tree, and to its left are some statues, including one of a river-god. Louis Vaudoyer (1961) rightly concludes that "this precious work was obviously a product of the painter's imagination," but this still does not explain the subject. A clue may be provided by what we know of its first owner.

Jean-Benjamin Delaborde (Boyer, 1962, pp. 148–49; see also Yves Durand, 1971), *Premier valet de chambre* to Louis XV, was one of Fragonard's close friends. Guimbaud (1928) mentions him, sometimes confusing him with his namesake, Jean-Joseph, who was also a *Fermier général* and an art collector. In any case, Jean-Benjamin was in Italy in 1774, like Fragonard and Bergeret, and in 1776 he published an illustrated book on Switzerland, *Tableaux de la Suisse,* which was not very successful. He entrusted his book on Italy to the Abbé de Saint-Non, and the result was the *Voyage pittoresque de Naples et de Sicile.* Perhaps it was Delaborde who commissioned the present work from Fragonard, guiding him in the choice of its subject. In any event, the large gondola at the right recalls those of Venice. A drawing, well known although unpublished before now (cat. no. 169, figure 2), shows not only the gondola, but also a very Venetian-looking street scene and architecture; this would tend to prove that the present work was painted upon Fragonard's return from the second trip to Italy, about 1775. This hypothesis is a tenuous one, for it is also possible that the picture was executed shortly before the Italian trip.

There is a magic to this painting; we can almost hear the rush of the waters and feel the cool of the shade and the gentleness of the sun. According to D. Wildenstein and G. Mandel (1972), and D. Sutton (1980; 1987), the great barren tree zigzagging across the composition that looks as if it had been struck by lightning may have been inspired by a work by Wu Zhen formerly in the collection of Bergeret (?), who was very fond of Chinese art, in the pagoda at the Château de Cassan; this hypothesis, however, has been rejected by Jacques Giès of the Musée Guimet. The tree contributes a golden note to the various blues and greens of the river, the dense groves, the thick hedges, and the manicured trees. The Gulbenkian picture—an ode to the forces of water in which the luxuriant vegetation triumphs—is enchanting, disquieting, and even somewhat frightening. The *Island of Love* is an "epic dream" that recalls Watteau, but the nostalgia and melancholy in his work have been replaced, here, by poetry and escape.

169   The Island of Love

Gouache, 26.7 x 35.6 cm.

Collection John W. Straus, New York

Provenance
The miniaturist A. Saint: sold (catalogued by Thoré), May 4, 1846, no. 287 (for 90 francs; 22 francs, according to P.); Eugène Tondu: sold posthumously, April 24–26, 1865, no. 127 (for 400 francs); F. de Villars: sold, March 13, 1868, no. 37 (for 820 francs, to Haro, who wrote the preface to the sales catalogue); Mme Périer; Sigismond Bar-

dac; Joseph Bardac, 1921; [Wildenstein]; Herbert N. Straus, 1926; John W. Straus.

Exhibitions
Paris, 1921, no. 112
Buffalo, 1935, no. 84, ill.
London, 1954–55, no. 603
Paris, 1958, no. 52, pl. 68
Washington, D.C., 1978, no. 51, ill. (with

complete list of the numerous exhibitions in which the work was included)

Bibliography
G. p. 339
P. pp. 303–4
R. pp. 185, 228, fig. 88, p. 175
A. 246
Massengale, 1979, p. 270, fig. 103

Related works
A bister wash drawing was formerly in the Forsyth Wickes collection (figure 1), and a study of a gondola accompanied by "marchands et leurs enfants sur un quai... avec construction à portes et fenêtres ogivales," in the Schiff collection (figure 2; A. 247, 248 confuses the provenances of the two works; see also A. 249, 250, the drawing from the Chabot sale of 1787, to be discussed below).
For the painting, see previous entry.

Figure 1. Fragonard. *The Island of Love.* Whereabouts unknown

Figure 2. Fragonard. *Gondola.* Private collection, New York

This is unquestionably Fragonard's most famous—and most beautiful—gouache: "a unique pearl in the master's jewel box" (Haro, preface to the Villars sales catalogue of 1868). This version of the *Island of Love* is a variant of the Lisbon painting (see previous entry for an explanation of the title) and of the two drawings reproduced here. The Schiff drawing (perhaps done during the artist's second visit to Venice, between July 19 and 31, 1774) seems to be the earlier of the two, but it is difficult to determine precisely the order of their execution. The Straus gouache and the Wickes drawing, which present many analogous details, may have been done after the painting in Lisbon.

Here, as in the latter painting, Fragonard played on the contrast between the somewhat disquieting energy of the water and the peacefulness of the grandiose and enchanting site. He gave free rein to his imagination and his fancy, the better to depict the elements—water, sun, light, and air—rendering them with an evident sensuality, so that Nature, not the spectator, becomes the true subject of this work.

170 The Little Swing

Oil on canvas, 52 x 71.2 cm.

Private collection, Paris

Provenance
Anonymous sale, April 15–17, 1844, no. 24; Marquise de Crillon, 1861; Duchesse de Polignac, *née* Crillon, 1883, 1889; Rodolphe Kann, 1900, 1907; [Wildenstein]; Comtesse de Béhague, 1926; Marquis de Ganay, 1956.

Exhibitions
Paris, 1883–84, no. 62
Amsterdam, 1926, no. 47, ill.
London, 1954–55, no. 214
Paris, 1956, no. 32

Bibliography
Horsin-Déon, 1861, p. 126 (*Annuaire des artistes...*) or p. 246 (*L'Artiste*)
P. p. 276
Bode, 1900, pp. XXXII–XXXIII, no. 97, ill.
E. Michel, 1901, pp. 504–5, ill.
Kann collection catalogue, 1907, vol. I, pp. XXV–XXVI, vol. II, no. 146, ill.
N. p. 121
D. and V. 133, ill.
R. p. 158
W. 438, fig. 186, p. 26 (French edition)
Wentzel, 1964, p. 214, fig. 161, p. 213
W. and M. 463, ill.
Posner, 1982, p. 88, fig. 18

This painting, which has just been restored, along with the *Island of Love* in Lisbon (cat. no. 168), occupies a unique place in Fragonard's oeuvre. Set against a bank of foliage that closes in the composition, leaving only a narrow opening through which the sky is visible, a young girl dressed all in pink disports herself on a swing in the presence of other young people gathered around a pool. At the right, the sunlight illuminates a stone statue of three Cupids, and below it, in the water, lead dolphins, all of which are ringed by hollyhock bushes; two of the Cupids are holding a heart, while the third aims his bow at the girl on the swing. The scene is animated by two well-placed sources of light: from the left, sunlight sparkles on the water in the fountain and on the young girl's dress, and, in the background, through an opening in the trees that lends depth to the composition, the milky blues of the sky, the trees, and the sunlight-bathed meadow are revealed.

The scene exudes peace, *joie de vivre*, and happiness. The only motion is that of the swing. While there is nothing innocent about the work, it is very far removed from the celebrated version in the Wallace Collection, which Fragonard painted ten years earlier. There, in an unusual departure for the artist, he included a wealth of detail, leaving nothing to chance. In the present work, with modesty and reserve he created an atmosphere of enchantment and love—a hymn in praise of Nature, the sun, and the joy of living.

VI

The Second Trip to Italy
(1773–74)

The reader may be surprised that the preceding chapter concluded with a discussion of some of Fragonard's most famous paintings: the *Fête at Saint-Cloud,* which belongs to the Banque de France; four paintings in the same style in Washington, D.C.; and the canvas—one of the jewels of the Gulbenkian Collection in Lisbon—titled (on the basis of a reference in an eighteenth-century sales catalogue) the *Island of Love.* We hesitated for some time before opting for this chronology, for we are not entirely convinced of the date of the dream-like Lisbon painting, and will delay making any decisions about its date until we have examined this master-piece of eighteenth-century landscape painting. We do not exclude the possibility that the *Fête at Saint-Cloud* was executed prior to Fragonard's departure for Italy in 1773.

For the artist, this voyage was no mere pleasure trip. Bergeret's offer was a tempting one, and it came at an opportune moment. Fragonard had suffered two heavy reverses—the failure of his commissions for Mme du Barry at Louveciennes and for Mlle Guimard's house in the Chaussée-d'Antin. These setbacks, which he wished to forget, must have affected him very deeply. He knew that since 1770—following the death of Boucher but prior to that of Louis XV, and well before d'Angiviller had taken over Marigny's duties—French art had sought new directions, and was leaning toward new models. His own style of art, which had never been officially accepted, but which, nonetheless, had had its devotees, was beginning to look "dated." It is therefore hardly surprising that Fragonard now wished to go back to the sources of the past, in Italy, to see more recent Italian works (those of Tiepolo, for example) and thus revive his own inspiration. It seems likely that the *Fête at Saint-Cloud* was not the first painting completed after Fragonard's return, but the crowning achievement of the long and fruitful development that had brought him from the *Coresus and Callirhoë* to the canvases painted for Louveciennes. When he arrived back in France, his break with the past was probably not yet complete, and many elements of his old style are discernible in the first paintings that he executed after 1774. Yet, Fragonard's desire to go on to new things, to explore new themes and techniques, is evident from then on. Italy had enabled him to cut the ties with his own past—the happy memories and the taste of success were now behind him.

On October 5, 1773, Fragonard left Paris for Rome. He had neglected to ask the Academy for authorization to make this trip, thus—once again—slighting the institution in which he held a membership. This was his second stay in Italy and lasted a much shorter time than the first; he returned to France in September 1774.

Fragonard's traveling companion was Pierre-Jacques-Onésyme Bergeret de Grancourt, a fifty-eight-year-old *fermier général* whom he had known for at least ten years (see G. Wildenstein, 1961; Terver, 1987). Bergeret had asked Mme Fragonard to join them, as well as a "former chambermaid" of the late Mme Bergeret named Jeanne Vignier (or Viguier: see Ananoff, 1983), who would later become the third Mme

Bergeret. A "son" from Bergeret's first marriage accompanied them "in a cabriolet, with a cook." Two coachmen and a valet completed the party.

Bergeret was one of the richest men in France, having inherited some eight million *livres* from his father in 1771 (Durand, 1971, p. 134). He had the excellent idea of keeping a journal of his trip with Fragonard; the original manuscript, which is now in the Bibliothèque Municipale, in Poitiers, was published in its entirety by Albert Tornézy in 1895 (and republished, in part, by Jacques Wilhelm in 1948). Bergeret's *Journal* is a fascinating document—perhaps even more fascinating than the one kept by the Abbé de Saint-Non. It has no literary pretensions, nor does it offer any particularly original insights into Italy; its one great merit is that it rings true. The details of the voyage (see the map below), the daily life of the Italians, the ceremonies and festivities the party encountered, are all conscientiously, and often acutely, described. The descriptions of plowing (Tornézy, p. 124), of Mardi Gras in Rome (ibid., p. 230), and of a visit to Pompeii (ibid., p. 314) give us a taste of Bergeret's style: he may have been "an honest but somewhat slow-witted gentleman," but he was a good observer, inquisitive about all the people and things that he saw, and much more intrigued by Italy's mores than by her glorious artistic past.

The famous portrait of Bergeret painted in Rome by François-André Vincent (figure 1) seems to emphasize the sitter's conceitedness, casting the man in a slightly ironic light: there is, doubtless, some truth in this portrayal. Yet, Bergeret's *Journal* is primarily interesting to us for its references to Fragonard, although the painter is very rarely quoted (see the Chronology for further details).

At some stage of the trip the two men seem to have quarreled—we do not know when or why—for, later on, there was a definite antipathy between Bergeret and the Fragonards. On the day of their departure, Bergeret was full of praise for them, but after his return he was bitterly critical of the couple, referring to them as "gens faux" ("false friends"). He calls Fragonard a coward, a poltroon, "who is afraid of everybody and dares not offer a forthright negative opinion, always saying things he does not believe." Bergeret's disdain for Mme Fragonard is even more harsh. However, his opinion of Fragonard as an artist is more interesting and more subtle: "His knowledge ... which is unquestionable ... [is] ... drowned in much fantasy." When Bergeret enlisted Fragonard for the Italian journey, he hoped that the painter would serve as a guide. Most writers agree that it was Bergeret who was responsible for the quarrel, which appears to have surfaced on their return from Italy, when the financier had tried to take possession of the drawings executed by Fragonard en route. In the eighteenth century, this was a legitimate step to take, but it is not known whether there were, in fact, legal proceedings against Bergeret that obliged him to buy or return the drawings that he had hoped to acquire for nothing (he opted for the first solution). The judgment set a precedent. (Unfortunately, we also have been unable to discover any records of this case; see the Chronology.)

As for Bergeret's judgment of Fragonard as a man, it is no doubt overly harsh, but it cannot be entirely dismissed since so many others have held similar views. Sadly, a great artist is not necessarily a great man, as well.

While he does not refer to Fragonard as frequently as we would like, Bergeret also does not mention the other artists that he met. We shall never find out what happened when Natoire, the aging director of the Académie de France, was reunited with Fragonard, his former pupil, nor shall we know what occurred during "the hour" spent "at the house of the famous Piranesi" on January 10, 1774. Jean-Simon Berthélemy and François-Guillaume Ménageot, two brilliant pensioners at the Palazzo Mancini, are quoted, along with P.-A. Pâris (see figure 2)—who served as Bergeret's

Figure 1. François-André Vincent. *Portrait of Bergeret*. Musée des Beaux-Arts, Besançon

Figure 2. François-André Vincent. *Portrait of P.-A. Pâris*. Musée Atger, Montpellier, Faculté de Médecine

guide in Rome, and remained Fragonard's lifelong friend. While François-André Vincent is mentioned twice for having surprised the financier by painting "deliciously" and presenting him with a portrait of "Diane, my white bitch," only passing allusions (to "my painting doctors") enable us to deduce that the young pensioner did, in fact, accompany Bergeret and Fragonard to Naples (on this point, see also Cuzin, 1983). Although Bergeret does not refer by name to his "guide" in Naples, it was doubtless the architect Bernard Poyet (Serbat, 1924, pp. 50–51).

Bergeret is relatively discreet in his comments on contemporary Italian painting, but his judgments are not banal: not only does he praise Tiepolo, but also Corrado Giaquinto—an unusual preference for a Frenchman at this time. This point seems to have eluded Tornézy, who failed to recognize in Bergeret's "Sorrado" the Neapolitan painter "who has many of M. Boucher's charms."

However, our main concern lies in Fragonard's artistic activity during his travels. His work from this period is abundant, varied, and limited entirely to drawing. The subject matter consists of landscapes, genre scenes (often linked to events that took place on the trip), portraits, and copies of old masters. These drawings differ from those executed during the first trip both in technique (bister wash, involving the use of a brush, rather than black or red chalk) and in the scope of the artist's ambition.

Fragonard's new inspiration is most clearly seen in his drawings of the countryside around Rome (see figures 3, 4). We have attempted to identify the sites and have questioned several experts on the matter, but with no appreciable results to date. Could the many "shaded" avenues, "Borghese" and "d'Este" villas, and clumps of umbrella pines be pure invention? Before we can conclude that these drawings have nothing whatsoever to do with Rome as it was at the time, further research should probably be undertaken. It now appears that Fragonard drew sites that he had chosen, usually covering the paper with a seemingly confused network of black lines, much as Bonnard would do 150 years later. When he returned to his studio, he completed the work with wash, and (unlike many of the other young pensioners) deliberately did not pay any further attention to the actual topography. What Fragonard sought to convey in these drawings was the coolness of a shaded avenue, the rustle of pine needles, and the shimmering heat—all of which he rendered most admirably.

Figure 3. Fragonard. *Italian Gardens*. National Gallery of Art, Washington, D.C., Samuel H. Kress Collection

Figure 4. Jean-Baptiste-Louis Lefaivre, after Fragonard. *Italian Gardens*. Musée des Beaux-Arts, Besançon

One other point should be mentioned in connection with these drawings: many of them are accompanied by crucial information as to the date and place of their execution (see figure 5). We believe that it was Bergeret, the suddenly (if temporarily) deprived owner, who supplied this information.

In Naples, on May 22, 1774, at four o'clock in the morning, "we hear [*sic*] the terrible news": Louis XV is dead. This event freed Fragonard of his obligation to hastily complete his official commissions. As it turned out, the Italian trip had brought him the renewed vitality that had hitherto been denied him.

Fragonard, just past forty years of age, seemed destined to become the greatest painter during the reign of Louis XVI.

Figure 5. Inscription on the *Half-length Portrait of a Neapolitan Woman* (cat. no. 192)

CHRONOLOGY

1773

October 5
Departure of Pierre-Jacques-Onésyme Bergeret (1715–1785) for Italy. The financier makes almost daily entries in his travel journal, for his nieces who remained in Paris. The manuscript, entitled *Voyage d'Italie (revu depuis mon départ)*, was first published in full by Tornézy in 1895, but the Goncourts had been familiar with it. Bergeret mentions Fragonard only rarely:

> Notre bagage est composé d'une berline dans laquelle nous sommes.[1] *M. et Madame Fragonard, peintre excellent pour son talens, qui m'est nécessaire surtout en Italie, mais d'ailleurs très commode pour voyager, et toujours égal,*[2] *Madame*[3] *se trouve de même, et comme il m'est très utile j'ai voulu le payer de reconnaissance,* en lui procurant sa femme qui a du talent et en état de goûter un pareil voyage rare pour une femme.[4] La 4ᵉ personne est une gouvernante à moy, ancienne femme de chambre de Madame B[ergeret]. Bien des raisons me l'ont fait emmener: elle n'est pas embarrassante en voyage, elle est forte et en état de rendre quelques services à des malades, et elle remplit le voeu que j'ai fait de tout temps, que plus je ferois tard ce voyage, plus j'y apporterois de commodité, et elle me seroit utile si je devenois malade, et enfin de plus je l'ai emmenée pour me garantir de toutes demandes dont j'ai été souvent persécuté par gens [*sic*] qui souhaitoient faire le voyage avec moy. *Par mon arrangement tout est d'accord; je me trouve le maître de ma bande et je suis sûr de faire un voyage agréable.*[5] Mon fils suit dans un cabriolet avec un cuisinier; mes deux grands cochers assis sur le siège, mon valet de chambre Loss courant avec le domestique de mon fils; tous ces derniers de meilleure volonté et avec espérance que cela durera tout le voyage (Tornézy, pp. 67–68).

The italicized passages above and below—see October 9, 1773—were deleted by Bergeret after his return from Italy (notes 1 to 5 follow

the Chronology). Mme Bergeret's former chambermaid was Jeanne Vignier, who became Bergeret's wife in 1777. His son was Pierre-Jacques (1742–1807), with whom Fragonard seems to have remained on excellent terms (see Portalis, pp. 18, 89, 223–24). We do not know who took care of Rosalie Fragonard, the artist's daughter, while her parents were away.

That very evening, the party reaches Orléans.

October 6
Vierzon

October 7
Argenton-sur-Creuse

October 8
Limoges

October 9
Uzerche: "Comme nous sommes arrivés de bonne heure dans l'endroit le plus affreux par la situation, sur une butte entourée de montagnes et terminée par une rivière meublée de chaussées et moulins qui occassionnent des chûtes et cascades d'eau nous avons, en peintres et amateurs, admiré avec extase ce que personne n'admire *et notre docteur M. Fragonard toujours laborieux et actif a projetté et exécuté un dessein de cette situation jusqu'à l'heure de notre dîner* ou souper qui s'est fait avant 6 heures" (Tornézy, p. 73).

October 10
Souillac

October 11
Cahors

October 12
Fragonard and Bergeret spent two weeks at Nègrepelisse (see cat. no. 171); Bergeret was the owner of the château, and *Receveur général des Finances de la Généralité de Montauban.*

October 26
Toulouse

October 27
Carcassonne

October 28
Béziers

October 29
Lunel

October 30
Tarascon and Nîmes

October 31
Aix-en-Provence

November 1
Aix and Marseilles

November 2
Marseilles

November 3–4
Toulon (see figure 1)

November 5
Le Luc (Var)

November 6
Fréjus

November 7–10
Antibes.
Fragonard appears to have been the only member of the party who was not seasick during the crossing from Antibes to San Remo by felucca. He recorded this episode in an amusing drawing (see figure 2).

November 11–12
San Remo (see cat. no. 173, figure 1)

November 13
Oneglia

November 14
Laigueglia

November 15
Finale.
Pierre writes to Ledoux on the subject of Mlle Guimard's *hôtel* (see June 5, 1770, and March 1773):

> Ce matin seulement Monsieur j'ay pu voir M. David après l'exposé de ma façon de penser sur son procédé; il s'est assés bien justifié, par le reçut des faits; et il est honnête. Il prétend que M. Fragonard étoit convenu de faire l'ouvrage pour six mille livres, qu'après l'ébauche il avoit exigé vingt mille livres, et quatre ans, que Mad^elle Guimard effrayée de la somme dernière avoit renoncé à son projet et n'étoit pas fachée d'en être quitte pour les autres louïs qu'elle avoit donné à M. Fragonard qui de son côté soit négligence soit dessin de suivre son second arrangement laissoit la salle imparfaite.
> M. Fragonard est parti et a trop rependu qu'il ne se souçioit pas de finir cet ouvrage de façon que le S. David ne luy a point écrit par les assurances qu'il a reçu de plusieurs personnes du dégoût de M. Fragonard.
> La première faute est d'avoir demandé six mille livres pour un ouvrage qui en vaut vingt et plus, soit même par en commençant, de là les tracasseries et les plaintes de part et d'autres.
> Que voulés vous faire Monsieur, si Mad^elle Guimard ne veut plus de M. Fragonard; et si M. Fragonard a renoncé tacitement à l'ouvrage. Sûrement Mad^elle Guimard est maîtresse de son choix et David ne paroît point dans le maintien d'un homme qui a des reproches à se faire. Bien loin de là; il croit fermement obliger M. Fragonard en le débarrassant d'une besogne dont son caractère

Figure 1. Fragonard. *The Fair at Toulon.* Musée Sainte-Croix, Poitiers

trop vif le dégoûte, et l'éloigne.
Je ne vois que la certitude des faits détruite qui puisse donner prise sur M. David, vous êtes plus à portée que moy de voir Mad^elle Guimard, et de juger ensuitte (Arch. Nat. 392, AP, folios 247–248, published by Régis Michel in *David e Roma,* Rome exhibition catalogue, 1981–82, pp. 238–39).

These decorations, which are lost today, were sold in 1844 (December 21–22, no. 16): "Quatre grands tableaux, les plus séduisants qu'on connaisse, décoraient autrefois le grand salon de l'hôtel de Mlle Guimard, depuis hôtel de M. le comte de Perregaux (. . .). Nous nous contenterons de dire que ces quatre compositions nous offrent des scènes idéales tirées de la mythologie, embellies par tout ce que l'imagination de l'auteur y a répandu d'esprit et de charme, par un coloris frais et brillant, par tout le prestige de l'art, qui captivent à la fois l'oeil, l'esprit et le coeur, et font naître de douces illusions.
"Deux de ces tableaux portent 3 mètres 9 cent. de hauteur sur 2 mètres 60 cent. de largeur. Les deux autres portent 3 mètres de hauteur sur 2 mètres 45 cent. de largeur."
The story told by Mme Fragonard to her grandson, and which was reported by the Goncourts (1865, p. 283), would seem to agree with the general tone of this letter, which contrasts somewhat with Meister's version of the affair: "ce fut Fragonard qui donna son congé au lieu de le recevoir. Il était fatigué des grands airs et du peu d'égards de la princesse. Un jour qu'elle lui répétait pour la centième fois: Monsieur le peintre, ça ne finira-t-il pas? C'est impossible!—C'est tout fini! lui dit Fragonard. Il prit la porte, et jamais la Guimard ne put le décider à revenir. Un détail fort curieux, c'est que plus tard, à l'heure où David n'était pas encore à Rome et *vanlootisait* à Paris, il vint trouver Fragonard et lui demanda son autorisation pour finir les peintures commencées par lui et dont la Guimard venait de lui commander l'achèvement. Fragonard se hâta de lui accorder sa demande, avec une grâce que n'oublia jamais, il faut le dire, la reconnaissance de David."

November 16
Savona (see cat. no. 173, figure 2)

Figure 2. Fragonard. *Interior of a Ship.* Private collection, New York

The Itinerary of Fragonard's Travels with Bergeret

Paris

Orléans

Vierzon

Argenton-sur-Creuze

Limoges

Uzerche

Souillac

Cahors

Nègrepelisse

Toulouse

Carcassonne

Béziers

Montpellier

Lunel

Nîmes

Tarascon

Aix-en-Provence

Le L

Marseilles

Toulon

Leipzig

Dresden

Naumburg

Gotha

Erfurt

Petrovice

Vacha

Veltrusy

Fulda

Prague   Planany

Schlüchtern

Frankfurt

Jihlava

Darmstadt

Heppenheim

Mannheim

Landau

Vienna

Strasbourg

Ganovitz

Ljubljana

Padua   Venice

Rovigo

Ferrara

Genoa

Cento

Savona   Sestri Levante

Bologna

Finale Ligure   Lerici

Laigueglia

Oneglia   Viareggio   Florence

San Remo   Pisa

Antibes

jus   Siena

Radicofani

Viterbo

Tivoli

Rome   Frascati

Albano Laziale

Velletri

Gaeta   Caserta

Naples   Portici

Pozzuoli

Figure 3. Fragonard, after Mattia Preti. *The Martyrdom of Saint Andrew*. Whereabouts unknown

Figure 4. Fragonard. *Landscape near Velletri*. Whereabouts unknown

November 17–22
Genoa

November 24–26
Sestri (see cat. no. 172)

November 27
Lerici

November 28
Viareggio

November 29
Pisa

November 31–December 1
Florence

December 2
Siena

December 3
Radicofani

December 4
Viterbo

December 5–31
Rome

December 9
At Sant'Andrea della Valle, Bergeret admires ''…un magnifique plafond du Dominiquain, superbe caractère, beaux angles de la coupole. Derrière le maître autel, trois tableaux du martyre et mort de saint André, de Calabraise, à fresque [see figure 3]. Ce sera à revoir plus d'une fois, beau dessein et belle couleur. Voilà deux auteurs bien capables de décider les jeunes gens qui vont à Rome pour se perfectionner'' (Tornézy, pp. 141–42).

December 16
Bergeret seems to prefer the architect Pierre-Adrien Pâris (1745–1819) as his guide, rather than Fragonard. At this time, Pâris was still living at the Académie de France in Rome, despite his failure to obtain the Prix de Rome. ''Le meilleur conducteur, qui connaît tout avec les anecdotes historiques. Il n'est pas indifférent d'être bien mené'' (Tornézy, pp. 154–55).

From Pâris's diary (now in the Bibliothèque Municipale, Besançon) —the entries for 1774 unfortunately are missing—Chipon (1906, p. 11) records the following: ''Déjeuner à Mme Fragonard et à la signora Martina 6 livres.''

In his *Lettres à un jeune artiste peintre pensionnaire à l'Académie royale de France à Rome* [Pierre-Charles Jombert] Cochin adds a footnote: ''Fragonard est à Rome, c'est un habile homme, mais gardez-vous bien de le prendre pour votre modèle, lui-même s'est gâté à Rome [following his first trip] par une imitation mal conçue de M. Mengs; avant que de partir pour l'Italie, il avait toute la couleur du fameux Lemoine; il a appris là les tons bleus, violets, aurores, verds, etc.'' (Cochin, 1849, p. 66; see also Locquin, 1914, p. 8).

December 27
Bergeret and his friends pay a visit to the painters Ménageot and Berthélemy, pensioners at the Académie de France in Rome (Tornézy, pp. 171–72).

1774

The *État des ouvrages de peinture ordonnés pour le Roy* (Arch. Nat. o¹ 1933) records the many commissions given to Fragonard, which he never completed: ''1765. Un tableau pour les Gobelins de même grandeur que celui de *Callirhoé*, 4,500 livres. 1767. À lui ordonné deux tableaux dessus de porte: 1° *Le Jour* sous la figure d'Apollon; 2° *La Nuit* représentée par Diane. Ces tableaux sont destinés pour Bellevue, 1,600 livres. 1770. À lui ordonné deux autres tableaux dont les sujets sont au choix de l'auteur. Ils sont destinés pour la salle à manger des petits appartements de Versailles, 1,600 livres. *Nota.* L'auteur ne paroît pas beaucoup s'occuper des trois articles cy dessus, il vient de retourner à Rome'' (Engerand, 1901, p. 195).

February 24
Not without a certain pride, Bergeret describes his artistic circle in the following terms: ''Quand je dirai que je vois icy tous les jours quelque chose de nouveau, je ne peux être entendu que d'un amateur de peinture. Tantôt c'est un joli dessein, une galanterie que me font quelques pensionnaires de l'Académie, tantôt, ma chienne Diane, levrette délicieusement peinte par M. Vincent, pensionnaire du Roy, qui m'en a fait l'agréable surprise, tantôt un dessein nouveau par mon camarade de voyage, M. Fragonard, quelquefois un morceau de porphire précieux, à bon marché, ou autre marbre granite, souvent faisant de fréquents voyages, inutiles, mené par un brocanteur qui nous vante des tableaux ou curiosités que nous jugeons infâmes dès le pas de la porte'' (Tornézy, pp. 239–40).

March 1–31
Rome

March 1
"Depuis plusieurs jours nous sommes plus occupés dans l'intérieur que dans l'extérieur, à des desseins et petites entreprises que nous suivons et qui se verront dans notre collection à Paris." This remark by Bergeret (Tornézy, p. 243) has often been mistakenly interpreted as an allusion to Fragonard's illustrations for La Fontaine's *Fables*.

March 6
Bergeret's collection is growing steadily. "Nous y fournissons, rangé dans mon cabinet, ce que mon camarade de voyage, M. Fragonard, a fait dans la semaine, ainsi que M. Vincent, pensionnaire du Roy à l'Académie, qui a un talent particulier et qui nous procure de quoy meubler notre petit sallon. Il s'y joint les petites emplettes de vases, de porphyre, granite" (Tornézy, p. 245).

April 2
Bergeret and his entourage visit Tivoli. Although he describes the Temple of the Sibyl and the Villa d'Este, he notes "rien à copier pour nous" (Tornézy, p. 281).

April 13
Bergeret and his party leave for Naples. The first stop is at Velletri (see figure 4). "Velletri est à 8 lieües de Rome environ; nous y voilà arrivés à 5 heures du soir par le plus beau tems. Presque toute cette route depuis Rome est de plaines incultes, pays plat; on y voit quelques tombeaux ruinés de côté et d'autre, mais qui n'ont pas de nom" (Tornézy, p. 290).

April 14
Gaeta

April 15
The group arrives in Naples, and remains there until June 12 (see cat. nos. 191, 192).
  Bellier de la Chavignerie (1865, p. 86) relates the following adventure, which befell Mme Fragonard and which was told to him by her grandson, Théophile:

> À Naples, nous nous arrêtâmes dans un des meilleurs hôtels de la ville; un matin, mon mari était sorti; on m'annonce un visiteur italien dont le nom m'était inconnu.—Mon mari n'y est pas, répondis-je.—C'est madame que l'on demande.—Faites entrer alors, mais ne me quittez pas, ajoutai-je à ma femme de chambre. Mon visiteur était un *signor* d'assez bonne mine, supérieurement vêtu; après trois saluts profonds, il me fit signe de m'asseoir, oubliant que j'étais chez moi. Je lui obéis, le regardant toutefois de tous mes yeux; alors il tira de sa poche un mouchoir de fine batiste qu'il déposa à mes pieds, et sur ce carreau improvisé il s'agenouilla respectueusement. Que signifiaient toutes ces cérémonies? Avais-je affaire avec un fou? Je me trouvais clouée sur mon fauteuil par la crainte et la surprise. Je regardai ma servante, qui conservait un imperturbable sang-froid; heureusement, l'explication ne se fit pas longtemps attendre; mon chevalier tira de sa poche une mesure et l'approcha de mon pied. (J'avais en effet demandé à mon hôtelier un cordonnier dont l'intervention m'était nécessaire; l'hôtelier avait averti le cordonnier de la cour!) Mon artiste, son opération terminée, recommença avec solennité ses révérences et disparut. Dès qu'il fut parti, je me pris à rire de lui et de moi.

April 23
Portici: "j'étois avec un peintre nommé M. Volaire qui réussit supérieurement à rendre l'horreur du Vésuve dont je rapporterai un tableau" (Tornézy, p. 303).

May 6
Visit to Pompeii (see cat. no. 189).

May 10
Death of Louis XV.

June
The party returns to Rome, and remains until June 28.

June 20
Bergeret is given an audience by Pope Clement XIV (1769–74) at which he seems to have been accompanied only by his son. Yet, Théophile (Valogne, 1847, p. 7) leads us to believe that Fragonard was also present: "On ne peut voir l'Italie sans voir le Pape; c'était le sentiment de notre financier: Fragonard demanda la faveur de lui être présenté avec son ami; le pape les reçut étant seul, dans son cabinet de travail, et comme suivant l'usage, mon grand-père mettait un genou en terre pour baiser la pantoufle sacrée, Ganganelli, car c'était lui, s'écria:—Laissez cela aux italiens. Fragonard, dans mes bras, dans mes bras." In the version supplied by Charles Blanc (1862, p. 8) the pope is reputed to have added: "mon cher artiste."

June 21–22
Frascati

June 29–July 7
Bergeret seems to have made no entries in his journal during this period.

July 8–12
Florence

July 14–16
Bologna

July 17
Ferrara

July 18
Padua

July 19–31
Venice

August 3
Ljubljana

August 4–5
Ganovitz

August 7–15
Vienna

August 10
"Le palais du Prince Lichtenstein, riche en beaux Rubens et superbes Vandyck. J'en rapporte des desseins faits par M. Fragonard. Mais Vienne n'a la réputation de rien renfermer de curieux. En cherchant bien, on peut trouver quelques cabinets, mais nous ne resterons que huitaine suffisante" (Tornézy, p. 400).

Figure 5. Fragonard, after Mattia Preti. *The Deliverance of Saint Peter.* Musée d'Art et d'Histoire, Narbonne

August 16
Jihlava

August 17
Planany.

Julien de Parme (1736–1799), in a letter to the Belgian painter Andries Cornelis Lens (1739–1822), refers to his hopes for success, in this ironic passage: "J'espère que mes productions galantes iront en foule orner les Quais de Paris, et faire nargue aux Fragonard, aux le Prince etc. On m'assure que je suis très capable de peindre en petit des sujets gracieux" (Rosenberg, 1984, p. 225).

August 18
Prague and Veltrusy

August 19
Petrovice

August 20–30
Dresden: "je suis retourné en carrosses aux galleries où est établi M. et Mme Fragonard dès le matin, pour y faire récolte de desseins. Je crois que l'on iroit exactement pendant un mois qu'il ne seroit pas possible de se faire un local suffisant de tout ce qu'il peut s'y voir" (Tornézy, p. 409; see cat. no. 193). Fragonard copies Mattia Preti's *The Deliverance of Saint Peter* (see figure 5).

September 1
Naumburg

September 2
Erfurt

September 3
Vacha

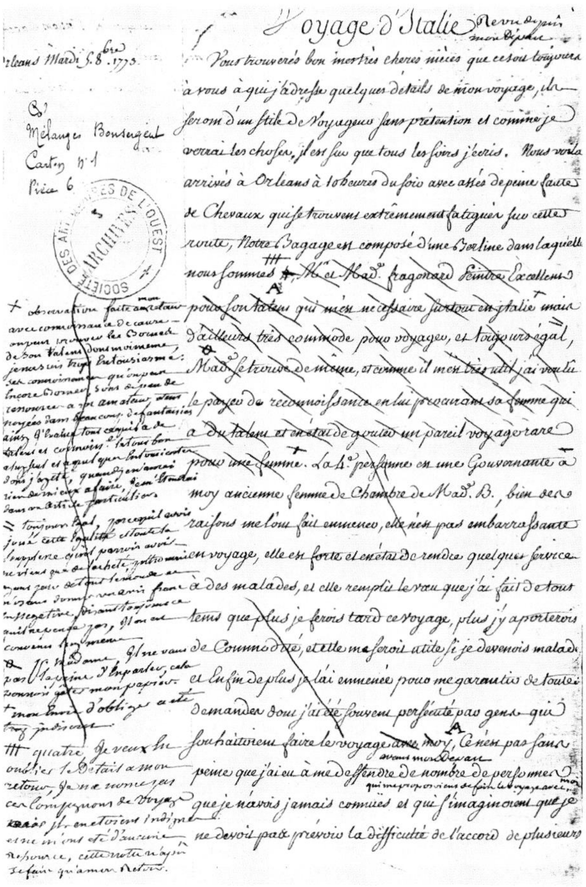

September 4
Schlüchtern

Séptember 5
Frankfurt and Darmstadt

September 6
Heppenheim

September 7
Landau

September 8
Mannheim

September 9
Strasbourg, and then Paris.

Once again, it is Théophile who tells us about Fragonard's differences with Bergeret at the end of their trip. "Dans ce voyage notre artiste réunit une grande quantité de matériaux, mais ses moindres croquis étaient eux-mêmes des petits chefs-d'oeuvre, ce n'est du moins ce qu'en pensait notre financier car, de retour à Paris, il pensa que s'il pouvait se les attribuer, il ferait une bonne affaire, au lieu d'un voyage agréable, mais fort coûteux—c'était pourtant un fermier-général? Mon grand-père réclama ses effets à son retour, on ne lui rendit que ses habits, il fallut plaider et des arbitres condamnèrent le fermier général à payer les dessins, ou à les rendre. Il aima mieux donner 30,000 livres, c'était une somme alors." Unfortunately, no record of this court case has yet been found in the Archives Nationales. However, in the inventory made after Bergeret's death, the following item appears: "Une liasse de vingt huit pièces qui sont mémoires et procédures relatif au procès contre le Sieur Chagonard [sic] peintre qui paraît terminé" (Paris, M.C., XVIII, 846, fol. 13, quoted by G. Wildenstein, 1961, p. 48).
Later on, the same inventory lists: "28 pièces qui sont quittances d'une somme de 3,000 livres données par M. Fragonard, peintre, audit feu sieur Bergeret pour ouvrages de peinture, tableaux et solde de tout compte et toutes les pièces, notes et mémoires relatifs à cette dette." Although paintings, not drawings, are at issue here, it is tempting to conclude, as Wildenstein implies, that this was the sum Bergeret was obliged to pay Fragonard; if so, the figure would differ by one zero from the sum recorded by Théophile.
Moreover, it was probably during this lawsuit that Bergeret crossed out certain entries in his *Journal* (see figure 6) and added the following notes in the margin (see October 5, 1773):

(1) Je veux en oublier le détail à mon retour; je ne nome pas ces compagnons de voyage, car ils en étoient indignes et ne m'ont été d'aucune ressource. Cette note n'a pu se faire qu'à mon retour.
(2) Toujours égal!—Parce qu'il avoit joué cette égalité et toute la souplesse qu'il paroît avoir ne vient que de lâcheté, poltronnerie, ayant peur de tout le monde et n'osant donner un avis franc en négative, disant toujours ce qu'il ne pense pas. Il en est convenu lui-même.
(3) Pour Madame il ne vaut pas la peine d'en parler, cela pourrait gâter mon papier. (With regard to this remark, Théophile told the Goncourts [1865, p. 28]: "Il n'y a rien d'étonnant à ce que M. Bergeret en voulût davantage à madame Fragonard qu'à son mari. Elle seule était chargée des affaires d'intérêt de la maison, *c'est ma caissière*, disait-il en parlant d'elle, l'artiste qui avait les chiffres en horreur, adressez-vous à elle.")
(4) Observation faite à mon retour avec connaissance de cause: On peut trouver les bornes à son talent, dont moi-même je me suis trop enthousiasmé. Ses connaissances, qu'on peut encore borner, sont de peu de ressources à un amateur, étant noyées dans beaucoup de fantaisies. Ainsi, j'évalue tout ce qu'il a de talent et de connaissance, le tout bon à luy seul et à quelques enthousiastes dont j'ay été. Quand je n'aurai rien de mieux à faire, je m'étendrai dans un article particulier.
(5) Oui, pour le moment et même tout le voyage en apparence pour moi, mais j'étois avec des gens faux.

Figure 6. Page from Bergeret's *Journal.* Bibliothèque Municipale, Poitiers

171 The Château de Nègrepelisse, near Montauban

Red chalk on paper, with traces of black chalk, 36.2 x 49.4 cm.

Museum Boymans-van Beuningen, Rotterdam, F-I-244

Provenance
M.C.: sold, November 21–23, 1895, no. 224, "Deux dessins à la sanguine ... Vieux château aux bords d'une rivière" (?); Mme de la Girennerie (Bergeret's descendant), Paris; Mrs. C. S. Hofer, Cincinnati (according to the Paris exhibition catalogue, 1952); Franz Koenigs (1881–1941; his stamp, Lugt 1023 a, is on the verso); acquired by D. G. van Beuningen, 1940; given to the Rotterdam museum, 1941.

Exhibitions
Paris, 1952, no. 90 (with a list of preceding exhibitions)
Amsterdam, 1974, no. 37, ill.

Bibliography
R. pp. 224, 225
Ananoff, 1961, p. 50, ill.
Méras, 1961, pp. 5–6, ill. between pp. 4 and 5
A. 381, fig. 132
Méras, 1972, p. 334, n. 3

Related works
A smaller version, dated October 1773, but in reverse and in bister wash, belonged to Prof. A. Chauffard in 1931 (see figure 1; Paris exhibition catalogue, 1931, no. 70).

For another drawing of the château, also in red chalk, once in a private collection in Essen, see A. 1488, fig. 400 (see figure 2).

On October 5, 1773, Fragonard and his wife left Paris in the company of Jacques-Onésyme Bergeret de Grancourt (1715–1785). They were on their way to Italy (see above), but Bergeret, who kept a diary, wished to make a detour to his estate at Nègrepelisse near Montauban, which he had bought from his father in 1751, along with the office of *Receveur général de la Généralité de Montauban* (G. Wildenstein, 1961, p. 43).

The party arrived on October 12, "at two o'clock in the afternoon, in excellent health and in fine summer weather. Ate well, and many speeches were later given in our honor." (This is the only allusion to the various festivities and toasts with which Bergeret was fêted on this visit [Tornézy, 1895, p. 76; see also p. 74].) The *Journal* provides no details about the stay at Nègrepelisse; in fact, it only resumes on October 26, when Bergeret's group is in Toulouse " ... after spend-

Figure 1. Fragonard. *The Château de Nègrepelisse.* Whereabouts unknown

Figure 4. Fragonard. *Le Four banal à Nègrepelisse.* Private collection, New York

Figure 2. Fragonard. *The Château de Nègrepelisse.* Whereabouts unknown

Figure 3. The belltower of the church at Nègrepelisse

ing exactly fifteen days at my Nègrepelisse estate, near Montauban.''

The Château de Nègrepelisse was already in a fairly dilapidated condition at this time, but was not actually demolished until 1845. It is certain that the château is the subject of the Rotterdam drawing; articles by Mathieu Méras, as well as documents given to us by M. A. Lombrail and Mme Deilhes (of Nègrepelisse) confirm this fact. The ruins of a tower, and the ramparts overlooking the Aveyron River are still recognizable today—as is the fifteenth-century octagonal Toulouse-style brick belltower (figure 3), which is almost unchanged since Fragonard's time.

Fragonard made a number of drawings at Nègrepelisse, many of them of the château itself (although Tornézy should be consulted with circumspection on this subject, pp. 41–42; see also Méras, 1972). Drawings of three views of the château are known, along with two representing the communal oven (see figure 4). The most famous of these (identifiable by a description perhaps by Bergeret himself) belonged to the Goncourts; in technique and effect it is quite different from the Rotterdam drawing.

This representation of the château is exact, and faithful in its detail: the towers, façade, narrow windows, and small cupola are all in evidence. In the foreground, under a vast cloudy sky, a cowherd bringing in his hay prods his oxen.

The importance of this drawing is not merely topographical; like the *Four banal,* it offers tangible evidence of Fragonard's style immediately prior to his second Italian trip.

172 View of the Ponte Santo Stefano at Sestri, near Genoa

Bister wash on paper, over an underdrawing in black chalk, 16 x 21.5 cm.

Musée des Beaux-Arts, Besançon, Inv. D. 2851

Provenance
Pierre-Adrien Pâris (1745–1819); bequeathed to the Bibliothèque Municipale, Besançon, 1819; transferred to the Besançon museum, 1843.

Exhibitions
Paris, 1925, no. 423
Besançon, 1956, no. 43

Bibliography
G. p. 340

P. p. 300
Martine, 1927, pl. 27
Bergeret, 1948, p. 157
R. p. 223
Cornillot, 1957, no. 45, ill. (with complete bibliography)
A. 1590

Related works
The Musée des Beaux-Arts, Lille, owns a second, larger version of this drawing (see figure

1), inscribed in the lower left-hand corner, "pont St. Stephano a Sestry le 26.9. ᵇʳᵉ 1773.,'' and in pencil ''rivière de Genes'' (see figure 2; bister wash and black chalk; 29.2 x 37 cm.; A. 1589; the drawing was formerly in the Bruun-Neergaard collection: sold, August 30, 1814, part of no. 129, and in the La Béraudière collection: sold, April 16–17, 1883, no. 116; see also London exhibition catalogue, Heim, 1974, no. 37, pl. 24).

From the inscription on the drawing in the Musée des Beaux-Arts, Lille (see *Related works,* above), which is too faded to be a later addition, we can affirm that the Besançon drawing is, indeed, of the Ponte Santo Stefano at Sestri Levante, near Genoa (see figure 3). This very old bridge—perhaps dating from Roman times—has barely changed since Fragonard's day. At its highest point there is a small aedicula dedicated to the Madonna del Carmine, which dates to the late seventeenth century (according to Fausta Franchini Guelfi). To the right of the Gromolo River is the church of Santo Stefano al Ponte.

Bergeret and Fragonard arrived at Sestri by sea on November 24, 1773. In his *Journal* (Tornézy, pp. 116–20), Bergeret describes this little town: "it is a beach, not a port ... consisting of a single street ... one sees pictures everywhere, both good and bad ... ," but he does not mention the bridge. "The sea was too rough" to permit the travelers to continue their journey before November 26.

This drawing, like the version in Lille that it seems to predate, has suffered somewhat. Fragonard was not content merely to depict the site; he enlivened the scene with washerwomen at their work, mules laden with laundry, and strolling passersby summarily indicated with one or two touches of bister wash, but perfectly recognizable just the same.

Figure 1. Fragonard. *View of the Ponte Santo Stefano at Sestri*. Musée des Beaux-Arts, Lille

Figure 2. Detail of figure 1

Figure 3. The Ponte Santo Stefano at Sestri Levante

173 View of the Coast near Genoa

Bister wash on paper, over an underdrawing in black chalk, 35.3 x 46.2 cm.
Signed at the bottom left: *fragonard*

Musée des Beaux-Arts, Besançon, Inv. D. 2850

Provenance
Pierre-Adrien Pâris (1745–1819), by 1806;
bequeathed to the Bibliothèque Municipale,
Besançon, 1819; transferred to the Besançon
museum, 1843 (the museum's stamp, Lugt
238 c, is at the bottom left).

Exhibitions
Paris, 1925, no. 421

Paris, 1935, no. 258
Besançon, 1956, no. 42
Grasse, 1957, no. 34
Paris, 1957, no. 148
London, 1977, no. 82

Bibliography
G. p. 340
P. p. 295

Martine, 1927, pl. 15
Bergeret, 1948, p. 33, pl. IV
R. p. 223
Cornillot, 1957, no. 44, ill. (with complete
bibliography)
Ananoff, 1961, p. 51, ill.
A. 1614, fig. 423
Sandoz, 1983, p. 40

Figure 1. Fragonard. *Cuisine à San Remo.*
Whereabouts unknown

Figure 2. Fragonard. *Le Chemin de Savone à
Gênes.* Private collection, France

The handwritten inventory of the collection of the architect P.-A. Pâris (1806, no. 119) mentions this work: "a beautiful drawing . . . executed on the coast of Genoa with a view of the sea," but it does not precisely identify the site. Bergeret wished to travel to Rome by sea, via Genoa (where he spent a week) and Pisa (where he arrived on November 29, 1773, according to his *Journal* [Tornézy, pp. 98–124]). He embarked from Antibes, with Fragonard and his other traveling companions, on November 11, but when they reached San Remo the sea had become so rough that Bergeret "decided to make his way to Genoa by an overland route."

Of the undoubtedly numerous drawings that Fragonard made on this first leg of the journey, very few have survived. One of them (see Chronology, figure 2) shows "the interior of a storm-battered vessel on which were messieurs Fragonard, Bergeret, Lubersac and Motion," all of them overcome by seasickness (see A. 272, fig. 91; A. 233, fig. 92). Frago-

nard also drew the *Cuisine à San Remo* (figure 1; A. 267, fig. 96) and the *Chemin de Savone à Gênes* (figure 2; A. 273, fig. 128); Bergeret and his party traveled this road by mule.

Attempts have been made to identify the massive rock overlooking the sea, which is the principal motif of Fragonard's drawing, by referring to Bergeret's *Journal*. For Cornillot and Bacou (London exhibition catalogue, 1977), the site was "Aiguilla" [Laigueglia; see November 14, 1773], but Bergeret mentions others at "Oneil" [Oneglia], where "the rocks take on a thousand different forms," and on the coast between Genoa and Sestri, where "the rocks [are of] an infinite variety."

The outlines of the travelers in the boat and the figures on the beach are indicated with just a few brushstrokes. Fragonard's prime intention was to render the solid mass of the rock, whose bizarre shape captured his full attention.

174 Man Seated in an Armchair

Bister wash on paper, over an underdrawing in light black chalk, 36.5 x 28.4 cm.
Inscribed at the lower center, slightly to the right, with the tip of the brush: *Rome 1774*

Musée du Louvre, Paris, Cabinet des Dessins, Inv. 23.586

Provenance
[Vassal de Saint-Hubert]: sold, March 29, 1779, no. 184: "un homme assis sur une pierre et un autre dans un fauteuil proche d'une table, ces deux dessins lavés au bistre sur papier blanc sont faits à Rome et datés de 1774. Hauteur chacun 13 pouces 3 lignes, largeur 10 pouces 2 lignes [about 36 x 27 cm.]"; seized during the Revolution, "3 prairial an II," from the home of the émigré Jean-Thérèse-Louis de Beaumont, Marquis

d'Autichamp, in the rue de Lille: " . . . n° 13. Deux dessins au bistre sur papier blanc représentant des Hommes assis par Fragonard" (Furcy-Raynaud, 1912, p. 254; see also the Archives du Louvre, IDD 6); entered the Louvre, at this time (the Louvre's stamp, Lugt 1886, is at the lower left).

Exhibitions
Paris, 1931, no. 40, ill.
Besançon, 1956, no. 50

Grasse, 1957, no. 42, pl. X
Paris, 1967, no. 87 (G. Monnier)

Bibliography
Guiffrey and Marcel, 1907, I, no. 90, ill. ("Étienne Aubry")
R. p. 212
A. 215, fig. 79
Bacou, 1971, colorpl. XXIV (French edition, 1976)
Coulon and Cornoy, 1971–76, p. 190

174   175

175   Man Seated on a Stone

Bister wash on paper, over an underdrawing in black chalk, 36.5 x 28.6 cm.
Inscribed in pen and ink, at the bottom left: *Rome 1774*

Musée du Louvre, Paris, Cabinet des Dessins, Inv. 23.587

Provenance
See the preceding entry (the Louvre's stamp,
Lugt 1886, is at the bottom left).

Exhibitions
Paris, 1931, no. 41
Paris, 1946, no. 374
Vienna, 1950, no. 121, pl. 6

Bern, 1954, no. 104
Vienna, 1966, no. 82
Paris, 1967, no. 86 (G. Monnier; with a
   complete list of exhibitions)

Bibliography
Guiffrey and Marcel, 1907, I, no. 91, ill.
   ("Étienne Aubry")

Lavallée, 1938, no. 8, pl. 8
Bergeret, 1948, p. 73, pl. X
Fosca, 1954, pp. 49–50, pl. 2
R. p. 212
A. 216, fig. 80

At the beginning of the nineteenth century, this drawing
and the one discussed in catalogue no. 174 were attributed
to Étienne Aubry (1745–1781); they were reascribed to
Fragonard by Louis Demonts, Eugène Rodriguès, and
Jacques Mathey (see the notations on the backs of the
mounts), as well as by Louis Réau (Paris exhibition catalogue, 1931) and Pierre Lavallée (1938). They already bore

this attribution in 1779, when they were sold by Vassal de
Saint-Hubert.

There can be no doubt whatsoever that the drawings were
executed in Rome in 1774, and it is now generally agreed
that they represent two of the traveling companions of
Jacques-Onésyme Bergeret de Grancourt. However, some
experts believe that the same model (Pierre-Jacques [1742–

1807], Bergeret's son) appears in both drawings, although the figures in question do not look alike, wear different clothes, and do not seem to be the same age. What is too often forgotten is that "two tall coachmen," a "cook," "my valet de chambre Loss," and "my son's servant" (Tornézy, p. 68) were also members of the party. Did the high boots of the man seated in the chair, his left foot resting on a basin, perhaps belong to the coachman, and was the cap worn by the man seated on the stone that of the cook?

The two drawings are related: Fragonard has played on the juxtaposition of an interior scene (represented by the chair) and one outdoors (indicated by the stone bench). The strong contrasts of the prevailing brown wash in the one are complemented by paler, more transparent and more luminous tones in the other. Following in the tradition of Bouchardon and of Greuze, his intention was to render "types" rather than portraits. The precision of the composition, the masterly execution, and the confident skill that Fragonard displays in these two drawings place them among the most accomplished works done during his second trip to Rome.

176   A Dwarf Conversing with a Young Woman

Bister wash on paper, over an underdrawing in black chalk, 36.6 x 28.6 cm.
Inscribed at the bottom right, in pen and ink, on a stone: *Rome 1774*; on the verso is the old inscription, in pencil:
      Bayoque mendiant de Rome/h. fragonard n° 422/du cabinet De La Reinière

Städelsches Kunstinstitut, Frankfurt am Main, Graphische Sammlung

Provenance
[Chabot and Duc de La Mure, or Desmarets]: sold, December 17–22, 1787, no. 174: "une Étude de deux figures représentant un Mendiant de taille raccourcie et grotesque, il est arrêté devant une jeune femme assise qui tient un chapeau sur elle" (for 72 *livres,* to Millioti); anonymous sale, May 31, 1790, no. 183: "deux dessins au bistre: l'un représentant le portrait d'un mendiant de Rome et celui de sa femme; il est connu sous le nom de Bajocco; pour pendant une femme Napolitaine" [43.2 x 35.1 cm.; probably the dimensions with the frame]; Grimod de La Reynière (see the inscription on the verso of the mount): sold, September 7–17, 1797 (according to Stuffmann) (?); part of the museum's original collection; inventoried (no. 1103), 1862; A., apparently in error, states that the stamp (Lugt 1085) is that of Glomy, who mounted the drawing.

Exhibitions
Frankfurt am Main, 1986–87, no. 125, ill. (entry by M. Stuffmann)

Bibliography
A. 262, fig. 88
Van Regteren Altena, 1965, pp. 140, 142, n. 9, fig. 88
Cuzin, 1983, p. 111, n. 37, fig. 15
Rome-Dijon exhibition catalogue, 1983, p. 102, n. 2 (entry by S. Laveissière)

Related works
The next numbered lot in the sale [Chabot ...] was "Une autre Étude d'après le même personnage, bien drapée et touchée aussi largement que la précédente." This drawing, also inscribed "Rome 1774," is in a private collection in Paris (see figure 1; A. 264, fig. 89).

Figure 1. Fragonard. *The Dwarf Bajocco.* Private collection, Paris

Figure 2. François-André Vincent. *The Dwarf Bajocco.* Statens Museum for Kunst, Copenhagen

Figure 3. Bénigne Gagneraux. *The Dwarf Bajocco.* Bibliothèque Nationale, Paris, Cabinet des Estampes

Figure 4. Fragonard. *Woman Leaning on a Milestone.* Fogg Art Museum, Harvard University, Cambridge, Massachusetts

377

176

The dwarf Bajocco was a popular and picturesque figure in Rome during the 1770s; a mendicant, bearded, and with a full head of hair, he posed for many artists, Italian as well as foreign, when they came to Rome (see figures 2, 3). Lists of these artists have been compiled by Van Regteren Altena (1965), Carlo Pietrangeli (1971), Brinsley Ford (1974), J.-P. Cuzin (1983), and Silvain Laveissière (1983). The dwarf's real name was Francesco Ravai, but he had been nicknamed Bajocco after the *baiocchi,* the coins that he solicited from passersby outside the Caffè Greco or in the Piazza di Spagna. Fragonard sketched Bajocco twice; in the Frankfurt drawing he leans on a crutch, before a young woman seated on a stone bench (Bajocco's wife, according to the author of the 1790 sales catalogue). The beggar's hat lies on the girl's knees, and she looks at him apprehensively. Behind the couple are two milestones (these also appear in a

second drawing by Fragonard—see figure 1—in which they frame the dwarf and emphasize his size, as well as in a third drawing, this one in the Fogg Art Museum: see figure 4; A. 2091, fig. 565; A. 2092 [?]; Washington exhibition catalogue, 1978, no. 32, ill.).

Fragonard posed and portrayed the beggar with respect, refraining from caricature. He is seen simply as he is, barefoot and in rags; the artist does not place undue emphasis on his picturesque attire. Fragonard is more concerned about the dwarf's conversation with his female companion than with his small stature. With a keen eye, Fragonard brings into play the subtle humor that enriches so much of his work, stressing the resemblance between his model and Socrates; the ironic expression of the dwarf recalls the portrait busts of the philosopher.

Bister wash on paper, over an underdrawing in black chalk, 36.8 x 25.5 cm.
Inscribed at the lower right (perhaps cut off by the mounter ?): *Rom*

Private collection, Paris

Provenance
Le Brun: sold, April 11, 1791, no. 311: "un
Jeune Homme assis, et tenant de la main
droite une bouteille. Ce dessin, lavé au bistre
sur papier blanc, est de l'effet le plus piquant
et de la touche la plus facile et la plus spirituelle" (for 39 *livres* 19; 45.9 x 37.8 cm.);
according to A., this drawing would seem to
have been confused with no. 735 in the
Vivant-Denon collection sale (1826): "un
jeune garçon assis et tenant une poële [*sic*]"
and no. 266 in the Brunet Denon collection
sale, February 2, 1846: "étude d'homme
assis, dessiné d'après nature à Rome," but it
does not bear the stamp of the collection (the
drawing may have been cut down); Hippolyte Walferdin: sold posthumously, April
12–16, 1880, no. 184 (for 350 francs, to
Haro); Jacques Doucet, by 1889: sold, June
5, 1912, no. 15, ill. (for 32,000 francs);
David-Weill (according to W.); private collection, Paris.

Bibliography
P. pp. 303, 309
W. p. 24, n. 3 (French edition)
Ananoff, 1961, p. 53, ill.
A. 220, fig. 83

Related works
A copy, inscribed at the bottom left "Fragonard 1779" (19.5 x 13.5 cm.) is in a private
collection in Belgium.

The drawing has, in all likelihood, been cut down at the sides and the bottom; this would seem to be confirmed by the dimensions given in the 1791 sales catalogue. Neverthe-less, it is among the most beautiful drawings Fragonard made in Rome.

The young man is seated on a shallow rectangular box; he wears a felt hat with a raised brim, and he faces to the right.

With nothing but bister wash, Fragonard succeeded in giv-ing volume to the sitter's body, folds and weight to his garments, and transparency to the flask in his hand. The model is placed in full sunlight; only his face is delicately shadowed. "The brush has the vivacity of a gesture ... a little water, some bister, a stroke of the hand, and the deed is done" (Goncourt, p. 298).

178 Head of a Man in a Turban

Bister wash on paper, over an underdrawing in black chalk, 32.2 x 26.4 cm.
Inscribed in pen and ink, at the bottom left: *Fragonard*

Musée des Beaux-Arts, Besançon, Inv. D. 2944

Provenance
Pierre-Adrien Pâris (1745–1819): featured
in the *Recueil des différents maîtres,* assembled by the artist, vol. I, no. 312;
bequeathed, at his death, to the Bibliothèque
Municipale, Besançon (the stamp, Lugt 238 c,
is at the bottom right); deposited in the
Besançon museum, 1843.

Exhibitions
(For a list, see Cornillot, 1957)
Washington, D.C.,..., 1952–53, no. 81
Zurich, 1955, no. 109
Besançon, 1956, no. 73
Munich, 1958, no. 272

Bibliography
P. p. 314
R. p. 215
Cornillot, 1957, no. 74, ill. (with complete
  bibliography)
Watelet, 1959, p. 126
A. 131

Related works
There is a study for the drawing formerly in
the Vivant-Denon collection from which a
lithograph was made by "Du Fi" (Dufourny?;
see figure 1), no. 729 in the catalogue of
the May 1–19, 1826, sale; sold, Christie's,
London, June 29, 1962, no. 46, ill. (see figures 2, 3; A. 758, fig. 209).

The present drawing is often compared
with a *Head of a Man in a Fur Cap* (A. 135,
fig. 341) in the Fitzwilliam Museum, Cambridge (see figure 4), and the *Head of a Man
in a White Turban* (A. 2054, fig. 558) in
Frankfurt am Main (see figure 5), both of
which are inscribed "Rome 1774" and
attributed by Cuzin (1983) to Vincent (see
Stuffmann, 1986–87).

The Besançon *Head of a Man in a Turban* is a study for a
drawing (lost since 1962) of an Oriental man seated before a
large book, which belonged to Dominique Vivant-Denon
and bore the usual inscription, "Rome 1774"—a place and
date that apply equally to the Besançon sketch.

In his customary way, Fragonard attempted, in this portrait, to render the three-dimensionality of the face without
lingering over the details. He wished to achieve a likeness,
but refrained from being overly meticulous. The moustache,
the heavy-lidded eyes, and the volume of the turban are
barely hinted at. The brushwork is sweeping and vigorous,
emphasizing the plasticity of the image. The result is
neither veristic nor altogether true to life; Fragonard's
study, although subjective, emerges as warm and human,
nonetheless.

Figure 1. Dufourny (?). *Un Oriental Assis devant un Grand Livre ("Le Sultan")*. Private collection, Paris

Figure 2. Fragonard. *Un Oriental Assis devant un Grand Livre.* Whereabouts unknown

Figure 3. After Fragonard. *Un Oriental Assis devant un Grand Livre.* The Metropolitan Museum of Art, New York

Figure 4. Attributed to Fragonard. *Head of a Man in a Fur Cap.* Fitzwilliam Museum, Cambridge

Figure 5. Attributed to François-André Vincent. *Head of a Man in a White Turban.* Städelsches Kunstinstitut, Frankfurt am Main

179 Head of a Monk

Red chalk on paper, 45 x 35.5 cm.
Inscribed on the mount, in pen and ink, at the bottom left (in the same hand as catalogue nos. 197–200):
. *fragonard-fecit romae.*
At the bottom right, on the drawing itself, is the dry mark of François Renaud (Lugt 1042), who mounted the drawing in the late 18th century.

Musée Atger, Montpellier, Faculté de Médecine, Inv. 146

Provenance
Xavier Atger (1758–1833); bequeathed to the Musée de la Faculté de Médecine, Montpellier, 1829 (the stamp of the museum does not appear on the drawing).

Exhibitions
Bern, 1954, no. 85

Bibliography
Atger catalogue, 1830, no. 146
Lagrange, 1860, p. 143 (?)
P. p. 314
Saunier, 1922, p. 164
Fosca, 1954, p. 64, no. 34, ill.
Claparède, 1955, no. XVIII, ill.
R. p. 215

Ananoff, 1961, p. 11, ill.
A. 137, fig. 58

179

Although the paper has yellowed slightly, the planes have become somewhat blurred (no doubt a counterproof was made from the drawing), and the eye has lost its brightness, this "fine life-size head of a bearded old man," as it is described in the 1830 Atger catalogue, is still an admirable work.

If we are to believe the author of the inscription on the mount, the drawing dates from 1773–74, and was executed during the artist's second visit to Rome.

The monk's head—with his cap, his cowl, and his flowing beard—covers the entire surface of the paper. We do not know if the drawing is a portrait, but it has more than just the unity of the conception and its monumentality to recommend it: its *vibrant* quality makes it exceptional.

180 Parc romain avec Tête colossale Crachant de l'eau

Bister wash on paper, over a light underdrawing in black chalk, 29 x 36.9 cm.
Inscribed at the bottom center: *Rome 1774*

Staatliche Kunsthalle, Karlsruhe, Kupferstichkabinett, 1976.54

Provenance
Dr. Peter Dalbert (according to the Karlsruhe exhibition catalogue, 1983): sold, Sotheby's, London, November 25, 1971, no. 34, ill. (for 4,400 pounds); [Cailleux]; acquired by the Karlsruhe museum, 1976. (On the verso

of the old mount is an unidentified collector's mark.)

Exhibitions
New York, 1974–75, no. 141, ill.
Karlsruhe, 1983, no. 34, ill. (entry by
   Eckart von Borries)

Bibliography
*Jahrbuch der Staatlichen Kunstsammlungen in
   Baden-Württemberg,* 1977, 14, p. 162,
   pl. 13

This landscape is part of a series of bister-wash drawings, all of which bear the same inscription: "Rome 1774." We have already given our reasons for believing that these inscriptions were made by Bergeret himself.

A fountain in the form of a colossal head spouts water into a broad, flat pond shaded by cypress trees. Other details may be distinguished: a pair of lovers, people strolling, a donkey drinking, and, on the hill to the right, the umbrella pines that so intrigued Fragonard.

We agree with Eckart von Borries that this site is purely imaginary, although the trees and the configuration of the park are reminiscent of many villas near Rome. The drawing itself was executed almost entirely with the tip of the brush; its lightness and precision evoke the beauties of the Roman countryside that so impressed eighteenth-century visitors from abroad.

181   Roman Park with a Fountain

Bister wash on paper, over an underdrawing in black chalk, 28.9 x 36.8 cm.
Inscribed at the bottom center, in bister: Rome 1774; at the right, in black chalk: levi; above right:
fragonard du Cabinet de Mr. De Lévi

Graphische Sammlung Albertina, Vienna, Inv. 12.736

Provenance
M. de Lévi (of the illustrious Lévi family whose members included Maréchal Duc François-Gaston [1720–1787], for example); Duke Albert of Saxe-Teschen (1738–1822; his stamp, Lugt 174, is at the lower left), who visited Paris in 1786.

Exhibitions
Paris, 1931, no. 76
London, 1932, no. 1018 (commemorative catalogue no. 679, pl. CLXXVI)
Paris, 1950, no. 153

Vienna, 1950, no. 124
Bern, 1954, no. 56

Bibliography
Meder, 1922, no. 32
Hempel, 1924, pp. 22, 21 fig. 8
Bergeret, 1948, p. 118, pl. XVIII
R. pp. 221, 222, 223
A. 2158, fig. 577
Benesch, 1964, no.223

Related Works
For a copy of the right side of the drawing,

with the fountain and the pruned trees, see Palais Galliéra, Paris, December 9, 1960, no. 61, plate XXIII (see figure 1). See also the drawing in the Pushkin Museum, Moscow (see figure 2; A. 2396; A. 906 attributes to Maréchal the copy that formerly belonged to Anatole France). The red-chalk drawing, from which the Besançon counterproof was made (A. 1552 a; Cornillot, 1957, no. 42), is now in the Musée des Beaux-Arts, Quimper (see figure 3; Pont-Aven exhibition catalogue, 1983, no. 17, pl. X).

Figure 1. Attributed to Fragonard. *Fountain*. Whereabouts unknown

Figure 2. *An Italian Park*. Pushkin Museum, Moscow

Figure 3. Attributed to Fragonard. *An Italian Park*. Musée des Beaux-Arts, Quimper

The inscription at the bottom center of the sheet attests that this drawing dates from Fragonard's second visit to Italy, but does it really represent Tivoli, as has so often been claimed? We know that Bergeret and Fragonard were at Tivoli on April 2, 1774 (Tornézy, pp. 279–81): "for many years now, no painter has left Rome without making many drawings in the gardens of the Villa d'Este." Bergeret is rather reserved on the subject: "On the whole, the gardens have many beauties, but nothing for us to copy; their main virtue is their plentiful water, which we tend to lack in France."

We believe that while Fragonard was inspired by the sites that he visited, and probably made rapid, succinct notes and sketches in black chalk in the course of his travels, he actually executed this type of drawing in the studio. Hence, his imagination played a not inconsiderable part in their composition—a part that we would like to understand more fully.

Benesch (1964) has correctly drawn attention to the "pointillist" technique of this drawing, and to its "magical, silvery light" ("silbrigen Lichtzauber").

182   Roman Park with Cypresses

Bister wash on paper, over an underdrawing in black chalk, 28.9 x 36.9 cm.
Inscribed at the top right, in black chalk: Levi a Rome

Graphische Sammlung Albertina, Vienna, Inv. 12.737

Provenance
See cat. no. 181 (the stamp, Lugt 174, is at the bottom left).

Exhibitions
Paris, 1931, no. 77

Paris, 1950, no. 149
Vienna, 1950, no. 123
Bern, 1954, no. 59

Bibliography
Meder, 1922, p. 13, pl. 62

Hempel, 1924, p. 22, fig. 2
Fosca, 1954, p. 67, pl. 41
R. p. 221
A. 2216, fig. 583

This drawing is obviously the pendant to the preceding one, and unquestionably dates from 1774. The people strolling near the entrance to the villa are depicted in a very reduced scale, in proportion to the cypress trees.

In marked contrast to the art of Hubert Robert, who was, above all, a topographer and "architect," and in whose works the human figure often played only a secondary—one might even say incidental—role, Fragonard depicts ordinary, everyday life, reveling in the chance encounter, or in children at play. For Robert, who constantly alludes to antiquity and to the inexorable destruction of its monuments, time is eternity; for Fragonard, it is but a fleeting moment.

183 A Garden near Rome

Bister wash on paper, over an underdrawing in black chalk, 34.8 x 46.2 cm.
Inscribed at the bottom left, in wash: *fragonard*

Musée du Petit Palais, Paris, Dutuit 965

Provenance
Hippolyte Walferdin (1795–1880): sold posthumously, April 12–16, 1880, no. 237 (for 3,120 francs, to M. Malinet); the brothers Eugène and Auguste Dutuit, Rouen, by 1889 (their stamp, Lugt 709 a, is at the bottom right); given to the Petit Palais, 1902.

Exhibitions
Paris, 1879, no. 580
Paris, 1934, no. 452
London, 1949–50, no. 419 (not 415), pl. 77
Amsterdam, 1951, no. 168, pl. XXXIII
Washington, D.C., ..., 1952–53, no. 88, pl. 29
Bern, 1954, no. 63
London, 1977, no. 83
Tokyo, 1982, no. 69, colorpl. 72 (with a list of exhibitions and a complete bibliography)

Bibliography
P. p. 316
Leclère, 1913, p. 105, ill.
Martine, 1927, pl. 13
Fosca, 1954, p. 60, pl. 24
R. p. 222
A. 2151, fig. 585 (see also A. 1547)
Sandoz, 1983, p. 40

Related works
Sometimes compared to A. 357, fig. 369, entitled in 1931 (Paris exhibition catalogue, no. 80) "les jardins de la villa d'Este à Tivoli" (see figure 1).
 See also A. 1547, illustrated in Fosca, 1954, p. 60, pl. 25.

Figure 1. Fragonard. *An Italian Park.*
Whereabouts unknown

All the experts seem to agree (with the exception of Fosca, 1954, who dates it 1760) that this splendid drawing was executed during Fragonard's second trip to Italy. However, identifying the site depicted is rather more problematical. In the nineteenth century, it was described as a "park enlivened by numerous figures," or else, as a "park decorated with statuettes [!] and people strolling." For subsequent scholars (such as Leclère, in 1913), the setting was the gardens of the Villa d'Este (see cat. nos. 30–36). More recently, R. Bacou (London exhibition catalogue, 1977) has suggested that this drawing is an imaginary view, *inspired* by the Villa d'Este—a proposal with which we agree.

 It is fascinating to compare Fragonard's views of gardens in the environs of Rome with the drawings that he made at Tivoli in the summer of 1760. First of all, in his later works,

Fragonard preferred bister wash to red chalk, and instead of pencil he used a brush, which he handled with dazzling skill. Secondly, he infallibly chose surprising angles of vision, which make the identification of his sites very difficult. And thirdly, the degree of inventiveness, imagination, and "poetic idealization" is greater than ever before.

 Particularly noteworthy in the present drawing are the ray of sunlight that illuminates the group of trees at the center of the composition; the strolling figures, who greet one another; and the children being urged by their parents to exchange kisses. A young man, sitting in the shadows on the steps of a well, is playing with his dog, while, in the foreground at the far right, an artist, seated on the ground, seems to be sketching the statue of the Farnese *Hercules.*

184 The Umbrella Pines at a Villa near Rome

Bister wash on paper, over a light underdrawing in black chalk, 44.7 x 33.7 cm.

Rijksmuseum, Amsterdam, Rijksprentenkabinet, 53.206

Provenance
David David-Weill, 1921; Fritz Mann-
heimer, before World War II; entered the
Rijksmuseum, 1953.

Exhibitions
Paris, 1921, no. 174
Paris, 1934, no. 457
Paris, 1946, no. 115
Paris, 1964, no. 111, colorpl. 94
London, 1968, no. 269, fig. 294
Amsterdam, 1974, no. 40, ill.

Bibliography
*Société de Reproductions de Dessins de
Maîtres,* 5th year, 1913, p. 13, ill.
Martine, 1927, pl. 46
Henriot, 1928, III, p. 169, ill.
Henraux, 1946, p. 9, ill.
R. p. 221
G. Wildenstein, 1961, p. 47, fig. 6
A. 2388, fig. 607
Roland Michel, 1983, p. 475

Figure 1. Fragonard. *View of a Villa near Rome.*
The Metropolitan Museum of Art, New York,
Robert Lehman Collection

This drawing is considered to be a representation of "the umbrella pines at the Villa Pamphili." Of the two villas by that name, one is celebrated for its Casino by Algardi, and for its gardens, and was described by Bergeret (Tornézy, p. 156) as "planted with nothing but pines, cypresses, ever-green oaks, and laurels"—hence, it was always green. The other, the Villa Pamphili near Frascati, also known as the Villa Aldobrandini, or the Villa Belvedere (Tornézy, p. 357), is vastly different architecturally from the building in Fragonard's drawing. Philippe Morel has suggested (ver-bally) that the subject may be the Villa Arrigoni-Muti, which is similar (see Rome exhibition catalogue, 1980, pp. 118 ff.). As explained before, this drawing, like so many of the others, is mostly imaginary in conception.

The building in the background is often compared with the one in a drawing that once belonged to the Goncourts (now in the Lehman Collection in the Metropolitan Museum, New York), sometimes entitled "View of the Villa Borghese" (see figure 1; A. 1441, fig. 736), but on closer examination the two villas are seen to have nothing in common.

The drawing depicts a sunny but cool day: only a few strollers take shelter under the umbrella pines. Groups of adults and children, placed at various distances, give the composition depth; in the foreground at the left, two pup-pies chase each other.

Much to be admired here is Fragonard's virtuosity in the use of wash, not least because this technique requires an extremely rapid execution, and leaves no room for second thoughts. Using a gradation of tone from the softest ocher to the deepest brown, he achieves extraordinarily sensitive effects of light and shadow.

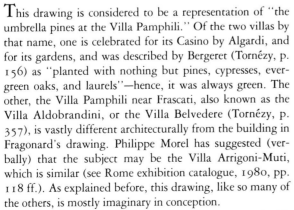

185 A Garden with Umbrella Pines in Rome

Bister wash on paper, over a light underdrawing in black chalk, 35.3 x 48.8 cm.

Musée des Beaux-Arts, Besançon, Inv. D. 2847

Provenance
At the bottom right, on the mount, is the stamp of the mounter of the drawing, J.-B. Glomy (Lugt 1085), from the second half of the 18th century; Pierre-Adrien Pâris (1745–1819), by 1806; bequeathed to the Bibliothèque Municipale, Besançon, 1819; transferred to the Besançon museum, 1843

(the museum's stamp, Lugt 238 c, is at the bottom left).

Exhibitions
Paris, 1925, no. 419
Amsterdam, 1951, no. 166
Washington, D.C., . . . , 1952–53, no. 89
Zurich, 1955, no. 111
Grasse, 1957, no. 36
Paris, 1957, no. 149

Bibliography
P. p. 303 (or 309)
Estignard, 1902, ill. between pp. 17 and 18
Martine, 1927, pl. 16
R. p. 222
Cornillot, 1957, no. 46, ill. (with a complete bibliography)
A. 2389, fig. 605

Figure 1. Fragonard. *"View of the Gardens of Rome."* Musée des Beaux-Arts, Besançon

In the inventory of the Pâris collection, 1806 (no. 118), this drawing was paired with another "view of the gardens of Rome in Bister done in Rome in 1773" (now also in the Besançon museum, but somewhat faded; see figure 1). We do not know whether this work came from the Bergeret collection, but Glomy, who mounted the drawing in the eighteenth century, did work for all the leading *amateurs* of the time, including the Abbé de Saint-Non.

The site is neither the Villa d'Este nor the Villa Pamphili, as have sometimes been suggested, and the specialists who have seen photographs of the drawing have not supplied any convincing identification.

Fragonard was "fascinated by umbrella pines" (Sollers, 1987, p. 324), which are the subject of this drawing and of a number of others from both his first and second trips to Rome. The statues; the clumps of trees; the stone steps at the right, flanked by lions; the wrought-iron gates at the entrance to the park; the people strolling; and the children playing are merely accessories to the two tall trees.

The drawing, executed almost entirely in brush and bister wash in tones ranging from very dark to very light, is one of the most beautiful evocations of Roman gardens, which were deeply admired by visitors to Italy in the eighteenth century, but which today are almost all abandoned or lost.

186   A Shaded Avenue

Bister wash on paper, over an underdrawing in black chalk, 45.5 x 34.7 cm.

Musée du Petit Palais, Paris, Dutuit 966

Provenance
Sireul: sold, December 3, 1781, no. 242: "un superbe dessin de ce maître, lavé au bistre sur papier blanc. Il représente une longue avenue en perspective. Ce dessin est d'un effet piquant et orné de figures analogues" (for 149 *livres* 19, to Paillet); the miniaturist Saint: sold, May 4, 1846, no. 13 (for 99 francs 50, to Mayor, of London); Hippolyte Walferdin: sold posthumously, April 12–16, 1880, no. 206 (for 1,810 francs, to Malinet); the painter Jean Gigoux (1806–1894): sold, March 20–23, 1882, no. 583 (for 2,030 francs, to Clement, the Dutuits' dealer; his stamp, Lugt 1164, is at the bottom left); the brothers Eugène and Auguste Dutuit, Rouen (their stamp, Lugt 709 a, is at the bottom right); given to the Petit Palais, 1902.

Exhibitions
Paris, 1879, no. 581
Paris, 1934, no. 460
London, 1949–50, no. 415
Amsterdam, 1951, no. 168, pl. 33
London, 1977, no. 84, ill.
Tokyo, 1980, no. 139, ill.

Bibliography
Bürger [Thoré], 1846, p. 371
G. p. 340
Eudel, 1884, p. 123
P. pp. 191, 293
Dorbec, 1905, pp. 79–80, n. 1
Martine, 1927, pl. 12
Wilhelm, 1951, p. 27
Sterling, 1955, p. 155
R. p. 216
A. 327, fig. 120, A. 365
Wrigley, 1981, p. 746, n. 11
Sandoz, 1983, p. 40

Figure 1. After Fragonard. *A Shaded Avenue*. Fogg Art Museum, Harvard University, Cambridge, Massachusetts

Figure 2. Fragonard. *A Shaded Avenue*. The Metropolitan Museum of Art, New York

Related works

An engraving of this drawing was made by Gustave-Marie Greux in 1882, for the Gigoux collection sales catalogue, and for the work by P. (illustrated between pages 40 and 41; see also p. 321, no. 3).

For a second version of this drawing, see the following entry.

Several versions of *A Shaded Avenue* were mentioned in the literature, between World Wars I and II: we are unfamiliar with the examples in the Groult collection (A. 329) and in the Fauchier-Magnan collection (A. 330, fig. 121). The authenticity of the one in the Joubin collection (today in the Fogg Art Museum; see figure 1; 1953.99; A. 1525) is doubtful. See also A. 331 (doubtful), A. 897 (unknown to us), A. 1451 (in red chalk; exhibited at Stein's, London, 1981, no. 53, ills.; perhaps it once belonged to P.-A. Pâris), and A. 1522 (formerly in the Seilern collec-tion; now in the Courtauld Institute Galler-ies; see the London exhibition catalogue, 1981, no. 166, ill.; the attribution is doubtful).

Finally, we cite the painting in The Metro-politan Museum of Art (see figure 2; on canvas, not panel, 29 x 24 cm.; see Sterling, 1955, pp. 155–56; W. 350, pl. 69), the pendant to which is the *View of an Italian Villa* (W. 349, pl. 68).

It is now generally agreed that this admirable *Shaded Ave-nue* dates from 1773–74 (only Portalis suggests that this drawing was done during Fragonard's first Italian trip, while Dorbec somewhat eccentrically attributes the work to Pierre Delaunay!). Again, there is much dispute as to the site depicted. Some experts favor the Château de Nègrepelisse (see cat. no. 171); others, the Château de Nointel (another of Bergeret's properties, near l'Isle-Adam; for views of this château and its park, see G. Wildenstein, 1961); and yet others (Réau) believe it is the Villa Mattei in Rome. Those who (like Sterling) identify the subject of Fragonard's draw-ing as an avenue of plane trees must opt for a location in the south of France, where such sights are common.

The question of whether Fragonard set out to produce a faithful rendering of an existing site, or, instead, followed his usual habit of giving free rein to his imagination, still remains.

Along the avenue of trees, strolling figures are pictured gossiping or playing with their children, while two dogs chase each other in the foreground, at the left (see cat. no. 184). At the right, near one of the statues, a couple is lean-ing on the balustrade of the terrace, contemplating the landscape.

Yet, the true subject of the drawing is the canopy of trees that covers the walkway. Exploiting all of the rich possibili-ties of bister, Fragonard describes the foliage and the branches of the trees shimmering in the sunlight. The plung-ing perspective of the tree trunks gives depth and monu-mentality to the composition, without in any way imitating Piranesi's visionary surrealism.

187 A Shaded Avenue

Bister wash on paper, over an underdrawing in black chalk, 44.5 x 34.4 cm.

Private collection, Paris

Provenance
Sigismond Bardac: sold, May 10–11, 1920, no. 4, ill. (for 143,000 francs, to Lucien Guiraud); Edward Esmond.

Exhibitions
Paris, 1921, no. 192
Paris, 1931, no. 69

London, 1932, no. 838 (commemorative catalogue, no. 689, pl. CLXXV)
Paris, 1937, no. 536
Paris, 1951, no. 48
London, 1954–55, no. 456
Grasse, 1957, no. 35, pl. VIII

Bibliography
R. G., 1920, pp. 296–98, ill. p. 297

Boucher and Jaccottet, 1952, p. 174, pl. 95
R. p. 216
A. 328 ("les rehauts de plume sont dus à une main étrangère")

Related works
See the preceding entry.

This drawing is similar in its dimensions to the Petit Palais version (see cat. no. 186), and considerably larger than the picture in the Metropolitan Museum (see cat. no. 186, figure 2). While there are fewer strolling figures in the latter, they closely resemble those in the Petit Palais drawing. The Petit Palais study appears to antedate the one in New York, which, in turn, seems to have been executed before the second *Shaded Avenue*. Fragonard has reduced the size of the figures to increase the importance of the trees. The rustling leaves, the brilliant light, the cool shade, and the use of perspective to create an impression of distance are achieved with a naturalness and a simplicity that belie the artist's deep knowledge of his craft.

188   View of an Italian Park

Bister wash on paper, over an underdrawing in black chalk, 35.5 x 46.5 cm.

Private collection, Paris

Provenance
In the same collection since the early nineteenth century. It might be the drawing [owned by Chabot and Duc de La Mure, or Desmarets] that was sold December 17–22, 1787, no. 173: "la vue d'une arcade soutenue par quatre colonnes au milieu desquelles est une statue sur un piedestal. Ce morceau touché avec un goût admirable, au bistre sur papier blanc, est orné de diverses figures rendue avec esprit" (for 79.19 *livres*, to Constantin ?). This reference is generally associated with the Stockholm drawing (see *Related works* below).

Bibliography
Unpublished

Related works
A second version, very similar in details and composition and inscribed "fragonard 1780," is in a New York private collection (see figure 1; P. p. 309; A. 1476).

Another drawing, which resembles the center part of the present composition (with a few variations) today is in the museum in Stockholm (see figure 2; A. 350, fig. 366; Bjurström, 1982, no. 954, ill., colorpl. p. XXiii).

Figure 1. Fragonard. *View of an Italian Park.* Private collection, New York

Figure 2. Fragonard. *View of an Italian Park.* Nationalmuseum, Stockholm

Figure 3. Fragonard. *View of an Italian Villa, with a Cascade.* The Metropolitan Museum of Art, New York

This drawing was directly inspired by Fragonard's landscape studies of the environs of Rome, executed during his second visit to Italy (1773–74). It is close to the vertical sketch in Stockholm (see figure 2), which, however, includes only the central motif of the present composition—the arch and the four columns surmounted by a balustrade and statues. There are parallels, too, with the *View of an Italian Villa, with a Cascade* in the Metropolitan Museum (see figure 3), and between the lush foliage of the tree at the right and that of the tree, also at the right, in the pendant to this picture, *A Shaded Avenue* (see cat. no. 186, figure 2).

Thick vegetation has overgrown an abandoned garden containing urns, sarcophagi, a statue, and an Egyptian-style fountain at which a flock of sheep has come to drink. Two passersby and a shepherd on horseback enliven the sunlit park that is shaded by the tall trees.

Here, Fragonard played on the contrast between the architectural elements and the animals, on the one hand, and, on the other, an all-pervasive, exuberant, and vibrant Nature, trembling with life.

189   "View of a Tomb Discovered at Pompeii near Vesuvius"

Bister wash on paper, over an underdrawing in black chalk, 28.5 x 36.8 cm.
Inscribed in pen and ink, at the lower right: *fait en 1774. pompeia près de portici, ville découverte./chambre ou on voit une feme [sic] qui s'est trouvé [sic] surprise par les cendres du Vésuve*

Musée des Arts Décoratifs, Lyons, Inv. 429

Provenance
M. Rabasse: acquired October 15, 1815, by "le chevalier" Alexandre Lenoir (an autograph inscription is on the verso of the drawing); Alexandre Lenoir: sold, December 11, 1837, no. 335, "vue de Pompeïa, par Fragonard; l'abbé de St. Non et sa soeur [sic] visitent une cave dans laquelle on voit une table et un squelette"; Laperlier: sold, December 22–23, 1856, no. 26 (for 19 francs); Tondu: sold posthumously, May 10–13, 1865, no. 231 (for 1 franc 50), "Pompéi. Vue d'une chambre où une famille fut surprise par l'éruption du Vésuve et ensevelie. On voit vers le milieu des [sic] squelettes et à gauche trois visiteurs" (?); acquired by the Musée des Arts Décoratifs, Lyons (the museum's stamp, Lugt 1699 a, is at the bottom left) from M. Rochoux, 1865.

Exhibitions
Besançon, 1956, no. 4

Paris, 1974–75, no. 45, ill. (entry by Jacques Vilain)
Detroit-Chicago, 1981–82, no. 99, ill.
Lyons, 1984–85, no. 84 (with complete list of exhibitions)

Bibliography
G. p. 339
Barazzeti, 1935, p. 2, ill.
Hennezel, 1938, p. 20 fig. 106
Ananoff, 1961, p. 54, ill.
A. 670, fig. 188

Related works
Étienne Fessard (see figure 1) made an engraving of the drawing (not in reverse), for the first volume of the Abbé de Saint-Non's *Voyage pittoresque ... de Naples et de Sicile,* which appeared in 1781 (see Pognon and Bruand, 1962, IX, p. 14, no. 86).

Figure 1. Étienne Fessard. *View of a Tomb Discovered at Pompeii near Vesuvius.* Bibliothèque du Louvre, Paris

393

189

"We left Naples at 8 o'clock in the morning and made our way to Pompeii, a curious city, discovered only a few years ago.... In one house, among others, in an underground room, where, doubtless, the laundry was done, one can see all the utensils, the furnace, the sink, etc...., and a pile of cinders on which lies the corpse of a woman in the position of someone who, having tried to flee from the liquid ash pouring in from all sides, finally fell backward and died. This we can surmise perfectly from her pose, and we are in ecstasy at the realization that this happened 1,700 years ago ... " (Tornézy, pp. 314–15).

There are few Fragonard drawings that so precisely illustrate a passage from the *Journal*. The visit to Pompeii took place May 6, 1774. Because the drawing has faded somewhat, it is difficult to identify the visitors; Fessard's engraving for the *Voyage pittoresque* remains much more detailed.

Two women (Mme Fragonard, and Jeanne Vignier, the future third wife of Bergeret ?) and four men (Bergeret, his son, Fragonard, and a guide, key in hand, who turns toward the visitors to note their astonishment) come upon a skeleton of a woman vividly illuminated by a ray of sunlight. (Perhaps one of the men is that "former pensioner of the king, an architect of much talent" [Tornézy, p. 292], who resided in Naples and gave advice to Bergeret's party.) Awe and surprise are clearly visible on the faces of the tourists, the "ecstasy"—to quote Bergeret—provoked by their glimpse into the distant past. It is this human presence, far more than the vestiges of antiquity in the foreground of the composition, that captures the visitors' attention.

Fragonard's drawing is not without humor in its parody of *Hamlet*: fascinated by what they see, the travelers appear to be lost in reverie about their own destiny.

190 The Oxcart

Bister wash on paper, over an underdrawing in black chalk, 27.3 x 36.6 cm.
Inscribed at the bottom right, partly hidden by the mount: *Naples 1774.*

Private collection

Provenance
[Chabot and Duc de La Mure, or Desmarets]:
sold, December 17–22, 1787, no. 177: "la
Vue d'un parapet ou passe un homme sur un
chariot [*sic*] attelé de deux Boeufs, on voit
aussi sur le devant de jeunes blanchisseuses"
(for 73 *livres*, to Desmarais); Count Eduard
Karolyi (1830–1885 ?), Füzer-Radvany castle, Hungary (according to A.); Count
Eduard's son, Count Istvan Karolyi, who
emigrated to France in 1944; anonymous
sale (no catalogue), May 21, 1951; [Cail-
leux]; private collection, Paris.

Exhibitions
Paris, 1954, no. 69, pl. 41
London, 1954–55, no. 273
Besançon, 1956, no. 106
Grasse, 1957, no. 43

Bibliography
Boucher and Jaccottet, 1952, p. 174, pl. 85
Ananoff, 1956, p. 41, ill.
R. pp. 223, 126 fig. 41
Ananoff, 1957, p. 515, ill.
A. 271, fig. 94

Although Fragonard and Bergeret stayed in Naples for
nearly two months, from April 15 to June 12, 1774, Bergeret's *Journal* (Tornézy, pp. 291–350) barely alludes to the
painter at all (see pp. 325, 340, 344, for these references).
Only rarely do the drawings executed in Naples and dated
by Fragonard illustrate entries in the *Journal* (see cat. no.
189). It is possible that the relationship between the two
men had already deteriorated at this time, and that they were
ignoring one another.

Thus, we have no way of knowing exactly when and
where Fragonard drew this oxcart. The oxen and their driver
(who stands in the cart, and turns and looks out at the
spectator, as he holds his goad in his right hand) are posi-
tioned as if on a stage, and are the true subject of this
drawing. There is much to admire: note the subtle play of
the curves of the wheels and the milestones, the straight lines
of the flight of steps leading to the washhouse, and the warm
light that bathes the entire scene.

Bister wash on paper, over an underdrawing in black chalk, 36.4 x 28.1 cm.
Inscribed in pen and ink, at the bottom center, on the stone: *Naples 1774 feme* [*sic*] *de S^{te}/Lucie*; on the mount, in pencil:
   Honoré Fragonard fec; on the verso of the mount, in pen and ink, in an 18th-century hand: honorée fragonard
   N° 422/N° 53 honoré fragonard

Städelsches Kunstinstitut, Frankfurt am Main, Graphische Sammlung, Inv. No. 1104

Provenance
Anonymous sale, May 31, 1790, no. 183
(see cat. no. 176); Grimod de La Reynière
(see cat. no. 176): sold, September 7–17,
1797 (according to Stuffmann) (?); part of
the museum's original collection; inventoried, 1862.

Exhibitions
Naples, 1979–80, no. 247, ill. (but not
   exhibited)

Frankfurt, 1986–87, no. 124, ill. (entry by
   M. Stuffmann)

Bibliography
Leporini, 1925, pl. 5
Ananoff, 1956, p. 41, ill.
R. p. 215, fig. 51, p. 100
W. p. 24 (French edition)
A. 181, fig. 71
Bacou, 1971, colorpl. XXV (French edition,
   1976)

Williams, 1978, p. 94
Cuzin, 1983, p. 110, n. 30
Zafran, 1983, p. 90, fig. III.7 ("Vincent")

Related works
François-André Vincent made at least two
drawings (see figure 1) and one painting (fig-
ure 2) of the same model, but full length (see
Cuzin, 1983; Zafran, 1983).
   See also the following entry.

Figure 1. François-André Vincent.
Portrait of a Neapolitan Woman.
Whereabouts unknown

Figure 2. François-André
Vincent. *Portrait of a
Neapolitan Woman.* Private
collection, United States

Figure 3. Massimo Stanzione.
Woman with a Rooster. The Fine Arts
Museums of San Francisco

On May 15, 1774, when he had spent one month in
Naples, Bergeret noted in his *Journal* (Tornézy, p. 324): "In
the afternoon, a little before sunset, the same number of
carriages jostle each other on the Strada Nuova and the
Chiaia and Santa Lucia roads as in Paris."

   The Passeggiata di Santa Lucia was (and still is) a favorite
place along which to stroll in Naples. The women of the
district—fishermen's wives, with ill-tempered natures—were
well known for their elegance. Their elaborate clothing (one
thinks of Massimo Stanzione's famous *Woman with a
Rooster*; see figure 3), was a blend of Islamic, Spanish, and
French influences, according to Nicola Spinosa (in a written

communication). The "Luciani" dressed with particular
splendor on feast days, favored costume jewelry (from the
Arab countries and Spain), and transacted all kinds of sea-
sonal business in the streets (in May, they grilled maize; in
November, chestnuts; and in all seasons they sold boiled
cuttlefish and octopus).

   Fragonard does not dwell on the picturesque and anecdotal details of the "Neapolitan costume," which might have
distracted our attention from his main theme: the reality and
the presence of the model. Once again, we can admire the
directness of the artist's execution, and his masterful balance
of volume and line.

192 Half-length Portrait of a Neapolitan Woman

Bister wash on paper, over an underdrawing in black chalk, 36.7 x 28.2 cm.
Inscribed in pen and ink, at the bottom right (slightly cropped): *Naples 1774; femē [de]/Sᵗᵉ Lu[cie]*

Collection Mr. and Mrs. Eugene V. Thaw

Provenance
M. [de Bièvres]: sold, March 10, 1790, no. 34, "trois belles études de têtes dont un buste de femme vu de face et richement ajusté"(?); Martial Pelletier: sold, April 29–May 4, 1867, no. 1315 (for 111 francs); M. Marmontel: sold, Paris, January 25–26, 1883, no. 103 (for 400 francs, bought in by the family), March 28–29, 1898 (not 1868), no. 24 (for 1,200 francs); E. M. Hodgkins: sold, Paris, April 30, 1914, no. 28 (bought in; still in this collection, 1921); Mrs. C. I. Stralem, from 1931; Donald S. Stralem (son of Mrs. C. I. Stralem); Mrs. Donald S. Stralem, until 1972.

Exhibitions
Paris, 1921, no. 173
Paris, 1931, no. 64

Paris, 1958–59, no. 50, pl. 63
London, 1968, no. 270, fig. 297
New York, 1972, no. 20
Washington, D.C., 1978, no. 33, ill.
New York, 1985, no. 11, ill.

Bibliography
P. p. 314
Bergeret, 1948, p. 102, pl. XIV
R. p. 215, fig. 13, p. 30
A. 119, fig. 495
Williams, 1979, p. 77, ill.
Cuzin, 1983, p. 110, n. 31, fig. 12
Zafran, 1983, p. 90, fig. III.6
Aaron, 1985, p. 18, fig. 2
Sutton, 1987, p. 88, fig. 8

Related works
See the preceding entry.

Figure 1. François-André Vincent. *Portrait of a Man.* 1775. Graphische Sammlung Albertina, Vienna

The model for the present work was undoubtedly the *"Woman from Santa Lucia,"* whom Fragonard had drawn before, seated and in profile (see cat. no. 191). In both drawings, her cap, her gaudy necklaces, her sumptuous embroidered dress, and even her earrings are exactly alike. Jean-Pierre Cuzin (1983) and Eric Zafran (1983) have shown that François-André Vincent, who seems to have been in Naples at the same time as Fragonard and Bergeret (see also the Introduction, pp. 362–63), made at least two drawings (now lost) and one full-length painting (now in a private collection in Georgia) of this same Neapolitan woman. Moreover, Vincent's sitter wears an almost identical costume, very close in its details to that depicted by Fragonard.

The authenticity of the present *Neapolitan Woman* is con-firmed not only by its provenance (it seems to have been in the unassailable de Bièvres collection, which was sold in 1790), but also by comparison with the—uncontested—drawings by Vincent, such as the *Portrait of a Man,* dated 1775, in the Albertina (see figure 1; previously unpublished). Although Vincent adopted Fragonard's manner of using wash, and sometimes achieved excellent imitations of his style, his work differs in its more detailed, diffuse, and meticulous technique. Fragonard goes beyond mere description; the attention that he pays to his subjects is not limited to their physical characteristics alone. With gentleness and delicacy, he renders the oval, slightly full face of the young Neapolitan woman so that it seems to melt into the surrounding space, its features conveying a tenderness that evokes our sympathy.

193 Satyr Pressing Grapes

Bister wash on paper, over an underdrawing in black chalk, 34.6 x 24.7 cm.
Inscribed at the bottom right, in two different hands: *h. frago-Dresden 1774 an ...*

The Art Institute of Chicago, Gift of Mr. and Mrs. Robert J. Hamman, in honor of Suzanne Folds McCullagh, 1982.500

Provenance
Sold, Paris, June 12, 1980, no. 32, ill.; [Cailleux]; given to the Art Institute of Chicago by Mr. and Mrs. Robert J. Hamman, 1982.

Exhibitions
Chicago, 1985, no. 42, ill. p. 101

Bibliography
Shestack, 1984, p. 46

192

193

Figure 1. Workshop of Peter Paul Rubens. *Satyr Pressing Grapes.* Staatliche Kunstsammlungen Dresden, Gemäldegalerie

Bergeret and his traveling companions arrived in Dresden August 20, 1774. On Monday, August 22, Bergeret went off "to the galleries, where M and Mme Fragonard had been established since the morning, making some drawings" (Tornézy, p. 409). The Elector of Saxony's collection made a very strong impression on Bergeret, who subsequently went to see it a number of times in the course of his travels.

Fragonard carefully copied a large painting then attributed to Rubens but now considered to be by the master's workshop (see figure 1). The painting shows a satyr pressing grapes, while a child collects the juice and, in the foreground, a tigress suckles her young (Gemäldegalerie catalogue, 1902, no. 974).

We have no way of knowing whether it was Fragonard or Bergeret who chose the paintings that were to be copied, but Bergeret recorded his admiration for the gallery and the way it was organized: "There is an inspector and guards, all of whom are very honest, giving total freedom to everyone to draw or copy there whatever they desire. Nothing can be more gratifying to a prince than to lend himself thus to the progress of the arts . . . " (Tornézy, p. 409).

We also can see how much Fragonard's work had improved since his first trip to Italy; instead of the black chalk that he used to make copies of old masters for the Abbé de Saint-Non, he now preferred the more pictorial technique of bister wash. In his copy of the Rubens, he managed to imitate the master's style without sacrificing his artistic personality; in fact, he achieved a tour de force of drawing, in his own style, but never betrayed his original model.

One senses from this work that Fragonard was fully aware of the vitality of the masterpieces around him. After all, he went to Italy a second time to find new energy and fresh inspiration, which he felt that he needed to maintain his position in Paris.

194 A Satyr Being Teased by Two Children

Bister wash on paper, over an underdrawing in black chalk, 46 x 34.9 cm.

Yale University Art Gallery, New Haven, Connecticut, The Paul Moore, Manson Collection, and Marie-Antoinette Slade Funds, 1981.37

Provenance
Feuchère *père:* sold, January 26, 1829, no. 87: "…un satyre et deux amours"; Baron Brunet Denon: sold, February 2, 1846, no. 267: "satyre lutiné par deux amours, dessin au bistre" (for 20 francs) (?); Hippolyte Walferdin, from 1862 ?: sold posthumously, April 12–16, 1880, no. 207 (for 490 francs, to Reboul) (?); at Reboul, 1889 (according to P.) (?); sold, Paris, January 23, 1980, no. 164, ill.; [David Carritt and Eugene V. Thaw]; acquired by Yale, 1981.

Exhibitions
London, *Artemis,* 1979–80, no. 14, colorpl.
New Haven, 1984, no. 8, ill. (entry by Alan Shestack)

Bibliography
Blanc, 1862, p. 15, ill. (?)
G. p. 325 (?)
Portalis, 1880, p. 26 (?)
P. p. 312 (?)

Related works
The drawing in the Museum Boymans-van Beuningen, in Rotterdam (F-I-107; see figure 1; A. 408, fig. 147) is believed to be the original, but in our view it is only a copy. It was first mentioned in 1927, in the Paris collection of Richard Owen, who sold it to Franz Koenigs (Paris exhibition catalogue, 1931, no. 7, ill.). The old "pedigree" cited in recent studies on Fragonard belongs—in our opinion—to the Yale drawing, not to the one in Rotterdam.

For a copy in red chalk reproduced by Dayot in 1907 (p. 146), which was formerly in the P. Decourcelle collection (sold, May 29–30, 1911, no. 95), see A. 409.

Two related paintings—one rectangular in format (see figure 2) and formerly in the Veil-Picard collection; the other, an oval (see figure 3)—can no longer be attributed to Fragonard.

A terra-cotta bas-relief attributed to Clodion was directly inspired by Fragonard's drawing (the child at the left of the composition differs slightly), but Anne Poulet (in a written communication) judges it to have been made in the late nineteenth century and Dean Walker (*idem*) considers it to be a fake. This bas-relief belongs to the Ackland Art Museum, in Chapel Hill (see figure 4). A sculpture group, formerly in the P. Decourcelle collection (same sale, no. 182, ill.) and today in the museum in Boulogne-sur-Mer (see figure 5), is also thought by A. Poulet to date from the late nineteenth century.

Figure 1. After Fragonard.
A Satyr Being Teased by Two Children.
Museum Boymans-van Beuningen,
Rotterdam

Figure 2. After Fragonard. *A Satyr
Being Teased by Two Children.*
Whereabouts unknown

Figure 3. After Fragonard.
A Satyr Being Teased by Two Children.
Whereabouts unknown

Figure 4. After Clodion.
A Satyr Being Teased by Two Children.
Ackland Art Museum, Chapel Hill,
North Carolina

Figure 5. After Clodion.
*A Satyr Being Teased by
Two Children.*
Musée des Beaux-Arts,
Boulogne-sur-Mer

Although this drawing is famous, few are familiar with it. Its history between 1829 and 1889 may be traced, but then it seems to have disappeared. In 1927, a drawing surfaced and was quickly purchased by Franz Koenigs; it is now in the Museum Boymans-van Beuningen, in Rotterdam, and has been assumed to be the original by Fragonard. In all good faith, the drawing was assigned the provenance of the first work—which only reappeared in 1980. A photographic comparison of the Yale and Rotterdam drawings (see figure 1) removes any doubt that only the former is genuine.

The composition, which was the subject of an engraving in Charles Blanc's short monograph on Fragonard (1862), quickly became popular. Anne Poulet believes that, at the time, it inspired the terra-cottas falsely attributed to Clodion (1738–1814). Clodion and Fragonard knew each other well, and the sculptor owned one of his friend's drawings (valued at 3 francs in the posthumous inventory of Clodion's effects! [Jules Guiffrey, 1893, p. 414; Furcy-Raynaud,

1912, p. 213]). A sale on December 9, 1811, featured a "terracotta ... by Claudion [*sic*] on a subject suggested by Fragonard, the Fountain of Love" (no. 128); this seems to confirm Fragonard's influence on the sculptor.

The drawing—which is reminiscent of the *Bacchanales* of 1763—probably dates from shortly after the artist's return from Italy in 1774. The influence of Rubens, whose work Fragonard had admired in Italy, but especially in Vienna and Dresden, is quite palpable. By 1880, Portalis was praising "the boldness, as well as the movement and the vitality" in this work; we would add dynamism and humor to its attributes. Two playful children are pictured tugging at the beard of an affable satyr while a couple, without displaying much surprise, observes the proceedings. We do not know where the satyr is taking the children, nor what his intentions are, but such is the joy implicit in the scene that we are scarcely more troubled by these thoughts than they are.

195 Young Girls Teasing a Satyr

Bister wash on paper, over an underdrawing in black chalk, 23.3 x 36.2 cm.
At the bottom left is an unidentified initial.

Private collection

Provenance
E. Lefèvre: sold, February 22–27, 1883, no.
466: "Nymphes et Satyres" (for 1,005
francs, to Clément) (?); Richard Lion: sold,
April 3, 1886, no. 41 (catalogue illustrated
with an engraving by Adolphe Lalauze) (for
4,900 francs, to Bouillon, for Muhlbacher);
G. Muhlbacher: sold, May 15–18, 1899,
no. 124, ill. (for 33,000 francs, to Boin);
Boin-Taburet, 1904; E. M. Hodgkins, Paris,
from 1907; private collection, Paris.

Exhibitions
Paris, 1888, no. 9
Brussels, 1904, no. 103, ill.
Paris, 1907, no. 186
Paris, 1950, no. 105, pl. XXVIII

Bern, 1954, no. 133
Paris, 1961, no. 17

Bibliography
P. p. 312
Fosca, 1954, pp. 60–61, pl. 26
A. 410, fig. 146 (and A. 413 ?)

Related works
The painting in the Sammlung Oskar Reinhart, in Winterthur, which has a similar composition (*The Burlington Magazine,* May
1970, fig. 76), is not by Fragonard (see figure 1).
   For Lalauze's engraving, see *Provenance*
above; P. p. 330, no. 152.

Figure 1. After Fragonard. *Young Girls Teasing a Satyr.* Sammlung Oskar Reinhart, Winterthur, Switzerland

Two scantily clad and smiling young girls pull on the beard
and the hair of a satyr whose hands are tied behind his back,
as their two companions look on.
   Fragonard loved this type of subject, in which mythology
is no more than a pretext. His imagination and verve are here
effortlessly expressed through the most delicate brushwork.

The composition, lightly sketched in with black chalk,
unfolds like a frieze—as is often the case with the work
executed by Fragonard after his second trip to Italy. With
humor, virtuosity, and youthful grace he expresses a joyous-
ness, spontaneity, and love of life.

196 Head of an Oriental Man

Bister wash on paper, over an underdrawing in black chalk, 34.5 x 25.5 cm.
Inscribed with a brush, in the center at the right: *frago 1775* [rather than 1773]

Musée du Louvre, Paris, Cabinet des Dessins, Inv. 26645

Provenance
Saint-Morys: confiscated during the Revolution; (the Louvre's stamps, Lugt 1886 and 2207, are at the bottom left and the bottom right, respectively).

Exhibitions
Paris, 1911, no. 157
Paris, 1921, no. 217
Paris, 1946, no. 377
Bern, 1954, no. 110, pl. XXII
Besançon, 1956, no. 74, pl. XVI
Munich, 1958, no. 270

Bibliography
P. p. 300
Guiffrey and Marcel, 1910, V, no. 4059
Martine, 1927, p. 8
Lavallée, 1938, no. 5, ill.
Lavallée, 1948, p. 82, pl. XLI
Fosca, 1954, p. 69, pl. 46
R. p. 215
A. 130, fig. 340

Related works
A copy of the composition, but in reverse, in black and red chalk (14.8 x 11.4 cm.), is in the Musée Fragonard, Grasse (see figure 1).

Figure 1. After Fragonard.
Head of an Oriental Man.
Musée Fragonard, Grasse

Figure 2. Giovanni Domenico Tiepolo. *Head of an Oriental Man.* Private collection, Paris

Figure 3. Giovanni Domenico (or Giovanni Battista) Tiepolo. *Head of an Oriental Man.* Pinacoteca Malaspina, Pavia

Figure 4. Abbé de Saint-Non, after Tiepolo. *Head of an Oriental Man.* Bibliothèque d'Art et d'Archéologie, Paris

This drawing is reminiscent of the art of Rembrandt, but even more so of the painted or engraved *teste* by the Tiepolos. During his first visit to Italy, Fragonard had copied the work of Tiepolo (Rosenberg and Brejon, 1986), whom he might also have met. Following his second visit to Rome, he returned via Venice, where Tiepolo's paintings made a strong impression on Bergeret: " . . . all is large, grand, and in very good taste, and made to please everyone," he wrote of the decorations at the Palazzo Labia (Tornézy, p. 388). It is not inconceivable that, en route, he acquired the drawings by Giovanni Domenico Tiepolo that are now in the Musée Atger in Montpellier (see Knox, 1970, n.p.).

The Louvre drawing was directly influenced by the first series of *Raccolta di Teste* published by Giovanni Domenico shortly after the death of his father in 1770 (Knox, 1970; see figures 2, 3, 4), but instead of copying one of the Oriental heads from this collection of Tiepolo's work, Fragonard took his inspiration from several engravings in order to create an image of his own invention.

Fragonard placed less emphasis on the picturesque aspect of his subject and on the clichés of "Orientalism" than did the Tiepolos. Doubtless, he made no attempt at an accurate psychological study of his model. Yet, the dynamism of his line and the solidity of the volumes that he achieved here, with but a few touches of the brush, are easily on a level with the work of his two great Venetian contemporaries. However, Fragonard could not compete with the elder Tiepolo, for he lacked the opportunity (and probably the capacity) to paint grand decorative programs like the ones in Udine, Milan, Würzburg, and Madrid that earned Giovanni Battista a reputation as Europe's foremost eighteenth-century painter.

Bergeret and His Friends

The four portraits included here all belong to the same series. Their technique (red chalk), their format, their composition especially, and the play on chairs and armchairs—all different, but with features in common from one drawing to the next—serve as unifying factors. Moreover, each of the works bears a similar inscription. At the left, there is usually a note in black chalk, strengthened with ink: "fragonard fecit" or "fragonard pere fecit," which probably dates from the time when Évariste's reputation carried more weight than that of his father. Other inscriptions appear either on the mount (which the *Portrait of Bergeret,* cat. no. 197, is missing) or partly on the mount and partly on the drawing. While we cannot say who was responsible for the first type of inscription, those in the latter category (which were added in jest) were doubtless by Xavier Atger, the Montpellier collector who owned the drawings at the beginning of the nineteenth century.

If the drawings once belonged to Jacques-Onésyme Bergeret de Grancourt ([1715–1785]; see Tornézy, 1895; G. Wildenstein, 1961; our Introduction; and cat. no. 197), it is not certain whether they are identical with the ones (lot no. 210) in the posthumous sale of the *fermier général*'s collection on April 24, 1786: "the Graces, Drawing in red chalk on white paper, and eight studies of figures and of landscapes, done in the same red and in black chalk." In addition, we do not know who had them mounted by François Renaud at the end of the eighteenth century; at what date (before 1776; see cat. no. 197) the drawings were executed; and even more importantly (in most cases), the identity of the models.

The *Seated Old Man,* in the Musée Atger (see figure 1; A. 225, fig. 353), and the famous, so-called *Postillon* in the same collection (see figure 2; A. 214, fig. 352)—the lower part has sustained an old tear, and the artist used a different color red chalk—appear to belong to a separate series. Xavier Atger also owned the beautiful red-chalk drawing *Head of a Monk* (see cat. no. 179), the only one whose inscription tells us that it was executed in Rome.

Figure 1. Fragonard. *Seated Old Man Holding a Staff.* Musée Atger, Montpellier, Faculté de Médecine

Figure 2. Fragonard. *Le Postillon.* Musée Atger, Montpellier, Faculté de Médecine

197 Portrait of Jacques-Onésyme Bergeret de Grancourt

Red chalk on paper, 44 x 33 cm.
Inscribed at the bottom left, in pencil strengthened with ink: *fragonard fecit*; at the bottom right, in black chalk:
c'est le dessin original

Musée Atger, Montpellier, Faculté de Médecine, Inv. M. 47, fol. 42

Provenance
Jacques-Onésyme Bergeret de Grancourt
(1715–1785), before 1776; Xavier Atger
(1758–1833); given to the museum of the
Faculté de Médecine, 1826 (its stamp, Lugt
38, is at the lower center; another stamp is at
the upper center; and a third [illegible] dry
mark is at the lower right). The drawing no
longer has its original mount.

Exhibitions
Bern, 1954, no. 80
Rome-Turin, 1961, no. 131

Bibliography
P. p. 295
Saunier, 1922, pp. 37, 162, 163, ill.
Bergeret, 1948, p. 157, frontispiece ill.
Fosca, 1954, pp. 64–65, pl. 36
Claparède, 1955, ill.
R. p. 210
Ananoff, 1961, p. 49, ill.
G. Wildenstein, 1961, p. 56, fig. 15, p. 59,
n. 29
A. 217, fig. 81

Related works
A copy in black chalk, signed Aubry, is
reproduced in a Prouté catalogue (1964,
no. 57; see figure 1).
The drawing "Du Cabinet de Monsieur
Bergeret" was the subject of an engraving
(figure 2), made to imitate red chalk (and
not in reverse), by Gilles Demarteau (1722–
1776) ("Fagonard [*sic*] inv. del"; see
Demarteau catalogue, 1788, no. 251; Portalis and Béraldi, 1880, p. 719; P. pp. 80
[ill.], 323, no. 31; Leymarie, 1896, p. 73,
no. 251; Roux, 1949, VI, no. 289).

Figure 1. After Fragonard (?).
*Portrait of Jacques-Onésyme
Bergeret*. Private collection, Paris

Figure 2. Gilles Demarteau.
Portrait of Jacques-Onésyme Bergeret.
Musée du Louvre, Paris,
Cabinet des Dessins,
Rothschild Collection

Who was the model for this drawing, to whom did it belong, and at what date did Fragonard execute it?

In 1788, Gilles-Antoine Demarteau brought out a "catalogue des estampes"—a collection of engravings by his uncle, Gilles Demarteau. Number 251 was the *Portrait of Bergeret*, a splendid engraving that imitated the look of red chalk (see figure 2). The description states that the original drawing was from the "collection of Monsieur Bergeret." Demarteau died in 1776, and hence it was before that date that Fragonard drew Bergeret's portrait. Was the work executed in Italy, as has so often been asserted? When he set out on his journey, in 1773, Bergeret was fifty-eight years old. He does

not look his age here, any more than he does in the portrait by François-André Vincent in Besançon (see page 362, figure 1), which was surely executed during the Italian trip; one well understands why Wildenstein dated the engraving to "about 1770."

In the drawing, Bergeret, wearing a wig, is seated in a chair. His left arm rests on the back of another chair; his smiling face is turned toward us. Fragonard does not flatter him, and makes no attempt to hide his corpulence. This is a portrait of a "brave homme," at peace with life, who has no great intellectual pretensions. Is this the Bergeret we envisage from reading his *Journal*?

198 Portrait of a Seated Man in a Three-cornered Hat

Red chalk on paper, 48.4 x 36.9 cm.
Inscribed at the bottom left, in black chalk strengthened with ink: *fragonard pere fecit*; on the mount, at the center, in ink: *philosophus meditans*.
At the lower right is the dry mark of François Renaud (Lugt 1042), who mounted the drawing in the second half of the 18th century.

Musée Atger, Montpellier, Faculté de Médecine, Inv. 148

Provenance
Bergeret (?); Xavier Atger (1758–1833); given to the Faculté de Médecine, Montpellier, 1829 (the museum's stamp, Lugt 38, is at the center).

Exhibitions
Bern, 1954, no. 79
Paris, 1974–75, no. 41 (with a list of exhibitions and a complete bibliography)

Bibliography
Atger catalogue, 1830, no. 148
Lagrange, 1860, p. 143, ill. p. 129
P. p. 310
Gonse, 1904, p. 272, ill.
D. and V., pl. 178 ("A. M. Montenard," in error, confused with A. 218, fig. 82)
Saunier, 1922, pp. 37, 162, 164
Fosca, 1954, p. 67, no. 40
Claparède, 1955, no. XII, ill.
R. p. 210
A. 219, fig. 350
Choppin de Janvry, 1975, p. 13, ill.
Terver, 1987, p. 171, n. 1, p. 173, ill.

Related works
M. Philippe Jennepin made available to us the photograph of an engraving, after the present Montpellier drawing, which proves that the sitter for the work was Adam Malet, "avocat en parlement, notaire royal et lieutenant de juge de la ville de Nègrepelisse." If the inscription turns out to be correct, then the drawing would certainly date to 1773.

philosophus meditans.

Figure 1. Unknown engraver. _Portrait of Adam Malet._ Private collection, Paris

This drawing—for no apparent reason—is supposed to be a portrait of Bergeret de Grancourt (1715–1785), but the younger and more robust sitter here bears no resemblance whatsoever to the model in the preceding drawing (cat. no. 197). The man, seated in a nail-studded armchair, leans forward slightly and stares fixedly ahead. He wears a three-cornered hat, and has slipped his right hand inside his waistcoat.

Perhaps the books on the table and the sitter's contemplative expression are the pretext for the Latin inscription "philosophus meditans," written in ink on the drawing's old mount. Almost certainly, this was added by Xavier Atger, who owned the drawing in the early nineteenth century.

Fragonard wanted to produce a portrait, and tried to capture a likeness of his model. As in his bister-wash drawings, his aim was to create a unified composition, and he omitted any detail that might distract from the overall effect. The composition is amazingly simple, but the drawing was executed with such a degree of precision that it achieves a striking monumentality nonetheless.

Seated Man Holding a Large Book

Red chalk on paper, 47.6 x 38 cm.
Inscribed at the bottom left, in black chalk strengthened with ink: *fragonard pere fecit*; at the bottom center, in red chalk: *f*; on the old mount, in ink: *L'avare Seul/gardant Son or*; on the verso: Portrait d'après nature
At the right is the dry mark of François Renaud (Lugt 1042), who mounted the drawing in the second half of the 18th century.

Musée Atger, Montpellier, Faculté de Médecine, Inv. 147

Provenance
Bergeret (?); Xavier Atger (1758–1833), given to the museum of the Faculté de Médecine, Montpellier, 1829 (the museum's stamp, Lugt 38, is at the lower center).

Exhibitions
Bern, 1954, no. 81
Rome, 1959–60, no. 84, pl. 41
Rome-Turin, 1961, no. 132
Paris, 1974–75, no. 43, pl. XVIII (with a complete list of exhibitions and bibliography)
Naples, 1979–80, no. 248, ill.
Detroit-Chicago, 1981–82, no. 100, ill.

Bibliography
Atger catalogue, 1830, no. 147
Lagrange, 1860, p. 143
P. p. 303
Gonse, 1904, p. 272, ill.
Saunier, 1922, pp. 161–62, ill. p. 162
Fosca, 1954, p. 54, no. 11, ill.
Claparède, 1955, no. XIII, ill.
R. pp. 211, 212
A. 223, fig. 351

This portrait is supposed to represent the Abbé de Saint-Non ([1727–1791]; see cat. no. 133), but we agree with Ananoff, who fails to see any reason why this should be so. The identification is a relatively recent one (Gonse, 1904), and the resemblance to Delvaux's engraving after Augustin de Saint-Aubin (1774), which is the only accepted portrait of the abbé (along with Fragonard's painting), is superficial, at best.

A tall, thin man is pictured in profile, seated in a chair and holding a large open book. Other books are placed around him; on the floor and on a table covered with a carpet are a bill (?) and some "sacks of gold" (?). These bags (we cannot be sure what they contain) are the reason for the inscription, in Atger's hand, on the old mount (see the preceding and the following drawings): "L'avare Seul gardant Son or" ("the

lonely miser, watching over his gold"). Clearly, Atger did not know the identity of the model any more than we do, and set out to describe him as La Bruyère would have done.

Those critics who believe that the model is, in fact, the Abbé de Saint-Non, whose generosity was well known, have some difficulty reconciling this fact with the "sacks of gold" and the "avarice" imputed to the sitter. Nor is there any agreement on the date of the drawing: François Fosca (1954) proposed 1759–61; Cailleux (1983), 1773–74, and (1978), 1780–85; and Lise Duclaux (1974–75 exhibition catalogue), 1789–91. In our opinion, this drawing belongs to a series of related monumental portraits, executed in red chalk. For the reasons why they cannot postdate 1776, see catalogue no. 197.

200　Portrait of a Magistrate

Red chalk on paper, 43.5 x 36 cm.
Inscribed at the bottom left, in black chalk strengthened with ink: *fragonard pere fecit.*
At the bottom right, in ink, in another hand (half on the drawing, half on the mount), is the inscription:
Est ne Canis aut volpes/Sub tabula positus?; the dry mark of François Renaud (Lugt 1042), who mounted the
drawing in the second half of the 18th century; and the stamp of the Galerie Cailleux.

Private collection, New York

Provenance
Bergeret (?); Xavier Atger (1758–1833):
sold, Dromont, December 6–9, 1871, no.
759; Laperlier: sold, February 17–18, 1879,
no. 67; Alphonse Kann: sold, December 8,
1920, no. 99, ill. (for 3,600 francs); O.
Lévy: sold, Paris, May 25, 1962, no. 33, pl.
I; [Cailleux]; private collection, New York.

Exhibitions
Paris-Geneva, 1978–79, no. 14, ill.
Paris, 1983, no. 31, ill.

Bibliography
A. 231, fig. 356

Related works
A. (231 a) catalogues a counterproof about
which we know nothing.

This drawing belongs unquestionably to the series of portraits in the Musée Atger, Montpellier (see the three preceding entries). Its technique and composition, and the inscriptions in ink in two different hands, confirm not only that these drawings were owned by the same collector (who had them mounted by François Renaud in the late eighteenth century), but also that they were conceived (undoubtedly, along with a number of others) as a series.

The inscription in pig latin, partly on the drawing and partly on the mount, is in Atger's hand, and is humorous in intent: "Is that a dog or a fox under the table?" The allusion is to the animal—indeed, difficult to identify—that is hiding behind the tablecloth. The magistrate has placed his cap on the table; he holds a pen in his left hand, and stares straight ahead with a somewhat distant expression. With a few strokes of chalk, Fragonard has captured the essence of this imposing figure, whose identity remains a mystery to us.

It is difficult to say when the portrait was executed. Cailleux (Paris-Geneva exhibition catalogue, 1978–79) originally suggested 1780–85, then (1983) changed his mind, dating it to Fragonard's second trip to Italy in 1773–74. While the drawing cannot postdate 1776 (see cat. no. 197), the direct, vigorous strokes, the attempt to reduce forms to their essentials, and the unity of vision it displays would seem to place it close in time to Fragonard's second Italian sojourn.

Red chalk on paper, 28.5 x 32.5 cm.
On the mount is the mark of François Renaud (Lugt 1042), who mounted the drawing in the late 18th century.

Museum Boymans-van Beuningen, Rotterdam, F-I 155

Provenance
Richard Owen, 1925; Franz Koenigs (1881–1941), before 1939 (his stamp, Lugt 1023 a, is on the verso); acquired by C. D. van Beuningen, 1940, and given to the Rotterdam museum, 1941.

Exhibitions
Paris, 1925, no. 443
Paris, 1950, no. 85
Paris, 1952, no. 89, pl. 23

Washington, D.C., . . . , 1952–53, no. 87, pl. 28
Bern, 1954, no. 44
Paris-Amsterdam, 1964, no. 109, colorpl. 98 (with a complete list of exhibitions)
Amsterdam, 1974, no. 36, ill.
Bremen, 1977–78, no. 187, ill.

Bibliography
Martine, 1927, p. 52

Bergeret, 1948, pl. XVI, p. 109, colorpl. cover
Boucher and Jaccottet, 1952, pl. 90
Fosca, 1954, pp. 65–66, pl. 37
Haverkamp-Begemann, 1957, no. 63, ill. (with complete bibliography)
Ananoff, 1961, p. 50, ill.
A. 334, fig. 364
Roland Michel, 1983, p. 475

Ever since its rediscovery in 1925, there has been general agreement that this drawing represents M. Bergeret and his traveling companions en route to Italy—stopped, here, for a picnic under some tall oak trees. Ananoff even goes so far as to date the drawing to October 11, 1773, and to identify the locale as "the Dordogne."

In our opinion, nothing could be less certain (see also Roland Michel, 1983): the presence of two *identical* carriages directly contradicts the description in the *Journal* (Tornézy, pp. 67–68). Bergeret specifically states that he is traveling in a *"berline"* with the Fragonards and his "gou-

vernante" (his housekeeper, the future Mme Bergeret!), and that his "son is following in a *cabriolet* with a cook" [the emphasis is ours]. Also, the style of the work would seem to place it slightly before 1773.

Fragonard clearly enjoyed drawing large trees; he used firmer strokes to indicate their trunks and the main branches, and utilized the white of the paper for an effect of glistening foliage. He succeeded admirably in communicating the poetry of the forest; the woods are neither frightening nor romantic, but have a special grandeur all their own.

202 Seated Old Man

Red chalk on paper, 25 x 27.8 cm.
Inscribed on the mount, in an old hand: fragonard portrait de son pere
At the lower right is the dry mark of François Renaud (Lugt 1042), who mounted the drawing in the 18th century.

The Israel Museum, Jerusalem, Gift of George Halphen and Mme Jacques Schumann in memory of
their parents, M. and Mme Fernand Halphen, Paris, 545-3-66

Provenance
Trouard (?): sold, February 22, 1779, no.
228: "deux dessins à la sanguine sur papier
blanc, l'un représente un vieillard assis et
l'autre un jeune garçon"; Pierre Decourcelle:
sold, May 29–30, 1911, no. 94 (for 1,305
francs, to Stettiner, for M. Fernand Halphen); Fernand Halphen: sold, December 8,
1964, no. 64, ill. (bought in by the family);
given to the Jerusalem museum by George
Halphen and Mme Jacques Schumann,
1966.

Exhibitions
Paris, 1951, no. 37
Jerusalem, 1986, no. 26, ill.

Bibliography
R. p. 210
A. 224, fig. 354
Chronique des arts, supplement to the
Gazette des Beaux-Arts, February 1967,
p. 121, no. 442, ill.

Figure 1. Fragonard.
A Beggar Leaning on a Stick.
Whereabouts unknown

From 1911 on, it has been agreed that this drawing represents "Fragonard's father," who died March 4, 1781, in
Grasse, where he lived in retirement, probably not having
seen his son since the latter's wedding in 1769. Hence, it is
more likely that the drawing depicts a beggar resting his
wounded leg.

Under a felt hat with a raised brim, the man wears a cap.
A porringer (or a warming pan) lies on the ground at the
right. The same beggar perhaps may be the subject of two
other red-chalk drawings by Fragonard: in one, he is seated
on the ground (A. 232 a, fig. 689: actually, a counterproof);
in the other, he is standing, leaning on a stick (see figure 1;

A. 259, fig. 97). The latter drawing may be identical with
one of the "old men standing and leaning on their canes,
each one begging," in the 1772 sale of the Huquier collection—in which case the Jerusalem drawing was done sometime before this date. In any event, we believe that it was
executed either just before or just after the series of red-chalk
drawings that date from Fragonard's second visit to Italy,
since it shares the same qualities of vibrant luminosity and
solidity of form.

Although perhaps less so than the *Beggar Leaning on a
Stick*, the present work was clearly influenced by Watteau's
drawings, in three colors, of chimney sweeps and beggars.

VII

"Through capriciousness and irresponsibility..." (1774–91)

"Through capriciousness and irresponsibility...." The quotation, which dates from December 23, 1788, is a cruel one. Barely three months earlier, Fragonard had lost his only daughter, Rosalie. Called upon to submit his reception piece, which would finally have given him the much-coveted title of Academician, Fragonard once again evaded the request. Although he was not the only one to do so, the members of the committee qualified his attitude as one of "capriciousness" and "irresponsibility."

Three years earlier, an anonymous author had produced a carefully nuanced account of the state of the arts in France. The page devoted to Fragonard is full of praise, but it concludes on a less happy note. "It is a matter for regret that M. Fragonard has not attained greater heights." What provoked this harsh judgment? What happened in the intervening years?

The long period of time covered by this chapter—seventeen years—was marked by three crucial events that profoundly affected Fragonard's private life. On his return from Italy—in 1775, as far as we can tell—a tall girl of fourteen, named Marguerite Gérard, came to share the lodgings of her sister and brother-in-law at the Louvre. She was the very image of Marie-Anne, only younger, more elegant, and also more charming. Among her shrewd descriptions of the occupants of the studios at the Louvre, Camille Vernet (the elder sister of Horace, who would later become Mme Hippolyte Lecomte) left us a delightful portrait of Marguerite. The two likenesses of Marguerite by Fragonard (cat. nos. 295, 296; the latter has just been acquired by the Louvre) do not in any way detract from this impression.

What place did Marguerite occupy in Fragonard's life and emotions? For many years, the view has prevailed that Marguerite took her sister's place in Fragonard's bed, Marie-Anne being sixteen years her senior. Nineteenth-century biographers—and even more recent ones—have tended to weave a love story around the relationship between Fragonard and his pretty young kinswoman, and on the artist's strange ménage à trois. According to these biographers, contemporary morals, the painter's own habits (he was reputed to have been the lover of the most famous dancers and actresses of the time), and even his paintings point to this conclusion. Yet, as we have already shown, no eighteenth-century sources confirm these liaisons, nor mention that Fragonard was his sister-in-law's lover—despite the fact that this was the age of "The Barber of Seville" (1775), when writers were not afraid to publish the most treacherous allusions and slanders.

There remains the problem of the letters: These consist of a group of notes discovered by Roger Portalis (today, in the Bibliothèque Doucet, Paris), all of which are in the hand of Marguerite Gérard. (The letters are published in their entirety, childish spelling mistakes and all, in the final chapter of this volume, which is devoted to Fragonard's final years.) They certainly date from the early nineteenth century, and were written by Marguerite to Jean-Honoré, when she was forty and he was seventy. All possess considerable delicacy and wit; there is no denying that they betoken a great intimacy and familiarity between the two artists—even tenderness—but we seriously doubt that there was a love affair between the two friends. Marguerite, who survived Fragonard by thirty years and lived on good terms with her sister after 1806, never married, nor did she ever discuss Jean-Honoré, at any time.

Very soon after her arrival at the Louvre, Marguerite became the pupil of her brother-in-law. In 1778, she helped him with his engravings (see cat. nos. 239–242). Her first paintings date from a few years later. A second debate now ensues as to what part Marguerite Gérard played in her brother-in-law's later paintings. In Sally Wells-Robertson, Marguerite has found a strong champion—an author who has published several articles resolutely and pertinently defending her thesis. Wells-Robertson's view of Marguerite is expansionist; she believes, for example, that *Le Premier Pas de l'enfance* (cat. no. 303) was executed entirely by Marguerite. Yet, Fragonard's participation in this work does not seem to have been limited to a few strokes of the brush, in one or two areas of the composition. The very concept of the painting was his, and his collaboration on several other late paintings also seems certain. In terms of painting, the worlds of Fragonard and Marguerite Gérard were diametrical opposites. Fragonard's vision is dynamic; it cannot function without expressing the movement, exuberance, and impulse that give life to the figures as well as the trees and plants in his work. Marguerite, by contrast, was more careful, more attentive to detail. She painted small. Undoubtedly, the fashion in her time was for a more refined, even "Dutch" effect, and she had no difficulty in adapting to the new aesthetic. Yet the "winks" exchanged by the two in their work prove their complicity as artists: The young woman in Marguerite Gérard's *L'Élève intéressante* (see figure 1), which dates from 1787, contemplates Fragonard's *Fountain of Love* (see cat. no. 283, figure 4). *La Nouvelle du retour,* after which Louis-Charles Ruotte made an engraving (figure 2), under the name of Fragonard (it was shown at the Salon of 1793, no. 429), was sold as a Fragonard in 1787 (with the Chamgrand collection, March 20–24, no. 223), and as the work of Marguerite Gérard in 1804 (with the Mesnard de Clesle collection, January 5, no. 12). Marguerite Gérard had her moment of glory, for which she deserves recognition. At the time that she wrote her letters, her reputation had eclipsed Fragonard's.

Five years after Marguerite arrived in Paris, her sister, Marie-Anne, gave birth to a son, Alexandre-Évariste (see cat. no. 294). The event took place in Grasse, but the baby's father was not present (this was not the first time; Jean-Honoré was away from Paris eleven years earlier when Rosalie was christened). Alexandre-Évariste's reputation as an artist cannot even benefit from the feminist enthusiasm that has rekindled interest in Marguerite Gérard. Precocious, protected (like a son!) by David, he was by no means the insipid Neoclassicist zealot he is made out to be (figure 3). He was tempted by the troubadour style, and then by romanticism, but his worst error was that of being born in the same year as Ingres, and not siding with him. Alexandre-Évariste was indecisive in his choices, too discreet in his tastes, and too distracted in his friendships: today, he is most undeservedly forgotten. When his father died, he was twenty-six years old. Like him, he seems to have almost entirely given up painting in his later years. "When he died in 1850, the public was very much surprised; people thought that he had been dead for twenty years," wrote the great Larousse in 1872. In 1850, Jean-Honoré was already beginning to enjoy a slight resurgence of glory. While Alexandre-Évariste seems to have kept on good terms with his aunt Marguerite, whom he survived by thirteen years, he too remained

Figure 1. Géraud Vidal, after Marguerite Gérard. *L'Élève intéressante.* Bibliothèque Nationale, Paris, Cabinet des Estampes

Figure 2. Louis-Charles Ruotte, after Fragonard (?). *"La Nouvelle du retour."* Musée Fragonard, Grasse

Figure 3. Alexandre-Évariste Fragonard. *Don Juan et la statue du Commandeur.* Musée des Beaux-Arts, Strasbourg

Figure 4. Fragonard. *A Boy Dressed as a Pierrot.* Wallace Collection, London

silent on the subject of his father. At the age of seventeen, he made a drawing entitled *Psyche Showing Her Riches to Her Sisters* (see cat. no. 9, figure 5), which he showed at the Salon, as if to remind the world that Jean-Honoré himself (when just over twenty) had made himself known forty-four years earlier with a—very different—work on the same subject (cat. no. 9). We await the young scholar who will restore Alexandre-Évariste to his place in the history of painting, and help to explain the son's debt to his father. In the paintings of Jean-Honoré, one senses such a deep love of children that one would be disappointed to learn that he had neglected Alexandre-Évariste.

While we know little of Fragonard's feelings for his son, we are certain of his deep love for his daughter, Rosalie (see cat. no. 293). Rosalie died at the age of eighteen at Cassan near l'Isle-Adam, while staying with the Bergerets, with whom the Fragonards had become reconciled after the death of Jacques-Onésyme in 1785. Rosalie's death was a terrible blow to Fragonard, and no doubt explains the reproach of the Academy. In all likelihood, his "capriciousness and irresponsibility" masked his deep grief. Also, Fragonard became gravely ill at this time, as Théophile recounted to the Goncourts. "He was so violently affected [by Rosalie's death] that he contracted a serious case of cholera morbus, which was then a very rare disease." (Perhaps it was the same deadly illness that swept through Europe in the nineteenth century.) The doctors consulted with one another, but Fragonard got no better, and they decided to send him to the country, to his native Grasse, to build up his strength.

Meanwhile, the Revolution had begun.

The death of Louis XV freed Fragonard from his obligations: now he could forget about his official commissions, for which he had no inclination anyhow. The champion of an edifying, educational style of painting (these qualifications were not well received, and did not take into account the exceptional role of the new *Surintendant*), d'Angiviller, Marigny's successor, was no lover of Fragonard's work. The history of France had officially replaced mythology as suitable subject matter. Tastes were changing, and Fragonard wanted to adapt, along with them. He continued to avoid exhibiting his work, except at the Salon de la Correspondance. He stood aloof, or was excluded, from the official art establishment, but once again—for three reasons—he allowed himself to believe that his moment of glory had come.

Figure 5. Fragonard. *Dites donc s'il vous plaît.* Wallace Collection, London

Figure 6. Fragonard. *Dites donc s'il vous plaît.* Whereabouts unknown

Never before had his paintings been so much in demand at public auctions. His *Visitation* (see cat. no. 231), in 1777; his *Adoration of the Shepherds* (cat. no. 234) and his *Verrou* (cat. no. 236), in 1785; and his drawings at the Varanchan de Saint-Geniès, Gros, and de Boynes sales (of 1777, 1778, and 1785, respectively) were all commanding very high prices.

The authors of the sales catalogues were partly responsible for this success, with their constant praise of his work. Not only was Le Brun a major ally, but Paillet and Rémy, the two greatest experts at the time, followed suit. (No one knows what became of the review of Fragonard's work by the mysterious Folliot, which is mentioned by a contemporary.) It may have been the role of these men to praise artists, but one senses a sincere admiration in their writing about Fragonard, an admiration that was shared by one or two avid collectors (some of whom were *fermiers généraux*). Fragonard had his clientele.

At about the same time, he began to acquire a second, less exclusive following. "Several [of his paintings] have been popularized by engravings, which the art enthusiasts have eagerly acquired," noted the *Mercure de France* in June 1784. Fragonard had always flirted with engraving. He practiced it himself, and furnished the Abbé de Saint-Non with a number of drawings to use for his aquatints, some of which were later published in his *Voyage pittoresque*. In 1778, he took a new (but short-lived) interest in engraving (see cat. nos. 239, 244); with an undeniable sense of publicity, he put his sister-in-law in charge of launching several plates dealing with familiar and allegorical topics (for example, *Au Génie de Franklin*, cat. no. 240).

Although, for some reason, he quickly gave up engraving, himself, he henceforth entrusted some of his compositions to a few of the most skillful engravers of the time—notably, Nicolas Delaunay. These specialists (see page 458, figures 6, 7) adroitly transcribed Fragonard's genre scenes, as well as his sometimes risqué drawings and paintings, both new and old. (It is a matter for regret that there has been no composite study of these engravings, partly due to the huge lacunae in the Bibliothèque Nationale in this area.) The work of Fragonard, or some of it, was popularized by these engravings (even today, hardly a week passes without some more or less mediocre proof of the *Verrou* being sold at the Hôtel Drouot); they expanded his clientele, and his wealth increased proportionately. The 8,000 *livres* that he paid for his house at Charenton in 1782, and the "fifteen to eighteen thousand *livres* of government annuity" that he possessed on the eve of the Revolution attest to it.

There was a third reason for Fragonard to believe that he was destined for success: he had adopted a new style. Of course, the style was still recognizably his own, but the subjects that he tackled were different, and he thus renewed both his technique and his inspiration. The *Visitation*, the *Adoration of the Shepherds*, *Le Verrou*, the *Invocation to Love* (cat. no. 280), the *Sacrifice of the Rose* (cat. no. 284), the superb *Réveil de la Nature* (of 1780), which was destroyed during World War II (see figure 18, p. 424), the *Fountain of Love* (cat. no. 283, figure 4), and the *Chiffre d'amour* (figure 7) are all examples of his new style. (The last two works belong to the Wallace Collection, London; see figure 8 for the *Serment d'amour* in the only version that seems convincingly autograph [in a private English collection; the Grasse version is badly damaged].)

All of these paintings are distinguished by a less obvious manner of execution, a pronounced taste for chiaroscuro, and colors ranging from golds to warm browns. They are also marked by a stylization and an intellectualization that are unfamiliar in Fragonard's oeuvre. He now seems to prefer images burning with desire to the reality of human bodies

Figure 7. Fragonard. *Le Chiffre d'amour*. Wallace Collection, London

Figure 8. Fragonard. *Le Serment d'amour*. Private collection, London

engaged in amorous combat; in effect, the sun has given way to the moon, and facts have been replaced by symbols. A final change, the importance and modernity of which have long been underestimated, is the shift in Fragonard's art from superficiality to deeper responses; henceforth, what his art loses in spontaneity, it gains in emotion.

The fall was a hard one. "It is true that the vogue for him was great, but it lasted for only a short period," wrote Théophile, adding, "one might say that he outlived his public by twenty-five years." (This places the end of the "vogue" somewhat early, in about 1780; it seems rather to have persisted until 1785.) Fragonard was ruined, although he was not, perhaps, the carefree financier of legend, especially with regard to his art (the practical advice he gave to Léonard Defrance on how to set a financial value on his work is that of a shrewd businessman). Afterward, he was obliged to fall back on illustrating the works of Ariosto, Cervantes, and La Fontaine.

There was nothing to be done, "and yet he had not compromised his talent. Then, after so much noise, a silence enveloped Fragonard; he and Greuze looked at each other and wondered where and how it had all happened." The death of Rosalie, and Fragonard's illness—was it an excuse?—ensued; he left for Grasse in 1790, taking with him (perhaps to reassure himself of his ability) the great compositions that he had painted for Louveciennes.

When he returned to Paris, it was a different place. The more fortunate of his clients had emigrated. Fragonard now gave up painting, and placed his talents at the disposal of the new Louvre.

CHRONOLOGY

1774

By the beginning of September, Fragonard is back in France after his journey to Italy with Bergeret.

1775

April 5
Julien de Parme reports on the dispersion of the collection of Du Tillot (the Marquis de Felino), on March 27: "j'y ai vû vendre des desseins de Robert, au nombre de deux, jusqu'à 1200, et une détestable esquisse de Fragonard 600" (letter to Andries Cornelis Lens; see Rosenberg, 1984, p. 227).

The sketch in question was n° 69 in the sale: "*Pan et Syrinx,* tableau esquisse de forme ovale, touché avec esprit: largeur 21 pouces, hauteur 17. T."; these dimensions coincide with those of a work with the same subject, currently on the Italian art market (see figure 6, p. 63).

July 12
Death in Grasse of Marie Gérard, née Gilette, mother of Marie-Anne and Marguerite Gérard (Grasse, Arch. Mun., G.G. 23).

Marguerite Gérard is generally assumed to have moved into the Fragonard household in Paris in this year, but there is no evidence to prove it, except for the fact of her mother's death—reason enough, perhaps, for a fourteen-year-old girl to take up lodgings with her sister (Doin, 1912, p. 430; Wells-Robertson, 1979, p. 179).

November 15
At the sale of the Mariette collection, Gabriel de Saint-Aubin sketches

Figure 1. Gabriel de Saint-Aubin. Detail of a page from the sales catalogue of the Mariette collection (1775). Museum of Fine Arts, Boston

Figure 2. Fragonard. *Saint Hubert adorant la croix.* Musée des Beaux-Arts, Orléans

Figure 3. Claude Hoin, after Fragonard. *The Death of a Hermit.* Bibliothèque Nationale, Paris, Cabinet des Estampes

Figure 4. Gabriel de Saint-Aubin. Detail of a page from the sales catalogue of the Pigache collection (1776). Bibliothèque Nationale, Paris, Cabinet des Estampes

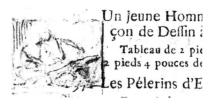

Figure 5. Gabriel de Saint-Aubin. Detail of a page from the catalogue of the Salon of 1777. Bibliothèque Nationale, Paris, Cabinet des Estampes

some works by Fragonard that are included there (an annotated copy of the catalogue is in the Museum of Fine Arts, Boston; see figure 1): we can recognize the *Saint Hubert adorant la croix* (see figure 2; in the Musée des Beaux-Arts, Orléans), and the *Death of a Hermit*, which was engraved in "L'an 4" by Claude Hoin (see figure 3). Henri Cohen (1912, I, p. 179) notes that, at the sale, Fragonard bought the series of sixty counterproofs of drawings by Edme Bouchardon for the latter's *Cris de Paris* for 600 *livres*.

1776

March 14
Liquidation of the estate of Jean Gérard, Mme Fragonard's brother, who died July 24, 1770. Present were Jean-Honoré, Marie-Anne, François Fragonard, and the three children, Pierre, Henri, and Marguerite Gérard, the wards of François (Minutier central, LXIV–441).

September 20
At the written request of Fragonard (we have been unable to trace this letter), he is relieved of the obligation to paint a ceiling for the Galerie d'Apollon, but, nonetheless, is still required to execute his "reception piece": "il a ensuitte été fait lecture d'une lettre de M. Fragonard, Agréé, adressée à M. le Directeur, par laquelle il suplie l'Académie de le dispenser de l'exécution du plafond pour la Gallerie d'Apollon, qui lui avoit été ordonné pour sa réception, qu'il craint de ne pouvoir faire assés promptement pour satisfaire la Compagnie. L'Académie a accordé sa demande, et il fera un autre tableau, dans la forme ordinaire de ceux de l'Académie" (*Procès-Verbaux*...,VIII, p. 242).
For his *Griffonis*, Saint-Non engraves *Taking Out the Flock*, after Fragonard's drawing (see cat. no. 82) and *S'il m'était aussi fidèle!* (cat. no. 119).

October 21
At the [Pigache] collection sale, Saint-Aubin sketches several works by Fragonard, which are to be sold, in the margin of his copy of the catalogue—among them is "un vieillard recevant ses enfans et petits-enfans" (see figure 4; A. 42).

1777

March
The *Mercure de France* (pp. 198–99) announces the publication of *Voyage de Naples et de Sicile* by the Abbé de Saint-Non, illustrated with "1,200 estampes gravées ... d'après les dessins de MM. Robert, Pérignon, Fragonard...."

March 19
At the sale of the Randon de Boisset collection, Fragonard's *Visitation* is sold for a huge sum, which prompts amused comment in the press (see cat. no. 231).

September
A work by François-André Vincent, *Un Jeune Homme donnant une leçon de dessin à une demoiselle*, is shown at the Salon, no. 196 (now in a New York private collection). Saint-Aubin noted in the margin of his copy of the Salon handbook (see figure 5; Dacier, 1910, II, p. 53): "commancé [*sic*] par Fragonard, dit-on." The painting, which belonged to Bergeret, is dated "10.III.1774." At this time, Fragonard and Vincent were both in Rome. On the presumed identity of the models in the work, see Cuzin, 1983, pp. 107–9.

At the same Salon, Delaunay exhibits *L'Heureuse fécondité* (no. 311), an engraving after Fragonard (see cat. no. 222), about which Bachaumont wrote: "on trouve un faire dans le moêlleux dans sa Complaisance maternelle et son heureuse fécondité d'après H. Fragonard" (*Mémoires secrets*, XI, p. 58).

September 27
Métra, in his account of the Salon (*Correspondance littéraire secrète*, no. 38), reproaches the painters for their wretched colors: "c'est ainsi que les enfants bien constitués de parens qui bégayent, bégayent à leur tour, et que tous les défauts, les vices même se perpétuent dans les familles. Voilà pourquoi les peintres qui se forment dans l'*attelier* des Vernets, des Hallé, peindront gris et toujours à travers un brouillard, ceux qui suivent les Brenets, les *Tragonards,* même les *Greuses,* seront voués au bleu, au violet, à l'olivâtre: voilà pourquoi les peintres les plus médiocres de l'école flamande sont encore excellens coloristes en ce moment où cette école est entièrement déchue. Au reste, M., avec de grands talens on fait rendre ces défauts supportables et les faire même oublier; vous n'en douterez pas en apprenant qu'on les reproches aux Vernets, aux Fragonards, aux *Greuses*."

October
An advertisement appears in the *Mercure de France* (vol. II, pp. 164, 167) for Nicolas Delaunay's engraving *L'Heureuse Fécondité* (see cat. no. 222) and Jean-François Janinet's engraving *Love the Sentinel* (figure 6), after paintings by Fragonard. Many versions of the latter painting are known. The principal ones are those in the Frick Collection (figure 7, p. 320) and in the National Gallery of Art in Washington (see W. 527, fig. 226; W. 320, fig. 143).

October 2
The *Journal de Paris* (no. 275, p. 3) announces Delaunay's engraving *L'Heureuse Fécondité* (see cat. no. 222): "elle a tout le piquant de l'effet du tableau original." The same advertisement appears in *Affiches, Annonces et Avis divers* of October 15, p. 167.

Figure 6. Jean-François Janinet, after Fragonard. *Love the Sentinel.* Musée du Louvre, Paris, Cabinet des Dessins, Rothschild Collection

Figure 7. Benoît-Louis Prévost, after Fragonard. *The Holy Family* (after Bartolomeo Schedoni). Bibliothèque du Louvre, Paris

Figure 8. Benoît-Louis Prévost, after Fragonard. *The Lamentation* (after Jusepe de Ribera). Bibliothèque du Louvre, Paris

Figure 9. Léonard Defrance. *Self-portrait*. Musées d'Archéologie et des Arts Décoratifs, Liège

November 24
Advertisement in the *Journal de Paris* (no. 328, p. 3) for Janinet's engraving *Love the Sentinel:* "cette estampe coloriée est très agréable et rend bien l'idée du coloris du maître."

December 22
François-Guillaume Ménageot's painting *Polyxena's Farewell to Hecuba* (in the Musée des Beaux-Arts, Chartres; see cat. no. 107, figure 3), on exhibition at the Salon (no. 202), is bought for 2,000 *livres* by the *Direction des Bâtiments* with a view to creating a tapestry of it at the Gobelins factory: "ce tableau, qui est fort beau, me paroîtroit fort propre à faire pendant à celuy de M. Fragonard, et servir à la manufacture royale des Gobelins qui a grand besoin d'être renouvelée en sujets neufs et en tableaux" (letter from d'Angiviller to Pierre, *A.A.F.*, 1905, p. 162). The painting by Fragonard to which allusion is made is, of course, the *Coresus and Callirhoë* (cat. no. 104).

December 29
The "avis" [notice] in the Varanchan de Saint-Geniès collection sales catalogue, which featured a number of Fragonards, states that the collection is especially valuable because of: "les plus belles esquisses et les plus beaux Dessins d'un de nos premiers Peintres [Boucher] toujours regretté, et recherché davantage depuis qu'il n'est plus: on verra avec plaisir beaucoup des pensées d'un de ses Élèves [Fragonard], devenu célèbre sans lui ressembler. Si les Tableaux soigneusement finis plaisent plus vulgairement, il est une certaine classe d'Amateurs qui jouissent suprêmement sur un seul croquis; ils recherchent l'âme et les pensées de l'homme de génie qu'ils savent voir et reconnoître."

Prévost makes engravings (see figures 7, 8) after drawings by Fragonard of *The Holy Family* by Schedoni (then in the Galleria di Capodimonte), and of Ribera's *Lamentation* (in the Certosa di San Martino), for the Abbé de Saint-Non's *Voyage pittoresque* (vol. I, facing p. 111).

1778

Appearance of the first engraving executed by Fragonard in collaboration with his young sister-in-law, Marguerite Gérard, *Le Chat emmailloté* (see cat. no. 239), inscribed in the margin: "première planche de mlle Gérard agée de 16 ans 1778." The painting by Fragonard after which this engraving was executed was exhibited the following year at the Salon de la Correspondance; it is now lost.

January
The *Mercure de France* (vol. II, pp. 171–72) announces Delaunay's engraving *Le Bonheur du ménage,* after Leprince (cat. no. 222, figure 5), the pendant to *L'Heureuse Fécondité* (see cat. no. 222), after Fragonard.

March 13
Léonard Defrance (a painter from Liège; 1735–1805; see figure 9) informs Abraham Fontanel (1750–1819), a dealer and keeper of drawings at the Société des Beaux-Arts, in Montpellier (see cat. no. 83), in a letter, that he has reworked two small paintings, "poliçons," identical to the ones given to Fragonard:

Monsieur,
J'ai toujours une singulière satisfaction d'aprendre des nouvelles de Mr. Fragonard à qui je vous prie, quand vous le verrez, de lui dire de ma part bien des choses agréables, ainsi qu'à Madame et tout ce qui lui appartient. Votre lettre, datée du quatre Mars courant, m'est parvenue le 12; elle a tardé au moins trois jours.
Depuis mon départ de Paris, je n'ai rien fait dont je puisse disposer aiant été contraint de peindre des sujets de nuit pour notre prince,[1] comme fonderie, clouterie, fenderie, etc., manufacture de fer de ce paijs. J'ai cependant fait à la dérobée deux petits tableaux dont je puis disposer, grand onze pouces et demi large, sur 8½ de haut.
L'un est à peu près le répété de la petite[2] qui quitte son ouvrage[3]...,que vous avez vu à Mr. Fragonard; il y a quelque changement dans le fond, et la tête qui regarde en face, au lieu que celui que vous avez vu regarde le ciel. L'autre est le pendant; c'est un garçon ou écolier qui, en faisant ses lectures de classe, les quitte. ... Un lit, une table, quelqu'accessoires, un chien, un écran compose le fond. Je crois qu'il n'y a pas tant de sécheresse que dans celui de Mr. Fragonard; ils sont généralement plus moëlleux; je puis me tromper, mais je ne le crois pas. S'ils peuvent vous convenir au prix de dix louis d'or les deux, je vous les ferai remettre, tant par égard pour M. Fragonard que pour lier connoissance, ainsi qu'en mémoire de votre pays où j'ai été si heureux. Ils pourront encore arriver à Paris avant la fin d'Avril, autrement je pourrai avec le tems vous en faire quelqu'autre moins poliçons; je n'aimerois pas même trop qu'ils fussent montré à personne de l'Académie royale. Cela pourroit me faire du tort. Vous sentez bien que n'est pas compris dans ce nombre Mr. Fragonard. Je suis en hâte votre très humble serviteur.

L. Defrance

1. The prince-bishop of Liège, François-Charles de Velbrick.
2. This word is repeated in the original text.
3. The remainder of the description proves that this was a free subject, like its pendant.

(This letter belonged to Jean Vallery-Radot and was annotated and published by him in 1926, pp. 25–26.)
Defrance's *Mémoires* (written during the Revolution and published by E. Wahle, 1980, p. 64) inform us that Fragonard assisted him in selling his work in Paris:

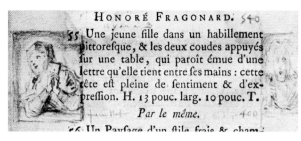

Figure 10. Gabriel de Saint-Aubin. Detail of a page from the sales catalogue of the Gros collection (1778). Musée du Petit Palais, Paris

Figure 11. Fragonard. *The Letter*. Private collection, United States

satisfait de mes essais en petit, je me mis à composer des tableaux; quoique je les finissais assez, je les peignais au premier coup, c'est-à-dire sans ébauche; je les envoyai à des marchands en Hollande. Ils furent acceptés et payés le prix demandé; je hasardai d'en emporter quelques-uns à Paris. Avant de les présenter à personne, je les montrai au citoyen Fragonard que j'avais connu à Rome. Cet aimable artiste m'en parut content. Je lui confiai que je venais tenter la fortune, il me demanda le prix des tableaux que je lui montrais et, le lendemain, ils étaient vendus; J'eus lieu d'être content de mon entreprise, et ce qui m'a le plus flatté, c'est que ce célèbre artiste m'en a demandés pour lui-même.

Je profitai de ce débouché, je fis des tableaux que je vendais aux marchands. Fragonard me conseilla de ne pas augmenter le prix; il faut, me dit-il, que le marchand gagne et attendre qu'il ait lui-même établi une valeur plus forte, parce qu'alors il est obligé de la soutenir pour ne pas passer pour avoir survendu.

April 13
In his copy of the Gros collection sales catalogue, Gabriel de Saint-Aubin sketches the drawings by Fragonard that are being sold (see cat. no. 83, figure 3). Among them was "Une jeune fille dans un habillement pittoresque," beside which Saint-Aubin noted in pencil, "il y en a trois," and he sketched two of them (figures 10, 11; see W. 382, pl. 79).

May 10
In the "État des tableaux et dessins composant le Cabinet de Hall" (the Swedish painter Peter Adolf Hall, 1739–1793), a number of works by Fragonard are mentioned (Villot, 1867, pp. 74–77).

June 24
The *Journal de Paris* (no. 175, p. 699) announces a new engraving by Jean-François Janinet, after Fragonard: *L'Amour folie* (figure 12), a pendant to *Love the Sentinel*.

July 4
At the Salon de la Correspondance, Fragonard exhibits a gouache "représentant un bosquet, au milieu duquel s'élève un pavillon entouré d'eau, dessiné par M. Boucher [doubtless Juste-Nathan, the son of François Boucher], architecte du Roi" (*Journal de Paris*, no. 185, p. 738).

November 15
An advertisement appears in the *Journal de Paris* (no. 319, pp. 1278–79) for an engraving entitled *Au Génie de Franklin* (see cat. no. 240). This engraving should not be confused with one by the Abbé de Saint-Non, after another drawing by Fragonard (see cat. no. 240, figure 3).

November 27
The *Journal de Paris* (no. 331, p. 1333) announces Fragonard's engraving *The Armoire*: "cette estampe a l'avantage rare d'être tout entière de la main de l'Auteur" (see cat. no. 238).

In the same year, Fragonard collaborated with Marguerite Gérard on engravings entitled *Les Traitants* and *Interior Scene* (cat. nos. 241, 242).

For the Abbé de Saint-Non's *Voyage pittoresque* (vol. 1, between pp. 112 and 113), Nöel Le Mire made engravings of *The Birth of the Virgin* and *L'Institution du Saint Rosaire* (figure 13) after Fragonard's copies of works by Luca Giordano. Gaucher made two engravings,

Saint Luke and *Saint Mark*, after paintings by Giovanni Lanfranco in the Chiesa dei Santi Apostoli, Naples, copied by Fragonard (see cat. no. 39, figure 4; cat. no. 40, figure 4).

1779

January 26
At the Salon de la Correspondance, the artist exhibits "*Au Génie de Franklin,* dessiné par M. Fragonard peintre du Roi et gravé par Mlle. Gérard, sa belle-soeur" (*Nouvelles de la République des lettres et des arts,* no. 1, p. 4).

April 13
Publication of the *Voyage pittoresque*. "M. l'abbé de Saint-Non (. . .) est, dit-on, le principal coopérateur de cette entreprise (. . .) Les sujets de la première livraison sont: No. 1 *Héliodore* (. . .) dessiné par M. Fragonard, gravé par M. Martini (. . .). N° 2 Un tableau de l'Espagnolet (. . .) un second (. . .) du Schedone, dessiné par M. Fragonard, gravé par M. Prévost" (*Nouvelles de la République des lettres et des arts,* pp. 64–65).

July 13
Fragonard exhibits at the Salon de la Correspondance "un tableau

Figure 12. Jean-François Janinet, after Fragonard. *L'Amour folie*. Musée du Louvre, Paris, Cabinet des Dessins, Rothschild Collection

représentant un enfant tenant entre ses bras un chat emmailloté, tandis qu'un autre enfant se réjouit de l'embarras du chat, par M. Fragonard, peintre du Roi: 3 pieds 6 po. de haut et 2 pi. 10 po. 6 lig. de large. Ce tableau très-gai et de la plus belle couleur, dans la manière vive de Rubens, a fait le plus grand plaisir'' (*Nouvelles de la République des lettres et des arts*, p. 173). The engraving appeared the previous year.

July 14
The *Journal de Paris* (no. 195, p. 795) announces ''*L'Armoire*, estampe gravée par Coron, d'après Fragonard'' (see cat. no. 236).

July 20
Mme Fragonard exhibits at the Salon de la Correspondance ''deux têtes de jeunes filles peintes en miniature (. . .) chacune de deux pouces et demi de haut sur deux pouces de large. Ces ouvrages d'une manière libre et très-pittoresque, et d'ailleurs d'un coloris charmant, ont été vus avec le plus grand plaisir'' (*Nouvelles de la République des lettres et des arts*, p. 181).

November 28
Announcement in the *Journal de Paris* (no. 332, p. 1352) of the publication of Delaunay's engraving *The Good Mother*, after Fragonard (see cat. no. 159). This print was exhibited at the Salon later that year (no. 288 in the Salon handbook).

The same newspaper notes, on December 3 (no. 337, p. 1373), that the print is dedicated to the *fermier général* Ménage de Pressigny.

Another print after Fragonard, *Love the Sentinel* (no. 268 in the Salon handbook; see figure 14), is exhibited at the same Salon by Simon-Charles Miger.

The economist Du Pont de Nemours (1739–1817), in a letter about the Salon addressed to the Margrave Caroline-Louise de Baden (Obser, 1908, pp. 100, 122), expresses amazement at Fragonard's absence from the Salon (see cat. no. 254), and praises the two engravings cited above: '' . . . Quant aux gravures, je n'y ai pas apporté la même attention. Elles courent partout. V.A. a peut-être déjà les meilleures. Je n'en ai bien regardé que deux, toutes deux d'après M. Fragonard, auxquelles les grands effets de lumière qui lui sont particuliers m'ont appelé et que la disette où nous sommes de ses tableaux m'a fait considérer plus soigneusement. L'une est *La Bonne Mère* gravée par de Launay (Salon, no. 288). L'autre est *L'Amour en sentinelle* (Salon, no. 268) où M. Miger me paraît avoir rendu tout l'éclat du charmant tableau qu'il a copié. . . . ''

Also at the Salon, Miger exhibits: ''270. Le Portrait de François de Bourbon, comte d'Enghien [see figure 15]. 271. Le Portrait de Louis de Bourbon, premier du nom, prince de Condé. 272. Le Portrait de Charles, troisième du nom, duc de Bourbon, Connétable de France [see figure 16]. Ces portraits ont été dessinés par M. Fragonard d'après les originaux.''

Figure 13. Nöel Le Mire, after Fragonard. *L'Institution du Saint Rosaire* (after Luca Giordano). Bibliothèque du Louvre, Paris

These engravings, illustrations for Desormeaux's *L'Histoire de la Maison de Bourbon* (5 vols., 1772–88), give the erroneous impression that Fragonard was also the author of the ''original'' portraits. For the attribution of this series (figure 17)—now at the Château de Chantilly—to Jean-Marie Ribou, see Seligmann and Ethlyne, 1958.

The Société des Beaux-Arts, Montpellier, organizes an exhibition featuring:
''Par M. Honoré Fragonard, Peintre du Roi.
60. *Un jeune Amour tenant une Marotte* (Du Cabinet de M. le Vicomte de Saint-Priest)
61. Un Dessein au bistre, représentant le *Triomphe du premier Prince d'Orange* (Du même Cabinet) (see cat. no. 83)
Par Madame Fragonard.
62. Le portrait d'une petite Fille, en Mignature (Du Cabinet de M. Boudet)
Par Mademoiselle Lusurier.
155. Copie du Tableau de M. Fragonard, appartenant à M. le Vicomte de Saint-Priest, représentant l'*Amour*'' (Stein, 1913, pp. 394, 400).

Figure 14. Simon-Charles Miger, after Fragonard. *Love the Sentinel*. Musée du Louvre, Paris, Cabinet des Dessins, Rothschild Collection

Figure 15. Simon-Charles Miger. *Portrait of François de Bourbon, Comte d'Enghien.* Bibliothèque Nationale, Paris, Cabinet des Estampes

Figure 16. Simon-Charles Miger. *Portrait of Charles de Bourbon, Duc de Vendôme*. Bibliothèque Nationale, Paris, Cabinet des Estampes

Figure 17. Jean-Marie Ribou. *Portrait of Charles de Bourbon, Duc de Vendôme*. Musée Condé, Chantilly

1780

January 1
Another announcement, this time in the *Mercure de France* (p. 45), for Delaunay's engraving *The Good Mother* (see cat. no. 159).

January 29
In Paris, Fragonard gives power of attorney to Claude Gérard in Grasse to sign the deed of emancipation that François Fragonard, the artist's father, wishes to register in favor of his only son (Nice, Arch. Dép. 3 E 76/226).

February 9
François Fragonard, "bourgeois demeurant au dit Grasse lequel désirant donner des marques de son affection au Sieur Jean honoré fragonard son filz unique, peintre agréé à l'académie royale demeurant à Paris, de son gré l'a émancipé comme par le présent acte il l'émancipe et le met hors de sa puissance et autorité paternelle à l'effet qu'il régisse et administre pour lui même ses biens et affaires . . ." (Nice, Arch. Dép. E 3 76/226). Claude Gérard, using Jean-Honoré's power of attorney, signs the deed of emancipation in his place. François dies the following year.

September 1
Jean-Honoré Fragonard pays a life annuity of 6,160 *livres* 16 *sols* 6 *deniers* for himself, his wife, Marie-Anne, and his sister-in-law, Marguerite Gérard; this will serve as Marie-Anne's income after Fragonard's death.
   On the same day, he pays another annuity of 14,814 *livres* 16 *sols* 4 *deniers* for his own benefit, after October 1, 1779, and for his wife, in the event of his death (Minutier central, XX-694).

October 17
Fragonard is represented by his father-in-law, Claude Gérard, at the settlement of a bequest by "dame Perrine Héligon, décédée épouse du sieur Christophe Isnard au sieur Augustin Héligon, son frère et à Guillaume françois et augustin Thomas-Benoît Héligon, ses neveux" (Minutier central, XX-694).

October 26
Birth and christening in Grasse of "Alexandre-Évariste Fragonard, fils de sieur Jean-Honoré fragonard peintre du Roy et de Marie anne Gérard son épouse. Le parrain sieur Alexandre Maubert négociant et la marraine dlle Marie Catherine Rose Mercurin épouse du sieur pierre Joseph Camatte negotian qui ont signé. Le pere se trouve absant. Le grand pere paternel a signé" (Nice, Arch. Dép. 70/15; see Sardou, 1865, p. 3; the copy of this document, Minutier central XCVI 568, erroneously gives October 20 as the date of birth).

The three documents cited above confirm that Fragonard was absent from Grasse at the time of his son's birth, contrary to the opinion of certain of his biographers.
   Fragonard dates *Le Réveil de la nature* "MDCCLXXX," on the pedestal of the statue. (This painting appears to have been destroyed during World War II [see figure 18; W. 490]; the photograph of the picture was kindly lent by Jacques Wilhelm.)
   H. W. Singer (1917, p. 309, no. 16) mentions a copy of Édouard Gautier-Dagoty's engraving *Dites donc s'il vous plaît*, after Fragonard's painting. The most famous version, which belongs to the Wallace Collection (W. 468, pl. 103), bears the handwritten inscription: "peint par fragonard. et gravée en/couleurs par Édouard/Dagoty 2me fils/1780." (Our illustration is of the copy in the Bibliothèque d'Art et d'Archéologie [see figure 19].)

November 27
Le Brun, the author of the Prault collection sales catalogue, appends to no. 27: "nous aurions pu à chacun des Tableaux de M. Fragonard que nous venons de décrire, mettre un éloge particulier; mais nous avons mieux aimé réserver pour un article séparé l'hommage qui est dû à ses talens. On y reconnoit par-tout le génie libre et facile et la touche neuve et piquante qui caractérisent ses productions." Alas, the "article" mentioned is unknown to us.

1781

March 4
Death, in Grasse, of François Fragonard, the artist's father, at the age of eighty-one. François was buried the following day. No member of his family is mentioned on his burial certificate (Nice, Arch. Dép. 2 E 70/16).

April 25
Métra, in his *Correspondance secrète* (p. 221), relates a curious anecdote on the subject of Mlle Colombe (Marie-Thérèse), the meaning of which partially escapes us (see cat. no. 245).

August 22
Fragonard exhibits "deux tableaux peints à l'aquarelle" at the Salon de la Correspondance: *The Good Mother* and *The Rest on the Flight into*

Figure 18. Fragonard. *Le Réveil de la nature* (1780). Probably destroyed

Figure 19. Édouard Gautier-Dagoty, after Fragonard. *Dites donc s'il vous plaît*. Bibliothèque d'Art et d'Archéologie, Paris

Egypt (see cat. nos. 160, 229), as well as a drawing of the interior of a stable (*Nouvelles de la République des lettres et des arts*, pp. 55, 56).

August 29
The Salon de la Correspondance shows "une vue du bois de Boulogne d'après M. Fragonard peintre du Roi, portant huit pouces de haut, un pied de large" (*Nouvelles de la République des lettres et des arts*, p. 63).

Fragonard still does not exhibit his original work at the Salon. A few lines from Louis Carmontelle (*La patte de velours*, p. 35) attest to the change in public taste: "—Le particulier: On voit au *Sallon* de cette année beaucoup moins de ces tableaux [de genre].—L'éditeur: J'en suis ravi; tout ce qui charme des caillettes, doit être soustrait au regard des hommes; car le goût du beau tient au bonheur comme aux vertus politiques. Un peuple sage et libre, est bien rebuté des minauderies de Boucher, des polissonneries de Fragonard, des simplicités de Wille."

1782

April 2
Announcement in the *Gazette de France* (no. 27, p. 130) of Delaunay's engraving of *The Swing* after the painting executed by Fragonard in 1767 (now in the Wallace Collection, London; figure 8, p. 226).

May
The *Mercure de France* (pp. 30–31) announces a new engraving by Delaunay, after Fragonard, *Les Beignets* (see cat. no. 222, figure 6). On May 2, the *Journal de Paris* (no. 122, p. 487) notes that this engraving was dedicated to "Mme la Présidente de Plaa"—as confirmed by the inscription.

June 12
Fragonard exhibits at the Salon de la Correspondance a "paysage dans lequel on voit sur un terrain élevé, un jeune homme jouant du flageolet, et une jeune fille qui gardent des moutons, par M. Fragonard, peintre du Roi" (see cat. no. 86; *Nouvelles de la République des lettres et des arts*, p. 171, no. 8).

June 19
The *Nouvelles de la République des lettres et des arts* (p. 180, no. 6) once again mentions the landscape by Fragonard at the Salon de la Correspondance: "M. Fragonard est en possession de plaire au public: la légèreté et l'esprit de sa touche sont étonnantes. On applaudit toujours au génie pittoresque qui préside à ses productions."

At the same Salon, Marie-Anne Fragonard exhibited (no. 29) "une tête de jeune fille, peinte en miniature." The *Nouvelles de la République des lettres et des arts* of June 26 (no. 13) noted: "cet artiste émule

de Rose-Alba, a fixé l'attention des Artistes et des Amateurs par la légèreté de sa touche et la couleur agréable."

July 4
Fragonard and his wife buy a house for 8,000 *livres*, from Edmée Anne Bouquet. The house is "en deux corps de logis, et une terrasse donnant sur la rivière, le tout scis aux carrières de Charenton avec les appartenances et dependances tenant presentement d'un costé à la maison où pend pour enseigne l'épée Royalle, d'autre costé au sieur Vaugeois et cidevant à Mde de Foussé aboutissant par derrière à la rivière et par devant sur le chemin des carrières. Ainsi que ladite maison se poursuit et comporte sans aucune exception, laquelle ledit sieur et dame fragonard ont dit bien connoître ainsi que ses apartennances et dépendances et en être contents" (Minutier central, XX-714; Archives de la Seine, DC 6 408, fol. 94 *v.*). Fragonard pays 2,000 *livres* in advance, and contracts to pay a further 3,000 *livres* in 3 months (confirmed, at the bottom of the deed, September 27), and the final 3,000 *livres* January 1, 1783.

Charenton is east of Paris on the banks of the Marne. At that time it was a popular place to stroll. Boucher, among other artists, painted the famous Moulin de Quinquengrogne (the picture is now in the Toledo Museum of Art).

August 21
Fragonard exhibits at the Salon de la Correspondance "un charmant paysage représentant une grotte ornée d'architecture, avec figures" (*Nouvelles de la République des lettres et des arts*, p. 253, no. 24; see cat. no. 168).

November 6
Victor-Marie Picot, in London, makes an engraving of a bust of a young girl "from a painting of M. Fragonard" (figure 20; see W. 418, fig. 176).

November 27
Fragonard exhibits at the Salon de la Correspondance "un tableau représentant un paysage orné d'arbres et d'eaux en cascade" (*Nouvelles de la République des lettres et des arts*, p. 271, no. 66; see cat. no. 168).

If we are to believe Théophile Fragonard (Valogne, 1955, p. 9), the Emperor of Russia, then traveling through France incognito, paid a visit to Fragonard in his studio at the Louvre: "Paul Ier, sous le nom de comte du Nord, vint chez lui plusieurs fois et fit un jour une belle révérence à son mannequin qui était habillé en dame."

Figure 20. Victor-Marie Picot, after Fragonard. *Bust of a Young Girl*. Bibliothèque Nationale, Paris, Cabinet des Estampes

Figure 21. Louis-Michel Halbou, after Fragonard. *L'Inspiration favorable*. Musée du Louvre, Paris, Cabinet des Dessins, Rothschild Collection

1783

February

The *Mercure de France* (pp. 137–38) once again advertises Delaunay's engraving *Dites donc s'il vous plaît*, which is exhibited along with that of the *Beignets* (cat. no. 222, figures 7, 6, respectively) at the Salon of 1783. See also the notices in the *Gazette de France*, February 21 (no. 15) and April 8 (pp. 72, 136).

May 8

Picot makes an engraving of *La Gimblette*, entitling it *New Thought* (see cat. no. 110, figure 8).

May 21

Fragonard exhibits a painting at the Salon de la Correspondance (no. 76), for which no title is given. (See also the *Nouvelles de la République*

des lettres et des arts, May 28 and June 4, pp. 168, 176, no. 112, p. 187, no. 131).

June

The *Mercure de France* (pp. 81–82) announces Louis-Michel Halbou's engraving, *L'Inspiration favorable*, after Fragonard (figure 21), the pendant to the *Messager fidèle*, after Jacques-Étienne Lallié. Several versions of Fragonard's painting, also entitled *Sapho inspirée par l'amour*, are known today (see W. 423–427; other advertisements appeared in the *Journal de Paris*, June 7, no. 158, pp. 660–61; the *Gazette de France*, June 10, no. 46, p. 210; and in *Affiches, Annonces et Avis divers*, June 11, no. 24, p. 96).

July 2

At the Salon de la Correspondance, Fragonard exhibits "N° 155. L'esquisse du tableau de Callirhoé qui est chez le Roi, à un anonyme Bergeret" (see cat. no. 104) and "N°ˢ 156–157 [*sic*]. Paysage avec figures d'hommes, d'animaux, à M. le comte de Choiseul-Gouffier" (see cat. no. 92; *Nouvelles de la République des lettres et des arts*, July 2, 1783, p. 246, cited by Wildenstein, 1960, p. 54).

July 3

Advertisement in the *Journal de Paris* for an engraving by Charles-François-Adrien Macret and Jacques Couché, *La Fuite à dessein* (figure 22), after a painting by Fragonard (see figure 23; a version of which is in Cambridge, at the Fogg Art Museum; W. 308, pl. 59), the pendant to *La Petite Thérèse*, after Jacques-Philippe Caresme. The print is dedicated to Mme la Marquise de Turpin de Crissé (a new advertisement appeared in the *Journal de Paris*, June 30, 1784, no. 182, p. 781; the *Gazette de France*, July 11, 1783, no. 55, p. 250; and in *Affiches, Annonces et Avis divers*, June 25, 1784, no. 78, p. 371, August 20, 1783, no. 34, p. 135).

November 26

Fragonard exhibits at the Salon de la Correspondance "l'intérieur d'un ménage où l'on voit un père caresser son enfant en présence de la mère, esquisse" (*Nouvelles de la République des lettres et des arts*, p. 313, no. 2). The painting is perhaps identical to W. 501, fig. 501 (another, more finished version is reproduced in figure 24; see W. 502, fig. 502), which seems to correspond to this description.

On December 10, the *Nouvelles de la République des lettres et des arts* (pp. 327–28) again mentions this painting: "À M. Vestier, peintre. Cette composition est remarquable par le mouvement de ses figures, et sur-tout par la grâce de l'enfant qui joue sur les genoux de son père."

Figure 22. Charles-François-Adrien Macret and Jacques Couché, after Fragonard. *La Fuite à dessein*. Musée du Louvre, Paris, Cabinet des Dessins, Rothschild Collection

Figure 23. Fragonard. *La Fuite à dessein*. Fogg Art Museum, Harvard University, Cambridge, Massachusetts

Figure 24. Fragonard. *The Happy Household*. Art market, United States

1784

May 8
Maurice Blot's engraving *Le Verrou* (see cat. no. 236, figure 5) is announced in *Affiches, Annonces et Avis divers*: "quant au sujet, il est de ceux dont la gaieté est un peu exagérée et il ne contribuera pas à la réforme des moeurs. Les Grâces toutes nues de l'Antique sont bien plus décentes que ce jeune homme et cette jeune fille, tout habillés qu'ils sont" (no. 56, p. 272).

May 22
The *Affiches, Annonces et Avis divers* (no. 62, p. 300) publishes a letter from a reader, M. de Saint Félix, dated May 16, which answers certain strictures in the same newspaper's May 8 issue (no. 56, p. 272), on the uniformity of the rendering of the fabrics in Blot's engraving *Le Verrou*: "le tableau a un effet piquant. Si M. Blot l'a exprimé; comme vous en devez convenir, il a rempli sa tâche. Je ne connois pas cet Artiste: mais j'ai vu son modèle, et enchanté de la belle et large manière avec laquelle il l'a imité, j'ai pris la liberté de vous adresser mon observation, d'après laquelle vous détruirez peut-être l'effet d'une censure rigoureuse." The response of the editor of *Affiches, Annonces et Avis divers* was swift: "nous admettons la distinction de Peintre d'histoire et de Bambochade, seulement par leurs productions. Or, comme l'Auteur du Verrou ne traitoit pas un sujet d'histoire, il auroit dû entrer dans tous les détails essentiels aux tableaux du genre inférieur" (see cat. no. 236).

June
Yet another announcement, this time in the *Mercure de France* (p. 37), for Blot's engraving: "on connoît la magie du pinceau de M. Fragonard, les grâces et la vérité qu'il a répandues dans ses tableaux; la gravure en a multiplié plusieurs que les amateurs se sont empressés d'accueillir. M. Blot vient d'en graver un qui offre une estampe charmante, intitulée le verroux; le sujet est galant et rendu de manière à produire l'effet le plus agréable."

Pierre-Philippe Choffard engraves a large *fleuron* for the *Voyage pittoresque* (vol. V), "Cérès vient d'allumer deux branches de Sapin à l'Etna" (figure 25), after a drawing by Fragonard.

1785

The *Discours sur l'origine, les progrès et l'état actuel de la peinture en France*, anonymously published in Paris, expresses disappointment at Fragonard's development (pp. 23–24):

M. Fragonard, né avec une forme de génie propre à former plusieurs artistes, ne nous paroît pas avoir rempli toute l'étendue de ses obligations envers la Nature. Loin de suivre la carrière sublime de son Art, où les plus grands succès lui étoient assurés, il s'est détourné dans de petits sentiers inconnus, pour se faire un genre plus favorable au délire de l'imagination qu'à l'exacte vérité. Nous devons avouer cependant que les compositions dans ce genre ont eu quelquefois des succès mérités; mais son ambition s'est bornée à faire briller quelques éclairs, dans une carrière où son génie pouvoit répandre une lumière plus grande et plus durable. Son tableau de *Callirhoé*, qui l'a fait agréer à l'Académie, autorise d'autant plus les reproches que nous lui faisons, qu'on le peut regarder comme un chef-d'oeuvre d'harmonie et d'expression. Malgré quelques incorrections de dessin, on regrettera toujours que M. Fragonard n'ait pas pris un vol plus élevé.

About this time, François-André Vincent bought two landscapes from Fragonard, as attested by a letter dated January 29, 1845, to the curators at the Louvre:

les tenant de mon père qui les avoit acheté à monsieur fragonard même dont il étoit l'ami, il y a de cela à peu près 60 ans, ils sont peu connus, n'ayant depuis ce tems nullement été vus du publique. Artiste moi même et connoissant leur mérite, j'ai pensée que le musée n'en ayant aucun qu'un peu remarquable de ce maître ils seroient comme je le crois digne d'y figurer honorablement. C'est dans cet espoir, monsieur, que je prends la liberté de m'adresser à vous pour vous prier de me permettre de les soumettre à votre jugement. Si donc messieurs, vous le trouviez convenable je les ferois porter à l'administration, ou vous voudrez bien je vous prie faire savoir votre détermination.

Mon père à l'époque que je vous ai dit, les a payés 1,200 livres quand à moi monsieur quoique que [*sic*] je les regarde comme deux, peut, être, des meilleurs de cet habile artiste, je borne mes prétentions à beaucoup moins, n'en demandant que la moitié c'est à dire 600 livres" (letter from the son of the painter Vincent, Archives du Louvre, P. 30).

The proposal was rejected.

March 14
The posthumous inventory of Bergeret's collection, compiled February 21, includes several works by Fragonard, "une esquisse," valued at 26 *livres*, and "cinq tableaux quatre dessus de porte et un devant de cheminée," valued at 24 *livres* (Minutier central, XVIII, 846, published by G. Wildenstein, 1961). The catalogue accompanying the sale of Bergeret's collection, April 24, 1786, affirms that the "esquisse" in question was identical to a study for the *Coresus and Callirhoë* (see cat. no. 104); G. Wildenstein, 1961 (p. 74), suggests that the "quatre dessus de porte" are, in fact, the four allegories of the arts (W. 57–60).

Also mentioned in the inventory are "quatre tableaux" valued at 26 *livres*, which perhaps belong to the series "Quatre Heures du jour" (W. 74–77).

March 29
The *Gazette de France* (no. 25, p. 104) announces Jacques Couché's engraving *La Coquette fixée* (cat. no. 5, figure 4), after Fragonard, the pendant to the *Sabots*, after Lavreince. See also the *Mercure de France*, June 11 (p. 93), which notes that this engraving was "terminée par Dambrun."

May 2
Advertisement in the *Journal de Paris* (no. 122, p. 497) for an engraving by Robert Delaunay, *La Cachette découverte* (in fact, *The Armoire*, cat. no. 238), after Fragonard. The *Gazette de France* of May 24 (no. 41, p. 178) and the *Mercure de France* of June 4 (pp. 46–47) also advertise this print.

July 14
Fragonard exhibits at the Salon de la Correspondance (no. 43) "une vue de jardin, dans lequel de haut arbres se joignent par les tiges... laissant apercevoir un château, différentes figures d'hommes..." (*Nouvelles de la République des lettres et des arts*, July 14, p. 215, quoted by Wildenstein, 1960, p. 54).

A PARIS.

Figure 25. Pierre-Philippe Choffard, after Fragonard.
Cérès. Bibliothèque du Louvre, Paris

Figure 26. Pierre-Philippe Choffard, after Fragonard.
The Rape of Proserpina. Bibliothèque du Louvre, Paris

December
The *Mercure de France* (p. 191) announces *The Fountain of Love*, engraved by Nicolas-François Regnault after Fragonard's painting (in the Wallace Collection; see cat. no. 283, figures 2, 3).

Choffard engraves a *fleuron* for the *Voyage pittoresque* (vol. IV) after Fragonard's drawing *The Rape of Proserpina* (figure 26).

December 12
Several works by Fragonard appear in the posthumous sale of the effects of the Marquis de Veri (see cat. nos. 157, 234, 236).

1786

Publication of volume one of Luc-Vincent Thiéry's *Guide des amateurs et des étrangers voyageurs à Paris*, which notes that at the residence of Monsieur de Courmont, *Régisseur général*, there is "une jolie esquisse de M. Fragonard" (p. 180); at the house of the Chevalier Lambert (see cat. no. 235) in the rue de Richelieu, there are "deux tableaux de monsieur Fragonard, dont la *Visitation*, tableau d'un effet et d'une magie de peinture au-dessus de tout éloge" (p. 189); and in the

collection of monsieur Le Noir Dubreuilh, in the rue Montmartre, there is a Fragonard landscape and a "nombre de dessins" (p. 461).

Also in 1786, Jacques-Antoine Dulaure publishes his *Nouvelle description des environs de Paris*, which mentions Mme du Barry's *Pavillon neuf* at Louveciennes: "le *sallon*, décoré très-richement, a des Dessus-de-portes, peints par M. Fragonard" (p. 19; see cat. nos. 152–153).

January 25
At the January 19 Salon de la Correspondance, Fragonard exhibits "un tableau représentant des Amours dans des nuages, qui jouent et se font des caresses; par M. Fragonard, Peintre du Roi; à M. Rémy, peintre. L'Artiste se montre, dans cet ouvrage, l'émule de Solimène. Ce Tableau est d'autant plus précieux, que la Gravure, qui a multiplié avec tant de satisfaction pour les Amateurs, des compositions de cet Artiste, pleines d'esprit ne peut rendre ni la couleur, ni la chaleur de ton qui caractérisent celle-ci" (see cat. no. 109; *Nouvelles de la République des lettres et des arts*, January 25, p. 45, no. 25).

July 22
Announcement of the engraving by Jean Mathieu, after Fragonard's

Figure 27. Jean Mathieu, after Fragonard.
Le Serment d'amour. Bibliothèque Nationale,
Paris, Cabinet des Estampes

Figure 28. Nicolas Delaunay, after Fragonard.
Le Chiffre d'amour. Bibliothèque Nationale,
Paris, Cabinet des Estampes

Figure 29. Angélique Papavoine, after Fragonard. *Sappho*. Bibliothèque Nationale, Paris, Cabinet des Estampes

Figure 30. Fragonard. *Sappho*. Private collection, Paris

painting *Le Serment d'amour* (figure 27), the pendant to Delaunay's *The Good Mother* (see cat. no. 159).

August 6
The *Journal de Paris* (no. 218, p. 903) announces "la foible résistance ou le verroux et l'Amant victorieux; deux estampes faisant pendant; coloriées au pinceau, 2 liv. 8 s. chaque. À Paris, chez le Sieur Le Beau, graveur."

October 11
Report concerning the demolition and rebuilding of a common wall between the house of Pierre Roustain de la Barolliere, parliamentary advocate and councillor to the king, and that of Fragonard, in Charenton (Arch. Nat. Z² 661ᴬ).

Claude Gérard, residing in Grasse, gives power of attorney to Fragonard, "peintre du Roy demeurant à Paris au Louvre paroisse St Germain Lauxerrois" to "en son nom recevoir les arreages echus et à échoir, des rentes perpetuelles qui luy appartiennent et de celles dont il a droit de jouir..." (Minutier central, XX-730, entered, December 13).

December 19
Advertisement in the *Gazette de France* (no. 101, p. 434, and December 22, no. 102, p. 438) for Delaunay's engraving *Le Chiffre d'amour* (figure 28). The engraving was shown at the Salon (no. 314); the original painting (W. 390) now belongs to the Wallace Collection (see also the *Journal général de France*, January 9, 1787, pp. 14–15).

1787

April
A letter from president Haudry to Aignan-Thomas Desfriches was probably written during this month (because of a reference at the end of the note to the recent sale of the Chevalier de Chamgrand's effects, March 20–24, 1787):

... ne croyez pas, Monsieur, qu'en fait de dessins, on ne paye que le nom de l'artiste; quelquefois l'engouement a lieu mais on en revient promptement. Quelque nom que porte un dessin, s'il est movais il se donne, s'il est médiocre, il se donne encore; s'il est bon, il se vend; s'il est excelent on se l'arrache.... Fragonard jouit de la plus grande réputation, ses bons dessins se payent au poids de l'or et ils le méritent; mais nous voyons tous les jours des Fragonards auxquels personne ne fait attention. Pourquoy cela? C'est que Fragonard ne peut pas toujours être sublime et qu'un aigle ne peut pas toujours être dans les airs; le bon Homère n'a-t-il pas quelquefois dormi? M. du Coudray vous a parlé d'une petite acquisition que j'ai faite, mais il auroit dû vous dire que ce n'est qu'un très petit échantillon du maître, agréable à la vérité mais peu conséquent. Quand on ne peut pas mettre des sommes considérables à la curiosité (surtout en fait

de tableaux), il faut se borner fortement à ces petites choses (published by Ratouis de Limay, 1907, pp. 26–27).

The "petit échantillon" may be identified with A. 284, which, according to the catalogue of the sale of March 17–19, 1823, no. 123, came from the "cabinet du président Haudry."

May 19
The *Journal de Paris* (p. 603) announces E. Guersant's engraving of "*La Chemise enlevée*, estampe faisant pendant à l'*Amour chatié par sa Mère*, gravée par Massard d'après M. Fragonard" (see cat. no. 72, figure 2). See also the *Mercure de France* (July 7, p. 47): "la *Chemise enlevée*, peinte par H. Fragonard, peintre du Roi, gravée par E. Guersant, prix. 3 liv. À Paris, chez Massard, Graveur du Roy (...). Cette Estampe fait pendant à celle de l'*Amour chatié par sa mère*."

June 17
Advertisement in the *Journal de Paris* (p. 745) for two engravings by Nicolas Ponce, *Le Pot au lait* and *Le Verre d'eau*, after paintings by Fragonard (see cat. no. 143; also, the *Journal général de France*, June 28, no. 77, p. 307; *Mercure de France*, August 25).

The Comte de Paroy exhibits an engraving (no. 287) at the Salon: "l'Hermite se faisant enlever par des Démons, pour courir après Angélique. Sujet de l'Arioste, d'après M. Fragonard. Gravure imitant le crayon" (see page 509).

December 17
The author of the [Chabot-La Mure] collection sales catalogue praises Fragonard's talents (p. 41): "tous les sujets de fantaisie y sont traités avec un charme et un agrément, qui n'appartiennent qu'à l'imagination de M. Fragonard, on retrouve ... dans les compositions de caractère toute l'âme et tout le sentiment qu'exige le grand genre..."

Publication of volume two of Thiéry's *Guide des amateurs...*, which notes two "délicieux" landscapes by Fragonard, one in the collection of the Duc de Chabot, at the Hôtel de La Rochefoucault, in the rue Mazarine (p. 494; on the *Hôtel* and the academy of drawing there, see cat. no. 277); the other, in the Comte de Vaudreuil's house in the rue de la Chaise. The count also owned several drawings (pp. 547, 549). Also mentioned is a painting (the subject is not given) in the collection of the Baron de Bezenval, in the rue de Bourgogne (p. 578).

Huber, in his *Notices générales des graveurs et des peintres*, published the same year, in Leipzig, writes (p. 661): "HONORAT FRAGONARD, reçu membre de l'Académie de Paris en 1765. Le Baiser dangereux, F. Flipart fc. Les Baignets, N. de Launay fc. Dites donc, s'il vous plait, id."

The Abbé Brizard, in his "Analyse du Voyage Pittoresque de Naples et de Sicile," pays homage not only to the Abbé de Saint-Non, but also to the entire team of artists who collaborated on his project: "pour employer à la fois tous les genres de séduction, l'Auteur du Voyage Pittoresque s'est entouré de tous les talens.... Fragonard ... reproduit les compositions des grands Peintres; morceaux neufs et piquans, dûs à l'amitié et à l'amour des Arts: tous les talens ont concouru pour élever un monument au génie" (p. 13). "On sent qu'une telle production ne pouvoit être le fruit des travaux d'un seul homme; M. l'Abbé de S.... aime à payer un juste tribut d'éloges et de reconnoissance à tous les talens qui l'ont secondé dans cette vaste entreprise, et qui ont contribué à sa perfection. À la tête des Artistes, il nomme MM. Fragonard et Robert, dont les dessins pleins d'esprit et d'imagination ont embelli cette collection" (p. 77).

1788

March 30
Announcement in the *Journal de Paris* (no. 90, p. 399) for Mlle Angélique Papavoine's engraving *Sappho* (figure 29), after Fragonard. This composition, entitled *L'Inspiration favorable*, had been engraved by Halbou (figure 21). (See figure 30 for a smaller version of the painting, in grisaille, previously unpublished.)

June 14
Announcement in the *Mercure de France* (p. 95; see also the *Journal de Paris*, June, p. 666; the *Journal général de France*, p. 274) for the engraving *Baiser à la dérobée* by Regnault, after the painting by Fragonard (see cat. no. 303).

July 26

Fragonard wins a lawsuit against "la dame Dufour et autres locataires d'une salle et dépendance," at his house at Charenton. The tenants, their rent one year in arrears, are ordered to pay 100 *livres* and "vingt cinq livres pour le terme courant qui echeoirois le premier octobre prochain afin de congé desdits lieux pour ledit jour premier octobre ... pour faciliter le payement de ladite somme de cent livres échue de vingt cinq livres à échoir, il seroit dit que les effets saisis et gagés par le procès verbal sus daté [12 juillet] seroient vendus sur la place du pont St Michel de la ville de Paris," the money thus obtained to be paid to Fragonard (Arch. Nat., Bailliage de Charenton Z² 661 B).

September 8

Legrand makes engravings of *L'Amour ingénieux* and *Telemachus and Eucharis* (figures 31, 32), after drawings by Fragonard.

Figure 31. Augustin-Claude-Simon Legrand, after Fragonard. *L'Amour ingénieux.* Bibliothèque Nationale, Paris, Cabinet des Estampes

Figure 32. Augustin-Claude-Simon Legrand, after Fragonard. *Telemachus and Eucharis.* Bibliothèque Nationale, Paris, Cabinet des Estampes

October 8

Death of Rosalie Fragonard at the Château de Cassan (figure 33): "le jeudi neuvième jour du mois d'octobre le corps de Rosalie fille de Sieur Jean honoré fragonard Peintre du Roi, et aggrégé [*sic*] à l'académie de Peinture et Sculpture, et de Marie Anne gérard sa femme, décédée hier chez monsieur Bergeret à Chateau-Pré dit Cassan âgé de dix huit ans, munie des sacrements de Pénitence et d'Extrême onction, a été inhumé dans le cimetiere par moi pretre soussigné en présence de Louis hubert Deaubonne concierge dudit Chateau Pré, soussigné et des soussignés. D'Eaubonne Joseph Culot Chevron prêtre" (L'Isle-Adam, Arch. Mun., town hall, registry of burials; see figure 34).

November 1

Augustin-Claude-Simon Legrand makes an engraving of "*Ma chemise brûle*" after Fragonard's drawing (see cat. no. 118, figure 1). The engraving is announced in the *Gazette de France,* December 23, no. 103, p. 456, and in the *Mercure de France,* January 3, 1789, p. 45.

December 17

The Academy summons two of its members who have not yet presented their reception pieces: "Déclaration faites par mrs. les Agréés au comité: 1765. Fragonard P. s'est présenté, mais est parti en disant qu'il allait revenir, et n'est point revenu" (Arch. Nat., O¹ 1925 B¹⁵). The declaration is certified by Antoine Renou, author of the 1773 *Dialogues.*

December 23

After the declaration of December 17, an injunction is served on the painters who have not yet presented their reception pieces: "mais on peut dès à présent prévoir qu'il y aura plusieurs agréés anciens qui ne satisferont pas et même sont dans l'impossibilité de fournir leur morceau de réception comme: M. Portier âgé de 72 ans, M. Courtois devenu aveugle, M. Fragonard par légèreté et insouciance, M. Strange à cause de son absence habituelle de France" (Arch. Nat. O¹ 1925 B¹⁵; cited by Locquin, 1978, p. 36).

1789

July 7

Fragonard signs a certificate requested by M. Mercier for Fiquet, guaranteeing the authenticity of two drawings from the Varanchan de Saint-Geniès sale, *Le Verrou* and *The Armoire* (see cat. nos. 236–238).

September 7

A session of the National Assembly is interrupted by the arrival of a delegation of wives and daughters of artists, who came to "offrir leurs bijoux à la patrie." Among these women are Mme Fragonard and Mlle Gérard (*Le Moniteur universel,* no. 54, p. 233; *Mercure de France,* pp. 202–3; see also the *Journal inédit ...* of Mme Moitte, published by Cottin, 1932, p. 2).

Figure 33. Jean-Antoine Alavoine. *Château de Cassan* (detail). Musée de L'Isle-Adam

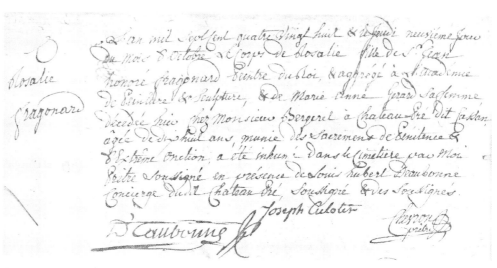

Figure 34. Burial certificate of Rosalie Fragonard. Archives Municipales, L'Isle-Adam

November 21
Greuze reminds Prince Yussupov of the commissions he has given to several French artists: "votre commission a été faite avec une telle indifférence, qu'il a fallu vous être attaché comme je vous le suis, pour m'en être occupé, et même je suis le seul, Fragonard m'a dit que personne ne lui en avait parlé, Mr Vincent est à peu près dans le même cas, Mme Lebrun ne l'a pas commencée, son mari m'a dit qu'elle le ferait à Rome, où elle est actuellement." He adds a postscript: "Mr Fragonard va commencer votre tableau ainsi que Mr Vincent" (Moscow Archives, published by Ernst, 1924, p. 267; the letter is dated to November 2 by Réau, 1922, p. 398). (On Greuze and Fragonard, see cat. no. 254.)

1790

January 12
Fragonard, his wife, and Marguerite Gérard (and Évariste?) arrive in Grasse, where they are to stay with their cousin Alexandre Maubert (Bibliothèque du Musée de Grasse, *Livre de compte de Maubert,* fol. 24). On the page of the account book on which he mentions their arrival, Maubert recorded the sum of 168 *livres* received from Fragonard each month from February 18, 1790, to February 12, 1791, very likely as payment for rent.

Contrary to what has been written (Wildenstein, 1960, p. 51), Fragonard does not seem to have belonged to the Masonic Lodge in Grasse. Perhaps there has been some confusion with Maubert, who, in fact, had been accepted as a member of the Loge maçonnique de Saint-Jean de la vraie humanité in 1782 (certificate in the Bibliothèque du Musée de Grasse).

As we have already noted (p. 417), Fragonard returned to Grasse to regain his health—not for political reasons.

April 20
Greuze informs Prince Yussupov that he has completed the commission for the painting *La Colombe retrouvée, ou la volupté* (now in the Pushkin Museum, Moscow), adding, "Mme Lebrun est toujours en Italie, son mari m'a assuré qu'elle travaille à votre tableau; Mr Fragonard n'est plus à Paris, il est en Provence, je ne sais où en est son ouvrage, dès qu'il sera fini on vous en donnera avis, de même que de celui de Mr Vincent" (Moscow Archives, published by Ernst, 1924, pp. 267–68; Zolotov, 1958, p. 147).

September 20
The painting for Prince Yussupov is sent off, and Greuze adds: "je n'ai point de nouvelles des tableaux, que vous m'avez chargé de vous faire faire par Mme Lebrun, Fragonard et Vincent. Je suis persuadé qu'ils ne manqueront pas de vous instruire lorsqu'ils seront terminés" (Moscow Archives, published by Ernst, 1924, p. 268). Nothing is known of the commission given to Fragonard.

1791

January 1
Announcement in the *Journal de Paris* (no. 1, p. 4) for two engravings by Delaunay, after Fragonard: *Education Does It All* and *The Little Preacher* (see cat. nos. 226, 227). The former is exhibited at the Salon (no. 538; see also *Mercure de France,* March 12, pp. 83–84).

March 10
Fragonard signs a receipt for the 3,600 *livres* given to him by Maubert; the receipt is generally associated with the canvases that the artist executed for Mme du Barry, which she subsequently rejected. These paintings were later installed by Fragonard in what is now the Musée Fragonard in Grasse (see figure 35): "j'ay reçu de mon cher cousin Maubert pour ouvrages de peinture la somme trois mille six cent livres dont quittance jusqu'a ce jour pour solde de tout compte à grasse ce dix mars 1791–signé—Fragonard peintre du ROY" (The Frick Collection, New York; figure 17, p. 322; published by Nolhac, 1907, p. 22).

April 19
Announcement in the *Journal de Paris* for Regnault's engraving, *The Warrior's Dream of Love,* after Fragonard (see cat. no. 283), the pendant to the *Fountain of Love.*

135 — GRASSE. Maison où habita le peintre Fragonard pendant la Révolution.   ND. Phot.

Figure 35. Villa Fragonard, Grasse

July 25
The *Journal de Paris* (no. 206, p. 832) announces an engraving by Antoine-Louis Romanet, *La Mère de famille,* after Fragonard (see cat. no. 222).

October 4
Delaunay's engraving *Les Regrets mérités,* after Marguerite Gérard (figure 36), "élève et soeur [*sic*] de M. Fragonard," is announced in the *Journal de Paris* (no. 277, p. 1129).

November 25
Death of the Abbé de Saint-Non. In his will (Minutier central, xx, 752, November 26, 1791, communicated by Mme Arquié Bruley), Saint-Non requests his brother, La Bretèche, "de choisir dans mes dessins ou estampes, et dans le nombre de mes tableaux, ceux qui auront été faits par moi, et les distribuer à son choix et comme des marques de souvenir et d'amitié à ceux et celles de nos parents et parentes et amis communs avec lesquels nous vivons le plus, et sommes liés le plus familièrement. Comme (. . .) M. Pâris, Robert et Fragonard (. . .)."

Figure 36. Nicolas Delaunay, after Marguerite Gérard.
Les Regrets mérités. Musée du Louvre, Paris, Cabinet des Dessins, Rothschild Collection

203 Jeune Fille vue de face

Red chalk on paper, 39.6 x 25.6 cm.
Inscribed at the bottom left, in ink: *frago . . . d*

Rijksmuseum, Amsterdam, Rijksprentenkabinet, 1953.207

Provenance
E. J. von Dalberg (?); Hessisches Landesmuseum, Darmstadt: sold about 1933; [Wildenstein]; Fritz Mannheimer, Amsterdam; entered the Rijksmuseum, 1953.

Exhibitions
London, 1968, no. 257, fig. 292 (confused with the drawing in the following entry)
Amsterdam, 1974, no. 47 a, ill.

Bibliography
Schrey, 1929, pl. 167, p. 11
A. 729, fig. 210
Roland Michel, 1983, p. 474
Schulz, 1984, p. 443, notes 1, 9

Related works
The following red-chalk drawings are comparable to those shown here: *Jeune Fille debout la main gauche sur la hanche, baissant les yeux* (A. 164, fig. 67; A. 724; there is a copy in Grasse, engraved [not in reverse] by Demarteau [1722–1776]; see figure 1); *Jeune Fille debout levant la tête* (engraved by Louis-Marin Bonnet; see Hérold, 1935, p. 128, no. 201; a copy was sold November 20, 1941, no. 10, ill.; see figure 2); *Jeune Fille debout vue de face* (A. 165, fig. 343; see figure 3); *Jeune Fille debout, vue de trois quarts et levant la tête* (A. 169, fig. 692; it is inscribed *frago,* apparently in the same hand as the inscription on the present drawing; see figure 4); *Jeune Fille debout, la main gauche sur la hanche, baissant les yeux* (A. 726, fig. 212; Williams, 1978, no. 30, ill.; figure 5); *Jeune Fille debout, tournée vers la droite, baissant les yeux* (A. 727, fig. 211; figure 6); *Jeune Fille debout, tournée vers la gauche, baissant les yeux* (Schulz, 1984; figure 7); *Jeune Fille assise* (A. 197, fig. 498; Williams, 1978, no. 31, ill.; figure 8).

For similar drawings in black chalk, see A. 166, fig. 68; A. 167, fig. 69; A. 168, fig. 50.

Figure 1. Gilles Demarteau. *Jeune Fille debout*. Bibliothèque Nationale, Paris, Cabinet des Estampes

Figure 2. Louis-Marin Bonnet. *Jeune Fille debout*. Bibliothèque d'Art et d'Archéologie, Paris

Figure 3. Fragonard. *Jeune Fille debout*. Whereabouts unknown

Figure 4. Fragonard. *Jeune Fille debout*. Whereabouts unknown

Figure 5. Fragonard. *Jeune Fille debout*. Fogg Art Museum, Harvard University, Cambridge, Massachusetts

Figure 6. Fragonard. *Jeune Fille debout*. Musée des Beaux-Arts, Besançon

Figure 7. Fragonard. *Jeune Fille debout*. Hessisches Landesmuseum, Darmstadt

Figure 8. Fragonard. *Jeune Fille assise*. The Pierpont Morgan Library, New York

Fragonard drew a series of standing young women, elegantly dressed, in varying poses. Engravings of some of these drawings were made in the eighteenth century.

Who do these drawings represent, and when did Fragonard execute them?

For many years, the model was assumed to be Marguerite Gérard (1761–1837), Marie-Anne Fragonard's young and pretty sister. After arriving in Paris (apparently) in 1775, she is believed to have posed for her brother-in-law between that date and 1780. Eunice Williams (1978) and Marianne Roland Michel (1983) have shown, however, that Fragonard did not always use the same model. The dresses change from one drawing to another, as one might expect, but the coiffures also differ and the features of the girls especially are not comparable. For these reasons, Roland Michel has proposed that the second Amsterdam drawing (see the following entry) is of Rosalie Fragonard (1769–1788), the painter's daughter, while Williams believes the same of the Cambridge drawing. In any case, the present drawing would seem to represent Marguerite Gérard—to whose beauty and elegance we have already referred.

These two specialists concur that the drawings in this group were executed over a relatively long period of time, between, approximately, 1775 and 1785; nothing about their attractive style would appear to contradict this.

204 Jeune Fille debout, la tête tournée vers la droite

Red chalk on paper, 38 x 24.2 cm.

Rijksmuseum, Amsterdam, Rijksprentenkabinet, 1953.208

Provenance
See the previous entry.

Exhibitions
Paris-Amsterdam, 1964, no. 115, pl. 97
Amsterdam, 1974, no. 47 b, ill.

Bibliography
Schrey, 1929, pl. 129
A. 730, fig. 705
Roland Michel, 1983, pp. 474–75
Schulz, 1984, p. 443, notes 1, 9

Related works
See the previous entry.

If we are to agree with Marianne Roland Michel (1983), this drawing represents not Marguerite Gérard, like the previously discussed work, but her niece, Rosalie Fragonard. The two young women have different hairstyles and different clothing. They were eight years apart in age. In spite of the shades of red chalk (it is burnt orange in the first drawing, and more like vermilion in this example), a number of other details confirm that the dates of the two drawings are roughly comparable: for example, the rough hatching in the backgrounds, the suggestion of balustrades by just a few parallel lines, and the intentionally stiff rendering of the girls' arms and hands.

Fragonard's goal was to produce a work of elegance: the shimmering satin, the model's pretty profile, her freshness, and her pose and bearing are charmingly described. She seems to rise up from the white background of the paper, a dream-like presence.

205 Jeune Fille debout, vue de profil

Red chalk on paper, 37.5 x 24.5 cm.

Musée des Arts Décoratifs, Paris, 23971

Provenance
Comte André Gaspard Parfait de Bizemont
H. Prunelé (1752–1837; his stamp, Lugt
128, is at the bottom right): sold, June 16,
1904, no. 18, ill. on cover of catalogue;
Houppe; bequeathed to the Musée des Arts
Décoratifs, 1923.

Exhibitions
Paris, 1931, no. 45
Bern, 1954, no. 116, pl. XXIII
Charleroi, 1957, no. 48
Grasse, 1957, no. 56

Bibliography
Fosca, 1954, p. 56, pl. 14
R. p. 215
A. 163, fig. 347

Related works
See catalogue no. 203.

Although it is faded, this drawing has a special charm. The model's slender, bare neck (is she Rosalie or Marguerite Gérard? see previous entries); her gathered hair; and her profile, delicately rendered, but in shadow are all drawn with an infectious tenderness. Of all Fragonard's red-chalk drawings, this is the one that, in feeling, most nearly recalls the art of Watteau.

206 Jeune Fille debout, vue de dos

Red chalk on paper, 37 x 24.5 cm.
Inscribed at the lower left, in red chalk: *fragonard*

Musée des Beaux-Arts, Orléans, Inv. 726

Provenance
Auguste-Lazare Belot: bequest to the Orléans
museum, 1872 (the museum's stamp, Lugt
1999 c, is at the lower right); entered the
museum, 1878.

Exhibitions
Paris, 1931 (*Province*), no. 89
Paris, 1931, no. 44
Vienna, 1950, no. 119
Washington, D.C., ..., 1952–53, no. 83
Bern, 1954, no. 113
Zurich, 1955, no. 108, pl. 9
Munich, 1958, no. 273, pl. 72
Orléans, 1975–76, no. 38, pl. XCIX (in fact
  IC; with a complete list of exhibitions)
Tokyo ..., 1983–84, no. 96, ill.

Bibliography
P. p. 305
Fosca, 1954, p. 56, pl. 15
R. p. 215
A. 725, fig. 521
Schulz, 1984, p. 441, pl. 42

Related works
See catalogue no. 203.

This drawing has correctly been linked by Barbara Schulz (1984) with those in Besançon and in Darmstadt (see cat. no. 203). These three red-chalk drawings are more meticulously executed and more detailed than the ones discussed in the preceding entries, and may well predate them—which would explain the curious dress of one of the models: "Fragonard's young woman wears a double skirt, pulled up to form three panels, exposing the petticoat. Two bands extending from the hips raise the skirt, creating wide openings. The sleeves are pleated and gathered above the elbows, and the cuffs form horizontal folds. Since there is no sash at the waist to hide the area between the hips and the bust, the dress is dominated admirably by the dynamic folds of the double skirt" (Fosca, 1954).

The girl (we suspect that she is very pretty) is walking in the country, among the wild grass. She is shown from the back, the better to display her elegant figure and the slender, delicate nape of her neck.

207 Seated Man, Reading

Red chalk on paper, 34 x 23.3 cm.
Inscribed at the bottom right, in pencil: *Fragonard* (followed by a stain in bister wash)

The Metropolitan Museum of Art, New York, Gift of Mrs. Howard J. Sachs and Peter G. Sachs, in memory of Miss Edith L. Sachs, 1978. 516.1

Provenance
Francis Abott (his dry mark, Lugt 970, is at the bottom right): sold posthumously, Dowell's, Edinburgh, January 22–26, 1894, part of no. 337: "Man Reading, and a Man in the attitude of Meditation, red chalk"; Camille Groult: anonymous sale, Galerie Georges Petit, Paris, June 21–22, 1920, no. 153 (for 3,600 francs); [Wildenstein]; Miss Edith Sachs.

Bibliography
A. 226, fig. 86
Bean and Turčić, 1986, no. 112, ill.

Related works
The École des Beaux-Arts owns a counter-proof of this drawing (see figure 1), slightly cut down at the top (Inv. 911).
See also the following entry.

Figure 1. Fragonard. *Seated Man, Reading.* Counterproof. École Nationale Supérieure des Beaux-Arts, Paris

This drawing is a late one, dating from after the artist's second trip to Italy; the line is as sensitive as ever, and the emphasis just as precise, but the forms are more strongly outlined, and their volumes are rendered with greater economy. Here again, Fragonard returns to the theme of reading, which figures so importantly in his work.

208 Seated Man

Red chalk on paper, 36.5 x 24 cm.

Musée d'Ixelles, Brussels

Provenance
Francis Abott (his dry mark, Lugt 970, is at
the bottom right): sold posthumously, Edinburgh, January 22–26, 1894, part of no.
337 (see the previous entry); given by Léon
Gauchez (bequest of Joseph-Benoit Willems,
in memory of his maternal grandfather) to
the Musée d'Ixelles, 1896.

Exhibitions
Brussels, 1925, no. 110

Bibliography
Musée d'Ixelles catalogue, 1921, no. 674
Lugt, 1956, p. 145

Related works
See the previous entry.

This drawing, which was known to and published by Frits Lugt in 1956, comes (like the one in the Metropolitan Museum) from the Abott collection, which was assembled in Edinburgh in the second half of the nineteenth century. It seems likely that the model is the same as the one in the New York drawing, but there is no conclusive proof of this—nor of his identity.

209   Young Boy with a Cat

Red chalk on paper, 35.6 x 49.2 cm.

Musée du Louvre, Paris, Cabinet des Dessins, R. F. 40.959

Provenance
Jean Masson (1856–1933), from 1921 (his
stamp, Lugt 1494 a, is at the bottom left):
sold, May 7–8, 1923, no. 77, ill. (for 16,700
francs); Mrs. Frank Jay Gould, Cannes;
gift of the Florence J. Gould Foundation to
the Louvre, 1984 (the Louvre's stamp, Lugt
1886, is at the lower right).

Exhibitions
Paris, 1921, no. 227

Bibliography
A. 10, fig. 5

Related works
Ananoff (1984, p. 13) reproduces a very
similar composition belonging to the "coll.
Y. A."; we cannot comment on this drawing's authenticity.

Figure 1. Fragonard. *An Artist Drawing.*
The Fine Arts Museums of San Francisco

This impressive red-chalk drawing portrays a young,
plump-cheeked, barefoot boy, lying rather than sitting on a
low wicker chair, with his head turned to his left. His
three-cornered paper hat, the fat cat hiding under his legs,
the barrel, the carafe with its canvas stopper, and the bowl (a
chamber pot?) attract our attention, but do not detract from
the main subject of the picture.

Fragonard loved to draw and to paint children: their
games, their moods, and their world occupy a significant
place in his work. The small boy who posed for him here
seems to find the session rather prolonged—as indicated by
his questioning look. He is set squarely in the foreground,
seen as if in close-up, and Fragonard has observed him with a
keen eye, captivating in its sureness.

This drawing is usually dated about 1775–80, but we
should not exclude the possibility that it may have been
done during Fragonard's second visit to Italy—like the San
Francisco sketch *An Artist Drawing* (figure 1).

210 The Sausage Vendor

Bister wash on paper, over an underdrawing in black chalk, 23.2 x 17.1 cm.

Graphische Sammlung Albertina, Vienna, Inv. 12.728

Provenance
At the lower right is the dry mark (Lugt 1042) of François Renaud, who mounted the drawing in the second half of the 18th century; [M. Sauzay]: sold, January 8, 1810, no. 129: "marchande de boudin. Sujet napolitain" (?); Albert, Duke of Saxe-Teschen (1738–1822; the dry mark of his collection, Lugt 174, is at the lower left); entered the Albertina at the time of its founding.

Exhibitions
Paris, 1935, no. 201, pl. XVIII
Bern, 1954, no. 86

Bibliography
Meder, 1922, pl. 23, *facsimile*
Fosca, 1954, p. 50, pl. 3
R. p. 106, pl. 69
A. 73, fig. 493

A young woman, seated in her shop, offers a blood sausage to two men who eye her leeringly. Her left hand is resting on other *boudins,* and a child plays under her petticoats. Sausages hang from the awning of her stall. If this drawing is identical to the one in the Sauzay collection sold in 1810, then is the scene really "Neapolitan," as described by the author of the catalogue? In any case, the drawing cannot postdate 1774—to judge from the liberal use of bister wash.

From a banal street scene Fragonard has contrived an amusing comedy of manners involving several small episodes, in which refined psychological observation is blended with humor as well as tenderness.

211   Head of a Young Man

Oil on canvas, 46 x 38 cm.

Musée des Beaux-Arts, Le Havre

Provenance
[Mme de Cossé]: sold, November 11, 1778, no. 95: "Joseph Vien et Honoré Fragonard. Une tête de vieillard et une tête de jeune homme, tableaux faisant pendans" [H. 43.2 x W. 35.1 cm.] (?); Hippolyte Walferdin (1795–1880): sold posthumously, April 12–16, 1880, no. 51 (for 610 francs); de Beurnonville: sold, May 9–16, 1881, no. 70 (for 400 francs); Mme Charras (according to P.); acquired by Le Havre, 1881 (for 480 francs).

Exhibitions
Paris, 1931 (*Province*), no. 17

New York, 1967, no. 71, ill.
Brussels, 1975, no. 42, ill. p. 83

Bibliography
P. p. 290
N. p. 115
Nicolle, 1931, p. 23
Réau, 1931, p. 92
R. p. 182
W. 483, pl. 110
Thuillier, 1967, p. 107, colorpl. p. 40

London exhibition catalogue, 1968, under no. 247
W. and M. 512, ill.

Related works
This painting is a study for the first version of the *Retour au logis* (see figure 1; W. 453, fig. 189); two other, later versions are known: W. 454, fig. 190 (see figure 2) and W. 455, pl. 99 (see figure 3). J. G. Huck also made an engraving of this composition (P. p. 328, no. 103), which dates from 1777.
   A drawing for the first version (see figure 4; A. 36, fig. 11) also exists.

Figure 1. Fragonard. *Le Retour au logis.*
Private collection, Paris

Figure 2. Fragonard. *Le Retour au logis.*
Private collection, Switzerland

Figure 3. Fragonard. *Le Retour au logis.*
Private collection, New York

Figure 4. Fragonard. *Le Retour au logis.*
Whereabouts unknown

This painting may have been included in the sale of the Cossé collection in 1778. It is curious that, according to the catalogue, Fragonard's *Head of a Young Man* was sold as the pendant to a *Head of an Old Man* by Vien. It will be remembered that the latter had taken over from Fragonard the commission to decorate the Comtesse du Barry's *Pavillon neuf* at Louveciennes. Thus, two styles, two concepts of painting, came face-to-face.

The Le Havre study was used by Fragonard for the first version of his painting *Le Retour au logis* (in a private collection, Paris), for the head of the young father, who bends, smiling, toward the cradle of his newborn son. The only modification is the broad felt hat, which is absent in the study but is taken directly from a drawing in the Musée des Beaux-Arts, Besançon (see the following entry).

Also of interest is the following note in the catalogue of the sale of the "M. de la Mure" collection in 1791 (April 19; no. 58), which included what seems to have been a preparatory drawing (we have been unable to trace this drawing): "a first version of a subject suggested by the Miss Sara novel, representing a loving mother and her husband contemplat-

ing their baby sleeping in a cradle." Allusions to the (then famous) sentimental tale by Saint-Lambert (the lover of Mme du Châtelet), *Sara Th,* published in 1765 and frequently reissued thereafter, are not rare in eighteenth-century sales catalogues. Thus, the sales catalogue of the Leroy de Senneville collection (April 5, 1780) featured the *Visit to the Nursery,* now in Washington (W. 459, pl. 101), "the subject of which was inspired by the Miss Sara Novel...." In the novel the young farmer and his wife lean tenderly over the cradle of their *fifth* child (see Réau, 1934, p. 4); however, this number is only correct with regard to the fine drawing now in the Fogg Art Museum (A. 37, fig. 16), *The Happy Family!*

The impact of the present study was considerable: in two later versions of the painting (an engraving of one was made in 1777), Fragonard refined the profile of the father, dispensed with his hat, and, in general, idealized the theme. This was a first step toward the *Fountain of Love,* of 1785 (now in the Wallace Collection). Against all expectations, in a sense, Vien had won!

212   Head of a Man Wearing a Hat

Bister wash on paper, over an underdrawing in black chalk, oval (vertical), 19.2 x 15.5 cm. (enlarged 2 cm. at the top)
Inscribed on the mat: Belle tête de Fragonard. peintre du Roi. N° 158

Musée des Beaux-Arts, Besançon, D. 2873

Provenance
Pierre-Adrien Pâris (1745–1819), before 1806 (date of the handwritten catalogue, no. 130); bequeathed to the city of Besançon, 1819; Bibliothèque Municipale; deposited at the Besançon museum, 1843 (the museum's stamp, Lugt 238 c, is at the bottom left).

Exhibitions
Besançon, 1956, no. 75
Charleroi, 1957, no. 44
Gray-Besançon, ..., 1977–78, no. 23, ill.

Bibliography
P. p. 314

Cornillot, 1957, no. 75, ill. (with detailed bibliography; not reproduced in Estignard, 1902)
A. 129, fig. 57

The drawing is mentioned in the handwritten inventory of the collection of Pierre-Adrien Pâris, compiled in 1806, no. 130: "Two medallions in bister by the same hand [Fragonard] ... the portrait of his wife [see cat. no. 291] ... and a head of a man wearing a hat...." This drawing must date from the artist's second Italian trip, or slightly after. Fragonard used the same long-haired model (but without the beard) for the father in his *Retour au logis* (W. 453, fig. 189); a preparatory study is included here (see the previous entry).

213 Une Vente publique sous les arbres

Bister wash on paper, over an underdrawing in black chalk, 25 x 38.1 cm.

Museum Boymans-van Beuningen, Rotterdam, MB 1953/T21

Provenance
[de Bièvres]: sold, March 10, 1790, no. 42:
"deux autres (dessins) dont une foire ou
vente publique..."(?); E. J. von Dalberg (?);
Grand Duke Louis of Hesse-Darmstadt
(1753–1830), from 1812; Hessisches Landesmuseum, Darmstadt, until 1933 (the
museum's stamp, Lugt 1257 e, is on the
verso); Fritz Mannheimer; entered the
Museum Boymans-van Beuningen, 1953.

Exhibitions
Paris, 1946, no. 126
Geneva, 1950, no. 92
Paris, 1950, no. 92
Amsterdam, 1951, no. 169
Bern, 1954, no. 94, pl. XX
Paris, 1964, no. 114, pl. 96
Bremen, 1977–78, no. 186, ill.

Bibliography
Stift und Feder, 1928, I, no. 11, ill., p. 4
Fosca, 1954, p. 63, no. 32 ill.
R. p. 224
A. 266, fig. 93

This drawing would seem to depict an open-air auction: a vendor standing on a table displays a length of fabric, while a clerk, seated under some tall trees, prepares to note the selling price. The drawing must be close in date to the artist's second visit to Italy (1773–74), and may well illustrate a scene observed along the way.

As was his custom, Fragonard sketched in the composition with a light underdrawing in black chalk. Then, using bister wash in varying strengths, he gave weight and consistency to the furniture, the foliage, and the branches of the trees, and bestowed life and authenticity upon the large number of buyers crowding round the auctioneer.

214 The Puppeteer

Light bister wash on paper, over an underdrawing in black chalk, 29.5 x 45 cm.

Private collection

Provenance
Anonymous sale, April 2, 1787, no. 75: "un catalan jouant de la musette et faisant avec son pied danser des marionnettes . . . Largeur 19 pouces hauteur 14 pouces [35.1 x 51.3 cm.]"; Frédéric Villot: sold, May 16–18, 1859, no. 110 (for 29 francs); Hippolyte Walferdin (1795–1880): sold posthumously, April 12–16, 1880, no. 178 (for 160 francs); Comte de La Béraudière: sold, April 16–17, 1883, no. 110 (for 145 francs); anonymous sale, March 29, 1884, no. 67; Dr. Suchet, 1889 (according to P.); Camille Groult: sold, March 21, 1952, no. 33, pl. X; private collection, Paris.

Exhibitions
Charleroi, 1957, no. 37
Grasse, 1957, no. 48

Bibliography
G. p. 298 (?)
P. p. 306
R. pp. 223–24
Ananoff, 1961, p. 11 (ill. of right side of drawing)
A. 256, fig. 357

With his left foot, a piper, wearing a large felt hat, is making two puppets dance; a dense crowd of children of every age surrounds him, watching the show.

In this work, which is difficult to date, the black-chalk underdrawing beneath the wash remains clearly visible. Broad strokes of bister wash indicate the ground, the awning over a window, the dress of a puppet, and the head of a dog (at the right of the composition).

Chalk is used to suggest outlines, without actually forming them, and to emphasize a detail in order to suggest a form or a pose—thus bringing the scene to life. It is all done with an astonishing economy of means, composed with an instinct for the essentials that is profoundly modern.

215 "Comical Scene with Two Cardplayers" ("La Perruque brûlée")

Bister wash on paper, over an underdrawing in black chalk, 35.1 x 46.2 cm.

Harvard University Art Museums (Fogg Art Museum), Cambridge, Massachusetts, Gift of Charles E. Dunlap, 1954.107

Provenance
M. de [Bièvres]: sold, March 10, 1790, no. 23: "deux sujets, l'un représentant des joueurs en colère, l'autre une étude de fleuve"(?) or no. 24: "deux autres sujets dont une scène comique entre des joueurs de cartes"(?); D....: sold, January 19, 1818, no. 124: "une famille groupée autour d'une table, s'amuse à jouer aux cartes" (?); Baronne de Ruble, 1889; Sigismond Bardac,
1907; [Wildenstein]; Charles E. Dunlap; given to the Fogg Art Museum, 1954.

Exhibitions
Paris, 1907, no. 159

Bibliography
P. p. 310, ill. between pp. 242 and 243
R. p. 198
A. 69, fig. 33

Related works
A second version of the same subject, only smaller, inscribed at the left *frago,* was sometimes entitled *L'Escamoteur* (1889), or *La Petite Bacchanale* (1907 Paris exhibition catalogue, no. 209); it is illustrated in D. and V., 1907, no. 171 (see also figure 1). From 1889, it belonged to the Marquis de Chennevières, and was formerly in the collection of Dr. Tuffier (A. 68).

Figure 1. Fragonard. *La Perruque brûlée.* Whereabouts unknown

Called *La Perruque brûlée* in 1907—a title which it has retained—this drawing depicts several cardplayers gathered around a table lit by a lamp. Fortune appears to be smiling on the player seated at the right, whereas his unlucky and enraged opponent, sitting on a chest, tosses out a card with one hand (or is he tearing it up with his teeth?), while setting fire to his wig with the other.

According to Ananoff, the "figure at the left could be M. Bergeret, and the one opposite him, Fragonard." The scene would seem to represent the two men "amusing themselves at an inn," during their travels in Italy in 1773–74.

The drawing may have been in the de Bièvres collection,
which was sold in 1790; a note in the sales catalogue explains that the collection of Fragonard drawings owned by M. de Bièvres "formed a portfolio of extremely valuable and interesting studies...executed by this Artist either during his trip to Rome or after his return."

The goings-on are entertaining the bystanders, who are shown roaring with laughter—all, except for a child playing with a dog. In this life-like scene, the artist's aim was to amuse. It gave him the chance to attempt a nocturnal setting with shadowy effects, which are especially well handled in the case of the central figure who raises his arms in delight.

216 The Tottering Chair

Bister wash on paper, over an underdrawing in black chalk, 23.4 x 36.3 cm.

Private collection, Paris

Provenance
Camille Groult, from 1921: sold, June
9–10, 1953, no. 5, pl. III (for 1,655,000
francs); private collection, Paris.

Exhibitions
Paris, 1921, no. 156
Paris, 1956, no. 115
Charleroi, 1957, no. 33
Grasse, 1957, no. 60

Bibliography
Ananoff, 1956, p. 41, ill.
R. p. 203, fig. 5, p. 11
A. 92, fig. 38

Related works
A copy in the Musée des Beaux-Arts, Orléans
(A. 686, vol. III, p. 293), belonged to Alexandre-Évariste Fragonard (1780–1850) (see
figure 1).

Figure 1. After Fragonard. *The Tottering Chair.*
Musée des Beaux-Arts, Orléans

A chair in which a young girl is seated is being tipped backward by an adolescent boy. Two accomplices observe the scene with amusement; one, under the table, peeks out from behind the tablecloth on top of which the other, who wears a broad felt hat, is seated. On the ground is another hat, and a basket of flowers. At the left, an Egyptian Canopic vase, surmounted by the head of a Sphinx (the same as the vase in François-André Vincent's portrait of Bergeret; see figure 1, p. 362) rests on a long stone shelf.

The surprise of the girl, whose bare feet seem to describe a dance step, the merry expressions on the faces of the three young men, and the liveliness of their poses give this spontaneously recorded scene a charming freshness. As was his wont, Fragonard takes pleasure in confusing and in mixing adolescents' games with those of children.

He began by rapidly sketching in his composition in black chalk, then developed it with the tip of the brush, and finally added gradations of light and shadow with random touches of bister wash.

217 Deianeira and Nessus

Watercolor on paper, highlighted with gouache and bister wash, over an underdrawing in black chalk, 42.6 x 34 cm.

Musée du Louvre, Paris, Cabinet des Dessins, R. F. 0025

Provenance
The watercolorist Louis-Marie Lanté (on the verso is his signature and the stamp, Lugt 1660 a); bequeathed to the Louvre, 1873.

Exhibitions
Paris, 1959, no. 51

Bibliography
Erdmann, 1929, p. 68

Mathey, 1933, p. 185
P[arker]., 1933, p. 106
Lugt, 1949, no. 1152, pl. LXVI
Ananoff, 1956, p. 38
A. 1103, fig. 292
London exhibition catalogue, 1968, under
    no. 250
Röthlisberger, 1971, p. 83, n. 44
Varshavskaya, 1975, p. 236, ill.

Related works
A second version of this watercolor, "ayant appartenue au petit-fils de Fragonard" (Mathey), is in the British Museum (see figure 1; A. 1104; Bergeret, 1948, p. 138, pl. XXII; reattributed to Fragonard by Sir Karl Parker, 1933).

Figure 1. Fragonard. *Deianeira and Nessus*. British Museum, London

Figure 2. Peter Paul Rubens. *Deianeira and Nessus*. The Hermitage, Leningrad

Figure 3. Christian Gottfried Schulze, after Peter Paul Rubens. *Deianeira and Nessus*. Bibliothèque du Louvre, Paris

The Louvre watercolor, which, for many years, was believed to be by Rubens, was finally reattributed to Fragonard by Mathey, while the London version was reascribed to him by Parker. In both cases, it was J. Byam Shaw who drew the attention of the specialists to these two fine works, whose attributions have not been seriously challenged since then.

It is evident that Fragonard copied the famous painting by Rubens, *Deianeira and Nessus,* but two questions remain: the first—whether the Louvre watercolor was executed prior to the London one, which appears so, since the latter is somewhat awkward, and much less spontaneous—is easy to resolve. The answer to the second—namely, which of the versions of Rubens's painting, known in the eighteenth century, did Fragonard copy, and when?—is more uncertain. The painting in Pommersfelden—still in the same princely collection, today—is often suggested as the source, but Fragonard did not pass through Pommersfelden in 1774, on his

return from Italy. In fact, all the evidence seems to show that he copied the example that is now in the Hermitage, Leningrad (see figure 2)—the one after which the dealer Le Brun had Christian Gottfried Schulze make an engraving, in 1778 (figure 3), and which he sold to Prince Alexander Stroganoff. Fragonard's copies appear to slightly predate Schulze's engraving.

While trying to abduct Deianeira, the centaur Nessus was mortally wounded by Hercules' arrow (previously steeped in the blood of the Hydra). Nessus gives Deianeira his tunic, which she will later use in her attempt to win back the love of Hercules.

The luminosity of the watercolor, along with its daring reds and blues, places it among Fragonard's finest copies. The work also demonstrates intelligence of a high order in its rendering of the warm and vibrant sensuality of the Antwerp master's original painting.

218 Les Petites Curieuses

Oil on panel, 16.5 x 12.5 cm.

Musée du Louvre, Paris, M.I. 860

Provenance
Anonymous sale, July 8, 1793, no. 18: "deux petites Études touchées avec intelligence; l'une offre la figure d'un Sultan sur des coussins, l'autre des jeunes filles qui jettent des roses par une fenêtre. Haut. 6 p. larg. 4.T. [16.2 x 10.8 cm. Canvas.] (?)"; given by Charles Sauvageot (1781–1860) to the Louvre, 1856.

Exhibitions
Paris, 1921, no. 37
Paris, 1974, no. 18

Bibliography
Sauzay, 1861, no. 1022
R. pp. 161–62
W. 279, fig. 132
G. Wildenstein, 1961, p. 249
W. and M. 297, ill., colorpl. XXXI
Clay, 1980, p. 17, ill.

Related works
A pastel (figure 1) of the same composition was sold with the Prault collection, November 27, 1780, no. 34: "...deux jeunes filles a demi cachées par un rideau vert et jettant des roses" (18.9 x 13.5 cm.). The drawing has undoubtedly been confused with a well-documented work that is today in the Edmond de Rothschild collection in Pregny (A. 48, fig. 23), attributed by W. and M. to the Abbé de Saint-Non.

Figure 1. Fragonard.
Les Petites Curieuses.
Private collection, Switzerland

This painting has been erroneously identified with a work in an anonymous sale in 1793, but that picture was on canvas, not panel; it was also smaller in size, and depicted the young girls throwing roses "out of a window." Its pendant was a "Sultan lying on some cushions," which would be the same work that was described as a Sultan "seated on a sofa" in the Leroy de Senneville collection sales catalogue of April 5, 1780 (no. 218; 15.6 x 12.9 cm.); the work, now lost (but see Tokyo, 1980, under no. 52), was considered to form a pair with the smallest of the *Sultanas* (W. 335, fig. 145; see cat. nos. 219, 220). The pastel (figure 1)—first mentioned in 1780—which we have not examined, is very similar in composition to the painting.

The little panel painting in the Louvre is hardly known, and has escaped the attention of the Fragonard experts; nonetheless, it was one of the first Fragonards to enter the Louvre (in 1856), well before those in the La Caze collection (1869). Doubtless because of its small size, and the fact that it was not hung in the galleries, it has barely been noticed. *Les Petites Curieuses* deserves a better fate.

The two young girls, hidden behind a pearl-gray curtain, which scarcely covers the breast of one of them, gaze at us with undisguised curiosity. The more smiling of the two is about to toss rose petals at us, which she has taken from the basket at the right. Fragonard wishes to give us the impression that we are both witnesses to this delightful spectacle, as well as the victims of the prank being played by these mischievous young girls. We observe, but we ourselves are being observed: there is a "reversibility of stares, [an] alternation of roles, [an] effect of giddiness" (J. Clay, 1980). Yet, the scene is approached with a sense of humor; there is no pedantry or didacticism about it.

The composition is skillful and bold; the execution, of an extreme delicacy; and the range of colors wonderfully refined. Only the pinks and reds of the hands, the breast, the cheeks, the lips, and the flowers stand out against the cold grays and whites of the curtain. Fragonard has treated this lighthearted subject with the light touch of a great master.

Oil on paper, mounted on panel, 32.2 x 24 cm. (panel, 33.5 x 25.2 cm.)

Ball State University Art Gallery, Muncie, Indiana, Permanent loan from the E. Arthur Ball Collection, Ball Brothers Foundation

Provenance

M[orel or Morelle], and others: sold, May 3, 1786, no. 178: "L'Esquisse de la Sultane, connue par le grand Tableau terminé qui était dans la collection de M. de Boisset . . . " (32.4 x 21.6 cm.; for 118 *livres*); Veil-Picard (according to the curators at the Muncie museum); [Wildenstein]; E. Arthur Ball, Muncie, since 1941; Ball State University Art Gallery, since 1951. (See also *Related works*.)

Exhibitions

New York, 1967, no. 68, ill.

Bibliography

G. p. 333
N. p. 145
Wilhelm, 1955, p. 372
W. 337, fig. 146
Posner, 1967, p. 363, fig. 48
Mesuret, 1972, p. 415
W. and M. 353, ill.

Related works

A version of this work (oil on canvas, 103.7 x 81.5 cm.) that has acquired considerable fame was sold with the Randon de Boisset collection (February 27, 1777, no. 227) and with the Vassal de Saint-Hubert collection (April 24, 1783, no. 64)—the first time, for the enormous sum of 4,200 *livres;* then, for 2,700 *livres.* It has just resurfaced in a sale at Sotheby's, London (December 10, 1986, no. 75, colorpl.), where it was bought by a New York dealer for £400,000 (see figure 1), and has now been restored. This painting was frequently mentioned in the eighteenth century; for example, the catalogues of the Morel (see

above) and Vieux-Viller (see below) sales allude to it. Three other "sultanes" were cited, in 1783, 1801, and 1803: one, in the collection of the Marquis de Fourqueveaux, was exhibited in the 1783 Salon de Toulouse (no. 146): "une femme assise, appuyée sur un coude par Fragonard" (Mesuret, 1972, no. 4645); another was in the collection said to belong to François-Louis-Joseph de Laborde Méréville (sold, Christie's, London, March 6–7, 1801, no. 2: "A sultana," for 4 guineas, to Fraser; on this collector, see Boyer, 1968); and a third was in the [Lespinasse, d'Arlet, de Langeac] collection, sold, July 11, 1803, no. 252 (no dimensions given; generally identified with the work in the following entry; see also P. p. 62, who claims that La Reynière also owned a *Sultana*).

Apart from the two paintings included here, and the one that has just been rediscovered (see figure 1), a small *Sultana* (see figure 2; 16 x 11 cm.; W. 335, fig. 145; Tokyo, 1980, no. 54, colorpl.) is also known today. This last work is assumed, without basis, to be the pendant to the "*Sultan assis sur un sopha*," which was sold in 1780 and 1793 (see cat. no. 218).

Finally, a drawing "au bistre" was sold with the V[ieux]-V[iller] collection, February 18, 1788, no. 242: "la Sultane dont le tableau était dans le Cabinet de M. de Boisset." Its dimensions (37.8 x 32.4 cm.) prevent it from being confused with the famous drawing in the Fauchier-Magnan collection (see figure 3; 22.3 x 16.1 cm.), sold, Sotheby's, London, December 4, 1935, no. 12, ill. (see A. 192, 740).

Figure 1. Fragonard. *The Large Sultana.* Private collection

Figure 2. Fragonard. *A Sultana Seated on an Ottoman.* Art market, New York

Figure 3. Fragonard. *The Sultana with a Letter.* Whereabouts unknown

Figure 4. Carle Vanloo. *A Sultana Taking Coffee.* The Hermitage, Leningrad

Figure 5. Carle Vanloo. *Two Sultanas Making a Tapestry.* The Hermitage, Leningrad

219

Four "Sultanas" are known today: the largest, which is over three feet high, and has just been rediscovered (see figure 1), caused a sensation in the eighteenth century. It was sold for a phenomenal sum in 1777 (with the collection of Pierre-Louis Randon de Boisset [1708–1776], *Receveur Général des Finances de Lyon*), and entered the collection of another *Fermier général* and Fragonard enthusiast, Vassal de Saint-Hubert. Perhaps not enough attention has been paid to the note affixed to the painting's (newer) frame, which reads, "Comtesse Violette de Vismes." The Vismes of Saint-Alphonse, rich financiers related to the Labordes, were favorites of Marie-Antoinette.

Did Fragonard set out to paint a portrait? None of the eighteenth-century sales catalogues specifically says so. Nev-

ertheless, the young woman's features are sufficently individualized to make this likely (Marguerite Gérard has been suggested as the model, but for no convincing reason). The author of the description in the Vieux-Viller collection sales catalogue (1786), which featured a study for the *Sultana*, notes that "Fragonard made several variations after...this first design." Two of these "variations" are included here (see the following entry). The drawing (figure 3), and the smallest painted version known (figure 2) have several aspects in common that set them apart from the others (for example, the two sultanas cross their legs in a similar fashion). In the larger version (figure 1), Fragonard has modified the inclination of the young woman's head, and has eliminated the customarily included letter.

Figure 6. Carle Vanloo. *A Sultana
Playing a Stringed Instrument.*
Private collection, Paris

Figure 7. Carle Vanloo. *A Pasha Having His
Mistress's Portrait Painted.* Virginia Museum of
Fine Arts, Richmond

The subject is a girl of barely sixteen, seated on an otto-man (this type of couch was very fashionable at the time of Louis XVI), with one elbow resting on a cushion at the back. She is dressed as a "sultana," in the traditional bouffant pantaloons, with a wide sash studded with cabochon glass beads. A double strand of pearls adorns her neck. The Turkish influence was very much in favor throughout the eighteenth century (see Boppe, 1911). The theater, in particular (Boppe, 1905, p. 229), was much preoccupied with "turqueries," as were painters. Carle Vanloo, Fragonard's master, executed for Mme de Pompadour his famous "*Sultane prenant du café, représentée sous les traits de madame de Pompadour*" (figure 4) and "*Deux sultanes travaillant à la tapisserie*" (figure 5) (shown at the Salon of 1755; today in the Hermitage), as well as a *Sultana Playing a Stringed Instrument* (figure 6), commissioned by the marquise for her

Château de Bellevue in 1754 (the last was sold at Christie's, London, April 2, 1976, no. 71, ill.). These works obviously differ considerably from Fragonard's paintings, but they belong to the same genre, midway between portrait and pure fantasy. Another such example is *A Pasha Having His Mistress's Portrait Painted,* exhibited at the Salon of 1737 (see figure 7).

The Muncie version, painted on paper, is—as the author of the 1786 sales catalogue of the Morel collection wrote—a work of the "most brilliant color and of the most fluid brushwork.... She seems to be reflecting with interest on the contents of the letter that she holds in her right hand."

The sultana's picturesque costume and her exotic, gaudy jewelry came to have an appeal for Fragonard, who, not without a certain humor, yielded to contemporary fashion.

220   The Sultana with Pearls

Oil on canvas, 47.5 x 38.5 cm.

Private collection

Provenance
See the *Related works*, in the previous entry, for a possible provenance for this painting; [Wildenstein, 1956]; Baronne von Cramm, New York, 1960: sold, Sotheby's, London, June 24, 1964, no. 40, ill.; [Wildenstein]; private collection.

Exhibitions
Tokyo, 1980, no. 52, colorpl.

Bibliography
R. p. 163 (with an old and erroneous provenance)
W. 336, pl. 67
W. and M. 352, ill.

Related works
See the previous entry.

Figure 1. Charles-Amédée Vanloo.
La Toilette d'une sultane. Musée du Louvre,
Paris

This *Sultana* is particularly remarkable for its skillful exe-cution. It is only a fraction larger than the Muncie version, and very similar in details of color and composition (it differs only in that the background contains the pedestals and shafts of two columns, and a gold-fringed, violet curtain). The lively brushwork of the first painting—its rapid-fire tech-nique, and the profusion of strokes that accent the forms and make them readable—is here supplanted by a more refined

execution that gives the painting surface the smoothness of porcelain, with all its nuances and gradations. In the present painting, every detail—the Oriental carpet, the fringes of the ottoman, and the pearls—is meticulously described. Har-mony is obtained through the contrasting effects of light with the half tints in those passages in shadow, as well as through the juxtaposition of turquoise greens with raspberry pinks.

220

Following a cherished habit that continued throughout his career, Fragonard treats the same composition and repeats the same subject in two radically different styles. It remains unclear whether these two works (which both, unquestionably, predate 1777) were painted before or after his second Italian trip in 1773. The technique of the New York painting, which anticipates that of *Le Verrou* (cat. no. 236), would suggest that the second hypothesis is the correct one. At the Salon of 1775, Carle Vanloo's nephew, Charles-Amédée Vanloo, exhibited four huge canvases representing sultanas, intended for the Gobelins; two of these are now in Nice, one is in the Louvre (see figure 1), and one is lost. The four works were commissioned for the king in 1772, through Mme du Barry.

221 The Pasha

Brush and bister wash on paper, with traces of black chalk at the top, 24.9 x 33.1 cm.

Musée du Louvre, Paris, Cabinet des Dessins, Inv. 26.660

Provenance
Chevalier de Saint-Morys; entered the Louvre during the Revolution, with the collections confiscated from the Émigrés (the Louvre's stamp, Lugt 1886, is at the bottom left).

Exhibitions
Paris, 1911, no. 158
Paris, 1921, no. 209
Paris, 1946, no. 376
Geneva, 1950, no. 90
Paris, 1950, no. 90
Washington, D.C., 1952–53, no. 80
Paris, 1962, no. 100

Bibliography
Guiffrey and Marcel, 1910, V, no. 4058, ill.
Foerster [1925], pl. V
Martine, 1927, pl. 7
Boucher and Jacottet, 1952, no. 86, ill.
R. p. 203, fig. 140, p. 280
A. 757
L. D[uclaux]., in Sérullaz, Duclaux, and Monnier, 1968, no. 58, colorpl.
Bryson, 1981, p. 108, fig. 45
Cuzin, Paris exhibition catalogue, 1986–87, p. 180

Related works
This drawing would appear to be a study for the *Pasha* formerly in the Waldeck-Rousseau and Charcot collections (W. 339, fig. 147), sold at Christie's, London, December 11, 1984, no. 138, colorpl. (see figure 1).
Two drawings in private collections are associated with this painting: one, in Paris (see figure 2; A. 50, fig. 24), and the other, in New York (see figure 3).

Figure 1. Fragonard. *The Pasha.*
Whereabouts unknown

Figure 2. Fragonard. *The Pasha.*
Private collection, Paris

Figure 3. Fragonard. *The Pasha.*
Private collection, New York

This drawing is both famous and exceptional. Executed in bister wash (with brush only), it is nothing if not surprising. Recently, Jean-Pierre Cuzin has suggested that it be re-ascribed to Jean-Baptiste Leprince (1734–1781; for a discussion of Leprince and Fragonard, see cat. no. 113). Quite apart from the fact that Leprince never attained this level of quality, the links between the Louvre drawing, the painting of the same subject (see figure 1), and, above all, the two preparatory drawings (figures 2, 3) would seem too close to overturn its traditional attribution.

Here, Rembrandt's influence is palpable, and the familiarity with Greuze's technique evident, but Fragonard also adds his own personal note. Using only the brush—like a Chinese calligrapher—he captures a gesture, indicates a volume, and emphasizes a fold. The *Pasha* is yet another example of the artist's virtuosity and range of talent; it is also one of the freest, most vigorous, and most inventive achievements among the whole body of his work.

222 L'Heureuse Fécondité

Oil on canvas, oval (horizontal), 54 x 64.8 cm.

Private collection

Provenance
[du Barry, Radix de Sainte Foy]: sold, February 17, 1777, no. 55: "un tableau touché avec beaucoup de feu et d'un effet excellent, il représente l'intérieur d'une chambre dans laquelle est une femme avec plusieurs enfans; on voit paroître à une croisée un homme qui semble les surprendre" (51.3 x 62.1 cm.; for 1,500 *livres,* to the goldsmith Aubert); or Servat (sometimes spelled Serval): sold, also in 1777 (?); "Paris, puis, vers 1800, Charpentier" according to W. and M.; "Adrien Pâris de Carpentier (c. 1800)" (according to Sutton [Tokyo, 1980]); private collection, Switzerland, 1972; private collection.

Exhibitions
Caracas, 1977, no. 20, ill.
Tokyo, 1980, no. 56, colorpl.

Bibliography
Blanc, 1862, p. 12 (?)
Renouvier, 1863, p. 168 (?)
G. pp. 331, 333 (?)
P. pp. 115, 279, 280 (?)
N. p. 130 (?)
R. pp. 167–68 (?)
W. and M. 392, ill., colorplates XXXVII, XXXVIII

Hallam, 1981, p. 619, fig. 2
Hoving, 1982, pp. 90–91, ill. (cover detail)

Related works
Several versions of this composition are known. The one in Washington (see figure 1; W. 368, fig. 157) is exactly the same size as the present picture—and may be identical with the version in the Servat collection (1777), or with that in the [du Barry] collection sale (1777).

A small, oval version in oil on canvas (see figure 2; 19 x 22 cm.; W. 366; W. and M. 389, ill.), formerly in the Marinescu collection, has been bequeathed to Palm Beach Atlantic College. Perhaps it is the same as no. 46 in the anonymous sale, April 29, 1790.

Wildenstein (W. 367) gives the dimensions of the Servat painting as 29 x 32 centimeters, but these are the dimensions of Delaunay's engraving, as confirmed by the text of *Affiches, Annonces et Avis divers,* October 15, 1777, p. 167 (see also the Amsterdam exhibition catalogue, 1926, no. 52; the Perregaux sales catalogue, December 8–9, 1841, no. 50).

For the drawings, see the following entry.

An engraving of the Servat painting, in an oval format, was made by Nicolas Delaunay (1739–1792) in 1777 (it was shown at the

Salon, no. 311; see Hébert and Sjöberg, 1973, XII, pp. 509–10, no. 159; see figure 3 for an illustration of the artist's proof). For the critics (*Affiches . . . , Mercure de France,* January 1778, pp. 171–72) this artist's proof confirmed that Delaunay's engraving, dedicated to Cochin, was after a *painting* by Fragonard. As a pendant, Delaunay made an engraving the following year of the *Bonheur du ménage,* after Leprince (see figure 5). Subsequent engravings by Delaunay include *Les Beignets,* after Fragonard (see figure 6), in 1782; *Dites-donc, s'il vous plaît,* after Fragonard (see figure 7); and the *Gaieté conjugale,* after Sigmund Freudeberg (see figure 8), the last two in 1783, followed, in 1791, by *The Little Preacher* (see cat. no. 227) and "*Education Does It All* " (see cat. no. 226). Also in 1791, Clément-Pierre Marillier made a rectangular engraving of the same composition, "terminée au burin par Romanet" (Portalis and Béraldi, 1882, III, p. 18; see figure 4).

L'Heureuse Fécondité, The Happy Family (W. 371, pl. 74; a drawing of this subject is illustrated here; see figure 9), and *The Donkey's Stable* (W. 369, pl. 75; see figure 10) are three separate works, and should not be confused with one another.

Today, two autograph versions of *L'Heureuse Fécondité* are known to us, both oval, and the same size. (We can say little about the Marinescu example, which we have not seen firsthand; see *Related works*.) It would seem that two examples of this work existed in 1777; the one after which Delaunay made his engraving, which belonged to "Monsieur Servat," and another, which was sold in the same year. We know the precise measurements of the latter painting, but not of the engraved version.

In any case, the composition, which is the earliest of the family scenes engraved by Nicolas Delaunay, must slightly postdate the artist's return from Italy in 1774. It marks a fresh interest on the part of Fragonard in children, children's games, and family life. "*L'Heureuse Fécondité*," wrote Charles Blanc, in 1862, "mirrors the manner of Greuze," adding— along with his commentary on the engraving made after the

painting—"Here Fragonard has painted a mother surrounded by her children; she plays with one of them while the others, who are older, are occupied with their own pursuits. Through an open window, the husband contemplates this scene of happy tranquillity. Sweet-tempered domestic animals complete the picture, seeming to blend in with the delightful eclogue as if they were part of the family. A spirituality and a delicacy shine through in the drawing of each figure, and in the facial expressions that Fragonard has bestowed on them. The children are especially charming...." Launay, in 1859, called attention to the change in Fragonard's choice of subject matter, and perhaps also in his manner of painting: "...but, at the same time, a revolution was under way in art and all the young painters pursued the violent reaction heralded by Vien. It was then that [Fragonard], in an attempt to accommodate his facile genius to the

457

Figure 1. Fragonard. *L'Heureuse Fécondité*.
National Gallery of Art, Washington, D.C.

Figure 2. Attributed to Fragonard. *L'Heureuse Fécondité*. Palm Beach Atlantic College, West Palm Beach, Florida

Figure 3. Nicolas Delaunay, after Fragonard. *L'Heureuse Fécondité*. Artist's proof. Musée du Louvre, Paris, Cabinet des Dessins, Rothschild Collection

Figure 4. Clément-Pierre Marillier and Antoine-Louis Romanet, after Fragonard. *L'Heureuse Fécondité*. Musée du Louvre, Paris, Cabinet des Dessins, Rothschild Collection

Figure 5. Nicolas Delaunay, after Jean-Baptiste Leprince. *Le Bonheur du ménage*. Bibliothèque Nationale, Paris, Cabinet des Estampes

Figure 6. Nicolas Delaunay, after Fragonard. *Les Beignets*. Musée du Louvre, Paris, Cabinet des Dessins, Rothschild Collection

Figure 7. Nicolas Delaunay, after Fragonard. *Dites-donc, s'il vous plaît*. Bibliothèque Nationale, Paris, Cabinet des Estampes

Figure 8. Nicolas Delaunay, after Sigmund Freudeberg. *La Gaieté conjugale*. Bibliothèque Nationale, Paris, Cabinet des Estampes

Figure 9. Fragonard. *The Happy Family*. Fogg Art Museum, Harvard University, Cambridge, Massachusetts

Figure 10. Fragonard. *The Donkey's Stable*. Private collection, Paris

Figure 11. Fragonard, after Antonio Federighi. *Pedestal of a Column in the Duomo, Siena*. British Museum, London

demands of the moment, sought new effects in purer and more intimate scenes of domestic life, producing these delicate compositions full of sentiment, charm, and—sometimes—naïveté, which we know as *L'Heureuse Fécondité, The Good Mother,* and *The Cradle,* and which have been reproduced so often, and so well, by engravers."

The pyramidal composition, inscribed within the oval format, unfolds like a frieze. Fragonard has modeled each figure by skillfully utilizing the light that enters from the left. While his art appears to have lost some of its softness,

with consummate mastery he balances passages lit from behind with areas of reflected light.

One other detail deserves attention: at the right of the composition is a kind of antique altar, adorned with a ram's head, on which some leeks have been placed. Fragonard had made a drawing of a very similar altar in the Duomo in Siena, during his first visit to Italy (see figure 11; Rosenberg and Brejon, 1986, no. 124, ill.). Although he sought fresh inspiration, Fragonard did not abandon the leitmotivs that he liked to introduce into his work.

223 L'Heureuse Fécondité

Watercolor on paper, heightened with gouache, over a faint underdrawing in black chalk and bister wash, oval (horizontal), 33.5 x 41.5 cm.

Musée Cognacq-Jay, Paris

Provenance

Chevalier de C[lesle]: sold, December 4, 1786, no. 111: "…l'exécution en est savante, et offre partout des richesses et de la *couleur*" [our emphasis; oval, 35.1 x 43.2 cm.; unsold ?]; de La Mure: sold, April 19, 1791, no. 56 (same description; unsold ?); Mesnard de Clesle: sold, 11 *nivôse an* XII [January 5, 1804], no. 22 (listed in the catalogue as a "*dessin sous verre*"); Comte de Charmaillé; entered the Musée Cognacq-Jay at its founding.

Exhibitions

Paris, 1946, no. 378
Grasse, 1957, no. 57

Bibliography

A. Hake, 1929, pp. 440, 434, ill.
R. p. 227, fig. 89, p. 176
A. 635, fig. 697
Burollet, 1980, no. 132, ill. (with a more complete bibliography and a list of exhibitions)

Related works

For paintings and engravings of the same subject, see the previous entry.

A second drawing "à l'encre de Chine sur papier blanc" was sold with the Montullé collection, November 19, 1787, no. 70 (see A. 1949). A copy was sold in Saint-Germain-en-Laye, February 23, 1969, no. 35 (ill.) and in Paris, May 31, 1972, no. 7.

A miniature of the central figure group, attributed to Marguerite Gérard, entered the Louvre with the Schlichting collection in 1914 (see figure 1).

There are almost no variations between the gouache and watercolor in the Musée Cognacq-Jay and the painting of the same subject included here (see cat. no. 222); all the evidence would suggest that Fragonard executed the watercolor version after—and from—the oil painting.

The moralistic theme of the composition is easily grasped: the couple, their five children, and the servant girl (or a younger sister) all exude happiness—as do the large dog and the donkey. The humbleness of the abode, and the meagerness of the fare—two leeks and some apples—matter not at all. The man and his wife are simple and hardworking; their lives are dedicated to their children's education, which is the source of their happiness. Clearly, Rousseau's moralizing lesson was immediately understood, but the sincerity and conviction with which Fragonard has passed on the message will doubtless upset some of our preconceived notions about him.

Figure 1. After Fragonard. *L'Heureuse Fécondité*. Musée du Louvre, Paris, Cabinet des Dessins

224 "Demandez pardon au grand-papa"

Bister wash on paper, over an underdrawing in black chalk, 33.9 x 44.2 cm.

The Armand Hammer Foundation, Los Angeles

Provenance

Louis-Antoine Auguste [de] Rohan-Chabot: sold, December 8, 1807, no. 43 (for 15 *livres* 5); Baron Vivant-Denon: sold, May 1–19, 1826, no. 732: "une scène familière rendue avec esprit et à l'effet, au lavis, au bistre représentant la réprimande du grand papa"; Baron Brunet Denon (nephew of Vivant-Denon): sold, February 2, 1846, no. 269: "la prière au grand papa"; Hippolyte Walferdin (1795–1880), from 1860: sold posthumously, April 12–16, 1880, no. 199 (for 850 francs); Comte de Jaucourt, 1889; Sigismond Bardac; George and Florence Blumenthal, 1921: sold, Paris, December 1–2,

1932, no. 30 (for 236,000 francs); [Jacques Seligmann]; Mrs. Jesse I. Straus: sold, Parke Bernet, New York, October 21, 1970, no. 34, ill.; acquired shortly afterward by Armand Hammer.

Exhibitions

Paris, 1860, no. 12
Paris, 1921, no. 133
Washington, D.C., 1978, no. 46, ill.

Bibliography

P. pp. 310 ("La Prière" and "La Prière au Grand-Père"), 311 ("La Réprimande du Grand Papa")

R. p. 206 ("La Visite au docteur")
A. 41, fig. 19
Dalevèze, 1977, p. 11, fig. 8
Armand Hammer catalogue, 1982, no. 79, colorpl. (a complete list of exhibitions in which the drawing was featured is on pp. 17–18)

The subject of this drawing has created much confusion over the years: in 1807, it was interpreted as "a Mother who appears to be telling her Child: *Ask Grandfather's pardon*"; in 1860, it was given the title "*La Prière*"; in 1921, it was called "*La Visite chez le docteur*"; and, today, it is known as "*La Réprimande du grand-père*." (In 1889, Portalis catalogued it three times, under three different titles.)

The first interpretation seems the most convincing: the little barefoot girl, held by the arms by her discontented mother, closes her eyes, and appears to be praying while making her excuses. The grandfather, who waits gravely with his fists on his hips, tries to seem cross. A young woman observes the scene with a smile, and a large dog lies sleeping at his master's feet. "It was the gift of this very sensitive

Artist to express all manner of feelings and all forms of natural behavior," noted the author of the 1807 sales catalogue; the comment is clumsy, but apt.

After his return from Italy, Fragonard made many drawings of family life; he was a past master at depicting these little dramas, successfully rendering each participant's moods and reactions, whether false or sincere. All the attitudes and gestures, along with the interplay of looks, expressions, and poses, are perfectly observed.

As was his custom, Fragonard covered the sheet of paper with a fine network of black-chalk lines, creating a first, abstract version of the work. Next, using bister wash with the mastery that he had achieved between 1775 and 1785, he painted, rather than drew, the finished composition.

225 The Donkey's Meal

Bister wash on paper, over an underdrawing in black chalk, 34 x 49 cm.

Harvard University Art Museums (Fogg Art Museum), Cambridge, Massachusetts, Gift of Theresa Kuhn Straus in memory of her husband Herbert N. Straus, Harvard Class of 1903, 1978.23

Provenance
[Chabot and Duc de La Mure, or Desmarets]: sold, December 17–22, 1787, no. 163: "la vue intérieure d'un ancien Temple habité par des villageois; on y compte huit figures, dont quatre enfans qui s'amusent à faire manger de l'herbe à un âne sur un autel antique; à la gauche au bas d'une statue, est placée une marmite sur un feu qui contribue à l'harmonie et à l'effet de ce sujet plaisant" (for 219 *livres,* to Carrière); Pierre-François Basan: sold, December 1–19, 1798, part of no. 94: "des Enfans jouant avec un âne près d'une vieille femme et d'une jeune fille, occupées de soins domestiques, des paysans partagent l'intérêt de cette scène" (for 36 francs, to Basan *fils*); Louis-Antoine Auguste [de] Rohan-Chabot: sold, December 8–9, 1807, no. 40: "famille villageoise dans l'intérieur d'une Étable" (for 30 *livres;* a handwritten note states that the drawing was sold with the Basan collection); E . . . : sold, June 4–5, 1874, no. 141 (for 259 francs; acquired by Rapilly, for Edmond de Goncourt); Goncourt (their stamp, Lugt 1089, is at the lower right): sold, February 15, 1897, no. 102, ill. (for 14,500 francs, to Mme A. Mayer); Noël Bardac, 1910; Mme Noël Bardac, 1921; [Wildenstein, 1925]; Mr. and Mrs. Herbert N. Straus, New York, 1931; given to the Fogg Art Museum, 1978.

Exhibitions
Paris, 1879, no. 587
Berlin, 1910, no. 180 (no. 170; small format edition)
Paris, 1921, no. 135
New York, 1925, no. 104
Paris, 1931, no. 35
Washington, D.C., 1978, no. 45, ill., detail ill.

Bibliography
Chennevières, 1880, p. 112
P. pp. 201, 298, 310
Foerster [1925], pl. 26
R. pp. 206, 209
A. 3, fig. 93 (see also A. 1949)
[Launay, 1983–84, no. 107]

Related works
A copy, with one or two variations (see figure 1), is in the Städelsches Kunstinstitut, Frankfurt (A. 4, fig. 4).

Figure 1. After Fragonard. *The Donkey's Meal.* Städelsches Kunstinstitut, Frankfurt

Figure 2. *Pandora.* Museo Capitolino, Rome

Figure 3. Fragonard. *The Donkey's Meal.* Graphische Sammlung Albertina, Vienna

Two children are pictured feeding a little donkey, from the base of an antique altar on which a sacrificial scene is depicted. Closer to the center of the composition, a caldron is boiling; behind it is a statue of Pandora (the original is now in the Museo Capitolino, Rome; see figure 2). At the left, a young woman is warming plates in the steam from the caldron.

The inclusion of Pandora is, once again, a reminder of Fragonard's knowledge of Greek mythology, as well as of his sense of humor. Pandora, the first woman, was endowed with all the gifts of the gods, but her curiosity led her to open the famous box containing every evil that could afflict mankind. The evils spread throughout the world: only Hope, as symbolized by this happy family, remained at the bottom of the box.

In this drawing, the artist employed less bister, and the tonality is grayer than that of most of his other drawings of this period; it postdates the artist's return from his second visit to Italy. The old woman in shadow, turning toward the young man who leans one hand on a column, figures in other drawings by Fragonard done at this time (see cat. no. 227).

The motif of the donkey's meal is also a frequent image in Fragonard's work; besides *L'Heureuse Fécondité* (cat. no. 222), two other paintings known today, *L'Heureuse Famille* (W. 371, pl. 74) and *The Donkey's Stable* (W. 369, pl. 75), are close to a drawing in the Albertina, also entitled *The Donkey's Stable* (see figure 3; A. 6, fig. 13). A fourth, oval painting (now lost) was sold with the Prault collection, November 27, 1780 (no. 23); "a child trying to climb onto the back of a donkey, while a little boy and a little girl are making it eat some grass." Perhaps the present drawing, one of Fragonard's happiest inventions, was inspired by this last work.

226   "Education Does It All"

Oil on canvas, 56 x 66 cm.

Museu de Arte de São Paulo

Provenance
Aubert: sold, March 2, 1786, no. 73:
" ... une jeune fille vue par le dos en corset et *juppe* blanche assise sur ses talons, faisant faire l'exercice à deux chiens épagneuls, pour amuser plusieurs enfans ... " (for 900 *livres,* to the expert Paillet); Nicolas Delaunay: sold posthumously, May 7, 1792, no. 5 (with its pendant; see the following entry); Count Constantin Stroganoff, Rome (according to the sales catalogue of the Roussel collection); Mme Eugène Roussel: sold, March 25–28, 1912, no. 7, ill. (for 250,000 francs); [Mr. Locke Agnew, 1913]; Walter Burns, London; [Wildenstein, 1924 (for sale at "quinze cent mille francs," according to Gimpel, 1963), 1926]; Baron Heinrich Thyssen-Bornemisza, Lugano, 1930; [Wildenstein]; acquired by Abbis de Châteaubriand, for the São Paulo museum, 1958.

Exhibitions
London, 1913, no. 39 (1914 ed., no. 72, pl. XXXVIII)
Detroit, 1926, no. 21, ill.
Munich, 1930, no. 112, pl. 130
Paris, 1953–54, no. 20, ill.
Tokyo, 1980, no. 76, colorpl.

Bibliography
G. p. 332
P. pp. 67, 114, 276
N. p. 128, ill. between pp. 128 and 129
Mayer, 1930, p. 320, ill.
R. p. 171, fig. 85, p. 170
W. 472, pl. 105, pp. 28, 40 (French edition)
Colombier, 1962, p. 70, ill.
Gimpel, 1963, p. 263
W. and M. 496, ill., colorpl. LVI

Related works
In 1791, Nicolas Delaunay made an engraving of this painting (horizontal and oval in format; see figure 1), entitling it *L'Éducation fait tout* (it was exhibited at the Salon of 1791, no. 538; see *Mercure de France,* March 1791, pp. 83–84; Hébert and Sjöberg, 1973, XII, p. 544, no. 264). There is another version of this engraving by Benedetto Eredi, dedicated to Giuseppe Rucellaï [*sic*], which we have been unable to trace.

A magnificent drawing, known since 1787, of the same composition but with several variations, is now at Waddesdon Manor (see figure 2; A. 11, fig. 6). There is another drawing, about which we can offer nothing definitive, which relates to the principal figure group in the composition; see, among others, the Versailles sales catalogue of November 19, 1978, no. 29, ill.

226

The painting was first mentioned in 1786, and the drawing, in 1787, but both works were evidently executed well before those dates—probably even prior to 1780.

To the delight of a group of adults and children, two spaniels are showing off for their young mistress, who is squatting on her heels. One of the dogs, wearing a cloak, grips a stalk of corn between his paws; the other sports a broad felt hat. According to the author of the Aubert collection sales catalogue, in 1786, they are "doing their exercises." The same critic admires "the brilliance, the intelligence and the harmony" that Fragonard demonstrates "in all his works," along with his "vigorous color tonali-

ties." The creamy whites, Pozzuoli reds, burnt siennas, ochers, golds, and yellows, in all their nuances, are enlivened by the shaft of light that strikes the shoulders of the young instructor.

This intimate scene was clearly intended to divert and to amuse, and confirms Fragonard's interest in the world of childhood and children at play. With tenderness, he observes both the young and the not so young. While Fragonard was less sensitive to the serious side of children than was Chardin, and did not share Greuze's concern with their moral instruction, the sympathy with which he depicted their wonder and their joy is nothing short of infectious.

Figure 1. Nicolas Delaunay, after Fragonard.
Education Does It All. Musée du Louvre, Paris,
Cabinet des Dessins, Rothschild Collection

Figure 2. Fragonard. *Education Does It All.*
Waddesdon Manor, Aylesbury, Buckinghamshire

227   The Little Preacher

Bister wash on paper, over an underdrawing in black chalk, 34.7 x 46.8 cm.

The Armand Hammer Foundation, Los Angeles

Provenance
Anonymous sale: May 31, 1790, no. 180:
"un dessin très capital et intéressant composé
de sept figures: Une jeune femme [*sic*] tient
un enfant sur une huche et le fait prêcher
devant la grand-mère et d'autres enfans [43.2
x 56.7 cm.]"; Marmontel: sold, Paris, January 25–26, 1883, no. 100 (for 1,500
francs, to Clément); Richard Lion: sold, April
3, 1886, no. 40; P. Ledoux: sold, March 5,
1918, no. 27 (for 36,500 francs); Adrien
Fauchier-Magnan, Paris; Arthur Veil-Picard;
[Lucien Guiraud, Paris]; Mrs. Jesse I. Straus:
sold, Parke Bernet, New York, October 21,
1970, no. 31, ill.; acquired by Armand
Hammer shortly after that date.

Exhibitions
Washington, D.C., 1978, no. 47, ill.

Bibliography
G. pp. 300–301 (the composition), 332
P. pp. 200, 310
Ananoff, 1956, p. 32, ill.
R. p. 205, fig. 79, p. 154
A. 40, fig. 18
Gimpel, 1963, p. 22
Dalevèze, 1977, p. 11, fig. 7
Armand Hammer catalogue, 1982, no. 80,
colorpl. (a complete list of exhibitions in
which the drawing was featured is on
pp. 17–18)

Related works
This drawing may be compared with the
painting of the same subject in the Veil-
Picard collection (see figure 1; W. 471, fig.
104; for its pendant, see the previous entry),
which is also mentioned as having been in the
Aubert collection sale, March 2, 1786
(no. 74). The present work and its pendant
were later sold under the same number (5)
with the Delaunay collection, May 7, 1792.

Like *"Education Does It All,"* an engraving
of *"The Little Preacher,"* horizontal and oval
in format, was made by Nicolas Delaunay
(see figure 2; Hébert and Sjöberg, 1973, XII,
p. 544, no. 263). We know nothing of the
engraving by "Batta Cecchi . . . [Giovanni
Battista Cecchi], dédiée au Baron Ricasoli,"
mentioned by the Goncourts (p. 332).

Figure 1. Fragonard. *The Little Preacher.*
Private collection, Paris

Figure 2. Nicolas Delaunay, after Fragonard.
The Little Preacher. Musée du Louvre, Paris,
Cabinet des Dessins, Rothschild Collection

227

In 1791, Nicolas Delaunay made engravings after Fragonard's *The Little Preacher* and "*Education Does It All*" (see the previous entry). Aside from their inscriptions, several details of these engravings confirm that they were based on the São Paulo and the Veil-Picard paintings, rather than on the Hammer collection and Waddesdon Manor drawings. Although it would seem logical that the two drawings preceded the paintings, we agree with Eunice Williams (1978) that Fragonard executed them *a posteriori,* as was his habit, about 1780—definitely before 1782, the year that Delaunay's engraving of *Les Beignets* appeared (see cat. no. 222, figure 6); the two works have several features in common, and, on the whole, are similar in composition.

The author of the Aubert collection sales catalogue (1786) describes this painting perfectly: "It represents a pretty child *en chemise,* with naturally curly blonde hair; he is standing on a large chest, delivering a little sermon with an air of charming gravity; a man, who seems to be his father, prompts him so that he will not make any mistakes; the grandmother, grandfather, mother, and two other small children make up the group of spectators at the left who observe with interest this simple and engaging scene." The Goncourts added their own colorful description: " ... a fair-haired, curly headed child with a doll in his arms, preaching from a buffet with the air of a little waxen Saint John."

Each of the participants is acutely observed, and each reacts according to his or her age. The picture is classical in composition, brilliantly executed, and original in theme; above all, the artist's intention was to divert and to amuse.

228   The Rest on the Flight into Egypt

Oil on canvas, oval (vertical), 55.2 x 44.5 cm.

The Barker Welfare Foundation through Yale University Art Gallery, New Haven, Connecticut

Provenance
Sometimes associated—without basis—with
the "Repos de la sainte Famille," in the A . . .
collection: sold, April 2, 1859, no. 15;
[Mme Oger de Bréart, "ancienne maîtresse de
Richard Wallace"]: sold, May 17–22, 1886,
no. 19 (for 2,550 francs); Charles Pillet
(according to P.); Chevalier, then Mme
Feuillet (according to W.); [Wildenstein];
Mr. and Mrs. Charles V. Hickox, 1956,
1968.

Exhibitions
New York, 1914, no. 20 (according to Chi-
cago, 1933, but it is probably a reference to
the Baltimore painting)
Chicago, 1933, no. 215
New Haven, 1956, no. 18, ill.
London, 1968, no. 224, fig. 282
Atlanta, 1983–84, no. 11, colorpl.

Bibliography
P. p. 287
N. p. 166
R. p. 142
W. 22, fig. 13
Rosenberg, 1969, p. 99
W. and M. 23, ill.

Related works

For the drawing, see the following entry.

The Yale painting is very close to the one in the Baltimore Museum of Art, which is slightly larger (66 x 55.9 cm.) (see figure 1; W. 23, fig. 14; Tokyo exhibition catalogue, 1980, no. 4, colorpl.).

There is also another version of the same composition that is even larger (187 x 124.5 cm.; see figure 2), which was deposited by the church of Saint-Nizier, Troyes, in the Troyes museum (Boutillier du Retail, 1913, pp. 19–23, ill.; W. 21, fig. 12; Tokyo exhibition catalogue, 1980, no. 3, colorpl.). Unfortunately, we have no information about this work prior to 1894 (Fichot, p. 487). As to the painting included in the posthumous sale of the painter Leprince's collection (November 28, 1781, no. 125), which is frequently mentioned—it was oval, but "en travers" (horizontal; measuring 89 x 92 cm.), and more likely can be associated with the Norfolk canvas (cat. no. 10).

These various versions of the *Rest on the Flight* may be compared with two drawings in the Musée des Beaux-Arts, Grenoble (figures 3, 4; Tokyo..., 1983, nos. 97, 98), both representing *Joseph's Dream*. The evidence would seem to show that Fragonard executed a large painting on this subject (3.33 x 1.70 m.): it was given to the church at Neuilly (sur Seine?), January 28, 1820 (Courajod, 1878, p. 383; we have been unable to trace this painting). The Grenoble drawings have certain points in common with the different versions of the *Rest on the Flight*. The step, the gourd, and the staff in the foreground of one of the drawings and in the painting are almost exactly identical.

Figure 1. Fragonard. *The Rest on the Flight into Egypt*. Baltimore Museum of Art

Figure 2. Fragonard. *The Rest on the Flight into Egypt*. Musée des Beaux-Arts, Troyes

Figure 3. Fragonard. *Joseph's Dream*. Musée des Beaux-Arts, Grenoble

Figure 4. Fragonard. *Joseph's Dream*. Musée des Beaux-Arts, Grenoble

The Yale study; the slightly larger version in Baltimore (see figure 1), which is both more highly finished yet sketchier, and in a worse state of preservation; the Troyes altarpiece, which has been heavily damaged and badly restored (see figure 2); and the preparatory drawings (see cat. no. 229) together underscore the importance for Fragonard of the theme of the Rest on the Flight into Egypt. Nonetheless, we have found no record of the commission, and no mention of the work prior to 1781—the date when the watercolor (cat. no. 229) was exhibited at the Salon de la Correspondance. There are very few variations among these works, even in terms of color. In the Troyes painting, Joseph (see also cat. no. 230) turns toward the Child Jesus, whom Mary has gently lifted up and is about to kiss. In the watercolor, Joseph wears the same kind of strange cap as does the sitter in the *Bust of an Old Man Wearing a Cap* in the Musée Jacquemart-André (see cat. no. 98; the Amiens *Head of a Bald Old Man* [cat. no. 102] could be a study for the figure of Joseph in the Baltimore and the Yale versions of the *Rest on the Flight*).

Works dealing with religious themes are rare in Fragonard's oeuvre (for a large *Saint Joseph,* see *Related works*), and are generally dated in his early period, prior to his departure for Rome (1756). This date, which Wildenstein and Sutton ascribe to the Yale canvas (Tokyo exhibition catalogue, 1980, but see Sutton, 1980; 1987, p. 102), is almost certainly correct for the Norfolk picture (cat. no. 10); however, the Yale version is definitely later.

The classical simplicity and the harmonious rhythms of the masterful composition—leading us to date it about 1775 —which is perfectly set within the oval format; the play of curves and straight lines; the assurance with which Fragonard arranges his figures; the sureness in the handling of light, which illuminates the Child Jesus, bathing him in its glow, as well as the face of his mother, and falls upon the edge of the stone bench on which she is sitting; the strange cloud of vapor from which Joseph is trying to extricate himself; the golden yellow tones of Joseph's robes; the exquisite contrast of the carmine red and teal blue of the Virgin's costume—all reflect the degree of accomplishment that Fragonard attained after his return from his second Italian sojourn.

The pentimenti, which are visible to the naked eye— Joseph's gourd, haversack, and staff originally occupied a more important position in the foreground of the composition—provide proof that the Yale canvas preceded the other versions.

468

229 The Rest on the Flight into Egypt

Pen and ink, black chalk, and bister wash on paper, heightened with watercolor, oval (vertical), 42.2 x 34 cm.

Musée du Louvre, Paris, Cabinet des Dessins, Kaufmann and Schlageter Gift, R. F. 40.439

Provenance
Probably Vassal de Saint-Hubert, from 1781: sold posthumously, April 24, 1783, no. 464: "la Sainte Vierge assise et caressant l'Enfant Jésus; Saint Joseph est vu à mi corps; trois têtes d'anges sont dans l'air. Ce Dessin, fait avec beaucoup d'art, a un coloris brillant; il est de forme ovale et porte 15 pouces 6 lignes de haut sur 12 pouces 6 lignes de large [41.9 x 33.8 cm.]"; M. D.: sold posthumously, Paris, May 26, 1909, no. 18 (for 14,000 francs, to Léonce Coblence); George and Florence Blumenthal, Paris and New York, before 1930; Mrs. Blumenthal, later Baronne von Wrangell: sold, Sotheby's, London, November 26, 1970, no. 72, ill. (to Othon Kaufmann and François Schlageter); given to the Louvre, with life interest, 1983.

Exhibitions

Paris, *Salon de la Correspondance,* 1781, no. 6
Paris, 1931, no. 4, ill.
Paris, *Kaufmann and Schlageter,* 1984, no. 3, ill.

Bibliography

(see Rosenberg, Paris exhibition catalogue, 1984)
Nouvelles de la République des lettres et des arts, VII, August 22, 1781, p. 55
Bellier de la Chavignerie, 1865, p. 84
G. p. 318
G. Wildenstein, 1926, pp. 18–19
Rubinstein-Bloch, 1930, V, n.p., pl. XXXI
R. pp. 142, 188, 227
A. 1773, fig. 438

Related works

Ananoff (A. 1774) catalogues a second, pen-and-ink and bister wash version of this work; according to him, it comes from the Vassal de Saint-Hubert (see above) and Denon collections (sold, May 1–19, 1826, no. 734). However, Ananoff provides no illustration, and we have been unable to locate this drawing. A.-N. Pérignon described the Denon drawing as "un croquis à la plume et au bistre représentant la Sainte Famille . . . de forme ovale." As for the Vassal de Saint-Hubert drawing, the fact that it was of a "coloris brillant," that it was the next lot (no. 465) in the sale, and was number 5 in the 1781 Salon de la Correspondance (see cat. no. 160) suggests that it may be identified with the present work. The Denon drawing does not appear to be the one in the collection of Gustave Déloye (1838–1899; Lugt 756), sold in Paris, June 10–11, 1899, no. 55 ("ex-coll. Loyeux") and December 5, 1964, at the Palais Galliéra (no. 2, ill.; 34 x 28 cm.).

Bruno de Saint-Victor has called our attention to a second version of the Kaufmann and Schlageter drawing—a watercolor, with similar measurements (see figure 1).

We should also mention that a "fuite en Égypte" was sold March 21, 1768, part of no. 190.

For related paintings, see the previous entry.

At the 1781 Salon de la Correspondance, which competed with the Salon du Louvre (reserved for members of the Academy), the organizer, Pahin de la Blancherie, exhibited three drawings by Fragonard: an *Intérieur d'une étable avec une femme endormie tenant un chien, et un taureau qui semble étonné et ému de ce spectacle,* and two "watercolors," *The Good Mother* (cat. no. 160), and a *Rest on the Flight into Egypt.*

The palm tree and, at the left, the head of the donkey, confirm that the subject of this drawing is, indeed, the Rest on the Flight. The Kaufmann and Schlageter watercolor (for its date, see the previous entry) is of value for its fine state of preservation, and especially for the freedom of its execution, the speed and assurance with which Fragonard applied the wash and placed the figures, and for the simplicity of his composition—all of which prove that the artist was as much at ease with religious themes as with any other genre.

Figure 1. Fragonard. *The Rest on the Flight into Egypt.* Private collection, France

230 Head of a Bald Old Man

Bister wash on paper, over an underdrawing in black chalk, 35.5 x 27.8 cm.

Private collection, Paris

Provenance
Anonymous sale: July 8, 1793, no. 70:
"deux belles Études de têtes de vieillard portant leur barbe; dessins très savans lavés au bistre" (?); Jacques Doucet: sold, May 16–17, 1906, no. 27, ill. (for 2,500 francs, to Marius Paulme); J. L.: sold, May 25–26, 1932, no. 12, pl. IV; sold: December 14, 1932, no. 96, ill. (for 30,000 francs); [does not appear to have been in the Walferdin collection].

Bibliography
Mathey, 1961, p. 304, fig. 5, p. 305
A. 312, fig. 59

This vigorous drawing recalls the heads of old men painted by Fragonard about 1767. However, it must have been executed rather later, since the fluidity of the wash resembles that of the artist's most perfect creations, which date from his second trip to Italy. Above all, this old man very much resembles Joseph, in the *Rest on the Flight into Egypt* in Troyes (see cat. no. 228, figure 2).

231 The Visitation

Oil on panel, 24 x 32 cm.

Collection Gertrude L. Chanler

Provenance

Carrier: sold, March 9–10, 1846, no. 91 (catalogue by Thoré, who provided no dimensions but, in 1860, confirmed that this painting was, indeed, the one that was later in the Walferdin collection) (for 172 francs, according to Lejeune, 1863, p. 296); Hippolyte Walferdin (1795–1880), by 1860: sold posthumously, April 12–16, 1880, no. 34 (for 2,400 francs, to Pilloy); de Beurnonville: sold, May 9–16, 1881, no. 71 (according to P., perhaps wrongly; the painting was referred to as on canvas) (for 1,000 francs); M. Peigné-Crémieux (according to P.); Félix Doistau, 1904: sold, June 9–11, 1909, no. 38, ill. (for 25,500 francs); Mme Brasseur, Lille: sold, June 1, 1928, no. 16, ill. (for 205,000 francs); [Wildenstein]; Mrs. Irving Laughlin, Washington; private collection, New York.

Exhibitions

Paris, 1860, no. 145
Brussels, 1904, no. 23
Paris, 1907, no. 103

Bibliography

Bürger [Thoré], 1860, p. 348
Gautier, 1860, p. 2
Saint-Victor, 1860, n.p.
Portalis, 1880, p. 10
P. p. 291
N. p. 165
D. and V. 121, ill. (in error, the drawing in the École Polytechnique)
Revue de l'art ancien et moderne, 1928, pp. 271–72, ill.
Wilhelm, 1955, p. 371
R. pp. 141–42, 188
W. 15, fig. 10
W. and M. 17, ill.

Related works

The finished work was included in the sales of the following collections: [Gramont], January 16, 1775, no. 81 (for 3,000 *livres*); Randon de Boisset, February 27, 1777, no. 226 (for 7,030 *livres*); [Chevalier] Lambert [and du Porail], March 27, 1787 (for 7,030 *livres*); [Vaudreuil], November 26, 1787, no. 109 (for 6,700 *livres*). If we are to believe the sales catalogues, the painting was transferred from canvas to panel sometime between 1777 and 1787; since that time, its whereabouts are unknown.

A sketch, mentioned in the eighteenth century, was sold with the collection of the Prince de Conti: April 8, 1777, no. 755 (for 2,501 *livres*); [Calonne]: April 21, 1788, no. 173, and again, in London, March 23–28, 1795, no. 24 (for 80 English pounds; no dimensions given; perhaps the finished painting; Calonne, according to the catalogue, would have acquired it for 250 *louis d'or*, 6,000 *livres*!). This work was an oil on canvas, and measured 24.3 x 32.4 centimeters.

Several *Visitation*s by Fragonard were mentioned in nineteenth-century sales (see *Provenance*, above, and the sales of the following collections: Laneuville, June 5–7, 1826, no. 147; Laperlier, February 17–18, 1879, no. 15 [25 x 32 cm.]; Beurnonville, May 9–16, 1881, no. 72 [originally, according to the catalogue, in the Laperlier collection; 25 x 32 cm.]; Alexandre Dumas, May 12–13, 1892 [the catalogue has not been found]; and Eugène Kraemer, May 5–6, 1913, no. 38. The catalogues accompanying these sales did not always distinguish between examples in oil on panel and in oil on canvas [the painting in the sale of the Robert de Saint-Victor collection, November 26, 1822–January 7, 1823—often cited—was an oil on panel representation of an "Annonciation"]).

W. reproduces two sketches—the one included here and a second (see figure 1; W. 14, fig. 9), which is not the same as that in the Kraemer collection sale (see figure 2) in 1913 (Wilhelm, 1955, p. 365, fig. 2)—and mentions another (see also W. and M. 16) that is perhaps the one sold December 12, 1966, no. 56, ill. (see figure 3).

P. (p. 291) refers to yet another, at the house of "M. Trumet de Fontarce."

Finally, we reproduce the École Polytechnique drawing (see figure 4; A. 1027, fig. 719), which was confiscated during the Revolution from the Prince de Condé at Chantilly; today, this drawing is in an extremely damaged and faded condition.

Figure 1. Fragonard. *The Visitation.* Whereabouts unknown

Figure 2. Attributed to Fragonard. *The Visitation.* Whereabouts unknown

Figure 3. Fragonard. *The Visitation.* Whereabouts unknown

Figure 4. Fragonard. *The Visitation.* École Polytechnique, Massy-Palaiseau

Of all of the compositions by Fragonard, *The Visitation* is one of the few that is mentioned by nearly all of his eighteenth-century biographers. The price commanded by this painting at the sale of the Randon de Boisset collection in 1777 caused a sensation. Le Carpentier, writing in 1821 (II, p. 282), remembered it well. Rémy, the expert at the sale, described it, in the style of the time: "This painting is of eminent merit, on account of the purity of the draftsmanship, the refinement of the brushwork, and the intelligence in the use of light." The more ambiguous reaction of the

Journal de Paris of Wednesday March 9, 1777, deserves mention, all the more so, as it is rarely quoted: "Well! Now they have sold *Honoré Fragonard's* Visitation for 7,030 *livres?* So much the better. A simpleton asked of me, Monsieur, is it meant to be night or day? What does it matter to you? Don't you see, idiot, that it is a heavenly light, a miraculous flash of lightning, that attends the cherubim, the watchful guardians of the precious tidings the Virgin bears in her breast? Can't you see that this is the whole point of the work, the very stuff of genius? *But the feet, the hands, the garments? . . .* Imbecile, be quiet. Doesn't it give you any pleasure? Do like me: I'm too entranced by its beauties to notice its defects. This painting has fetched a high price and it is well worth the money. And what charms me even more is that I am told the Author himself is sufficiently modest to be astonished by its glory. A good sign. For those geniuses fattened on pride are quite often men of very lean talent."

The painting had been acquired for the "chevalier Lambert"—actually, Sir John Lambert (1728–1799), an English merchant based in Paris, who was director of the Compagnie des Mers du Sud. Lambert was the "Englishman" to whom several early biographies refer (Landon, 1832, p. 93). Lauded by Thiéry (1786, I, p. 189: "a painting the effect of whose magical execution cannot be too highly praised") as well as by John Trumbull, the American colonel-*cum*-painter (1953, pp. 119–20: "a most striking picture, small;

The effect aerial, mystical, etc. . . . cost three hundred pounds"), it is regrettable that the picture is now lost.

The present fine sketch is some consolation for the disappearance of the finished painting. When this was displayed to the public in 1860, it, too, provoked much admiration. Théophile Gautier saw in it "the light, the refinement and the charm of a Tiepolo." Thoré found it "a small masterpiece of extreme delicacy and of the most harmonious color," while Paul de Saint-Victor called it "a pearl, radiating an aureole of light." All of the critics of the past are profuse in their praise of the *Coresus and Callirhoë,* which was exhibited at the Salon of 1765. Like Lenoir (1816, p. 420), they mostly go on to say: " . . . next he painted the *Visitation of the Virgin* for the Duc de Gramont" (doubtless, Antoine-Antonin, Choiseul's brother-in-law). From this reference, and from similar passages in other writings, a serious misunderstanding has arisen concerning the chronology of Fragonard's work. Hence, Wildenstein places the *Visitation* at the beginning of the artist's career, between 1748 and 1752—but it was more likely executed after Fragonard's return from his second visit to Italy. The admiration of the public must have convinced Fragonard that he had achieved an artistic rebirth, not only by returning to religious painting, but also with regard to his technique and his inspiration. In the presence of this little jewel, who would doubt that Fragonard was still a great painter.

Oil on panel, 28.8 x 23.2 cm.

The Armand Hammer Foundation, Los Angeles

Provenance
The expert Le Brun: sold, "par cessation de commerce," September 26, 1806, no. 150: "L'Éducation de la Vierge par Sainte-Anne, en présence de plusieurs chérubins . . . " (31 x 22 cm., on wood; for 60 *livres*, to Constantin); (the architect?) Fontaine (according to the catalogue of the Hammer collection); Camille Groult (according to P. p. 276, and N. p. 164, doubtless, confused with the work in the following entry); does not appear to have been in the 1880 Walferdin collection sale; Charles T . . . , 1921; [Wildenstein]; Mr. and Mrs. Henry R. Luce, 1956; acquired by Armand Hammer, 1969.

Exhibitions
New Haven, 1956, no. 19, ill.

Bibliography
P. p. 276 (?)
N. p. 164
Paris exhibition catalogue, 1921, under no. 27
Paris exhibition catalogue, Musée Carnavalet, 1950, under no. 17 (the author speaks of an "esquisse sur toile"!)
R. p. 141 (?)
W. 18, pl. 1
Sterling, 1964, n. 23
W. and M. 20, ill.
Lee, 1980, p. 219
Sutton, 1980; 1987, p. 102
Tokyo exhibition catalogue, 1980, ill. under entry 2 of the Japanese text
Armand Hammer catalogue, 1982, no. 7, colorpl. (with a complete list of exhibitions; see also no. 77)

Related works
A large "Éducation de la Vierge, esquisse très librement peinte sur toile, hauteur 5 pieds 10 pouces [189 cm.], largeur, 4 pieds 10 pouces [157 cm.]" was sold with the collection of the painter and connoisseur Folliot (see cat. no. 150), April 15–16, 1793, no. 48.

A "charmante esquisse du sujet terminé plus en grand par cet habile Peintre [Fragonard], représentant l'Éducation de la Vierge par Sainte Anne. T. [oil on canvas]," was sold with the [Aubert] collection, April 17, 1806, no. 13 (for 20 *livres,* to Brunet).

Three versions of the *Education of the Virgin* were featured in nineteenth-century sales: those of March 17, 1852, no. 37; January 27, 1853, no. 6; and December 13–15, 1853, no. 28, but no mention was made in the catalogues of either the dimensions or the supports.

Three paintings by Fragonard of this subject are extant today: the Hammer version; the Bérard example (see figure 1; oil on canvas, 90 x 72 cm.; W. 17, fig. 11; now in a private collection in Paris, and definitely the picture sold with the Walferdin collection [no. 66], and perhaps also with the Aubert collection); and, finally, the San Francisco picture (see figure 2; oil on canvas; 84 x 115 cm.; W. 19, pl. 2). The last painting was also in the Walferdin collection sale (no. 65); if it is to be identified with the Folliot painting, it must have been considerably reduced at the sides and especially at the top and bottom (by about 40 inches!).

For other drawings by Fragonard on the same theme, see the following entry.

The Abbé de Saint-Non copied an *Education of the Virgin:* "tableau sur toile, esquisse d'après Fragonard" (G. Wildenstein, 1959, p. 239).

Figure 1. Fragonard. *The Education of the Virgin.* Private collection, Paris

Figure 2. Fragonard. *The Education of the Virgin.* The Fine Arts Museums of San Francisco

Figure 3. Giovanni Battista Tiepolo. *The Education of the Virgin.* Santa Maria della Fava, Venice

Figure 4. Fragonard, after Giovanni Battista Tiepolo. *The Education of the Virgin.* Norton Simon Collection, Pasadena

Figure 5. Abbé de Saint-Non, after a drawing by Fragonard, after Tiepolo. *The Education of the Virgin.* Aquatint. Bibliothèque d'Art et d'Archéologie, Paris

The idea of Fragonard as a painter of religious subjects seems incongruous, but, nonetheless, it was paintings of this type that made him known, provoking widespread reaction to his work among the critics and the general public. This was the case with *The Adoration of the Shepherds* and its pendant, *Le Verrou*, with *The Visitation* (cat. no. 231), and, as we will see, with *The Education of the Virgin* as well.

Three paintings and several drawings with the same subject as the present picture are extant today (see the following entry, and *Related works*), but it is also known that Fragonard painted a large composition, more than six and a half feet in height, of which the San Francisco picture (figure 2) may be a fragment.

While experts agree on the relationship between these different works, they differ strongly on the dates. In 1960, Wildenstein placed all of them in the period between 1748

and 1752. At the other extreme is Marianne Roland Michel (New York exhibition catalogue, 1983), who dates the San Francisco painting between 1780 and 1785. Without going into further detail, we would mention Sterling, who, in 1964, compared *The Education of the Virgin* with some of Fragonard's *figures de fantaisie* (of 1769); and Wildenstein, who, in 1921, dated the painting "about 1764." Wilhelm (1950) concurs. (See also Lee, and Sutton.)

A passage that has gone unnoticed until now (and which should still be accepted with caution) has enabled us to propose a solution to this problem. The text in question is from the *Dialogues sur la peinture,* published in 1773 and attributed to Antoine Renou—whom we have already quoted abundantly in relation to the Louveciennes paintings. It consists of a note accompanying one of "Milord"'s violent diatribes against artists who dare not paint ceilings, or risk their reputations at the Salon: "these gentlemen, who in their own circles are always acclaimed as the century's greatest men, would soon be convinced of the reverse by the catcalls of the public, if they ever descended to earth." Against whom, and against what works, is "Milord" inveighing? "This unedifying picture is an education of the Holy Virgin, and it is surely the most clumsy and disgraceful painting since the decline of the arts and of the Roman Empire" (Renou, p. 30, note n). Could this "disgrace" be the *Education of the Virgin* that was sold with the Folliot collection in 1793, "a very freely painted sketch," or is the reference to the San Francisco painting—or, at least, to what remains of it? Further confirmation is provided by the fact that, during Fragonard's first trip to Italy, he copied Giovanni Battista Tiepolo's *Education of the Virgin* in Santa Maria della Fava, Venice (see figures 3, 4; Rosenberg and Brejon, 1986, no. 214, ill.). In 1774, Saint-Non (who, in turn, copied Fragonard's painting!) made an aquatint of his friend's drawing (see figure 5). In reverse, Fragonard's composition is very close to that of Tiepolo.

However, it is difficult to date the Hammer painting prior to Fragonard's return from his second visit to Italy; the same applies to the Saint Louis drawing (see cat. no. 233). Yet, it does not seem impossible that, after 1774, Fragonard may have returned to a composition that was important to him, reinterpreting it within the framework of his new style. He had, in any case, seen Tiepolo's painting in Venice a second time, and Bergeret (1895, p. 389) praises its "most pleasing composition and very beautiful color."

Nor was Tiepolo Fragonard's only source of inspiration. Le Brun, commenting on Fragonard's painting a few days after the artist's death in 1806, noted: "The effect and harmoniousness of this composition are worthy of Rembrandt, whose genius Fragonard so well understood."

In spite of its size, the work is a monumental one, composed with classical precision. A mysterious, celestial light enlivens the colors, the raw whites, the warm browns, and especially the yellows: *the* Fragonard color *par excellence*. The simple daring with which the artist repeats the theme elicits admiration, as do the beauty of the faces—the pensive Saint Anne, her features marked by age and experience, meditating over her bible, and the Virgin, whose expression blends confidence and questioning—and the quality of the dialogue that unites mother and daughter.

233   The Education of the Virgin

Bister wash on paper, over an underdrawing in black chalk, 39.5 x 29.4 cm.

The Saint Louis Art Museum, 146:1986

Provenance
[de Ghendt]: sold, November 15, 1779, no. 268: "l'Éducation de la Vierge, sujet en hauteur d'une charmante composition, au bistre, du plus grand effet" (?); Duc de Ch[abot or Choiseul]: sold, December 10–15, 1787, no. 268: "l'Éducation de la Sainte Vierge, par Sainte Anne; on voit en haut un groupe d'Anges. Dessin capital d'un grand effet, lavé de bistre sur papier blanc" (?); François Marcille *père*: sold, March 4, 1857, no. 66: "l'éducation de la Vierge. Dessin à l'encre de Chine" (?); Camille Groult, 1889 (according to P., who noted that it was acquired from Féral in 1884 for 120 francs); [Groult]: sold, June 9–10, 1953, no. 6, pl. IV (bought in); sale of works "provenant de la collection Camille Groult," February 23, 1979, no. 1, ill.; [Cailleux]; acquired by Saint Louis, through the Sidney and Sadie Cohen Print Purchase Fund, 1986.

Figure 1. Fragonard. *The Education of the Virgin*. Whereabouts unknown

Figure 2. Attributed to Fragonard. *The Education of the Virgin*. Musée des Beaux-Arts, Rouen

Figure 3. Attributed to Fragonard. *The Education of the Virgin*. The Armand Hammer Foundation, Los Angeles

Exhibitions
New York, Cailleux and Colnaghi, 1983,
  no. 5, ill.

Bibliography
P. p. 299
Connaissance des arts, August 15, 1953,
  no. 18, p. 34, ill.
R. p. 187
A. 1769, fig. 441
Connaissance des arts, January 1979,
  no. 323, p. 103, fig. 3
Lee, 1980, p. 219

Related works
For paintings of the same subject, see the previous entry.

Two versions of the *Education of the Virgin* in bister wash are known today: in addition to the Saint Louis example, there is another, larger one (see figure 1; 55 x 44 cm.), illustrated by P. (between pp. 130 and 131), which unquestionably belonged to the Norblin and Walferdin collections (A. 1770, fig. 440). It is impossible to determine which of these drawings was in the 1779 and 1787 sales mentioned above.

Two drawings "à la pierre noire" were included in the [Trouard] sale, February 22, 1779, no. 227 a, and in the sale of the collection of the [Duc de Chabot and de La Mure, or Desmarets], December 17, 1787, no. 167, but we hesitate to identify these as the drawings in the Musée des Beaux-Arts, Rouen (see figure 2; A. 1771, fig. 746), or in the Hammer collection (see figure 3; Armand Hammer catalogue, 1982, no. 77), neither of which is very convincing.

An *Education of the Virgin* was in the Hall collection in 1778 (Villot, 1867, p. 77), and one was in an anonymous sale, May 31, 1790, as part of no. 326 (see also A. 1767, 1768, 1772).

For information on the date of this drawing, and on the sources that inspired it, see the previous entry. We believe that Fragonard developed a first version of the composition before 1773, of which the San Francisco painting and the Rouen and Hammer drawings are manifestations. He took up the subject again after his return from Italy in 1774; the Hammer painting (see cat. no. 232), the Bérard picture, and the second bister-wash drawing are part of this second group of works, which may be tentatively dated about 1776–78. In the earlier works, as in the painting by Tiepolo, the Virgin and Saint Anne both look at the Bible, while, in those in the second group, the Virgin's confident yet inquiring glance is directed at her mother.

Oil on canvas, 73 x 93 cm.

Private collection

Provenance
Louis-Gabriel, Marquis de Veri Raionard (1722–1785): sold posthumously, December 12, 1785, no. 36: "... la Sainte Famille y est représentée dans un lieu où paroit descendre toute la gloire et toute la lumière des cieux, dont le principal effet se porte sur la figure de l'Enfant Jésus: près de lui est assise la Vierge sa mère dans l'attitude la plus gracieuse et la plus intéressante, et dans le fond on entrevoit à peine la figure de saint Joseph, qui paroit enveloppée sous l'éclat de la lumière céleste; sur le devant sont placés les Bergers, les uns prosternés contre terre, les autres dans l'attitude du respect et de l'adoration ..." (72.9 x 91.8 cm.; for 9,501 *livres,* to Paillet, the expert at the sale); Heurtault and Henri Leroux, Versailles (according to W. and the Tokyo exhibition catalogue, 1980); [Wildenstein, 1962]; private collection, New York.

Exhibitions
London, 1962, no. 44, ill.
Tokyo, 1980, no. 24, colorpl.

Bibliography
(see also the *Bibliography* of *Le Verrou,* cat. no. 236)
Lenoir, 1816, pp. 421–22
Landon, 1832, p. 93
Blanc, 1862, p. 10
G. pp. 258, 323
P. pp. 62–63, 123–24, 269
N. p. 165
Locquin, 1912, p. 265, n. 10
G. Wildenstein, 1921, p. 357
R. p. 142
W. 90, fig. 64
Brookner, 1962, p. 173

W. and M. 98, ill.
L'Œil, November 1974, no. 232, p. 67, ill.
Rosenberg and Compin, 1974, p. 277, fig. 22
Sutton, 1980; 1987, p. 105
Bailey, 1985, pp. 75, 78, n. 2, p. 72, fig. 5

Related works
A copy (figure 1) in the same format as the painting belonged to Bruant (sold by his widow, June 18–20, 1908, no. 228, ill.) and Marius Paulme (sold, November 22, 1923, no. 40, ill.). Exhibited in 1921 (no. 13), this copy was included in the sale of the Florence Gould collection in New York at Sotheby's, April 25, 1985, no. 73, ill.

None of the other versions of the *Adoration of the Shepherds* sometimes attributed to Fragonard (in Lille, or the Musée Magnin, Dijon) are, in fact, by him. (See also W. and

M. 98 A, a painting sold in Paris, December 14, 1960, no. A, ill., that later belonged to the Marshall collection, Sotheby's catalogue, 1974, no. 43, ill.)

An *Adoration of the Shepherds* was sold with the Villars collection, March 13, 1868, no. 35 (for 1,400 francs; see G. p. 323; N. p. 165); it is similar in description to that of the Veri painting (oil on canvas), but has different dimensions (34 x 45 cm.), and, perhaps, was a preparatory sketch.

A painting entitled "Adoration des Bergers" was included in the sale of Comte Castellani's collection, February 28–March 1, 1859, no. 120, but no additional information was given.

As to the drawing, see the following entry.

No engravings of the painting have been made.

For the pendant, see cat. nos. 236, 237.

Figure 1. After Fragonard. *The Adoration of the Shepherds.* Whereabouts unknown

Figure 2. Charles Le Brun. *The Adoration of the Shepherds.* Musée du Louvre, Paris

At the sale of the Marquis de Veri's collection, in 1785, the *Adoration of the Shepherds* caused a sensation. Its selling price of 9,501 *livres* was the highest bid for a Fragonard in the eighteenth century, but less than the 21,000 *livres* paid for Greuze's *Fils puni* and *Fils ingrat.* The expert at the sale (who also bought the painting, although probably on behalf of a collector) expressed his enthusiasm in the catalogue: "this Painting, which is as marvelous as it is sublime, is one of the finest compositions of its type ever produced by the painter's Art.... The effect of such a masterpiece is more easily felt than described, for on it M. Fragonard has lavished all the wealth of his brilliant and vivid imagination. Each individual figure has as magical an effect as that of the ensemble, so the eye scarcely knows where to alight...." While this work was cited by Fragonard's first biographers, who, no doubt, recalled the impression that it made at the

Veri collection sale, by the nineteenth century it was no longer known. Thus, for half a century the copy (figure 1)—only recently, sold with the Florence Gould collection, and formerly owned by a collector with fine taste, Marius Paulme—was considered to be the original work. Today, however, there is no doubt whatsoever that the true original is the present canvas.

When the *Adoration* was exhibited for the first time in London, in 1962, it gained the admiration of Anita Brookner, who described it as: "a smoky masterpiece, recognizably Italian in origin but with a Rembrandtesque softness and chiaroscuro."

The painting had been commissioned by the Marquis de Veri, brother of the more famous abbé, a commissioner in Rome prior to 1772, a distinguished *amateur,* and a friend of artists (Greuze, Hubert Robert, the Lagrenées, and, espe-

cially, Fragonard—ten of whose paintings he possessed; for another work by Fragonard once in his collection, see cat. no. 157). From Colin Bailey (1985), we have some idea of de Veri's activity: "De Veri's acquisitions were made with less fanfare [than those of La Live de Jully] and were concentrated in the years between 1775 and 1779." These dates seem to support perfectly our hypothesis that the *Adoration* was painted shortly after 1776—in any event, prior to its pendant, *Le Verrou* (cat. no. 236).

Fragonard gave new life to what was, in fact, a common theme (see figure 2). The composition is planned on two levels: In the foreground are the lamb, and the kneeling shepherd. At the center, on a stone platform almost like a stage, are the Virgin and the Child Jesus, the latter bathed in the celestial light that also illuminates the golden-haired Joseph. A group of shepherds is clustered at the right side of

the canvas, and, at the left, the donkey's saddle along with the horns and muzzle of the ox are visible against the scumbled background. All of these elements bear witness to Fragonard's determination to free himself from contemporary artistic formulas. The work, as a whole, is monumental —skillfully blending realism and stylization. Above all, the artist wanted us to be as excited and touched by the marvelous and mysterious vision of the Virgin and Child as are the shepherds.

We agree with the expert quoted earlier, who concludes: "We presume, with pleasure, that this painting will be viewed at exhibitions with the same enthusiasm that it elicited in M. le Marquis de Veri, and, above all, with sufficient zeal to prevent it from passing into foreign collections." On this final point, Paillet's admonition has gone unheeded.

Bister wash on paper, over an underdrawing in black chalk, 36 x 46.9 cm.

Musée du Louvre, Paris, Cabinet des Dessins, R. F. 31.875

Provenance
Duc de Chabot: anonymous sale, December 10–15, 1787, no. 273: "l'adoration des Bergers, composition de sept figures. Ce dessin d'une touche facile et pleine d'esprit, est au crayon lavé de bistre" (for 180 *livres,* to Desmavert?); anonymous sale, April 22–23, 1830, no. 86: " … étude de son tableau de l'adoration des bergers"; Hippolyte Walferdin (1795–1880): sold posthumously, April 12–16, 1880, no. 219 (for 550 francs, to Malinet); Dr. Suchet, 1889; Sigismond Bardac; George and Florence Blumenthal, Paris and New York, 1921: sold, Paris, December 1–2, 1932, no. 29, ill. (for 107,000 francs);

acquired by the Cabinet des Dessins, 1968 (the Louvre's stamp, Lugt 1886, is at the lower right). (In the lower right there is a red oval seal that we have been unable to identify.)

Exhibitions
Paris, 1921, no. 202

Bibliography
(see also the previous entry, and the following entry, *Le Verrou*)
G. p. 323
Portalis, 1880, p. 27
P. p. 293

Rubinstein-Bloch, 1930, V, n.p., no. XXXII
R. p. 186
A. 460, fig. 160
Gazette des Beaux-Arts, supplement, February 1969, p. 66, no. 63, ill.
Rosenberg and Compin, 1974, p. 277, fig. 23

Related works
For the painting of the same subject, see the previous entry.
For the pendants, see cat. nos. 236, 237.
For the drawing in Vienna (A. 462), see Ananoff, 1968 (and also A. 461, A. 1035).

The superb *Adoration of the Shepherds* in the Louvre is virtually identical to the painting of the same subject commissioned by the Marquis de Veri (see the previous entry). Nevertheless, in the painting, Fragonard modified the group of shepherds somewhat, placing the figure in the foreground kneeling before the Virgin at a farther remove and increasing the importance of the cottony cloud that separates him from the others. This sketch appears to be a very advanced study for the final composition, and must have preceded it by only a very short period.

Oil on canvas, 73 x 93 cm.

Musée du Louvre, Paris, R. F. 1974.2

Provenance
Louis-Gabriel, Marquis de Veri Raionard
(1722–1785): sold posthumously,
December 12, 1785, no. 37: "…il est
connu et gravé sous le titre *du Verrou*: il
représente un intérieur d'appartement dans
lequel sont un jeune homme et une jeune fille;
celui-ci fermant le verrou de la porte, l'autre
s'efforçant de l'en empêcher. La scène se passe
auprès d'un lit, dont le désordre indique le
reste du sujet… [72.9 x 91.8 cm.]" (for
3,950 *livres*, to Le Brun); the *Fermier général*
Laurent Grimod de La Reynière (1734–
1793): sold, November 1792 (in fact, April 3,
1793), no. 28: "…le verrouil…" (for
3,010 *livres*, again to Le Brun); may have
been offered to the Louvre, for purchase, by
"Mr. d'Arjuzon" [Gabriel d'Arjuzon (1761–
1851)], in 1817 (Archives des Musées
Nationaux, P. 5, April 8, 1817); Marquis A.
de Bailleul, Château de Rouville, Alizay
(Eure), 1887 (according to François Heim,
the work was listed in a posthumous inventory of the marquis's collection, dated June 7,
1887); Mme de La Potterie (daughter of the
Marquis de Bailleul), until her death in
1921; offered to the Louvre, for purchase, by
the expert Georges Sortais, 1922 (Archives
des Musées Nationaux, P. 5, June 14, 1922);
Mme Le Pelletier (mother-in-law of one of
the La Potterie heiresses), 1927 (see D. Wildenstein, 1975, p. 21); André Vincent: sold,
Galerie Charpentier, Paris, May 26, 1933,
no. 21, ill.; Lebaron-Cotnareanu; Spoturno
Coty: sold, Palais Galliéra, Paris, March 21,
1969, no. 166, ill.; [Galerie Heim]; acquired
by the Louvre, through a generous subsidy
from the Ministère de l'Économie et des
Finances, 1974.

Exhibitions
Paris, 1974, no. 22, ill.
Paris-Detroit-New York, 1974–75, no. 59,
ill., colorpl.
Paris, 1980–81, no. 52, colorpl.

Bibliography
(The present work is cited by all of Frago-
nard's biographers)
Lenoir, 1816, pp. 421–22
G. pp. 272, 329

P. pp. 62, 118, 192, 290–91
N. pp. 59, 124
R. p. 161
W. 495, fig. 204 (the engraving, now lost)
W. and M. 506 (ill.: engraving)
L'Œil, November 1974, no. 232, pp. 59–67
Rosenberg and Compin, 1974, pp. 263–78,
colorpl.
Thuillier, in Paris exhibition catalogue, 1974,
p. 1
D. Wildenstein, 1975, pp. 13–24, p. 15,
fig. 4
Ananoff, 1979, pp. 211–18
Bailey, 1985, pp. 71, 75, 78, n. 2, fig. 6,
p. 72

Related works
Paintings
For the pendant to this painting, see cat.
no. 234.
For the sketch, see the following entry.
Many copies of *Le Verrou* were made and
sold in the nineteenth century (for a list of
these, see Rosenberg and Compin, 1974,
p. 272, n. 50; D. Wildenstein, 1975, p. 22;
for an excellent photograph of the Penon
painting, see *L'Œil*, November 1974,
p. 65).
A copy on panel, 13 x 16 *pouces*, the pendant to an "armoire," was confiscated on 25
vendémiaire, *an* II, from the émigré Bhoir
Lantenay (Arch. Nat., F¹⁷ 372, p. 111).
For other copies, see the sales at Versailles,
February 14, 1971, no. 28, ill., and at Christie's, London, May 24, 1985, no. 63. The
version in the Baroda Museum and Picture
Gallery, in India, is cited by Wilenski, 1949,
p. 145.

Drawings
A drawing (see figure 1) was sold with the
Varanchan de Saint-Geniès collection,
December 29–31, 1777, no. 61 (for 800
livres, to Mercier; see A. 2002, fig. 549).
This is the drawing for which Fragonard
signed a certificate of authenticity (see figure
2) on July 7, 1789 (see Rosenberg and Compin, 1974, p. 267, fig. 10); the drawing was
formerly in the collection of Baron Edmond
de Rothschild (see also cat. no. 238).
Another drawing was included in the M.…
sale, November 15, 1784 (postponed from
the 11th), no. 155 (for 96 *livres*). According
to the sales catalogue, the drawing was
squared (see A. 2005; for its pendant, see
cat. no. 238).

A third drawing was sold with the Morel
collection, April 19, 1786, no. 377 (for 300
livres), and, perhaps, with the Boyer de Fons
Colombe collection, January 18, 1790, no.
190 (see A. 2003).
The drawing from the Walferdin and the
Beurdeley collections (A. 2004, fig. 550),
sold in New York, at Sotheby's, January 16,
1985 (no. 149, colorpl.) is today on the
London art market (see figure 3).
A "huile et gouache sur papier collé sur
carton" was included in the exhibition in
Bern (no. 103; see A. 2006; a photograph of
this work is in the Courtauld Institute of Art,
London). See figure 4 for A. 2007, which is
reproduced in Rosenberg and Compin, 1974,
p. 269, fig. 14. For other drawings on this
subject by or after Fragonard, see Rosenberg
and Compin, 1974, p. 272, n. 50.

Engravings
Maurice Blot (1753–1818) made an engraving (see figure 5) after the painting in 1784
(Roux, 1934, III, pp. 59–60, no. 10); it was
announced in the May 1, 1784, *Journal de
Paris*, in the May 11 *Gazette de France*, and
in the June 5 *Mercure de France* (p. 37).
See also a text by the director of *Affiches,
Annonces et Avis divers*, the Abbé de Fon-
tenai, of Saturday May 8, 1784 (p. 272); the
letter written by a reader, M. de Saint Félix;
and the director's response (*Affiches…*,
May 22, p. 300). Portalis (p. 331) catalogues
no less than five states of Blot's engraving.
He mentions the oval engravings by Louis
Binet and Pierre-Adrien Le Beau (entitled la
Faible Résistance; see *Journal de Paris*,
August 6, 1786, p. 903; Sjöberg and Gardey, 1974, XIII, p. 326, no. 12), and the
aquatints by Noipmacel (anagram of J. A. Le
Campion; see Sjöberg and Gardey, 1974,
XIII, p. 413, no. 1), and those attributed to
Jean-Marie Mixelle. In addition, aquatints
were made by A. M. de Gouy (see Hébert,
Pognon, and Bruand, 1968, X, p. 449, no.
21) and Laurent Guyot ([1756–1808];
reproduced in D. Wildenstein, 1975, p. 17,
fig. 5), and there were innumerable more-or-
less mediocre nineteenth-century prints. See
also the very interesting entries in *Aimer en
France 1780–1800*, the Clermont-Ferrand
exhibition catalogue, 1977, nos. 11–17,
plates 16 ("*Nous avons la clef il a trouvé la
serrure*"), 17 ("*L'Inutile Résistence*" [*sic*]).
See figures 6, 7, for two engravings that
prove the popularity of the composition.

Figure 1. Fragonard. *Le Verrou.*
Whereabouts unknown

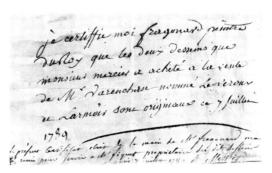

Figure 2. Certificate of authenticity signed by Fragonard.
Whereabouts unknown

Figure 3. Fragonard. *Le Verrou*. Art market, England

Figure 4. Fragonard. *Le Verrou*. Private collection, France

Figure 5. Maurice Blot, after Fragonard. *Le Verrou*. Bibliothèque Nationale, Paris, Cabinet des Estampes

Figure 6. Mlle David. *À bas le Verrou*. Bibliothèque Nationale, Paris, Cabinet des Estampes

Figure 7. Pierre-Adrien Le Beau, after Jacques-Louis-François Touzé. *L'Amant victorieux. Suite du Verrou*. Bibliothèque Nationale, Paris, Cabinet des Estampes

Le *Verrou* was acquired by the Louvre in 1974, and published by us in the same year. Almost immediately, a violent controversy broke out, which focused on the following points: Is the provenance of the painting, which we meticulously (and prudently) reestablished—it is summarized above in the *Provenance*—open to criticism? The only subsequent objections have been on questions of detail. Is the painting original? Is it *the* original? The November 1974 *L'Œil* contains an excellent résumé of the various points of view taken up by the press at the time, but in the December 1974 and January 1975 editions of *Galerie Jardin des arts*, and in the December 1974 *Connaissance des arts*, André Parinaud and François Duret-Robert, respectively, cast further light on the matter. An article by Daniel Wildenstein in the *Quotidien de Paris* of October 9, 1974, "*Le Verrou* du Louvre est un faux," will give some idea of the tone of these attacks. Even today, they have not entirely ceased, although the adversaries of the painting are now greatly reduced in number, and some of them prefer to regard this work as invented by Fragonard, and "very inferior" to the sketch (D. Wildenstein, 1975, p. 13).

As to the question of whether the Louvre should have bought *Le Verrou*, the correctness of the decision is even more evident today than it was in 1974. The painting gives the impression of having always been in the national collections; it completes—and crowns—the ensemble of Fragonard's work in the Louvre.

A comparison of the *Adoration of the Shepherds* (cat. no. 234), which is unanimously accepted as the original work by Fragonard, and its pendant, *Le Verrou*, should definitively end this controversy—much of which is also due to a lack of understanding of Fragonard's later works, and of the radical and very visible change that took place in his style of painting. From 1774 onward, the artist's choice of colors, his use of chiaroscuro, his artistic concepts, and his compositions evolved in surprising ways.

The Goncourts' description of *Le Verrou* is memorable: "This is the famous composition, this couple ardently and languidly embracing, the man in his shirt and underwear, stretching a bare, muscular arm toward the bolt of the door, which he pushes closed with the tips of his fingers; his head is turned toward the woman cradled in his right arm [*sic*], whom he envelops with a glance of burning desire; and the distracted woman, with averted face and a terrified and supplicating gaze, despairingly pushes away her lover's mouth with an already yielding hand . . . her fall is inevitable; nor has Fragonard forgotten to include in the background of his painting that which he knew so well how to open and unmake: the bed."

After Fragonard painted the *Adoration of the Shepherds* for the Marquis de Veri (see the previous entry); "and since the *amateur* requested a second [painting] to serve as a pendant to the first, the artist, believing that he was proving his genius, by way of bizarre contrast produced for him a freely executed painting full of passion, known as *Le Verrou*," wrote Alexandre Lenoir in 1816, in a frequently quoted text (in Lenoir's first draft, which D. Wildenstein, who owns the manuscript, published in 1975, Lenoir had written [p. 16],

236

"so that the painting serving as the pendant might offer a pronounced contrast, he executed *Le Verrou*").

This "contrast," and the reasons that may have induced the painter and the man who commissioned his paintings to juxtapose two works, at first glance, of such widely different subject matter will be discussed subsequently.

The first engraving of Fragonard's painting (of all his works, *Le Verrou* was the most widely popularized by such reproductions) was made by Blot in 1784. This was a full year before the original work was sold, following de Veri's death. In view of the success of this engraving, Blot decided, in 1786, to make another engraving, of a second Fragonard composition, which, however, did not appear until 1792. This was *The Contract* (see figure 8; W. 522). The original might have been the picture included in the Hautpoul collection sale, June 29, 1905, no. 42, ill., and, perhaps, was identical with the canvas in the Radziwill collection sale, June 8, 1967, no. 6, ill.: "attributed to Marguerite Gérard."

One salient detail stands out in *The Contract*: on the wall of the room in which the young man and the young woman in the satin dress meet, two paintings—or, rather, two drawings, to judge by the frames—are represented: *Le Verrou* (see figures 9, 10) and *The Armoire* (see cat. no. 238). Hence, Fragonard and Blot, by alluding in one of the three compositions to the other two, established a link among them, presenting them like the three chapters of a novel: the "seduction" (*Le Verrou*), the lovers surprised (*The Armoire*), and the resolution (*The Contract*). Yet, another engraver, who was a contemporary of Blot, wished to give *Le Verrou* a less "moralistic" pendant than *The Contract*. With this in mind, in 1788, Nicolas-François Regnault made an engraving of *Le Baiser à la dérobée* (the painting is in the Hermitage, Leningrad; see cat. no. 304).

The appearance of Blot's engraving led to the exchange of letters between the director of *Affiches, Annonces et Avis divers*, the Abbé de Fontenai, and a reader, M. de Saint Félix (see *Related works*, above), who wrote: "If you had been familiar with the painting after which he [Blot] made his engraving, you would have seen that this work is by a History Painter." Thus, for M. de Saint Félix the "contrast" appeared less surprising than it did to Lenoir. Certain allu-

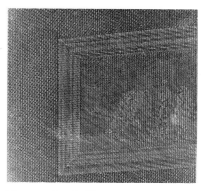

Figure 8. Maurice Blot, after Fragonard. *The Contract*. Bibliothèque Nationale, Paris, Cabinet des Estampes

Figure 9. Detail of figure 8

Figure 10. Detail of figure 8

sions, such as the overturned pitcher, and, especially, the apple, can hardly be fortuitous. Fragonard's intent was to juxtapose sacred and profane love. "The profane theme is antithetical to the religious one, as is sexual passion to childish innocence.... The parallel, far from diminishing the work, may well reveal its deeper significance" (Thuillier, 1974).

Fragonard pays homage to Rembrandt in his use of a rich chiaroscuro, but he also simplifies the composition, and reconstructs it by way of reduction, focusing on the strong diagonal that extends from the bolt to the apple and skims over the surfaces of the two faces on the way. All superfluous detail is dispensed with. The influences of Rubens and Boucher are both present, but, at the same time, Fragonard has preserved his own special vitality and élan. He

attempted to modify his artistic concepts, and gave the work that he created an unaccustomed seriousness, gravity, and emotional force. Like the *Bathers*—indeed, like all of Fragonard's masterpieces—the effect of *Le Verrou* is a cross between a pulsing reality and a sensuous dream. Yet, it is also more than this, because, in painting *Le Verrou*, Fragonard strengthened his artistic personality, changing from a prodigious virtuoso into a true creator, capable of renewing his talents. With *Le Verrou*, he attained an equilibrium that he was never again to equal: a balance between composition and execution, between sensuality and the poetry of his subject.

Not until the Salon of 1785, when David exhibited his *Oath of the Horatii*, would one encounter a more revolutionary painting in all of French art.

237   Le Verrou

Oil on panel, 26 x 32.5 cm. (the panel was enlarged by 1.7 cm. at the bottom)

Collection Mr. Akram Ojjeh

Provenance
Confiscated during the Revolution from "Coigny, émigré" (Marie-François, Duc de Coigny, Maréchal de France [1739–1821]); inventory of the national repository at Nesle, drawn up by Le Brun, 27 *germinal*–30 *prairial, an* II [April 16–June 18, 1794], no. 6: "Esquisse du Verrou, sur bois, haut 8 p°. larg 12 p°. [21.6 x 32.4 cm.] de fragonard" (Arch. Nat. F¹⁷ 372, p. 314; "Jourdan" is written in the margin; the confiscation order, signed by Lemonnier, is dated April 23); Jourdan: sold, April 4, 1803, no. 13: "l'esquisse du sujet agréable, déjà connu dans la curiosité..." (for 80 francs); B. G. Sage (of the Royal Academy of Sciences): sold posthumously, February 8, 1827, no. 43; Abel Remusat: sold, April 1–3 (actually, April 22–23), 1833, no. 17 (or 11, according to the catalogue): "Le Verroux [*sic*]. Esquisse faite avec beaucoup d'esprit [no

dimensions given]"; B[ertrand].; sold, Saint-Germain-en-Laye, March 17, 1854, no. 7 (for 40 francs, to Georges; probably bought in); Bertrand ("calligraphe académicien"): sold again, November 16–17, 1855, no. 387 (to H. D.); Adrien Fauchier-Magnan; [Wildenstein]; Baronne von Cramm, New York, 1960: sold, Sotheby's, London, June 24, 1964, no. 41, ill.; [Knoedler]; private collection: sold, Sotheby's, Monte Carlo, February 14, 1983, no. 645, colorpl.

Exhibitions
Cambridge, Mass., 1931
Hartford, 1934, no. 28
San Francisco, 1934, no. 27
Glens Falls, N.Y., 1941, no. 9 (we have not been able to verify the exhibition catalogues mentioned in the 1964 London sales catalogue)

Bibliography
(see the previous entry)
Lejeune, 1863, pp. 295, 296
P. p. 291
N. p. 124
Wilenski, 1949, p. 153
R. p. 161
W. 494, pl. 61, pp. 21, 36 (French edition)
W. and M. 507, ill.
Rosenberg and Compin, 1974, p. 268, fig. 11
D. Wildenstein, 1975, p. 14, fig. 2
Roland Michel, New York exhibition catalogue, 1983, p. 21, ill.
Figaro Magazine, "Arts" supplement, June 22, 1985
Gazette des Beaux-Arts, supplement, November 1985, pp. 20–21

Related works
See the previous entry.

In a number of its details, the sketch for *Le Verrou* (see the previous entry) differs from the preparatory drawings that have been recovered, as well as from the finished painting. In the preparatory drawings, a richly worked, oval portrait of a man, along with a sketch, or an engraving, adorns the wall of the room; a three-cornered hat, some clothes, and a fan are

lying on the floor. There is a carved wooden headboard, and two elaborate Louis XV-style armchairs occupy the foreground. In the painted sketch, by contrast, many of these details—such as the paintings on the wall and the three-cornered hat—have been eliminated; the overturned armchair has been replaced by one of more restrained design, and its mate, by a folding chair. The overall simplification is carried even further in the finished painting. All peripheral elements have been dispensed with, save those with symbolic significance: the apple on the table (which, in the drawings, has rolled to the floor, and does not exist at all in the sketch), an upset jug, and a few flowers abandoned on the ground. There are two other major differences between the sketch and the Louvre painting: the muscular, black-haired youth has become a frail, scantily dressed, fair-haired lover, while the more serious, inward-looking expression of the "victime" has given way to a wide-eyed stare.

A comparison of the color scheme of the sketch and that of the final painting reveals a striking difference in their respective chromatic range. The cool tones of the sketch have given way to warmer, saturated colors: deep oxblood is used, instead of a salmon pink verging on brown; golden yellow replaces the acid, lemon yellow; and the whites are creamy, not harsh. Another fundamental difference lies in the use of light, which, in the sketch, has no important role, but, in the Louvre painting, creates the sweeping diagonal that links the bolt with the apple, via the faces and the entwined bodies of the lovers.

There is general disagreement about when the sketch, the drawings, and the original composition were executed. Marianne Roland Michel (1983) dates the sketch to 1778. For D. Wildenstein (1975, p. 13), "Fragonard made a drawing of this subject [*Le Verrou*] about 1765–70; then, one year later, completed a painting, which was called a *sketch* on account of its freedom of execution. Finally, about 1780–84, he, or his 'atelier,' took up the subject again, adopting an erotic approach that was very different from that of the sketch, and very much in fashion at the time, and this new painting was the one engraved by Blot in 1784."

It does not seem likely that Fragonard gradually developed his compositions over a long period of time, but, rather, that he was capable of changing his technique, adapting it to suit either a sketch or a finished painting. *Le Verrou* (a drawing for which was sold in 1777), or at least the versions of *Le Verrou* known to us all appear to have been executed between 1776 and 1779. The many drawings and the magnificent oil sketch in any case indicate the importance that Fragonard attached to this work, and bear witness to the extent of his ambition.

238 The Armoire

Bister wash on paper, over an underdrawing in black chalk, 34 x 46.5 cm.

Kunsthalle, Hamburg, Kupferstichkabinett, Inv. 24005

Provenance
Part of the Hamburg museum's collections, from the end of the nineteenth century (after 1869, but before 1913).

Bibliography
Unpublished

Related works
Paintings
W. and M. (no. 508) do not exclude the possibility that Fragonard could have executed a painting on this theme, and mention a copy in a private collection. A copy on panel, 13 x 16 *pouces*, was confiscated the 25 *vendémiaire, an* II, from the émigré Bhoir Lantenay (Arch. Nat. F¹⁷ 372, p. 111; see cat. no. 236).

Drawings
Ananoff catalogues several drawings that are identical, or nearly the same as the one in Hamburg. The most celebrated of these, which varies in several respects from the engraving, belonged to the Varanchan de Saint-Geniès collection, sold, December 29–31, 1777, no. 66, "un dessin fort plaisant et spirituellement composé, on le connoît sous le titre du jeune garçon surpris dans l'Armoire [37.8 x 24.3 cm.]" (for 900 *livres*, to Mercier). This is the drawing for which Fragonard signed a certificate of authenticity on July 7, 1789 (see cat. no. 236, figure 2), and which formerly belonged to the Edmond de Rothschild collection (see figure 1; A. 1987, fig. 542).

Another drawing, of a curiously square format (10 x 10 *pouces*), was sold November 15 (postponed from the 11th), 1784, no. 156: "un autre . . . sous le nom de l'Armoire" (the pendant to a *Verrou*; see A. 1986).

There are four additional drawings: one (A. 1985) today in the Ian Woodner collection, New York, on which we can offer no opinion; A. 683 (see Tokyo exhibition catalogue, 1980, no. 131, ill.); A. 684; and a drawing sold, June 10, 1975, no. 11, ill.; the attribution to Fragonard of these last three works has been rejected by Ananoff.

Engravings
Fragonard himself made an engraving of this composition (see G. Wildenstein, 1956, no. XXIII, ill., who mentions four states, the last of which is in the Baltimore . . . exhibition catalogue, 1984–85, no. 76, ill., with an entry by Victor Carlson). The engraving (figure 2), signed and dated 1778 (the second state), was announced by the *Journal de Paris*, November 27, 1778, no. 331, p. 1333; it was copied by Coron (Roux, 1946, V) in 1779, by Robert Delaunay (1749–1814) in 1785 (Hébert and Sjöberg, 1973, XII, p. 574, no. 73), by Laurent Guyot (Portalis and Béraldi, 1881, II, p. 367, no. 2), and by Campion [or Le Campion] without the hat! (see P. p. 322, no. 15; G. Wildenstein, 1956), among others.

For the inclusion of *The Armoire* in *The Contract*, see cat. no. 236.

Figure 1. Fragonard. *The Armoire.*
Whereabouts unknown

Figure 2. Fragonard. *The Armoire.*
Musée du Louvre, Paris,
Cabinet des Dessins, Rothschild Collection

Of the many preparatory drawings for *The Armoire*, the one in Hamburg (previously unpublished) seems to us the finest, as well as the most authentic; the same could perhaps be said of the version formerly in the Rothschild collection. It varies only in some details from Fragonard's engraving, "entirely by the Artist's own hand," as the *Journal de Paris* noted November 27, 1778. "The anger of the Father and the Mother who open the wardrobe where the Lover has hidden is expressed with as much force as are the grief of the young woman and the fear of the young man ... who senses a whipping in the offing." The *Journal de Paris* also expresses its appreciation of the "spice and wit liberally distributed" by the artist "in fistfuls." Portalis and Béraldi (1881, II, p. 210) were not the only critics to note that "there is something in the way that the scoundrel holds his hat that testifies to [the artist's] freedom of invention" (see Posner, 1982, p. 85, on this exact point), adding: "but what extraordinary virtuosity in the execution! What a skillful distribution of light, what verity of expression, and what mischievousness!"

The Armoire became famous and was much popularized by the engraving. Fragonard's aim, here, was to amuse: unlike the compositions executed by Greuze in the same years—with which *The Armoire* is often compared (*Le Fils ingrat* was exhibited at the Salon of 1778, and the features of the mother in *The Armoire* are like those of Greuze's figures)—this picture has no moralizing undertones. Fragonard does not take sides; he neither approves nor condemns, nor does he draw any conclusions. He only presents the essentials of a comic scene, but he does not judge, and, above all, does not appeal to sentiment.

Composed with impressive skill, as evidenced by the interplay between the two open doors, *The Armoire* is also a brilliant exercise in sheer artistic virtuosity. Note also the copper caldron, and the branches curiously placed above the wardrobe; the artist was to include these details once again in the contemporary *Visit to the Nursery* in Washington (see W. 459, pl. 101).

239   Le Chat emmailloté

Etching, in two states: first state, 22.8 x 17 cm.; copperplate, 26 x 19 cm.

Musée Fragonard, Grasse

Provenance
"M. Maurice Fenaille" or "M. Fix-Masseau," 1921.

Exhibitions
Paris, 1921, no. 269 (?)

Bibliography
G. Wildenstein, 1956, pp. 38–39, no. XXVI (with details on the examples that were sold, an earlier bibliography, etc.)
Pognon and Bruand, 1962, IX, pp. 290–91, no. 26
Hébert, Pognon, and Bruand, 1968, X, p. 107, no. 2

Related works
In 1779, Fragonard had exhibited "un Enfant tenant un chat emmailloté," at the Salon de la Correspondance. A painting (W. 474) with the same subject, included in the sales of the de Ghendt collection, November 15, 1779, no. 37; the [Silvestre] collection, April 17, 1780 (not 1778), no. 55; and in an anonymous sale, November 25, 1782, no. 54, is now lost.

A drawing of the same subject was formerly in the Edmond de Rothschild collection (see figure 1; A. 15, fig. 9).

Figure 1. Fragonard. *Le Chat emmailloté.*
Whereabouts unknown

This etching, which is very rare, bears an inscription of which one cannot help but be skeptical: "première planche de Mlle Gérard agée de 16 ans en 1778." Marguerite Gérard, Mme Fragonard's younger sister, had left her native Grasse in 1775 after the death of her mother. She went to live with her brother-in-law at the Louvre, and he taught her the rudiments of drawing and engraving. Her etching must date from early in 1778—for Marguerite entered her seventeenth year on January 24.

The real question concerns how large a part Marguerite played in the preparation of this etching, and how great a hand Fragonard had in it, for there can be no doubt that he was the "inventor" of the composition (see *Related works*). In 1778, Fragonard again took up engraving, which he had abandoned fifteen years earlier. The sureness of the execution compels us to share Georges Wildenstein's view, which he advanced in 1956: "If we closely examine the technique of this work, which was composed in close collaboration, it becomes clear that the teacher's hand most often prevails over the delicate work of his young pupil."

To judge from the engraving, which exhibits greater sympathy for the two dogs than for the wretched trussed cat, one can only regret that the original painting has been lost, for it must have been among Fragonard's most piquant offerings.

239

240   Au Génie de Franklin

Etching, in two states: second state, 47.8 x 37.4 cm.; copperplate, 55.5 x 47.8 cm.

Bibliothèque Nationale, Paris, Cabinet des Estampes

Exhibitions
Paris, 1976–77, no. 206, ill. (the Bibliothèque Nationale example)

Bibliography
G. Wildenstein, 1956, pp. 40–41, no. XXVII (with a detailed list of the collections that own a proof of the composition, a list of sales in which this etching was included, and a complete bibliography)
Pognon and Bruand, 1962, IX, p. 291, no. 27
Betz, 1966, pp. 111–14
Hébert, Pognon, and Bruand, 1968, X, p. 107, no. 3
Sheriff, 1983, pp. 180–93

Related works
The preparatory drawing (figure 1; A. 450, fig. 156), which varies considerably, belongs to the White House in Washington, D.C.

This drawing is sometimes confused with another drawing by Fragonard (figure 2), after which the Abbé de Saint-Non made an aquatint (figure 3) in the presence of Benjamin Franklin (A. 451, fig. 157; Guimbaud, 1928, pp. 166–67, 186–87).

We share certain reservations as to the authenticity of the Chicago drawing (figure 4; A. 138, fig. 60), which resembles the famous bust by Houdon (figure 5), bequeathed to the Louvre by Hippolyte Walferdin in 1880.

Figure 1. Fragonard.
Au Génie de Franklin.
White House, Washington, D.C.

488

ERIPUIT COELO FULMEN SCEPTRUM QUE TIRANNIS.

AU GENIE D. FRANKLIN.

Figure 2. Fragonard. *The Bust of Franklin Crowned by Liberty.* Whereabouts unknown

Figure 3. Abbé de Saint-Non, after Fragonard. *The Bust of Franklin Crowned by Liberty.* Bibliothèque Nationale, Paris, Cabinet des Estampes

Figure 4. Attributed to Fragonard. *Franklin.* The Art Institute of Chicago

Figure 5. Jean-Antoine Houdon. *Franklin.* Musée du Louvre

240

The drawing is by Fragonard, but the etching is said to be the work of his sister-in-law Marguerite Gérard. As with the etching discussed in the previous entry (see also G. Wildenstein, 1956; Victor Carlson, Baltimore ... exhibition catalogue, 1984–85), Fragonard's participation was far from negligible. The *Journal de Paris* of November 15, 1778 (p. 1278), confirms this, noting that the work was "engraved by Mlle Gérard after drawings by Fragonard, and under his guidance." Walferdin owned an example of the etching—as we know from the expert Féral (sale, April 22–24, 1901, no. 198 a)—annotated by Marguerite Gérard herself, who acknowledged the help of "mon maître et bon ami M. Frago."

The etching, versions of which exist in both bister and in black, bears the title "Au GENIE De FRANKLIN," and, below the image, the following line in Latin: ERIPUIT COELO FULMEN SCEPTRUMQUE TIRANNIS ("He has torn the lightning from the sky and the scepter from the tyrant"). This echoes a line from *Anti-Lucretius*, "Eripuitque jovi fulmen Phoebusque sagittas," by Turgot, which exists in several translations (see Sheriff, 1983). The allusion is, of course, to Franklin's invention of the lightning conductor. During "bonhomme Franklin's" triumphant stay in Paris between 1776 and 1785, the American politician was greeted with

open arms by everyone of note in the capital. It is likely that he met Fragonard, but there is no proof of this. However, we do know that the Abbé de Saint-Non gave Franklin a demonstration of the aquatint process, while the "tea was being prepared," "engraving a second Fragonard drawing right before his eyes" (figures 2, 3).

The composition of *Au Génie de Franklin* is not unambitious: "The painter represented him [Franklin] holding up the shield of Minerva against the lightning, which he had tamed with his conductors, and, with the other hand, commanding Mars to do battle with avarice and tyranny. Meanwhile, America, leaning nobly upon him, and bearing a fasces to symbolize the United Provinces, tranquilly contemplates her vanquished enemies" (Pahin de la Blancherie, *Nouvelles de la République des lettres et des arts*, January 26, 1779, no. 1, p. 4). An analogous text appeared in the *Journal de Paris*, November 15, 1778 (p. 1278): "The purpose was to render by means of the etching needle the bold and lively effect of the original drawing: with the same rapidity with which the drawing itself was executed. It seems to us that this was successfully accomplished." Is the success attributable to Marguerite Gérard or to Fragonard? From the above critique, one might assume that its author knew the answer well.

241 Les Traitants

Etching, in one state, 23.3 x 17.5 cm.
Signed and dated at the center: *fragonard 1778* (with the stamp of the Cabinet des Estampes, Lugt 249)

Musée du Louvre, Paris, Cabinet des Dessins, Rothschild Collection

Exhibitions
Tokyo, 1980, no. 171, ill. (the example in
   the Metropolitan Museum)

Bibliography
Lafuente Ferrari, 1947, p. 108, fig. 17
G. Wildenstein, 1956, p. 34, no. XXIV
   (with a list of collections, sales, and a
   detailed bibliography)
Pognon and Bruand, 1962, IX, p. 290,
   no. 24

Related works
A drawing, a copy after the etching by Fragonard, is in the Worcester Art Museum
(1952.5; see figure 1)—perhaps, A. 79?

Figure 1. After Fragonard.
Les Traitants. Worcester Art Museum

P. L. B. 1

That this work is dated is a rarity in Fragonard's oeuvre. The year 1778 marked the artist's phenomenal but brief return to engraving. Yet, the subject of the etching remains enigmatic. An old man, wearing boots and an odd cap, places a small bag (of gold?) on a table. A black man (with white hands!) stares intently at a seated man (a magistrate?), from whom he awaits a response. Is this a scene of usury? In what trade are the three typecast characters engaged? Contrary to Guimbaud's assertion (1928, pp. 167, 211, no. 18), the etching does not appear to copy a work by the elder Tiepolo. Nonetheless, it was clearly inspired by the world of the Venetian master (and also by the etching technique of his son, which involved simple lines with no cross-hatching).

Did Fragonard attempt to bend the technique of etching to his habitual rapid execution? Was he dissatisfied with the results? Cursorily dismissed by Guimbaud as "a hasty, discouraged sketch," the work has found a strong supporter in Victor Carlson (1984). In any case, it occupies an important place here, where the aim is to present every facet of Fragonard's diverse talent.

Etching, in one state, 23.2 x 17.3 cm.

Staatliche Museen Preussischer Kulturbesitz, Berlin-Dahlem, Kupferstichkabinett

Bibliography
G. Wildenstein, 1956, p. 36, no. XXV (see also p. 35)

Pognon and Bruand, 1962, IX, p. 290, under no. 25
Hébert, Pognon, and Bruand, 1968, X, p. 107, under no. 1

Related works
The preparatory drawing for this etching (figure 1; A. 795, fig. 704) belonged to Camille Groult.

Figure 1. Fragonard.
Interior Scene.
Whereabouts unknown

Figure 2. Fragonard.
Interior Scene.
Bibliothèque Nationale, Paris, Cabinet des Estampes

Georges Wildenstein (1956) has shown that two distinct plates existed of this composition. Illustrated here, in addition to the very rare proof of the second plate in Berlin, is the example in the Bibliothèque Nationale of the first plate (in a second state; see figure 2), which has the merit of being signed by Fragonard, and dated (once again) 1778.

As in the case of the etchings discussed above, questions have arisen about the subject and the participation of Marguerite Gérard. Can one affirm (see G. Wildenstein, 1956) that, by comparison with the *First Riding Lesson* (see cat. no. 243, figure 3), the Berlin version of the *Interior Scene* is by Marguerite Gérard, while the example in Paris is entirely by the hand of Fragonard? The problem of the collaboration between the two artists appears far from being resolved. Moreover, the quality of the Berlin proof would suggest that it was not executed very long after *Les Traitants* (see previous entry).

The subject is puzzling: three men are involved in an animated discussion; a woman, whose face registers her surprise, leans over toward a young girl who rests one bare foot on the wooden chest between them while appearing to listen in on the proceedings. A small child raises both hands to its mouth. Perhaps Fragonard's intention here was simply to improvise, and to describe a scene from life, with no perceptible subject to speak of.

243 The First Riding Lesson

Bister wash on paper, over an underdrawing in black chalk, 34.8 x 45.2 cm.

The Brooklyn Museum, New York, Gift of Mr. and Mrs. Alastair Bradley Martin, 57.189

Provenance
Duc de Ch[abot or Choiseul]: sold, December 10–15, 1787, no. 274: " ... c'est une jeune femme qui fait asseoir son enfant sur un dogue, qu'un homme retient par le museau ... " (for 60 *livres*, to Le Brun); [Le Brun]: sold, July 8, 1793, part of no. 69: "une jeune femme et son mari promenant leur enfant sur le dos d'un chien" (the drawing was identified with one called "*Dites-donc s'il vous plaît*," probably A. 600, fig. 190); Baron de Silvestre: sold, December 4–6, 1851, no. 258 (for 19 francs 50); Hippolyte Walferdin (1795–1880), by 1860: sold posthumously, April 12–16, 1880, no. 224 (for 950 francs, to Lacroix); Baron Edmond de Rothschild, 1889, 1907; Maurice de Rothschild (son of Baron Edmond); Mr. and Mrs. Alastair Bradley Martin (The Guennol Collection); given to The Brooklyn Museum, 1957.

Exhibitions
Paris, 1860, no. 8
Paris, 1907, no. 198
Paris, 1958, no. 54, pl. 72
Washington, D.C., 1978, no. 44, ill.
Tokyo, 1980, no. 129, ill.

Bibliography
G. p. 332
Portalis, 1880, p. 22
P. pp. 114, 199, 310, ill. between pp. 118 and 119
N. p. 83
D. and V. 164, ill.
R. p. 205
G. Wildenstein, 1956, p. 43
A. 12, fig. 2
Mrozińska, 1960, p. 10, fig. 2

Related works
Photographs exist of two other versions of this drawing: the first (see figure 1) also came from the Walferdin collection (no. 223 of the 1880 sale) and was rejected by Ananoff (A. 13); the second (figure 2), much smaller than the Brooklyn drawing, belonged to Ignace Paderewski, and is now in the Muzeum Narodowe, Warsaw (see Heim Gallery, London, 1980, no. 29, pl. 41). See also A. 14, 1943.

An engraving of the drawing, in reverse, was made by Marguerite Gérard (with the help of Fragonard ?), probably in 1778 (see figure 3). We know of three states of this work (the second is illustrated here; see G. Wildenstein, 1956, XXVIII, p. 291, no. 28; Pognon and Bruand, 1962, IX, p. 291, no. 28; Hébert, Pognon, and Bruand, 1968, X, p. 107, no. 4). Vivant-Denon (figure 4) also made an engraving after the Warsaw drawing (Roux, 1949, VI, p. 553, no. 189).

Figure 1. After Fragonard (?). *The First Riding Lesson.* Whereabouts unknown

Figure 2. Fragonard. *The First Riding Lesson.* Muzeum Narodowe, Warsaw

Figure 3. Marguerite Gérard, after Fragonard. *The First Riding Lesson.* Bibliothèque Nationale, Paris, Cabinet des Estampes

The subject of this drawing requires no special explanation. The bulldog, with his bell, is not unique in the work of Fragonard—who may well have been the owner of the animal—nor is the young father's curious cap. The same cap is worn by one of the figures in the rare etching, rather vaguely titled *Interior Scene* (see cat. no. 242), that is signed by Fragonard and dated 1778 (see cat. no. 242, figure 1)—thus, satisfactorily resolving the much-debated question of this drawing's date.

To a greater extent, perhaps, than in the other drawings and graphic works that he produced during this prolific period of creativity, Fragonard here uses the tip of his brush to indicate volumes and to outline faces. In the case of the mother and child, this technique proved successful, but the father's face is twisted into an unfortunate grimace.

The composition is more simplified and abbreviated than usual. Fragonard eliminated all superfluous detail in order to concentrate fully on his subject, making the best use of the white areas of the paper.

Figure 4. Dominique Vivant-Denon, after Fragonard. *The First Riding Lesson.* Bibliothèque Nationale, Paris, Cabinet des Estampes

244 ''Mosieur Fanfan''

Etching, 23.2 x 17.8 cm.; 26 x 19.2 cm. (copperplate)
Three plates of this composition exist. The first, of which only one state and one example are known, was published in 1971 by A. Ananoff (see figure 1). The second, also known in only one state, is inscribed *épreuve avant la lettre* (the example from the Rothschild Collection is illustrated). As to the third, although G. Wildenstein (1956) mentions only three states (see figures 2, 4, 5), we know of a fourth (see figure 3; sold, Paris, May 31, 1962, no. 341, ill.).

Musée du Louvre, Paris, Cabinet des Dessins, Rothschild Collection

Bibliography
G. Wildenstein, 1956, pp. 44–45, nos. XXIX, XXX (with all the information on the different states, the sales, the collections with examples of the etching, an earlier bibliography, and a list of exhibitions)
Pognon and Bruand, 1962, IX, pp. 291–92, nos. 29–30
Hébert, Pognon, and Bruand, 1968, X, p. 108, nos. 5, 6
Ananoff, 1971, pp. 179–82

Related works
A painting with the same subject (now lost) was included in the sale of the Leroy de Senneville collection, April 5, 1780, no. 54: ''un jeune enfant représenté debout en chemise tenant un polichinel [*sic*] avec lequel il paroit s'enfuir et deux petits chiens qui le suivent, cherchant à mordre une poupée qu'il tient sous son bras ... '' (W. 475; see also the Reber sale, Basel, 1809, no. 953).

For a drawing that we have not examined and thus cannot authenticate, see A. 623, fig. 196.

For a miniature after the engraving, attributed to Marguerite Gérard, see the catalogue of the Palais Galliéra sale, Paris, December 5, 1975, no. 59, ill. (see figure 6).

Figure 1. Fragonard. *Monsieur Fanfan* (first plate; illustration after Ananoff)

Figure 2. Fragonard. *Monsieur Fanfan* (third plate, first state). Musée du Louvre, Paris, Cabinet des Dessins, Rothschild Collection

Figure 3. Fragonard. *Monsieur Fanfan* (third plate, second state). Whereabouts unknown

Figure 4. Fragonard. *Monsieur Fanfan* (third plate, third state). Bibliothèque Nationale, Paris, Cabinet des Estampes

Figure 5. Fragonard. *Monsieur Fanfan* (third plate, fourth state). The Metropolitan Museum of Art, New York

Figure 6. After Fragonard. *Monsieur Fanfan.* Whereabouts unknown

244

The plate is entitled "Mosieur [*sic*] Fanfan jouant avec Monsieur Polichinelle et Compagnie." It is often claimed that the model was Alexandre-Évariste, Fragonard's son, born in Grasse in 1780 (see cat. no. 296), but this is definitely not the case. In fact, only the latest states (see figures 4, 5) of the last of the three plates bear this inscription. In addition, the painting of this subject was sold over

six months *before* Alexandre-Évariste's birth: although now unfortunately lost, it was described in detail in the catalogue (see *Related works*), and was most certainly the inspiration for the different versions of the etching.

On the basis of Alexandre-Évariste's age—since the model appears to be about two—the etching has generally been dated to 1782, but we believe that the plate was executed in 1778, like the others included here (see cat. nos. 239–242). The same question arises as to the respective participation of Fragonard and of his sister-in-law in this work. Once again, we would unquestionably ascribe the concept and the composition to Fragonard, while it would appear that Marguerite Gérard played a substantial part in the technical aspects of the execution, and in the handling of the materials—as confirmed by the notation on the examples of the first state. No satisfactory answer has yet been put forward as to why Fragonard and Marguerite Gérard suddenly gave up engraving after 1778.

The subject is deliberately a sentimental one: a very young child is trying to escape from two determined spaniels bent on stealing his doll. "Fanfan" seems to be taking his misfortune in stride—all the more so because his "polichinelle," whom he hugs firmly against his chest, appears to be safe from the clutches of the two dreadful little dogs.

Fragonard's was a fresh approach to the theme of childhood, which was very much in fashion following the publication of *Émile* in the last quarter of the eighteenth century. Effortlessly, the artist penetrated the psychology of his model, whom he portrays with tenderness and sympathy. The humor and delicacy of this work make us smile.

245 Girl Holding a Dove

Oil on canvas, diameter, 65 cm.

Private collection, Tel Aviv

Provenance

"Il y a quinze ans," wrote René Gimpel, on January 29, 1921 (published, 1963, p. 182), "un chercheur passionné d'objets d'art, lisant le guide Baedeker, vit qu'à Saint-Brice, au nord de Saint-Denis, existait encore une maison de plaisance ayant appartenu à Mlle Colombe qui fut la maîtresse de Fragonard. Il s'y rendit et y trouva deux portraits de Mlle Colombe. Je les achetai avec lui. Ils sont aujourd'hui dans la collection du baron Édouard de Rothschild"; Baron Édouard de Rothschild; [Wildenstein]; private collection, Israel.

André Vassal, the brother of Jean-Antoine Vassal de Saint-Hubert, had had a folly built at Saint-Brice for his mistress, Marie-Catherine Riggieri (1751–1830), on land that he had acquired in 1769. She sold it in 1805, along with the furnishings, to "sieur Revenaz" (Revenez, according to W.), who subsequently resold it to M. de Guy, the mayor of Saint-Brice. The mayor's son-in-law, Colonel de Mondonville, later inherited the house. The portrait was found in the bedroom: "dans un panneau qui faisait face à la cheminée, on voyait encastrée dans la boiserie" the picture of the girl with a dove in her arms. "Au dessus de la cheminée, et faisant pendant au portrait de Marie-Catherine, on remarquait un portrait rond de sa soeur Adeline [*sic*]" (Stern, 1923; see also W., for the changes of ownership in the nineteenth century).

Exhibitions

Paris, 1907 (not in catalogue)
Paris, 1946, no. 17

Bibliography

N., ill. between pp. 56 and 57 ("Mademoiselle Colombe")
Dayot, 1907, ill. p. 151
D. and V., pl. 90
Stern, 1923, pp. 51–52, 59, 283, ill. opp. p. XII
R. p. 177
Andia, 1960, p. 23, ill.
Cailleux, 1960, pp. iii–v, p. ii, fig. 1
W. 411, fig. 170
W. and M. 436, ill.

Related works

Réau, then W. and M. mention a replica that was formerly in the Davies collection before entering the Los Angeles County Museum of Art. This is, in fact, W. 416, fig. 175 (W. and M. 442!), which was sold, June 21, 1982, no. 37, at Sotheby's, Los Angeles, to a Los Angeles private collector. If any other work by Fragonard can be associated with the painting included here, it is W. 420, fig. 179, which is currently on the art market in New York (see figure 1).

For a panel attributed to Pieter Joseph Sauvage, probably from Saint-Brice, see the Béziers catalogue (Lugand, 1976, p. 34, ill.).

Figure 1. Fragonard. *Head of a Girl.* Art market, New York

Each of these admirable paintings is believed to represent one of the Colombe sisters, because the canvases were discovered at the beginning of the twentieth century in a house near Paris, at Saint-Brice-la-Forêt, on the outskirts of the Forêt de Montmorency; this house had been given to the oldest of the three sisters, Marie-Catherine, by her lover (see *Provenance,* above).

The Colombe sisters, Venetian-born actresses with the Comédie Italienne (their real name was Riggieri-Romboccoli), were the toast of Paris in the second half of the eighteenth century. Marie-Thérèse (1754–1837) was known as Marie-Thérèse Théodore, or Colombe *l'aînée,* since she was the first in the family to go on the stage; most critics agree that she is the model in the second painting (see the following entry). Marie-Madeleine (1760–1841) led as adventurous a life as her two older sisters (see Stern, 1923). The Colombe sisters (or at least some of them) were thought —groundlessly—to have been the mistresses of Fragonard, and, also for no plausible reason, attempts have been made to identify them with the sitters in many of his paintings (see Cailleux, 1960). This is partly due to the artist's habit—not uncommon among painters—of always depicting the same types of faces. In reality, we know nothing whatsoever about the relationship between Fragonard and the Colombe sisters; in the eighteenth century, their names were only linked on a single occasion, as far as we can discover. François Métra, in his *Correspondance secrète, politique, et littéraire,* April 25,

1781 (XI, p. 221), records the following doubtful and equally ambiguous anecdote: "Mlle Colombe [Marie-Thérèse], that pretty actress whose adventures I have already recounted for you once or twice, has fallen in love with the comedian Dugazon [a well-known actor, of the time]... after seeing him play the comic role of the *Roi de Cocagne.* To make herself known to him, she decided to send him her portrait. She inquired after a skillful painter, and M. Fragonard was recommended. She hurried to him, and begged him to make a perfect likeness of her. *I am very sorry, Mademoiselle,* the artist told her, *but I only do history paintings, and noble subjects. Well Monsieur,* she replied, *let us begin: we can leave the rest to someone else."*

Despite the presence of the doves, which are associated with Venus, we consider this painting a work of pure imagination, rather than a faithful portrait of the actress. The young woman who holds a dove in her arms watches a second one fluttering close by her. Fragonard magisterially juxtaposes the white of the girl's chemise and the birds' feathers with the pinks of her cheeks and lips, of the draperies, and of the feet, beaks, and eyes of the doves. A warm sunlight suffuses the scene, which is composed of a series of curves that are perfectly inscribed within the circular format. The flapping wings of the doves, the happy expression on the girl's face, and the gracefulness of her pose make this one of Fragonard's most perfect and most successful works.

246 Girl Holding a Cat and a Dog

Oil on canvas, diameter, 65 cm.

Private collection, Tel Aviv

Provenance
See the previous entry.

Exhibitions
Paris, 1907 (not in catalogue)
Paris, 1946, no. 16

Bibliography
N., ill. between pp. 112 and 113 ("Portrait de jeune fille")
Dayot, 1907, ill. p. 151

D. and V., pl. 92
Stern, 1923, pp. 52, 167, 168, 288–89
R. p. 177
Andia, 1960, p. 23, ill.
Cailleux, 1960, pp. iii–v, p. ii, fig. 2
W. 410, fig. 169
W. and M. 435, ill.

Related works
For the pendant, see the previous entry.

Figure 1. Fragonard. *Girl Leaning on a Worktable.* Private collection, Paris

This painting is believed to represent one of the Colombe sisters; some scholars, such as Cailleux (1960), have identified the sitter as Marie-Thérèse (1754–1837); others—the majority—as Marie-Madeleine (1760–1841), the youngest of the three. Like the previously discussed picture, this one, too, is not a portrait, but a work of fantasy. In contrast to the range of whites and pinks in the *Girl Holding a Dove,* here Fragonard creates a harmony of blues and whites. A blue ribbon holds the girl's powdered hair in place, a simple blue string admirably sets off her neck, and she is swathed in blue draperies. Even the white cat who claws at the puppy has bright blue eyes.

While the dating of this painting, and of the one discussed in the previous entry, is problematic, a drawing (see figure 1)

that was recently sold in Paris (November 29, 1985, no. 60, ill.; colorpl. on cover of catalogue) provides a clue. In the background of this fine red-chalk drawing of a girl leaning on a worktable there is a round painting. Resting on the floor, and unframed, it is a distinct yet hasty copy of our young woman holding a dog and a cat in her arms. This drawing is believed to represent Marguerite Gérard (born 1761), and, from the style of the work, would seem to date from between 1775 and 1780. The soft, almost pastel, colors, and the mellower effect of the more subtle brushwork in the present painting argue for a comparable dating. The sitter, seen in profile, appears to be enjoying the tussle between the two little animals that she holds in front of her, at some distance.

247 The Kiss

Bister wash on paper, over an underdrawing in black chalk, 45.3 x 31 cm.

Graphische Sammlung Albertina, Vienna, Inv. 12.726

Provenance
Albert, Duke of Saxe-Teschen (1738–1822; his stamp, Lugt 174, is at the bottom left); part of the original collection of the Albertina.

Exhibitions
Paris, 1931, no. 11
Vienna, 1950, no. 127
Bern, 1954, no. 98

Bibliography
Meder, 1922, pl. 22

Leporini, 1925, pl. 1
Fosca, 1954, p. 61, pl. 27
Panofsky, 1955, pp. 319–20, fig. 95
R. pp. 192, 198, 261, fig. 135
A. 449, fig. 372
Thuillier, 1967, colorpl. p. 130
Bacou, 1971, colorpl. XXVII (French edition, 1976)

Related works
There is another version of this drawing (figure 1), which can be dated to 1767 (repro-duced by D. and V., pl. 173; see A. 2455; see also 2456, formerly in the collection of Dr. Tuffier).

An engraving (figure 2) was made by Jean-Philippe-Guy Le Gentil (1750–1824), Comte de Paroy, a "graveur amateur" and an "associé libre" of the Academy, September 3, 1785 (*Procès-Verbaux . . .*, IX, p. 255; see Portalis and Béraldi, 1882, III, p. 276; P. p. 331, who reproduces the engraving on p. 224; Delteil, 1910, pp. 234–35; and Bellier and Auvray, II, p. 206).

Figure 1. Fragonard. *The Kiss.* Whereabouts unknown (after D. and V.)

Figure 2. Comte de Paroy, after Fragonard. *The Kiss.* Bibliothèque Nationale, Paris, Cabinet des Estampes

"Spirat adhuc Amor, vivunt commissi calores" ("Love still breathes, and passions still smolder..."). This verse by Horace (Book IV, Ode IX, lines 10–11) accompanies the engraving by the Comte de Paroy, executed after a horizontal version of Fragonard's composition.

Love is shown plunging his torch into the remains of an ancient sarcophagus, while an embracing couple is reborn from the ashes in a funeral urn. Cupids look on in wonder. Two large, dense trees, lit by the glare of the torch, envelop the scene in mystery.

Fragonard, here, takes up the "eternal theme of the bed and the tomb, of death and love," treating it with sensuality, but also with unaccustomed seriousness and emotion. This admirable blend of imagination, reverie, and morbid imagery is reminiscent of works by Goya, Fuseli, and their more daring nineteenth-century contemporaries—of whom Fragonard sometimes seems to have been the forerunner.

248   Girl Consulting a Fortune-Teller

Bister wash on paper, over an underdrawing in black chalk, 32 x 26 cm.

Musée Marmottan, Paris

Provenance
M. [de Bièvres]: sold, March 10, 1790, no. 27: "deux autres, une étude de saint Jérôme et une Jeune fille consultant un Nécromancien"; anonymous sale, November 26–27, 1793, no. 28: "la Bonne Aventure et St. Jérôme..." (this *Saint Jérôme* may be identified with A. 457, fig. 161, or with A. 1082, recently sold in Paris, April 14, 1986, no. 54, ill.); François-Martial Marcille: sold posthumously, March 4–7, 1857, no. 63: "L'Horoscope" (for 83 francs); M. E. N[orblin].: sold, March 16–17, 1860, no. 57 (for 42 francs, to Gigoux, according to Lejeune, 1863, p. 297); Eudoxe Marcille, 1889 (according to P., who, no doubt, has confused the father and the son); Georges de Bellio (1828–1894); Ernest Donop de Monchy (the son-in-law of de Bellio; no. 199 in the handwritten catalogue of the collection, established before 1897); bequeathed to the Académie des Beaux-Arts by Mme Victorine Donop de Monchy, the daughter of Georges de Bellio, 1957.

Exhibitions
Tokyo, 1980, no. 119, ill.

Bibliography
P. p. 305 (?)
Musée Marmottan catalogue, 1965, p. 15, no. 726
Niculescu, 1970, p. 72
Cannon-Brookes, 1980, p. 471, fig. 2

Related works
Two versions of this drawing are catalogued by Ananoff (A. 35, fig. 78; A. 1980, fig. 538; see also A. 1324), but we can make no pronouncements about them.

An owl is perched on a book of spells, which a fortune-teller is consulting with the aid of a magnifying glass. The young man casually rests his hand on the knee of the girl who has come to consult him. The girl, whose face has a dreamy yet attentive expression, anxiously awaits his prognosis.

Fragonard treats this theme with typical humor. He does not belabor his point, criticize, nor condemn; his aim is simply to amuse us and to evoke a smile.

The originality of this composition deserves mention; the interplay of curves and straight lines lends the drawing rhythm, while the bister wash gives the forms depth. The ensemble serves to focus our attention on the owl, which is set off against the dark vault, and on the fortune-teller's wandering hand.

249   The Death of a Hermit

Bister wash on paper, over an underdrawing in black chalk, 33.9 x 44.8 cm.

Graphische Sammlung Albertina, Vienna, Inv. 12.730

Provenance
Albert, Duke of Saxe-Teschen (1738–1822; his stamp, Lugt 174, is at the lower left); in the collection of the Albertina since its founding. Two references in eighteenth-century sales catalogues seem unrelated to the Vienna drawing: those of the Le Brun collection sale, December 23, 1771–January 7, 1772, no. 377: "la Mort d'un Hermite..." (probably A. 459), and the M. [de Bièvres] collection sale, March 10, 1790, no. 31: "... un sujet de Diogène, une composition d'après le Calabrese."

Exhibitions
Bern, 1954, no. 129

Bibliography
A. 2485, fig. 618

The identity of the hermit is by no means evident. According to Jennifer Montagu, he could be Diogenes, who allowed himself to die by voluntarily ceasing to breathe, only to be discovered by his friends. Diogenes is frequently represented with a jar and a dog, who, here, is shown howling in grief.

Hermits occur often in the work of Fragonard, who enjoyed drawing their emaciated bodies (and not only those of pretty young women!). Several of these representations of hermits were mentioned in various eighteenth-century sales (of the Mariette collection, for example), and a number are still extant today. The Vienna drawing is unquestionably the most beautiful, yet, it is also the strangest, on account of the astonishing setting of the composition (one is tempted to call it a "stage set"). The philosopher lies abandoned in a rock-strewn landscape. In front of him, in the foreground, are his stick and a wicker basket; at the left is a group of old men, two of whom contemplate the spectacle in fascination.

The Vienna drawing is a late work—from after the artist's second Italian trip—that can be dated between 1775 and 1780.

250 The Attack

Bister wash on paper, over an underdrawing in black chalk, 34.5 x 46 cm.
Inscribed at the bottom left, in pen and ink: *E. Le Sueur.*

Pushkin Museum, Moscow, Inv. 5636

Provenance
State Museum collections; State Pushkin
Museum of Fine Arts, Moscow, since 1925.

Exhibitions
Moscow, 1927, no. 60
Moscow, 1955, p. 85
Leningrad, 1956, p. 98
Moscow, 1959, pp. 8, 39
Moscow-Leningrad, 1966, n.p. [p. 68], ill.

Bibliography
Sidoroff, 1929–30, I, p. 224, ill.
Sidoroff, 1940, pp. 120–21, ill.
A. 1978, fig. 537
Pushkin catalogue, 1977, no. 158, colorpl.

This drawing is exceptional: as three old men look on—Fragonard's usual bearded types, with flowing hair—another man, bare to the waist, strikes a young man on the chin with his right fist, causing him to recoil.

What attracts Fragonard in such scenes is not so much their violence, but the rapidity of the action. He addresses a problem that has always fascinated artists: how to capture a gesture and describe it—how to depict movement without arresting it.

The drawing contains one curious detail: the hand on the victim's right shoulder. To whom does it belong?

251 A Priest Stabbing a Young Woman on an Altar

Bister wash on paper, over an underdrawing in black chalk, 38.8 x 47.2 cm.
Inscribed at the bottom left, in black chalk strengthened with ink: *fragonard fecit*

Musée Atger, Montpellier, Faculté de Médecine, Inv. 145

Provenance
Mounted in the eighteenth century (the dry mark ARD, Lugt 172, appears on the mount); anonymous sale, October 13–14, 1828, no. 134: "le sacrifice d'Iphigénie" (?); given by Xavier Atger (1758–1833) to the Montpellier museum, 1829 (his stamp, Lugt 38, is at the bottom center).

Exhibitions
Bern, 1954, no. 130
Paris, 1974–75, no. 44, pl. XVII

Bibliography
Musée Atger catalogue, 1830, no. 145 ("dessin plein d'expression et de force fait au pinceau et au bistre")

P. p. 315
Saunier, 1922, p. 164
Fosca, 1954, pp. XXII, 58, pl. 20
Claparède, 1955, plates XIX, XX
R. p. 192
A. 1681, fig. 431
Wilson, 1981, p. 149, fig. 42

The theme of this drawing remains something of a mystery, and Atger was wise and prudent to entitle it "unknown subject." It cannot represent the Sacrifice of Abraham, as Portalis thought, in spite of the Tablets of the Law included in the composition—nor is it the Sacrifice of Iphigenia, as Saunier, Réau, and Ananoff maintain; the Sacrifice of Jepthah, as Ananoff suggested; or the Massacre of the Innocents, as proposed by Fosca.

A priest (?) holds a young girl ruthlessly by the hair on an altar, as he prepares to cut her throat. On the ground lie the corpses of two babies and a man.

The drawing cannot date from before 1767 (Wilson), and is probably much later, since Fragonard's mastery of the handling of bister wash is already apparent, and the frieze-like composition has taken on a neoclassical feeling. The impact of the drawing lies in its vitality and in the violence that it displays. The strong diagonal, which extends from the raised knife to the victim's open hand; the illuminated, expressive faces; the pivoting, almost cinematic, movements of the figures; and the strange close-up effect all contribute to the extraordinary power that characterizes this work.

252 A River-god

Bister wash on paper, over an underdrawing in black chalk, 32 x 22 cm.
Signed at the lower left, in pen and slightly darker ink: *Par h. fragonard*.

Private collection

Provenance
Formerly, Sir Robert Abdy collection.

Bibliography
Unpublished

River-gods were especially favored by Fragonard: a "river" was included in the sale of the de Bièvres collection, March 10, 1790 (part of no. 23), and several others are reproduced by Ananoff (390, pl. D; 391, fig. 141; 392, fig. 142).

This river-god is the most unnerving and the most grandiose of these representations—and also the latest in date. The god, seated on a rock, seems to have emerged from the waves, which he appears to be blessing, as a serpent looks on. A brilliant light illuminates his grave, majestic face, his torso, and his right leg.

Romantic in concept, the drawing's strong evocative power brings to mind the art of George Romney. It is yet another example of the importance of water and aquatic themes in Fragonard's work.

253 Plutarch's Dream

Bister wash on paper, over an underdrawing in black chalk, 35.1 x 48.9 cm.

Private collection, Paris

Provenance
[Chabot and Duc de La Mure, or Desmarets]:
sold, December 17–22, 1787, no. 168: "une
Figure de vieillard entouré de tous les accessoires d'un savant et dont le sujet ingénieux
paraît indiquer une vision allégorique dont
nous ne pouvons rendre plus de compte" (?)
(for 74 *livres,* to Paillet); Dr. G.: sold posthumously, May 15–17, 1883, no. 76: "un
historien de l'antiquité" (for 25 francs, to M.
André); Charles André: sold posthumously,
May 18–19, 1914, no. 51, ill. (to Léo Dal-
ligny); Mme Fernand Halphen, 1931, 1951.

Exhibitions
Paris, 1931, no. 9
Paris, Galerie Cailleux, 1951, no. 36

Bibliography
R. p. 195
A. 453, fig. 154
Roland Michel, 1961, p. iii, fig. 4

Related works
For a study, see the following entry.
  In the Rouen museum there is a painting of
this same subject (figure 1). Smaller than the
drawing (oil on panel, 24.3 x 31.5 cm.; see
W. 85, fig. 62; Tokyo exhibition catalogue,
1980, no. 20, colorpl.), and unfortunately
much damaged, it was formerly in the collection of the painter Jean-Baptiste Descamps
(1742–1836), known as Descamps *fils.*
Appointed as the museum's first curator in
1806, Descamps catalogued the picture
beginning in 1809 (Rouen museum catalogue, no. 195).

We doubt that this drawing was included in the Chabot collection sale of 1787, as has so often been asserted, because it would seem that the author of the catalogue would surely have noted the inscription in capital letters on the large book in the picture: VIE DES HOMMES ILLUSTRES. The figure in the painting is Plutarch, who is present, as a philosopher, to witness the victory of MEDIOCRITY over GRANDEUR.

Interestingly, the catalogue entry by Descamps on the panel painting in Rouen is instructive as to Fragonard's intentions: "The subject of this little painting gives some idea of the painter's nature," he begins, before offering this lengthy description: " ... a scale ... which, at each end ... terminates in a ball; the higher one is inscribed GRANDEUR; it is topped with a crown of thorns; the crown of immortality awaits it in heaven. The lower ball is inscribed MEDIOCRITE; it is crowned with roses over which is the cap of Liberty"!

Figure 1. Fragonard. *Plutarch's Dream.*
Musée des Beaux-Arts, Rouen

The rest of Descamps's entry deserves to be quoted in full: "The artist concludes his dream by comparing mankind on earth to reptiles emitting their venom into a vessel placed over a fire; he maintains that when this poison reaches a certain temperature, it evaporates and unleashes trouble throughout the world."

Descamps adds: "The execution of this little painting is handled in the manner of Rembrandt. There is a sense of burning enthusiasm; the brushwork is smooth and thick, with that magical chiaroscuro that so characterizes the art of this most original of painters."

This description, written only a few months after the death of Fragonard, by an artist who probably knew him, applies also to the present drawing (executed between 1778 and 1780, as Marianne Roland Michel has aptly shown). We should not view either the painting or the drawing as antirevolutionary statements, but they do serve to enlighten us as to Fragonard's philosophical ideals—insofar as we can trust Descamps—his elitist sympathies, and his deep pessimism.

Who would have guessed that Fragonard, the painter of joyous, exuberant, and vibrant life, was really a skeptic and a misanthrope?

254 Study for *Plutarch*

India ink wash on paper, over an underdrawing in black chalk, 32 x 33 cm.
Traces of ink (for example, around the figure's left hand) appear to be later additions.

Musée Greuze, Tournus

Provenance
Acquired by the Société des Amis des Arts de Tournus at a "vente Tinardon" (which we have been unable to trace), in Paris, in 1897 (according to Martin and Masson [1907], in the catalogue of the Musée Greuze, 1910—not in 1927).

Bibliography
Martin and Masson [1907], no. 14
Musée Greuze catalogue [Jean Martin], 1910, no. 28
Rosenberg, in the Paris-Detroit-New York exhibition catalogue, 1974–75, p. 457

Related works
See the previous entry.

Figure 1. Jean-Baptiste Greuze. *Le Donneur de chapelets.* Private collection

This drawing, which is damaged, and was perhaps "over-restored" in the nineteenth century, has always been attributed to Greuze, and associated with his *Donneur de chapelets* (figure 1). It is definitely by Fragonard, however, and is a preparatory study for the principal figure in the preceding drawing, *Plutarch's Dream.*

Fragonard's drawings are not always as radically different from those of Greuze as one would think. The two men worked for a different clientele, and had different ambitions, but the techniques that they employed (despite Greuze's preference for gray wash) can sometimes lead to confusion.

The following curious texts associate the two men. In his account of the Salon of 1779, at about the time that Fragonard was painting *Plutarch's Dream,* the economist Dupont de Nemours wrote to Margrave Caroline-Louise of Baden (Obser, 1908, p. 100): "but two great artists who seriously shun the Academy are Fragonard and Greuze. Both have a great deal of style, the former brilliant and daring, employing with the most vivid contrasts all the magic of color...." A few years later, the tone changes: "then, after so much noise, silence surrounded Fragonard; he and Greuze looked at each other and wondered where and how it had all gone by" (Théophile Fragonard, 1847; see Valogne, 1955).

255   Ariosto Inspired by Love and Folly

Bister wash on paper, over an underdrawing in black chalk, 33.4 x 45.4 cm.

Musée des Beaux-Arts, Besançon, Inv. D. 2862

Provenance
Pierre-Adrien Pâris (1745–1819): listed in the handwritten inventory of his collection, 1806, no. 120: "autre beau dessin au bistre du même, représentant Arioste composant ses Poëmes, inspiré par l'amour et la folie"; bequeathed to the Bibliothèque Municipale, Besançon; deposited in the Musée des Beaux-Arts, 1843 (the museum's stamp, Lugt 238 c, is at the lower left).

Exhibitions
Besançon, 1956, no. 80, pl. XIV

Bibliography
P. p. 294
Martine, 1927, pl. 34
Cioranescu, 1939, II, pl. XIV
Mongan, Hofer, and Seznec, 1945,
   pp. 20–21, ill. between pp. 8 and 9
Friedlaender, 1947, p. 215
Bouchot-Saupique, 1956, p. 17
R. p. 226
Cornillot, 1957, no. 80, ill. (with more
   details)

A. 452, fig. 159
Roland Michel, 1961, pp. i–iii, fig. 3, p. ii
Wakefield, 1976, pp. 14–15, 61, fig. 39 a
Wakefield, 1978, n.p.
Williams, 1978, p. 153
Michine, 1980, p. 188
Bjurström, 1982, no. 956

Related works
Fragonard dealt with the theme of inspiration on several occasions, in a number of comparable works—among them: *The Inspiration of the Poet* (figure 1; A. 454, fig. 155), and *Homage to Gluck* (figure 2; A. 455, fig. 158; in a New York private collection), a fine drawing that M. Roland Michel (1961, p. ii, n. 4) suggests may be identified with no. 239 in the sale of the Sireul collection (December 3, 1781: "La peinture dédiant ses crayons à Homère, Virgile et Mécène").

See also A. 456; Tokyo exhibition catalogue, 1980, no. 141, ill.

Figure 1. Fragonard. *The Inspiration of the Poet.* Whereabouts unknown

Figure 2. Fragonard. *Homage to Gluck.* Private collection, New York

The title of this famous drawing comes from the inventory of the Pâris collection, but it is not, strictly speaking, a portrait of Ariosto. Our knowledge of the poet's features (see, on this subject, Gronau, 1933) is based on the bearded portrait by Titian, after which an engraving was made for the frontispiece of the 1532 edition of *Orlando Furioso*; it was reprinted in the many subsequent editions.

The Besançon drawing is more concerned with the source of the poet's inspiration. Only the presence of Love and of Folly alludes directly to the central theme of Ariosto's epic poem: Orlando, who is in love with Angelica, loses his mind at the news of his beloved's betrothal to Medoro (canto XXIII). The possibility of a link between the Besançon drawing and the series of illustrations for *Orlando Furioso* has often been raised (see cat. nos. 256–265), and it has sometimes been suggested that this drawing may have been intended as a frontispiece for a projected new edition of the book. However, this hypothesis is ruled out by the fact that the Besançon drawing is much larger than Fragonard's series of illustrations, and, unlike them, is horizontal in format.

Although the present drawing displays obvious affinities with *Plutarch's Dream* (cat. no. 253), all evidence would seem to indicate that the "Orlando Furioso" series was executed slightly later—closer to 1788 than to 1780.

The furnishings depicted in the drawing are most original, and include a broad-backed chair, a table whose base is ornamented with sphinxes—one thinks of Jacob —and the lyre and the globe, both frequently found in Fragonard's work.

Ariosto, crowned with laurels, is leaning on his worktable. His eyes are closed, and he is trying to concentrate, while Love and Folly—the latter, shaking a cap and bells—attempt to distract him.

Fragonard treats his hero in the same offhand manner that Ariosto used, to ridicule his own protagonists—for which he was often reproached (see Seznec, 1945, p. 37)—but, as Walter Friedlaender correctly noted (1947, p. 215), underlying Fragonard's satirical humor there is deep sympathy, and perhaps even a secret complicity with the great, unhappy poet.

Fragonard as Illustrator: Fragonard and Ariosto

It is well known that Fragonard's paintings were sometimes inspired by famous literary works. Torquato Tasso's *Gerusalemme liberata* was the source of the marvelous canvases in the Veil-Picard collection (see cat. no. 71 a), and Jean-François Marmontel's *Annette et Lubin* and La Fontaine's *Perrette et le pot au lait* gave rise to still other works (see cat. nos. 87, 143, respectively). Yet, Fragonard's work as an illustrator of novels, stories, and poems is still relatively misunderstood; in fact, only his drawings for La Fontaine's fables have received close study.

Halbou, Patas, Aliamet, and Duclos made engravings, after Fragonard's lively drawings, for Didot the Elder's edition of the *Contes,* begun in 1795 but never completed. Three series of drawings, probably dating from well before the projected edition of Didot, are known today. The most famous of these is the series in the Béraldi collection in the Musée du Petit Palais, Paris, which includes fifty-seven black-chalk counterproofs heightened with bister wash. It was based on the forty-two black-chalk sketches now in the Schiff collection, along with a number of others that remain to be found. The third series, which is dispersed among several collections, is composed of much more finished drawings, probably prepared for engravings. (For a summary of this subject, see Roland Michel, 1970, pp. i–v; E. Williams, 1978, no. 53.)

Fragonard was busy with still other projects toward the end of his career. The drawings for Mme de Genlis's *Les Veillées du château* (A. 2668) we have seen only in reproduction (P. p. 218; sold, March 21, 1922, no. 39), and they do not seem to be the work of the master. On the other hand, the illustrations for Cervantes's *Don Quixote* and for Ariosto's *Orlando Furioso* deserve attention. According to Théophile Fragonard (1847; see Valogne, 1955, p. 9): "David and his school gave so different an impetus to the tastes of artists and *amateurs* that the vogue for Fragonard's work ceased before he reached the age of fifty. One could say that he outlived his public by some twenty-five years, because he was seventy-five when he died in 1806. Nonetheless, he had done nothing unworthy of his talent. It was during this time that he executed several hundred drawings for *Orlando Furioso,* and equally as many large and magnificent drawings for *Don Quixote.* M. Denon owned some of these, which he had set aside, intending to use them himself to make etchings. At the sale of Denon's collection, these drawings were bought by a rich English *amateur,* who had a folio edition of the Spanish classic printed in a single copy, to accommodate the drawings. It must be admitted that Fragonard's talent was always valued more highly in England than in France."

This very important passage, which is rarely quoted, is indispensable for a number of reasons: Most scholars date the Ariosto drawings in the 1780s, for stylistic reasons, and here is solid confirmation that they are correct. Hence, a close reading of Théophile's statement, together with a stylistic analysis of the drawings, reinforces the supposition that Fragonard executed these works "at the time" that the "vogue for his work ceased."

We have no knowledge of the unique copy of Cervantes published by the "rich Englishman," and question whether it really existed. It is true that many of the drawings for *Don Quixote* are today in the British Museum, or in the Ashmolean Museum, Oxford (see figure 1). Their attribution to Fragonard has been challenged by Ananoff (1961, pp. 155–57), who, having compared them with the notebooks of sketches in the museum in Grasse, believes that they are more likely by his son, Alexandre-Évariste. Like Eunice Williams (1978, p. 148), we do not accept Ananoff's view. While the thirty-odd surviving drawings do not possess the power of the "Orlando Furioso" series— some of the contours seem to have been strengthened, perhaps by Évariste—they are, beyond any doubt, Jean-Honoré's conceptions. Théophile's statement, along with Vivant-Denon's eight engravings (figure 2)

Figure 1. Fragonard. *Scene from* Don Quixote. Ashmolean Museum, Oxford

after the drawings in his collection, would seem to confirm this.

Orlando Furioso is the most famous work by Ludovico Ariosto (1474–1533), poet at the court of Duke Alfonso I d'Este of Ferrara. Published in 1516, the work was continually being revised by its author, until the definitive edition appeared in 1532. The long, epic poem of forty-six cantos, which relates the struggles between the Christians and the pagans, was based on the *Chanson de Roland*. Orlando (Roland), the nephew of Charlemagne, is in love with the beautiful Angelica, an Oriental princess: he succumbs to madness when she marries the Saracen Medoro. Around this principal theme revolve various episodes of gallantry, in which the chivalrous obligations and the religious convictions of the protagonists are brought into conflict with their sentiments.

Fragonard's decision to illustrate this celebrated poem was an ambitious undertaking: over one hundred and sixty drawings have been identified, to date. In 1945, Elizabeth Mongan, Philip Hofer, and Jean Seznec published 137 of these, accompanied by very detailed commentaries. All of the drawings came —via the Roederer and Rosenbach collections—from the collection of Hippolyte Walferdin (sold posthumously, April 12–16, 1880, no. 228: "136 compositions"; five more drawings for this series had already been sold on April 3, 1880, no. 65). It is generally thought that Walferdin bought them from the Fragonard family. Many other drawings were later added to this magnificent ensemble, which was kept intact until 1922, but is now dispersed among a number of museums and private collections. A single lot of about sixty of these drawings, the property of Norton Simon, was placed on the market at Agnew's, London, in 1978.

As Seznec points out (1945, p. 41), of the poem's forty-six cantos, only the first third are consistently illustrated by Fragonard. Canto V is omitted altogether, and drawings for the other two-thirds of the poem are very sporadic. Do many drawings still remain to be found? Although Théophile mentions several hundred, perhaps it would be more reasonable to suppose that Fragonard—as was so often the case—simply failed to complete his project.

We know nothing of the origin of this undertaking, who commissioned it, or why. The "honoré fragonard" generally inscribed at the top of some of the sheets, which we believe to be in the painter's own hand (see cat. no. 263), and the black-chalk lines that mark the boundaries of some of the compositions would seem to indicate that the artist did not execute

Figure 2. Dominique Vivant-Denon, after Fragonard. *Scene from* Don Quixote. Bibliothèque Nationale, Paris, Cabinet des Estampes

Figure 3. Fragonard. *The Hermit, the Donkey and the Demons.* Thomas Agnew & Sons Ltd., London

Figure 4. Jean-Baptiste Greuze. *Illustration for Canto XXIX of* Orlando Furioso. Städelsches Kunstinstitut, Frankfurt am Main, Graphische Sammlung

the drawings for his own pleasure, but definitely intended them to be used for engravings. This was the case, as far as we know, for only one drawing, after which an engraving was made by the Comte de Paroy that was exhibited (no. 287) at the Salon of 1787 (see cat. no. 247): "L'hermite se faisant enlever par des Démons, pour courir après Angélique. Sujet de l'Arioste, d'après M. Fragonard. Gravure imitant le crayon."

Unfortunately, we have been unable to trace this engraving. It must have been a copy of *The Hermit, the Donkey and the Demons* (figure 3; Agnew's, London), an illustration of lines 31–32 of canto VIII (Mongan, Hofer, and Seznec, 1945, pl. 42). The hermit who pursues Angelica abandons his sluggish donkey, and appeals to the demons to carry him more swiftly to his prey.

Ariosto's poem was a huge success, from its first publication in 1516, but, as Cioranescu notes (1939, II, p. 174), "the level of interest it aroused in France reached its height about 1780." The translation by d'Ussieux (1775–83; see the copy now in the Bibliothèque Nationale, Réserve, Yd 256–259) included forty-six plates by Nicolas Ponce, after Cochin, to which forty-six more were added, after drawings by Cipriani, Moreau, Eisen, Monnet, Cochin, and Greuze (figure 4); these had previously been used for the Baskerville edition published in 1773.

Some of the criticism of this edition was very harsh: "our beautiful edition of Ariosto by Baskerville: now

they've polluted it with wretched vignettes by that pitiful Eis[en]...." The author of this passage—none other than the redoubtable author of the *Dialogues sur la peinture,* whom we have already quoted on several occasions—went on to add, apropos of Cochin: "in (...) the Ariosto that I was telling you about a moment ago, there are one or two nice ideas and a few pleasant compositions. But, for the rest, the transition from the mediocre to the great distorts everything... this, precisely, is the origin of the trouble: in your country [France—it is "Milord" who is speaking] the men who can draw are a class apart. Your great Artists should be made to draw. If I had a book I wanted to have embellished, I would not address myself to your Mar[illiers], your Mon[nets], your Co[chins] but to your leading Painters and Sculptors..." (Renou, 1773, pp. 90–91, 94–95). Did Fragonard take this comment literally, and attempt to rival the professional vignettists? In any event, his venture came too late, for the Baskerville and d'Ussieux editions of Ariosto had "saturated" the market.

Not enough attention has been paid to Fragonard's extraordinarily innovative approach to the concept of illustration. In contrast to most books illustrated with engravings, he did not group several episodes on a single sheet, thus, increasing the number of drawings per canto, which would have made the project very expensive. Nor could his drawings be engraved exactly as they were, since the profusion of black-chalk lines and the large areas of light bister wash would have proved difficult to translate into the medium of engraving.

Included here is a selection of little-known drawings, some of them never before published, alongside the more famous examples. According to Jean Seznec, Fragonard must have read Ariosto in the Italian, so faithfully does he render the details of the smallest nuances of the original text.

Bister wash on paper, over an underdrawing in black chalk, 39.4 x 26 cm.

The Rosenbach Museum and Library, Philadelphia, 54.99

Provenance
Hippolyte Walferdin (1795–1880): sold
posthumously, April 12–16, 1880, part of
no. 228 (to Louis Roederer, Reims); after the
death of Louis, passed to his nephew, Léon
Olry-Roederer; bought by Dr. A. S. W.
Rosenbach, for the Rosenbach Company,
1922; Rosenbach Museum and Library.

Bibliography
Mongan, Hofer, and Seznec, 1945, pl. 32
Rorschach and Taylor, 1985, no. 43, ill.

Figure 1. Nicolas Ponce, after Cochin.
Engraving for Roland (chapter VII,
1775–85 ed.). Bibliothèque
Nationale, Paris, Département des
Imprimés (réserve)

Canto VII, 21:
  Tolte che fur le mense e le vivande,
  Facean, sedendo in cerchio, un giuoco lieto,
  Che nell'orecchio l'un l'altro domande,
  Come più piace lor, qualche secreto.
  Il che agli amanti fu commodo grande
  Di scoprir l'amor lor senza divieto:
  E furon loro conclusioni estreme
  Di ritrovarsi quella notte insieme.

"The tables were removed; the guests, gathered in a circle, began to play games invented by Love to encourage tender and discreet avowals. Many secrets were whispered, but the sweetest, most mysterious pledges were those exchanged by Ruggiero and Alcina: in the fever of their mutual desire, they agreed to meet later that night."

The Saracen Ruggiero is momentarily distracted from his passion for Bradamante by the charms of Alcina. Fragonard depicts the pair as they arrange their tryst; putti play at the foot of the ottoman on which they are seated, while, around them, little cloud-borne cupids flutter through the palace.

Fragonard's illustrations are rarely of the same episodes that were depicted in the engravings in earlier editions of *Orlando*; thus, it is interesting to compare this drawing with Ponce's engraving, dated 1776 (figure 1), after Cochin, for chapter VII of the d'Ussieux edition (1775–83) of Ariosto.

In contrast to Cochin's profusion of characters, with their stiff poses, Fragonard filled the foreground with only two figures. Behind them he rapidly sketched in a fanciful decor, paying little heed to the exigencies of engraving. Fragonard was hardly a vignettist!

257 Alcina and Ruggiero Are United

Bister wash on paper, over an underdrawing in black chalk, 38.5 x 23.5 cm.

Private collection, Paris

Provenance
Th. H[ertzog]: sold, April 3–8, 1876, no.
1420: "jeune femme suppliée par son
amant"(?); Groult (?); anonymous sale,
March 26, 1953, no. 91, ill.; Dormeuil; private collection, Paris.

Bibliography
A. 485, fig. 166

Canto VII, 27–29:
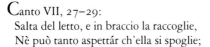
Salta del letto, e in braccio la raccoglie,
Nè può tanto aspettár ch'ella si spoglie;

Benchè nè gonna nè faldigia avesse,
Che venne avvolta in un leggiér zendado,
Che sopra una camicia ella si messe
Bianca e sottíl nel più eccellente grado.
Comme Ruggiero abbracciò lei, gli cesse
Il manto, e restò il vel sottile e rado,
Che non copría dinanzi nè di dietro,
Più che le rose o i gigli un chiaro vetro.

Nè così strettamente édera preme
Pianta, ove intorno abbarbicata s'abbia,
Come si stríngon li due amanti insieme,
Cogliendo dello spirto in sulle labbia
Söave fior, qual non produce seme
Indo o Sabéo nell'odorata sabbia.

"He leapt from his bed; and dressed though Alcina still was, he gathered her in his arms. Fortunately, she had wrapped herself in nothing more substantial than a cloak, which a playful cupid, a party to this blissful moment, has let fall from her shoulders. The light veil that still covered her body revealed no more of her charms to Ruggiero than the purest crystal dew hides the lovely contours of lilies and roses. No ivy ever clung more closely to the tree that supports and feeds it than were the arms of these two happy lovers ent-wined around each other: and no flower from the sands of India or the plains of Sheba ever gave forth such sweet perfume as the mingled breath that escaped their burning lips."

Fragonard's oeuvre includes many studies of lovers embracing (see, for example, cat. nos. 145, 147). Here, Ariosto's poem presents him with another opportunity to address this theme. Ruggiero, seated on the edge of the bed, passionately clasps Alcina, who has just come to join him. The half-open door (the contrast with *Le Verrou* is potent) admits a draft, which makes the bed curtains billow. With rapid strokes of the brush and the chalk, the canopy is transformed into garlands of ivy.

Bister wash on paper, over an underdrawing in black chalk, 40.5 x 25.3 cm.
Recently restored.

Musée d'Art et d'Histoire, Narbonne

Provenance
Bequeathed to the Narbonne museum by
Maurice Peyre (1800–1859), a politician
from that city. Not inventoried.

Bibliography
Paris exhibition catalogue, 1974–75, p. 147

Canto VII, 31:
  Non è diletto alcún che di fuor reste,
  Che tutti son nell'amorosa stanza;
  E due e tre volte il dì mútano veste,
  Fatte or ad una or ad un'altra usanza.
  Spesso in conviti, sempre stano in feste,
  In giostre, in lotte, in scene, in bagno, in danza.

"The two lovers left no pleasure untried. In the course of a single day, they changed their clothes two and even three times. They whiled away the hours jousting, tussling, dancing, and in play."

The setting of the present work is similar to that of the drawing discussed in catalogue no. 256, but it is more precisely indicated; columns with Corinthian capitals frame a gallery, which contains an attentive audience among whom, doubtless, are Ruggiero and Alcina, there to amuse themselves. In the background are arcades resting on large pillars. To the sound of a small orchestra of horns, trumpets, flutes, and other instruments, several girls are dancing in a circle. Fragrant vapors rise from an incense burner in the right foreground. The sportive atmosphere is adeptly rendered by the blending of chalk and wash and by the supple lines that merely sketch in the forms, yet never sacrifice the clarity of the composition. We begin to recognize from one drawing to the next the various characters, settings, and objects, all of which are faithfully taken from Ariosto's celebrated narrative.

Bister wash on paper, over an underdrawing in black chalk, 40 x 24.8 cm.

Musées de Langres, 880–7

Provenance
From the collection of Hippolyte Walferdin
(1795–1880), who was originally from
Langres; given to the Langres museum by his
family, at his death in 1880.

Bibliography
*Bulletin de la Société Historique et Archéolo-
    gique de Langres,* July 1880, p. 14
Langres museum catalogue, 1886, no. 79
Sérullaz and Volle, 1976, pp. 77–78, ill.

Figure 1. Fragonard. *Melissa
and Ruggiero.* Whereabouts
unknown

Figure 2. Fragonard. *Alcina Appears to Ruggiero in Her True Guise*. Musée du Louvre, Paris, Cabinet des Dessins

Figure 3. Fragonard. *Alcina Appears to Ruggiero in Her True Guise*. Art market, Paris

Canto VII, 40–41:

> E ben sapéa che sta in gioco e in ballo,
> E in cibo, e in ozio molle e delicato;
> Nè più memoria avéa del suo signore,
> Nè della donna sua, nè del suo onore.
>
> E così il flor de' più begli anni suoi
> In lunga inerzia avér potría consunto
> Sì gentíl cavalier, e per dovér poi
> Pérdere il corpo e l'ánima in un punto;
> E quell'ódor che sol rimán di noir,
> Poscia che 'l resto frágile è defunto,
> Che trae l'uom del sepolcro, e in vita il serba,
> Gli saría stato o tronco, o svelto in erba.

"She saw, to her grief, that this brave Paladin was now leading a dissolute life of pleasure and idleness, never thinking of his beautiful mistress, his king, or even his honor; she could not bear the thought that such a man, who should have been a hero, was wasting his finest days in this shameful inertia, and that, at the end of his life, his reputation already tarnished in his youth, he would be remembered without honor by his fellowmen."

Of the various interpretations of the subject of this drawing that have been suggested (see Sérullaz and Volle, 1976), only the above passage seems to fit perfectly. In her ardent desire to further the union of Ruggiero and Bradamante, the sorceress Melissa, leaning imperiously on her staff, conjures up the image of Ruggiero and Alcina, who are locked in an embrace. The portrait of Melissa is rendered with scrupulous fidelity to Ariosto's description: "half naked, barefoot, her hair coming undone" ("discinta e scalza e sciolta avéa le chiome," canto III, 8). The lovers' rapture is in sharp contrast to the strange and disturbing world of the sorceress, inhabited by the serpent, the sphinx, and all sorts of monsters.

Later on, Melissa will break the spell cast over Ruggiero by slipping a magic ring on his finger (see figure 1; sold at Christie's, London, March 19, 1975, no. 134, ill.). She thus forces him to see the reality of his former life of debauchery. Alcina appears in her true guise—that of a frightful old crone (canto VII, 72). This final episode is illustrated in a drawing now in the Louvre (R. F. 24.318; see figure 2). Alone among the works in the series, there exists a much smaller copy of this latter drawing (25.7 x 22.3 cm.), which was recently sold and is on the Paris art market (see figure 3).

260 Angelica Is Abducted by the Inhabitants of the Isle of Ebuda

Bister wash on paper, over an underdrawing in black chalk, 39 x 25 cm.

Musée des Beaux-Arts, Dijon, CA 857

Provenance
His de la Salle (1795–1878; the stamp, Lugt 1333, is at the bottom left); given to the Dijon museum between 1862 and 1865.

Exhibitions
Dijon, 1960, no. 32
Dijon, 1974, no. 68, ill.

Bibliography
Dijon museum catalogue, 1883, no. 857
Lavallée, 1947, p. 117 ("l'attribution à Fragonard ne peut être conservée, on penserait plutôt à Deshays")
Paris exhibition catalogue, 1974–75, p. 147

Canto VIII, 64:
    La bella donna di gran sonno oppressa
    Incatenata fu, prima che desta:
    Portaro il frate incantatór con essa
    Nel legno pien di turba afflitta e mesta.

"Still in a deep slumber, she was bound in chains by the Ebudians; she did not come to her senses until she was carried aboard the vessel with the hermit-sorcerer, there to lament her new misfortunes."

In the story, Angelica, fleeing from Renato, is cast up on a rocky shore, at the mercy of an unsavory hermit. The inhabitants of the isle of Ebuda, who were seeking a young girl to offer as a sacrifice to Proteus—god of the denizens of the sea—come across the sleeping Angelica, and, as shown in the drawing, carry her off. From a cloud on high, a winged creature, armed with a dagger and a trident, watches the abduction. This allegorical figure, who fills the upper part of the sheet—as is frequently the case in the series of drawings—here serves as an allusion to the cruelty of Proteus.

261 Angelica Is Menaced by the Killer Whale

Bister wash on paper, over an underdrawing in black chalk, 39.3 x 25.8 cm.

National Gallery of Art, Washington, D.C., Gift of Edith G. Rosenwald, 1978.10.2

Provenance
Hippolyte Walferdin (1795–1880): sold posthumously, April 12–16, 1880, part of no. 228 (to Louis Roederer, Reims); after the death of Louis, passed to his nephew, Léon Olry-Roederer; bought by Dr. A. S. W. Rosenbach, for the Rosenbach Company, 1922; bought by Mrs. Lessing J. Rosenwald, Jenkintown, Pennsylvania, 1945; given to the National Gallery, 1978.

Exhibitions
Washington, D.C., *Master Drawings*, 1978, pp. 84–85, ill.

Bibliography
Mongan, Hofer, and Seznec, 1945, pl. 66
National Gallery Annual Report, 1978, p. 30

Figure 1. Jean-Auguste-Dominique Ingres. *Ruggiero and Angelica*. Musée du Louvre

Canto X, 94–95:
La fiera gente inospitale e cruda
Alla bestia crudel nel lito espose
La bellissima donna così ignuda,
Come natura prima le compose.
Un velo non ha pure, in che richiuda
I bianchi gigli e le vermiglie rose,
Da non cader per luglio o per dicembre,
Di che non sparse le polite membre.
Vi fu legata pur quella mattina,
Dove venia per trangugiarla viva
Quel smisurato mostro, orca marina,
Ché di abborrévol esca si nutriva.
Dissi di sopra come fu rapina
Di quei che la trovaro in sulla riva
Dormire al vecchio incantatore accanto
Ch'ivi l'avéa tirata per incanto.

"Angelica had been chained to the rock that very morning, to await the killer whale who would come to devour her. In this same canto, I also told how this rare beauty had been surprised by the Ebudians, after being put to sleep under the spell of a wicked hermit, and how she was lying on the sand alongside this aged sorcerer when the Ebudians came upon her: The barbaric islanders had thus exposed Angelica to the monster's deadly jaws. This young princess, naked as the day she was born, had not a single veil to cover the brightly colored roses and the lilies, placed so that their brilliance would enhance so perfect a body."

In Fragonard's drawing, two men are lifting Angelica from the boat, while a third hammers the shackles that will pin her to the side of a rock. An allegorical figure like the one in the previously described drawing is here accompanied by a lion. Ruggiero will arrive just in time to save the beautiful Angelica from the attack of the whale. This would serve as the theme of one of Ingres's most famous paintings (see figure 1).

Bister wash on paper, over an underdrawing in black chalk, 39.4 x 26 cm.

The Rosenbach Museum and Library, Philadelphia, 54.105

Provenance
Hippolyte Walferdin (1795–1880): sold
posthumously, April 12–16, 1880, part of
no. 228 (to Louis Roederer, Reims); at the
death of Louis, passed to his nephew, Léon
Olry-Roederer; bought by Dr. A. S. W.
Rosenbach for the Rosenbach Company,
1922; Rosenbach Museum and Library.

Exhibitions
Philadelphia, 1950–51, no. 71, ill.

Bibliography
Mongan, Hofer, and Seznec, 1945, pl. 78
Rorschach and Taylor, 1985, no. 49

Canto XI, 44, 46:
> Fuor della grotta il vecchio Proteo, quando
> Ode tanto rumór, sopra il mar esce;
> E visto entrare e uscír dell'orca Orlando,
> E al lito trar sì smisurato pesce,
> Fugge per l'alto océano, obbliando
> Lo sparso gregge; e sì 'l tumulto cresce,
> Che fatto al carro i suoi Delfini porre,
> Quel dì Nettuno in Etïopia corre.
>
> Con Melicerta in collo Ino piangendo,
> E le Neréide coi capelli sparsi,
> Glauci, e Tritoni, e gli altri, non sapendo
> Dove, chi quà chi là van per salvarsi.
> Orlando al lito trasse il pesce orrendo,
> Col qual non bisognò più affaticarsi,
> Che pel travaglio e per l'avuta pena,
> Prima morì che fosse in sull'arena.
>
> Dell'ísola non pochi érano corsi
> A riguardár quella battaglia strana.

"When he heard all the noise, old Proteus emerged from his deep grotto and rose above the surface of the water; but having seen Orlando going in and out of the killer whale's mouth, and then hauling the monstrous animal up onto the shore, he was seized with panic, and abandoned the rest of his scattered flock. The noise and the tumult of the waves grew so loud that Neptune himself quickly harnessed his dolphins to his chariot, and, terrified, fled to the Ethiopian seas. The weeping Ino, with Melicertes clinging to her neck; the wild-haired Nereids; Glaucus; the Tritons; and the rest of the court of the god of the sea escaped in every direction. Yet, brave, good Orlando began to pull the whale with greater ease, as its strength ebbed, and, indeed, the monster was dead even before it reached the shore. The people of the island came forth from all over to witness this strange battle."

Orlando, in turn, sails past the isle of Ebuda, where he spies a young girl tied to a tree. This time it is Olympia, whom the whale is about to devour. Orlando decides to kill the beast, and, by means of an anchor that he has thrust into its gaping jaws, he is depicted—in the middle ground, at the left—dragging the animal out of the sea. The trumpet of Fame celebrates his exploits.

In the foreground the denizens of the ocean are fleeing in terror.

263 Caligorante Chained to a Tree

Bister wash on paper, over an underdrawing in black chalk, 43.5 x 28.7 cm.
Inscribed in the center, at the top, in black chalk: *honoré fragonard*

Staatliche Museen Preussischer Kulturbesitz, Berlin-Dahlem, Kupferstichkabinett, KdZ 4553

Provenance
[Roger Portalis, 1889]: sold, February 2–3, 1911, no. 93: "un géant enchaîné" (to the Berlin Kupferstichkabinett).

Bibliography
P. p. 311, ill. between pp. 296 and 297
Wescher, 1934, p. 357
Mongan, Hofer, and Seznec, 1945, p. 22
A. 1918, fig. 763

Related works
The Berlin museum owns another drawing for *Orlando Furioso* (A. 1912, fig. 487, ill.) that illustrates canto XIII (see figure 1) and also comes from the Portalis collection (the stamp, Lugt 2232, is at the lower right).

Figure 1. Fragonard. *Orlando Putting the Prisoners in Chains.* Staatliche Museen Preussischer Kulturbesitz, Berlin-Dahlem, Kupferstichkabinett

Figure 2. Fragonard. *Astolfo Overpowering Caligorante.* Musée d'Art et d'Histoire, Narbonne

Canto XV, 77:

Fan legare il gigante alla verdura
Con un'altra catena molto grossa
Ad una quercia di molt'anni dura,
Che non si romperà per una scossa;

E da dieci sergenti averne cura,
Chè la notte discior non se ne possa,
Ed assalirli e forse far lor danno,
Mentre sicuri e senza guardia stanno.

"With a second, strong chain, Astolfo carefully attached the giant to the trunk of a tough, old tree that he could not topple for all his struggles. For greater security, ten guards were charged with watching over him, since the sudden movements and changes of mood of such a giant were always to be dreaded."

Astolfo, having overwhelmed the giant Caligorante (canto XV; see the previously unpublished drawing in the Narbonne museum: figure 2), decides not to kill him, but to carry him off as a prisoner. On his arrival at the mouth of the Nile, he encounters Griffone and Aquilante, who are eager for revelry; but first they make sure to chain up the bearded giant with the blank stare.

With a few touches of wash and considerable humor, Fragonard describes the impressive musculature and the huge feet of Caligorante. Around him are the silhouettes of the Lilliputian figures who attempt to bind him to the tree trunk, before the eyes of a vigilant watchman.

264 Griffone, Aquilante, and Astolfo Charge Caligorante

Bister wash on paper, over an underdrawing in black chalk, 37.5 x 25 cm.

Musée Grobet-Labadie, Marseilles, GL 4999

Provenance
Hippolyte Walferdin (1795–1880): sold posthumously, April 12–16, 1880, part of no. 228 (to Louis Roederer, Reims); at the death of Louis, passed to his nephew, Léon Olry-Roederer; bought by Dr. A. S. W. Rosenbach for the Rosenbach Company, 1922; Norton Simon, 1955: bought, along with fifty-nine other drawings in the series; bought by Thomas Agnew & Sons, London, 1978; sold by the Galerie Cailleux, Paris, to the Musée Grobet-Labadie, 1984.

Bibliography
Mongan, Hofer, and Seznec, 1945, pl. 118
La Revue du Louvre . . . , 1984, no. 4, p. 290, ill.

Canto XV, 93–94:
Acqua si trova ed arba in questa via:
Di tutti gli altri ben v'è carestia.

Si che prima ch'entrassero in viaggio,
Ciò che lor bisognò fecion raccorre;
E carcar sul gigante il carrïaggio,
Ch'avria portato il collo anco una torre.

"Although they knew that they would find nothing but water, meadows, and a few trees, this was the one [the road] that they preferred. It is true that they had plenty of provisions, and that they had quickly assembled everything that might be necessary, even commodious, for the journey. They loaded all of this heavy baggage onto the shoulders of Caligorante; indeed, had they so desired, they could even have taken the tower of Orrile with them, transporting it by the same means."

Astolfo, who wanted to visit the Holy Land, decided to continue his travels in the company of Griffone and Aquilante. Against a background of balusters, colonnades, and pediments (which, apart from a single obelisk, has nothing to do with Egypt), Fragonard's figures load the supplies needed for their trip onto the back of the giant Caligorante, whose arms are tied behind him.

The network of black-chalk lines alternating with areas of bister wash is characteristic of Fragonard's drawings for *Orlando Furioso,* and would have been extremely difficult for an engraver to reproduce.

This drawing was recently acquired by the museum in Marseilles.

Bister wash on paper, over an underdrawing in black chalk, 36.5 x 23.6 cm.

Musée du Louvre, Paris, Cabinet des Dessins, MNR-CD 90

Provenance
Assigned to the Louvre by the Office des
Biens privés, 1950.

Figure 1. Fragonard. *Ruggiero Prepares to Write to Bradamante*. Nationalmuseum, Stockholm

Canto XXV, 85–86, 90:

Poi che più cose immaginate s'ebbe,
Pensa scriverle alfin quanto gli accada;
E bench'egli non sappia come debbe
La lettera invïar, si che ben vada,
Non però vuol restar; chè ben potrebbe
Alcun messo fedel trovar per strada.
Più non s'indugia, e salta delle piume:
Si fa dar carta, inchiostro, penna e lume.

I camerieri discreti ed avveduti
Arrecano a Ruggier ciò che comanda.
Egli comincia a scrivere, e i saluti,
Come si suol, nei primi versi manda:
Poi narra degli avvisi che venuti
Son dal suo re, ch'aiuto gli domanda;
E se l'andata sua non è ben presta,
O morto o in man degl'inimici resta.
(...)
Voglio, lo soggiunga, quando vi piaccia,
L'assedio al mio signor levar d'intorno,
Acciò che l'ignorante vulgo taccia,
Il qual direbbe, a mia vergogna e scorno:
Ruggier, mentre Agramante ebbe bonaccia,
Mai non l'abbandonò notte nè giorno;
Or che fortuna per Carlo si piega,
Egli col vincitor l'insegna spiega.

"'Do give me leave, oh dear and sovereign mistress of my life, to go and rescue Agramante's besieged camp, and to silence the slander: men must no longer dare to say that I served this emperor when all France trembled before his might, but that I switched my allegiance to Charles when I saw that he was the victor. If only a letter, a message could be sent, to reassure her and obtain her pardon!' Finally, he decided to write, although he had no idea how the letter could reach her. Perhaps he would encounter a faithful messenger. He leapt from his bed and asked that a candle be brought to him. First, he paid his mistress the customary compliments, and then he told her about Agramante's plea for his assistance. If he did not hurry, the prince would lose his life or his liberty."

This previously unpublished drawing is similar to the one in the Stockholm museum (see figure 1; Mongan, 129), which represents Ruggiero preparing to write to Bradamante, in order to justify his delay. Ruggiero, torn between love and duty, approaches a desk, on which there is a quill and an inkwell. Inspiration, in the form of a winged spirit, appears to him. The Louvre drawing immediately follows this scene. Ruggiero wears the same costume, with its slit sleeves and ruffled collar, and shoes with large bows. The hat, the inkwell, and the shield in the Stockholm drawing have been dispensed with, but the armchair—which is not unlike the one in the drawing of *Ariosto Inspired by Love and Folly* (cat. no. 255)—and the desk, with the pile of thick large books underneath it, are exactly the same.

The allegorical figure in the upper part of the drawing makes it easy to guess the contents of the letter: Slander, bearing in one hand the mask of Untruth and, in the other, a purse filled with money (?), is being stabbed by an attacker. In fact, Ruggiero is about to embrace Catholicism, in order to marry Bradamante, but not without first bringing help to his besieged king—so as not to be accused of abandoning him in favor of the victorious Charlemagne, and of converting to another faith out of cowardice.

266   The Letter

Bister wash on paper, over an underdrawing in black chalk, 39.9 x 29 cm.

The Art Institute of Chicago, Gift of Tiffany and Margaret Blake, 1945.32

Provenance
Anonymous sale, May 31, 1790, no. 323: "un jeune homme par une croisée remet une lettre à une femme qui est dans un appartement"; Le Brun: sold, April 11, 1791, no. 347: "une femme assise sur un sopha, surprise de l'arrivée d'un homme qui lui apporte une lettre: ils sont vêtus dans un costume pittoresque et un peu espagnol" (for 24 *livres*); Saint: sold, May 4, 1846, part of no. 18: "l'intrigue à la fenêtre"; Duc de Montesquiou-Fezensac (according to the 1921 exhibition catalogue); [we do not believe that it was in the Hippolyte Walferdin collection]; David David-Weill, before 1913; [Wildenstein, 1938]; Tiffany and Margaret Blake; given to the Art Institute, 1945.

Exhibitions
Paris, 1921, no. 126
London, 1932, no. 808 (no. 687 in the commemorative catalogue)
Paris, 1958, no. 49, pl. 64
Paris, 1976–77, no. 18, ill.
Washington, D.C., 1978, no. 43, ill. (with a complete list of the exhibitions in which this drawing has been included)

Bibliography
Société de Reproductions des Dessins de Maîtres, 1913, vol. 5
P. p. 300
G. Wildenstein, 1921, p. 359, ill.
Foerster [1925], pl. 10
Martine, 1927, pl. 39
Henriot, 1928, III, p. 117, ill. p. 119
R. p. 203
A. 74, fig. 32 (see also A. 1955)
Munhall, 1971, p. 404, fig. 8
Meder, 1978, II, pl. 207

Figure 1. Augustin de Saint-Aubin and Noël Pruneau, after Jean-Baptiste Leprince. *L'Amour à l'Espagnole.* Musée du Louvre, Paris, Cabinet des Dessins, Rothschild Collection

This "highly important" drawing (it was referred to this way in the 1791 sales catalogue) is dated decidedly after 1770 by E. Williams (1978). It seems to have been executed just before the famous *Two Young Women Conversing, La Lecture,* and *La Rêveuse* (see cat. nos. 269–271). The "picturesque costumes" are described as "un peu espagnol" because of the young man's cuffs and broad starched collar.

The story is simple: a young woman receives a love letter delivered by a young messenger, who appears at her window. She turns toward the gallant young man, who looks at us ironically. The subject is an ordinary one: Leprince's painting *Amour à l'Espagnole,* after which an engraving was made in 1783 by Augustin de Saint-Aubin and Noël Pruneau (see figure 1), offers a number of similarities with the Chicago drawing.

With his fine narrative skill, Fragonard captured the figures' facial expressions, which help explain the event taking place. He depicts his theme objectively, but takes pleasure in including the spectator in on the joke. Here, his technical virtuosity is perfectly complemented by an exceptionally lively gift for observation.

267 Young Woman Reading

Bister wash on paper, over an underdrawing in black chalk, 44.6 x 33.9 cm.

Graphische Sammlung Albertina, Vienna, Inv. 12732

Provenance
Varanchan de Saint-Geniès: sold, December 29–31, 1777, no. 56: "une très belle étude de jeune personne coëffée à l'anglaise et assise devant un livre. Ce dessin lavé au bistre sur papier blanc, est d'un caractère noble et d'un excellent effet" [45.9 x 33.8 cm.]" (for 100 *livres*); Desmarets: sold, March 17, 1797, no. 87: "deux dessins, au bistre sur papier blanc, répresentans [*sic*] l'un une femme qui dessine, l'autre une qui lit [45.9 x 33.8 cm.]";

Albert, Duke of Saxe-Teschen (1738–1822) (the dry mark of his collection, Lugt 174, is at the lower left); entered the Albertina at the time of its founding.

Exhibitions
Paris, 1931, no. 59
London, 1932, no. 1007 (no. 691 in the commemorative catalogue)
Paris, 1950, no. 155
Bern, 1954, no. 76, cover ill.

Bibliography
P. p. 306 (the Varanchan drawing)
Schönbrunner and Meder, 1896–1908, III, pl. 255
Meder, 1922, pl. 27
Fosca, 1954, p. 51, pl. 5
R. p. 211
Mrozińska, 1960, p. 17, fig. 6
A. 178, fig. 695

Related works
See the following entry.

The evidence would seem to confirm that this drawing is identical with the one in the sale of the Varanchan collection in 1777 (see the following entry)—in which case it was obviously executed before then. Nothing in its style contradicts this dating; from the time of his second visit to Italy, Fragonard liked to draw (one might just as easily say paint) with bister wash over a delicate underdrawing in black chalk—here, virtually invisible.

A young woman, seated on a cushion atop a chest, is reading—or, at least, it appears as if she is reading, for she gives the impression of striking a pose—from a book placed on a moon-shaped lectern. Other books, whose edges are visible, lie scattered on the floor, or are on top of a wardrobe. The sitter may be Marguerite Gérard (1761–1837), Mme Fragonard's younger sister. Although there is no absolute proof, it is believed that Marguerite went to live at her brother-in-law's, in the Louvre, in 1775. What we know of Marguerite's beauty would seem to corroborate this identification—to which the Varanchan collection sales catalogue, however, makes no allusion.

The originality of the drawing is due, in part, to the shape of the lectern, against which the girl's delicate profile is effectively set off.

268 Young Woman Drawing

Bister wash on paper, over an underdrawing in black chalk, 45.1 x 33.8 cm.
Inscribed at the lower right: *H. Fragonard*
A damaged area at the lower center of the paper has been restored.

Graphische Sammlung Albertina, Vienna, Inv. 12731

Provenance
Desmarets: sold, March 17, 1797, part of no. 87 (see the previous entry); Albert, Duke of Saxe-Teschen (1738–1822) (the dry mark of his collection, Lugt 174, is at the lower left); entered the Albertina at the time of its founding.

Exhibitions
Paris, 1931, no. 58

Paris, 1950, no. 154
Bern, 1954, no. 75
Washington, D.C., 1984–85, no. 72, color-pl. (entry by Christine Ekelhart)

Bibliography
Schönbrunner and Meder, 1896–1908, VII, pl. 749
Meder, 1922, pl. 26
Fosca, 1954, pp. 50–51, pl. 4

R. p. 211
A. 1965, fig. 536
Benesch, 1964, no. 224, ill.

Related works
See the previous entry.

This drawing clearly is the pendant to the Albertina's *Young Woman Reading* (see the previous entry). It was probably executed slightly earlier than 1777, and may also represent Marguerite Gérard, Mme Fragonard's younger sister.

The young woman is seated on a low stool, and is resting a drawing board on her knees. She is sketching from life (an antique bust lying on the floor is an allusion to her previous works) a man in his prime, with a full head of hair and a beard, and a stern expression, as well as a baby and its mother. The models, standing behind a low wall (a chest?), pose for a *Holy Family,* not unlike the figure group in the painting of the *Rest on the Flight,* in Troyes (see cat. no. 228, figure 2). The mother and child resemble their counterparts in *L'Heureuse Fécondité* (see cat. no. 222), but Fragonard did not only wish to include references to his own oeuvre. Skillfully blending the sacred and the profane, and reality and fiction, he drew his inspiration directly from a painting by Schedoni that he had copied in Naples in 1761 (see figure 1). In this Emilian artist's *Holy Family* (then in the Capodimonte, and now in the Palazzo Reale; see Rosenberg and Brejon, 1986, no. 6), the Child Jesus is standing on the carpenter's bench in a pose that Fragonard would remember —and utilize—fifteen years later.

The composition breaks down into two triangles, linked by the gaze of the young woman toward her models. Her intense concentration gives a tension to the drawing, whose shimmering luminosity invites our admiration.

Figure 1. Fragonard, after Bartolomeo Schedoni. *The Holy Family.* Graphische Sammlung Albertina, Vienna

269　Two Young Women Conversing

Bister wash on paper, over an underdrawing in black chalk, 28 x 21 cm.

Museum Boymans-van Beuningen, Rotterdam, F-1-228

Provenance
[Chabot and Duc de La Mure or Desmarets]: sold, December 17–22, 1787, no. 171: "deux Études de figures de femmes, assises et bien drappées; l'une coeffée d'un chapeau est très ressemblante à un habile artiste dans le genre de la miniature" (for 60 *livres,* to Millioty ?); anonymous sale, July 8, 1793, no. 66: "deux autres dessins lavés au bistre; l'un représente une jeune fille tenant un livre à la main, l'autre deux femmes qui causent ensemble" (?); Desmarets: sold, March 17, 1797, no. 88: "deux dessins, au bistre, l'un une femme endormie devant une glace, l'autre deux femmes conversant" [29.7 x 21.6 cm.] (?); Baron Brunet Denon: sold, February 2, 1846, no. 264: "la confidence" (for 46 francs) (?); Marius Paulme, from "la

fin de 1925" (his stamp, Lugt 1910, is at the bottom right): sold posthumously, May 13, 1929, no. 86, pl. 58 (for 560,000 francs, to F. Lugt); Franz Koenigs (1881–1941), Haarlem, from 1929 (his stamp, Lugt 1023 a, is on the verso); acquired by D. G. van Beuningen, 1940, and given to the Rotterdam museum the following year.

Exhibitions
Paris, 1931, no. 53
Paris, 1937, no. 541, pl. 95 of the album
Paris, 1950, no. 87, pl. 6
Paris, 1952, no. 93
Paris-Amsterdam, 1964, no. 116, pl. 95 (with a complete list of exhibitions and a bibliography)
Amsterdam, 1974, no. 45, ill.

Bibliography
P. p. 296 (?)
R. pp. 211–12, 23 fig. 10
Haverkamp-Begemann, 1957, no. 65, ill. (with a detailed bibliography)
A. 722, fig. 204 (and A. 60)

Related works
The slightly larger drawing of the same subject, formerly in the National Gallery of Canada, Ottawa (A. 721, fig. 203; Paris exhibition catalogue, 1969–70, no. 44, fig. 21), is now considered by curators to be a fake (G. Norman, *The Times,* March 8 and 9, 1978, illustrated on March 9). For the verso of this sheet, see catalogue no. 270.

Is this drawing identical with one of the two included in the Chabot and de La Mure sale in 1787? The entry in the sales catalogue states that in one of these, one of the "seated women ... strongly resembles a skillful painter of miniatures." This "artiste" cannot be anyone else but Mme Fragonard, who enjoyed a wide reputation for her works in this period mention her name and attribute miniatures to her (whereas today they are usually ascribed to her husband!).

Unfortunately, the 1787 sales catalogue also notes that the "skillful *artiste* ... is wearing a hat." In our opinion, the lady wearing the hat—elegantly topped with black feathers —is not Mme Fragonard, but her sister, the beautiful Marguerite Gérard (born, 1761), who was sixteen years her junior. This is neither the place to recount Marguerite's artistic career nor to speculate on the supposed love affair between Jean-Honoré and his sister-in-law. We do not

267

268

exclude the possibility, however, that the Rotterdam drawing may represent the two sisters about 1780.

The two women are seated in front of a table, covered with a cloth, on which one can (barely) discern some books, drawings (?), a blank canvas (?), and a feather duster. (Might this be Fragonard's studio?) The younger of the women wears an elegant low-necked dress decorated with ruching, with short frilled sleeves and a ruffle around neck. Her companion, whose arms are crossed over her knees, wears a city dress and a black hooded mantle; on her head is a small white lace cap. The women lean toward each other and look out at us as if their gaze were fixed on the artist who was drawing them. Are they "exchanging confidences," as implied by the title given to the work by Marius Paulme, who rediscovered it, in 1925 (and by which it was known in 1846, if it is the same drawing as no. 264 in the sale of the Brunet Denon collection)? This is doubtful, even though the attitudes of the two young women suggest that they are about to share some gossip. They are chatting, but they are also posing.

269

270 La Lecture

Bister wash on paper, over traces of an underdrawing in black chalk, 28.1 x 21 cm.

Musée du Louvre, Paris, Cabinet des Dessins, Inv. 26.651

Provenance
For the possible provenance of the Louvre drawing, see catalogue no. 267; Chevalier de Saint-Morys, whose collection entered the Louvre at the time of the Revolution with those confiscated from the Émigrés (the Louvre's stamps, Lugt 1886 and 2207, are at the lower left and center).

Exhibitions
Paris, 1921, no. 127
Amsterdam, 1926, no. 150
Paris, 1931, no. 54
London, 1932, no. 690 (no. 839, ill., in the commemorative catalogue)
Paris, 1937, no. 540
Paris, 1946, no. 375
Paris, 1950, no. 88, pl. 36
Paris, 1962, no. 99

Bibliography
G. pp. 297, 331
P. p. 307, ill. between pp. 224 and 225
N., ill. between pp. 94 and 95
Guiffrey and Marcel, 1910, V, no. 4053
Foerster [1925], pl. 19
Leporini, 1925, pl. III
Nolhac, 1933, ill. between pp. 192 and 193
Lavallée, 1938, no. 7, ill.
Claudel, 1946, p. 152, ill. on opp. page
Wilhelm, 1951, p. 24, ill.
R. p. 212
A. 61, fig. 27
Starobinski, 1964, p. 125, ill. p. 123
Fried, 1980, p. 138, ill. p. 137

Related works
Two other versions of this drawing are known. One, very likely by Fragonard, formerly in the Walferdin and Heseltine collections, is in the Hammer collection, Los Angeles (see figure 1; A. 62, fig. 28; Jacquemart-André–Louvre catalogue, 1977, no. 67, colorpl.). The other, probably after Fragonard, belongs to the Museum of Art at the Rhode Island School of Design, in Providence (see figure 2; A. 63).

There is also a version of *La Lecture* on the verso of *La Confidence,* formerly in Ottawa (see *Related works,* catalogue no. 269).

Jules de Goncourt made an engraving (see figure 3) of the Louvre drawing, which served as the frontispiece of his study on Fragonard published in 1865.

Figure 1. Attributed to Fragonard.
La Lecture.The Armand Hammer
Collection, Los Angeles

Figure 2. After Fragonard (?).
La Lecture. Museum of Art,
Rhode Island School of Design,
Providence

Figure 3. Jules de Goncourt,
after Fragonard. *La Lecture*.
Bibliothèque Nationale, Paris,
Cabinet des Estampes

This drawing is justly famous. It is difficult to decide whether it was intended as the pendant to the Rotterdam drawing (cat. no. 269) or to a version of *La Rêveuse* (cat. no. 271), but, in any event, certain common motifs are discernible from one drawing to the next, such as the armchair, the satin dresses, the mantle, the ruffles, and even details of the hairstyles. There is no question but that the two women are Marguerite Gérard (1761–1837) and her sister, Marie-Anne Fragonard (1745–1823).

With a considerable economy of means and his usual technical virtuosity in the use of light and dark bister wash, Fragonard located his two figures in the pictorial space with a solidity and a feel for the rhythm of the composition that are astounding.

Moreover, he was able to capture the atmosphere of contemplative silence and of reverie that surrounds the reader, who "turns her back squarely on reality. It is her burgeoning dream, on the contrary, that we are directly presented with, but through the figure seated in the foreground: I am referring to her dress, with its wide pleats and glimmering iridescence, but also to the regard of this pensive young woman, whose shadowy profile indicates her absolute concentration on some imaginary place in which she cannot decide whether to stay. She leans, or rather hangs, over the baluster of an invisible pool'' (Paul Claudel, written at Brangues, July 8, 1941, in *L'Œil écoute,* 1946).

271   La Rêveuse

Bister wash on paper, over an underdrawing in black chalk, 30.5 x 21.5 cm.

The Metropolitan Museum of Art, New York, Robert Lehman Collection, 1975.1.627

Provenance

According to Thirion (1895), a version of *La Rêveuse* belonged to one of the Roslins, a powerful family of *fermiers généraux*; perhaps, the ''Jeune fille tenant un livre à la main'' in an anonymous sale, July 8, 1793, no. 66 (see also *Related works,* and cat. no. 269); Baronne de Ruble, 1889; Alfred Beurdeley (his stamp, Lugt 421, is at the bottom right): sold, Paris, March 13–15, 1905, no. 71 (for 20,000 francs, to E. Cognacq); (on the purchase of the drawing by E. Cognacq, who believed for a while, on the advice of a ''charitable ami,'' that the drawing was a fake: ''c'est Groult qui l'a fait,'' see the anecdote reported by Eudel, 1908); Ernest Cognacq, 1921; Gabriel Cognacq, 1931: sold, May 14, 1952, no. 1, ill.; [Feilchenfeld, Zurich]; acquired by Robert Lehman, and entered the Metropolitan Museum along with the rest of his collection, 1975.

Exhibitions

Paris, 1907 (not in catalogue)
Paris, 1921, no. 145
Paris, 1931, no. 26
Bern, 1954, no. 77, pl. XVII
Zurich, 1955, no. 102
Stockholm, 1958, no. 250
Washington, D.C., 1978, no. 48, ill.
New York, 1980, no. 14, ill.

Bibliography

P. p. 305, ill. between pp. 140 and 141
Thirion, 1895, p. 332
D. and V., pl. 169, ill.
Eudel, 1908, pp. 428–29
Foerster [1925], pl. 20
Fosca, 1954, p. 61, pl. 28
R. p. 216
A. 58, fig. 682

Related works

A second version of this drawing exists, with variations (figure 1; see A. 59). It was given to the Boston museum with the Forsyth Wickes collection in 1965.

A copy of this drawing (A. 734) is in the Musée des Beaux-Arts, Orléans.

Figure 1. Fragonard. *La Rêveuse.*
Museum of Fine Arts, Boston

Figure 2. Jean-Baptiste-Siméon Chardin.
The Amusements of Private Life.
Nationalmuseum, Stockholm

The Boston version (figure 1), also autograph, differs somewhat from the New York drawing, mostly with regard to the placement and the pose of the central figure, who is closer to the picture plane, and turns farther to the left. We are in agreement with Eunice Williams (1978) that the much more beautiful—and better preserved—Boston version predates the New York drawing (what has happened to the sitter's feet in the latter?). We also believe that if one of these two versions is the pendant to the *Two Young Women Conversing* in Rotterdam (cat. no. 269), it can only be the Boston drawing.

A girl sitting on the edge of an armchair before a mirror partially covered with drapery (perhaps this is her dressing table), an open book in her hand, appears to be dozing. Is she asleep, or has her reading induced a pleasant daydream? A young woman stands nearby, with one finger raised to her lips to enforce silence on her companion, who turns in her direction and points ironically to the sleeping figure. Can we deduce from her dress and her hat that she is Marguerite

Gérard, and that the woman in the lace cap is her sister, Marie-Anne Fragonard? Since the eighteenth century, certain compilers of sales catalogues did not hesitate to propose such an identification (see cat. no. 267).

Lost in her book, the pretty girl seems to be unmindful of her uncomfortable position leaning on the back of the armchair, for she is far from the real world. In an intentional contrast on the part of the artist, her two companions bring us back to earth.

This drawing has often been compared to Chardin's *Amusements of Private Life* (see figure 2; Stockholm; Rosenberg, 1983, no. 123, ill.); like Chardin, Fragonard explored the theme of escape through reading. In Chardin's picture, the sitter is alert, even though she has the look of someone who has just put down a book and is still preoccupied with what she has read. However, for Fragonard, his sleeping model is the point of departure for a little scenario that is guaranteed to make us smile.

272 The Village Fête

Gray wash on paper, with traces of bister, over an underdrawing in black chalk, 34.8 x 43.3 cm.

Rijksmuseum, Amsterdam, Rijksprentenkabinet, 1953:205

Provenance
Duc de Feltre: sold posthumously, May 6–9, 1867, no. 89 (for 430 francs, to Basset; no dimensions given); anonymous sale, May 15–17, 1883, no. 78: "un marché de village. Fête de village. Deux jolis dessins à la sépia"(?); Baronne Mandraut (according to Henriot); Baronne de Ruble, 1889 (according to P. and A.—erroneously, in our opinion); David

David-Weill, 1927; Fritz Mannheimer; entered the museum in Amsterdam, 1953.

Exhibitions
Paris, 1946, no. 120
Amsterdam, 1951, no. 170
Paris-Amsterdam, 1964, no. 112, pl. 93
Amsterdam, 1974, no. 42, ill.

Bibliography
P. p. 301
Martine, 1927, pl. 47
Henriot, 1928, III, p. 141, ill. p. 143
A. 815, fig. 522 (see also—erroneously—A. 253, 254)
Roland Michel, 1983, p. 475

272

Since at least 1867—and, very likely, as early as the eighteenth century—this drawing has been associated with the *Children Dancing in a Park* (cat. no. 273). Three separate divertissements may be distinguished in the scene: at the left, a child is carrying a processional banner on which the Virgin and Child and two saints are depicted; at the center, there is a public fountain surmounted by a statue of the Three Graces, and, below, female figures are bearing water; and, at the right, is a traveling show, complete with a puppet theater, toy stalls ("À LA BELLE ... "), and a crêpe seller. In the background is the village church: we can discern its pointed

bell tower, and the columns on its classical façade. Fragonard has included numerous picturesque details, such as the two women locked in combat on the ground; the terrified dog that is fleeing, at the extreme left; and, at the right, the three elegant ladies and their male companion, who are visiting the fair.

The costumes, the architecture of the church, and the technical delicacy of the handling of this gray wash drawing confirm the late date—sometime between 1775 and 1780—proposed by Marianne Roland Michel for this work.

273　Children Dancing in a Park

Gray wash on paper, with traces of bister wash, over an underdrawing in black chalk, 34.8 x 43.3 cm.

Rijksmuseum, Amsterdam, Rijksprentenkabinet, 1953:204

Provenance
Duc de Feltre: sold posthumously, May 6–9, 1867, no. 88 (for 450 francs, to Basset; no dimensions given); sold, 1883 ? (see the previous entry); Baronne Mandraut (according to Henriot); Baronne de Ruble, 1889 (according to P. and A.—but in our view the drawing in question is our cat. no. 274); David David-Weill, 1927; Fritz Mannheimer; entered the museum in Amsterdam, 1953.

Exhibitions
London, 1932, no. 788 (no. 684 in the commemorative catalogue)
Paris, 1946, no. 119
Paris, 1950, no. 89
Amsterdam, 1951, no. 171 (not 170), pl. 34
Paris-Amsterdam, 1964, no. 113, pl. 92
Amsterdam, 1974, no. 43, ill.

Bibliography
P. p. 311

Martine, 1927, pl. 45
Henriot, 1928, III, p. 125, ill. p. 127
A. 817, fig. 523 (see also—erroneously—A. 253, 254)
Williams, 1978, p. 107, fig. 4
Roland Michel, 1983, p. 475

Related works
For the drawing in the Lehman Collection at The Metropolitan Museum of Art, see catalogue no. 274.

For the pendant to this drawing, see the previous entry.

We do not believe that the setting of the *Children Dancing in a Park,* any more than that of the *Village Fête,* depicts a real place—nor do we believe any longer that it is a study for one of Fragonard's paintings.

Directly in the center of the composition, at the foot of a flight of steps, two very young children are performing some dance steps, as a group of elegant people look on. The cascade, the orange trees in their box-like planters, the statue of Amour under the tall trees, and the parasols gleaming in the sunshine, all evoke the tranquillity of a happy summer afternoon.

274 Two Young Children Dancing in a Park

Gray wash on paper, with traces of pink and green, over an underdrawing in black chalk, 34.3 x 42.5 cm.
On the verso is a study in black chalk for the drawing in Amsterdam: catalogue no. 273 (see figure 1).

The Metropolitan Museum of Art, New York, Robert Lehman Collection, 1975.1.628

Figure 1. Verso of catalogue no. 274

Provenance
Baronne de Ruble, 1889 (see P. 1889, p. III); Alfred Beurdeley (his stamp, Lugt 421, is at the lower left and right): sold, Paris, March 13–15, 1905, no. 80, ill. (for 9,000 francs, to Walter Gay); [André Weil, 1938]; Robert Lehman, after World War II: entered the Metropolitan Museum along with the rest of his collection, 1975.

Exhibitions
Paris, 1921, no. 114
Paris, 1931, no. 66
London, 1932, no. 798 (no. 677 in the commemorative catalogue)
Paris, 1946, no. 122
Paris, 1957, no. 97
Washington, D.C., 1978, no. 39, ill.
New York, 1980, nos. 13 a and b, ill.
Bordeaux, 1981, no. 160, ill.

Bibliography
P. p. 301, ill. p. 81
R. p. 228
Ananoff, 1957, p. 520, ill.
G. Wildenstein, 1960, p. 47, p. 50, n. 7, p. 46, fig. 2
A. 790, fig. 706
Williams, 1979, p. 76, ill.
Gaehtgens, 1983, p. 33, fig. 21
Roland Michel, 1983, p. 475

Related works
For the drawing in Amsterdam, see catalogue no. 273.
For the Banque de France painting, see catalogue no. 161.

This drawing has always been associated with the *Fête at Saint-Cloud* (which belongs to the Banque de France; see cat. no. 161), but we do not consider it a preparatory study for that painting, so great are the differences between the two works. Moreover, the practice of creating a preparatory drawing, in the true sense of the term, was completely alien to Fragonard's usual working methods.

The study on the verso of the sheet, in black chalk only, to our knowledge has been reproduced just once, in 1980. It is very close in its details to the drawing in Amsterdam *Children Dancing in a Park* (cat. no. 273), and, in spite of the freedom of its execution, Eunice Williams (1978) considers it—rightly, we believe—to be a "souvenir" of the Amsterdam composition, rather than a study for it.

Once again, the question of the dates of these three drawings arises. We believe that, on the basis of their technique and of the fashions depicted, they must have been executed between 1775 and 1780.

The importance of the Lehman watercolor lies in its freedom of invention, its improvised character, and, above all, in its evocation of the gardens and the parks so beloved by eighteenth-century society.

275 The Children's Lessons

Gray wash on paper, over an underdrawing in black chalk, 43.4 x 34.7 cm.
Inscribed in ink (barely legible), in the left foreground: *fragonard*

Private collection

Provenance
Laurent Laperlier, from 1860: sold, April 11–13, 1867, no. 60 (for 700 francs, with its pendant); Eudoxe Marcille; has remained in the collection of Marcille's descendants.

Exhibitions
Paris, 1860, no. 14
Paris, 1879, no. 573

Paris, 1884, no. 272
Paris, 1921, no. 129
Paris, 1931, no. 24

Bibliography
G. p. 341, n. 1
Burty, 1879, p. 147
Chennevières, 1880, p. 108
P. p. 296, ill. between pp. 92 and 93

Tornézy, 1895, pp. 53–54, 56
Foerster [1925], pl. 31
R. p. 204
A. 26, fig. 14

Related works
For the pendant, see the following entry.
  For the study, see catalogue no. 277.

276 The Return of the Victor

Gray wash on paper, over an underdrawing in black chalk, 43.4 x 34.7 cm.
Inscribed on the stool at the right, in pen and ink: *fragonard*

Private collection

Provenance
See the previous entry (no. 61 in the Laperlier collection sale).

Exhibitions
Paris, 1860, no. 15
Paris, 1879, no. 574
Paris, 1884, no. 273
Paris, 1921, no. 130
Paris, 1931, no. 25

Bibliography
G. pp. 341–42, n. 1
Burty, 1879, p. 147
Chennevières, 1880, p. 108
P. p. 296, ill. between pp. 158 and 159
Tornézy, 1895, pp. 53–54, 56
N., ill. between pp. 88 and 89
R. p. 204
Ananoff, 1957, p. 522, ill.
A. 27, fig. 15

Related works
For the pendant, see the previous entry.
  For the study, see catalogue no. 278.

While this drawing and catalogue no. 275 reveal an unaccustomed side of Fragonard's talent, they have yet to disclose all their secrets.

What do they represent? The titles by which they are usually known, *Le Concours* (The Competition) and *La Récompense* (The Reward), do not seem to us entirely satisfactory. In catalogue no. 275, elegantly dressed men and women, along with a number of children, crowd attentively around a table. Two governesses—their curls topped by magnificent hats—tend to the children; one of them is making a little girl recite her lessons, while the other is teaching a small boy how to write. In the foreground, another girl is

engrossed in reading, while her young classmate, who has abandoned his book and his plumed hat on the ground, turns to look at the two dogs who are observing the scene. In the present drawing, which is sometimes entitled "Il a gagné le prix," a small boy is being carried in triumph by a couple—perhaps his governess and his tutor. He is welcomed with open arms by his parents, who are surrounded by a large and happy audience. The two dogs, who have recognized their mistress, are running along, ahead of her. While there is no apparent "reward" in the present drawing, in the previous one we fail to understand what kind of "competition" is taking place among the children.

In the nineteenth century, and in certain recent catalogues, some critics proposed that the Bergeret family served as the models for these drawings, and that the Folie Beaujon or Cassan was the site depicted, but there is little to support these hypotheses.

Perhaps we can find the beginnings of an explanation in the very old inscription on the verso of the drawing—more freely executed, but just as widely studied—in Frankfurt (see cat. no. 277): "instruction d'enfans fait chez le Duc de Chabost." Swarzenski was the first to recall that the Duc de Chabot—Louis-Antoine-Auguste de Rohan Chabot (1733–1807), one of the heroes of the Seven Years' War, Comte, and then Duc de Chabot (he did not assume the title of Duc de Rohan until 1791)—and the Duchesse (née Élisabeth Louise de la Rochefoucault [1740–1786]) maintained a popular drawing academy in Paris in their home, the *hôtel* de la Rochefoucault, in the Faubourg Saint-Germain. Hubert Robert (see Carlson, *Robert* exhibition catalogue, Washington, D.C., 1978, p. 22, n. 73), Vien, and Lagrenée, but also Taraval, Durameau, Pierre, Desfriches, and many other artists taught there (see Ratouis de Limay, 1907, pp. 6–7, n. 1, p. 51). Moreau the Younger was an important presence at

the school; Mahérault (1880, p. 481, no. 467) catalogues a work by this artist "drawn at the Duc de Chabot's 1777." Wâtelet and other *amateurs* attended classes assiduously, and the duchess herself was known to draw (works by her may be seen in Besançon and in San Francisco; see Hattis, 1977, no. 73, ill.). "After which she sat down and began to draw, for a whole hour, in the company of several Gentlemen, who were all seated in a circle around a large table..." wrote Mozart. "To cut the session short, I finally began to play on the wretched and detestable pianoforte. But most vexing of all was that Madame and all her Gentlemen would not interrupt their drawing for a single instant..." the young prodigy continued, in a letter of May 1, 1778 to his father (published by Curzon, 1928, p. 187).

That Fragonard also visited the Duchesse de Chabot's academy seems highly probable, and that he made drawings there is very likely (one would like to imagine that he was among those who so gratified Mozart with "a bunch of praise"!). However, it remains to be determined whether the two scenes represented in these drawings refer to specific events—in which case, one hopes that we will uncover the details one day—or whether, once again, they are products of Fragonard's fertile imagination and his talent for invention, which were given free rein.

The style of the clothing, the architecture, the few pieces of furniture, the gray wash, and the narrative quality of the scenes all seem to indicate that these two drawings postdate 1780. At a time when he himself was tempted by illustration, Fragonard was perhaps trying to prove that he could compete fearlessly with Moreau the Younger, in a genre that was then becoming increasingly popular.

277 The Children's Lessons

Gray wash on paper, heightened with color, over an underdrawing in black chalk, 43.4 x 34.4 cm.
Inscribed on the front of the mount: *Honoré Fragonard fec.*, and on the verso, in ink: *n° 52 honoré Fragonard*; in black chalk, and in ink in an old hand: *honorée* [sic] *fragonard invᵗ fecit*; in ink: *fragonard 304*; and, again in ink, in an old hand: *fragonard 304/instruction d' enfans fait chez le Duc de Chabost*

Städelsches Kunstinstitut, Frankfurt am Main, Graphische Sammlung, Inv. 1233

Provenance
Part of the museum's original collections; listed in the first inventory, 1862.

Exhibitions
Frankfurt am Main, 1986–87, no. 127, colorpl.

Bibliography
Swarzenski, n.d., pp. 3–14
A. 604, fig. 192
Williams, 1978, p. 166

Related works
For the pendant, see catalogue no. 278.
 For the finished drawing, see catalogue no. 275.
 See also the three preceding entries.

This drawing and the one in New York (cat. no. 278) have never been brought together with the versions in Paris (cat. nos. 275, 276), which share the same format but are more finished. The New York drawing has been incised with a stylus—from which we may deduce that Fragonard used his first drawing as a model for the second, much more meticu-lous version, in which he included a greater variety of detail. The touches of color in the Frankfurt sheet give it a liveliness and a spontaneity that are less evident in the Paris version. Here, one admires the rendering of light, as well as the way in which Fragonard creates a feeling of distance between the groups of figures.

278 The Return of the Victor

Gray wash on paper, over an underdrawing in black chalk, 42.9 x 34.2 cm.
The drawing was incised with a stylus, according to Eunice Williams (1978).

The Pierpont Morgan Library, New York, Purchased as the gift of the Fellows with the assistance of several Fellows, 1955.5

Provenance
Hippolyte Walferdin (1795–1880): sold posthumously, April 12–16, 1880, no. 261 (for 165 francs); Camille Groult, in 1889; anonymous sale, December 19, 1941, no. 46, pl. III (acquired by Ancel); Mme Mottart: sold by her estate, Galerie Charpentier, Paris, February 8, 1945, no. 38, pl. XXV; [de Bayser, before 1955]; acquired by The Pierpont Morgan Library with the support of Walter C. Baker, Mme Renée de Becker, Francis Kettaneh, Mrs. Paul Moore, John S. Newberry, Jr., Mr. and Mrs. Carl Stera, Mrs. Herbert N. Straus, and Forsyth Wickes, 1955.

Exhibitions
Baltimore, 1959, no. 48
London, 1968, no. 278, fig. 293
New York, 1974, no. 29, ill.
Washington, D.C., 1978, no. 58, ill.

Bibliography
G. p. 342
P. p. 311
R. p. 204
Ananoff, 1957, p. 522, ill.
Stampfle, 1957, pp. 76–79
A. 605, fig. 193
Pierpont Morgan catalogue, 1981, no. 106, ill.

Related works
See the three previous entries.

279 La Lecture

Bister wash on paper, over an underdrawing in black chalk, 34 x 47.5 cm.

Private collection

Provenance
In the same family since the beginning of the nineteenth century.

Bibliography
Unpublished

Related works
A drawing, although with variations, of the left side of the composition was formerly in the Walferdin collection (see figure 1; A. 45, fig. 22); another, also with variations, of the central figure group (see figure 2; A. 52, fig. 26), was formerly in the Beurdeley collection. The little girl seated on the ground at the extreme right of the present drawing may be seen as well at the right of the one shown in figure 1.

For a first version of the composition, see catalogue no. 136, figure 2.

Figure 1. Fragonard. *Woman Reading*. Whereabouts unknown

Figure 2. Fragonard. *Woman Cooking*. Whereabouts unknown

A very elegant young woman is about to read a book aloud: Two young people listen to her attentively, while, at the far left, an old man appears to be dozing. Near him, a small boy waits impatiently, and, at the right, two children are playing —one, with a cat; the other, with an apple. At the center, another young woman, seated on the ground and stirring the contents of a cooking pot with a ladle, looks out at us with the same curiosity as the bulldog to her right.

Here, Fragonard treats the theme of reading, which was very fashionable in the eighteenth century, in a typically personal manner, taking special care to study the behavior of each figure, in light of the individual's age and social condition. Whether he is depicting the short cape worn by the reader or the steam rising from the pot, Fragonard makes use of all of the nuances and the possibilities afforded by the bister wash, never forgetting his composition, which is constructed with barely concealed precision.

The drawing is a late one, from about 1780.

280   The Vow to Love

Oil on canvas, 52 x 63 cm.

Private collection

Provenance
François-Alexandre-Frédéric, Duc de la Rochefoucault-Liancourt (1747–1827): sold posthumously, March 20–23, 1827, no. 23: "ce joli tableau représente une jeune fille venant prier l'Amour de lui accorder un amant plus constant" [Oil on canvas, 51.4 x 62.1 cm.]; Duc de Polignac; Duchesse de Polignac, née Crillon (according to the 1921 Paris exhibition catalogue); [Wertheimer, London]; L. Neumann, London (according to the 1921 Paris exhibition catalogue); Mrs. Ferris-Thompson (according to W.); [Wildenstein]; Jean Bartholony, 1921, [Wildenstein]: acquired by Mortimer Schiff, 1923 (according to Gimpel); John M. Schiff, 1933, 1960; private collection.

Exhibitions
Paris, 1921, no. 65, ill.
London, 1933, no. 115, pl. 27
Paris, 1937, no. 164
New York, 1940, no. 198
Pittsburgh, 1951, no. 94, ill.
New Haven, 1960, no. 26, ill.

Bibliography
N. p. 116
R. p. 164

Pantheon, September–October 1960,
    p. LXXX, ill.
W. 491, pl. 113, p. 29 (French edition)
Gimpel, 1963, p. 238
Vermeule, 1964, p. 129
W. and M. 520, ill.
Sutton, 1980; 1987, pp. 112–13
Hallam, 1986, p. 183

Related works
For the sketch, see the following entry.

For the drawings, see catalogue no. 282.
    A version of this painting is in the Musée
des Beaux-Arts, Orléans (see figure 1; Oil on
canvas, 35 x 45 cm.; W. 492, fig. 203;
Tokyo exhibition catalogue, 1980, no. 82,
colorpl.; O'Neill, 1981, no. 55, colorpl.). In
spite of the variations, this appears to be an
interesting copy, dating from the late eighteenth century (see also the painting sold
March 24, 1952, no. 43).

Figure 1. After Fragonard. *The Vow to Love.*
Musée des Beaux-Arts, Orléans

Figure 2. Louis-Jean-François Lagrenée
the Elder. *The Invocation to Love.*
Art market, Paris

Figure 3. Jean-Baptiste Greuze.
The Offering to Love.
Wallace Collection, London

This painting, which is very famous, has recently been magnificently restored. Its date (1780, at the latest) is virtually incontestable, for the following year, a drawing for (or after) the same composition was put up for sale. As noted above, the canvas originally belonged to the Duc de la Rochefoucault-Liancourt, and was sold in 1827, after his death. In 1775, Louis-Jean-François Lagrenée the Elder (1725–1805) had painted an *Invocation to Love* for the duke (see figure 2; Sandoz, 1983, pp. 245–46, no. 285, pl. XXXVIII), which confirms that Fragonard did not invent the theme, although he made it his own. Greuze had painted the *Offering to Love* (see figure 3) for Choiseul by 1767.

This work is one of a group of allegories on the subject of love, which became Fragonard's specialty, from 1775 on. The series was a huge success, to judge by the engravings— many of which were hand colored—that were made after it; not only were they among the most popular in the course of the eighteenth century, but they remain so, even today.

Curiously enough, the *Vow to Love* was the exception (see *Related works*, catalogue no. 282) and did not share the success of the engravings of *The Sacrifice of the Rose* (cat. no. 284), *The Fountain of Love* (cat. no. 283, figure 2), *Le Chiffre d'amour* (figure 7, p. 418), or *Le Serment d'amour* (figure 8, p. 418).

With eyes closed, and her head thrown backward in rapture, a blonde and rosy-cheeked young girl extends her right arm toward a statue of the blindfolded Amour, atop a broad pedestal. The girl, whose body is veiled in diaphanous white and gold draperies, seems to rise up, in an attitude of supplication, from the mysterious half light.

The neoclassical, frieze-like composition is romantic in tone, and succeeds admirably in conveying a sense of passionate excitement. Fragonard has created an abstract, timeless image of the dreams and longings of love—one that is in direct contrast to the risqué tableaux that are all too often associated with his name.

281 The Vow to Love

Oil on panel, 24 x 32.5 cm.

Musée du Louvre, Paris, R. F. 1722

Provenance
Hippolyte Walferdin (1795–1880), by
1848: sold posthumously, April 12–16,
1880, no. 28, ill. (for 10,000 francs, to
Brame); L. Tabourier, by 1883: sold posthumously, June 20–22, 1898, no. 92, ill. (for
18,500 francs, to Huchez); given to the
Louvre by Dr. Maurice Audéoud, with life
interest, 1898; entered the Louvre, 1907.

Exhibitions
Paris, 1848, no. 30
Paris, 1860, no. 144
Paris, 1883–84, no. 59, ill.

Amsterdam, 1926, no. 50, ill.
Paris, 1974, no. 23, ill.

Bibliography
Clément de Ris, 1848, p. 194
Bürger [Thoré], 1860, p. 348
Gautier, 1860, p. 2
Saint-Victor, 1860, n.p.
Portalis, 1880, p. 16, ill. p. 17
P. pp. 73, 280, 292
N. p. 116
Le Prieur, 1909, pp. 78–80, ill.
Gillet, 1929, pp. 83–84, pl. 88, p. 85
R. p. 163

W. 493, fig. 205, p. 29 (French edition)
Sterling, 1964, n.p.
Thuillier, 1967, pp. 55, 136–37, colorpl.
p. 133
W. and M. 522, colorpl. LX
D. Wildenstein, 1975, p. 19 ("très vraisem-
blablement les *Égarements de l'Amour*
d'Évariste Fragonard, exposé au Salon de
1795 [no. 204] par le jeune artiste, âgé de
quatorze ans"!)
Haskell, 1976, p. 63, pl. 155

Related works
See the previous and the following entries.

The sketch for *The Vow to Love* (for the painting, see the previous entry) was first exhibited to the Parisian public in 1848, at which time it belonged to Hippolyte Walferdin. In 1860, it caused a sensation at the legendary exhibition in the boulevard des Italiens organized by Philippe Burty. The following quotations from the "reactions" by Paul de Saint-Victor, Théophile Thoré, and Théophile Gautier reveal not only the admiration of these writers for Fragonard, but also their amazement at a work of such extraordinary poetic force.

"*Le Voeu à l'amour* is the work of a poet, rather than of a painter. It is not even a sketch, hardly a smudge. If the Shades could paint, they would do it like this. A girl, or rather a cloud in the form of a woman, throws herself upon an altar plunged in darkness. Come no closer! The slightest breath would dissolve this vaporous apparition! But what soul carries away this ethereal form? It is the incarnation of a burning sigh" (Saint-Victor).

"*Le Voeu à l'amour* is a trifle, a marvel! a vague smear on a small canvas, a masterpiece of poetry! Only in Sappho and the Greek lyric poets does one find inspiration to equal that of the painter of this inimitable sketch. What does it represent? A girl rushing headlong toward a statue of Amour. What spirit, like an eagle in flight! She appears to fly, her feet no longer touch ground; she is certain to catch hold of Amour, this violent creature! But to what fantastic world has she been transported? Around her, all sense of reality has vanished; she seems to be enveloped in I know not what intoxicating and consuming incense that surrounds those who abandon themselves to the son of Venus.—In this simple sketch, Fragonard—like his subject—has transcended the limits of the painter's art, and he has entered the realm of rhythmic poetry. André Chénier might have written a fine verse on this *Voeu à l'amour*" (Thoré).

"Under the title of *Voeu à l'amour* we find one of the most astonishing sketches that ever escaped from the brush of Fragonard.—In this little canvas there is a passion as intense as that of Sappho's immortal ode.—Art has disappeared, and the heat of desire emerges with such force that the brush no longer indicates the forms, out of fear that it will not keep pace. Never has sudden motion been rendered as swiftly.—A girl with windblown hair, caught up in a whirl of floating draperies, runs toward a statue of Amour, offering herself to him, body and soul, with frenetic abandon. In the background are confused and indistinguishable forms, such as those one catches a glimpse of during a fast race; it is mysterious, stormy, almost sinister, full of an inviolable horror. In the shadows there seem to be misshapen and terrifying figures, pursuing the girl. Amour himself, on his pedestal, has a fierce and sardonic expression, like one of those gods who demand human beings to be sacrificed to them. It is difficult to depict so much with so little: a few touches of white, in a jumble of gray, black, and bitumen, blended together with feverish excitement! Whoever would have thought that the 18th century was as susceptible to so much poetry and passion, in the person of its most frivolous painter, Honoré Fragonard?" (Gautier).

Twenty years later, Roger Portalis voiced his enthusiasm for this "vaporous vision in silvery-gray tones." Jacques Thuillier, writing in 1967, noted that the *Vow to Love* "contains all the best of Prud'hon" (Correggio also comes to mind). "A pallid ray of light falls upon the rounded cheeks of a girl, whose complexion is heightened with a few touches of vermilion; she seems to have escaped from a canvas by Rubens. But what is her strange dream? Here again, there are no smiles or theatrical gestures; only a kind of levitation, which transports the body, like an absolute gift. Is this rapture physical or spiritual, or both? Who is this all-conquering Eros, half hidden in the shadows, and what potion does he offer to lovers? There is no answer save for the affirmation of this secret, as if that were the true nature of love. This lyricism, which exalts passion while protecting its mystery, gives us some measure of Fragonard's renunciation of the clarity of vision (to the point of spiritual aberration, delight, even melancholy) that characterized art in the century after Watteau—and, in many ways, has continued to do so ever since. The painter has come a long way since *L'Escarpolette* and *L'Orgie*."

282 The Vow to Love

Bister wash on paper, over an underdrawing in black chalk (lightly squared for transfer), 33.5 x 41.6 cm.

The Cleveland Museum of Art, Grace Rainey Rogers Fund, 43.657

Provenance

See *Related works*. The dry mark FR (Lugt 1042) of François Renaud, a mounter of drawings in the second half of the 18th century, is at the lower right; François-Martial Marcille: sold posthumously, March 4–7, 1857, part of no. 416: "prière à l'amour et scène de famille 2 dessins lavés au bistre" (? perhaps the Princeton drawing); anonymous sale, Paris, June 1–2, 1875, no. 333: "Invocation à l'amour, à l'encre de chine rehaussé de bistre" (no dimensions given); the painter Pierre-Désiré-Eugène Franc Lamy (1855–

1919): his stamp, Lugt 949 b, is on the verso of the mount; [Wildenstein]; Grace Rainey Rogers: sold, Parke Bernet, New York, November 18–20, 1943, no. 46, ill.; acquired in the same year by The Cleveland Museum of Art.

Exhibitions

Montreal, 1950, no. 73
Paris, 1958, no. 51, pl. 67
Los Angeles, 1961, no. 46, ill.
Toronto . . . , 1972–73, no. 50, pl. 112

Providence, 1975, no. 56, ill.
Washington, D.C., 1978, no. 50, ill.
Tokyo, 1980, no. 156, ill.

Bibliography

P. pp. 64–65, 305 (the drawing in the Sireul sale)
Francis, 1945, p. 88, ill. p. 91
A. 2422, fig. 612
Vermeule, 1964, p. 129, fig. 108
Williams, 1979, p. 75, ill.
Ross, 1983, p. 18

Related works

For the paintings, see the previous entries.

Two eighteenth-century sales catalogues mention works relating to the *Vow to Love*: that of the Sireul sale, December 3, 1781, no. 241: "... une jeune fille invoquant l'Amour, au pied de sa Statue; le fond présente une intention de Paysage ... " (35.1 x 45.9 cm.; sold for 60 *livres*), and that of an anonymous sale (cited by O'Neill in 1981), March 24, 1783, no. 39: "... une jeune fille se jetant au pied de la statue de l'Amour dans un bosquet ... " (no dimensions given). The Sireul drawing, cited by P. (pp. 305, 315), is sometimes identified with no. 185 in the Walferdin sale because of its dimensions (35.4 x 46.3 cm.). It was owned by Comte Arthur de Vogüé, and then by Sigismond Bardac. Mme Bardac, who later married Debussy, sold the drawing to René Gimpel May 11, 1918, for "quinze mille francs" (1963, p. 36). Today, it is part of the Margaret Mower collection at The Art Museum, Princeton University (figure 1; see A. 2421, fig. 611; Ross, 1983, p. 18, ill.).

See also A. 1630, and 688, a gouache, that perhaps was in a Brussels collection in 1950 (figure 2).

Finally, we cite a rare anonymous engraving, from about 1800 (figure 3; P. 328, no. 111).

Figure 1. Fragonard. *The Vow to Love*. The Art Museum, Princeton University

Figure 2. After Fragonard. *The Vow to Love*. Whereabouts unknown

Figure 3. Anonymous. *The Vow to Love*. Whereabouts unknown

As Eunice Williams has shown, and according to Fragonard's usual practice, the Cleveland drawing is a faithful copy of the New York painting (cat. no. 280). The Princeton drawing (figure 1) is more problematical: Williams (1978) is in doubt as to whether it is a preparatory study or a copy. The weakness of this work, as pointed out by Ross in 1983 (for example, the girl's left foot), appears to be due to the condition of the drawing, which has suffered from prolonged exposure to light, and should not call into question its authenticity.

The Cleveland drawing, which also represents passionate love, is more precise and meticulous than the painting in the observation of detail. The girl offers herself blindly to Amour, who himself is blindfolded. At the left, a small winged putto leans nonchalantly on a globe, as if to emphasize his influence over it.

As we have noted above, from 1775 onward Fragonard tackled new themes; in his paintings, as well as in his sketches, he modified his technique: his brushwork became smoother, mistier, and more vaporous; his compositions more frieze-like; and his palette more monochromatic, with greater emphasis on chiaroscuro. Yet, he continued to employ bister wash, even in his more finished drawings, and always with the same extraordinary virtuosity.

283 The Warrior's Dream of Love

Oil on canvas, 61.5 x 50.5 cm.

Musée du Louvre, Paris, R. F. 2149

Provenance
François-Martial Marcille: sold posthumously, January 12–13, 1857, no. 55: "le rêve du bonheur" (for 150 francs); Jules Burat: sold posthumously, April 28–29, 1885, no. 70: "le Songe d'amour.... Il provient de la vente Marcille, 1857" (for 3,300 francs, to the Marquis de Talleyrand, Duc de Dino); Baron Basile de Schlichting, by 1907; bequest of Baron Schlichting, 1915.

Exhibitions
Paris, 1883–84, no. 61
Paris, 1907, no. 136
Bregenz-Vienna, 1968–69, no. 213, pl. 117
Paris, 1974, no. 21, ill.

Bibliography
Horsin-Déon, 1861, p. 129 (same text, but no author's name given, in L'Artiste, 1861, XII, p. 247)
Mantz, 1885, p. 294
Eudel, 1887, p. 366
P. pp. 71, 289
N. p. 117
D. and V. 106, ill.
Tourneux, 1907, p. 100
Pigler, 1956, II, p. 571
R. p. 163
W. 211, pl. 21, p. 14 (French edition)
Carpenter, 1962, p. 361
Thuillier, 1967, p. 132
W. and M. 221, ill. and colorpl. XV (see also 518 A)
Augsburg-Cleveland exhibition catalogue, 1975–76, pp. 127, 182, fig. 173
Sutton, 1980; 1987, p. 110

Related works
An "esquisse," on panel, is mentioned in the catalogue of the sale of the Chevalier de C[lesle] collection, December 4, 1786, no. 81: "... le sujet nous a semblé représenter un guerrier endormi, couronné par l'Amour et rêvant à une femme qui lui apparaît en songe, portée sur des nuages et accompagnée de plusieurs Amours..." (31 x 23 cm.; sold for 100 livres).

A stipple engraving of the painting (or the sketch, according to W.) was made by Nicolas-François Regnault (1746–about 1810), in 1791 (see figure 1), according to the Journal de Paris, of April 19, 1791, p. 440, as a pendant to the engraving of the Fountain of Love (see figure 2), which had appeared in 1785 (P. p. 331, no. 158, mentions four states of the engraving, and illustrates it between pp. 232 and 233; see also G. pp. 267–68, 327, and the 1977 Clermont-Ferrand exhibition catalogue, pp. 64–65); the latter engraving was after Fragonard's famous, and very successful painting, of the same title, now in the Wallace Collection, London (see figure 4).

The engraving of the present work was adapted for the lid of a snuffbox sold at Christie's, London, October 9, 1975 (?).

Figure 1. Nicolas-François Regnault, after Fragonard. The Warrior's Dream of Love. Bibliothèque Nationale, Paris, Cabinet des Estampes

Figure 2. Nicolas-François Regnault, after Fragonard. The Fountain of Love. Bibliothèque Nationale, Paris, Cabinet des Estampes

Figure 3. Detail of craquelure, catalogue no. 283

Photographed before restoration

Figure 4. Fragonard. *The Fountain of Love*. Wallace Collection, London

keep watch at his feet. "From his slumber...dreams of love rise up like a Jacob's ladder...crowned by the Assumption of Venus" (Goncourt, pp. 267–68). Using a putto as an intermediary (there are thirteen or fourteen in the picture), Venus—or, rather, Volupté—offers a goblet to the warrior. (Fragonard represented a blindfolded Venus, but Regnault removed this detail.)

That Regnault made engravings of the present painting (see figure 1) and, as a pendant, of the *Fountain of Love* (figure 2), raises the question of whether Fragonard conceived of these two paintings to complement one another. Their dimensions are certainly similar, as is the inspiration underlying their respective themes, but here the resemblance ends—which leads us to believe that the two works were painted independently of one another.

In what year? Wildenstein dates the present painting between 1761 and 1765, but this has been wisely contested by Carpenter (1962) and Thuillier (1967). The sketch was sold in 1786 (see *Related works*), and Regnault, as we have said, published his engraving of the *Fountain of Love* in 1785. Hence, Fragonard's two paintings must date from before this. While the *Fountain of Love* predates the engraving by a short time, we cannot rule out the possibility that the *Warrior's Dream* may have been executed several years earlier than that. The vivid colors—strident blues and sumptuous, warm reds—and the jewel-like quality of the paint surface are reminiscent, in effect, of *Le Verrou* (see cat. no. 236).

With the *Fountain of Love*, even more than with the *Warrior's Dream*, Fragonard seems to have broken new ground. The poses of the figures are now frozen, and their profiles have become classical; moonlight bathes the scene in an otherworldly glow; and passion has given way to intellect, poetry to literature, and sensuality to allegory. In this masterpiece, love is described with a seriousness that we would hardly expect of the eighteenth-century sensibility.

The decision to restore this painting was made after much—understandable—hesitation. A network of deep craquelure—the individual cracks several millimeters wide—covered most of its surface (see figure 3). Once the repaints had been removed, several intact areas were revealed, but other areas remained disfigured. It took all the talents of the restorer, Mme Le Pavec, to make the painting legible, and suggest its original brilliance.

What does the picture represent? Regnault entitled his engraving *Le Songe d'Amour*, and employed a stipple technique—imported from England, and in fashion since about 1770—which he had been one of the first in France to practice. The engraving bore the caption "L'Amour et la Volupté charment le sommeil du guerrier par la douce illusion des plaisirs." A soldier is dozing on an antique bed, his helmet and sword beside him. He dreams, while his dogs

284   The Sacrifice of the Rose

Oil on panel, 54 x 43 cm.

Private collection, France

Provenance
Godefroy: sold, December 14, 1813, no. 46: "le sacrifice de la rose. Une jeune fille entièrement nue, la tête doucement inclinée sur l'épaule gauche, les yeux fermés, et la bouche entrouverte dans un moment de langueur et d'abandon est assise près d'un autel; l'Amour, les deux ailes déployées, sous la figure d'un bel adolescent la soutient et brûle au feu de son flambeau la rose dont elle vient de lui faire le sacrifice. Un essaim de petits Amours jouant dans les nuages, célèbrent son triomphe. Tableau gracieux dont la couleur mystérieuse et l'exécution suave répondent à l'idée heureuse du peintre. Bois 19 p sur 15 p. ½" (51.3 x 42 cm.; for 355 francs); Baron Vivant-Denon: sold, May 1, 1826, no. 153 (oil on panel, same dimensions [19 *p. sur* 15 *p.*]; the sales catalogue states that the painting was "gravé sous le titre le Sacrifice de la rose"; for 245 francs, according to G.); Brunet Denon, nephew of Baron Vivant-Denon: sold, February 2, 1846, no. 329 (no doubt the one in the Vivant-Denon collection, as the sales catalogue confirms); A. A. estate: sold, March 30, 1882, no. 18 (oil on panel, 51 x 41 cm.; for 3,050 francs, to Daupias, according to W.); Count Daupias, Lisbon: sold, May 16–17, 1892, no. 14 (oil on panel, 54 x 42 cm.; for 6,000 francs); M. S.: sold, June 14, 1900, no. 5, ill. (for 18,000 francs); Deutsch de la Meurthe (according to W.); [Wildenstein, 1906]; David Weill (according to W.); Jean Bartho-loni, 1921; Paul Dutasta: sold, June 3–4, 1926, no. 64, ill. (for 200,000 francs, to Lesieur); R. R.: sold, June 5–6, 1946, no. 14, ill.

Exhibitions
Marseilles, 1906, no. 534
Paris, 1921, no. 66, ill.

Bibliography
G. p. 327
P. p. 288
N. p. 117
Dorbec, 1921, pp. 26, 27
W. 497, pl. 115
W. and M. 527, ill.
Haskell, 1976, p. 43, n. 91

Related works

See the following entry.

There is a painting in a Los Angeles private collection (see figure 1; oil on canvas, 65 x 54 cm.) that was acquired at a sale at Christie's, London, April 10, 1981, no. 64, ill., which perhaps may be identified with the painting from the collection of Senator Eugène Mir, exhibited in 1921 (no. 93) and mentioned by R.; on the subject of this painting, see also the excellent study by David Carritt, which appeared in the Artemis catalogue, 1982, no. 13, colorpl.

Another painting, formerly in the collection of Comte Charles de Gramont (see figure 2; oil on canvas, 59.5 x 49.5 cm.; W. 498, fig. 207; sold at Christie's, London, June 25, 1971, no. 20, ill.; Tokyo exhibition catalogue, 1980, no. 83, colorpl.), has been known since 1860 (no. 140) and the Walferdin sale (no. 57).

The Wildenstein painting (see cat. no. 286, figure 3; oil on canvas, 31 x 24 cm.; W. 499, fig. 208) definitely came from the Marcille collection, sold, January 12–13, 1857, no. 54: "offrande à l'Amour," and from the Walferdin collection, sold, April 12–16, 1880, no. 58. Is it the same picture described as "Le sacrifice de la Rose. Cette gracieuse composition est un des meilleurs ouvrages de ce savant peintre" (no dimensions given), which was sold February 11–12, 1842, no. 1 (on this sale, see Wells-Robertson, 1979, p. 186, n. 26), with the collection "de feu M. Destouches, peintre," March 4–5, 1847, no. 6: referred to as the "tableau qui a précédé la composition du même sujet, connue par la gravure," and which figured in an anonymous sale February 27–28, 1852, no. 36: "le Sacrifice à l'Amour. Première pensée du maître"?

In 1824, Marguerite Gérard owned a *Sacrifice of the Rose* (Wells-Robertson, 1979, pp. 183, 189).

In the sale of the Walferdin collection, April 12–16, 1880, no. 59, there was a "Tête d'étude pour le Sacrifice de la Rose" (oil on panel, 19 x 15 cm.; see Portalis, 1880, under p. 16).

According to Sutton (Tokyo exhibition catalogue, 1980, no. 83), the composition was copied by Prud'hon.

A stipple engraving of the painting (see figure 3)—probably of this version—was made by Henri Gérard (1755–about 1835) in 1790 for the Société des Amis des Arts (see Hébert, Pognon, and Bruand, 1968, X, p. 103, no. 4; Clermont-Ferrand exhibition catalogue, 1977, no. 65, ill.). Saint-Non owned a proof of this engraving (G. Wildenstein, 1959, p. 241, nos. 128–137).

For the related drawings, see cat. no. 286.

Figure 1. Fragonard. *The Sacrifice of the Rose*. Collection Mr. and Mrs. Stewart Resnick

Figure 2. Fragonard. *The Sacrifice of the Rose*. Whereabouts unknown

Figure 3. Henri Gérard, after Fragonard. *The Sacrifice of the Rose*. Bibliothèque Nationale, Paris, Cabinet des Estampes

Figure 4. Pierre-Paul Prud'hon. *The Abduction of Psyche*. Musée du Louvre

"**M.** Fragonard *père* died on Friday morning, following a short illness. He was seventy-four and a half years old, and extremely stout. The French school has lost a justly admired painter: *Callirhoé*, the *Fontaine d'Amour*, the *Sacrifice de la Rose* and many of his other subjects, copied and disseminated in the form of engravings, have associated the very idea of the Graces with the name Fragonard." With these words, the *Journal de Paris* on Monday, August 25, 1806, recorded Fragonard's passing. The paintings mentioned (two of which are late works) "brought him enormous sums of money," as Landon noted (1832, p. 93).

Today, five paintings on the theme of the Offering to Love (or of *The Sacrifice of the Rose*, to borrow the title of Henri Gérard's 1790 engraving) are known to us.

The two sketches (see figure 2; cat. no. 286, figure 3), which belonged to Hippolyte Walferdin, were the subjects of lengthy studies in 1860 and 1880. The first, which is very close to the Minneapolis drawing (cat. no. 286), dates from well before the other versions; the second sketch, a preparatory study for the painting, represents the unconscious young woman being carried to the altar in the arms of Amour.

Of the three finished versions, only the one in Buenos Aires (cat. no. 285)—which we have never seen firsthand!—shows the girl completely naked (although she was very likely depicted nude in the present painting, before the addition of her "veils of modesty"). The Argentina painting may well be the same one that was sold in 1849, even though the description in the sales catalogue leaves room for doubt. The example included in the sale of the Godefroy collection in 1813 was an oil on panel, like the present painting. The third version, which may be the finest of all (see figure 1)—and has also suffered considerable damage—is perhaps the canvas that was owned by Marguerite Gérard, Fragonard's sister-in-law and the engraver's sister, in 1824; today, it is in a private collection in Los Angeles.

It is difficult to determine which of these versions was the source of Henri Gérard's 1790 engraving. We do not rule out the possibility that it may have been the one that has remained in France. In any case, it is the version that differs the least from the engraving.

The painting must have been executed before 1788, and probably slightly after 1785—the date of the Wallace Col-

lection's *Fountain of Love* (see cat. no. 283, figure 4), which was the subject of an engraving that year. We are not the first to have been tempted to compare these two works, in order to determine whether they were designed as pendants, or merely were conceived in the same spirit. The subject of the painting, a young woman "swooning before the altar of love" (Thoré, 1860, p. 348), requires no explanation: it is an allegory of the loss of virginity and of the ecstasy of love, but as a result of Fragonard's genius, the least overtone of lewdness, sentimentality, or lack of taste has been avoided. Again, it was the Goncourts (p. 269) who best described this intensely lyrical work, which, in its strangeness and originality, surpasses even the best of Prud'hon (see figure 4) and is on a par with the art of Correggio: "thrust forward, almost carried off the ground by little putti, who attempt to trans-

port her while they play amid her transparent veils, a woman emerges from two slanting rays of light that rise upward before her, along the path of which putti fly, quivering in their immobility. A smile on her face, the young woman is about to faint, and, as if overcome by the light's caress, she lets fall a rose, which a winged spirit sets on fire with his torch. Thus, the *Sacrifice de la Rose*: a hint of Saint Teresa, in a scene worthy of Parny!"

One other important detail deserves mention: the altar on which the rose is burning is copied, as Vermeule (1964, p. 129) has shown, from a circular cinerarium that formerly belonged to the Museo Capitolino in Rome. Fragonard used it before, in the *Swing* in the Wallace Collection. What a distance he had come in twenty years!

285 The Sacrifice of the Rose

Oil on canvas, 65 x 54 cm.

Museo Nacional de Arte Decorativo, Buenos Aires

Provenance
Forbin-Janson: sold, June 12, 1849, no. 28:
"une jeune fille entièrement nue brûle sur
l'autel de l'Amour la rose qu'elle tient à la
main. Un nuage voluptueux l'entoure à
demi, une molle langueur est dans ses yeux.
Le tableau est gravé. T. H. 65 cent. L. 54
cm" (for 130 francs) (?); Constanzo Santamarina, Buenos Aires: given to Manuel
Quintana, President of the republic of
Argentina, 1890; Susana Rodrigues de
Quintana, widow of Manuel Quintana: sold,
J. C. Naony Cia., Buenos Aires, November
28, 1930, no. 46; acquired by Matías Errázuriz, a wealthy Chilean collector; acquired
by the Museo Nacional de Arte Decorativo,
Buenos Aires, with the Errázuriz collection,
1937.

Exhibitions
Buenos Aires, 1893, catalogue unavailable
Buenos Aires, 1968, no. 13

Bibliography
N. p. 117
Schiaffino, 1933, pp. 342, n. 2, 343, ill.
  (reproduces, in error, the painting from the
  collection of Senator Eugène Mir, which is
  today in Los Angeles; information supplied
  by Mariano Aldao)
Buenos Aires museum catalogue, 1947,
  no. 53
R. p. 164 (states that the painting came from
  the collection of Eugène Mir)
W., under no. 497, fig. 206
W. and M. 526, ill.

Related works
See the previous entry.

There are several interesting variations among the Buenos Aires painting—which, as we have noted, we had never seen firsthand—the engraving, and the oil on panel version discussed in the previous entry. Here, the heroine is completely naked, represented without her usual transparent "veils of modesty." Her expression is more saccharine and affected.

She does not swoon, and the strange, ecstatic, and almost terrifying smile on her face, in the engraving, is gone. We will not know whether this is a less-inspired replica, a later version, or an autograph variation on the theme until the work is exhibited alongside another example of the same composition, and the two are compared.

286   The Sacrifice of the Rose

Bister wash on paper, heightened with watercolor, over an underdrawing in black chalk, 42.2 x 33 cm.
Inscribed at the lower left: *fragonard*

The Minneapolis Institute of Arts, Gift of Mr. and Mrs. Clinton Morrison, 83.109

Provenance
The painter of miniatures Saint: sold, May 4,
1846, no. 17: "le sacrifice à la rose, charmant et gracieux dessin lavé à l'encre de chine
et mêlé d'aquarelle" (for 90 francs); Hippolyte Walferdin (1795–1880), by 1860: sold
posthumously, April 12–16, 1880, no. 189
(for 2,600 francs, to Bartholdi); Bartholdi,
1889; Baron de Neuflize; Roberta, Countess
of Bessborough; Desmond Browne, Esq.
(according to the Christie's sales catalogue):
sold, Christie's, London, July 5, 1983, no.
34, colorpl. (acquired by The Minneapolis
Institute of Arts, through Artemis, 1983).

Exhibitions
Paris, 1860, no. 7
Minneapolis, 1985–86, ill., n.p.

Bibliography
G. pp. 269 (?), 327
Portalis, 1880, pp. 16, 20
P. pp. 199, 312
R. p. 204
A. 2427, 988
Gazette des Beaux-Arts, supplement, March
1984, p. 29, no. 182, ill.

Related works
For the paintings and the engraving, see catalogue nos. 284–285.

A horizontal drawing exists of the same
subject (see figure 1; A. 2424, fig. 616),
which was also exhibited in 1860 (no. 17),
but whose whereabouts are now unknown. It
is perhaps identical with the "nymphe qui est
venue offrir sa rose dans le temple de
l'Amour et à laquelle rose l'Amour met le
feu; elle est sur des nuages soutenue par un
groupe de plaisirs. Ce dessin *colorié* [our
emphasis] est d'un effet piquant, et est un des
beaux dessins de ce maître" [32.4 x 40.5
cm.; see A. 1619, and also A. 2426, and
L'Estampille, January 1984].

In the museum in Karlsruhe there is a preliminary version of this composition, in black
chalk (see figure 2; A. 2425, fig. 617).

Figure 1. Fragonard. *The Sacrifice of the Rose.* Whereabouts unknown

Figure 2. Fragonard. *The Sacrifice of the Rose.* Staatliche Kunsthalle, Karlsruhe

Figure 3. Fragonard. *The Sacrifice of the Rose.* Whereabouts unknown

This drawing, recently acquired by The Minneapolis Institute of Arts, is very close in the details of the composition to a study for the *Sacrifice of the Rose* (which we have never seen firsthand) that was formerly in the Wildenstein collection (see figure 3; W. 499, fig. 208). This painted sketch, smaller than the drawing, appears to be a preparatory study, probably dating from before 1780.

Two other drawings—one, in black chalk; the other, in bister wash—deal with the same theme. Both horizontal in format, they are of different dates, and reveal Fragonard's longstanding interest in this subject.

In the Minneapolis drawing—which successfully blends bister wash and watercolor—a figure of Amour, with large wings, sets fire with his torch to the rose proffered to him by the young woman in an ecstatic trance. Various putti smile on the scene. The allegory is clear, but the passionate intensity; strange, evocative power; otherworldly moonlight; and the emotional energy of the painting are all conspicuously absent here.

287 Self-portrait, Seen Full Face

Black chalk on paper, heightened with colored pencil on the lips and the cheeks, round, diameter, 12.9 cm.
The drawing is glued to a second sheet of paper, and encircled by a double black-chalk line.
Inscribed on the verso, in pencil: *son portrait dessiné par lui-même*

Musée du Louvre, Paris, Cabinet des Dessins, R. F. 41.192

Provenance
Huot-Fragonard: sold, May 19–20, 1876, part of no. 26: "sous ce numéro qui sera divisé seront vendus les sept dessins suivants: Trois portraits de l'artiste . . . " (for 50 francs, with the portrait of Alexandre-Évariste: see catalogue no. 294); Camille Groult; Jean Groult: sold, May 24, 1955, no. 125 C, pl. III (for 450,000 francs, for the seven drawings); René Hinzelin, Paris; donated to the Cabinet des Dessins by the Société des Amis du Louvre, 1986 (the Louvre's stamp, Lugt 1886, is at the lower right).

Exhibitions
Paris, 1921, no. 118

Bibliography
P. pp. 138, 267, frontispiece ill.
R. p. 210
G. Wildenstein, 1959, no. 192, fig. 1
Lamy, 1961, p. 47, ill.
A. 123, fig. 53

Related works
For three other self-portraits, see the three following entries; for still other self-portraits,

and portraits of Fragonard, see entry below. For other round or oval portraits, see entry below.

In the Besançon museum (Cornillot, 1957, no. 86, ill.), there is a portrait of a man that appears to be part of the series of seven drawings in the Louvre (see figure 1). This portrait bears the date "Xbre 1787" and the name "Mlle. Gerard." Ananoff, who formerly attributed this work to Fragonard (A. 125, fig. 54), now believes it is by Marguerite Gérard (1979, p. 215, fig. 5). We cannot yet accept this attribution.

The Louvre has recently received from the Société des Amis du Louvre three self-portraits drawn by Fragonard, along with portraits of Mme Fragonard, Rosalie, Alexandre-Évariste Fragonard, and Marguerite Gérard, which came from the Huot-Fragonard, Groult, and Hinzelin collections (see cat. nos. 288, 289, 292–294, 296). From a direct descendant of M. Huot-Fragonard, M. Pierre Huot (in a written communication), as well as from the Goncourt brothers, we can now affirm that the seven drawings sold in four lots in 1876 did, indeed, originally come from the collection of Théophile Fragonard, who died in 1876—as did his mother, the former Julie Fournier, wife of Alexandre-Évariste. The same Huot-Fragonard sale included a portrait of Fragonard that the Goncourts (p. 286, n. 1) acknowledged having seen at Théophile's house (and attributed to Marguerite Gérard!).

In our introduction to this catalogue we have attempted to describe Fragonard's appearance: later in life he was short, exceedingly fat, with "very disheveled gray hair," but "always active, always cheerful." Nonetheless, he did not often paint or draw his own likeness, and the numerous attempts to identify his features in the canvases in Grasse (attributed by Cuzin, 1983, p. 104, fig. 1, to François-André Vincent), in the former M. C. collection in Neuilly (Lamy, twice, in 1961), in the former Groult collection (W. 376, pl. 76; Tokyo exhibition catalogue, 1980, no. 58, colorpl.), and in the San Francisco museum (W. 486, pl. 111; Tokyo exhibition catalogue, 1980, no. 80, colorpl.) have been notably unsuccessful.

Fragonard definitely painted his self-portrait before the cascades at Tivoli (sale of the Baché collection, April 22, 1776, no. 92), but this picture is now lost. Only the painting attributed to Marguerite Gérard (by Portalis, as well, p. 138), mentioned above (sold at Christie's, London, December 10, 1982, no. 14, ill.), seems to us beyond question to represent him (see figure 2), as does the "miniature in oil" by Marguerite Gérard (in the Walferdin collection sale, April 12–16, 1880, no. 103), after which, according to the catalogue, an engraving was made "by Charpentier" (ibid., no. 360; see also P. p. 319) and, in any case, by Paul-Edme Le Rat (see figure 3). We, in turn, would suggest that the Washington painting (see figure 4), which is regarded as a portrait of Hubert Robert and is frequently attributed to Fragonard, is, in fact, the artist himself—a young and impertinent Fragonard—but we have no substantiating proof. Among the drawings that are considered to be self-portraits by Fragonard, not one (with the exception of the four included here: cat. nos. 287–290) is actually his work—neither the Louvre drawing (formerly in the Péreire collection; A. 120), which is, in fact, by Claude Hoin, nor even less so the drawing (A. 124) from the collection of Gustave Deloye (1839–1899; the sculptor of the bust of Fragonard now at Versailles)—but this is not the case with the rare engraving by Charles-Louis-François Le Carpentier (1744–1822), which dates from 1803 (see figure 5), in the artist's lifetime (Sjöberg and Gardey, 1974, XIII, pp. 446–47, no. 27). One will recall that this same Le Carpentier published a *Life* of Fragonard in 1821, which is an essential document for anyone wishing to understand the painter's career and ambitions. Another engraving, less frequently reproduced, is still of interest: it is a copy of a drawing dated 1797 by a certain Émmanuel Lemoine (see figure 6) that at one time belonged to Walferdin (sold, April 12–16, 1880, no. 325; it had been acquired by the collector at the sale of the Silvestre collection, December 4–6, 1851, no. 262). For Walferdin, as for Tourneux (1907, p. 100), Lemoine's drawing was unquestionably of Fragonard. They were absolutely correct, for, in 1798, Jacques-Antoine-Marie Lemoine (1751–1824), another native of Rouen, exhibited at the Salon (part of no. 269) a "Portrait in black chalk of C. Fragonard"!

Figure 1. Attributed to Fragonard. *Portrait of a Man*. Musée des Beaux-Arts, Besançon

Figure 2. Attributed to Marguerite Gérard. *Fragonard.* Whereabouts unknown

Figure 3. Paul-Edme Le Rat, after Marguerite Gérard. *Fragonard* (according to Portalis, 1880)

Figure 4. Unknown painter. *Fragonard* (?). National Gallery of Art, Washington, D.C.

Figure 5. Charles-Louis-François Le Carpentier. *Fragonard* (1803). Bibliothèque Nationale, Paris, Cabinet des Estampes

Figure 6. Tiburce de Mare, after Émmanuel Lemoine (1797). *Fragonard*. Bibliothèque Nationale, Paris, Cabinet des Estampes

Figure 7. Unknown painter. *Fragonard* (?). Musée Fragonard, Grasse

Finally, there is the famous, so-called bald portrait of Fragonard (from the Walferdin collection), lent to the museum in Grasse by the Louvre (R. F. 422; see figure 7), for which we are unable to arrive at an attribution.

Two questions remain: when, and on what occasion, did Fragonard decide to execute this self-portrait?

The man depicted is about fifty years old (this is true in all three drawings, so that we cannot be certain of the order in which they were made). It is known that Fragonard executed a whole series of similar portraits in black chalk, either oval or round, of the members of the Bergeret family (A. 115, fig. 686; A. 126, fig. 688; A. 2036, fig. 553; A. 127, fig. 55; see also A. 2037, fig. 555; A. 104, fig. 685, which is very similar to a painting sold at Versailles December 14,

1969, no. 159, as the work of Fragonard; and, more recently, at Sotheby's, Monte Carlo, January 20, 1987, no. 404, colorpl., as by M. Gérard, but judged by Léger, London, in 1954, to be by Frédéric Schall). We also know that, after the quarrel of 1774, Fragonard was reconciled with Bergeret and, especially, with his son Pierre-Jacques (see cat. no. 175). Jacques-Onésyme Bergeret, who died in 1785, had acquired property at Cassan, near L'Isle-Adam, in 1778, where the Fragonards stayed on several occasions, and where Rosalie died in 1788. In our opinion, it was just before this date, and at Cassan, that Fragonard drew his own portrait, for he seems to be in good health, and, with a smile, confidently returns our gaze.

288   Self-portrait in Three-quarter View, Facing Left

Black chalk on paper, round (slightly elongated), 13 x 12.8 cm.
Enlarged at the left by a strip of paper 11 millimeters wide, and, at the right, by a strip of paper, colored with wash, 14 millimeters wide.
The drawing is glued to the mount.
Inscribed on the verso, in ink: *fragonard Peintre*; in pencil: *son portrait dessiné par lui même*

Musée du Louvre, Paris, Cabinet des Dessins, R. F. 41.191

Provenance
See the previous entry; Huot-Fragonard: sold, May 19–20, 1876, part of no. 26 (for 75 francs, with the portrait of Marguerite Gérard: see catalogue no. 296); Jean Groult: sold, May 24, 1955, no. 125 B, pl. III; donated to the Cabinet des Dessins by the Société des Amis du Louvre, 1986 (the Louvre's stamp, Lugt 1886, is at the lower right).

Exhibitions
Paris, 1921, no. 117

Bibliography
P. pp. 138, 267, ill. p. 268
Lamy, 1961, p. 46, ill.
Lamy, 1961 (*B.S.H.A.F.*), p. 80, ill.

A. 121, fig. 52
W. and M., p. 83, ill.
Tokyo exhibition catalogue, 1980, fig. 21 (accompanies entry 58 in the Japanese text)

Related works
See the previous entry.

The smile on Fragonard's face is more ironic, here, than in the preceding drawing. One senses that Fragonard is scrutinizing himself in the mirror.

288   289

289   Self-portrait, Facing Slightly to the Right

Black chalk on paper, round (slightly elongated), 12.9 x 12.8 cm.
At the right, a strip of the paper is colored with wash.
The drawing is glued to the mount.
Inscribed on the verso, in ink: *Fragonard peintre*

Musée du Louvre, Paris, Cabinet des Dessins, R. F. 41.193

Provenance
See catalogue no. 287; Huot-Fragonard:
sold, May 19–20, 1876, part of no. 26 (for
22 francs; separately); Jean Groult: sold, May
24, 1955, no. 125 D; donated to the Cabinet
des Dessins by the Société des Amis du
Louvre, 1986 (the Louvre's stamp, Lugt
1886, is at the lower center).

Bibliography
P. p. 138
A. 122, fig. 687

Related works
See catalogue nos. 287–288.

Of the three self-portraits, this one appears closest to the portrait and the miniature by Marguerite Gérard (see cat. no. 287, figures 2, 3). "Round, fat, high-spirited, always active, always cheerful, he had fine rosy cheeks, twinkling eyes, and very disheveled gray hair, and he was seen in the galleries [of the Louvre] always dressed in a long, loose-fit-ting mottled gray greatcoat...." Such is the description of Fragonard supplied by Mme Hippolyte Lecomte (née Camille Vernet, 1788–1858) at the beginning of the nine-teenth century (see Delaroche-Vernet, 1923, p. 224; and P. p. 242). The three drawings in the Louvre illustrate her words almost to the letter.

290 Portrait of Fragonard Seated in an Armchair

Black chalk on paper, round, diameter, 17.5 cm.
Inscribed at the bottom, in Latin, in black chalk: *se ipsum delineabat frago/apud de Bergeret/anno 1789.*

Fondation Custodia (F. Lugt Collection), Institut Néerlandais, Paris, Inv. 3943

Provenance
Apparently, Colonel de la Girennerie, a descendant of Bergeret (see the Walferdin collection sales catalogue, no. 272); Hippolyte Walferdin (1795–1880): sold posthumously, April 12–16, 1880, no. 274 (for 415 francs, to Lefilleul); Camille Groult (?), according to the 1974 exhibition catalogue; Eugène Paillet, 1889; anonymous sale, December 19, 1928, no. 5 (for 25,500 francs, to Féral); acquired by Frits Lugt (Lugt 1028), 1929; Institut Néerlandais.

Exhibitions
Paris, 1935, no. 250
Paris, 1964, no. 108, pl. 89
Amsterdam, 1974, no. 35, ill.

Bibliography
G. p. 322
Gonse, 1889, p. 75, ill.
P. p. 268, ill. p. 221
Guimbaud, 1928, ill. between pp. 92 and 93
R. p. 210
W. p. 31 (French edition)
A. 1315, fig. 386
W. and M., p. 84, ill.
Tokyo exhibition catalogue, 1980, ill., n.p.

Related works
In the museum in Grasse there is an anonymous engraving after this drawing (see figure 1). A second engraving (see figure 2) by Adolphe-Théodore-Jules Martial Potémont (known as Martial) is included in an 1891 edition of the *Contes* of La Fontaine. In the latter engraving, Fragonard's head was "remplacée" by the likeness in the Le Carpentier engraving (see cat. no. 287, figure 5), which, itself, was considerably altered.
See also the three preceding entries.

Colonel de la Girennerie was the grandson of Jacques Oné-syme Bergeret. Hippolyte Walferdin bought from him several lots of Fragonard drawings, executed at La Folie Beaujon, the Paris residence of Bergeret's son Pierre-Jacques, whose subjects included "Fanfan between Mlle Gérard and her father," "Frago giving a drawing lesson to M. de la Gérénerie [*sic*]," or "M. Frago goes through the wrong door by mistake and falls down in a place where there is no commode and sprains his ankle dreadfully at thirty minutes and two seconds after eight o'clock"! (see the Walferdin collection sales catalogue of April 12–16, 1880, nos. 272, 273; Portalis, 1880, p. 22).

All the evidence suggests that the drawing in the Lugt collection belonged to M. de la Girennerie; as the inscription notes, Fragonard made this self-portrait in 1789 at Bergeret's home, but whether it was in Cassan, Nointel, or Paris we do not know. It should be recalled, however, that the

Figure 1. Unknown artist. *Fragonard.* Musée Fragonard, Grasse

Figure 2. Martial, after Fragonard. *Fragonard.* Bibliothèque Nationale, Paris, Cabinet des Estampes

painter's daughter, Rosalie, died in Cassan in 1788, and that Fragonard was "so violently affected by this that he suffered a serious attack of cholera morbus"—as related by the Goncourts (note p. 293), based on information supplied by Fragonard's grandson Théophile.

In the present drawing, Fragonard shows no signs of suffering from this "then rare disease." However, there is no reason to doubt the veracity of the inscription, which was probably written by Pierre-Jacques Bergeret—in any case,

not by Fragonard himself, who knew no Latin, and, as we have mentioned before, was practically illiterate.

Unlike the three self-portraits in the Louvre, here, Fragonard did not attempt to provide an exact rendering of his facial features. He seems to have observed himself, merely making a quick note of a gesture or an expression. The result is by no means a great drawing, but, as the work of an artist who was about to renounce the artistic scene forever, it takes on an especially moving significance.

291 Portrait of Mme Fragonard

Bister wash on paper, over a light underdrawing in black chalk, oval, vertical, 19.5 x 15.7 cm.
Inscribed on the verso, in ink: *Portrait de Madame Fragonard faite* [sic] *par son mari, peintre du Roi*

Musée des Beaux-Arts, Besançon, Inv. D. 2872

Provenance
Pierre-Adrien Pâris (1745–1819), from 1806: handwritten catalogue of the collection, no. 130: "deux médaillons au Bistre du même" [Fragonard] "le portrait de son épouse ... "; bequeathed to the city of Besançon; Bibliothèque Municipale, Besançon; Musée des Beaux-Arts, Besançon, from 1843 (the museum's stamp, Lugt 238 c, is at the lower left).

Exhibitions
Paris, 1921, no. 120
Besançon, 1956, no. 65, pl. XI

Bibliography
Bellier de la Chavignerie, 1865, p. 86
G. 288, notes 1, 322
P. p. 302, ill. between pp. 110 and 111
Bouchot, 1906, p. 207, ill.
N., ill. between pp. 78 and 79
D. and V., pl. 143
Foerster [1925], pl. 1
Martine, 1927, pl. 31
Bergeret, 1948, pl. XXIII, p. 143
Wilhelm, 1951, p. 28, ill.
R. p. 211, fig. 3, p. 10
Cornillot, 1957, no. 76, ill. (with a complete list of exhibitions and bibliography)

A. 109, fig. 684
Terver, 1987, p. 93, ill.

Related works
Théophile Fragonard copied a drawing made in 1793 and representing Mme Fragonard, which he presented to Edmond de Goncourt; it was included in the Goncourts' *L'Art du dix-huitième siècle* (part of the Audéoud gift to the Bibliothèque Nationale, Rés. 2, Audéoud, 281; see figure 1).

See catalogue no. 292, and the text below.

Figure 1. Théophile Fragonard. *Marie-Anne Fragonard.* Bibliothèque Nationale, Paris, Département des Imprimés (réserve)

Figure 2. Marguerite Gérard. *Marie-Anne Fragonard.* Musée Fragonard, Grasse

Figure 3. Marguerite Gérard. *Marie-Anne Fragonard and Her Grandchildren.* Whereabouts unknown

This is not the place to provide a biography of Marie-Anne Gérard (1745–1823), who became Mme Fragonard in 1769. The two drawings of her by her husband, and the two portraits of her by her sister, Marguerite (one is in the Musée Fragonard, Grasse: see figure 2; the other was formerly in the Marcel Fragonard collection: see figure 3), represent her as a woman of authority: "my treasurer," as Fragonard called her. To Mme Hippolyte Lecomte (Delaroche-Vernet, 1923, p. 224; P. p. 242), we owe this scathing description of Mme

Fragonard, dating from the early nineteenth century: "Mme Fragonard was rather tall, heavyset, and quite common. And what taste! She spoiled the few charms that had survived her youth by the most extravagant incongruities in her attire.... From Grasse she had kept ... a terribly strong accent...." Yet, on the contrary, there is no evidence that the Fragonard household was not a happy one (even if Mme Fragonard was over three inches taller than her husband!), and that the couple's relationship left anything to be desired.

Mme Lecomte, who described the inhabitants of the studios in the Louvre, continued: "a painter of miniatures, she was considered very skillful in that minor art and, not infrequently, some of her works were attributed to her husband." The private exhibitions, the Salon de la Correspondance of 1783, and, especially, the eighteenth-century sales catalogues (thirty miniatures were sold at sixteen different sales, between 1778 and 1785 !) confirm the importance of her accomplishments in this genre. The miniatures that can be attributed to her (most of which have been ascribed to her more famous husband; see P. pp. 316–18, and W. and M., p. 112, who reaffirm her authorship, as well as the excellent summary by Eunice Williams, 1982, pp. 210–12) prove the originality of her talent (see figure 4); a study of her work that relied on the sales catalogues would produce several surprises.

The attribution of the Besançon drawing to Fragonard dates from 1806. Marie-Anne, wearing the distinctive lace cap by which she may be recognized in several other famous studies by her husband (for example, the *Two Young Women Conversing*: cat. no. 269; *La Lecture*: cat. no. 270; and *La Rêveuse*: cat. no. 271), is still young; she looks out at the spectator with a faint smile on her lips. Her dark eyes, finely drawn eyebrows, and well-shaped mouth make her very attractive. The drawing has sustained some damage from exposure to light and dampness, making certain passages difficult to read, but it appears to precede by several years the birth in 1780 of Alexandre-Évariste, Marie-Anne's second child.

In this portrait, Fragonard employed the brush almost exclusively—continuing a practice that characterizes his late drawings.

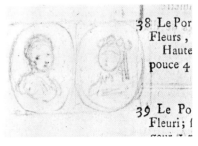

Figure 4. Gabriel de Saint-Aubin, after Marie-Anne Fragonard. Detail of a page from the Calvière collection sales catalogue (1779). Bibliothèque Nationale, Paris, Cabinet des Estampes

292 Portrait of Mme Fragonard

Black chalk on paper, round (slightly elongated), 12.9 x 12.6 cm.
At the right, a strip of the paper is colored with wash.
The drawing is glued to the mount.
Inscribed on the verso, in ink: *Mme Fragonard*

Musée du Louvre, Paris, Cabinet des Dessins, R. F. 41.194

Provenance
See catalogue no. 287; Huot-Fragonard:
sold, May 19–20, 1876, part of no. 26:
"portrait de Madame Fragonard" (for 137
francs, with the portrait of Mlle Fragonard:
see catalogue no. 293); Hippolyte Walferdin:
sold, April 3, 1880, part of no. 67; Camille
Groult; Jean Groult: sold, May 24, 1955,
no. 125 F; donated to the Cabinet des Dessins

by the Société des Amis du Louvre, 1986 (the
Louvre's stamp, Lugt 1886, is at the lower
right).

Exhibitions
Paris, 1921, no. 121

Bibliography
G. pp. 287–88 (?)

P. pp. 138, 302
R. p. 211
Ananoff, 1961, p. 49, ill.
A. 111, fig. 49

Related works
See the previous entry.

This may well be the drawing to which the Goncourts alluded, when they wrote: "a portrait of her, which is owned by M. Théophile Fragonard, shows her aged about forty, with strong features composed of sensuous planes; piercing black eyes under thick eyebrows; a broad, stubby nose; a wide mouth; dark coloring; and lustrous brown hair." In any case, the description could hardly be more precise, and continues, without mincing words: "[she has something of the] pleased and impassioned air of a Dutch matron warmed by the sun of Provence."

Fragonard's portrait of his wife nevertheless reveals a genuine tenderness.

293 Portrait of Rosalie Fragonard

Black chalk on paper, round (slightly elongated), 12.8 x 12.7 cm.
At the right, a strip of the paper is colored with wash.
The drawing is glued to the mount.
Inscribed on the verso, in ink: *Mlle Fragonard*

Musée du Louvre, Paris, Cabinet des Dessins, R. F. 41.195

Provenance
See catalogue nos. 287, 292; Huot-Fragonard: sold, May 19–20, 1876, part of no. 26: "portrait de Mademoiselle Fragonard" (for 137 francs, along with the portrait of her mother, Marie-Anne Gérard: see catalogue no. 292); Hippolyte Walferdin: sold, April 3, 1880, part of no. 67; Jean Groult: sold, May 24, 1955, no. 125 E; donated to the Cabinet des Dessins by the Société des Amis du Louvre, 1986 (the Louvre's stamp, Lugt 1886, is at the bottom, slightly to the left).

Bibliography
P. pp. 138, 302, 311
R. p. 211

A. 112, fig. 50
Williams, 1978, p. 136

Related works
For several portraits supposedly of Rosalie, see catalogue nos. 297–299.

In the Louvre, there is a famous drawing (R. F. 3880; A. 188, fig. 502) from the Goncourt collection that is believed to represent Rosalie. This identification was confirmed for the Goncourts by Théophile Fragonard, who inscribed the drawing itself "ma tante Rosalie." In our opinion, this very fine drawing (see figure 1) is not by Fragonard, and the sitter is hardly likely to be his daughter.

Figure 1. French School, 18th century. *Portrait of a Woman.* Musée du Louvre, Paris, Cabinet des Dessins

Rosalie Fragonard was born in 1769, and died in 1788. We know that her early death deeply affected her father, for whose work she often served as the inspiration (although perhaps less often than Fragonard's biographers would have it, so eager have they been to recognize Rosalie in every one of his little girls at play, or in each of the elegant young women in the costume of a "Savoyarde").

Judging from this drawing, Rosalie and her mother looked very much alike. Her slightly heavy chin, her dark eyes and arched eyebrows, and her stubby nose resemble Marie-Anne's features. Nonetheless, one senses that the personality of the placid young woman in the picture remains undefined.

294 Portrait of Alexandre-Évariste Fragonard

Black chalk on paper, round (slightly elongated), 13 x 12.8 cm.
Inscribed on the verso, in ink: *Fragonard fils peintre*

Musée du Louvre, Paris, Cabinet des Dessins, R. F. 41.196

Provenance
See catalogue no. 287; Huot-Fragonard:
sold, May 19–20, 1876, part of no. 26:
"portrait d'Alexandre Fragonard enfant"
(for 50 francs, with a portrait of his father:

see catalogue no. 287); Jean Groult: sold,
May 24, 1955, no. 125 G; donated to the
Cabinet des Dessins by the Société des Amis
du Louvre, 1986 (the Louvre's stamp, Lugt
1886, is at the bottom, slightly to the left).

Bibliography
P. pp. 138, 302
R. p. 212
A. 103, fig. 48

Born in 1780 (the same year as Ingres)—like his father—in Grasse, Alexandre-Évariste Fragonard also had a highly successful career as an artist. During his lifetime, he enjoyed greater fame than did his father, who had soon been forgotten. When Alexandre-Évariste died in 1850, his work was completely out of fashion, while a new crop of collectors (notably, Walferdin, Thoré, Renouvier, Saint, Carrier, Burty, Gautier, Saint-Victor, and Blanc, among others) began, happily, to discover and to enthusiastically acquire the works of Jean-Honoré.

Practically nothing is known of the relationship between Fragonard and his son (although we tend to doubt that it was a close one). Having learned the rudiments of his profession from Jean-Honoré, the extremely precocious Alexandre-Évariste then studied with Jacques-Louis David, the master of Neoclassicism (David, writing to his pupil Alexandre-Évariste, never forgot to ask that he be remembered to his parents). However, the younger Fragonard did not imi-

tate the works of his teacher any more than he did those of his father. One awaits the results of much of the research that has been undertaken, in recent years, on this "flamboyant" painter (Jal, 1872, p. 606), attracted by the troubadour style, who attempted to reconcile the aesthetic of David with that of the burgeoning Romanticism. There is little doubt that one day Alexandre-Évariste will occupy a well-deserved and important place in the history of early-nineteenth-century painting, quite independent of the reputation of his father.

The present drawing, recently acquired by the Louvre, shows the boy aged about five. There is no evidence that any of the other portraits of children painted by Fragonard during much of his career represent Alexandre-Évariste, nor that he was the model for *The Little Preacher* (cat. no. 227) or for those other scenes of childhood that his father so cherished.

Bister wash on paper, over a very light underdrawing in black chalk, 18.6 x 13 cm.

Musée des Beaux-Arts, Besançon, D. 2945

Provenance
Pierre-Adrien Pâris (1745–1819): bequeathed to the city of Besançon; inventoried, 1806, no. 163: "le portrait de Mlle Gérard au Bistre par Fragonard"; Bibliothèque
Municipale, Besançon (its stamp, Lugt 238 c,
is at the lower right); entered the museum,
1919.

Exhibitions
Paris, 1933, no. 151
Paris, 1950, no. 86
Besançon, 1956, no. 68, pl. XII
Grasse, 1957, no. 53
Bordeaux, 1958, no. 174

Bibliography
P. p. 314
Estignard, 1902, ill. between pp. 126 and
   127
Bouchot, 1906, p. 215, ill. p. 205
Martine, 1927, pl. 32
Cornillot, 1957, no. 78, ill. (with a list of
   exhibitions and a comprehensive
   bibliography)
Mrozińska, 1960, p. 16, fig. 5
A. 2039, fig. 560
Harris, 1979, p. 61, n. 22, fig. 8

Related works
See catalogue no. 296.
   Théophile Fragonard copied an 1814 self-
portrait by Marguerite Gérard, and made a
gift of this drawing to Edmond de Goncourt
(it may be seen in the example of the Goncourts' *L'Art du dix-huitième siècle*, part of
the Audéoud gift to the Bibliothèque
Nationale, Rés. 2, Audéoud, 281; see
figure 1).
   A "portrait de l'habile Artiste Mlle Gérard,
fait au crayon rouge," by Fragonard, was
sold July 8, 1793, no. 73.

Figure 1. Théophile Fragonard.
Marguerite Gérard. Bibliothèque
Nationale, Paris, Département des
Imprimés (réserve)

Marguerite Gérard (1761–1837), sixteen years younger
than her sister, Mme Fragonard, was the victim of her own
good fortune. The fact that she lived with the Fragonards—
very likely, from 1775 on—has provoked much calumny,
and many of the painter's biographers have given free rein to
their imaginations regarding the relationships of this supposed "ménage à trois" (which Fragonard's work does much
to reinforce). However, there is nothing—not even the letters
that Marguerite wrote to her brother-in-law in the early
nineteenth century; these are printed in their entirety in
chapter VIII, below—to prove that the painter and his pupil
were anything other than close friends. Yet, one thing

remains certain: for a long time, this "love story" has obscured Marguerite's reputation as an artist.

Marguerite Gérard's other misfortune was her position as a woman. Feminists today believe that she was unjustly victimized both in her own time—having been denied the recognition that she deserved—and, more recently, by modern art historians, who uphold the superior creativity of male artists.

Yet, Marguerite Gérard was, in fact, famous, and although she may have since been forgotten, she has shared that fate with her highly talented nephew. (It is a pity, in this regard, that Sally Wells-Robertson's excellent thesis has not yet been published.) Like Alexandre-Évariste, as an artist Marguerite Gérard was thrust into the background by the advocates of a rigid Neoclassicism; and, also like him, her talent, originality, and imagination made her work stand out; it was as different from Fragonard's as from David's.

The damage sustained by this drawing—from exposure to light—may perhaps explain why it was recently attributed to Marguerite Gérard (by Wells-Robertson, and Williams; see Harris, 1979), and assumed to be a self-portrait. In any event, for Pâris, as early as 1806, there was no doubt that the sitter was, indeed, Marguerite Gérard—sketched by her brother-in-law. The date of 1778 first suggested by Henri Bouchot (1906) for the work seems all the more plausible, especially since it is very possible that the portrait of Marguerite is contemporary with that of her sister (see cat. no. 291).

It is known that Marguerite Gérard was beautiful (see the following entry). On several occasions, she was a source of inspiration to her brother-in-law—serving as his model, for *La Lecture* and *La Rêveuse* (see cat. nos. 270, 271). Fragonard scarcely seems to have noticed that she was also a very talented artist in her own right.

296 Portrait of Marguerite Gérard

Black chalk on paper, round (slightly elongated), 12.9 x 12.8 cm.
At the right, a strip of the paper is colored with wash.
The drawing is glued to the mount.
Inscribed on the verso, in ink: *Melle Gérard—peintre*

Musée du Louvre, Paris, Cabinet des Dessins, R. F. 41.197

Provenance
See catalogue no. 287; Huot-Fragonard: sold, May 19–20, 1876, part of no. 26: "portrait de Mademoiselle Gérard" (for 75 francs, with a self-portrait: see catalogue no. 288); Jean Groult: sold, May 24, 1955, no. 125 A, ill.; donated to the Cabinet des Dessins by the Société des Amis du Louvre, 1986

(the Louvre's stamp, Lugt 1886, is at the lower right).

Exhibitions
Paris, 1921, no. 923

Bibliography
P. pp. 138, 267

Algoud, 1936, p. 246, ill.
R. p. 211
Mrozińska, 1960, p. 19, fig. 8
A. 113, fig. 51

Related works
See the previous entry.

"From Grasse she [Mme Fragonard] had kept ... a terribly strong accent, and, curiously enough, while it was so disagreeable when she spoke, this same accent took on a seductiveness in the case of her sister, Mlle Gérard. Then, it sounded harmonious and enchanting. She [Mlle Gérard] was as tall as Mme Fragonard, but was possessed of an elegance and a presence besides, while, in terms of distinction, she was second to none. In short, she was the absolute antithesis of her sister," wrote Mme Hippolyte Lecomte, early in the nineteenth century, describing the artists at the Louvre (see Delaroche-Vernet, 1923, p. 224; P. p. 242).

The judgment is amply confirmed by this drawing recently acquired by the Louvre.

As on a medallion, the young artist is shown in profile, from the left. Her long neck, and her delicate features are seen to advantage. We believe that this drawing also dates from about 1785, and that the series is a homogeneous one. Moreover, we do not rule out the possibility that Fragonard may have had it in mind when he painted the solemn profile of the young woman in the *Fountain of Love* (cat. no. 283, figure 4) but whether consciously or not we shall never know.

297 La Jeune Fille à la marmotte

Watercolor and bister wash on paper, over an underdrawing in black chalk, 25.9 x 21.2 cm.

Graphische Sammlung Albertina, Vienna, Inv. 12.543

Provenance
Albert, Duke of Saxe-Teschen (1738–1822; the dry mark of his collection, Lugt 174, is at the lower left); entered the Albertina at the time of its founding.

Exhibitions
Paris, 1931, no. 61, ill.
London, 1932, no. 1020 (no. 692 in the commemorative catalogue)
Vienna, 1950, no. 120
Bern, 1954, no. 78, pl. XVIII

Bibliography
Schönbrunner and Meder, 1896–1908, V, pl. 362
Meder, 1922, pl. 25
Fosca, 1954, p. 51, pl. 5 a
R. pp. 181, 211
A. 2066, fig. 561
Benesch, 1964, no. XXV, colorpl.

Related works
The pendant to *La Jeune Fille à la marmotte* is entitled *Enfant à la curiosité*. Several versions of these works are known:

A painting on copper (see figure 1), in the Pushkin Museum, Moscow (32 x 24 cm.; see W. 508, fig. 212), was originally in the collection of the Marquis de Veri, sold December 12, 1785, no. 41; we do not know the present whereabouts of its pendant (see figure 2), which belonged to Prince Yussupov (see W. 509, fig. 213).

There is a painting on canvas, in the Portland Art Museum, Oregon (see figure 3; 39.8 x 32 cm.; W. 507, pl. 119), which, according to W., originally belonged to the Ménage de Pressigny collection; its pendant (figure 4) is in the same museum (see W. 506, pl. 118).

An oval picture (40 x 32 cm.), formerly owned by René Gimpel, was on the Paris art market in 1969 (see figure 5); its pendant (see figure 6) has been included in several sales: at Versailles, June 11 and 13, 1968,

no. 207, colorpl.; and at the Palais Galliéra, Paris, June 13, 1969, no. 9, pl. V; the attribution of these two paintings is often disputed.

For two pastels (figures 7, 8; 40 x 31 cm.), see the H. Michel Lévy sale, May 25, 1905, nos. 37, 38, ill. The Abbé de Saint-Non owned "deux ... dessins coloriés par M. de St Non représentant un jeune savoyard qui montre la curiosité et une marmotte copies d'après Fragonard," whose value was estimated at twelve *livres* in the inventory made after the abbé's death (G. Wildenstein, 1959, p. 239, nos. 35–37).

For the full-length versions, known as *Rosalie en fanchon* or *La Vielleuse*, see figure 9; W. 505, fig. 211; and also W. 42, 43, fig. 30. For this last, highly doubtful painting, see Rosenberg, 1983, no. 89 A; the work, which belongs to the Fogg Art Museum, exists in a version attributed to Marguerite Gérard that was sold at Versailles May 27, 1973, no. 251.

Figure 1. Fragonard. *La Jeune Fille à la marmotte*. Pushkin Museum, Moscow

Figure 2. Fragonard. *Enfant à la curiosité*. Whereabouts unknown

Figure 3. Fragonard. *La Jeune Fille à la marmotte*. Portland Art Museum, Oregon

Figure 4. Fragonard. *Enfant à la curiosité*. Portland Art Museum, Oregon

Figure 5. Attributed to Fragonard. *La Jeune Fille à la marmotte*. Whereabouts unknown

Figure 6. Attributed to Fragonard. *Enfant à la curiosité*. Whereabouts unknown

Figure 7. Fragonard. *La Jeune Fille à la marmotte*. Pastel. Whereabouts unknown

Figure 8. Fragonard. *Enfant à la curiosité*. Pastel. Whereabouts unknown

Figure 9. Fragonard. *La Vielleuse*. Whereabouts unknown

This appealing work is very famous; nonetheless, many questions remain as to its date, its link with the various existing painted versions, and the identity of the model.

We shall confine our comments to one or two of these points. First of all, it should be noted that the pendant to the painting—a connection that dates to the eighteenth century —was first described as a "petit garçon à la curiosité" in the catalogue accompanying the sale of the Marquis de Veri's collection in 1785. (The "curiosité" was a box containing geological artifacts or precious objects.) We would add that there was no mention of the Albertina watercolor in Fragonard's lifetime. However, we do know that the Abbé de Saint-Non made "color" copies of these two paintings by Fragonard. For a while we believed the Albertina watercolor to be one of these copies: the detached look of the girl, and

the somewhat frozen quality of the composition had seemed to confirm this. Yet, in light of the enthusiasm expressed by Benesch, for whom the present work was among Fragonard's "most valuable," we must set aside this hypothesis. In addition, none of the works by the Abbé de Saint-Non with which we are familiar (with the exception of his aquatints) is of high quality.

Was the model for this drawing the artist's daughter, Rosalie (1769–1788)—in which case the "garçonnet" would be Alexandre-Évariste, her brother, born in 1780? We do not think so, since the resemblance between the young woman depicted here and in the "joueuse de vielle" (hurdy-gurdy player) included in the 1774 sale of Vassal de Saint-Hubert's collection (a signed replica of this work exists; see figure 9; W. 505, fig. 211) definitely rules out

such an identification. The sitter for the "joueuse de vielle" is believed to have been Françoise Chemin, whose looks were well known in Paris at the end of the eighteenth century. Moreover, it is known that Fragonard's picture had "been painted" as a "pendant" to a work by Chardin, the "Aveugle des Quinze-vingts." This commission (by Vassal himself?) was the occasion for yet another association between the two artists, and facilitated a comparison of their respective merits.

The young woman wears an elegant scarf tied under her chin; her lips are too red, her cheeks are too pink, and the bodice of her dress is too revealing. She holds a half-open box, set atop a stone, containing a marmot of the type that Savoyard women used to display in the streets of Paris. Is this simply a genre scene, or—according to certain interpretations now in fashion (see, for example, Vada Dunifer, 1985, p. 177)—is it rich in sexual connotations that would have been understood by all in the eighteenth century?

There is no question that Fragonard has considerably embellished reality. Not all Savoyard women were pretty; and the pretty ones doubtless were not always content with merely displaying their marmots. However, Fragonard's work does not lend itself to such attempts at overinterpretation.

The artist's wish was to charm, to win over the spectator, to demonstrate his skills, but he did not set out to render a faithful likeness of the sitter. Fragonard was not a critic of the moral climate of his day, but a poet.

298 Young Woman Seated on the Ground

Red chalk on paper, 22 x 17 cm.
Inscribed at the bottom left, in ink: *frago.1785.*

Private collection, New York

Figure 1. Fragonard. *Young Woman Seated in a Chair.* Courtauld Institute of Art, London, Seilern Collection

Provenance

François-Martial Marcille (1790–1856): sold posthumously, March 4–7, 1857, no. 65: "jeune femme assise" (?) (this information may relate to the other drawing of the same subject [see figure 1], which was in the collection of the Goncourt brothers; the latter, in an unpublished notebook quoted by E. Launay, note that they bought this drawing for 15 francs—no. 65 in the Marcille sale brought 42 francs!); Edmond and Jules de Goncourt: sold, February 15, 1897, no. 84 (for 2,400 francs, to Homberg; does not seem to bear the stamp of the Goncourt brothers' collection, Lugt 1089); Joseph Homberg: sold, May 11, 1923, no. 14, ill. (for 15,100 francs, to Mrs. Gould); Florence J. Gould, near Nice: sold, Sotheby's, New York, April 24, 1985, no. 3, colorpl.; private collection, New York.

Exhibitions

New York, Zangrilli, Brady and Co., 1986, no. 17, ill.

Bibliography

E. de Goncourt, 1881, p. 78
P. p. 305
W. p. 30 (French edition)
A. 191, fig. 78
Williams, 1978, p. 136
[E. Launay], 1983–84, no. 94, pl. 117

In 1857, the Goncourts had acquired two drawings, very similar in format and both in red chalk. Along with the Seilern collection, the second of these drawings (see figure 1) recently entered the Courtauld Institute of Art in London (A. 199, fig. 77; London exhibition catalogue, 1981, no. 135, ill.). The importance of these two drawings lies in the inscription that each bears in its bottom left corner: *frago. 1785.* (not *1765*, as has sometimes been read); although not signatures, there is no reason to doubt their authenticity. Because dated works are rare in Fragonard's oeuvre, such information is valuable to those interested in the evolution and the vicissitudes of the master's style.

These two drawings are unquestionably portraits—but is the sitter the same in each, and is Eunice Williams (1978) correct in identifying both models as Rosalie Fragonard, the painter's daughter (1769–1788)? We prefer to reserve judgment, because the resemblance between the two young ladies seems questionable. Of the two, only the present drawing may perhaps represent Rosalie (on this point, see cat. no. 293).

The young woman, her legs crossed under her, wears a small cap and a short cape over her dress. She is set off against a white cloth draped over the table behind her. Her pensive, dream-like expression is the source of the work's special charm.

Red chalk on paper, 24.1 x 18.8 cm.

Private collection, New York

Provenance
M. E. N[orblin].: sold, March 16–17, 1860,
no. 58: "très joli dessin, spirituellement exécuté à la sanguine, représentant une jeune
femme assise" (?); the architect Hippolyte
Destailleur: sold, April 27–28, 1866, no. 70:
"jeune fille assise" (for 8 francs 50) (?); private collection, New York.

Exhibitions
Washington, D.C., 1978, no. 54, ill.
New York, 1984, no. 16, fig. 24

Bibliography
A. 2068, fig. 562

Related works
An engraving of the drawing, with some
variations, was made by Martel (in imitation
of red chalk), and entitled *La Reflection* (see
figure 1), and one was also made by Alexandre Briceau ("Briceau Direxit"!) (see figure
2). Both of these follow the format of the
drawing (the composition is not reversed).

Figure 1. Martel, after
Fragonard. *"La Reflection."*
Bibliothèque d'Art et
d'Archéologie, Paris

Figure 2. Alexandre Briceau. *Young
Woman Dozing.* Bibliothèque d'Art
et d'Archéologie, Paris

Figure 3. Fragonard. *Young Woman
Seated.* Whereabouts unknown

Eunice Williams (1978) is convinced—perhaps rightly—
that the model for this portrait was Rosalie Fragonard, who
died at an early age. In any case, the date of the red-chalk
drawing must be very close to that of the preceding one:
1785. The same sitter appears in another red-chalk drawing,
which was exhibited in London in 1968 (no. 183) as the
work of David; we reattributed the sheet to Fragonard in
1969 (p. 99; see figure 3; see also A. 1177, fig. 732). In this
last drawing, instead of dozing in a chair, the young woman
is seated on the ground, turned toward the spectator.

The harmoniousness of the present work derives from the
refinement of the execution and the delicacy of the
cross-hatching.

300 Young Girl Beside a Fireplace, Holding a Bellows

Red chalk on paper, 24.1 x 20.9 cm.

Private collection

Provenance
François-Martial Marcille (1790–1856): sold posthumously, March 4–7, 1857, no. 67: "Cendrillon. Dessin à la sanguine"; Hippolyte Walferdin (1795–1880): sold posthumously, April 12–16, 1880, no. 193 (for 465 francs, to M. de Turenne); Comte Arthur de Vogüé, 1889; Camille Groult (according to the London exhibition catalogue, 1968); Stanley Shaw Bond, London, 1932: sold, Christie's, London, June 9, 1944, no. 57 (for 550 guineas, to Hatvany); Baron Paul Hatvany, 1950: sold, Christie's, London, June 24, 1980, no. 47, colorpl.; private collection.

Exhibitions
London, 1932, no. 818 (no. 688 in the commemorative catalogue)
London, 1950, no. 27, ill.
London, 1968, no. 280

Bibliography
P. p. 295
A. 748

Related works
A similar drawing, but in bister wash, inscribed "Rome 1774," on which we must reserve judgment, is catalogued by A. (195, fig. 76). For a drawing of a young woman (the same one ?) crouching on her heels and leaning her right arm on a bellows, see A. 196, fig. 75, and the Grasse exhibition catalogue, 1957, no. 55, pl. XIII (see figure 1).

Figure 1. Fragonard. *Young Girl Crouching, and Leaning on a Bellows.* Whereabouts unknown

One can easily understand how both Walferdin and, later, Portalis were tempted to give this charming drawing the fanciful title of "Cendrillon." However, we believe that Fragonard simply represented a young woman crouching before a fire, kindling its flames with the aid of her bellows.

With a minimum of pressure applied to his pencil, Fragonard describes the exact gesture of the girl and the attentive expression on her face, skillfully rendering the reflection of the firelight on her face. Although rapidly executed, the appeal of this drawing lies, above all, in the poetic delicacy of its intimate subject.

301 Landscape with a Double Flight of Steps

Bister wash on paper, over an underdrawing in black chalk, 47 x 33 cm.

Private collection

Provenance
In the collection of the same family since the beginning of the nineteenth century.

Bibliography
Unpublished

Related works
A preparatory study in black chalk (16.5 x 21 cm.; A. 1517) was sold in Paris May 23, 1928, no. 54, pl. X (see figure 1). It would seem to have belonged to the Walferdin collection (part of no. 275 of the April 12–16, 1880, sale).

Figure 1. Fragonard. *Landscape with a Double Flight of Steps*. Whereabouts unknown

This fine drawing gives rise to two questions: can it be dated, and what is the site represented?

The drawing clearly was inspired by Roman parks and gardens, but we cannot be certain whether Fragonard represented an actual place, or let his imagination run free. We tend to favor the second interpretation, although we do not rule out the possibility that the drawing may considerably postdate the artist's return from his second trip to Italy in 1774.

About 1780, Fragonard began to use bister wash almost exclusively for detailed compositions of this type. He began with a rapidly executed sketch in black chalk, like the one in figure 1, and then employed only the brush to achieve these highly evocative imaginary views, at which he would become a master. This seems to confirm—along with the vast output of Hubert Robert, who, even more than Fragonard, preferred red chalk and architectural subjects—that there was a ready clientele in Paris for works of this type.

302   Park in the Italian Style, with Portrait Busts and Strollers

Bister wash on paper, over an underdrawing in black chalk, 23.8 x 38 cm.
Inscribed in ink, at the lower right: *frago 1786*

Crocker Art Museum, Sacramento, 1871.407

Provenance
Judge Edwin Bryant Crocker (1818–1875);
given to the Sacramento museum by his
widow, Margaret E. Rhodes, 1885.

Exhibitions
Sacramento, 1940, no. 63 a, pl. 9
Berkeley, 1968, no. 5:82, ill.
Claremont, California, 1976, no. 24, ill.
Washington, D.C., 1978, no. 52, ill.

Bibliography
A. 947
Crocker Art Museum catalogue, 1964, p. 89,
   no. 407, ill.
Rosenberg, 1970, p. 35, no. 16, pl. 34
Crocker Art Museum catalogue, 1971, no.
   88, pl. p. 129

Related works
A drawing (A. 946, fig. 260) with a composition similar to that of the Sacramento sheet

was sold in Paris December 9, 1981, no. 42,
ill. It is dated 1774, but we prefer to reserve
judgment on its authenticity.
   For other, comparable drawings, see A.
364, fig. 133 (today in the Thaw collection,
New York); A. 1445, fig. 394; A. 1580, fig.
741; A. 1598, fig. 422; A. 2362, fig. 601;
see also A. 361, fig. 135, acquired by the
Stanford museum, and a drawing sold at
Sotheby's, London, November 26, 1970, no.
74, ill.

The Sacramento drawing may perhaps be called unexcep-
tional, but, apart from the fact that it was one of the first
works by Fragonard to enter an American public collection,
it is dated. The "1786" that is clearly visible in the lower
right confirms that, twelve years after his return from Italy,
Fragonard was still deriving inspiration from his memories
of the trip.
   Feathery touches of bister wash are scattered across the
page: Fragonard's artistic vision has become more all

encompassing, more "impressionistic," sacrificing the
restraints imposed by the composition.
   In a park dominated by a Roman villa, strollers wander
among the tombs, columns, and sculptured busts from
antiquity. Pines, cypresses, and other trees cast their shadows
over the scene. This description could apply just as well to
many other drawings by Fragonard, but the artist never
repeats himself, nor tires of his subject.

Oil on canvas, 44 x 55 cm.

Harvard University Art Museums (Fogg Art Museum), Cambridge, Massachusetts, Gift of Charles E. Dunlap

Provenance
O.: sold, December 16–17, 1839, no. 88 (with *L'Enfant chéri*); de Rigny: sold, June 2, 1857, no. 40; Pillot: sold, December 6–8, 1858, no. 43 (for 1,605 francs, to Morens); Lord Rosebery; (Wells-Robertson, 1974–75, doubts that the Fogg painting is the same as the one included in the de la Roncière collection sale, March 28, 1859, no. 25); [Wildenstein]; Charles E. Dunlap; given to the Fogg museum, 1961.

Exhibitions
Paris-Detroit-New York, 1974–75, no. 71, pl. 16 (entry by Sally Wells-Robertson, who cites other exhibitions)

Bibliography
Doin, 1912, p. 432
Wilhelm, 1951, p. 22
W. 540, fig. 234
W. and M. 561, ill.
Rosenberg and Compin, 1974, p. 276, n. 59, fig. 24
Rosenberg, in Paris-Detroit-New York exhibition catalogue, 1974–75, p. 416

Gaehtgens, 1975, p. 46
Wells-Robertson, 1979, pp. 185–86, notes 34, 35
Berezina, 1983, p. 221

Related works
An engraving of the painting was made by Géraud Vidal and Nicolas-François Regnault (1746–about 1810) in 1786 (?), or perhaps 1792, which bore the notation, "Peint par M. Fragonard et Mlle Gérard. Retouché par Regnault et G. Vidal. Dédié aux bonnes mères" (P. p. 330, no. 139; Doin, 1912, p. 433, ill.; and Toulouse exhibition catalogue, 1951, no. 412). The print is very rare, and we have not seen an example of it firsthand, but we illustrate the "second edition" from the Musée Paul-Dupuy, Toulouse (see figure 1).

The pendant, *L'Enfant chéri*, was also the subject of an engraving (see figure 2), in 1792 (*Mercure de France*, May 26, 1792, p. 108); it also belongs to the Fogg Art Museum (see figure 3; W. 541, pl. 125). At the sale of the Pillot collection, December 6–8, 1858, no. 46, the painting was cata-

logued jointly as by Fragonard and Mlle Gérard: "figures par Mlle Gérard, paysage par Fragonard." Marguerite Gérard returned to the composition in a more Neoclassical work —now in the Hermitage—after which her brother, Henri Gérard, made an engraving in 1788 entitled *L'Élant [sic] de la nature* (see figure 4). Another, larger version, signed (and dated ?), is now in the Hillwood Museum, Washington, D.C. (see figure 5).

The sketches for the painting and for its pendant were included in the Van Leyden collection sale in Amsterdam, September 10, 1804, no. 131: "Fragonard: Deux charmantes Esquisses, dont les sujets en grand ont été gravés sous le titre des Premiers Pas de l'Enfance...."

At a conference in honor of Ian Woodner in Cambridge, Massachusetts, E. Williams presented a drawing, belonging to a French private collector (see figure 6), which she believed was related to the Fogg painting. She is of the opinion—as are we—that this drawing was executed by Fragonard alone. Her publication on the subject is forthcoming.

Figure 1. Nicolas-François Regnault and Géraud Vidal. *Le Premier Pas de l'enfance*. Musée Paul-Dupuy, Toulouse

Figure 2. Nicolas-François Regnault and Géraud Vidal. *L'Enfant chéri*. Musée Paul-Dupuy, Toulouse

Figure 3. Marguerite Gérard and Fragonard. *L'Enfant chéri*. Fogg Art Museum, Cambridge, Massachusetts

Figure 4. Henri Gérard, after Marguerite Gérard. *L'Élan de la nature*. Bibliothèque Nationale, Paris, Cabinet des Estampes

Figure 5. Marguerite Gérard. *L'Enfant chéri*. Hillwood Museum, Washington, D.C.

Figure 6. Fragonard. *Le Premier Pas de l'enfance*. Private collection, France

303

This painting has become a bone of contention between the defenders of Fragonard and the advocates of his beautiful pupil, Marguerite Gérard: but, in any case, its subject requires little explanation. Observed by a large, three-colored cat, a baby toddles toward its mother, while its little sister, nurse, and grandmother look on. The engraving of the work, made by Regnault and Vidal (see figure 1, and *Related works*), was entitled *Le Premier Pas de l'enfance*, and bore an inscription stating that it was "Painted by M. Fragonard and Mlle Gérard." Despite this notation, on several occasions, Sally Wells-Robertson has tried to prove that the painting was executed entirely by Marguerite Gérard (1761–1837), at the very most, "under the eye of her master" and brother-in-law. For Wells-Robertson, the caption on the print was intended to "favor" the "commercial

prospects" of the engravers, "by presenting the charming domestic scenes of the young artist, under the aegis of the famous painter from Grasse." More recently (1979), this same critic indicated that another state of the engraving once existed (it is now lost), which attributed the composition "to Mlle Gérard alone."

We willingly acknowledge that a large portion of the painting was executed by Mademoiselle Gérard; but, as we noted in 1974 and in 1974–75, we believe that certain sections of the picture—the grandmother and the baby, most certainly—are by Fragonard. The warm, predominantly yellow tones, and a pronounced taste for thick, heavy brushstrokes seem to us to be undeniable evidence of the master's hand. At the same time, we do not now rule out the possibility that, in the pendant, *L'Enfant chéri* (in Sally Wells-Rob-

Figure 7. Fragonard and Marguerite Gérard. *Young Woman Playing the Guitar, near a Sleeping Child.* Staatliche Kunsthalle, Karlsruhe

Figure 8. Fragonard and Marguerite Gérard. *La Liseuse.* Fitzwilliam Museum, Cambridge

Figure 9. Fragonard and Marguerite Gérard. *The Sleeping Child.* Whereabouts unknown

Figure 10. Fragonard. *Portrait of an Old Woman,* called *Portrait of Sophie.* Musée des Beaux-Arts, Besançon

ertson's view, this is not the pendant at all)—or, at least, in the version in Cambridge (see figure 3)—the foliage and the trunks of the trees may be by Fragonard.

Our opinion was supported by the inclusion of *Le Premier Pas* in the "David to Delacroix" exhibition in Paris, in Detroit, and in New York in 1974–75. When the canvas was juxtaposed with *Le Verrou* (cat. no. 236) and *Le Baiser à la Dérobée* (cat. no. 304), it was easy to distinguish the passages by Fragonard and those by his sister-in-law in the Fogg painting (see the remarkable account by Gaehtgens, 1975). That the two artists worked together is attested both by early sales (the Villers collection sale, December 2, 1795, included four such paintings, two of which are known to us—they are now in the Karlsruhe museum; see figure 7—and there was also a sale in London, March 6, 1957, no. 86, ill.), and by recent scholarship (Hallam, 1986, p. 177). Paintings such as *La Liseuse* (in the Fitzwilliam Museum, Cambridge; see figure 8), and *L'Enfant endormi* (included in the Clos collection sale, November 18–19, 1812, no. 9, and on the art market in London in 1962; see figure 9), to cite just two examples, provide further proof of a collaboration.

A further note about the "grandmother": we have already encountered this figure in a drawing by Fragonard (cat. no.

225), and she served as a model for him on several other occasions—notably, for the superb drawing *Les Sept Âges de la vie* in the Lauder collection (Williams, 1978, no. 41, ill.). An admirable pastel by Fragonard, one of the few that has been identified to date (see figure 10; P. p. 313; A. 2041; Cuzin, 1986, p. 65, fig. 10, in color), seems to be a portrait from life of a certain old woman, the artist's "housekeeper," Sophie, if we are to believe Théophile Fragonard, according to an inscription on the verso of the mount.

Marguerite Gérard favored cool tones, silvery whites, and stiff, meticulously drawn drapery folds in her work. "The *Premier Pas de l'enfance* is an early affirmation of the artist's preference, which she displayed throughout her life, for elegant mothers, aristocratic or bourgeois, always beautifully dressed and coiffed, as opposed to Fragonard's taste for more ordinary female types. Simplicity of composition; frozen, theatrical poses; and a porcelain-like perfection in the rendering of the mother and the nursemaid are characteristic of the static and controlled style of Marguerite Gérard," Sally Wells-Robertson aptly wrote in 1974–75. The "dynamism of the baby," the tender, delighted expression on the face of "Sophie"—at once, so natural and so touching—remind us of the genius of Mlle Gérard's master.

304   Le Baiser à la dérobée

Oil on canvas, 45 x 55 cm.

The Hermitage, Leningrad

Provenance
Formerly, Stanislaw II Augustus Poniatowski, King of Poland (1732–1798; valued at 200 ducats in the handwritten catalogue of the collection: see Réau, 1928, p. 188, no. 102; Ryszkiewicz, 1975); at the Lazienki

Summer Palace, Warsaw, 1851, on the second floor, in the king's apartments; would have had to have been returned to Poland according to the terms of the Treaty of Riga; entered the Hermitage in exchange for *La Polonaise,* a copy after Watteau, in 1895.

Exhibitions
(For a detailed list, see the Hermitage catalogue, 1985)
Paris, 1937, no. 165, pl. 61 of the album
Moscow-Leningrad, 1955–56, p. 60
Bordeaux, 1965, no. 21, with pl.

304

Paris, 1965–66, no. 19, with pl.
Paris-Detroit-New York, 1974–75, no. 60,
 pl. 33 (entry by Pierre Rosenberg)
Washington-Detroit-Los Angeles, 1975–76,
 pp. 49–52, ill., and color details
Tokyo, 1980, no. 89, colorpl.

Bibliography
Gault de Saint-Germain, 1808, p. 233
Landon, 1808, p. 9
Revue universelle des arts, 1856, III, p. 58
P. pp. 72, 271 ("Le Baiser")
N., ill. between pp. 124 and 125
Schmidt, 1909, pp. 52–53, colorpl.
Réau, 1932, ill. between pp. 98 and 99
Gerson, 1942, p. 102, pl. 29 (reissued in
 1983)
Wilhelm, 1951, p. 22, ill. p. 17
R. pp. 52, 70, 108, 157, pl. 59, p. 117
Sterling, 1957, p. 52, colorpl.
W. 523, pl. 124, p. 30 (French edition; the
 painting is dated between 1789 and 1806)

Carpenter, 1962, p. 361
Thuillier, 1967, pp. 12, 54, 72, 73, colorpl.
Watson, 1971, pp. 88, 87, ill.
W. and M. 546, ill.
Rosenberg and Compin, 1974, p. 274,
 fig. 21
Gaehtgens, 1975, p. 46
Ryszkiewicz, 1975, p. 18
Wells-Robertson, in Los Angeles exhibition
 catalogue, 1976, p. 198
Ananoff, 1979, pp. 215–16, 218, n. 23
Wells-Robertson, 1979, p. 187, n. 33
Hermitage catalogue, 1985, pp. 92–93,
 no. 48, ill. (with detailed bibliography)

Related works
Paintings
A copy after the engraving was sold at the
Galerie Charpentier in Paris as the work of
Marguerite Gérard, on June 24, 1937, no.
25, pl. V. Also, a "signed" copy on panel was
sold at the Palais Galliéra, Paris, November
29–December 3, 1965, no. 105 (see figure
1). Ananoff (1979, p. 218, n. 23) mentions
"trois ventes (1837, 1863, 1867, à la vente
Boitelle du 10–11 janvier, no. 89) où passe
un *Baiser à la dérobée* de Marguerite Gérard
d'après Fragonard."

Engravings
A stipple engraving was made by Nicolas-
François Regnault (1746–about 1810) in
1788 (P. p. 322, no. 25, ill. between pp. 128
and 129; we know of two states, and illustrate an example of the first: see figure 2). In
1790, Jean-Charles Charpentier made an
engraving of just the central group of the
composition in a medallion. The Regnault
engraving was announced in the *Mercure de
France*, June 14, 1788, p. 95; in the *Journal
de Paris*, June 1788, p. 666; and in the *Journal général de France*, 1788, p. 274.

Figure 1. After Fragonard and Marguerite Gérard (?). *Le Baiser à la dérobée*. Whereabouts unknown

Figure 2. Nicolas-François Regnault, after Fragonard and Marguerite Gérard (?). *Le Baiser à la dérobée*. Bibliothèque Nationale, Paris, Cabinet des Estampes

The success that he achieved with the engraving of *Le Verrou* (cat. no. 236) induced Nicolas-François Regnault to produce a pendant to it. He chose to make an engraving of a composition by (?) Fragonard, *Le Baiser à la dérobée*, with a totally different feeling. In this painting, a young man gives a chaste kiss to a young woman who has come to fetch a shawl, while delicately clasping her hand. She appears willing, but somewhat anxious at being taken by surprise. In the background, at the right, in another room, we can discern two women and a man huddled around a table, playing cards.

Regnault's engraving dates from 1788. How then are we to explain the huge differences in style, technique, and spirit between this painting and *Le Verrou*, which cannot, however, have been executed more than ten years earlier? *Le Verrou* is a passionate, lyrical work, while *Le Baiser à la dérobée*, "like a Boilly, but a Boilly of genius" (Sterling, 1957), is competent and bourgeois. It seems odd that the evolution of Fragonard's style appears to have led him to imitate the minor Dutch masters of the seventeenth century, Metsu and ter Borch, so admired at the close of the eighteenth century: "This cold and wretched fashion of the time? Here ... is the white satin dress of ter Borch, always the same dress, which everyone will soon quarrel over and on which one will no longer know whose signature to read: Fragonard's or Boilly's. Here, too, commences ... the cold, polished, miniaturist manner of Fragonard, so different from the lively technique of his painted sketches that one scarcely recognizes his hand in the original, and it appears to us to be merely a copy" (Goncourt, p. 272).

As early as 1974 (in the *From David to Delacroix* exhibition catalogue—although Gerson had already mentioned the possibility of a collaboration in 1942!), we questioned whether these late paintings were the work of Marguerite Gérard, Fragonard having provided the original idea for the composition. This hypothesis has since attracted the attention of Sally Wells-Robertson and Alexandre Ananoff. To Wells-Robertson (writing in 1976 and 1979), *Le Baiser à la*

dérobée, like *Le Contrat* (W. 522; see cat. no. 236, figure 8), appears to have been painted by Fragonard, "in the style of Marguerite Gérard." Ananoff does not hesitate to see in *Le Contrat*, in any case, and "undoubtedly" in *Le Baiser à la dérobée*, the hand of Fragonard's accomplished sister-in-law. Yet, perhaps Thomas Gaehtgens (1975) has best set the problem to rest; he reminds us that *Le Verrou* was exhibited between *Le Premier Pas de l'enfance* and *Le Baiser à la dérobée* at the "David to Delacroix" exhibition in Paris: "the comparison of these three paintings clearly proves that the Leningrad canvas can be accepted only with the greatest difficulty as part of Fragonard's oeuvre. Moreover, the fine but meticulous rendering of the silk dresses, and the undramatic construction of the painting, in the Dutch style, makes one think, rather, of Marguerite Gérard."

The painting may represent a completely new departure by a painter who was never locked into a single style, and who was able to adapt (under pressure from the expert Le Brun, the great champion of the seventeenth-century Dutch masters) to the requirements of a new clientele for bourgeois scenes, delicately handled and painted with a jewel-like precision. The second possibility is that it marked the decline of a prematurely aged artist who allowed his name to appear at the bottom of an engraving after a painting for which he had merely suggested the idea. As in 1974, we hesitate to make a determination, but despite the refinement of the color, and the basic intelligence of the composition, we would now favor—with discretion—the second hypothesis. (When will there be an exhibition of the works of Marguerite Gérard?)

One final point: Fragonard has accustomed us to his habit of drawing inspiration from, and copying or emulating the old masters. Yet, he never effaced his own talents, always imposing on a work his stamp and his very personal touch, which are so easily discernible in pictures of this type. Would he, at so late a stage in his career, have renounced this practice?

305 Portrait of a Man

Oil on canvas, 64.5 x 52.5 cm.

Private collection, Paris

Provenance
From the "chambre à coucher de M. Malvilan," maternal grandfather of Alexandre Maubert, Fragonard's cousin, in Grasse, 1889 (according to P.); Rodolphe Kann, Paris, 1907; [Duveen]; [Wildenstein]; David David-Weill; private collection.

Exhibitions
London, 1908, no. 136
Paris, 1921, no. 74, ill.

Bibliography
P. pp. 135–36, 273
Nevill, 1903, p. 293
Kann collection catalogue, 1907, I, pp. XXV–XXVI (by W. Bode); II, no. 147, ill.
Henriot, 1926, I, pp. 133–34, ill. p. 135
R. p. 173
W. 525, pl. 122
W. and M. 548, ill.

Figure 1. Fragonard. *Presumed Portrait of Honoré-Léopold-Germain Maubert*. Whereabouts unknown

This painting was admired by Roger Portalis during one of his frequent visits to Grasse to see the Louveciennes paintings, which were then in the house of M. Malvilan (see his letter to Edmond de Goncourt, dated January 8, 1888, Bibliothèque Nationale, ms. fr. 22.473). It was in the bedroom of M. Malvilan, a grandson, on his mother's side, of Alexandre Maubert, who was a cousin of the Fragonards and served as their host in 1790–91, that Portalis discovered this portrait. "There was a traditional belief in the house that [the picture] was a likeness of Chardin ... but of a young Chardin, wearing a cap set on the back of his head, without a wig, and with closely cropped hair; strong, bony features; a prominent nose; and a generally pleasing face." This "tradition," which does not seem to have convinced Portalis—farther on, he writes, "whoever the model may be ... "—is now unanimously discounted.

In the same house, there was a second portrait, of the same format, which was also catalogued by Portalis (p. 283). "M. Maubert . . . Brother of Fragonard's host in Grasse." This painting, now in a private collection (see figure 1; Tokyo exhibition catalogue, 1980, no. 90, colorpl.), is now thought to represent Honoré-Léopold-Germain Maubert, the son of Alexandre Maubert, at the age of fifteen. If this is the case, it is possible that the present painting may, in fact, be a portrait of Alexandre Maubert.

To accept this hypothesis, we would have to assume that both canvases were painted in Grasse during Fragonard's stay in 1790–91 (otherwise, he would have had to have brought them with him from Paris—as he did the Louveciennes paintings).

The execution of these two works—especially of the present one—is curious. The hands are summarized with bold and vigorous brushstrokes, and the costume is rendered with a frankness bordering on brutality. Color is reduced to essentials, and the facial features are analyzed with severity and unaccustomed psychological insight. Instead of a likeness, the artist attempted to reveal the personality of the sitter. Is this Fragonard's final painting?

VIII
Fragonard:
Functionnaire at the Louvre

In Anatole France's *Les Dieux ont soif,* the hero of the novel, Évariste Gamelin, provided a disagreeable portrait of Fragonard: "I ran into him some time ago, that wretched old man, strolling under the arcades of the Palais-Égalité, powdered, gallant, fidgety, dissolute, hideous. At the sight of him, I wished that some stalwart friend of the arts would, like Apollo, string this Marsyas up to a tree and flay him as an eternal example to bad painters."

Anatole France's condemnation of Fragonard through Évariste Gamelin—who was modeled on Alexandre-Évariste Fragonard, on Philippe-Auguste Hennequin, and, especially, on Claude-Louis Châtelet, who collaborated on the illustrations for the *Voyage pittoresque* and lost his life by the guillotine—seems to be categorical.

The facts, however, are not so one-sided, and are even paradoxical, for Fragonard's chief defender was none other than David, the leading representative of the new aesthetic. David spoke out on Fragonard's behalf on three occasions: in 1792, 1793, and 1805.

In 1792, David commended Fragonard to the Minister of the Interior, Roland, to try to obtain lodgings for him at the Louvre after his escapade in Grasse, where he seems to have recovered his health; David wanted Fragonard to be given new and more spacious lodgings in the "galeries" at the Louvre, below the Grande Galerie: "What is less well known is the way in which he and his respectable family live. I recently described them to you in terms of the simple and patriarchal values of our forefathers." One year later—Roland having committed suicide in the meantime—there was more praise of Fragonard in the very official "rapport sur la suppression de la commission du Muséum par le citoyen David imprimé par ordre de la Convention Nationale" (p. 5): "warmth and originality are what characterize him; being both a connoisseur and a great artist, he will devote his old age to the preservation of the masterpieces whose number he helped to increase in his youth." This time, David was trying to obtain for Fragonard a curatorial position in the future Musée du Louvre.

His last clients had been dispersed by the Revolution, a new type of painting was in vogue, and Fragonard bowed to his fate. He appealed to David—his son Alexandre-Évariste's master—to help him obtain a position as *conservateur* in order to make ends meet. David—who could not have forgotten the time that Fragonard relinquished to him the commission to decorate Mlle Guimard's *hôtel* in the Chaussée-d'Antin—acceded to his request.

For several years Fragonard worked as an administrator, and played an essential role in the founding of what is now the Louvre. It is difficult to determine the exact nature of this role—this time, because of the sheer abundance of documents; not a week went by without Fragonard signing some official document. He was one of the six members of the Commission du Muséum Central, created in 1792, and he served on the committee until 1797, weathering many a storm—some of which were violent, indeed. He attended to every aspect of the museum: the wages of the guards; the works of art that were seized, and their transport between the various repositories and the Louvre; keys and closets; opening hours; the installation of the paintings; minor privileges; the inventory of drawings in what would become the Cabinet des Dessins; petitioners; the first catalogues; and the creation of the special museum of the École française at Versailles.

What was Fragonard's position in relation to the other commissioners? Can his role be defined? Did he have a special domain all to himself? What was his personal contribution to the museum policies that were being laid down? What were his ideas, his conception of the role of the museum in the new revolutionary society? Guillaume, Tuetey, Christiane Aulanier, Yveline Cantarel-Besson, and especially Georges Wildenstein (1959) have examined these questions, but it is still too early for any definitive answers. The history of the Louvre during the Revolution remains to be written.

In 1797, Fragonard was relieved of his duties—whether for reasons of health or of ideology is not known. In 1805, he lost his lodgings at the Louvre, as did the other artists and the scholars who lived there, but was given a pension for life as compensation. Marguerite Gérard sent him tender letters, which must have consoled him in his old age. It is unlikely that he painted any more. He died suddenly on August 22, 1806, one week after Napoleon's thirty-seventh birthday, one year after his friend Greuze, two years after Giovanni Domenico Tiepolo, and two years before Hubert Robert.

His death went virtually unnoticed. On December 31, 1806, the *Journal de Paris* published its yearly obituary; the editor, a certain "De L. Lande" (the same La Lande who had announced Fragonard's death in *Le Publiciste* on August 25, and in *Le Moniteur Universel* on the 26th), listed the artists who had died that year in what he considered to be "the order of their importance and merit": "Bachelier, Fragonard, Dumarest engraver, Ledoux, Renou, Mme Vien." Fragonard occupied an honorable second place between Bachelier, the founder of the free school of drawing, who devoted himself to floral and animal subjects, and to encaustic painting, and Rambert Dumarest, the engraver of the great men of France.

David had his own opinion—that of a great artist. One year earlier, he had thanked Évariste for having sent him a book (quite possibly the *Tableaux historiques de la Révolution française,* the last volume of which had just appeared) that he had taken "an incredible pleasure in looking through." David also sent warm regards to Évariste's "loving mother" and to Marguerite Gérard, and asked him to "congratulate" his "fine father": "[who] was clever enough to sense that there was more than one way to arrive at one's goal, and the name of Fragonard will be hailed in all of the genres."

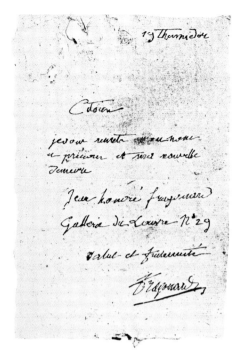

Figure 1. Note from Fragonard in which he gives his new address. Private collection, Paris

CHRONOLOGY

(Dates from the "Calendrier républicain" appear in parentheses)

1792

Assemblée Législative (October 1, 1791–September 20, 1792)

January 21
The posthumous inventory of the collection of the Abbé de Saint-Non, who had died November 25, 1791, listed many works by Fragonard, as well as copies made by Saint-Non after Fragonard's paintings (see G. Wildenstein, 1959).

February 4
Announcement in the *Mercure de France* (p. 60) for Maurice Blot's engraving *The Contract*, after Fragonard—the pendant to *Le Verrou* (cat. no. 236).

May 19
Announcement in the *Mercure de France* (p. 108) for Géraud Vidal's

engraving *L'Enfant chéri*, "d'après le Tableau peint par M. Fragonard et Mlle. Gérard (...) faisant suite au *Présent* et celle dite *Je m'occupois de vous* (...). Cette estampe, gravée avec beaucoup de soin, est faite pour plaire à toutes les mères qui nourrissent et élèvent leurs enfans" (see cat. no. 303).

August 15
Fragonard and his wife, who are back in Paris, on this date buy a bond for 90 *livres* from the "Caisse d'épargnes et de bienfaisance du sieur Lafarge" for the benefit of their son Alexandre-Évariste. This document was countersigned in 1793 and until 1814 (a photocopy of the document is in the library of the Musée Fragonard, Grasse).

September 19
Alexandre-Évariste is admitted at the age of twelve into the École des élèves protégés as a pupil of David (*Liste des élèves,* Bibliothèque de l'École des Beaux-Arts, ms. 95, fol. 171).

Convention nationale (September 1792–October 1795)

October 24
David intercedes with Roland, Ministre de l'Intérieur, on behalf of various artists to obtain lodgings for them at the Louvre:

> Tout récemment encore, vous avez à ma sollicitation, donné à M. Moreau, graveur, dessinateur, un logement aux Galeries du Louvre. Ce qu'il vous reste à faire, ce que votre coeur s'empressera de saisir, c'est d'aller chercher le mérite qui se cache, de l'exposer au grand jour, de le récompenser; mon devoir, à moi, comme artiste, c'est de vous le faire connnaître.
>
> Les vertueux artistes dont je veux parler sont Fragonard et Taillasson, l'un de Marseille [*sic*], l'autre de Bordeaux. Le premier est bien connu par ses talents, mais ce que l'on ne connaît pas, ce sont ses moeurs, celles de sa respectable famille; je vous en fis dernièrement la peinture, en les comparant aux moeurs simples et patriarcales de nos premiers pères (...)
>
> Eh bien, ces artistes estimables, on les a laissés dans l'oubli comme à dessein. Mais ils ont un ami, mais cet ami connaît enfin un ministre vertueux [un ministre vertueux!]. Liberté, voilà de tes fruits! peintres, sculpteurs, artistes, tous tant que vous êtes, séchez vos larmes: vous allez occuper le palais des rois; mais ne dédaignez jamais ces greniers; ils vous ont donné les premiers l'hospitalité.

In a postscript he added: "Fragonard ayant un logement au Louvre, il l'échangerait pour un aux galeries de Louvre. Ainsi, vous voyez par ce changement un logement de plus au Louvre, et Taillasson, qui est peintre, pourrait l'occuper" (letter published by Perroud, 1900, pp. 364–66; D. and Guy Wildenstein, 1973, p. 44).

A note dated "19 thermidor" [August 6, no year is mentioned; see figure 1; the Goncourts, 1865, p. 314, published another example] confirms the change of lodgings:

Jean honoré fragonard-Gallerie du Louvre n° 29
Salut et fraternité. Fragonard

The "Tableau général de la distribution des logements du bâtiment National et de la galerie du muséum, avec des observations particulières" dated "24 pluviose an III" [February 12, 1795], published by d'Argé in 1858 (pp. 250, 300), described the lodgings: "porte du côté de la colonnade...le peintre David, trois pièces au premier étage et un atelier (un citoyen employé aux postes et une femme de confiance); -le peintre Fragonard atelier commun avec le citoyen David...[and] galerie du muséum: le peintre Fragonard, huit pièces, cuisine, cabinets et cave" (for floor plans of Fragonard's lodgings, see Arch. Nat. O¹ 1675-72; see figure 2).

In 1792, Jean-Claude Gorjy published his *Ann'quin Bredouille ou le petit cousin de Tristram Shandy,* which described the changes in taste: "les charmants sujets de Boucher, les jolies gaietés de Fragonard, les petites libertés de Lawrence [Lavreince], les compositions érotiques de Lagrenée ont fait place à des caricatures aussi plates que révoltantes sur les événements du jour, caricatures dont l'esprit de parti a charbonné les traits. Une représentation de citadelle détruite a remplacé le groupe de Léda. Un autel sermentaire a succédé à la gentille chiffonnière sur laquelle on signait des billets à la Châtre" (quoted by the Goncourts, 1854, p. 93).

Brizard publishes his book on Saint-Non, which discusses the relationship between the abbé and Fragonard (see page 95).

1793

March 10
The expert Le Brun writes to the minister Garat to suggest that a commission be created with the following tasks: "[de] constater l'état actuel des dépôts des arts...[de] faire un choix des objets dignes d'attention...[et de] mettre à part les tableaux médiocres à l'effet d'en débarrasser les dépôts, et enfin pour que l'on ne s'occupe de restaurer que les tableaux qui en vaudront la peine, et qu'il soit dressé un catalogue des tableaux qui doivent orner le Musée." Fragonard is at the top of the list of names that he proposes in connection with this plan (Tuetey and Guiffrey, 1909, III, pp. 102–3).

April 1
The restorer Picault also suggests to Garat the creation of this commission, and mentions the name of Fragonard (Tuetey and Guiffrey, 1909, III, pp. 116–17).

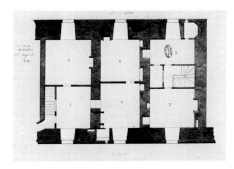

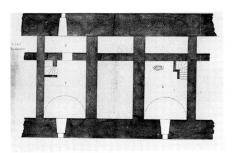

First floor

Figure 2. Floor plans of Fragonard's lodgings. Archives Nationales, Paris

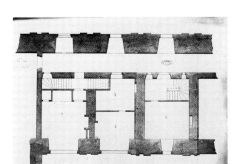

Mezzanine

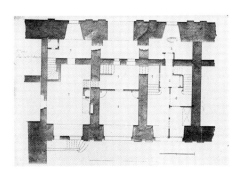

Ground floor

Cellar

July 24
The *Journal de Paris* (no. 42, supplement to no. 205, p. 1) announces the sale of Henri Gérard's engraving *The Sacrifice of the Rose,* after Fragonard's painting, the pendant to *L'Art d'aimer,* after the painting by Marguerite Gérard, also engraved by her brother (cat. no. 284).

August 10
The decision is taken to open the Muséum.

November 4
Fragonard and Henri Gérard are admitted into the Commune des Arts (list of the artists referred by the Société Républicaine des Arts to the Comité d'instruction publique, quoted in G. Wildenstein, 1960, p. 52, French edition).

November 10
Fragonard and his wife sell their house in Charenton to their cousin Honoré Fragonard, director of the École Vétérinaire in Alfort, for 9,000 *livres* (Minutier central, LXIV, 441, quoted in G. Wildenstein, 1960, p. 52, French edition).

November 15
The Convention establishes a contest for prizes in sculpture and in painting, and Fragonard is chosen to be among the fifty members of the jury, along with his cousin, the anatomist Honoré Fragonard. The subject of the painting was to be "Brutus, mort dans un combat et ramené à Rome par les chevaliers." There is a record of Fragonard's opinion of the painting (now lost) by Fulchran-Jean Harriet (1778?–1805) that was awarded the second prize: "motivé sur des expressions liées à la scène et heureusement senties, des formes qui tiennent à la bonne école, un principe de couleur qui dérive d'un ton vrai. Quelque manque de goût arrête avec justice ce que les autres parties prononcent à une plus haute faveur" (Renouvier, 1863, p. 17).

November 18
The Muséum des Arts is opened to the public.

December 18
David, in his "rapport sur la suppression de la commission du Muséum," proposes to the Convention the creation of a new conservatory;

Fragonard is at the top of his list of candidates: "[il] a pour lui de nombreux ouvrages; chaleur et originalité, c'est ce qui le caractérise; à la fois *connaisseur* et grand artiste, il consacrera ses vieux ans à la garde des chefs-d'oeuvre dont il a concouru dans sa jeunesse à augmenter le nombre" (Tuetey and Guiffrey, 1909, III, p. 358; D. and Guy Wildenstein, 1973, p. 78).

"Deux...gravures, d'après Fragonard [possibly cat. no. 143] et la Citoyenne Gérard" by Ponce (no. 403), and "une femme tenant une lettre à la main," by Louis-Charles Ruotte, after Fragonard (no. 429), are exhibited at the Salon (figure 2, p. 416).

Using etchings prepared by Antoine-Jean Duclos, Jean-Louis Delignon engraves *Le Cocu battu et content* (figure 3) and *La Matrone d'Éphèse,* after drawings by Fragonard, for Didot's edition of La Fontaine's *Contes.*

Among the property seized from the émigrés were many works by Fragonard. Certain of the documents related to these seized pictures were published by Tuetey (1901–2) and by Furcy-Raynaud (1912). G. Wildenstein (1960, p. 37) quoted from much of the archival material, but a systematic search of the Archives Nationales and the archives of the Louvre remains to be conducted.

1794

January 16–(27 *nivôse*)
The Commission du Muséum is dissolved by decree. It is replaced by a Conservatoire, of which Fragonard is a member; for his duties, the artist receives an annual stipend of 2,400 *livres* (Arch. Nat. AD XVIII^22, published by Tuetey and Guiffrey, 1909, III, pp. 372–73).

January 31–(12 *pluviôse*)
The first session of the Conservatoire is held. Since the minutes were not signed, we can only presume that Fragonard attended. The proceedings of the Conservatoire (Archives du Musée du Louvre, I BB1, I BB2) were published by Yveline Cantarel-Besson in 1981 [referred hereafter as Cantarel-Besson].

February 7–(9 *pluviôse*)
Fragonard presides, provisionally, over the morning session of the Conservatoire. The order of the day includes security problems at the Muséum, and surveillance rounds are scheduled: "Fragonard premier inscrit sur la liste dud. rapport, serait de garde aujourd'hui." At the evening session, Fragonard is elected president by five votes to three over Varon, who is appointed vice-president (Cantarel-Besson, I, pp. 6–8).

February 8–12–(20–24 *pluviôse*)
Fragonard presides over the daily sessions of the Conservatoire (Cantarel-Besson, I, pp. 8–12).

February 13–(25 *pluviôse*)
Fragonard signs a report by the Conservatoire submitted to the Comité d'instruction publique announcing the compilation of a "catalogue raisonné de tous les objets appartenant au Muséum" (Tuetey and Guiffrey, 1909, III, pp. 375–79).

At Naigeon's request, the Commission temporaire des Arts appoints Fragonard, Jean-Baptiste-Joseph Wicar, and Charles-Jean-Baptiste Lelièvre to examine the national repository in the rue de Beaune of which Naigeon is in charge (Tuetey, 1912, I, p. 71).

February 14–21–(26 *pluviôse*–3 *ventôse*)
Fragonard presides over the daily sessions of the Conservatoire (Cantarel-Besson, I, pp. 13–17).

February 24–(6 *ventôse*)
Dardel is named president of the Conservatoire in Fragonard's place (Cantarel-Besson, I, pp. 17–18).

February 27–(9 *ventôse*)
Fragonard, Wicar, and Lelièvre are appointed to verify the scientific and art objects in the Nesle (rue de Beaune) repository (G. Wildenstein, 1960, p. 52, French edition).

Figure 3. Jean-Louis Delignon, after Fragonard. *Le Cocu battu et content.* Bibliothèque Nationale, Paris, Cabinet des Estampes

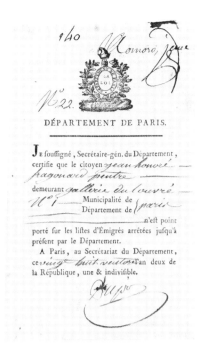

Figure 4. Certificate of non-emigration.
Bibliothèque d'Art et d'Archéologie, Paris

March 1–(11 *ventôse*)
Presentation at the session of the Conservatoire of: "Un état d'inventaire des trente-deux tableaux remis par l'ancienne commission du Muséum provenant de Notre-Dame et Saint-Gervais, dont lui [Le Sueur], Wicard [*sic*] et Fragonard, ses collègues ont donné décharge" (Cantarel-Besson, I, p. 20).

March 5–(15 *ventôse*)
Naigeon and Fragonard are appointed by the Commission temporaire des Arts to examine paintings at the residence of "citoyen" Gané, rue de Cléry, which belong to "citoyen" Forestier (Tuetey, 1912, p. 91).

The Comité d'instruction publique establishes the definitive list of the members of the Commission temporaire des Arts: Bonvoisin, Fragonard, Le Sueur, Naigeon, Picault (Guillaume, 1897, III, p. 503).

March 8–(18 *ventôse*)
The Conservatoire delegates Picault, Fragonard, and Bonvoisin to help Vincent receive the drawings seized from the émigrés (Cantarel-Besson, I, p. 24).

March 9–(19 *ventôse*)
"Les cit. Fragonard, Dupasquier, Wicar et Bonvoisin sont nommés commissaires pour faire le triage des plus beaux desseins qui, avant leur exposition, seront soumis à l'examen du Conservatoire" (Cantarel-Besson, I, p. 24).

March 10–(20 *ventôse*)
For the first time, Fragonard signs the attendance book of the Commission temporaire des Arts (G. Wildenstein, 1960, p. 52, French edition). Lenoir is opposed to Fragonard's wish to remove the paintings from the repository of the Petits-Augustins (Guillaume, 1901, IV, p. 693).

March 14–(24 *ventôse*)
Fragonard and Le Sueur are designated to prepare a celebration on the occasion of the planting of a Liberty tree (Cantarel-Besson, I, p. 26).

The Ministre de l'Intérieur, Paré, empowers Fragonard, in his capacity as member of the Conservatoire and of the Commission temporaire des Arts, to draw up an inventory of the paintings, art objects, and scientific instruments seized from religious and public institutions, and from the émigrés (a photocopy of the document is in the library of the Musée Fragonard, Grasse).

March 18–(28 *ventôse*)
Fragonard, "demeurant gallerie du Louvre n° 1," is issued a certificate of non-emigration (figure 4; Bibliothèque d'Art et d'Archéologie, *carton* 14, published by Portalis, 1889, pp. 236–37).

Fragonard, Le Sueur, and Picault are delegated by the Conservatoire to examine art objects in the possession of the art expert Le Brun (Cantarel-Besson, I, pp. 27–28).

March 19–(29 *ventôse*)
Fragonard is delegated, along with other *conservateurs,* to transfer to the Muséum paintings "provenant de la maison du duc de Wurtembourg [*sic*] à Montbéliard," which had been entrusted to the Comité de Salut Public, and to remove from the repository of the Petits-Augustins the landscape paintings by Champaigne (these large compositions from the Val-de-Grâce are today divided between the Louvre and the museums in Mayence and Tours) for transport to the Muséum (Cantarel-Besson, I, p. 28).

March 21–(1er *germinal*)
Fragonard and his wife give power of attorney to Henri Gérard to inquire into the estate of the Robins, of which they are heirs, as representatives of Marie Gilette, Marie-Anne Fragonard's mother (G. Wildenstein, 1960, p. 53, French edition).

March 24–(4 *germinal*)
Fragonard, Bonvoison, Picault, and Varon are delegated by the Conservatoire: "pour faire part au Comité d'instruction publique du refus qui a été fait aux commissaires de leur délivrer les objets qu'on les avait chargés de recueillir" (Cantarel-Besson, I, p. 31).

March 28–(8 *germinal*)
Fragonard and Bonvoisin visit "citoyen" Amant to see a painting (Arch. Nat. F17 1231).

March 31–(11 *germinal*)
The Conservatoire disapproves of Fragonard's removal of a painting "contre son arrêté portant qu'aucun changement ne serait fait dans le Muséum sans un arrêté du Conservatoire (. . .) lequel [tableau] sera remis à la place qu'il occupait" (Cantarel-Besson, I, p. 34).

April 6–(17 *germinal*)
Fragonard and several other commissioners are delegated by the Conservatoire to examine and bring back to the Muséum some paintings in storage at the national repository of the Petits-Augustins (Cantarel-Besson, I, p. 36).

April 8–(19 *germinal*)
Report by Fragonard, Bonvoisin, and Picault on the stained-glass windows of the Abbaye d'Autrey (Arch. Nat. F17 1231).

April 10–(21 *germinal*)
Henri Gérard and Fragonard give power of attorney to Antoine Dousons to enquire into the Robin estate (G. Wildenstein, 1960, p. 53, French edition).

April 13–(24 *germinal*)
A certificate of residency (figure 5) is issued to Fragonard: "âgé de soixante-deux ans taille de quatre pieds onze pouces; cheveux et sourcils gris front haut, nez ordinaire yeux gris bouche moyenne menton rond marqué de petite verole; demeure actuellement à Paris, rue des orties gallerie du Louvre dans l'étendue de cette section, et qu'il y réside depuis dix-huit mois sans interruption." Fragonard's witnesses are the painters François Dumont and Horace Vernet (Bibliothèque d'Art et d'Archéologie, *carton* 14, published by Portalis, 1889, pp. 237–38).

That same day a certificate of residency is also issued to Marguerite Gérard (figure 6): "âgée de trente-deux ans taille de cinq pieds un pouce cheveux et sourcils bruns yeux bruns nez bien fait bouche petite menton pointu visage ovalle, teint vif animé, demeure actuellement à Paris, rue Gallerie du Louvre n° 1 dans l'étendue de cette section et qu'il [*sic*] y réside depuis dix-huit mois sans interruption." Same witnesses as for Fragonard (Bibliothèque d'Art et d'Archéologie, *carton* 14, published by Portalis, 1889, p. 250; Doin, 1912, p. 440).

April 15–(26 *germinal*)
Inventory of the paintings owned by the Noailles family is drawn up in the presence of Fragonard (Arch. Nat. F17 1190–91).

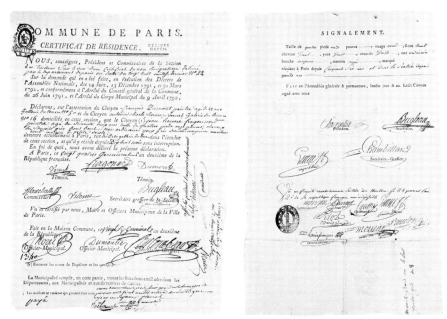

Figure 5. Fragonard's certificate of residency. Bibliothèque d'Art et d'Archéologie, Paris

April 23–(4 *floréal*)
"Le Conservatoire arrête que les Cns Fragonard, Wicart [*sic*], Lannoy et Le Sueur se transporteront au dépôt de Nesle rue de Beaune, à l'effet d'extraire les tableaux qu'ils jugeront devoir être placés au Muséum des arts" (Cantarel-Besson, I, p. 40).

April 25–(6 *floréal*)
"Le Conservatoire arrête que Fragonard et Picault sont nommés commissaires pour faire transporter les tableaux et vases de porcelaine, demain matin, dans les dépôts fermant à clef" (Cantarel-Besson, I, p. 40).

April 28–(9 *floréal*)
Marguerite Gérard gives to the notary Doillot copies of her birth certificate and those of Jean-Honoré, Marie-Anne, and Évariste Fragonard, "tirées des registres de Bapteme de la ville de Grasse," which had been issued February 4, 1793 (Minutier central, XCVI, 568).

May 5–(16 *floréal*)
Fragonard and Le Sueur report on the mission that had been entrusted to them on April 25, and sign the minutes (Cantarel-Besson, I, pp. 44–45).

May 8–(19 *floréal*)
Fragonard and Bonvoisin are delegated to examine a painting by Teniers at the home of the painter Petit-Coupray (Cantarel-Besson, I, p. 46).

May 14–(25 *floréal*)
A "certificat de civisme" is issued to Fragonard: "peintre avant et depuis la Révolution actuellement conservateur du muséum (...). Taille de quatre pieds onze pouces visage rond, front haut cheveux gris, yeux gris, sourcils gris, nez ordinaire, bouche moyenne, menton rond, marqué, résidant à Paris depuis cinquante-six ans et dans la section depuis quinze ans" (see figure 7; Bibliothèque d'Art et d'Archéologie,

Figure 6. Marguerite Gérard's certificate of residency. Bibliothèque d'Art et d'Archéologie, Paris

Figure 7. "Certificat de civisme." Bibliothèque d'Art et d'Archéologie, Paris

carton 14, published by Portalis, 1889, pp. 261–62; Nolhac, 1906, p. 180).

May 22–(3 *prairial*)
Bonvoisin and Fragonard are delegated by the Conservatoire to remove the seals from the repository of the Muséum to make available to "citoyen" Dabos a painting by Rembrandt that he wishes to copy (Cantarel-Besson, I, p. 51).

May 24–(5 *prairial*)
Fragonard and Bonvoisin return two paintings by Raphael and one by Rembrandt to the repository (Cantarel-Besson, I, p. 52).

May 30–(11 *prairial*)
Rectification of the death certificate of Fragonard's daughter, whose complete name is Henriette-Rosalie. The witnesses are the painter Pierre-Antoine Demachy and André Dalbeau (possibly the same Dalbeau who was Fragonard's pupil; see May 1768), described as a "limonadier" (Minutier central, XCVI, 568).

June 4–5–(16–17 *prairial*)
Fragonard supervises the transfer of paintings from the Salon to the Salle du Conseil (Cantarel-Besson, I, p. 56).

June 15–(27 *prairial*)
At the session of the Conservatoire, Fragonard and Bonvoisin are delegated to examine a painting attributed to Lebrun, and: "le Conservatoire arrête que les trois clefs de la cloison de chêne au pied de l'escalier seront tirées au sort; le sort est tombé sur les cns Dupasquier, Fragonard et Dardel, lesquels les garderont pendant un mois" (Cantarel-Besson, I, p. 57–58).

June 17–(29 *prairial*)
Fragonard reads his report (Arch. Nat. F¹⁷ 1231) on the so-called Lebrun: "d'où il résulte que le tableau n'est pas de Le Brun, mais de Stella (...) trop médiocre pour qu'on s'en occupe" (Cantarel-Besson, I, p. 59).

June 19–(1ᵉʳ *messidor*)
Fragonard and Bonvoisin are delegated to take down the paintings that will not be included in the Contest intended to replace the "prix d'encouragements" (Cantarel-Besson, I, p. 60).

June 21–(3 *messidor*)
Fragonard is appointed vice-secretary of the Conservatoire, and signs the minutes. The following day, along with five other *conservateurs,* he must appear before the executive Commission to discuss the problem of the museum guards' wages (Cantarel-Besson, I, p. 60).

June 28–(10 *messidor*)
Fragonard receives 28 *livres* and 14 *sols* from the Commission temporaire des Arts (Tuetey, 1912, I, p. 255).

July 7–(19 *messidor*)
Fragonard is delegated, along with three other *conservateurs,* to present to the Comité de Salut Public a report designed to obtain "les salles de la cidevant académie de peinture qui doivent faire partie du Muséum" (Cantarel-Besson, I, p. 65). The Académie Royale had been dissolved August 8, 1793.

July 16–(28 *messidor*)
Fragonard and the architect Lannoy present to Granet (deputy from the Var), Fourcray (chemist), and David the decree of the Comité du Salut Public "qui les mettent en possession des différentes salles de l'académie," which will permit the Muséum to expand (Cantarel-Besson, I, p. 70).

July 19–(1ᵉʳ *thermidor*)
Fragonard, Varon, and David Le Roy apprise the Conservatoire of the favorable reception of their report on the enlargement of the Muséum (Cantarel-Besson, I, p. 66).

Fragonard, Wicar, Picault, and Bonvoisin are named "commissaires," and are delegated to check on the condition of the paintings "propres au concours de restauration" (Cantarel-Besson, I, p. 70).

July 21–(3 *thermidor*)
A "citoyen" Robin reclaims a marble base; Fragonard is delegated to return it to him (Cantarel-Besson, I, p. 71).

July 22–August 6–(4–19 *thermidor*)
Fragonard serves as secretary of the Conservatoire (Cantarel-Besson, I, pp. 72–78).

July 25–(7 *thermidor*)
Fragonard and five other *conservateurs* present before the Comité d'instruction publique a report proposing that the Muséum be kept open all day without interruption (Cantarel-Besson, I, p. 73).

July 31–(13 *thermidor*)
Fragonard and Bonvoisin are delegated to examine a report from Dumarest, and to see a painting by Primaticcio owned by "citoyen" Lanos, and a Pourbus in the possession of the jeweler Roux (Cantarel-Besson, I, pp. 75–76).

August 1–(14 *thermidor*)
Fragonard and Bonvoisin give an account of the report by Dumarest, who is summoned to appear before the Comité d'instruction publique (Cantarel-Besson, I, p. 76).

August 2–(15 *thermidor*)
Fragonard, among others, is delegated to remove the paintings hung beneath the cartoons by Giulio Romano and to replace them with paintings from the repositories (Cantarel-Besson, I, p. 77).

The Comité d'instruction publique deliberates on the purge of the Conservatoire following the "provisoire" arrest of David (Robespierre had been executed July 28). Fragonard was supposed to be excluded from the Commission temporaire des Arts. This decree, read before the Conservatoire on September 7, never went into effect (Cantarel-Besson, I, pp. 88–89, II, n. 209).

August 7–(20 *thermidor*)
Fragonard is replaced by Dupasquier in his duties as secretary (Cantarel-Besson, I, p. 78).

August 12–(25 *thermidor*)
Fragonard and Bonvoisin are delegated to examine a painting by Valentin owned by the architect Girard (Cantarel-Besson, I, p. 80).

August 16–(29 *thermidor*)
"Le Conservatoire arrête que Fragonard sera président par intérim pour signer les arrêtés de ce jour qui doivent être portés au Comité d'instruction publique" (Cantarel-Besson, I, p. 81).

August 17–(30 *thermidor*)
Report by Fragonard, Bonvoisin, and Picault on the Livois collection in Angers (Arch. Nat. F 1270 B, F¹⁷ 1231). There were several works by Fragonard in this collection, including three miniatures (nos. 331–333 in the Livois catalogue), the sketch for the *Coresus and Callirhoë* (cat. no. 105; today in Angers), and the *Pierrot* (now in the Wallace Collection).

"D'après le rapport fait par les citoyens Dardel, David Le Roy, Varon, Fragonard, [et] Dupasquier, Scellier est autorisé à faire transporter dans les dépôts les monuments qu'ils ont notés et mis en réserve dans la maison d'Orsay" (Tuetey, 1912, I, pp. 347–48).

August 22–(5 *fructidor*)
Fragonard, as well as the other possessors of the three keys (see June 15), must return them at the next session (Cantarel-Besson, I, p. 84).

August 28–(11 *fructidor*)
"Fragonard et [Bonvoisin] sont nommés commissaires pour aller examiner un tableau dit de Rubens proposé par des Liégeois rue Jacques" (Cantarel-Besson, I, p. 86).

August 30–(13 *fructidor*)
Negative report by Fragonard and Bonvoisin on the "Rubens," which is not considered worthy of the Muséum (Cantarel-Besson, I, p. 86).

September 4–(18 *fructidor*)
Fragonard signs the final list of paintings chosen for the Muséum (G. Wildenstein, 1959, p. 193).

September 5–(19 *fructidor*)
Fragonard returns to "citoyen" Lannoy two of the three keys to the repository (Cantarel-Besson, I, p. 88).

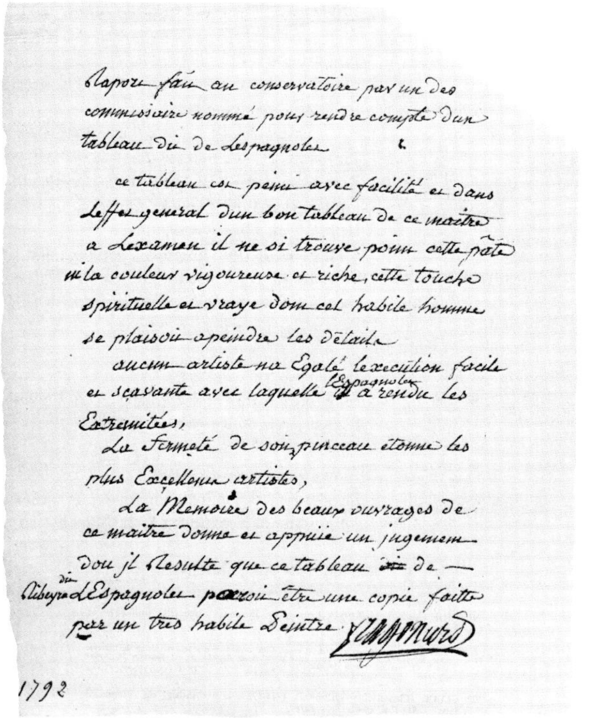
Raport fait au conservatoire par un des
commissaire nommé pour rendre compte d'un
tableau dit de Lespagnolet
ce tableau est peint avec facilité et dans
Leffet general d'un bon tableau de ce maître
a Lexamen il ne si trouve point cette pâte
ni la couleur vigoureuse et riche, cette touche
spirituelle et vraye dont cet habile homme
se plaisoit a peindre les détails
aucun artiste na Egalé lexecution facile
et sçavante avec laquelle Lespagnolet a rendu les
Extremitées,
La Fermeté de son pinceau étonne les
plus Excellens artistes,
La Memoire des beaux ouvrages de
ce maître donne et appuie un jugement
dont il Resulte que ce tableau de
Ribeyra dit Lespagnolet paroit être une copie faitte
par un tres habile peintre Fragonard
1792

Figure 8. Report signed by Fragonard on a painting by Ribera. Whereabouts unknown

September 16–(30 *fructidor*)
Le Brun, Fragonard, and Varon are delegated to sort the paintings and prints in the various repositories in Paris and Versailles (Tuetey, 1912, I, p. 403).

September 17–(1[er] *sans-culotide*)
Fragonard and Bonvoisin are delegated to go and examine a painting by Ribera, and to send a picture by Philippe de Champaigne to be restored (Cantarel-Besson, I, p. 92).

The Jury des Arts meets at the Gobelins manufactory to select the works that will be adapted and woven as tapestries: "N° 52—*Corésus et Callirhoé* par Fragonard.—Sujet à rejeter comme ne rappellant que des idées superstitieuses" (Jules Guiffrey, 1897, pp. 364, 366, 383; see cat. no. 104).

September 19–(3 *sans-culotide*)
"Fragonard et Picault rendent compte que s'étant trouvés au Muséum lorsque l'on a annoncé l'arrivée d'un chariot chargé de tableaux venant de la Belgique, ils ont accueilli le C[ns] Barbier, lieutenant d'hussards nommé par les représentants du peuple à l'armée du Nord pour veiller au transport de ce dépôt, et ont partagé les fatigues de sept de leurs frères volontaires venans aussi de l'armée du Nord pour escorter ce précieux convoi. Lesdits C[ns] Fragonard et Picault ont cru devoir, au nom du Conservatoire, faire donner à dîner aux 7 volontaires par le C[n] Bosset, traiteur et portier de l'enceinte du Muséum. Le Conservatoire approuve la conduite de leurs collègues Fragonard et Picault."

The report on the Ribera painting is also read (Cantarel-Besson, I, pp. 92–93). An autograph document in the sale of the Robert Schuman collection, March 4–5, 1965 (no. 89), may quite possibly be related to this report (see figure 8):

Raport fait au conservatoire par un des commissaire[s] nommé pour rendre compte d'un tableau dit de Lespagnolet ce tableau est peint avec facilité et dans l'effet général d'un bon tableau de ce maître a l'exament il ne si trouve point cette pâte ni la couleur vigoureuse et riche, cette touche spirituelle et vraye dont cet habile homme se plaisoit à peindre les détails

aucun artiste na Egalé lexecution facile et sçavante avec laquelle l'Espagnolet a rendu les Extrémitées,

La fermeté de son pinceau étonne les plus Excellens artistes,

La Mémoir des beaux ouvrages de ce maître donne et appuie un jugement dont il Resulte que ce tableau de Ribeyra dit l'Espagnolet paroit être une copie faitte par un très habile peintre

Fragonard 1792

The date of 1792, however, is improbable.

September 22–(1er *vendémiaire*)
Fragonard and Bonvoisin read their report on "quatre tables de bois pétrifié" purchased at Versailles, "à la vente des effets provenant de la liste civile." At the end of the session, Fragonard is again elected president (Cantarel-Besson, I, pp. 95–96).

He presides over the session of September 23, and is replaced then by Bonvoisin: "le citoyen Fragonard, président, ayant été obligé de se retirer, le citoyen Bonvoisin, ex-président, le remplace," was noted at the session of October 22 (Cantarel-Besson, I, p. 105).

October 4–(13 *vendémiaire*)
Fragonard serves as vice-president of the session of the Conservatoire. In the company of Picault, he returns to the office of the Conservatoire the key to a repository of frames (Cantarel-Besson, I, pp. 100–101).

October 6–(15 *vendémiaire*)
Fragonard and Picault are delegated by the Conservatoire to choose paintings from the repositories, to be placed in the Muséum (Cantarel-Besson, I, p. 101). Along with Le Brun, they sign the inventories of the art objects from Avignon, Aix, and Marseilles, as well as that of the Choiseul-Gouffier collection, and also an inventory of flower paintings (Arch. Nat. F[17] 1231).

October 13–(22 *vendémiaire*)
Fragonard, Langlier, Picault, and Naigeon sign a report favorable to Le Brun's proposal to offer paintings in payment of his debt to the Republic (G. Wildenstein, 1960, p. 54, French edition).

October 20–(29 *vendémiaire*)
Fragonard, Picault, and Dupasquier verify the objects brought to the Muséum by the marble carver Scellier. At the end of this session of the Conservatoire, Fragonard is reelected president (Cantarel-Besson, I, p. 105). He presides at the sessions of October 22 and 24.

October 22–(1er *brumaire*)
The inventory of the objects assembled in the district of Arras by "citoyen" Doncre is presented to Fragonard, Picault, and Bonvoisin (Arch. Nat. F[17] 1270 B; published by Tuetey, 1912, I, p. 486, n. 1).

October 24–(3 *brumaire*)
Fragonard and Picault issue to "citoyen" Madaye a release from storage of damaged "bordures dorées," which are to be repaired (Cantarel-Besson, I, p. 106).

The copy of the release given to "citoyen" Madaye is filed at the Conservatoire on October 26 (ibid., p. 107).

October 30–(9 *brumaire*)
Fragonard serves as president of the Conservatoire until November 5 (Cantarel-Besson, I, pp. 108–11).

November 3–(13 *brumaire*)
Fragonard and Picault are delegated by the Conservatoire to prepare a report on a damaged crate of paintings from Liège (Cantarel-Besson, I, p. 109).

November 5–(15 *brumaire*)
Fragonard and Picault read their report on the paintings from Liège. Several curators, Fragonard among them, form a delegation to appear before the Commission exécutive de l'instruction publique: "pour porter les diverses demandes relatives à la garde et au chauffage du Muséum." Fragonard and Picault are delegated to return to Vien the *Triomphe de la République*, a drawing that he had exhibited in the Muséum (Cantarel-Besson, I, p. 111).

November 9–(19 *brumaire*)
Fragonard and Dardel transfer from the repository in the rue de Beaune to the Muséum a *Concert* by Caravaggio (today attributed to Giordano; inv. 56). Fragonard and Picault also report on their appearance before the Commission exécutive de l'instruction publique (Cantarel-Besson, I, p. 112).

November 10–(20 *brumaire*)
The Commission temporaire des Arts asks Fragonard to join Picault and Dardel: "[pour] y constater l'urgence du travail à faire dans la ci-devant galerie [the Galerie des Glaces in the Palais de Versailles] de cette commune" (Tuetey, 1912, I, p. 544).

November 11–(21 *brumaire*)
Fragonard presides at the session of the Conservatoire (Cantarel-Besson, I, pp. 112–13).

November 13–(23 *brumaire*)
"Fragonard et Picault annoncent au Conservatoire qu'ils ont fait transporter de chez le condamné Durvey treize tableaux au Muséum dont il[s] donneront la notte à la prochaine séance" (Cantarel-Besson, I, p. 113).

November 15–(25 *brumaire*)
The curators delegated by the Commission temporaire des Arts to go to Versailles (see November 10, 1794) are also asked to travel to Marly to see: "le groupe représentant *Le Temps relevant les arts*" (Tuetey, 1912, I, p. 557).

November 20–(30 *brumaire*)
Le Brun submits to the Commission temporaire des Arts the inventory of objects from the "liste civile du Garde-Meuble," drawn up October 2 in the presence of Nitot, Besson, Fragonard, Picault, and Fleury (mentioned by Tuetey, 1912, I, p. 575, n. 4).

November 23–(3 *frimaire*)
Fragonard presides at the session of the Conservatoire; he is invited, along with Picault, to appear before the Commission de l'instruction publique to present proposals to resolve the conflict with the museum guards (Cantarel-Besson, I, pp. 114–15).

November 25–(5 *frimaire*)
Fragonard, Picault, and Dardel submit to the Commission temporaire des Arts their report on the condition of the works of art at Versailles and in Marly (Tuetey, 1912, I, p. 581, n. 2, pp. 673–78).

November 29–(9 *frimaire*)
The request by "citoyen" Taunay to open a window in the gallery of the Muséum is rejected by Fragonard on behalf of the Conservatoire (Cantarel-Besson, I, p. 117).

November 30–(10 *frimaire*)
A report by "citoyen" Goupy on "l'état des bibliothèques, dépôts d'objets d'art et de science, monuments qu'il a visités...," counter-signed by Picault, Le Brun, and Fragonard, among others, is submitted to the Commission temporaire des Arts (Tuetey, 1912, I, p. 604).

December 7–(17 *frimaire*)
Fragonard is elected vice-secretary of the Conservatoire. He signs the minutes of the session, as well as those of December 9 (Cantarel-Besson, I, pp. 118–19).

December 13–(23 *frimaire*)
Fragonard, Picault, and Bonvoisin sign the report on the paintings assembled in the district of Châlons-sur-Marne (Arch. Nat. F¹⁷ 1231).

December 14–(24 *frimaire*)
Fragonard is to serve on the jury for the sculpture, painting, and architecture contests, which is to meet December 20 (Szambien, 1986, p. 185).

December 15–(25 *frimaire*)
Three curators, including Fragonard, are delegated to collate the accounts of the rue de Beaune repository kept by Naigeon (Cantarel-Besson, I, p. 122).

December 16–(26 *frimaire*)
The statement of expenditures for the trip to Versailles made by Fragonard, Varon, and Le Brun is accepted by the Commission temporaire des Arts (G. Wildenstein, 1960, p. 54, French edition).

December 21–(1er *nivôse*)
Fragonard signs the minutes of the Conservatoire (Cantarel-Besson, I, pp. 123–26).

1795

January 2–6–(13–17 *nivôse*)
Fragonard signs the minutes of the Conservatoire (Cantarel-Besson, I, pp. 127–28).

January 9–(20 *nivôse*)
Report signed by Fragonard, Bonvoisin, Picault, and Dardel concerning Charlemagne's jewel cabinet, designed by Labarre (Tuetey, 1917, II, p. 42, n. 3).
Fragonard, Bonvoisin, and Lannoy sign a petition in favor of a raise in wages for the museum guards (G. Wildenstein, 1960, p. 54, French edition). According to G. Wildenstein (1959, p. 196), the salary of the curators was also increased.

January 11–(22 *nivôse*)
Fragonard signs the statement on the art objects seized in the district of Senlis (Arch. Nat. F¹⁷ 1231).

January 12–(23 *nivôse*)
Report by Fragonard, Bonvoisin, and Picault on the objects seized in the district of Versailles (Arch. Nat. F¹⁷ 1270 B).

January 14–(25 *nivôse*)
Fragonard, along with many other artists—Suvée, Regnault, Vien, Vernet, Robert, the Lagrenées—signs a petition to preserve the part of the Bois de Boulogne adjacent to Auteuil, the rest of the forest being sufficient to provide firewood. "Il paraît intéressant pour les études des artistes et même pour les propriétés de la République, de conserver la petite partie qui longe le petit village d'Auteuil" (Bibliothèque municipale du XVIe arrondissement, ms. Parent de Rosan, XXVIII, p. 258).

January 16–(27 *nivôse*)
Fragonard is delegated by the Conservatoire to supervise the transport from Ville d'Avray to Paris of wood for the heating of the Muséum (Cantarel-Besson, I, p. 131).

January 18–(29 *nivôse*)
Picault and Fragonard deliver to the Conservatoire a report on a painting attributed to Leonardo da Vinci that they examined in the workshop of the restorer Hacquin (Cantarel-Besson, I, p. 132).

January 24–(5 *pluviôse*)
Report signed by Fragonard on the paintings seized in the district of Quimper (Arch. Nat. F¹⁷ 1231).

January 29–(10 *pluviôse*)
The "citoyens" Leblanc, Le Brun, Dardel, and Fragonard are delegated to report on: "l'adjonction de la Commission des Arts de Versailles à celle de Paris. Ils s'attacheront principalement à démontrer l'utilité d'une commission ambulante chargée de surveiller la conservation des objets de sciences et d'arts" (Tuetey, 1917, II, p. 89).

February 1–(13 *pluviôse*)
Fragonard and Picault must visit the Château de Choisy to examine the painted ceiling decorations (Arch. Nat. F¹⁷ 1231; see also G. Wildenstein, 1959, p. 196, n. 53, p. 201, who mistakenly dates the report January 1).

February 3–(15 *pluviôse*)
Report by Fragonard, Bonvoisin, and Picault on a drawing requested by Percier (G. Wildenstein, 1960, p. 55, French edition).

February 5–19–(17 *pluviôse*–1er *ventôse*)
Fragonard serves as secretary of the Conservatoire (Cantarel-Besson, I, pp. 135–39).

February 5–(17 *pluviôse*)
Fragonard signs a report concerning a request for employment by "citoyen" Gly (Arch. Nat. F¹⁷ 1231).

February 13–(25 *pluviôse*)
Fragonard and Picault visit the church of Saint-Germain-des-Prés to remove the paintings by Lemoyne and by Jean-Baptiste Vanloo (G. Wildenstein, 1959, p. 196, n. 54, p. 201).

February 19–(1er ventôse)
Fragonard contracts for a life annuity of 650 livres for his wife and an annuity of 500 livres for Marguerite Gérard (G. Wildenstein, 1960, p. 55, French edition).

February 21–(3 ventôse)
Fragonard, Bonvoisin, and Picault sign the report concerning the state of the paintings in the district of Vitry-sur-Marne (Arch. Nat. F¹⁷ 1231).

February 28–(10 ventôse)
Fragonard, Le Brun, Bonvoisin, and Picault receive a list of paintings to be mounted on stretchers (Arch. Nat. F¹⁷ 1231).

March 7–(17 ventôse)
Fragonard is appointed to be vice-secretary of the Conservatoire (Cantarel-Besson, I, p. 145).

March 13–(23 ventôse)
Fragonard witnesses the opening of a crate of objects from Maestricht (G. Wildenstein, 1960, p. 55, French edition).

March 16–(26 ventôse)
Fragonard, vice-secretary, reads the report that he prepared with Bonvoisin on the appraisal of two paintings by François Gérard and Gioacchino Giuseppe Serangeli: "représentant la mort de Bara et celle de Viala" (Cantarel-Besson, I, p. 147).

March 20–(30 ventôse)
Fragonard, Bonvoisin, and Picault: "envoient trente rapports à la Commission temporaire des Arts" (G. Wildenstein, 1960, p. 55, French edition), and eighteen more reports March 21.

March 21–April 4–(1er–15 germinal)
Fragonard is appointed secretary of the Conservatoire (Cantarel-Besson, I, pp. 149–53).

April 8–(19 germinal)
Lannoy is authorized by the Conservatoire to entrust Fragonard with the two keys to the "porte aux trois serrures" of the repository (Cantarel-Besson, I, p. 154).

April 16–(27 germinal)
Bonvoisin and Fragonard address their reply to the Commission exécutive d'instruction publique, which "demande au Conservatoire la liste des vues des ports de la République, peints par Joseph Vernet qui décorent le Muséum" (Cantarel-Besson, I, p. 155).

April 18–(29 germinal)
Robert, Fragonard, Pajou, Picault, and de Wailly are appointed curators of the Muséum by a decree of the Comité d'instruction publique (Cantarel-Besson, I, p. 156).
    The new Conservatoire thus constituted holds its first session April 20, but the original Conservatoire continues to meet until June 22 (Cantarel-Besson, I, p. 165, II, p. 392, n. 395).

April 22–(3 floréal)
Fragonard serves as president of the Conservatoire until May 8 (Cantarel-Besson, I, pp. 156–60).

April 24–(5 floréal)
"Fragonard et Picault rendent compte que l'inventaire des objets d'art qui décorent les travées de la gallerie du Muséum est terminé"; on April 26, they will proceed with the verification (Cantarel-Besson, I, p. 157).
    At the session of the new Conservatoire, Fragonard and Picault report that they have received from the Comité d'instruction publique a: "boëtte mutilée... dont il manque vingt-cinq pierres de différentes grosseurs" (Cantarel-Besson, I, p. 166).
    At the session of the Commission temporaire des Arts, Fragonard suggests that until the departmental museums are opened, certain objects should be assigned to the Commission des travaux publics, as per its request (Tuetey, 1917, II, p. 230).

May 4–(15 floréal)
An extract from the deliberations of the recently dissolved Conserva-

toire is read at the meeting of the new Conservatoire. The document is signed by Fragonard: "à dater de ce jour, il [the former Conservatoire] ne s'occupera que de la reddition [sic] de ses comptes et il n'ouvrira aucun paquet à lui adressé [qui] seront remis aux nouveaux conservateurs..." (Cantarel-Besson, I, p. 168).

May 11–(22 floréal)
Fragonard and Picault submit to the Conservatoire "citoyen" Chotard's bills for the restoration of some frames (Cantarel-Besson, I, p. 160).

May 14–(25 floréal)
Fragonard and Picault are delegated to verify the bill presented by the marble carver Scellier (Cantarel-Besson, I, p. 161).

June 4–(16 prairial)
Fragonard is elected acting president (Cantarel-Besson, I, p. 163).

July 6–(18 messidor)
"Les citoyens de Wailly, Pajou et Fragonard font leur rapport du recollement qu'ils ont fait au garde-meuble des objets d'art qu'il renferme, assez précieux pour être recueillis au Muséum" (Cantarel-Besson, I, p. 196).

July 9–(21 messidor)
Fragonard goes to the Nesle repository in the rue de Beaune to choose: "les cages de verre [vitrines] qui seront propres à l'usage du Muséum et de suite les y fera transporter" (Cantarel-Besson, I, p. 198).

August 16–(29 thermidor)
Fragonard signs a letter from the Commission des Arts addressed to the curators, which specifies that the Muséum will meet the expense of transporting the paintings to the annual exhibition of works by living artists September 10 ("extrait du Registre des délibérations du Conservatoire," Bibliothèque d'Art et d'Archéologie, Paris).

August 18–September 21–(1er fructidor–5e jour complémentaire)
Fragonard is unanimously elected president of the new Conservatoire (Cantarel-Besson, I, pp. 219–38).

August 22–(5 fructidor)
Fragonard and Pajou finish "le tri des volumes de dessins qui font partie des 177 volumes de dessins et d'estampes venus de Cologne et déposés au Muséum des Arts" (Cantarel-Besson, I, p. 222).

September 5–(19 fructidor)
Fragonard and Picault proceed with the transport from the Gardemeuble of the frames and curtain rods needed by the Muséum (Cantarel-Besson, I, p. 229).

Directoire (October 1795–November 1799)

November 10–(19 brumaire)
Fragonard and Picault prepare to present themselves before the Commission de l'organisation et du mouvement des armées to retrieve canvas intended for uniforms that will be used for the restoration of paintings (Cantarel-Besson, I, p. 272).

November 12–(21 brumaire)
"[Fragonard] annonce qu'il va faire porter à l'étude, dans la gallerie du Muséum, un tableau de Rembrandt n° 168 provenant du Stadthouder." During the same session, premises vacated by a carpenter are assigned to Évariste Fragonard (Cantarel-Besson, I, p. 273).

November 28–(7 frimaire)
Fragonard invests 600 livres in a life annuity for Marguerite Gérard (G. Wildenstein, 1960, p. 55, French edition).

December 18–(27 frimaire)
Fragonard and Robert visit "citoyen" Duquenne, at his request, to examine a painting attributed to Raphael that he wishes to sell. Fragonard and Picault certify that they have received the canvas necessary for the restoration of paintings (Cantarel-Besson, I, p. 291).
    Publication by Didot of the second volume of La Fontaine's Contes (the first was published the year before; two more volumes were

planned, but they were never published). The two volumes contain sixteen engravings after drawings by Fragonard.

In "l'an 4" (1795 or 1796) Claude-Jean-Baptiste Hoin makes an engraving of *La Mort d'un moine franciscain*, "à la manière du lavis," after Fragonard (see p. 419, figure 3).

1796

January 3–(13 *nivôse*)
Fragonard and Picault announce that they have received the remainder of the canvas needed for the restoration of paintings (Cantarel-Besson, I, p. 300).

January 4–(14 *nivôse*)
Fragonard signs the curators' petition in support of the museum guards' wage demands (G. Wildenstein, 1960, p. 55, French edition).

January 21–(1er *pluviôse*)
Fragonard presides at the sessions of the Conservatoire until February 18 (Cantarel-Besson, I, pp. 9–32).

At the January 21 session, Robert and Fragonard state that they have examined the enamels from the collection of Jean Petitot received from the Bibliothèque Nationale (Cantarel-Besson, II, p. 9).

January 31–(11 *pluviôse*)
The inventory of the painting collection of the Stadtholder is drawn up in the presence of Fragonard (Cantarel-Besson, II, p. 18).

February 15–(26 *pluviôse*)
Fragonard signs the Conservatoire's report on the wages of the museum personnel (G. Wildenstein, 1960, p. 55, French edition).

February 18–(29 *pluviôse*)
Fragonard supports the demands of the invalid veterans employed by the Muséum (G. Wildenstein, 1960, p. 55, French edition).

March 21–(1er *germinal*)
Fragonard invests in several life-annuity contracts: for the sum of 900 *livres*, for himself; 3,400 *livres*, for Marie-Anne; 800 *livres*, for Marguerite Gérard; and 900 *livres* each, for Marguerite and Évariste (G. Wildenstein, 1960, p. 55, French edition).

May 20–(1er *prairial*)
Fragonard and Robert report on the objects that they found at the Mint "lesquels conviennent à la collection du Muséum" (Cantarel-Besson, II, p. 70).

May 26–(7 *prairial*)
Fragonard invests in a new life-annuity contract to benefit his wife, his sister-in-law, and Henri Gérard, his brother-in-law (G. Wildenstein, 1960, pp. 55–56, French edition).

May 28–(9 *prairial*)
Fragonard signs the document to requisition a portrait by Mme Vigée-Le Brun stored in the Nesle repository (G. Wildenstein, 1960, p. 56, French edition).

June 3–(15 *prairial*)
Fragonard and Pajou, after having sorted the drawings in the Nesle repository over the previous weeks, transport them to the Muséum to be stamped with the Louvre's "RF" mark (Cantarel-Besson, II, p. 74).

June 5–(17 *prairial an* IV)
Fragonard invests 37 *livres* in life annuities for his wife; his sister-in-law, Marguerite; as well as for Madeleine and Henri Gérard (G. Wildenstein, 1960, p. 56, French edition).

June 19, 21, 27, July 1, 3, 7, 9, 11–(1er–23 *messidor*)
Fragonard presides at the sessions of the Conservatoire (Cantarel-Besson, II, pp. 80–88).

July 15–(27 *messidor*)
"Avis sur une réclamation du citoyen Verrier Huin," concerning the work in the Galerie d'Apollon, is signed by Fragonard (G. Wildenstein, 1960, p. 56, French edition).

July 22–(4 *thermidor*)
A document for the removal of paintings from the rue de Beaune repository is signed by Fragonard (G. Wildenstein, 1960, p. 56, French edition).

July 29–(11 *thermidor*)
At the session of the Conservatoire, a letter addressed to Fragonard from "citoyen" Tolosan is read, offering works in his possession (a Jean-Baptiste Santerre, and sculptures by Laurent Guiard) in exchange for paintings that the Muséum cannot keep (Cantarel-Besson, II, p. 95).

August 6–(19 *thermidor*)
At the request of the Conservatoire, Fragonard and Pajou visit the Nesle repository to make a final selection of objects to be retained for the Muséum (Cantarel-Besson, II, pp. 98–99).

August 9–(22 *thermidor*)
Fragonard signs an authorization for Norblin de la Gourdaine to copy a painting (catalogue of autographs, Maison Charavay, December 1967, n° 32129).

August 13–(26 *thermidor*)
The receipt for art objects from the collections of the stadtholder is signed by Fragonard (G. Wildenstein, 1960, p. 56, French edition).

August 24–(7 *fructidor*)
Fragonard and Picault transfer three crates of objects and the inventory of their contents from the Garde-meuble to the Muséum (Cantarel-Besson, II, p. 109).

August 26–(9 *fructidor*)
Fragonard and Picault again transfer objects from the Garde-meuble (Cantarel-Besson, II, p. 110).

The *Journal de Paris* (no. 339, p. 1358) announces Fragonard's election to participate "au jury du concours de la demi-figure, de grandeur naturelle et de la tête d'expression."

August 31–(14 *fructidor*)
Letter from the curators to the Ministre du département Intérieur concerning the opening of the Salon on "10 vendémiaire" (G. Wildenstein, 1960, p. 56, French edition).

September 2–(17 *fructidor*)
Rocks and precious stones from the Garde-meuble are transferred to the Muséum (G. Wildenstein, 1960, p. 56, French edition).

September 26–(5 *vendémiaire*)
Fragonard presents to the Conservatoire a letter from "citoyen" Senez of Bordeaux, who offers a painting that he believes to be by Guido Reni and requests 14 *sols* for postage for the letter (Cantarel-Besson, II, pp. 124–25).

November 23, 25, 29, December 1, 3, 13–(3–23 *frimaire*)
Fragonard presides at the sessions of the Conservatoire (Cantarel-Besson, II, pp. 146–53).

December 1–(11 *frimaire*)
Fragonard and Pajou are appointed by the Conservatoire to verify the Muséum's accounts (Cantarel-Besson, II, pp. 148–49).

December 17–(27 *frimaire*)
Fragonard and Pajou are delegated by the Conservatoire to remove objects from the Mint (Cantarel-Besson, II, p. 155).

December 19–(29 *frimaire*)
Fragonard presides at the session of the Conservatoire and presents his report on his assignment at the Mint (Cantarel-Besson, II, p. 155).

In 1796, the painter Jacques-Luc Barbier (1769–1860), also called Barbier-Walbonne (see Brière, 1920), who brought many works of art from Belgium that were intended for the Muséum, expresses his wish to embark upon "la carrière des arts." Fragonard intercedes on his behalf in a report to the Commission temporaire des Arts (sale of autographs, A. Dupont collection, December 3–4, 1958, no. 107):

vous connaissez, citoyens, le zèle qu'a mis le citoyen Barbier à remplir la mission dont il a été chargé: vous l'en avez même félicité lorsqu'il vint vous annoncer l'arrivée à Paris des premiers trophées de nos victoires dans la Belgique, consistant en chefs d'oeuvre de Rubens et autres peintres célèbres, lesquels avaient été encaissés et conduits par lui avec le plus grand soin et la surveillance la plus active. Après avoir fait et accompagné plusieurs envois de ce genre; après avoir, surtout, fait la guerre pendant quatre ans sans relâche, il sollicite une réquisition auprès du comité d'Instruction publique pour rentrer dans la carrière des arts.... C'est au moment où ses braves frères d'armes triomphent de toute part; c'est au moment où nos ennemis presque vaincus nous offrent le rameau d'olivier, qu'il se sent animé du désir de transmettre sur la toile les combats et les actions héroïques dont il a été témoin.... Nous pensons donc que la Commission temporaire des Arts doit s'empresser d'appuyer la demande du citoyen Barbier ... mais à condition qu'il continuera de prendre les mêmes soins qu'exigent le transport à Paris des tableaux qui vous ont été désignés comme faisant partie de l'inappréciable collection des chefs d'oeuvre en peinture que possédaient les Belges et que la République s'empressera d'offrir à l'admiration de tous les peuples comme l'un des plus beaux fruits de ses conquêtes....

A "contrôle du 2e bataillon de la 2e brigade" (Arch. de la Seine, Affaires militaires, V Dx 2694–2721) mentions Fragonard: "Jean honoré; age: 64/grade: volontaire/domicille: gallerie, no 1/Peintre."

1797

January 10–(21 *nivôse*)
Reading of Fragonard's and Hubert Robert's report on a painting owned by "citoyen" l'Espinasse Darlet, who wishes to exchange it for objects in the Muséum (Cantarel-Besson, II, p. 162).

January 18–(29 *nivôse*)
Fragonard and Pajou verify the Muséum's accounts (Cantarel-Besson, II, p.166).

January 20–(1er *pluviôse*)
Fragonard and Pajou are reimbursed two francs "pour voiture prise pour le service du Musée" (Cantarel-Besson, II, p. 168).

January 27–(8 *pluviôse*)
At the session of the Conservatoire, letters are read from the Ministre de l'Intérieur, dated January 22, dealing with the reorganization of the Muséum, renamed the Musée central des Arts. Fragonard is to be replaced by Suvée on the future council; he is asked, along with Picault (whose duties will be taken over by Jollain), to give all the necessary accounting information to the new council (Cantarel-Besson, II, pp. 171–72).

January 28–(9 *pluviôse*)
Along with Picault, Robert, Pajou, de Wailly, and Foubert, Fragonard signs the audit of the Conservatoire's books (Cantarel-Besson, II, p. 173).

January 30–(11 *pluviôse*)
Fragonard and Picault return the keys to the main doors of the Muséum (G. Wildenstein, 1960, p. 56, French edition).

February 10–(22 *pluviôse*)
Fragonard serves as a member of the jury formed to select the works slated for the Musée spécial de l'École française in Versailles and for the Muséum (G. Wildenstein, 1960, p. 56, French edition).

February 11–(23 *pluviôse*)
The council asks the Ministère de l'Intérieur to entrust Fragonard with the surveillance of the transport of paintings between Paris and Versailles (G. Wildenstein, 1960, p. 56, French edition).

February 21–(3 *ventôse*)
Fragonard is delegated by the Conseil, along with David, Vincent, Vien ... and others, to decide which works are to remain in the Muséum and which are to go to the Musée spécial in Versailles (Arch. du Louvre, *Procès-verbaux du Conseil*, I, pp. 21–22).

April 7–(18 *germinal*)
Fragonard and Picault receive compensation as former curators (Arch. du Louvre, *Procès-verbaux du Conseil*, I, p. 41).

April 30–(11 *floréal*)
First session of the Jury des Arts, of which Fragonard is a member (Arch. du Louvre, *Procès-verbaux du Conseil*, I, p. 48).

May 2–27–(13 *floréal*–8 *prairial*)
The Conseil entrusts Fragonard with the supervision of the transport of paintings between Paris and Versailles (Arch. du Louvre, *Procès-verbaux du Conseil*, I, pp. 51–52, 64).
The first shipment leaves August 2. Fragonard will supervise thirteen shipments between then and September 25, 1799.

August 12–(25 *thermidor*)
Fragonard, his wife, and Marguerite Gérard buy a house at Évry-Petit-Bourg [today, Évry], in the Essonne district (G. Wildenstein, 1960, p. 57, French edition).

1798

January 4–(15 *nivôse*)
In response to the government's loan drive to finance the war against England, the Conseil offers to contribute the 70th part of its members' annual salaries; Fragonard makes a gift of 51 *livres* out of his annual 3,600 *livres* (Arch. du Louvre, *Procès-verbaux du Conseil*, I, p. 174; see also June 16, 1798, pp. 275–76).

January 15–(26 *nivôse*)
Fragonard signs a receipt for "quatorze pièces d'or de vingt quatre livres pour deux dessins des contes de La Fontaine ayant pour titre *Le petit chien qui secoue des pierreries* et *La fiancée du roy de garbe* ..." (Institut Néerlandais, Paris; see figure 9).

February 28–(10 *ventôse*)
Fragonard signs another receipt for "deux cent cinquante livres pour à compte sur le prix de quatre dessins, destinés à l'illustration des *Contes* de La Fontaine, à lui avancée par le citoyen Tilliard, éditeur" (inventory of autographs in the collection of Benjamin Fillon, July 15, 1879, no. 1762, published by Charavay, 1879, Vol. II).

March 4–(14 *ventôse*)
The Jury des Arts, meeting at the Gobelins, decides to transfer Fragonard's *Coresus and Callirhoë* to Versailles (Arch. du Louvre, *Procès-verbaux du Conseil*, I, p. 213).

March 18–(28 *ventôse*)
In the presence of Fragonard, the administrator of the Musée spécial de l'École française acknowledges the receipt of 88 paintings (G. Wildenstein, 1960, p. 57, French edition).

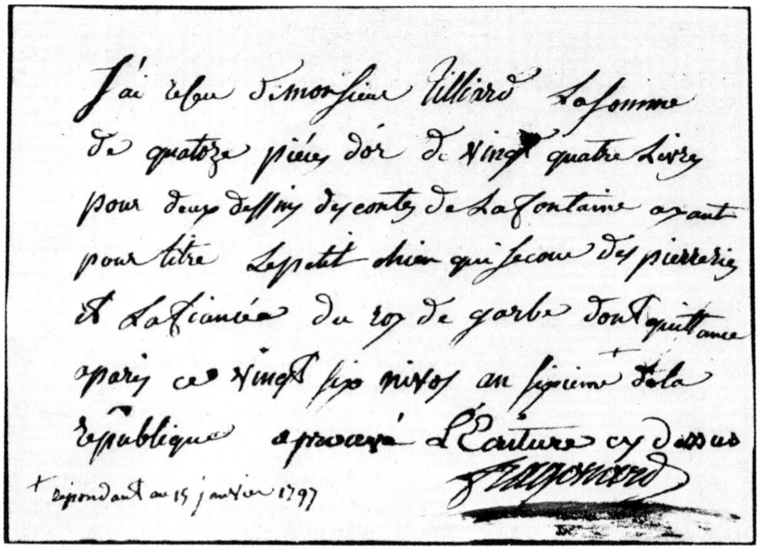
J'ai reçu de monsieur Tilliard la somme
de quatorze pièce d'or de vingt quatre livres
pour deux dessins des contes de La fontaine ayant
pour titre Le petit chien qui secoue des pierreries
et La fiancée du roy de garbe dont quittance
paris ce vingt six nivos an sixième de la
république approuvé l'écriture cy dessus
Fragonard
+ répondant au 15 janvier 1797

Figure 9. Receipt signed by Fragonard. Institut Néerlandais, Paris

1799

The list of paintings with floral and animal subjects in the Musée de Versailles and the Musée Central is to be sent to Fragonard because these works are to be transferred to the École de dessin in Lyons (Arch. Nat., F¹⁷ 1062 *dossier 2*).

April 25–(6 *floréal*)
Fragonard serves as a member of the Jury des Arts, entrusted with the distribution of prizes (*Journal de Paris*, no. 216), to be held April 30 (*Le Rédacteur*, 12 *floréal*, published by Aulard, 1902, V, pp. 493–94).

July 26–(8 *thermidor*)
Fragonard signs the famous petition of 254 artists (among them, David, Greuze, Prud'hon, Vernet, Suvée, Brongniart, and Houdon), in favor of the return to France of Mme Vigée-Le Brun, whose name appears on the list of émigrés (published by Tuetey, 1911, p. 180; reproduced by Girodie, 1927, pl. XLV).

1800

June 2–(13 *prairial*)
The administrator reminds the Conseil that Fragonard's duties end with the shipments from Paris to Versailles (G. Wildenstein, 1960, p. 58, French edition).

June 12–(23 *prairial*)
The Ministre de l'Intérieur informs Fragonard that starting on the "1ᵉʳ *messidor*" he will be released from his duties (G. Wildenstein, 1960, p. 58, French edition).

1801

January 8–(18 *nivôse*)
Fragonard requests a reimbursement of 36 *livres* from the Conseil for the purchase of a bas-relief for the Galerie d'Apollon (G. Wildenstein, 1960, p. 58, French edition).

1802

January 1–(12 *nivôse an* X)
Marguerite Gérard sends her best wishes for the New Year to her sister, Marie-Anne, and her brother-in-law, Jean-Honoré (figure 10). The following is an excerpt from that letter with the original spelling [for the entire text, see below]: "Vous soétérége. de la guété. de lesprit. du talant. du genie. de la mabilite. des amies. une amie. Vous posedéz tout cella. mai que soietez a M. quelques ducas de plus. deux ou trois petites filles pour jouer folatrer. rouler secouer soter ouspiller toutes. la journée."

There are several other letters from Marguerite Gérard to her brother-in-law that have lent credence to the idea that she was once his mistress (Bibliothèque d'Art et d'Archéologie, Paris; published by Portalis, 1889, pp. 226–33; Nolhac, 1906, pp. 103–4; Doin, 1912, pp. 443–44). They are published here in their entirety, but with standard spelling and punctuation:

Mon bon ami veut savoir si j'ai du plaisir quand je lui dis quelque chose d'agréable. Eh bien! je l'avoue, c'est ma seule jouissance; mon coeur reconnaissant et sensible n'est heureux que quand il s'occupe de son ami et lui dit tout ce qu'il lui inspire d'agréable. Mais quand la manière de s'exprimer a pu plaire à mon ami, je suis plus heureuse, je crois que je l'aime mieux, croyant que je lui plais davantage. Mon bon ami, l'on pourrait comparer l'amitié et l'amour à deux femmes, l'une jolie, l'autre figure agréable et ordinaire. La jolie plaît, enchante par sa fraîcheur printanière, passe comme une fleur, ne dure qu'un instant; l'autre reste toujours la même; quelquefois elle s'embellit en vieillissant. Je crois que c'est l'image de la nôtre. N'es-tu pas de mon avis, mon bon ami?

Quand mon bon ami me dit qu'il ne saurait trouver du plaisir dans aucun lieu que quand il s'y trouve avec moi, mon coeur enchanté voudrait ne le quitter qu'un instant et devenir son ombre pour le rendre heureux. Si je disais à mon bon ami que le désir de lui plaire et celui du travail me livrent tour à tour des combats pénibles; qu'il m'en coûte de résister à ses désirs, d'opposer mes goûts à ses plaisirs?

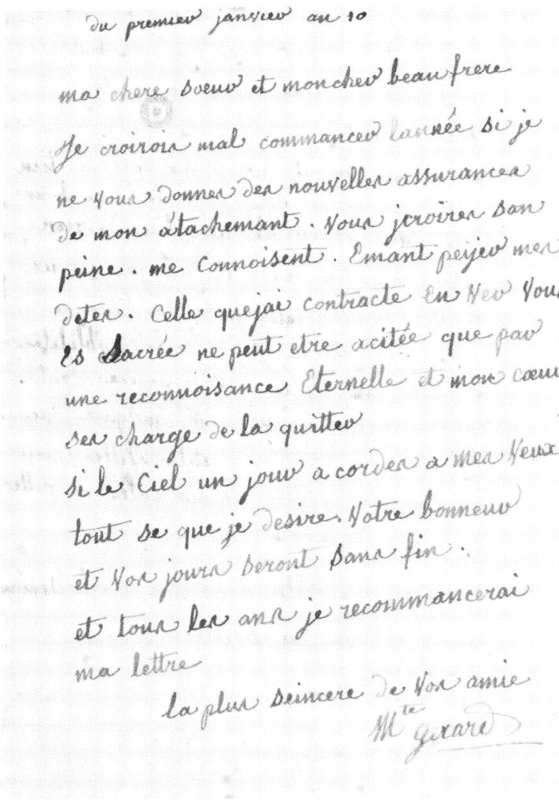

Figure 10. Letter from Marguerite Gérard to Marie-Anne and Jean-Honoré Fragonard. Bibliothèque d'Art et d'Archéologie, Paris

revenant à la comparaison de l'amour et de l'amitié, que ton fils n'a pas trouvée juste, en voici une autre. Je compare l'amour à une rose printanière dont la couleur éblouissante séduit; son parfum pénètre tous les sens. On la cueille non sans blessure, elle se fane, elle n'est plus;—l'amitié à la modeste violette dont le maintien tranquille n'attire point les regards; on ne la découvre que par son parfum, on la cueille sans crainte, elle est sans épine, et par conséquent sans danger.

Mon bon petit papa, tu veux que je te parle de tes défauts et tu fais cette demande à ton amie. Tu sais que l'amitié, soeur aînée de l'amour, a la vue basse, cela tient de famille. Ce n'est donc pas à moi qu'il faut t'adresser, car je ne vois rien que ton esprit aimable, qu'un enfant qu'un rien chagrine, qu'un rien apaise; un vrai nourrisson du caprice. Le caprice nourrit la coquetterie; la coquetterie séduit, quand elle est conduite par l'esprit. Chez toi, elles sont toujours ensemble.

Quand mon ami me demande que je lui écrive quelque chose d'agréable, je ne connais qu'un sujet, c'est de lui que je parle. De lui, parce qu'il me paraît le plus aimable des sujets. Si je voulais peindre d'un enfant la joie, la gaieté et le caprice, les caresses, le bonheur, je le prendrais pour modèle. Si je voulais peindre de l'amitié les caractères, la douceur, la complaisance, les soins, la tendresse, je le prendrais encore pour modèle d'un philosophe le plus aimable, des peintres le plus ingénieux et le plus gracieux, des maris le meilleur, d'un ami le plus tendre et le plus constant, des maîtres le plus soigneux et le plus attentif. Voilà le portrait de mon ami: je suis glorieuse de le nommer ainsi, sa constance m'assure que c'est pour la vie et mon bonheur est parfait.

Mon bon ami, tu ne saurais croire combien je suis malheureuse quand je te vois indisposé. Figure-toi une colombe à qui l'on a ravi son tourtereau. Quand elle le voit en gêne, combien elle est inquiétée! Elle ne peut quitter l'endroit où son ami se trouve détenu, croyant par sa présence, soulager ses ennuis, et par ses soins lui rendre sa liberté plus vite. Elle voit voltiger autour d'elle ses aimables compagnes avec qui elle passait tant de jours heureux, cela n'a plus de charme pour elle. Son ami souffre, ne peut partager ses plaisirs: il n'y en a plus pour elle. Mais quand son ami lui sera rendu, plus aimable que jamais, son bonheur, sa joie, son délire même la paieront des ennuis qu'elle aura éprouvés. Ah! mon ami, que nous ne sentons notre bonheur vivement que quand nous avons eu peur de le perdre!

Du premier janvier an 10
Ma chère soeur et mon cher beau-frère,
Je croirais mal commencer l'année si je ne vous donnais de nouvelles assurances de mon attachement. Vous y croirez sans peine, me connaissant. Aimant payer mes dettes, celle que j'ai contractée envers vous est sacrée, ne peut être acquittée que par une reconnaissance éternelle et mon coeur s'est chargé de l'acquitter. Si le ciel un jour accorde à mes voeux tout ce que je désire, votre bonheur et vos jours seront sans fin et tous les ans je recommencerai ma lettre.
La plus sincère de vos amies.
Il est fort heureux pour moi, voulant vous souhaiter la bonne année, de m'y être prise la veille. L'on dit ordinairement que bonne volonté tient lieu de tout. Je me suis prouvée que bonne volonté sans esprit ne tient lieu de rien. Pourtant, mon bon ami, il faut que je vous la souhaite. Vous souhaiterais-je de la gaieté, de l'esprit, du talent, du génie, de l'amabilité, des amis, une amie? Vous possédez tout cela. Mais que souhaiter à Monsieur? Quelques ducats de plus, deux ou trois petites filles pour jouer, folâtrer, rouler, secouer, sauter, houspiller toute la journée.
S'il ne faut que cela pour être parfaitement heureux, je vous le souhaite accompagné de plusieurs autres.

Mon bon ami veut que je lui dise pourquoi j'ai refusé de lui donner ce qu'il me demande. Eh bien mon bon ami voici la raison. Vous possédez une petite somme qui doit vous suffire pour longtemps.
Mon bon ami sait qu'il faut être raisonnable il sait encore qu'en nourrissant les fantaisies on les augmente sans en être plus heureux. Je sais bien qu'on peut appeler ce raisonnement folie, mais chacun doit raisonner comme sa situation l'exige. Une coquette vante les plaisirs et la variété, une femme laide la constance, une vieille la sagesse, une guerrière les beaux exploits. Nous devons vanter l'économie. Cela tient lieu de fortune quand on est sage.

Mon bon ami désire que je lui fasse compagnie, et que je l'entretienne par une conversation agréable. Combien je serai heureuse de pouvoir satisfaire à ses désirs. L'on dit vulgairement, babiller comme une femme. Je suis femme. Mais je t'avoue que l'ignorance qui s'est mise à califourchon sur mes épaules me bride et m'empêche de parler. Je sens, non sans chagrin, que pour la vie je suis condamnée à traîner ce fardeau insipide pour moi et pour....

Eh bien mon bon ami comment as-tu trouvé la journée? Si j'en juge par ta gaieté, elle t'a paru agréable. L'influence d'un beau jour ranime et donne l'empreinte du plaisir à tout ce qui respire.
Tel l'on entend les oiseaux au commencement du printemps chanter leur amour et le retour de la belle saison. J'ai vu, mon bon ami par sa joie et ses aimables folies ramener la gaieté dans toute la société et éloigner la froide mélancolie. Compagne inséparable de l'âge que l'on appelle raison. Toi seul a le droit de la faire fuir par ta présence. Voilà pourquoi l'on te voit partir avec regrets. Tu t'éloignes, elle revient presque aussitôt. Personne n'a le droit de s'en défendre. Elle déplaît, elle ennuie, l'on s'y habitue, l'on vit avec elle comme avec un voisin inopportun que l'on ne peut renvoyer. Je désire que cette ennuyeuse ne s'empare jamais de toi, car elle tue tous ceux dont elle a fait choix. La gaieté et la santé sont deux compagnes inséparables. Cela vaut bien mieux.

March 17–(26 ventôse)
Fragonard, his wife, and Marguerite Gérard buy a house at 57, rue de l'Oursine (today 29, rue Broca, Paris, 5ᵉ arrondissement; Minutier central, LXXVIII, 1042).

April 4–(14 germinal)
For 4,000 francs, François Louette, a former cabinetmaker, sells to Fragonard and his wife—who will have life interest—and to Marguerite Gérard, who will retain eventual ownership, a plot of land of 364 toises, near the rue Saint Hyppolite and the rue de l'Oursine, in the faubourg Saint-Marceau, Paris, and an adjacent lot, of 948 toises, on which there are buildings (Minutier central, LXXVIII, 1043).

1803

December 13
Henry Castel, a twenty-year-old painter from Grasse, enters the École

des Beaux-Arts as Fragonard's pupil (Bibliothèque de l'École des Beaux-Arts, ms. n° 95, fol. 297 a).
Charles-Louis-François Le Carpentier engraves a portrait of Fragonard (figure 5, page 555).

1804

April 7
In his journal, the English painter Joseph Farington (1747–1821) relates a conversation that he had with Loutherbourg (1740–1812), a French painter who settled in England in 1771: "He spoke of Fragonard as having very fine talents for painting, but He soon lost at Paris a great deal of that excellence which he shewed in Italy" (Greig, 1923, II, p. 122).

1805

April 1–(11 germinal)
Napoleon issues a decree calling for the eviction of all the artists with lodgings in the Louvre (Arch. Nat., IV-968).

April 10–(20 germinal)
Fragonard signs a petition addressed to Napoleon concerning the issue of lodgings in the Louvre (Bibliothèque d'Art et d'Archéologie, carton 14, architect Vaudoyer).

July 9–(20 messidor)
Fragonard receives a life pension of 1,000 francs half-yearly as compensation for the loss of his lodgings. The notification was addressed to him "au Palais royal, Maison Very" (Bibliothèque du Musée Fragonard, Grasse), indicating that, by that time, he had left the Louvre for the Palais-Royal, where (according to G. Wildenstein, 1960, p. 33) he lived in the house of the restaurateur Véry, arcades 83 and 85 (today, the restaurant Grand Véfour). A letter dating from November 20 and signed by Fragonard, in which he notes this change of address, has come down to us: "Monsieur, Fragonard [Jean honoré] artiste peintre d'histoire, cy devant logé gallerie du Louvre et de present 2ᵉ arrondissement palais Royal chez Very Restaurateur. Requiert nomme Rentier et peintre un numero pour chaque billet de banque de france de 500 francs n° 508. Je suis avec Respect et reconnoissance Fragonard. Ce 20 9 bre" (published by Levy, 1982).

October 15–(23 vendémiaire)
David thanks Évariste Fragonard for an "ouvrage" that he received from him:

je suis bien sensible, mon bon ami, à votre tendre souvenir; il me prouve que je suis présent à votre mémoire. J'ai reçu avec bien de la satisfaction votre ouvrage et j'ai eu un plaisir incroyable à le parcourir. Continuez, mon bon ami; vous êtes né pour aller loin; quand on fait à vingt-quatre ans une pareille oeuvre, on doit s'estimer heureux. Je félicite votre brave père et je me mets à sa place. Qu'il jouisse complètement de la liberté qu'il vous a laissée dans les arts; car il a senti, en habile homme, qu'il n'y avait point une seule route pour arriver au but, et le nom de Fragonard sera distingué dans tous les genres. J'embrasse bien votre tendre mère, et je n'oublie pas mademoiselle Gérard; la postérité m'en ferait trop de reproches.
Votre ami sincère,
David

(introduction to the sales catalogue of the collection of Alexandre-Évariste Fragonard, December 6, 1850; excerpt quoted by D. and Guy Wildenstein, 1973, p. 169).

1806

February 25
Three "certificats de vie" are issued to Fragonard (Minutier central, répertoire, LXVIII-13).

July 5
Fragonard receives 500 francs for the first six months of the year—part of his compensation for losing his lodgings at the Louvre (Arch. Nat., O² 838, dossier 6, E 1719).

August 22

The traditional version of Fragonard's death, as recounted by the Goncourts (1865, p. 308), is that he died after a walk in the Champ-de-Mars, where he had eaten an ice cream that proved fatal.

The death certificate (Minutier central, LXXVIII, 1080) states: "du vendredy 22 août 1806. Acte de décès de M. Jean-Honoré Fragonard, peintre de la ci-devant Académie, âgé de 74 ans 5 mois, né à Grasse, département du Var, décédé ce jourd'hui à 5 heures du matin, palais du Tribunat, maison de Veri, restaurateur, division de la Butte-des-Moulins, époux de d^e Marie Gérard.

Les témoins ont été MM. Alexandre-Évariste Fragonard, peintre d'histoire, demeurant rue Verdelet, n° 4, division de la Halle-au-Bled, fils du défunt, et Jean-Baptiste Alezard, propriétaire demeurant rue St Thomas du Louvre n° 30. Division des Tuilleries, ami du décédé; lesquels ont signé avec M. André, Docteur en médecine qui a constaté ledit décès . . . " (excerpt published by Piot, 1873, p. 48).

The *Journal de Paris* (no. 237, p. 1742) reported the artist's death in these terms: "M. Fragonard père est mort vendredi matin, à la suite d'une assez courte maladie. Il étoit âgé de 74 ans et demi, et extraordinairement replet. L'école française perd en lui un peintre justement estimé. *Callirhoé, La Fontaine d'Amour, Le Sacrifice de la Rose* et divers autres sujets reproduits et multipliés par la gravure, ont attaché au nom de Fragonard l'idée même des Grâces. Cet excellent homme laisse un fils qui promet de soutenir le nom qu'il porte; il compose et peint le bas relief avec une grâce toute particulière et une imagination heureuse et brillante. On connoît aussi Mll. Gérard, qui, élève de M. Fragonard, est la rivale de son talent, en même tems qu'elle fut, jusqu'à son dernier moment, l'amie constante de sa vieillesse."

The *Mercure de France* (August 30, p. 434) noted: "M. Fragonard, l'un des peintres de l'ancienne école qui a eu le plus de réputation, est mort, le 22 août, à la suite d'une maladie très-courte. Il étoit âgé de 74 ans."

The *Revue philosophique, Littéraire et politique* (no. 29, 4th trimester, October 11, p. 123) was equally concise: "enfin, M. Fragonard, peintre, de l'ancienne Académie, qui réussissait dans les sujets érotiques et galans, est mort, il y a quelques jours, dans la 74e année de son âge. Il laisse un fils qui jouit d'une réputation méritée dans les arts."

August 24

The burial certificate reads: "le dimanche 24 août a été présenté le corps de feu Jean Honoré Fragonard, Peintre de la cy-devant académie, âgé de 74 ans 5 mois, Palais du Tribunat, rue d'arcole n° 11" (Register of the parish of Saint-Roch, fol. 25).

An affidavit issued on September 27 (Minutier central, LXXVIII, 1080) mentions that no posthumous inventory was drawn up after Fragonard's death, and that he left "pour son seul et unique héritier M. Alexandre Évariste Fragonard son fils."

Marguerite Gérard exhibits at the Salon (no. 218): "La Rosière recevant le baiser de protection de la dame du lieu." This painting (now lost) was reviewed by the *Pausanias français* (pp. 217–18): "je reviens au titre du sujet. Qu'est-ce qu'un baiser de protection de la dame du lieu? J'ai le malheur de ne pas saisir le sens de ces mots. Les Amis des Arts, de la grace ingénieuse, et de tout ce qu'il y a d'aimable avec abandon, retrouvent ici avec un vif plaisir le portrait du vieux Fragonard, dans celui du Bailly. Il fut le Maître de mademoiselle Gérard, et elle semble hériter de son pinceau."

Marie-Anne Fragonard died in 1823 (not 1824; Wells-Robertson, 1979, p. 187). Her sister, Marguerite Gérard, died in 1837, and her son, Évariste, in 1850. Théophile, Évariste's son, was born the year of his grandfather's death, and died in 1876.

List of Exhibitions

This list does not include the exhibitions held in the eighteenth century (at the Salon du Louvre, the Salon de la Correspondance, in Montpellier, Versailles ...). A small dot precedes the most important exhibitions.

Amiens, 1860
"Notice des tableaux et objets d'art, d'antiquité, et de curiosité," Hôtel de Ville
Amsterdam, 1926
"Exposition rétrospective d'art français," Rijksmuseum
Amsterdam, 1951
"Het Franse landschap van Poussin tot Cézanne," Rijksmuseum
Amsterdam, 1964
See Paris–Amsterdam, 1964
Amsterdam, 1974
"Franse tekenkunst van de 18ᵈᵉ eeuw uit Nederlandse verzamelingen; French Drawings of the Eighteenth Century from Dutch Collections," Rijksprentenkabinet, Rijksmuseum
Atlanta, 1983–84
"The Rococo Age," The High Museum of Art (Catalogue by E. Zafran)
Augsburg–Cleveland, 1975–76
"Johann Liss," Rathaus; The Cleveland Museum of Art

Baltimore, 1959
"Age of Elegance: The Rococo and Its Effect," The Baltimore Museum of Art
Baltimore–Boston–Minneapolis, 1984–85
"Regency to Empire: French Printmaking," The Baltimore Museum of Art; Museum of Fine Arts; The Minneapolis Institute of Arts
Berkeley, 1968
"Master Drawings from California Collections," University Art Museum
Berlin, 1910
"Ausstellung von Werken französischer Kunst des XVIII. Jahrhunderts," Königliche Akademie der Künste (Large-format catalogue)
Berlin, 1973
"Vom späten Mittelalter bis zu Jacques-Louis David," Staatliche Museen Preussischer Kulturbesitz
Berlin, 1983
"Bilder vom irdischen Glück: Giorgione, Tizian, Rubens, Watteau, Fragonard," Schloss Charlottenburg
Bern, 1954
• "Fragonard," Kunstmuseum
Besançon, 1956
• "J.-H. Fragonard: Peintures et dessins," Musée des Beaux-Arts
Besançon, 1977
"Dessins français du XVIIIᵉ siècle," Musée des Beaux-Arts
Biot, 1985
"Images du travail," Musée National Fernand Léger

Bordeaux, 1882
"Exposition de la Société Philomatique."
Bordeaux, 1956
"De Tiepolo à Goya," Galerie des Beaux-Arts
Bordeaux, 1958
"Paris et les ateliers provinciaux au XVIIIᵉ siècle," Galerie des Beaux-Arts
Bordeaux, 1964
"La Femme et l'artiste, de Bellini à Picasso," Galerie des Beaux-Arts
Bordeaux, 1965
"Chefs d'oeuvre de la peinture française dans les musées de l'Ermitage et de Moscou," Galerie des Beaux-Arts
Bordeaux, 1967
"La Peinture française en Suède," Galerie des Beaux-Arts
Bordeaux, 1980
"Les Arts du théâtre de Watteau à Fragonard," Galerie des Beaux-Arts
Bordeaux, 1981
"Profil du Metropolitan Museum of Art de New York: De Ramsès à Picasso," Galerie des Beaux-Arts
Bourg-en-Bresse, 1982
"Jérôme de Lalande," Centre Culturel Albert Camus
Bregenz–Vienna, 1968–69
"Angelika Kauffmann und ihre Zeitgenossen," Vorarlberger Landesmuseum; Österreichisches Museum für Angewandte Kunst
Bremen, 1977–78
"Zurück zur Natur," Kunsthalle
Breteuil, 1986
"Un Grand Collectionneur sous Louis XV: Le Cabinet de Jacques-Laure de Breteuil, Bailli de l'Ordre de Malte, 1723–1785," Château de Breteuil
Brunswick–Coburg, 1982
"Zeichnungen alter Meister aus polnischen Sammlungen," Herzog Anton Ulrich-Museum; Kunstsammlungen der Veste Coburg
Brunswick, 1983–84
See Rotterdam–Brunswick, 1983–84
Brussels, 1904
"L'Art français au XVIIIᵉ siècle," Palais des Beaux-Arts
Brussels, 1912
"Exposition de la miniature."
Brussels, 1925
"Exposition d'art français du XVIIIᵉ siècle," Musée Royal des Beaux-Arts de Belgique
Brussels, 1975
"De Watteau à David: Peintures et dessins des musées de province français," Palais des Beaux-Arts
Buenos Aires, 1893
"Exposición artística," Palacio Hume
Buenos Aires, 1968
"El arte de vivir en Francia del siglo XVIII en las colecciones argentinas," Museo Nacional de Arte Decorativo
Buffalo, 1935
"Master Drawings, Selected from the Museums and Private Collections of America," Albright Art Gallery

Cambridge, Mass., 1931
"Loan Exhibition of Eighteenth Century French Art," Fogg Art Museum, Harvard University
Cambridge, Mass., 1980
"French Drawings from a Private Collection: Louis XIII to Louis XVI," Fogg Art Museum, Harvard University
Cambridge, Mass., 1984
"Master Drawings and Watercolors: The Hofer Collection," Fogg Art Museum, Harvard University
Caracas, 1977
"Cinco siglos de arte francès," Museo de Bellas Artes
Charleroi, 1957
• "Fragonard–David–Navez," Palais des Beaux-Arts
Chicago, 1933
"A Century of Progress: Exhibition of Painting and Sculpture," The Art Institute of Chicago
Chicago, 1978
"European Portraits, 1600–1900, in The Art Institute of Chicago," The Art Institute of Chicago
Chicago, 1985
"Great Drawings from The Art Institute of Chicago: The Harold Joachim Years, 1958–1983," The Art Institute of Chicago
Claremont, Calif., 1976
"Eighteenth Century Drawings from California Collections," Montgomery Art Center
Clermont-Ferrand, 1977
"Aimer en France," Bibliothèque Municipale
Cleveland, 1956
"The Venetian Tradition," The Cleveland Museum of Art
Compiègne–Aix-en-Provence, 1977
"Don Quichotte vu par un peintre du XVIIIᵉ siècle: Natoire," Musée National du Château; Musée des Tapisseries
Copenhagen, 1935
"L'Art français au XVIIIᵉ siècle," Charlottenbourg Palace

Detroit, 1926
"Loan Exhibition of French Paintings," The Detroit Institute of Arts
Detroit–Chicago, 1981–82
"The Golden Age of Naples: Art and Civilization under the Bourbons, 1734–1805," The Detroit Institute of Arts; The Art Institute of Chicago (See vol. 2 of the catalogue)
Dijon, 1960
"Dessins français, XVIIᵉ et XVIIIᵉ siècles, des collections du Musée de Dijon," Palais des États de Bourgogne
Dijon, 1974
"Dessins de la collection His de la Salle," Musée des Beaux-Arts
Dijon, 1977
"J.-B. Greuze, 1725–1805," Palais des États de Bourgogne
Dijon, 1982–83
"La Peinture dans la peinture," Musée des Beaux-Arts

Ferrara, 1985
"Torquato Tasso tra letteratura, musica, teatro, e arti figurativi," Castello Estense, Casa Romei
Florence, 1968
"Mostra di disegni francesi da Callot a Ingres," Gabinetto dei Disegni e Stampe degli Uffizi
Frankfurt am Main, 1925
"Ausstellung von Meisterwerken alter Malerei aus Privatbesitz," Städelsches Kunstinstitut
Frankfurt am Main, 1986–87
"Französische Zeichnungen im Städelschen Kunstinstitut, 1550 bis 1800," Städtische Galerie, Städelsches Kunstinstitut

Geneva, 1949
"Trois Siècles de peinture française, XVIᵉ–XVIIIᵉ siècle: Chefs-d'oeuvres des musées de France," Musée Rath
Geneva, 1951
"De Watteau à Cézanne," Musée d'Art et d'Histoire
Glens Falls, N.Y., 1941
"Drawings and Paintings of the XVIIIth Century," Crandall Library
Grasse, 1957
• "Oeuvres de Fragonard," Musée Fragonard
Gray–Besançon–Belfort–Dôle, 1977–78
"Peintures et dessins de 1750 à 1830: Collections des Musées de Gray, Besançon, Belfort, Dôle," Musée Baron Martin; Musée des Beaux-Arts; Musée d'Art et d'Histoire; Musée Municipal

Hartford, 1934
"Loans in Honor of the Ancry Memorial," Wadsworth Atheneum
Houston, 1986–87
"A Magic Mirror: The Portrait in France, 1700–1900," The Museum of Fine Arts

Ipswich, England, 1927
"Bicentenary Memorial Exhibition of Thomas Gainsborough, R.A.," Ipswich Museum

Jerusalem, 1986
"100 Works on Paper from the Collections of the Israel Museum," The Israel Museum

Karlsruhe, 1983
"Di französischen Zeichnungen, 1570–1930," Kupferstichkabinett, Staatliche Kunsthalle

Lausanne, 1986
"A. L. R. Ducros (1748–1810): Paysages d'Italie à l'époque de Goethe," Musée Cantonal des Beaux-Arts
Leningrad, 1956
"French Art of the 15th–20th Centuries," The Hermitage
Leningrad–Moscow, 1975
"100 Paintings from The Metropolitan Museum," The Hermitage; Pushkin Museum
Lille, 1960
"Le Paysage en Orient et en Occident."
Lille, 1985
"Au temps de Watteau, Fragonard, et Chardin," Musée des Beaux-Arts
Lisbon, 1951
"Rotéiro das pinturas," Museu Nacional de Arte Antiga
Lisbon, 1961
"Pinturas da colecçào da Fundaçào Calouste Gulbenkian," Museu Nacional de Arte Antiga

Lisbon, 1966
"Rotéiro da pintura estrangeira," Museu Nacional de Arte Antiga
London, 1898
"Roman d'amour de la jeunesse," Thomas Agnew & Sons Ltd.
London, 1908
Exhibition, Royal Academy of Arts
London, 1913
"Pictures, Drawings . . . of the French School of the Eighteenth Century," Burlington Fine Arts Club
London, 1928
"Drawings Made in Rome and Florence by Fragonard," The Warren Gallery
London, 1932
"French Art, 1200–1900," Royal Academy of Arts
London, 1933
"Three French Reigns . . . ," 25 Park Lane
London, 1937
"Pictures from the Gulbenkian Collection," National Gallery
London, 1949–50
"Landscape in French Art," Royal Academy of Arts
London, 1950
"French Master Drawings of the Eighteenth Century," Matthiesen Gallery
London, 1954–55
"European Masters of the Eighteenth Century," Royal Academy of Arts
London, 1962
"Religious Themes in Painting," Wildenstein & Co.
London, 1968
• "France in the Eighteenth Century," Royal Academy of Arts
London, 1974
"From Poussin to Puvis de Chavannes," Heim Gallery
London, 1977
"French Landscape Drawings and Sketches of the Eighteenth Century," British Museum
London, 1978
"18th Century French Paintings, Drawings, and Sculptures," Artemis David Carritt Ltd.
London, 1978
"Fragonard Drawings for *Orlando Furioso*," Thomas Agnew & Sons Ltd.
London, 1979–80
"Sèvres Porcelain from the Royal Collection," Queen's Gallery, Buckingham Palace
London, 1981
"The Princes Gate Collection," Courtauld Institute Galleries
London, 1982
"Mantegna to Cézanne: Master Drawings from the Courtauld, a Fiftieth Anniversary Exhibition," Courtauld Institute Galleries
London, n.d.
"La Douceur de vivre," Wildenstein & Co.
Long Beach, Calif., 1979
"French Drawings from the Fr. B. Crocker Collection," Long Beach Museum of Art
Los Angeles, 1961
"French Masters: From Rococo to Romanticism," University of California
Los Angeles, 1976
"Old Master Drawings from American Collections," Los Angeles County Museum of Art
Los Angeles, 1976
"Women Artists, 1550–1950," Los Angeles County Museum of Art
Lyons, 1984–85
"Dessins du XVIᵉ au XIXᵉ siècle de la collection du Musée des Arts Décoratifs de Lyon," Musée Historique des Tissus

Marseilles, 1906
"Catalogue des ouvrages exposés au Grand Palais dans la Section de l'Art Provençal," Exposition Coloniale
Marseilles, 1969
"Donation Maurice et Pauline Feuillet de Borsat," Musée Borély
Marseilles, 1971
"Dessins des Musées de Marseille," Musée Cantini
Marseilles, 1984
"Techniques du dessin," Musée Grobet-Labadie
Minneapolis–New York, 1954
"French XVIIIth Century Painters," The Minneapolis Institute of Arts; Wildenstein & Co.
Minneapolis, 1985–86
"The Art of Collecting," The Minneapolis Institute of Arts
Montpellier, 1980
"De Raphael à Matisse: 100 Dessins du Musée Fabre," Musée Fabre
Montreal, 1950
"The Eighteenth Century Art of France and England," The Montreal Museum of Fine Arts
Moscow, 1927
"French Drawings of the 16th–19th Centuries," Pushkin Museum
Moscow, 1955
"French Art of the 15th–20th Centuries," Pushkin Museum
Moscow–Leningrad, 1955–56
"French Art of the 15th–19th Centuries," Pushkin Museum; The Hermitage
Moscow, 1959
"Le Dessin et l'aquarelle," Pushkin Museum
Moscow–Leningrad, 1966
"Masterpieces of Drawing from the Collection of the Museum of Fine Arts," Pushkin Museum; The Hermitage
Moscow, 1972
"French Drawings of the 16th–18th Centuries," Pushkin Museum
Munich, 1930
"Sammlung Schloss Rohoncz," Neue Pinakothek
Munich, 1958
"Europaïsches Rokoko," Residenzmuseum

Nantes–Lausanne–Rome, 1985
"Les Frères Sablet," Musées Départementaux de Loire-Atlantique; Musée Cantonal des Beaux-Arts; Palazzo Broselie
Naples, 1979–80
"Civiltà del '700 a Napoli, 1734–1799," Museo e Gallerie Nazionali di Capodimonte
Naples, 1984–85
"Civiltà del Seicento a Napoli," Museo e Gallerie Nazionali di Capodimonte
New Haven, 1956
"Pictures Collected by Yale Alumni," Yale University Art Gallery
New Haven, 1960
"Paintings, Drawings, and Sculptures Collected by Yale Alumni," Yale University Art Gallery
New Haven, 1984
"French Drawings: Acquisitions, 1970–84," Yale University Art Gallery
New York, 1914
"Fragonard," E. Gimpel and Wildenstein
New York, 1914
"Loan Exhibition of the J. Pierpont Morgan Collection," The Metropolitan Museum of Art
New York, 1922
"Notable Paintings by Great Masters," P. Jackson Higgs Galleries
New York, 1926
"Fragonard," Wildenstein & Co.

New York, 1937
"Pictures from the David-Weill Collection," Wildenstein & Co.
New York, 1940
"European and American Paintings, 1500–1900," New York World's Fair
New York, 1958
"Fifty Masterworks from the City Art Museum of Saint Louis," Wildenstein & Co.
New York, 1967
"Masters of the Loaded Brush: Sketches from Rubens to Tiepolo," M. Knoedler & Co.
New York, 1968
"The Artist and the Animal," M. Knoedler & Co.
New York, 1972
"French Drawings and Prints," The Metropolitan Museum of Art
New York–Los Angeles–Indianapolis, 1973
"Woodner Collection, II: Old Master Drawings from the XV to the XVIII Century," William H. Schab Gallery; Los Angeles County Museum of Art; Indianapolis Museum of Art
New York, 1974
"Major Acquisitions of the Pierpont Morgan Library, 1924–1974: Drawings," The Pierpont Morgan Library
New York, 1974–75
"The Grand Gallery," The Metropolitan Museum of Art
New York, 1977
"Paris–New York: A Continuing Romance," Wildenstein & Co.
New York, 1980
"Seventeenth and Eighteenth Century French Drawings from the Robert Lehman Collection," The Metropolitan Museum of Art
New York, 1981
"European Drawings, 1375–1825," The Pierpont Morgan Library
New York, 1983
"18th Century French Drawings," Cailleux and Colnaghi
New York, 1984
"French Master Drawings," Didier Aaron Gallery
New York, 1985
"Drawings from the Collection of Mr. and Mrs. Eugene Victor Thaw," The Pierpont Morgan Library
New York, 1985
"French and Italian Eighteenth Century Master Drawings," Spencer A. Samuels & Co.
New York–New Orleans–Columbus, 1985–86
"The First Painters of the King," Stair Sainty Matthiesen; New Orleans Museum of Art; Columbus Museum of Art
New York, 1986
"15th–18th Century French Drawings in The Metropolitan Museum of Art," The Metropolitan Museum of Art
New York, 1986
"French and English Drawings, 1700–1875," Zangrilli Brady & Co.
New York, 1987
"Chez elle, chez lui: At Home in 18th Century France," Rosenberg & Stiebel, Inc.
New York–Edinburgh, 1987
"The Art of Drawing in France, 1400–1900," The Drawing Center; National Gallery of Scotland
Notre Dame, Ind., 1972
"Eighteenth Century France: A Study of Its Art and Civilization," Art Gallery, O'Shaughnessy Hall, University of Notre Dame

Oporto, 1964
"Arts plastiques français de Watteau à Renoir: Collection de la Fondation Calouste Gulbenkian," Museu Nacional de Soares dos Reis
Orléans, 1975–76
"Le Dessin français du XVIe au XVIIIe siècle," Musée Historique, Hôtel Cabu
Orléans, 1978
"Dessins français du XVIe au XVIIIe siècle," Musée Historique, Hôtel Cabu
Ottawa, 1976
"Dessins européens des collections canadiennes, 1500–1900; European Drawings from Canadian Collections, 1500–1900," The National Gallery of Canada

Paris, 1848
"Explication des ouvrages de peinture exposés à la Galerie Bonne Nouvelle," Association des Artistes, Galerie Bonne Nouvelle
Paris, 1860
"Catalogue de tableaux et dessins de l'École française, principalement du XVIIIe siècle tirés de collections d'amateurs," Galerie Martinet, 26 boulevard des Italiens (Catalogue by Ph. Burty)
Paris, 1866
"Tableaux anciens empruntés aux galeries particulières," Palais des Champs-Élysées
Paris, 1874
"Ouvrages de peinture exposés au profit de la colonisation de l'Algérie par les Alsaciens-Lorrains," Palais de la Présidence du Corps Législatif (Palais Bourbon)
Paris, 1878
"Portraits historiques (Exposition universelle)," Palais du Trocadéro
Paris, 1879
"Catalogue descriptif des dessins de maîtres anciens exposés à l'École des Beaux-Arts," École des Beaux-Arts
Paris, 1880
"Exposition de tableaux anciens de décoration et d'ornement," Musée des Arts Décoratifs
Paris, 1883
"Portraits du XVIIIe siècle (1783–1883)," École des Beaux-Arts
Paris, 1883–84
"L'Art du XVIIIe siècle," Galerie Georges Petit
Paris, 1884
"Catalogue des dessins de l'École Moderne," École des Beaux-Arts
Paris, 1885
"Exposition de tableaux, statues, et objets d'art au profit de l'oeuvre des orphelins d'Alsace-Lorraine," Salle des États, Musée du Louvre
Paris, 1885
"Portraits du siècle," École des Beaux-Arts
Paris, 1887
"Exposition de tableaux de maîtres anciens au profit des inondés du midi."
Paris, 1888
"L'Art français sous Louis XIV et sous Louis XV (au profit de l'oeuvre de l'Hospitalité de Nuit)," Maison Quentin
Paris, 1888
"Exposition internationale de blanc et noir."
Paris, 1889
"Exposition centennale de l'art français (Exposition universelle)," Section des Beaux-Arts
Paris, 1894
"Marie-Antoinette et son temps," Galerie Sedelmeyer
Paris, 1897
• "Catalogue de portraits de femmes et d'enfants," École des Beaux-Arts
Paris, 1907
"Chardin–Fragonard," Galerie Georges Petit

Paris, 1909
"Exposition de cent portraits de femmes des écoles anglaise et française du XVIIIe siècle," Musée du Jeu de Paume
Paris, 1911
"La Turquerie au XVIIIe siècle," Musée des Arts Décoratifs
Paris, 1913
"Catalogue de dessins de l'École française du dix-huitième siècle," Galerie Georges Petit
Paris, 1921
• "Exposition d'oeuvres de J.-H. Fragonard," Musée des Arts Décoratifs (Catalogue by G. Wildenstein)
Paris, 1923
"L'Art français au service de la science française," Chambre Syndicale de la Curiosité
Paris, 1925
"Le Paysage français de Poussin à Corot," Musée du Petit Palais
Paris, 1926
"Soixante-huit Dessins de Fragonard: Souvenirs de son voyage à Rome et à Florence," Geoffroy Dodge et Cie
Paris, 1928
"La Jeunesse vue par les maîtres du XVIe au XIXe siècles," Galerie Jean Charpentier
Paris, 1928
"La Vie parisienne au XVIIIe siècle," Musée Carnavalet
Paris, 1931
"Chefs d'oeuvre des musées de Province," Musée de l'Orangerie
Paris, 1931
• "Dessins de Fragonard," Jacques Seligmann et fils (Catalogue with a foreword by L. Réau)
Paris, 1933
"Exposition du pastel français du XVIIe siècle à nos jours," Jacques Seligmann et fils
Paris, 1933
"Hubert Robert," Musée de l'Orangerie
Paris, 1934
"Les Artistes français en Italie, de Poussin à Renoir," Musée des Arts Décoratifs
Paris, 1934
"Cent Ans de portraits français (1800–1900)," Galerie Bernheim Jeune
Paris, 1934
"Esquisses, maquettes, projets, et ébauches de l'école française du XVIIIe siècle," Galerie Cailleux
Paris, 1934
"Le Siècle de Louis XV vu par les artistes," *Gazette des Beaux-Arts*
Paris, 1935
"Le Dessin français dans les collections du XVIIIe siècle," *Gazette des Beaux-Arts*
Paris, 1937
"Chefs d'oeuvre de l'art français," Palais National des Arts
Paris, 1939
"Les Chefs d'oeuvre du Musée de Montpellier," Musée de l'Orangerie
Paris, 1943
"Jardins de France," Galerie Charpentier
Paris, 1943
"Le Portrait français," Galerie René Drouin
Paris, 1946
"Chefs d'oeuvre de la peinture française du Louvre," Musée du Petit Palais
Paris, 1946
"Les Chefs d'oeuvre des collections privées françaises retrouvés en Allemagne," Musée de l'Orangerie
Paris, 1946
"Les Goncourt et leur temps," Musée des Arts Décoratifs
Paris, 1948
"La Douceur de vivre," Galerie Bernheim Jeune

599

Paris, 1950
"Cent Cinquante Chefs d'oeuvre de l'Albertina de Vienne," Bibliothèque Nationale
Paris, 1950
"Chefs d'oeuvre des collections parisiennes," Musée Carnavalet (Catalogue by J. Wilhelm)
Paris, 1950
"Le Dessin français de Fouquet à Cézanne," Musée de l'Orangerie
Paris, 1951
"Le Dessin français de Watteau à Prud'hon," Galerie Cailleux
Paris, 1951
"Plaisir de France," Galerie Charpentier
Paris, 1952
"Chefs d'oeuvre de la collection D. G. van Beuningen," Musée du Petit Palais
Paris, 1952
"Musée Boymans de Rotterdam: Dessins du XVᵉ au XIXᵉ siècle," Bibliothèque Nationale
Paris, 1953
"Chefs d'oeuvre du musée d'art de São Paulo," Musée de l'Orangerie
Paris, 1953
"Figures nues de l'école française," Galerie Charpentier
Paris, 1953
"Monticelli et le baroque provençal," Musée de l'Orangerie
Paris, 1954
"Le Nu à travers les âges," Galerie Bernheim Jeune
Paris, 1956
"De Watteau à Prud'hon," *Gazette des Beaux-Arts*
Paris, 1957
"Besançon, le plus ancien musée de France," Musée des Arts Décoratifs
Paris, 1957
"Cent Chefs d'oeuvre de l'art français, 1750–1950," Galerie Charpentier
Paris, 1957–58
"Le Portrait français de Watteau à David," Musée de l'Orangerie
Paris, 1958
"Portraits dans le dessin français du XVIIIᵉ siècle," Cabinet des Dessins, Musée du Louvre
Paris, 1958–59
"De Clouet à Matisse: Dessins français des collections américaines," Musée de l'Orangerie
Paris, 1959
"Dessins de Pierre Paul Rubens," Cabinet des Dessins, Musée du Louvre
Paris, 1960
"Fragonard et les grands maîtres italiens, 1760–1761," Galerie Beauvau (Catalogue by A. Ananoff)
Paris, 1960
"Tableaux de la collection Gulbenkian," Fondation Calouste Gulbenkian
Paris, 1961
"Les Français à Rome," Hôtel de Rohan
Paris, 1962
"Première Exposition des plus beaux dessins du Louvre et de quelques pièces célèbres des collections de Paris," Musée du Louvre
Paris–Amsterdam, 1964
"Le Dessin français de Claude à Cézanne dans les collections hollandaises," Institut Néerlandais; Rijksprentenkabinet, Rijksmuseum
Paris, 1965–66
"Chefs d'oeuvre de la peinture française dans les musées de Leningrad et de Moscou," Musée du Louvre
Paris, 1967
"L'Académie de France à Rome," École des Beaux-Arts

Paris, 1967
"Dessins français du XVIIIᵉ siècle: Amis et contemporains de P.-J. Mariette," Cabinet des Dessins, Musée du Louvre
Paris, 1968
"Édouard Vuillard, K.-X. Roussel," Musée de l'Orangerie
Paris, 1969
"Hommage à Louis La Caze," Musée du Louvre
Paris, 1971
"François Boucher," Cabinet des Dessins, Musée du Louvre
Paris, 1973
"Autour du Néoclassicisme," Galerie Cailleux
Paris, 1974
"Louis XV: Un Moment de perfection de l'art français," Hôtel de la Monnaie
Paris, 1974
• "Tableaux de Fragonard et meubles de Cressent," Musée du Louvre (*Petit Journal des grandes expositions*, no. 10)
Paris, 1974–75
"Dessins du Musée Atger de Montpellier," Cabinet des Dessins, Musée du Louvre
Paris, 1974–75
"Le Néoclassicisme français: Dessins des musées de province," Galeries du Grand Palais
Paris–Detroit–New York, 1974–75
"De David à Delacroix: La Peinture française de 1774 à 1830; French Painting, 1774–1830: The Age of Revolution," Galeries du Grand Palais; The Detroit Institute of Arts; The Metropolitan Museum of Art
Paris, 1976
"Dessins français de l'Art Institute de Chicago: De Watteau à Picasso," Cabinet des Dessins, Musée du Louvre
Paris, 1976–77
"L'Amérique vue par l'Europe," Galeries du Grand Palais
Paris, 1977
"La Collection Armand Hammer," Musée Jacquemart-André
Paris, 1978
"Défense du patrimoine national," Musée du Louvre
Paris–Geneva, 1978–79
"Sanguines," Galerie Cailleux
Paris, 1979
"Un Album de croquis d'Hubert Robert," Galerie Cailleux
Paris, 1979
"Ch. de Wailly," Caisse Nationale des Monuments Historiques
Paris, 1980–81
"Cinq Années d'enrichissement du patrimoine national, 1975–80," Galeries du Grand Palais
Paris, 1980–81
"Des Monts et des eaux: Paysages, 1715–1850," Galerie Cailleux
Paris, 1981
"La Rue de Varenne," Musée Rodin
Paris, 1981
"Collection Thyssen-Bornemisza: Maîtres anciens," Musée du Petit Palais
Paris, 1983
"Dessins français conservés à la Bibliothèque de l'École Polytechnique," Maison des Polytechniciens
Paris, 1983
"Raphaël et l'art français," Galeries du Grand Palais
Paris, 1983
"Rome, 1760–1770: Fragonard, Hubert Robert, et leurs amis," Galerie Cailleux
Paris, 1984
"Acquisitions du Cabinet des Dessins, 1973–

1983," Cabinet des Dessins, Musée du Louvre
Paris, 1984
"La Donation Kaufmann et Schlageter au département des Peintures," Musée du Louvre (Catalogue by P. Rosenberg)
Paris, 1984–85
"Diderot et l'art de Boucher à David," Hôtel de la Monnaie
Paris, 1985
"Graveurs français de la seconde moitié du XVIIIᵉ siècle," Cabinet des Dessins, Collection E. de Rothschild, Musée du Louvre
Paris, 1985
"Oeuvres de jeunesse, de Watteau à Ingres," Galerie Cailleux
Paris, 1986
"Les Concours d'esquisses peintes, 1816–1863," École des Beaux-Arts
Paris, 1986–87
"La France et la Russie au siècle des Lumières," Galeries du Grand Palais
Paris–Detroit–New York, 1986–87
"François Boucher, 1703–1770," Galeries du Grand Palais; The Detroit Institute of Arts; The Metropolitan Museum of Art
Philadelphia, 1950–51
"Masterpieces of Drawing," Philadelphia Museum of Art
Philadelphia, 1985
"Eighteenth Century French Book Illustration: Drawings by Fragonard and Gravelot from the Rosenbach Museum and Library," The Rosenbach Museum and Library
Pittsburgh, 1951
"French Painting, 1100–1900," Carnegie Institute
Pont-Aven, 1983
"Cent Dessins des Musées de Quimper," Musée de Pont-Aven
Portland, Ore., 1956
"Paintings from the Collection of Walter P. Chrysler, Jr.," Portland Art Museum
Princeton, 1977
"Eighteenth-Century French Life-Drawing," The Art Museum
Providence, 1975
"Rubenism," Museum of Art, Rhode Island School of Design

Rennes–Dijon–Chambéry–Saint-Étienne–Avignon, 1964–65
"Peintures françaises du XVIIIᵉ siècle au Musée du Louvre."
Richmond, 1981
"Three Masters of Landscape: Fragonard, Robert, and Boucher," The Virginia Museum of Fine Arts
Rome, 1959
"Il Settecento a Roma," Palazzo delle Esposizioni
Rome, 1959–60
"Il disegno francese da Fouquet a Toulouse-Lautrec," Palazzo Venezia
Rome–Turin, 1961
"L'Italia vista dai pittori francesi del XVIII e XIX secolo," Palazzo delle Esposizioni; Galleria Civica d'Arte Moderna (Catalogue cited is the Turin edition)
Rome, 1962
"Il ritratto francese da Clouet a Degas," Palazzo Venezia
Rome, 1980
"Ville e paese," Palazzo Venezia
Rome, 1981–82
"David e Roma," Académie de France à Rome, Villa Medici
Rome–Dijon, 1983
"Bénigne Gagneraux," Galleria Borghese; Musée des Beaux-Arts

Rotterdam, 1957
"Tekeningen van Europese meesters in het Museum Boymans te Rotterdam," Museum Boymans-van Beuningen
Rotterdam–Brunswick, 1983–84
"Schilderkunst uit de eerste hand: Olieverfschetsen van Tintoretto tot Goya; Malerei aus erster Hand: Ölskizzen von Tintoretto bis Goya," Museum Boymans-van Beuningen; Herzog Anton Ulrich-Museum
Rouen, 1970
"Choix de dessins anciens," Bibliothèque Municipale

Sacramento, 1940
"Three Centuries of Landscape Drawing," E. B. Crocker Art Gallery
Saint-Paul-de-Vence, 1973
"André Malraux," Fondation Maeght
Saint Petersburg, Fla., 1982–83
"Fragonard and His Friends: Changing Ideals in Eighteenth Century Art" (Catalogue by M. L. Grayson)
San Francisco, 1934
"French Painting from the Fifteenth Century to the Present Day," California Palace of the Legion of Honor
San Francisco, 1949
"Rococo Masterpieces of Eighteenth-Century French Art from the Museums of France," California Palace of the Legion of Honor
Shanghai, 1982
"250 Years (1620–1870) of French Painting."
South Bend, Ind., 1972
"Eighteenth Century France: A Study of Its Art and Civilization," The South Bend Art Center
Stockholm 1958
"Fem seckler fransk Konst," Nationalmuseum
Sydney, 1980–81
"French Painting: The Revolutionary Decades, 1760–1830," Art Gallery of New South Wales

Tokyo, 1978
"European Landscape Paintings," National Museum of Western Art
Tokyo–Kyoto, 1980
• "Fragonard," National Museum of Western Art; Municipal Museum (Catalogue by D. Sutton)

Tokyo, 1982
"Masterpieces from the Petit Palais," Idemitsu Art Gallery
Tokyo–Yamaguchi–Nagoya–Kamakura, 1983–84
"Exhibition of XVIIth–XIXth Century French Painting," Isetan Museum; Yamaguchi Prefectural Museum; Aïchi Cultural Center; Kanagawa Prefectural Museum of Modern Art
Toledo–Chicago–Ottawa, 1975–76
"The Age of Louis XV: French Painting, 1710–1774," The Toledo Museum of Art; The Art Institute of Chicago; The National Gallery of Canada
Toronto–Ottawa–San Francisco–New York, 1972–73
"Dessins français des XVIIᵉ et XVIIIᵉ siècles des collections américaines; French Master Drawings of the 17th and 18th Centuries in North American Collections," Art Gallery of Toronto; The National Gallery of Canada; California Palace of the Legion of Honor; New York Cultural Center (Catalogue by P. Rosenberg)
Toulon, 1985
"La Peinture en Provence," Musée de Toulon
Toulouse, 1951
"Les Graveurs en taille-douce de 1600 à 1800," Musée Paul-Dupuy
Toulouse, 1954
"Le Dessin toulousain de 1730 à 1800," Musée Paul-Dupuy
Troyes–Nîmes–Rome, 1977
"Charles-Joseph Natoire," Musée des Beaux-Arts; Musée des Beaux-Arts; Villa Medici

Versailles, 1981
"Dessins français XVIIIᵉ et XIXᵉ siècles du Musée Lambinet et de la Bibliothèque Municipale de Versailles," Musée Lambinet
Vichy, 1941
"Dessins, gravures, et pastels de maîtres français du XVIIIᵉ siècle," Galerie Sévigné
Vienna, 1950
"Meisterwerke aus Frankreichs Museen," Graphische Sammlung Albertina
Vienna, 1966
"Kunst und Geist Frankreichs im 18. Jahrhundert," Österreichische Galerie im Oberen Belvedere
Vienna, 1967
"Meisterzeichnungen aus den Museum der schönen Kunste in Budapest," Graphische Sammlung Albertina
Vienna, 1969
"200. Jahre Albertina," Graphische Sammlung Albertina

Washington, D.C., 1950
"European Paintings from the Gulbenkian Collection," National Gallery of Art
Washington, D.C.–Cleveland–Saint Louis–Cambridge, Mass.–New York, 1952–53
"French Drawings: Masterpieces from Five Centuries," National Gallery of Art; The Cleveland Museum of Art; City Art Museum; Fogg Art Museum; The Metropolitan Museum of Art
Washington, D.C.–Detroit–Los Angeles, 1975–76
"Master Paintings from the Hermitage and the State Russian Museum, Leningrad," National Gallery of Art; The Detroit Institute of Arts; Los Angeles County Museum of Art
Washington, D.C., 1978
• "Drawings by Fragonard in North American Collections," National Gallery of Art (Catalogue by E. Williams)
Washington, D.C., 1978
"Hubert Robert: Drawings and Watercolors," National Gallery of Art
Washington, D.C., 1978
"Master Drawings from the Collection of the National Gallery of Art," National Gallery of Art
Washington, D.C., and other cities, 1981
"French Master Drawings from the Rouen Museums: From Caron to Delacroix," National Gallery of Art
Washington, D.C., 1982
"Eighteenth-Century Drawings from the Collection of Mrs. Gertrude Laughlin Chanler," National Gallery of Art (Catalogue by M. Morgan Grasselli)
Washington, D.C.–New York, 1984–85
"Old Master Drawings from the Albertina," National Gallery of Art; The Pierpont Morgan Library
Williamstown, 1964
"Portrait of a Man (The Warrior), Jean-Honoré Fragonard," The Sterling and Francine Clark Art Institute (Catalogue by Ch. Sterling)

Zurich, 1955
"Schönheit des 18. Jahrhunderts," Kunsthaus

Bibliography

This selected bibliography includes only those works referred to in the catalogue. A small dot precedes the most important sources.

A

A. *See* Ananoff, A. 1961–70.

Aaron, D. *Dessins insolites du XVIIIe siècle français.* Lausanne, 1985.

Abécédario. See Mariette, P.-J.

Adhémar, J. "Lettres adressées aux Goncourt concernant les Beaux-Arts, conservées à la Bibliothèque Nationale." *Gazette des Beaux-Arts,* Nov. 1968, pp. 229–36.

Adhémar, J., and J. Lethève. *Inventaire du fonds français: Graveurs après 1800.* Vol. VIII. Paris, Bibliothèque Nationale, Cabinet des Estampes, 1954.

Adhémar, J., and J. Seznec. *See* Seznec, J., and J. Adhémar.

Alauzen, A. *La Peinture en Provence.* Marseilles, 1962.

Alexandre, A. "La Collection Henri Rouart." *Les Arts,* no. 132 (Dec. 1912), pp. 2–32.

Alexeyeva, V., and N. Vodo. *See* Pushkin Museum, Moscow. 1977.

Alfasa, P. "L'Exposition Fragonard." *La Revue de Paris,* July 1, 1921, pp. 190–200.

Algoud, H. "Marguerite Gérard au Musée Fragonard de Grasse." *Revue de l'art ancien et moderne* 70 (1936), pp. 239–46.

———. *Fragonard.* Monaco, 1941.

Allemagne, H. R. d'. *Récréations et passe-temps.* Paris [1905].

———. *Histoire des jouets.* Paris, n.d.

Alvin-Beaumont, V. "Jean-Honoré Fragonard: La Vérité sur la *Bonne Mère.*" *Le Pedigree: Erreur et vérité en art,* July 1913, pp. 25–31.

———. "La *Bonne Mère* de Fragonard." *Le Temps,* Dec. 1, 1913, p. 5.

Ananoff, A. "Des révélations sensationnelles sur Fragonard." *Connaissance des arts,* no. 54 (Aug. 1956), pp. 38–43.

———. "Comment dessinait Fragonard." *Jardin des arts,* no. 33 (July 1957), pp. 515–22.

———. "Identification de deux dessins de Fragonard ayant figuré au Salon de 1765." *Gazette des Beaux-Arts,* Jan. 1959, pp. 61–63.

———. "La Réalité du voyage de Fragonard aux Pays-Bas." *Bulletin de la Société de l'Histoire de l'Art Français* 1959 (1960), pp. 15–22.

———. "Différentes séries de dessins exécutés par Fragonard pour les 'contes' de La Fontaine." *Bulletin de la Société de l'Histoire de l'Art Français* 1960 (1961), pp. 7–17.

———. "La Technique des dessins de Fragonard." *La Vitrine* 1961, pp. 8–15.

———. "En authentifiant ses dessins...." *Connaissance des arts,* no. 113 (July 1961), pp. 49–55.

• ———. *L'Oeuvre dessiné de Jean-Honoré Fragonard.* 4 vols. Paris, 1961–70.

———. "Alexandre-Evariste Fragonard et son père."

Bulletin de la Société de l'Histoire de l'Art Français 1961 (1962), pp. 155–57.

———. "Identification d'un personnage représenté sur un dessin de Fragonard." *Bulletin de la Société de l'Histoire de l'Art Français* 1961 (1962), pp. 153–54.

———. "Fragonard et Ango, collaborateurs de Saint-Non." *Bulletin de la Société de l'Histoire de l'Art Français* 1962 (1963), pp. 117–20.

———. "Deux Peintures inédites de Jean-Honoré Fragonard." *Bulletin de la Société de l'Histoire de l'Art Français* 1964 (1965), pp. 113–14.

———. "Attributions et identifications nouvelles de quelques dessins de François Boucher et de Gabriel de Saint-Aubin." *Bulletin de la Société de l'Histoire de l'Art Français* 1965 (1966), pp. 169–76.

———. "Identification d'un dessin de Saint-Non." *Bulletin de la Société de l'Histoire de l'Art Français* 1967 (1968), pp. 137–39.

———. "Drawings by J. H. Fragonard for *Jerusalem Delivered.*" *Connoisseur,* no. 671 (Jan. 1968), pp. 12–16.

———. "Effets d'aquarelle et de gouache." *Connaissance des arts,* no. 197–98 (July–Aug. 1968), pp. 96–103.

———. "*Mosieur Fanfan:* Découverte d'une nouvelle gravure." *Gazette des Beaux-Arts,* Mar. 1971, pp. 179–82.

———. "Propos sur les peintures de Marguerite Gérard." *Gazette des Beaux-Arts,* Dec. 1979, pp. 211–18.

———. "Bergeret, son hôtel de la rue du Temple et sa troisième femme." *Gazette des Beaux-Arts,* July–Aug. 1983, pp. 8–10.

———. "Fragonard: Quelques dessins d'une collection." *L'Estampille,* no. 165 (Jan. 1984), pp. 10–17.

———. "Alexandre-Évariste et Jean-Honoré Fragonard, son père." *L'Œil,* no. 344 (Mar. 1984), pp. 70–75.

Ananoff, A., and D. Wildenstein. *François Boucher.* 2 vols. Lausanne and Paris, 1976.

Andia, B. de. "Les 'Folies' de Paris au XVIIIe siècle." *Médecine de France,* no. 113 (1960), pp. 17–32.

André, E. "Honoré Fragonard." *L'Art décoratif,* July–Dec. 1907, pp. 1–12.

Anonymous. "Chronique." *Revue universelle des arts* 1858, pp. 78–96.

Antonsson, O. *Sergels Ungdom och Romtid.* Stockholm, 1942.

Apollinaire, G. *Fragonard and the United States.* Paris, 1914.

———. "Chroniques d'art." In *Oeuvres complètes.* Paris, 1966.

Aptchinskaïa, N. V. *Fragonard* (in Russian). Moscow, 1982.

Arbaud, L. "Mademoiselle Godefroid." *Gazette des Beaux-Arts,* Jan. 1869, pp. 39–52.

Argé, Ch. d'. "Une Page de l'histoire du Louvre." *Revue des Beaux-Arts* 1858, pp. 247–50, 298–301.

Armand Hammer Collection Exhibitions. Los Angeles, 1982.

Arnason, H. H. *Jean-Antoine Houdon.* Paris, 1975.

Arnaud, O. "Subleyras, 1699 à 1749." In *Les Peintres français du XVIIIe siècle...,* vol. II, pp. 49–92. Paris, 1930.

Asplund, K. *P. A. Hall: Sa Correspondance de famille.* Uppsala, 1955.

Assézat, J., and M. Tourneux. *See* Diderot, D. 1875–77.

Aulanier, Ch. *Histoire du Palais et du Musée du Louvre.* 10 vols. Paris [1947–69].

Aulard, A. "Correspondance: A propos de Fragonard et de Robespierre." *La Révolution française,* Sept. 14, 1900, pp. 278–79.

———. *Paris pendant la réaction thermidorienne et sous le Directoire.* Vol. V. Paris, 1902.

Auvray, I. *See* Bellier de la Chavignerie, E., and L. Auvray.

Axilette, J. A. "François Casanova: Sa Vie, ses oeuvres." Thesis, École du Louvre, 1929.

B

Bachaumont, L. Petit de. *Mémoires secrets pour servir à l'histoire de la République des Lettres en France depuis 1762 jusqu'à nos jours.* 31 vols. London, 1777–89.

Bachstitz, K. W. *The Bachstitz Gallery Collection.* 3 vols. Berlin [1921].

Bacou, R. *Il settecento francese.* Milan, 1971; French ed. Paris, 1976.

Baetjer, K. *European Paintings in The Metropolitan Museum of Art by Artists Born in or before 1865: A Summary Catalogue.* 3 vols. New York, 1980.

Bailey, C. "Le Marquis de Véri, collectionneur." *Bulletin de la Société de l'Histoire de l'Art Français* 1983 (1985), pp. 67–83.

Baker Collection. *See* Virch, C.

Bapst, G. "Tableaux de Fragonard pour Bellevue." *Nouvelles Archives de l'art français* 8 (1892), p. 126.

Barazzetti, S. "Le 23 août...." *Beaux-Arts,* no. 138 (Aug. 23, 1935), p. 2.

Barbery, B. "L'Enfance de Fragonard: Un Roman des Goncourt." *Mercure de France,* June 1934, pp. 296–315.

———. "Les Origines de Fragonard." *Le Temps,* July 7, 1938; Sept. 14, 1938.

———. "Les Fragonard de Grasse à New York." *Mercure de France* 1949, pp. 21–646.

Barotte, R. "Fragonard au pays de Renoir." *Le Journal des arts,* Sept. 25, 1957.

———. "Au Musée du Louvre: 700 Chefs d'oeuvres redeviennent visibles." *Plaisir de France,* no. 263 (1960), pp. 68–69.

Barzel, Ch. "Le Vrai Fragonard." *Comoedia,* Apr. 27, 1932.

Baudicour, P. de. *Le Peintre-graveur français.* 2 vols. Paris, 1859–61.

Bazin, G. "Fragonard et Gabriel de Saint-Aubin." *L'Amour de l'art,* no. 9 (Sept. 1931), p. 365.

———. *Trésors de la peinture au Louvre.* Paris, 1957; new eds., 1960; 1962.

Bean, J., and L. Turčić. *15th–18th Century French Drawings in The Metropolitan Museum of Art.* New York, 1986.

Beau, M. *La Collection des dessins d'Hubert Robert au Musée de Valence.* Lyons, 1968.

Beaucamp, F. *Le Peintre lillois Jean-Baptiste Wicar (1762–1834).* 2 vols. Lille, 1939.

Beaumont, E. de. "Deux Mobiliers d'autrefois." *Gazette des Beaux-Arts,* Feb. 1872, pp. 129–39.

Bédarida, H. *Parme et la France de 1748 à 1789.* Paris, 1928.

Bellier de la Chavignerie, E. *Les Artistes français du XVIIIᵉ siècle oubliés ou dédaignés.* Paris, 1865. Extracted from *La Revue universelle des arts.*

Bellier de la Chavignerie, E., and L. Auvray. *Dictionnaire général des artistes de l'école française.* 2 vols. 1882–85.

Bellocchi, U., and B. Fava. *L'interpretazione grafica dell'Orlando furioso.* Reggio Emilia, 1961.

Benesch, O. *Meisterzeichnungen der Albertina: Europäische Schulen von der Gotik bis zum Klassizismus.* Salzburg, 1964.

Benoît, A. *L'Histoire de la peinture de toutes les époques et tous les peuples.* Vol. 4. Saint Petersburg, 1912.

Benoît, F. *L'Art français sous la Révolution et l'Empire.* Paris, 1897; reprint, Geneva, 1975.

———. "Quelques tableaux français du Musée de Lille." *Bulletin de la Société de l'Histoire de l'Art Français* 1907, pp. 141–57.

Béraldi, H. *See* Portalis, R., Baron, and H. Béraldi.

Berezina, V. N. *French Painting: Early and Mid-Nineteenth Century.* Moscow and Florence, 1983.

• Bergeret de Grancourt, P. J. O. "Voyage d'Italie." Published with the article by M. A. Tornézy, "Bergeret et Fragonard: Journal inédit d'un voyage en Italie, 1773–1774." *Bulletin et mémoires de la Société des Antiquaires de l'Ouest, 1894,* 17 (1895).

———. *Voyage d'Italie, 1773–1774.* [Abridged ed.]. Introduction and notes by J. Wilhelm. Paris, 1948.

Bernard, Ch. "Le Musée du Louvre s'enrichit." *La Belle France,* Aug. 1946, pp. 40–41.

Bernier, G. *L'Art et l'argent: Le Marché de l'art au XXᵉ siècle.* Paris, 1977.

Besançon. Musée de Besançon. *Catalogue des peintures, dessins, et antiquités,* by J.-F. Lancrenon and A. Castan. 6th ed. Besançon, 1879.

———. *Catalogue des peintures, dessins, et antiquités,* by A. Castan. 7th ed. Besançon, 1886.

———. 1929. *See* Magnin, J.

Betz, J. "Dem völkerverbindenden Genie: Zu einer Apotheose Franklins von Fragonard." *Die BASF,* Mar. 1966, pp. 111–14.

Béziers. Musée des Beaux-Arts. *See* Lugand, J. 1976.

Biebel, F. M. "Fragonard's 'Progress of Love': A Study of Artistic Taste." In *Actes du XIXᵉ Congrès International d'Histoire de l'Art, 1958,* pp. 110–11. Paris, 1959.

• ———. "Fragonard and Madame du Barry." *Gazette des Beaux-Arts,* Oct. 1960, pp. 207–24.

Binai, P. "Printmaking in France, 1700–1800." *Carnegie Magazine* 49, no. 7 (1975), pp. 304–12.

Bizet, R. *La Double Vie de Gérard de Nerval.* Paris, 1928.

Bjurström, P. "Fragonard och Ariosto." *Kontakt med Nationalmuseum* 1976, pp. 15–27.

———. "Drawings by Jean-Honoré Fragonard in Nationalmuseum." *Nationalmuseum Bulletin* (Stockholm) 2, no. 1 (1978), pp. 37–49.

———. *French Drawings: Eighteenth Century. Drawings in Swedish Public Collections, no. 4.* Stockholm, 1982.

Blanc, Ch. *Le Trésor de la curiosité tiré des catalogues de vente.* 2 vols. Paris, 1857.

———. *Histoire des peintres de toutes les écoles depuis la Renaissance jusqu'à nos jours.* Vol. II. Paris, 1862.

Blum, A. "L'Estampe satirique et la caricature en France." *Gazette des Beaux-Arts,* Oct. 1910, pp. 275–92.

Blumenthal Collection. *See* Rubinstein-Bloch, S.

Bocher, E. *Les Gravures françaises du XVIIIᵉ siècle.* Part 5, *Augustin de Saint-Aubin.* Paris, 1879.

Bode, W. *La Galerie de tableaux de M. Rodolphe Kann à Paris.* Vienna, 1900.

———. *Collection R. Kann.* 2 vols. Vienna, 1907.

Boerlin-Brodbeck, Y. *Antoine Watteau und das Theater.* Basel, 1973.

———. "La Figure assise dans un paysage." In *Antoine Watteau (1684–1721): Le Peintre, son temps, et sa légende. Colloque Watteau, 1984,* pp. 163–71. Paris, 1987.

Boisjolin, C. A. Vieilh de. *Biographie universelle des contemporains.* 4 vols. Paris, 1830.

Bon, S. "La Danse et les peintres des fêtes galantes au XVIIIᵉ siècle." *Jardin des arts,* no. 35 (Sept. 1957), pp. 643–50.

Bonnefon, P. "Fragonard et Robespierre." *Bulletin de l'art ancien et moderne,* no. 107 (Aug. 3, 1901), pp. 213–14.

Bonnefoy, Y. *L'Improbable et autres essais.* Paris, 1983.

Boppe, A. "Les Peintres de turcs au XVIIIᵉ siècle." *Gazette des Beaux-Arts,* July 1905, pp. 43–55; and Sept. 1905, pp. 220–30.

———. *Les Peintres du Bosphore au XVIIIᵉ siècle.* Paris, 1911.

Bordeaux, J.-L. *François Le Moyne and His Generation, 1688–1737.* Paris, 1984.

Borenius, T. "The Fragonard Exhibition in Paris." *Burlington Magazine,* no. 221 (Aug. 1921), pp. 94–99.

Bouchard, M.-A. "Une Famille d'artistes français du XVIIIᵉ siècle: Les Gautier d'Agoty." *Mémoires de la Commission des Antiquités du Département de la Côte d'Or* 1937, part 2, pp. 135–40.

Boucher, F. *Fragonard.* [Paris, 1966].

Boucher, F., and Ph. Jaccottet. *Le Dessin français au XVIIIᵉ siècle.* Lausanne, 1952.

Bouchot, H. "Fragonard et l'architecte Pâris." *Revue de l'art ancien et moderne* 19 (Mar. 1906), pp. 203–16.

Bouchot-Saupique, J. "Tiepolo—Goya." *Cahiers de Bordeaux* 1956, pp. 15–18.

———. "Les Miniatures et émaux de la collection David-Weill." *Jardin des arts,* no. 26 (Dec. 1956), pp. 114–19.

Boudet, M. "Le Château de Crécy et la salle La Caze." *Mémoires de la Société Archéologique d'Eure-et-Loir* 16 (1936), pp. 89–118.

Bouleau, Ch. *Charpentes: La Géométrie secrète des peintres.* Paris, 1963.

Boulenger, M. "La Maison de Fragonard à Grasse." *Le Figaro,* May 10, 1914.

Bourcard, G. *Les Estampes du XVIIIᵉ siècle, école française: Guide-manuel de l'amateur.* Paris, 1885.

Bourland-Collin, S. *Donation Maurice et Pauline Feuillet de Borsat.* Marseilles, 1969.

Boutillier du Retail, M.-A. "Un Fragonard à Troyes." *Annuaire administratif, statistique, et commercial du département de l'Aube* 1913, pp. 19–24.

Bouvy, E. "L'Abbé de Saint-Non." *L'Amateur d'estampes* 1928, pp. 65–72.

Bouyer, R. "Les Expositions: De Fragonard à Boudin." *Bulletin de l'art ancien et moderne,* no. 734 (Jan. 1927), pp. 18–25.

Boyer, F. "Les Collections et les ventes de Jean-Joseph de Laborde." *Bulletin de la Société de l'Histoire de l'Art Français* 1961 (1962), pp. 137–52.

———. "Les Collections de François de Laborde-Méréville (1761–1802)." *Bulletin de la Société de l'Histoire de l'Art Français* 1967 (1968), pp. 141–52.

Boymans-van Beuningen Museum, Rotterdam. *See* Haverkamp-Begemann, E. 1957.

Brejon de Lavergnée, B. *See* Rosenberg, P., and B. Brejon de Lavergnée.

Brière, G. "Catalogue critique des oeuvres d'artistes français réunies à l'exposition de cent portraits de femmes du XVIIIᵉ siècle, ouverte à la salle du Jeu de Paume des Tuileries (avril–juillet 1909)." *Bulletin de la Société de l'Histoire de l'Art Français* 1909, pp. 118–44.

———. "Le Peintre J.-L. Barbier et les conquêtes artistiques en Belgique (1794)." *Bulletin de la Société de l'Histoire de l'Art Français* 1920, pp. 204–10.

———. 1924. *See* Musée du Louvre, Paris, 1924.

———. "L'Exposition des chefs-d'oeuvre des musées de province." *Bulletin de la Société de l'Histoire de l'Art Français* 1931, pp. 189–217.

———. "Deux Vues de Paris identifiées." *Société d'Iconographie Parisienne* 1932, pp. 69–72.

———. "L'Art français du XVIIIᵉ siècle dans les musées des États-Unis." *Musées de France,* suppl. 1949, pp. 16–27.

Brière-Misme, C. "La Résurrection de la salle à manger de Louis XV au Petit Trianon." *Bulletin de la Société de l'Histoire de l'Art Français* 1967 (1968), pp. 217–40.

Briganti, G. *Les Peintres de "Vedute."* Paris, 1971.

Brinton, Ch. *Modern Artists.* New York, 1908.

Brizard, Abbé G. "Analyse du *Voyage Pittoresque de Naples et de Sicile.*" *Mercure de France,* Feb. 1787

———. *Notice sur Jean Claude Richard de Saint-Non.* Paris, 1792; reprint, Geneva, 1973, with the "Analyse . . ." of 1787.

Broglie, G. de. *Madame de Genlis.* Paris, 1985.

Brookner, A. "French Painting at the Royal Academy." *Connoisseur,* no. 543 (Mar. 1955), pp. 40–44.

———. "French Pictures at Waddesdon." *Burlington Magazine,* no. 676 (July–Aug. 1959), pp. 271–73.

———. "*The Paintings of Fragonard,* by Georges Wildenstein." *Burlington Magazine,* no. 696 (Mar. 1961), pp. 111–12.

———. "Current and Forthcoming Exhibitions." *Burlington Magazine,* no. 709 (Apr. 1962), pp. 170–77.

Brosses, Ch. de. *Lettres familières sur l'Italie.* Edited by Y. Bézard. 2 vols. Paris, 1931.

Brouwer, J.-W. "Jean-Honoré Fragonard." *Tableau,* Feb. 1982, pp. 341–45.

Brown, C. *Mercury and Argus,* by Carel Fabritius: A Newly Discovered Painting." *Burlington Magazine,* no. 1004 (Nov. 1986), pp. 797–99.

Brown, R. "Fragonard's *Mademoiselle Colombe as Venus.*" *Los Angeles County Museum Bulletin* 9, no. 1 (1957), pp. 3–5.

Bruand, Y. "Un Grand Collectionneur marchand et graveur du XVIIIᵉ siècle, Gabriel Huquier (1695–1772)." *Gazette des Beaux-Arts,* July–Sept. 1950, pp. 99–114.

Bruand, Y., and M. Hébert. *Inventaire du fonds français: Graveurs du XVIIIᵉ siècle.* Vol. XI. Paris, Bibliothèque Nationale, Cabinet des Estampes, 1970.

Brunon-Guardia, G. "L'Exposition Fragonard." *Beaux-Arts,* no. 5 (1931), p. 9.

Bryson, N. *Word and Image: French Painting of the Ancien Régime.* Cambridge, Eng., 1981.

Bukdahl, E. M. *Diderot, critique d'art.* 2 vols. Copenhagen, 1980–82.

Bulletin de la Société Fragonard à Grasse. Exercice, 1925–26. Cannes, 1926.

Bulletin de la Société Historique d'Auteuil et Passy 7, no. 2 (1910), p. 40.

Bulletin du bi-centenaire de Jean-Honoré Fragonard à Grasse, 1732–1932. Cannes, 1932.

Bürger, W. [Th. Thoré]. *See* Thoré, Th.

Burollet, Th. *Musée Cognacq-Jay: Peintures et dessins.* Paris, 1980.

Burty, Ph. *Eaux-fortes de Jules de Goncourt.* Paris, 1876.

———. "Profils d'amateurs." Part 1, "Laurent Laperlier." *L'Art* 1879, pp. 147–51.

C

Cabanne, P. "Fragonard: Le Plaisir de vivre." *Lecture pour tous,* Aug. 1958, pp. 54–59.

Cailleux, J. *See* Cayeux, J. de.

Cailleux (galerie). *See* Galerie Cailleux, Paris.

Cain, G. "La Maison de Fragonard à Grasse." *Le Figaro,* May 10, 1914, p. 1.

Cambry (citoyen). *Description du département de l'Oise.* 2 vols. 1803.

Cannon-Brookes, P. "The World as Illusion: Fragonard in Japan." *Apollo,* June 1980, p. 471.

Cantarel-Besson, Y. *La Naissance du Musée du Louvre.* 2 vols. Paris, 1981.

Cardinal, C. *Catalogue des montres du Musée du Louvre.* Vol. I, *La Collection Olivier.* Paris, 1984.

Cariou, A. *See* Quimper. Musée des Beaux-Arts. 1985.

Carlson, V. *See* exhibitions, Baltimore–Boston–Minneapolis, 1984–85.

Carmontelle, L. *La Patte de velours.* Paris, 1781.

Carotti, J. *See* Chambéry. Musée de Chambéry.

Carpenter, R. B. "The Dutch Sources of the Art of J.-H. Fragonard." Ph.D. diss., Harvard University, 1955.

———. "G. Wildenstein, *The Paintings of Fragonard* (Complete Edition) (book review)." *Art Bulletin* 44 (Dec. 1962), pp. 358–62.

Carritt, D. *See* exhibitions, London, Artemis, 1978.

Castan, A. 1879. *See* Besançon. Musée de Besançon. 1879.

———. 1886. *See* Besançon. Musée de Besançon. 1886.

———. "Bibliothèque de la ville de Besançon: Inventaire des richesses d'art de cet établissement." In *Inventaire des richesses d'art de la France,* vol. II. Paris, 1887.

Caste, L. "Provansal et sa famille." *Mémoires de l'Institut Historique de Provence* 14 (Jan.–June 1937), pp. 58–106.

———. "Les Origines de Fragonard." *Le Temps,* June 8, 1938.

Catton-Rich, D. "French School." In *European Paintings in the Collection of the Worcester Art Museum.* Worcester, Mass., 1974.

Cayeux, J. de [J. Cailleux, pseud.]. "Le Pavillon de Madame du Barry à Louveciennes." Thesis, Paris, 1933.

———. "Le Pavillon de Madame du Barry à Louveciennes et son architecte C.-N. Ledoux." *Revue de l'art ancien et moderne* 67 (Jan.–May 1935), pp. 213–24; 68 (June 1935), pp. 35–48.

———. "Fragonard as Painter of the Colombe Sisters." *Burlington Magazine,* no. 690, supp. no. 4 (Sept. 1960), pp. i–ix.

———. "New Facts about Fragonard and the Colombe Sisters." *Burlington Magazine,* no. 694, supp. no. 6 (Jan. 1961), pp. i–iii.

———. "A Note on the Pedigree of Paintings and Drawings." *Burlington Magazine,* no. 714, supp. no. 12 (Sept. 1962), pp. i–iii.

———. "Introduction au catalogue critique des *Griffonis* de Saint-Non." *Bulletin de la Société de l'Histoire de l'Art Français* 1963 (1964), pp. 297–384.

———. "Dessins d'Hubert Robert." *Revue de l'art,* no. 7 (1970), pp. 100–103.

———. "Les Artistes français du XVIIIᵉ siècle et Rembrandt." In *Études d'art français offertes à Charles Sterling,* pp. 287–305. Paris, 1975.

———. 1978. *See* exhibitions, Paris-Geneva, 1978–79.

———. 1983. *See* exhibitions, Paris, 1983.

———. *Les Hubert Robert de la collection Veyrenc au Musée de Valence.* Valence, 1985.

Caylus, Comte de. 1802. *See* Sérieys, A.

———. 1877. *See* Nisard, Ch.

Cervinara collection. *See* Lavagnino, E.

Chambéry. Musée de Chambéry. *Catalogue raisonné,* by Jules Carotti. Chambéry, 1911.

Champeaux, A. de. "L'Art décoratif dans le vieux Paris." *Gazette des Beaux-Arts,* Nov. 1890, pp. 394–415; Dec. 1890, pp. 467–92; Sept. 1891, pp. 252–64; Sept. 1892, pp. 218–39; Sept. 1893, pp. 238–47; Sept. 1895, pp. 187–200; Nov. 1895, pp. 401–16.

———. *L'Art décoratif dans le vieux Paris.* Paris, 1898.

Charavay, E. *Inventaire des autographes et documents historiques réunis par M. Benjamin Fillon.* Vol. II. Paris, 1879.

Charensol, G. "Fragonard." *Médecines-peintures,* no. 79 (n.d.).

Châtelet, A., and J. Thuillier. *La Peinture française de Le Nain à Fragonard.* Geneva, 1964.

[Chaussard, P.]. *Le Pausanias français: État des arts du dessin en France à l'ouverture du XIXᵉ siècle: Salon de 1806.* Paris, 1806.

Chennevières, H. de. "Silhouettes de collectionneurs: M. Eudoxe Marcille." *Gazette des Beaux-Arts,* Sept. 1890, pp. 217–35; Oct. 1890, pp. 296–310.

Chennevières, Ph. de. 1851–60. *See* Mariette, P.-J.

———. *Les Dessins de maîtres anciens exposés à l'École des Beaux-Arts en 1879.* Paris, 1880.

———. "Une Collection de dessins d'artistes français," part 19. *L'Artiste* 13 (1897), pp. 175–85. For the index, *see* Prat, L. A.

Chipon, M. "Le Cabinet Adrien Pâris à l'exposition rétrospective de Besançon." *L'Art,* Apr.–July 1906, pp. 1–34.

Choppin de Janvry, O. *Le Pavillon chinois de Cassan à l'Isle-Adam.* Paris, 1975.

Cioranescu, A. *L'Arioste en France des origines à la fin du XVIIIᵉ siècle.* 2 vols. Paris, 1939.

Claparède, J. *Les Dessins de Tiepolo et de Fragonard du Musée Atger de la Faculté de Médecine de Montpellier.* Journées médicales de Montpellier. Toulouse [1955].

Clapp, F. M. "The Du Barry Fragonards in the Frick Collection" (Summary). *Actes du XIIIᵉ Congrès International d'Histoire de l'Art* 1933, pp. 182–83.

Claudel, P. *L'Œil écoute.* Paris, 1946.

Clay, J. *Le Romantisme.* Paris, 1980.

Clay, M. "L'Épopée des Wildenstein." *Réalités,* no. 158 (Mar. 1959), pp. 77–83, 102.

Clément de Ris, L. "Troisième Exposition de l'Association des Artistes." *L'Artiste,* Jan. 30, 1848, pp. 193–96.

———. *Les Musées de province: Histoire et description.* 2d ed. Paris, 1872.

Clément-Janin, N. "Les Fragonard de Grasse et leur graveur." *La Renaissance de l'art français,* no. 3 (Mar. 1922), pp. 136–40.

Cochin, Ch.-N. *Voyage pittoresque d'Italie; ou, Recueil de notes sur les ouvrages de peinture et de sculpture qu'on voit dans les principales villes d'Italie.* Paris, 1756.

———. *Voyage d'Italie; ou, Recueil de notes....* 3 vols. Paris, 1758; reprint, Geneva, 1972.

———. *Essai sur la vie de M. Deshays.* Paris, 1765; new ed. Paris, 1977.

———. "Lettres inédites de Charles-Nicolas Cochin." Edited by Du Broc de Segange. *L'Art et l'archéologie en province* 1849, pp. 1–6, 47–51, 61–66. *See also* Locquin, J. 1914.

Coffin, D. R. *The Villa d'Este at Tivoli.* Princeton, 1960.

Cohen, H. *Guide de l'amateur de livres à vignettes et à figures.* 4th ed. Edited by C. Mehl. Paris, 1880.

———. *Guide de l'amateur de livres à gravures du XVIIIᵉ siècle.* 2 vols. 6th rev. ed. Edited by S. de Ricci. Paris, 1912.

Colette. *En camarade.* 1919; reissued in *Oeuvres complètes.* Paris, 1973.

Collé, C. *Journal et mémoires de Charles Collé (1748–1772).* Edited by H. Bonhomme. 3 vols. Paris, 1868.

Colombier, P. du. "Nouvelle jeunesse pour Fragonard." *Connaissance des arts,* no. 120 (Feb. 1962), pp. 66–73.

Compin, I. *See* Rosenberg, P., and I. Compin.

Conisbee, Ph. "*Gabriel François Doyen, 1726–1806,* by Marc Sandoz; *Fragonard,* by David Wakefield" (book review). *Burlington Magazine,* no. 892 (1977), pp. 511–12.

———. *Painting in Eighteenth-Century France.* Oxford, 1981.

———. "London and Paris: French Artists at Home and Abroad." *Burlington Magazine,* no. 1000 (July 1986), pp. 532–34.

Coolus, R. "Fragonard et son élève." *Opéra,* Mar. 27, 1946, pp. 1, 7.

Cooper, D. *Great Private Collections.* London, 1963. French translation, *Les Grandes Collections privées.* Paris, 1963. Includes an article by J. Leymarie.

Cornillot, M.-L. *Collection Pierre-Adrien Pâris, Besançon.* Inventaire général des dessins des musées de province, no. 1. Paris, 1957.

Correspondance des Directeurs de l'Académie de France à Rome. Edited by A. de Montaiglon and Jules Guiffrey. 17 vols. Paris, 1887–1907.

Corvisier, A. *Arts et société dans l'Europe du XVIIIᵉ siècle.* Le Puy, 1978.

Cottin. *See* Moitte, Madame.

Coulon, R. "Dix-neuf Dessins du XVIIIᵉ siècle." *Vie de Bordeaux,* Jan. 29, 1977.

Coulon, R., and J.-M. Cornoy. "Pierre-Jacques Bergeret fils, 1742–1877." *Bulletin et mémoires de la Société Archéologique de Bordeaux,* 1971, 68 (1976), pp. 178–208.

Coupin, M. P. A. *Essai sur J. L. David, peintre d'histoire.* Paris, 1827.

Courajod, L. *L'École royale des élèves protégés.* Paris, 1874.

———. "Objets d'art concédés en jouissance par la Restauration." *Nouvelles Archives de l'art français* 1878, pp. 371–99.

Courboin, F. *La Gravure en France des origines à 1900.* Paris, 1923.

Couturier, M.-A. *La Vérité blessée.* Paris, 1984.

Cresp, A.-H. *La Vie d'un grassois: Fragonard.* Cavaillon, 1984.

Crocker Art Museum, Sacramento, Calif. *Catalogue of Collections,* by F. W. Kent. Sacramento, 1964.

——. *Master Drawings from Sacramento....* Sacramento, 1971.

Crow, T. E. *Painters and Public Life in Eighteenth-Century Paris.* New Haven and London, 1985.

Culot, P. "Dessins et eaux-fortes de la suite des Bacchanales de Jean-Honoré Fragonard." *De Gulden Passer* 52 (1974), pp. 67–68.

Curzon, H. de. *See* Mozart, W. A.

Cuzin, J.-P. "Vincent: De l'Académie de France à l'Institut de France." *Études de la Revue du Louvre,* no. 1 (1980), pp. 93–100.

——. "De Fragonard à Vincent." *Bulletin de la Société de l'Histoire de l'Art Français* 1981 (1983), pp. 103–24.

• ——. "Fragonard dans les musées français: Quelques tableaux reconsidérés ou discutés." *Revue du Louvre,* no. 1 (1986), pp. 58–66.

——. "Vincent reconstitué." *Connaissance des arts,* no. 409 (Mar. 1986), pp. 39–46.

Czwiklitzer, Ch. "Lettres autographes de peintres et sculpteurs." In *Die Handschrift der Maler und Bildhauer.* Basel, 1976.

D

D. and V. *See* Dayot, A., and L. Vaillat. 1907.

Dacier, E. *Catalogues de ventes et livrets de Salons illustrés par Gabriel de Saint-Aubin.* 6 vols. Paris, 1909–21.

——. *L'Oeuvre gravé de Gabriel de Saint-Aubin.* Paris, 1914.

——. *La Gravure de genre et de moeurs.* Paris and Brussels, 1925.

——. "Le Chef-d'oeuvre de l'abbé de Saint-Non." *Revue de l'art ancien et moderne,* June–Dec. 1928, pp. 266–69.

——. *Gabriel de Saint-Aubin.* 2 vols. Paris, 1929–31.

——. "Les Dessins de Fragonard de la collection Henri Béraldi pour les *Contes* de La Fontaine: L'Histoire et la légende." *Bulletin de la Société de l'Histoire de l'Art Français* 1934, pp. 267–79.

——. *Le "Livre de croquis" de Gabriel de Saint-Aubin.* Paris, 1944.

——. "Le *Livre de Croquis* de Gabriel de Saint-Aubin du Cabinet des Dessins." *Revue des Beaux-Arts de France* 9 (Feb.–Mar. 1944), pp. 147–54.

——. "Catalogues de ventes et livrets de Salons illustrés et annotés par Gabriel de Saint-Aubin." Part 12, "Catalogue de la vente Verrier (1776)." *Gazette des Beaux-Arts,* Jan.–June 1953, pp. 297–334.

Daintrey, A. *Fragonard's "Le Billet doux."* London, 1969.

Dalevèze, J. "Trois Maîtres du dessin français du XVIIIᵉ siècle dans la collection Armand Hammer." *L'Œil,* no. 261 (1977), pp. 4–11.

Damécourt, A. "Un Fragonard." *Le Cousin Pons,* Dec. 15, 1916, pp. 141–42.

——. "A propos d'un Fragonard." *Le Cousin Pons,* Mar. 1, 1917, p. 182.

Darras, E. "La Famille Bergeret de l'Isle-Adam et de Trouville (Seine-et-Oise)." *Mémoires de la Société Historique et Archéologique de l'Arrondissement de Pontoise et du Vexin* 1933, pp. 65–92.

Daulte, F. *See* Fosca, F. 1954.

Davenport, B. "A Fragonard Rediscovered." *American Art News,* Mar. 7, 1917, p. 5.

David, P. M. "Fragonard, peintre varois: Sa Vie, ses oeuvres." *Bulletin de la Société des Amis du Vieux Toulon,* no. 57 (Apr. 1938), pp. 69–94.

David-Weill, D., collection. *See* Henriot, G.

Davidson, B. *See* Munhall, E., and B. Davidson.

Dayot. A. *La Peinture française du XVIIIᵉ siècle.* Paris, 1911.

Dayot, A., and L. Vaillat. *L'Oeuvre de J.-B.-S. Chardin et de J.-H. Fragonard.* Paris, 1907.

——. "Fragonard." *L'Art et les artistes* (special issue) 5, no. 27 (June–July 1907), pp. 141–58.

Defrance, L. *Mémoires.* Annotated edition by F. Dehousse and M. Pauchen. Liège, 1980.

Delage, J. *See* Mannlich, Ch. von. 1948.

Delaroche-Vernet, H. "Mémoires inédits sur les Vernet." *Revue de l'art ancien et moderne* 49 (June–Dec. 1923), pp. 223–24.

Delécluze, E.-J. *Louis David: Son École et son temps.* Paris, 1855; new ed. by J.-P. Mouilleseaux, Paris, 1983.

Delteil, L. *Manuel de l'amateur d'estampes du XVIIIᵉ siècle.* Paris, 1910.

——. 1913. *See* Grappe, G. 1913.

Denon, D. Vivant. *Monuments des arts du dessin chez les peuples tant anciens que modernes.* 4 vols. Paris, 1829.

Déon, S. *See* Horsin-Déon, S.

Derschau, J. von. *Sebastiano Ricci.* Heidelberg, 1922.

Desanlis, J. "Jean Claude Richard de Saint-Non." *Bulletin de la Société Archéologique et Historique du Châtillonnais,* no. 2 (1949–50), pp. 2–7.

Dialogues sur la peinture. See Renou, A.

Diderot, D. *Oeuvres complètes de Diderot.* Edited by J. Assézat and M. Tourneux. 20 vols. Paris, 1875–77.

——. *Essais sur la peinture. Oeuvres esthétiques, 1766.* Edited by P. Vernières. Paris, 1959; Paris, 1968.

——. *Correspondance (avril–décembre 1771).* Edited and annotated by G. Roth. Vol. XI. Paris, 1964.

——. *Diderot Salons. See* Seznec, J., and J. Adhémar.

Dilke, Lady. *French Painters of the XVIIIth Century.* 2 vols. London, 1899.

Dimier, L. "Fragonard." *Le Mois littéraire et pittoresque* 1907, pp. 25–38.

——. *Faits et idées de l'histoire des arts.* Paris, 1923.

——. *L'Art français.* Edited by H. Zerner. Paris, 1965.

Discours sur l'origine, les progrès, et l'état actuel de la peinture en France. Paris, 1785.

Doin, J. "Marguerite Gérard, 1761–1837." *Gazette des Beaux-Arts,* Dec. 1912, pp. 429–52.

Dorbec, P. "L'Exposition de la jeunesse au XVIIIᵉ siècle." *Gazette des Beaux-Arts,* July 1905, pp. 77–86.

——. "L'Exposition Fragonard au pavillon de Marsan." *Gazette des Beaux-Arts,* July 1921, pp. 23–32.

Downs, J. "Benjamin Franklin and His Circle." *Bulletin of The Metropolitan Museum of Art* 31, no. 5 (May 1936), pp. 98–104.

Du Broc de Segange. *See* Cochin, Ch.-N. 1849.

Duclaux, L. 1968. *See* Sérullaz, M., L. Duclaux, and G. Monnier.

——. 1974. *See* exhibitions, Paris, 1974–75.

Duguet, R. *Louis David: Les Contemporains.* 1899.

Dulaure, J.-A. *Nouvelle Description des environs de Paris.* Paris, 1786.

Dulwich Picture Gallery, London. *Catalogue of the Collection of Pictures, Bequeathed to Dulwich College by the Late Sir Francis Bourgeois,* by R. Cockburn. London [1816?].

——. *The Dulwich Picture Gallery,* by P. Murray. London, 1980.

Dumolin. "Notes sur le lotissement de la Grange Batelière." *Le Vieux Montmartre,* Sept. 1926, pp. 34–50.

Dumont-Wilden, L. *Le Portrait en France.* Brussels, 1909.

Dumoulin, M. "Honoré Fragonard." *Le Petit Journal,* no. 16 (Apr. 14, 1907), p. 179.

Dunifer, V. "Two Veterans Playing Piquet." *Konsthistorisk tidokrift,* no. 4 (1985), pp. 170–80.

Duparc, F. J. "A *Mercury and Aglauros* Reattributed to Carel Fabritius." *Burlington Magazine,* no. 1004 (Nov. 1986), pp. 799–802.

Duplessis, G. *See* Wille, J.-G.

Durand, Y. *Les Fermiers généraux au XVIIIᵉ siècle.* Paris, 1971.

Duret-Robert, F. "La Vérité derrière *Le Verrou.*" *Connaissance des arts,* no. 274 (Dec. 1974), pp. [5–11].

Duval, A. *Monuments des arts du dessin recueillis par Vivant Denon.* 4 vols. Paris, 1829.

Duvivier, A. "Liste des élèves de l'ancienne école académique et de l'école des Beaux-Arts." *Archives de l'art français* 5 (1857–58), pp. 273–333.

E

Einstein, L. "Looking at French Eighteenth Century Pictures in Washington." *Gazette des Beaux-Arts,* May–June 1956, pp. 213–50.

Eisler, C. *Paintings from the Samuel H. Kress Collection: European Schools Excluding Italian.* London, 1977.

Ellenberger, M. *L'Autre Fragonard.* Paris, 1981.

Engerand, F. *Inventaires des tableaux commandés et achetés par la direction des Bâtiments du Roi (1709–1792).* Paris, 1901.

Erdmann, K. "Peter Paul Rubens *Nessus und Dejanira.*" *Zeitschrift für bildende Kunst* 1929–30, pp. 65–71.

Ergmann, R. "La Collection inédite du Bailli de Breteuil." *Connaissance des arts,* no. 413–14 (July–Aug. 1986), pp. 70–75.

Ernst, S. *See* Yussupov Gallery, Leningrad. 1924.

Errera, I. *Répertoire des peintures datées.* 2 vols. Brussels, 1920–21.

Estignard, A. *A. Pâris: Sa Vie, ses oeuvres, ses collections.* Paris, 1902.

Ethlyne, J. *See* Seligman, G., and J. Ethlyne.

Eudel, P. *L'Hôtel Drouot et la curiosité en 1883.* Paris, 1884.

——. *L'Hôtel Drouot et la curiosité en 1885–86.* Paris, 1887.

——. *L'Hôtel Drouot et la curiosité en 1886–87.* Paris, 1888.

——. *Trucs et truqueurs.* Paris, 1908.

F

Fajol, A. "Fragonard." *Art méridional,* Nov. 1937, pp. 6–9.

Farington, J. *The Farington Diary.* Edited by J. Greig. 8 vols. London, 1923–28.

Farnarier, J. *Contribution à la connaissance de la ville de Grasse.* Vol. II, *La Cathédrale.* Vol. III, *L'Évêché de Grasse.* Grasse, 1981.

Fava, B. *See* Bellocchi, U., and B. Fava.

Fels, F. *Éros, ou l'amour peintre.* Monte Carlo, 1968.

Fenaille, M. *État général des tapisseries de la Manufacture des Gobelins, depuis son origine jusqu'à nos jours (1600–1900).* 6 vols. Paris, 1903–23.

Fenwick, K.-M. *See* Popham, A. E., and K.-M. Fenwick.

Feuillet, M. *Les Dessins d'Honoré Fragonard et d'Hubert Robert des Bibliothèque et Musée de Besançon.* Paris, 1926.

———. "Causerie d'un amateur d'art. Avec Fragonard en Italie." *Le Gaulois artistique,* Dec. 20, 1926, pp. 31–33.

Fichot, Ch. *Statistique monumentale du département de l'Aube Troyes.* Troyes, 1894.

Filangieri di Candida, A. *Gallerie Nazionali italiane.* Vol. V. Rome, 1902.

Florisoone, M. "Les Artistes français en Italie." *Formes,* June 1934, pp. 3–4.

———. *Le Dix-huitième Siècle.* Paris, 1948.

Flynn Johnson, R. *See* Johnson, R. F.

Foerster, C. F. *Jean-Honoré Fragonard.* Berlin [1925].

Fogg Art Museum, Harvard University, Cambridge, Mass. *Drawings in the Fogg Museum of Art,* by A. Mongan and P. J. Sachs. 3 vols. Cambridge, Mass., 1940.

Fontaine, A. *Les Collections de l'Académie Royale de Peinture et de Sculpture.* Paris, 1910; 2d ed. Paris, 1930.

Ford, B. "William Constable, an Enlightened Yorkshire Patron." *Apollo,* June 1974, pp. 408–15.

Fosca, F. *Le Dix-huitième Siècle de Watteau à Tiepolo.* Geneva, 1952.

———. *Les Dessins de Fragonard.* With notes by F. Daulte. Paris and Lausanne, 1954.

Foster, J. J. *A Dictionary of Painters of Miniatures (1525–1850).* London, 1926.

Foucart, J. *See* exhibitions, Lille, 1985.

Foucart Borville, J. "La Notion d'attribution en matière d'oeuvre d'art devant les tribunaux français." *Revue de l'art,* no. 42 (1978), pp. 107–12.

Fourcaud, L. de. "Honoré Fragonard." *Revue de l'art ancien et moderne* 21 (Jan.–June 1907), pp. 5–20, 95–110, 209–28, 287–392.

Fragonard, Th. *See* Valogne, C.

Francastel, P. *Histoire de la peinture française du Moyen-Âge à la fin du XVIIIᵉ siècle.* Vol. I. Paris, 1955; new ed. Paris, 1984.

France, A. *Les Dieux ont soif.* Paris, Mercure de France, 1912.

Francis, H. S. "A Drawing by Jean-Honoré Fragonard." *Bulletin of The Cleveland Museum of Art* 32 (June 1945), p. 88.

———. "Jean-Honoré Fragonard: Morpheus." *Bulletin of The Cleveland Museum of Art* 53 (Mar. 1966), pp. 66–73.

Fraser, A. I. *See* Janson, F., and A. I. Fraser.

Fred, W. *Fragonard.* Berlin, n.d.

Freedberg, D. *Rubens: The Life of Christ after the Passion.* Corpus Rubenianum, Ludwig Burchard, part 7. New York, 1984.

Frick Collection, New York. *See* Munhall, E., and B. Davidson.

Fride, P. "Iconographie de Denis Diderot." Master's thesis, Paris I, 1984–85.

Fried, M. *Absorption and Theatricality: Painting and Beholder in the Age of Diderot.* Berkeley, 1980.

Friedlaender, W. "Fragonard Drawings for Ariosto." *Art Bulletin* 29 (Sept. 1947), pp. 214–15.

Furcy-Raynaud, M. "Correspondance de M. de Marigny avec Coypel, Lépicié, et Cochin." *Nouvelles Archives de l'art français* 19 (1903); 20 (1904).

———. "Correspondance de M. d'Angiviller avec Pierre." *Nouvelles Archives de l'art français* 21 (1905); 22 (1906).

———. "Les Tableaux et objets d'art saisis chez les émigrés et condamnés, et envoyés au muséum central." *Archives de l'art français* 6 (1912), pp. 245–343.

G

G. *See* Goncourt, E. and J. de. 1865.

Gabillot, G. *Hubert Robert et son temps.* Paris, 1895.

Gachons, J. des. "Fragonard." *Je sais tout* 6 (July 15, 1906), pp. 623–30.

Gaehtgens, T. W. "De David à Delacroix: La Peinture française de 1774 à 1830." *Kunst-Chronik,* Feb. 1975, pp. 41–59.

———. 1983. *See* exhibitions, Berlin, 1983.

Gaehtgens, T. W., and J. Lugand. J.-M. Vien monograph. Forthcoming.

Galerie Cailleux, Paris. *Album jubilaire.* Paris, 1962.

Gallet, M. *Ledoux.* Paris, 1980.

Gardey, F. *See* Sjöberg, Y., and F. Gardey.

Gauguet, N. *See* Quimper. Musée des Beaux-Arts. 1873.

Gault de Saint-Germain, P.-M. *Les Trois Siècles de la peinture en France.* Paris, 1808.

———. *Choix des productions de l'art les plus remarquables exposées dans le salon de 1819.* Paris, 1819.

Gautier, Th. "Tableaux de l'école française ancienne." *Le Moniteur universel,* Nov. 16, 1860, pp. 1–2.

———. *Guide de l'amateur au Musée du Louvre.* Paris, 1882.

Gazier, G. "La Salle Adrien Pâris du Musée de Besançon." *La Renaissance de l'art français et des industries de luxe,* no. 1 (Jan. 1920), pp. 11–19.

Geffroy, G. *La Vie artistique.* Vol. VI. Paris, 1900.

———. "Chardin et Fragonard." *Staryé Gody* 1907, pp. 497–508.

Gemäldegalerie, Dresden. *Catalogue of the Royal Picture Gallery in Dresden,* by K. Woermann. 5th ed. Dresden, 1902.

Genlis, Madame de. *See* Maugras, G. *See also* Broglie, G. de.

Georgel, P., and A.-M. Lecoq. *See* exhibitions, Dijon, 1982–83.

Gerson, H. *Ausbreitung und Nachwirkung der holländischen Malerei.* Amsterdam and Haarlem, 1942; reprint, Amsterdam, 1983.

Gerspach. "Prix d'ouvrages de peinture payés par la manufacture des Gobelins au XVIIIᵉ siècle à Fragonard, Tessier, et Jacques." *Nouvelles Archives de l'art français* 4 (1888), pp. 120–21.

Getreau-Abondance, F. "Inventaire des collections publiques: Catalogue raisonné des peintures et dessins de l'école française, Musée Jacquemart-André." Master's thesis, Paris, 1976.

Gide, A. *Journal, 1889–1939.* Paris, 1948; Paris, 1955.

Gillet, L. *See* Musée du Louvre, Paris. 1929.

Gimpel, R. *Journal d'un collectionneur.* Paris, 1963.

Girod de l'Ain, G. *Les Thellusson: Histoire d'une famille.* Neuilly-sur-Seine, 1977.

Girodie, A. *Jean-Frédéric Schall.* Strasbourg, 1927.

Godard, L. "Exposition de peinture: L'École française du dix-huitième siècle au boulevard des Italiens." *Les Beaux-Arts revue nouvelle* 1 (1860), pp. 328–37.

Goldstein, C. "Towards a Definition of Academic Art." *Art Bulletin* 57 (Mar. 1975), pp. 102–9.

Goldyne, J. R. *See* Johnson, R. F., and J. R. Goldyne.

Goncourt, E. de. *La Maison d'un artiste.* 2 vols. Paris, 1881.

———. *La Guimard.* Paris, 1893.

Goncourt, E. and J. de. *Histoire de la société française pendant la Révolution.* Paris, 1854.

———. "Fragonard." Paris, 1865. Republished in *L'Art du XVIIIᵉ siècle,* 1906.

• ———. *Fragonard.* Paris, 1865. With 4 etchings by J. de Goncourt.

• ———. "Fragonard." *Gazette des Beaux-Arts,* Jan. 1865, pp. 32–41; Feb. 1865, pp. 132–62.

———. *L'Art du XVIIIᵉ siècle.* 3 vols. Paris, 1906.

———. *Journal mémoires de la vie littéraire.* 9 vols. Paris, n.d.

Gonse, L. "Honoré Fragonard par M. le baron Roger Portalis." *Gazette des Beaux-Arts,* Jan. 1889, pp. 74–77.

———. *Chefs d'oeuvre des musées de France.* Vol. II, *Sculpture, dessins, objets d'art.* Paris, 1904.

Gordon, K. K. "Madame de Pompadour, Pigalle, and the Iconography of Friendship." *Art Bulletin* 50 (Sept. 1968), pp. 249–62.

Göthe, G. *Johan Tobias Sergel.* Stockholm, 1919.

———. "Nagra mindre kända arbeten av sergel." *Nationalmusei Arsbok* 1919, pp. 59–74.

Graphische Sammlung Albertina, Vienna. *See* Benesch, O.

Grappe, G. H. *Fragonard: Peintre de l'amour au XVIIIᵉ siècle.* 2 vols. Paris, 1913. With the appendix, "Liste des estampes exécutées d'après les oeuvres d'Honoré Fragonard," by L. Delteil.

———. *La Vie de J.-H. Fragonard.* Paris, 1923.

———. *La Vie et l'oeuvre de Fragonard.* Paris, 1929.

———. "L'Abbé de Saint-Non, amateur des arts." *Le Figaro, supplément artistique,* no. 231 (May 2, 1929), pp. 358–59; no. 234 (May 23, 1929), pp. 476–78.

———. "Le Mariage de Fragonard." *L'Illustration,* Dec. 6, 1930. Unpaged.

———. *La Vie de Jean-Honoré Fragonard.* Paris, 1942.

———. *Fragonard: La Vie et l'oeuvre.* Monaco, 1946.

Grayson, M. L. "Fragonard's *La Bonne Mère* and the Symbolism of the Spacious Cradle." *Pharos* 17, no. 2 (Dec. 1980), pp. 20–26.

———. 1982. *See* exhibitions, Saint Petersburg, 1982–83.

Greig, J. *See* Farington, J.

Grenier, R. *La Fiancée de Fragonard.* Paris, 1982.

Grigaut, P. L. "A Realistic Landscape by Fragonard." *Bulletin of The Detroit Institute of Arts* 1 (1948), pp. 14–17.

Grimm. *Correspondance littéraire, philosophique, et critique par Grimm, Diderot, Raynal, Meister, etc.…* Edited by M. Tourneux. 16 vols. Paris, 1877–82.

Gronau, G. "Titian's Ariosto." *Burlington Magazine,* no. 366 (Nov. 1933), pp. 194–203.

Grunchec, Ph. *See* exhibitions, Paris, École des Beaux-Arts, 1986.

Gueorguievskaïa, E. *See* Pushkin Museum, Moscow. 1980.

Guerry-Brion, L. *Fragonard.* Milan, 1952.

Guiffrey, Jean. "L'Exposition Chardin-Fragonard." *Revue de l'art ancien et moderne* 22 (Aug. 1907), pp. 93–106.

———. 1909. *See* Tuetey, A., and Jean Guiffrey.

———. "The Fragonards of the John W. Simpson Collection." *Art in America* 2, no. 1 (Dec. 1913), pp. 29–44.

Guiffrey, Jean, and P. Marcel. *Inventaire général des dessins du Musée du Louvre et du Musée de Versailles.* Vol. I, Paris, 1907; Vol. V, Paris, 1910.

Guiffrey, Jules, 1887–1907. *See Correspondance des Directeurs.*

———. "Le Sculpteur Clodion." *Gazette des Beaux-Arts,* Feb. and May 1893, pp. 164–76, 392–417.

———. "Les Modèles des Gobelins devant le jury des arts en septembre 1794." *Nouvelles Archives de l'art français* 13 (1897), pp. 349–89.

———. *Liste des pensionnaires de l'Académie de France à Rome*. Paris, 1908.

———. "Les Expositions de l'Académie de Saint-Luc et leurs critiques (1751–1774)." *Bulletin de la Société de l'Histoire de l'Art Français* 1910, pp. 77–124.

———. "Inventaire après décès de Clodion (30 avril 1814)." *Archives de l'art français* 6 (1912), pp. 210–44.

Guillaume, M. J. *Procès-Verbaux d'instruction publique de la Convention Nationale*. Vol. III. Paris, 1897; vol. IV, Paris, 1901.

Guillerm, A. "Les Illustrations de Fragonard pour les *Contes* de La Fontaine." *Gazette des Beaux-Arts*, Mar. 1977, pp. 99–106.

Guimbaud, L. *Saint-Non et Fragonard d'après des documents inédits*. Paris, 1928.

———. *Fragonard*. Paris, 1947.

———. "Fragonard: Le Peintre des Grâces." *Jardin des arts*, no. 159 (Feb. 1968), pp. 74–85.

H

H. *See* Hake, A.

Hake, A. "Das Musée Cognacq in Paris." *Pantheon*, Oct. 1929, pp. 434, 438–40.

Hake, H. "Fragonard's *Quatre Bacchanales*." *Apollo*, June 1926, pp. 346–48.

Hall, P.-A. *See* Asplund, K.

Hallam, J. S. "The Two Manners of Boilly." *Art Bulletin* 63 (Dec. 1981), pp. 618–33.

———. "Boilly et Calvet de Lapalun: De la sensibilité chez le peintre et l'amateur." *Bulletin de la Société de l'Histoire de l'Art Français* 1984 (1986), pp. 177–92.

Harcourt, Duc d'. *Guide du château de Champ-de-Bataille*. Paris, n.d.

Harris, M. A. W. "The Abbé de Saint-Non and His Pastel Copy of a Painting by Fragonard." *Apollo*, July 1979, pp. 57–61.

Haskell, F. *Rediscoveries in Art*. New York, 1976. French translation, *La Norme et le caprice*. Paris, 1986.

Hattis, Ph. *Four Centuries of French Drawings in the Fine Arts Museums of San Francisco*. San Francisco, 1977.

Hautecoeur, L. "Les Arts à Naples au XVIIIᵉ siècle." *Gazette des Beaux-Arts*, May 1911, pp. 396–411; Aug. 1911, pp. 156–71.

———. *Le Louvre et les Tuileries de Louis XIV*. Paris, 1927.

———. *Histoire du Louvre … des origines à nos jours, 1200–1928*. Paris, *L'Illustration* [1929?].

Haverkamp-Begemann, E. *Vijf eeuwen tekenkunst: Tekeningen van Europese meesters in het Boymans Museum te Rotterdam*. Rotterdam, 1957.

———. *Drawings from the Clark Art Institute*. 2 vols. New Haven, 1964.

Hébert, M., E. Pognon, and Y. Bruand. *Inventaire du fonds français: Graveurs du XVIIIᵉ siècle*. Vol. X. Paris, Bibliothèque Nationale, Cabinet des Estampes, 1968.

Hébert, M., and Y. Sjöberg. *Inventaire du fonds français: Graveurs du XVIIIᵉ siècle*. Vol. XII. Paris, Bibliothèque Nationale, Cabinet des Estampes, 1973.

Hell, H. "Fragonard: Premier des impressionnistes." *Réalités*, Mar. 1956, pp. 64–71.

Hellman, G. S. "Fragonard's Long Lost Italian Drawings Come to Light." *Art Digest* 6 (Feb. 15, 1932), pp. 21, 32.

Hempel, E. "Fragonard und Robert in ihrer römischen Studienzeit." *Die graphischen Künste* 47, no. 1 (1924), pp. 9–24.

Hennezel, H. d'. *Chambre de commerce de Lyon, Musée Historique des Tissus, Musée des Arts Décoratifs*. Angers, 1938.

Henraux, A. S. "L'Exposition des chefs d'oeuvre des collections françaises retrouvés en Allemagne." *Bulletin des musées de France*, July 1946, pp. 8–9.

Henriot, G. *Collection David Weill*. 3 vols. Paris, 1926–28.

Hercenberg, B. *Nicolas Vleughels, peintre et directeur de l'Académie de France à Rome, 1668–1737*. Paris, 1975.

Herluison, H. *Actes d'état-civil d'artistes français*. Orléans, 1873; reprint, Geneva, 1972.

Hermitage, Leningrad. 1957. *See* Sterling, Ch. 1957.

———. *Katalog zhivopisi* (Catalogue of paintings). Vol. I. Leningrad and Moscow, 1958.

———. 1975. *See* Varshavskaya, M.

———. *Zapadnoevropeĭskaia zhivopis: Katalog; Peinture de l'Europe occidentale: Catalogue* (in Russian, with index of artists and portraits in French). Leningrad, 1976.

———. *Catalogue of Western European Painting: French Painting, Eighteenth Century*, by I. S. Nemilova. Moscow and Florence, 1986. First published in Russian, Leningrad, 1985.

Hérold, J. *Louis-Marin Bonnet (1736–1793): Catalogue de l'oeuvre gravé*. Paris, 1935.

Hiesinger, K. B. "The Sources of François Boucher's Psyche Tapestries." *Bulletin of the Philadelphia Museum of Art* 72 (Nov. 1976), pp. 7–23.

Hind, A. M. *Fragonard, Moreau le Jeune, and French Engravers, Etchers, and Illustrators of the Later XVIII Century*. London, 1913; Paris, 1914.

Hix. "La Galerie La Caze au Louvre." *La Vie parisienne*, Apr. 23, 1870, pp. 330–31.

Hofer, Ph. "Don Quixote and the Illustrators." *Dolphin*, no. 4 (Winter 1941), pp. 135–43.

———. 1945. *See* Mongan, E., Ph. Hofer, and J. Seznec.

Hoffmann, E. "Fragonard at the Louvre." *Burlington Magazine*, no. 855 (June 1974), pp. 354–57.

Hohenzollern, J. G., Prinz von. "Jean-Honoré Fragonard, Mädchen mit Hund." *Weltkunst* 47, no. 5 (1977), p. 393.

Holck Colding, T. *Aspects of Miniature Painting, Its Origins and Developments*. Copenhagen, 1953.

Hombron, H. *See* Quimper. Musée des Beaux-Arts. 1873.

Horsin-Déon, S. *De la conservation et de la restauration des tableaux*. Paris, 1851.

———. "Les Cabinets d'amateurs à Paris: Le Cabinet de M. le Comte d'Hautpoul." *Annuaire des artistes et des amateurs* 1860, pp. 156–70.

———. "Les Cabinets d'amateurs à Paris: Le Cabinet de M. Lacaze." *Annuaire des artistes et des amateurs* 1861, pp. 117–41.

———. "Les Cabinets d'amateurs à Paris: Cabinets de MM. Lavallard et Eudoxe Marcille." *Annuaire des artistes et des amateurs* 1862, pp. 137–38, 143–48.

Hourticq, L. *La Peinture française du XVIIIᵉ siècle*. Paris, 1939.

Hourticq, L., et al. *Le Paysage français de Poussin à Corot*. Paris, 1926.

Houssaye, A. *Galerie du XVIIIᵉ siècle*. 6th ed. Paris, 1858.

———. *Histoire de l'art français au dix-huitième siècle*. Paris, 1860.

Hoving, T. "The Best of the Best." *Connoisseur*, no. 850 (Dec. 1982), pp. 90–101.

Huber, M. *Notices générales des graveurs et des peintres*. Leipzig, 1787; reprint, Geneva, 1972.

Huisman, P. *French Watercolors of the 18th Century*. New York, 1969.

Hussman, G. C. "Boucher's *Psyche at the Basketmakers*: A Closer Look." *J. Paul Getty Museum Journal* 4 (1977), pp. 45–50.

I

Indianapolis Museum of Art. *See* Janson, F., and A. I. Fraser.

Ivanoff, N. "Francesco Algarotti e gli artisti francesi a Venezia nel settecento." *Arte veneta* 20 (1966), pp. 203–6.

J

Jaccottet, Ph. *See* Boucher, F., and Ph. Jaccottet.

Jal, A. *Dictionnaire critique de biographie et d'histoire*. 2d ed. Paris, 1872.

Janson, F., and A. I. Fraser. *100 Masterpieces of Painting: Indianapolis Museum of Art*. Indianapolis, 1980.

Jarey, P. "Mademoiselle Guimard et son hôtel de la chaussée d'Antin." *Le Vieux Montmartre*, Sept. 1926, pp. 21–33.

Jeannerat, C. "Rectification d'attribution d'une toile présumée de F. Boucher." *Bulletin de la Société de l'Histoire de l'Art Français* 1952 (1953), pp. 94–95.

Joachim, H. "Three Drawings by Fragonard." *The Art Institute of Chicago Quarterly* 56, no. 4 (1962–63), pp. 68–71.

Johnson, R. F., and J. R. Goldyne. *Master Drawings from the Achenbach Foundation for Graphic Arts, the Fine Arts Museums of San Francisco*. San Francisco, 1985.

Josz, V. "Le Prix de Rome de Fragonard." *Mercure de France*, Oct. 1900, pp. 95–125.

———. "Les Trois Femmes de Fragonard." *Mercure de France*, Dec. 1900, pp. 642–703.

———. *Fragonard, moeurs du XVIIIᵉ siècle*. Paris, 1901.

———. "Fragonard, de la Pompadour à la du Barry." *Mercure de France*, Feb. 1901, pp. 299–354.

Jouin, H. *Inventaire général des richesses d'art de la France. Province: Monuments civils*. Vol. III (Musée d'Angers). Paris, 1885.

Joullain, C.-F. *Réflexions sur la peinture et la gravure*. Paris, 1786; reprint, Geneva, 1973.

Journal. *See* Rosenberg, P., and B. Brejon de Lavergnée. 1986.

Jullian, R. "Le Thème des ruines dans la peinture de l'époque néo-classique en France." *Bulletin de la Société de l'Histoire de l'Art Français* 1976 (1978), pp. 261–72.

K

Kahn, G. "H. Fragonard." *L'Art et le beau*, special issue, 1907, pp. 1–36.

Kann, R., collection. *See* Bode, W.

Kaye, W. J. *Grasse (Riviera) and Its Vicinity*. Nice, 1912.

Kirby, L. "Fragonard's *The Pursuit of Love*." *Rutgers Art Review* 1982, pp. 58–79.

Knox, G. *Domenico Tiepolo: Raccolte di teste*. Udine, 1970.

Kouznetsova, I. 1980. *See* Pushkin Museum, Moscow. 1980.

———. 1982. *See* Pushkin Museum, Moscow. 1982.

Kunsthalle, Hamburg. *Katalog der alten Meister der Hamburger Kunsthalle.* 5th ed. Hamburg, 1966.

L

Labande, L.-H. "L'Hôtel de Matignon à Paris." *Gazette des Beaux-Arts,* Nov.–Dec. 1935, pp. 257–70, 347–63.

Labat, G. *Étude sur quelques miniatures de 1750 à 1815.* Bordeaux, 1907.

Lachaise, Dr. *Manuel pratique et raisonné de l'amateur de tableaux.* Paris, 1866.

Lafenestre, G., and E. Michel. *Inventaire général des richesses d'art de la France: Provinces, monuments civils.* Paris, I, 1878.

Laffon, J. *Catalogue sommaire illustré des peintures: Musée du Petit Palais.* 2 vols. Paris, 1981–82.

La Fizelière, A. de. *L'Oeuvre originale de Vivant Denon.* 2 vols. Paris, 1873.

La Fontaine, J. de. *Contes.* 2 vols. New Firmin Didot edition. Paris, 1794–95.

Lafuente Ferrari, E. *Antecedentes, coincidencias, e influencias del arte de Goya.* Madrid, 1947.

Lagrange, L. "Musées de Province: Collection Atger à Montpellier." *Gazette des Beaux-Arts,* Feb. 1860, pp. 129–45.

———. "Notes de voyage." *Gazette des Beaux-Arts,* Aug. 1867, pp. 188–92.

Lamb, C. *Die Villa d'Este in Tivoli: Ein Beitrag zur Geschichte der Gartenkunst.* Munich, 1966.

Lamouzèle, E. "Catalogue de la collection du cardinal de Bernis à l'archevêché d'Albi." *Bulletin de la Société de l'Histoire de l'Art Français* 1909, pp. 281–91.

Lamy, P. "Le Vrai Visage de Fragonard." *Bulletin de la Société de l'Histoire de l'Art Français* 1960 (1961), pp. 79–81.

———. "Fragonard: Une Découverte capitale et des inédits révélateurs." *Connaissance des arts,* no. 113 (July 1961), pp. 52–54.

Lancrenon, J.-F. *See* Besançon. Musée de Besançon. 1879.

Landon, C. P. *Salon de 1808.* 2 vols. Paris, 1808.

———. *Salon de 1822.* Paris, 1830.

———. *Annales du musée: École française moderne.* 2d ed. Paris, 1832.

Laprade, J. de. "Musée National de Pau." *Revue des arts,* no. 4 (1957), pp. 182–85.

Larguier, L. *En compagnie des vieux peintres.* Paris, 1927.

Larousse, P. "Fragonard." In *Grand Dictionnaire universel du XIXᵉ siècle.* Vol. VIII, pp. 699–700. Paris, 1872.

La Sizeranne, R. de. "Le Double miroir du XVIIIᵉ siècle, Chardin-Fragonard." *La Revue des deux mondes,* July 1, 1907, pp. 171–91. Reprinted in *Le Miroir de la vie: Essais sur l'évolution artistique.* 2 vols. Paris, 1909.

Latil, J.-Ph. *Histoire civile et religieuse de Grasse pendant la Révolution.* Grasse, 1905.

———. *Histoire civile et religieuse de Grasse.* Part 1, *La Révolution.* Grasse, 1907.

Launay, A. de. "Les Musées intimes: Fragonard." *Les Salons de Paris,* Apr. 19, 1859, pp. 4–5.

Launay, E. "Les Goncourt collectionneurs: Les Dessins français du XVIIIᵉ siècle du cabinet d'Auteuil." Thesis, 3d cycle, Paris IV, 1983–84.

Lauts, J. "Marchese Gregorio Agdollo's Gemäldesammlung: Ein Verzeichnis aus dem Jahre 1762." In *Interpretazioni Veneziane: Studi di storia dell'arte in onore di Michelangelo Muraro,* pp. 457–64. Venice, 1984.

Lavagnino, E. *I quadri italiani e francesi della collezione del Duca di Cervinara.* Rome, 1962.

La Vaissière, P. de. "Peintres méconnus qui se cachent sous Parrocel et Fragonard: Les Delarue." *L'Estampille,* no. 146 (1982), pp. 44–56.

Lavallée, P. *J.-H. Fragonard: Quatorze Dessins du Louvre.* Paris, 1938.

———. "Sur quelques dessins français des XVIIᵉ et XVIIIᵉ siècles conservés au Musée de Dijon." *Bulletin de la Société de l'Histoire de l'Art Français* 1941–44 (1947), pp. 114–18.

———. *Le Dessin français.* Paris, 1948.

———. *Les Techniques du dessin.* Paris, 1949.

Laveissière, S. *See* exhibitions, Rome–Dijon, 1983.

Laver, J. *Fragonard (1732–1806).* London, 1955.

Lavice, A. *Revue des musées de France.* Paris, 1870.

Le Carpentier, Ch. *Galerie des peintres célèbres.* 2 vols. Paris, 1821.

Leclère, T. *Hubert Robert et les paysagistes français du XVIIIᵉ siècle.* Paris, 1913.

Le Coat, G. "La Fonction dialectique de la représentation animale dans la peinture pré-révolutionnaire." *Actes du Colloque International de Clermont-Ferrand* 1977 (1980), pp. 47–53.

———. "Watteau et l'imaginaire social: La Représentation animale comme étude de cas." In *Antoine Watteau (1684–1721): Le Peintre, son temps, et sa légende. Colloque Watteau, 1984,* pp. 181–84. Paris, 1987.

Lee, R. W. *Ut Pictura Poesis: The Humanistic Theory of Painting.* New York, 1967. First published in *Art Bulletin* 20 (Dec. 1940), pp. 197–269.

——— *Names on Trees: Ariosto into Art.* Princeton, 1977.

Lee, T. P. "Recently Acquired French Paintings: Reflection on the Past." *Apollo,* Mar. 1980, pp. 212–23.

Lefort, P. "La Collection de M. B. Narischkine." *Gazette des Beaux-Arts,* Mar. 1883, pp. 219–25.

Le Hir. "Compte-rendu de la vente du 11–13 avril 1867." *Journal des amateurs d'objets d'art et de curiosité* 1867, pp. 125–31.

Lejeune, T. *Guide théorique de l'amateur de tableaux.* 2 vols. Paris, 1863.

Lemoisne, P. A. "Les Collections de MM. G. et H. Pannier." *Les Arts,* no. 63 (Mar. 1907), pp. 10–29.

———. "Augustin de Saint-Aubin et les dessins de Fragonard pour l'édition des *Contes* de La Fontaine." *Byblis,* no. 2 (1922), pp. 68–74.

Lenoir, A. "Fragonard." In *Biographie universelle, ancienne et moderne (Biographie Michaud).* Vol. XV. Paris, 1816.

Le P[aon]. *Critique des peintures et sculptures des Messieurs de l'Académie Royale.* 1765.

Le Petit, J. "Les *Contes* de La Fontaine illustrés par Fragonard." *Le Livre* 1880, pp. 217–20.

Leporini, H. *Fragonard.* Vienna and Leipzig, 1925.

Leprévots, R. "Une Allégorie de la ville de Paris à l'occasion de l'année jubilaire du règne de Louis XV." *Bulletin du Musée Carnavalet,* no. 2 (1977), pp. 21–26.

Le Prieur, P. "Les Récentes Acquisitions du Département des Peintures au Musée du Louvre (1907–1908)." *Gazette des Beaux-Arts,* Jan. 1909, pp. 65–84.

Lespinasse, P. "Le Portraitiste Roslin et les artistes suédois en France pendant la seconde moitié du XVIIIᵉ siècle." *Bulletin de la Société de l'Histoire de l'Art Français* 1927, pp. 234–97.

———. *La Miniature en France au XVIIIᵉ siècle.* Paris, 1929.

Lévêque, J.-J. *Fragonard.* Paris, 1983.

Levetine, G. "Marguerite Gérard and Her Stylistic Significance." *The Baltimore Museum of Art Annual* 3 (1968), pp. 20–31.

Levey, M. *Rococo to Revolution.* New York and Washington, D.C., 1966.

Levey, M., and W. Kalnein. *Art and Architecture of the Eighteenth Century in France.* Baltimore, 1972.

Lévy, P. *L'Art et l'argent.* Paris, 1982.

Leymarie, J. *See* Cooper, D.

Leymarie, L. de. *L'Oeuvre de Gilles Demarteau l'aîné, graveur du Roi.* Paris, 1896.

Lhote, A. *La Peinture, le coeur, et l'esprit.* Published with *Parlons peinture.* Paris, 1933.

———. *Parlons peinture.* Paris, 1936.

L'Hote, E. "Les Cabinets d'amateurs à Paris." *L'Artiste* 22 (1861), pp. 243–52.

Lièvre, P. "La Leçon de Fragonard." *L'Amour de l'art,* July 1921, pp. 197–201.

Livchits, N.-A. *Jean-Honoré Fragonard* (in Russian). Moscow, 1970.

Locquin, J. *La Peinture d'histoire en France de 1747 à 1785.* Paris, 1912; new ed. Paris, 1978.

———. "Les Éditions des lettres à un jeune artiste peintre, pensionnaire à l'Académie Royale de France à Rome, par C.-N. Cochin." *Bulletin de la Société de l'Histoire de l'Art Français* 1914, pp. 6–9.

Lossky, B. "Fragonard en Bohême." *Revue française de Prague,* Sept. 15, 1936, pp. 1–8.

———. "Fragonard sur les routes de Slovénie." *Zbornik Zaumetnostno Zgodovino* 9 (1972), pp. 139–44.

Loyrette, H. "Séroux d'Agincourt et les origines de l'histoire de l'art médiéval." *Revue de l'art,* no. 48 (1980), pp. 40–56.

Lugand, J. "De la folie de Louveciennes au château des ducs de Savoie." *Revue de Savoie,* no. 4 (1956), pp. 251–58.

———. *Catalogue du Musée des Beaux-Arts de la ville de Béziers.* Vol. II, *1960–1976.* Montpellier, 1976.

Lugt, F. *Les Marques de collections de dessins et d'estampes.* Amsterdam, 1921. *Supplément.* The Hague, 1956.

———. *Musée du Louvre. Inventaire général des dessins des Écoles du Nord: École flamande.* Vol. I. Paris, 1949.

Luynes, Duc de. *Mémoires sur la Cour de Louis XV (1735–1758).* Edited by L. Dussieux and E. Soulié. 17 vols. Paris, 1860–65.

M

Mabuchi, A. *Les Grands Maîtres de la peinture.* No. 20, *Fragonard.* Tokyo, 1983.

McAllister-Johnson, W. M. "La Visite du grand-duc de Russie, 1782." *Nouvelles de l'estampe,* no. 45 (May–June 1979), pp. 21–24.

MacFall, H. "Fragonard." *Connoisseur,* May 1905, pp. 3–12.

McGregor, N. "Le Voyage pittoresque de Naples et de Sicile." *Connoisseur,* no. 788 (Oct. 1977), pp. 131–38.

Madonna, M. L. "Pirro Ligorio e la villa d'Este: La scena di Roma e il mistero della Sibilla." In *Il giardino storico italiano: Atti del convegno di studi Siena-San Quirico d'Orcia, 1978,* pp. 173–96. Florence, 1981.

Magnin, J. *Les Dessins du XVIIIᵉ siècle au Musée de Besançon.* Besançon, 1929.

Mahérault, M. J. F. *L'Oeuvre de Moreau le Jeune.* Paris, 1880.

Mandel, G. *See* Wildenstein, D., and G. Mandel.

Mannlich, Ch. von. *Mémoires du chevalier Christian de Mannlich.* Edited by J. Delage. Paris, 1948.

———. *Rokoko und Revolution: Lebenserinnerungen des Johann Christian v. Mannlich (1741–1822).* Stuttgart, 1966.

Mantz, P. "Exposition de Chartres." *L'Artiste* 4 (June 6, 1858), pp. 70–73.

———. "Exposition d'Amiens, tableaux de l'école française, écoles étrangères: Sculpture, dessins de maîtres anciens, gravure." *L'Artiste* 1860, pp. 4–8.

———. "La Collection La Caze au Musée du Louvre." *Gazette des Beaux-Arts,* July 1870, pp. 5–25.

———. "La Collection Burat." *L'Artiste* 1 (1885), pp. 287–96.

Marcel, P. 1907–10. *See* Guiffrey, Jean, and P. Marcel.

———. "La Collection de dessins de Gabriel Lemonnier au Musée de Rouen." (Mélanges offerts à Henry Lemonnier). *Archives de l'art français* 1913, pp. 467–95.

———. *Les Peintres et la vie politique en France au XVIIIe siècle.* Paris, 1914.

Marie, A. *Gérard de Nerval, le poète, l'homme....* Paris, 1914.

Mariette, P.-J. *Abécédario de P.-J. Mariette.* Edited by Ph. de Chennevières and A. de Montaiglon. 6 vols. Paris, 1851–60. See especially vol. II, 1853–54.

Marigny, Marquis de. *See* Furcy-Raynaud, M. 1903–4.

Martin, J. *See* Musée Greuze, Tournus.

Martin, J., and Ch. Masson. *Catalogue raisonné de l'oeuvre peint et dessiné de J.-B. Greuze.* Paris, 1907.

Martin, N. "Les Dessins de la collection Feuillet de Borsat: Musée Borély, Marseille." *L'Estampille,* no. 134 (June 1981), pp. 36–51.

Martine, Ch. *Dessins de maîtres français.* Vol. VI, *Honoré Fragonard.* Paris, 1927.

Massengale, J. Montague. "Drawings by Fragonard in North American Collections." *Burlington Magazine,* no. 913 (Apr. 1979), pp. 270–72.

———. "Fragonard Élève: Sketching in the Studio of Boucher." *Apollo,* Dec. 1980, pp. 392–97.

Mathey, J. "Greuze et Fragonard, copistes de Rubens." *Bulletin de la Société de l'Histoire de l'Art Français* 1933, pp. 183–87.

———. "Un Dessin de Fragonard au Musée de Besançon." *Gazette des Beaux-Arts,* Jan.–June 1949, pp. 373–400.

———. "Fantasy in Boucher's Landscapes and Fragonard's Figures." *Connoisseur,* no. 594 (June 1961), pp. 302–5.

Mathon de la Cour, Ch. J. *Lettres à Monsieur, sur les peintures, les sculptures, et les gravures exposées au Sallon du Louvre en 1765.* Paris, 1765.

Mauclair, C. *Les Grands Artistes: Fragonard.* Paris, 1904.

———. "Fragonard." *L'Art et les artistes* 3 (Apr. 1906), pp. 187–200.

———. *Greuze.* Paris [1907].

———. *Histoire de la miniature féminine française: Le XVIIIe Siècle, l'Empire, la Restauration.* Paris, 1925.

———. *Un Tableau de Fragonard.* N.p. [1929?].

Maugras, G. *L'Idylle d'un "gouverneur": La Comtesse de Genlis et le duc de Chartres.* Paris, 1904.

Mauray, R. "A propos des 'scènes familiales' de Fragonard." *Revue de l'art ancien et moderne* 47 (1925), pp. 154–66.

Mayer, A. L. "Die Gemälde der Sammlung comtesse de La Béraudière." *Pantheon* 1 (1928), pp. 275–83.

———. "Die Austellung der Sammlung 'Schloss Rohoncz' in der Neuen Pinakothek, München." *Pantheon,* July 1930, p. 320.

Mayor, J. "L'Hôtel de la chancellerie d'Orléans à Paris." *Gazette des Beaux-Arts,* Aug. 1916, pp. 333–59.

Mazars, P. *L'Univers de Fragonard.* Paris, 1971.

Meaudre de Lapouyade. *Lonsing, 1739–1799.* Paris, 1911.

Meder, J. 1895–1908. *See* Schönbrunner, J., and J. Meder.

———. *Handzeichnungen alter Meister aus der Albertina und aus Privatbesitz.* Vienna, 1922.

———. *Albertina Facsimile.* 4 vols. Vienna, 1922–23.

———. *Die Handzeichnungen (ihre Technik und Entwicklung).* Vienna, 1923.

———. *The Mastery of Drawing.* Vols. I and II. New York, 1978.

Meier-Graefe, J. "Correspondance d'Allemagne: L'Exposition d'art français du XVIIIe siècle à Berlin." *Gazette des Beaux-Arts,* Mar. 1910, pp. 262–72.

Méjanès, J. F. "A Spontaneous Feeling for Nature: French Eighteenth Century Landscape Drawings." *Apollo,* Nov. 1976, pp. 396–404.

Mémoires secrets.... See Bachaumont, L. Petit de.

Méras, M. "Fragonard à Nègrepelisse." *Bulletin de la Société Archéologique du Tarn-et-Garonne* 87 (1961), pp. 1–8.

———. "Deux Tableaux retrouvés des collections Bergeret de Grancourt au château de Nègrepelisse." *Gazette des Beaux-Arts,* Dec. 1972, pp. 331–34.

Merson, O. "Les Logements d'artistes au Louvre." *Gazette des Beaux-Arts,* Mar. 1881, pp. 264–70; Sept. 1881, pp. 276–88.

Mesuret, R. 1954. *See* exhibitions, Toulouse, 1954.

———. *Les Expositions de l'Académie Royale de Toulouse de 1751 à 1791.* Booklets edited and annotated by R. Mesuret. Toulouse, 1972.

Métra. *Correspondance secrète, politique, et littéraire.* 18 vols. London, 1788.

Metropolitan Museum of Art, New York. *French Paintings: A Catalogue of the Collection of The Metropolitan Museum of Art.* Vol. I, *XV–XVIII Centuries,* by Ch. Sterling. Cambridge, Mass., 1955.

———. 1956. *See* Salinger, M.

———. 1980. *See* Baetjer, K.

———. 1986. *See* Bean, J., and L. Turčić.

Michaud. *See* Lenoir, A.

Michaud, J.-L. "Portraits dans le dessin français du XVIIIe siècle au Musée du Louvre." *Le Peintre,* Mar. 1, 1958, pp. 4–5.

Michel, A. "Les Fragonard de la Collection Wallace." *Les Arts,* no. 6 (July 1902), pp. 2–5.

———. *Histoire de l'art depuis les premiers temps chrétiens jusqu'à nos jours....* Vol. VII, *L'Art en Europe au XVIIIe siècle,* part 2. Paris, 1925.

Michel, R. "La Galerie de M. Rodolphe Kann." *Gazette des Beaux-Arts,* June 1901, pp. 493–506.

Michel, R. *See* exhibitions, Rome, 1981–82.

Michine, V. "Fragonard as Interpreter of Ariosto" (in Russian). *Sovétsoyé Iskoussotvozanie* 79, no. 2 (1980), pp. 170–92.

Miette de Villars, M. *Mémoires de David.* Paris, 1850.

Mirimonde, A. P. de. "Scènes de genre musicales de l'école française au XVIIIe siècle dans les collections nationales." *La Revue du Louvre et des musées de France,* no. 1 (1968), pp. 13–26.

———. *L'Iconographie musicale sous les rois Bourbons: La Musique dans les arts plastiques, XVIIe–XVIIIe siècles.* 2 vols. Paris, 1975–77.

Moir, A. *Caravaggio and His Copyists.* New York, 1976.

Moitte, Madame. *Journal inédit de Madame Moitte, femme de Jean-Guillaume Moitte, 1805–1807.* Edited by Cottin. Paris, 1932.

Molinier, E. *Le Mobilier royal français au XVIIe et XVIIIe siècles.* Vol. III. Paris, n.d. [between 1896 and 1911].

Mongan, A. and E. *European Paintings in the Timken Art Gallery.* San Diego, 1969.

Mongan, A., and P. J. Sachs. *See* Fogg Art Museum, Harvard University, Cambridge, Mass.

Mongan, E., Ph. Hofer, and J. Seznec. *Fragonard Drawings for Ariosto.* London, 1945.

Monnier, G. *See* Sérullaz, M., L. Duclaux, and G. Monnier.

Montaiglon, A. de. 1851–60. *See* Mariette, P.-J.

———. "Notice sur Greuze et sur ses ouvrages par Madame de Valori." *Revue universelle des arts* 1860, pp. 248–61.

———. 1875–92. *See Procès-Verbaux....*

Montaiglon, A. de, and J. Guiffrey. *See Correspondance des Directeurs....*

Morand, L. *Une Famille d'artistes: Les Naigeon.* Paris, 1902.

Morgan Grasselli, M. *See* exhibitions, Washington, D.C., 1982.

Mornet, D. *Le Sentiment de la nature en France de J.-J. Rousseau à Bernardin de Saint-Pierre.* Paris, 1907; reprint, Geneva, 1980.

[Mosser, M.]. "Le Libertinage du décor ou le lit peintre." In *Catalogue triennal.* Milan, 1985.

Mouilleseaux, J.-P. *See* Delécluze, E.-J.

Moulidars, T. de. *Grande Encyclopédie ... des jeux....* Paris, 1888.

Mozart, W. A. *Lettres de W. A. Mozart.* Translated by H. de Curzon. 2 vols. Paris, 1928.

Mrozińska, M. "Dwa rysunki J. H. Fragonarda na tematy z zycia rodzinnego rocznik." *Muzeum Narodowego w Warszawie* 5 (1960), pp. 7–22.

Munhall, E. "Fragonard's Studies for *The Progress of Love.*" *Apollo,* May 1971, pp. 400–407.

Munhall, E., and B. Davidson. *The Frick Collection, An Illustrated Catalogue.* Vol. II, *French, Italian, and Spanish Paintings.* New York, 1968.

Munière, L. "Jean-Honoré Fragonard: Les Blanchisseuses." *L'Estampille,* Apr. 1985, pp. 61–62.

Muñoz, A. "Chardin et Fragonard." *Arte retrospettiva* 1907(?), pp. 257–74.

Murray, P. *See* Dulwich Picture Gallery, London. 1980.

Musée Atger, Montpellier. *Notices des dessins sous verre, tableaux, esquisses ... réunis à la Bibliothèque de la Faculté de Médecine de Montpellier.* Montpellier, 1830.

———. 1955. *See* Claparède, J.

Musée Cognacq-Jay, Paris. *See* Burollet, Th.

Musée des Beaux Arts, Béziers. *See* Lugand, J. 1976.

Musée Greuze, Tournus. *Catalogue du Musée de Tournus (Musée Greuze),* by J. Martin. New ed. Tournus, 1910.

Musée d'Orléans. *See* O'Neill, M.

Musée du Louvre, Paris. 1855. *See* Villot, F. 1855.

———. *Catalogue des peintures exposées dans les galeries.* Vol. I, *École française,* by G. Brière. Paris, 1924.

———. *La Peinture au Musée du Louvre: École française, XVIIIe siècle,* by L. Gillet. Paris, 1929.

———. 1949. *See* Lugt, F. 1949.

———. 1957. *See* Bazin, G. 1957.

———. 1968. *See* Sérullaz, M., L. Duclaux, and G. Monnier.

———. 1984. *See* Cardinal, C.

Musée du Petit Palais, Paris. *See* Laffon, J.

Musée Turpin de Crissé, Angers. *Catalogue-guide,* by A. Recouvreur. Angers, 1933.

N

N. See Nolhac, P. de. 1906.

Naquet, F. *Les Artistes célèbres: Fragonard.* Paris, 1890.

National Gallery of Canada, Toronto. See Popham, A. E., and K.-M. Fenwick.

Nemilova, I. S. *Zagadki starykh kartin* (The riddles of old paintings). Moscow, 1973.

——. "Contemporary French Art in Eighteenth Century Russia." *Apollo,* no. 160 (June 1975), pp. 428–42.

——. "The Probability of J. H. Fragonard's Authorship of the Painting, *Head of a Girl*" (in Russian). *Soobcheniya Gosoudarstvennogo Ermitage,* no. 43 (1978), pp. 12–13.

——. 1986. See Hermitage, Leningrad. 1986.

Neveu, B. "Le Voyage de l'abbé de Saint-Non dans l'Italie du Sud." *Journal des savants,* Oct.–Dec. 1973, pp. 295–300.

Nevill, R. "Jean-Honoré Fragonard." *Burlington Magazine,* no. 7 (Sept.–Oct. 1903), pp. 51–57; no. 9 (Dec. 1903), pp. 286–93.

Nicaise, A. *L'École française du XVIII* siècle.* Châlons-sur-Marne, 1883.

Nicolle, M. "Une Anthologie de la critique d'art en France." *Gazette des Beaux-Arts,* Jan. 1931, pp. 45–63.

——. "Chefs d'oeuvre des musées de Province: École française, XVII* et XVIII* siècles." *Gazette des Beaux-Arts,* Aug. 1931, pp. 98–127. Also issued as an offprint, pp. 1–30.

Niculescu, R. "Georges de Bellio: L'Ami des impressionnistes." *Paragone* 1, no. 247 (Sept. 1970), pp. 25–66; 2, no. 249 (Nov. 1970), pp. 41–85.

Nisard, Ch. *Correspondance inédite du comte de Caylus avec le P. Paciaudi.* 2 vols. Paris, 1877.

• Nolhac, P. de. *J.-H. Fragonard, 1732–1806.* With a catalogue of paintings sold at auction from 1770 to 1905, by H. Pannier. Paris, 1906.

——. "Un Pensionnaire du Roi à Rome au XVIII* siècle: Fragonard." *Le Correspondant,* Oct. 10, 1906, pp. 29–50.

——. "A propos des Fragonard de Grasse." *Musées et monuments* 1 (1907), pp. 3–4.

——. [Communication de M. de Nolhac]. *Bulletin de la Société de l'Histoire de l'Art Français* 1907, pp. 11–12.

——. "Deux Questions sur Fragonard." *Revue de l'art,* no. 124 (July 1907), pp. 19–24.

——. "Fragonard et Chardin." *Les Arts,* July 1907, pp. 37–46.

——. "Une Danseuse de Fragonard." *Les Arts,* no. 101 (May 1910), p. 2.

——. *Fragonard,* 1918; 2d ed. Paris, 1931.

——. "L'Abbé de Saint-Non et Fragonard." *La Renaissance,* Jan. 1932, pp. 35–38.

——. *Portraits du XVIII* siècle.* Paris, 1933.

——. *Peintres français en Italie.* Paris, 1934.

Norman, G. "More than 30 Fragonard Drawings May be Fakes." *The Times,* Mar. 8, 1978.

——. "When a Fragonard Copy Looks Just Too Good to Be True." *The Times,* Mar. 9, 1978.

O

Obser, K. "Lettres sur les Salons de 1773, 1777, et 1779 adressées par Du Pont de Nemours à la margrave Caroline-Louise de Bade." *Archives de l'art français* 1908, pp. 1–123.

Ochsé, M. "Fragonard: Des tourbillons de volupté." *Jardin des arts,* May 1972, pp. 4–43.

O'Neill, M. *Les Peintures de l'école française des XVII* et XVIII* siècles: Catalogue critique du Musée d'Orléans.* 2 vols. Orléans, 1981.

Oppé, A. P. "Honoré Fragonard." *Old Master Drawings,* June 1927, pp. 8–9.

Osborne, C. M. "Pierre Didot the Elder and French Illustration, 1785–1822." Ph.D. diss., Stanford University, June 1979.

Oulmont, Ch. *68 Dessins de Fragonard: Souvenirs de son voyage à Rome et à Florence.* With notes by Ch. Oulmont. Paris, 1926.

Oursel, H. See exhibitions, Lille, 1985.

P

P. See Portalis, R. 1889.

Paciaudi, père. See Nisard, Ch.; *and see* Sérieys, A.

Pannier, H. 1906. See Nolhac, P. de. 1906.

——. "Catalogue manuscrit des dessins de Fragonard passés en vente publique, avec croquis de Pannier." MS., n.d. Paris, Bibliothèque Nationale, Cabinet des Estampes.

Panofsky, E. *Meaning in the Visual Arts.* New York, 1955.

Pâris, P.-A. "Catalogue de mes livres ainsi que des autres objets qui composent mon cabinet tels que les marbres et bronzes antiques … tableaux et dessins en bordure.…" MS., 1806. Bibliothèque Municipale de Besançon.

Pariset, F.-G. *Les Arts graphiques en France autour de 1778.* Vol. XI. Paris, 1979.

P[arker], K. T. "A Drawing by Fragonard after Rubens." *British Museum Quarterly* 7, no. 4 (May 1933), pp. 105–6.

Pays, A. J. du. "Exposition de tableaux et de dessins de l'école française (Boulevard des Italiens, 26)." *L'Illustration,* Sept. 29, 1860, pp. 222–23.

Pérignon, A. N. *Description des objets d'art qui composent le cabinet de feu M. le Baron V. Denon.* Paris, 1826.

Perroud, Cl. "A propos de deux lettres de David en octobre 1792." *La Révolution française,* Apr. 14, 1900, pp. 359–71.

Pichon, Baron J. "Mémoires de Pajou et de Drouais pour Mme du Barry." In *Mélanges de littérature et d'histoire recueillis et publiés par la Société des Bibliophiles Français.* Paris, 1856.

Pidansat de Mairobert. *Anecdotes sur M.* [sic] *la comtesse du Barry.* London, 1775.

Pierpont Morgan Library, New York. *European Drawings, 1375–1825,* by C. D. Denison and H. B. Mules. New York, 1981.

Pietrangeli, C. *Il museo di Roma.* Bologna, 1971.

Pigler, A. "Fragonard et l'art napolitain." *Gazette des Beaux-Arts,* Mar. 1931, pp. 192–97.

——. *Barockthemen.* 2 vols. Budapest, 1956; 2d ed., 3 vols., Budapest, 1974.

Pilgrim, Lord. "Mouvement des arts." *L'Artiste,* June 1849, p. 72.

Pilon, E. *L'Art et les moeurs en France.* Paris, 1909.

Pinault, M. "Diderot et les illustrateurs de l'*Encyclopédie*." *Revue de l'art,* no. 66 (1984), pp. 17–38.

——. "Les Chapitres artistiques des volumes de planches de l'*Encyclopédie*." In *Diderot: Les Beaux-Arts et la musique (Colloque, 1984),* pp. 67–91. Aix-en-Provence, 1986.

Piot, E. *État-civil de quelques artistes français (extrait des registres des paroisses des anciennes archives de la Ville de Paris).* Paris, 1873.

Pizon, P. "A propos des portraits de Fragonard." *Argus de la presse,* May 15, 1974, pp. 3–8.

Plantier, J.-F. "Une Bacchanale inédite de Fragonard." *Le Cousin Pons,* no. 108 (Apr.

1925), pp. 5–6.

Pognon, E., and Y. Bruand. *Inventaire du fonds français: Graveurs du XVIII* siècle.* Vol. IX. Paris, Bibliothèque Nationale, Cabinet des Estampes, 1962.

Popham, A. E., and K.-M. Fenwick. *European Drawings (and Two Asian Drawings) in the Collection of the National Gallery of Canada.* Toronto, 1965.

Portalis, R., Baron. *Les Dessinateurs d'illustrations au dix-huitième siècle.* Paris, 1877.

——. "La Collection Walferdin et ses Fragonard." *Gazette des Beaux-Arts,* Apr. 1880, pp. 297–322. Also issued as an offprint, pp. 5–30.

——. "Les Peintures décoratives de Fragonard et les panneaux de Grasse." *Gazette des Beaux-Arts,* Dec. 1885, pp. 481–93.

• ——. *Honoré Fragonard: Sa Vie, son oeuvre.* 2 vols. Paris, 1889.

——. *Scènes de la vie champêtre: Panneaux décoratifs de Fragonard.* Paris, 1902.

Portalis, R., Baron, and H. Béraldi. *Les Graveurs du dix-huitième siècle.* 3 vols. in 6. Paris, 1880–82.

Posner, D. "Baroque and Rococo Oil Sketches." *Burlington Magazine,* no. 771 (June 1967), pp. 360–63.

——. "The True Path of Fragonard's *Progress of Love.*" *Burlington Magazine,* no. 833 (Aug. 1972), pp. 526–34.

——. Review of *François Boucher,* by A. Ananoff and D. Wildenstein. *Art Bulletin* 60, no. 3 (Sept. 1978), pp. 560–62.

——. "The Swinging Women of Watteau and Fragonard." *Art Bulletin* 64, no. 1 (Mar. 1982), pp. 75–88.

Posner, D., and J. S. Held. *17th and 18th Century Art: Baroque Painting, Sculpture, Architecture.* Englewood Cliffs, N.J., n.d.

Pouthas, Ch. H. "Technique de la couleur des peintres anciens et des peintres modernes." *L'Art et les artistes,* no. 186 (Mar. 1938), pp. 223–29.

Prajoux, J., Abbé. *Histoire de Coteau depuis son origine jusqu'à nos jours.* Roanne, 1924.

Prat, L. A. "Une Collection de dessins d'artistes français par Philippe de Chennevières: Index." *Bulletin de la Société de l'Histoire de l'Art Français* 1977 (1979), pp. 275–95.

Procès-Verbaux de la Commission des Monuments. See Tuetey, L. 1901–2.

Procès-Verbaux des séances de l'Académie royale de 1648 à 1792. Edited by A. de Montaiglon. 10 vols. Paris, 1875–92.

Pupil, F. *Le Style troubadour.* Nancy, 1985.

Pushkin Museum, Moscow. *Catalogue de la galerie des tableaux du Musée Pouchkine,* by L. Réau. Moscow, 1948.

——. *Frantsuzskiĭ risunok shestnadtsatogo–vosemnadtsatogo vekov; Le Dessin français des XVI*–XVIII* siècles* (in Russian, captions and summary also in French), by V. Alexeyeva and N. Vodo. Moscow, 1977.

——. *La Peinture française au Musée Pouchkine,* by I. Kouznetsova and E. Gueorguievskaïa. Paris and Leningrad, 1980.

——. *Frantsuzskaia zhivopis' XVI–pervoĭ poloviny XIX veka* (French painting of the 16th–first half of the 19th century), by I. Kouznetsova. Moscow, 1982.

Q

Quimper. Musée des Beaux-Arts. *Catalogue des tableaux exposés dans les galeries du Musée de la*

ville de Quimper, dit Musée de Silguy, by N. Gauguet and H. Hombron. Brest, 1873.
——. *Musée des Beaux-Arts de Quimper,* by A. Cariou. Quimper, 1985.

R

R. *See* Réau, L. 1956.
R. G. "Les Grandes Ventes du mois de mai: La Collection Sigismond Bardac." *Revue de l'art,* no. 216 (May 1920), pp. 293–98.
Rabbe, F. "Un Portrait de Robespierre par Honoré Fragonard." *La Révolution française,* Mar. 14, 1900, pp. 256–57.
Ratouis de Limay, P. *Un Amateur orléanais au XVIIIᵉ siècle, Aignan-Thomas Desfriches (1715–1800).* Paris, 1907.
——. "Le Président Robert de Saint-Victor" (Mélanges offerts à H. Lemonnier). *Archives de l'art français* 1913, pp. 422–39.
——. *Le Pastel en France au XVIIIᵉ siècle.* Paris, 1946.
——. "Un Chanteur de l'opéra, graveur, et collectionneur au début du XIXᵉ siècle." *Bulletin de la Société de l'Histoire de l'Art Français* 1949 (1950), pp. 70–78.
Raynard, J. "Une Collection russe." *L'Art* 1883, pp. 53–56, 68–70.
Réau, L. "Lettres de Greuze au prince Nicolas Borisovitch Iousoupov." *Bulletin de la Société de l'Histoire de l'Art Français* 1926, pp. 395–99.
——. "Les Colin-maillard de Fragonard." *Gazette des Beaux-Arts,* Mar. 1927, pp. 148–52.
——. "Catalogue de l'art français dans les musées russes." *Bulletin de la Société de l'Histoire de l'Art Français* 1928, pp. 167–314.
——. "Grimou." In *Les Peintres français du XVIIIᵉ siècle,* vol. II, by L. Dimier. Paris and Brussels, 1930.
——. "Quelques peintures de Fragonard (Amiens et Rouen)." *Bulletin des musées de France* 1931, pp. 30–32.
——. "Les Dessins de Fragonard." *Bulletin de l'Académie des Beaux-Arts,* Jan.–June 1931, pp. 66–73.
——. "Les Influences flamandes et hollandaises dans l'oeuvre de Fragonard." *Revue belge d'archéologie et d'histoire de l'art* 2, no. 2 (Apr. 1932), pp. 97–104.
——. *Histoire de l'expansion de l'art français: Le Monde latin.* Paris, 1933.
——. "Ce qu'on vendra: A propos de *L'Heureuse Famille* de Fragonard." *Beaux-Arts,* July 1934, p. 4.
——. "L'Influence de Fragonard." *La Renaissance,* no. 1–2 (Jan.–Feb. 1935), pp. 1–8.
——. "Honoré Fragonard." *Beaux-Arts,* May 6, 1938.
——. *Le Rayonnement de Paris au XVIIIᵉ siècle.* Paris, 1946.
——. *Trésors de la peinture française: Fragonard.* Geneva, 1948.
——. 1948. *See also* Pushkin Museum, Moscow. 1948.
——. "Documents sur Watteau et Fragonard." *Bulletin de la Société de l'Histoire de l'Art Français* 1947–48 (1949), pp. 113–14.
——. "Fragonard." *Connoisseur,* no. 512 (June 1949), pp. 69–74.
——. *Fragonard.* Brussels, 1956.
——. *Iconographie de l'art chrétien.* Vol. II, *L'Ancien Testament.* Paris, 1956.
——. "L'Influence de Fragonard en Espagne."

Cahiers de Bordeaux 1956, pp. 19–23.
——. "Les Dessins de Fragonard du musée de l'Île-de-France (Fondation Ephrussi de Rothschild) à Saint-Jean-Cap Ferrat." *Académie des Beaux-Arts* 1960–61, pp. 75–81.
Reboul, R. *Biographie et bibliographie de l'arrondissement de Grasse.* Grasse, 1887.
Recouvreur, A. "Honoré Fragonard, ici et à côté." *La Province d'Anjou* 7 (1932), pp. 247–60.
——. 1933. *See* Musée de Crissé, Angers.
Regteren Altena, J. Q. van. *See* Van Regteren Altena, J. Q.
Reinach, S. *Répertoire de reliefs grecs et romains.* Vol. III. Paris, 1912.
[Renou, A.]. *Dialogues sur la peinture.* 2d ed., with added notes. Paris, chez Tartouillis, 1773; reprint, Geneva, 1973.
Renouvier, J. *Histoire de l'art pendant la Révolution.* 2 vols. Paris, 1863.
Rey, R. "La Peinture française pendant la deuxième moitié du XVIIIᵉ siècle." Course given at the École du Louvre, 1938.
——. "Le Voyage de l'abbé de Saint-Non et de Fragonard à Tivoli et à Rome." *Revue des voyages,* Mar. 1955, pp. 20–23.
Reynolds, G. *Catalogue of Miniatures: Wallace Collection.* London, 1980.
Ricci, S. de. *The Roederer Library of French Books: Prints and Drawings of the Eighteenth Century.* Philadelphia, 1923.
——. "Un Cabinet de dessins français: La Bibliothèque Roederer." *Beaux-Arts,* no. 17 (Oct. 15, 1923), p. 272.
Rice, P. *Man as Hero.* New York and London, 1987.
Richardson, J. *The Collection of Germain Seligman.* New York and London, 1979.
Röbels, H. *Katalog ausgewählter Handzeichnungen und Aquarelle im Wallraf-Richartz-Museum.* Cologne, 1967.
Roberts, K. "Current and Forthcoming Exhibitions." *Burlington Magazine,* no. 903 (June 1978), pp. 409–14.
Robertson, S. Wells. *See* Wells-Robertson, S.
Rochefort, H. "La Collection de M. Henri Rochefort." *Les Arts,* no. 43 (July 1905), pp. 2–22.
Roederer, P.-L., Comte. *Journal du comte P.-L. Roederer.* Edited by M. Vitrac. Paris, 1909.
Roederer Library, Philadelphia. *See* Ricci, S. de.
Roger-Milès, L. "La Collection Lehman." *Bulletin de l'art ancien et moderne* 19 (Jan.–May 1925), pp. 161–76.
Rogers, M. R. "*The Wash Women,* by Jean-Honoré Fragonard (1732–1806)." *Bulletin of the City Art Museum of Saint Louis* 23, no. 3 (July 1938), pp. 30–31.
Roland Michel, M. "The Themes of 'the Artist' and of 'Inspiration' as Revealed by Some of Fragonard's Drawings." *Burlington Magazine,* no. 704 (Nov. 1961), suppl. no. 9, pp. i–iii.
——. "Fragonard, Illustrator of the *Contes* of La Fontaine." *Burlington Magazine,* no. 811 (Oct. 1970), suppl. no. 25, pp. i–vi.
——. "Fragonard, illustrateur de l'amour." *Actes du colloque international de Clermont-Ferrand* 1977 (1980), pp. 25–32.
——. "Sous le signe de l'abbé de Saint-Non." *Études de la Revue du Louvre,* no. 1 (1980), pp. 88–93.
——. "Des Monts et des eaux." *Burlington Magazine,* no. 933 (Dec. 1980), suppl. no. 39, pp. i–v.
——. "Un Peintre français nommé Ango...." *Burlington Magazine,* no. 945 (Dec. 1981), suppl. no. 40, pp. i–viii.
——. "La Fête de Watteau." *Revue de l'art,* no. 62

(1983), pp. 71–74.
——. "French Eighteenth Century Drawings." *Apollo,* June 1983, pp. 469–75.
——. "A propos de portraits de famille." *Burlington Magazine,* no. 1000 (July 1986), pp. 546–52.
Romard, D. "La Cote des peintres: Jean-Honoré Fragonard." *Gazette de l'Hôtel Drouot,* Sept. 24, 1971, p. 57; Nov. 26, 1971, pp. 14–15; Dec. 3, 1971, pp. 18–19.
Rorschach, K. "Fragonard at the Rosenbach Museum and Library." *Apollo,* June 1985, pp. 418–19.
Rorschach, K., and S. B. Taylor. *See* exhibitions, Philadelphia, 1985.
Rosenberg, P. "Une Esquisse inédite de Suvée." *Revue du Louvre,* no. 1 (1967), pp. 33–34.
——. "La Peinture française en Suède" (Exhibition review). *Revue de l'art,* no. 1–2 (1968), p. 137.
——. "Le XVIIIᵉ Siècle français à la Royal Academy" (Exhibition review). *Revue de l'art,* no. 3 (1969), pp. 98–100.
——. "Twenty French Drawings in Sacramento." *Master Drawings* 8, no. 1 (Spring 1970), pp. 31–39.
——. 1972–73. *See* exhibitions, Toronto, 1972–73.
——. "La Fin d'Ango." *Burlington Magazine,* no. 949 (Apr. 1982), pp. 236–39.
——. *Tout l'oeuvre peint de Chardin.* Paris, 1983.
——. "Une Correspondance de Julien de Parme (1736–1799)." *Archives de l'art français,* n.s. 26 (1984), pp. 197–245.
——. Review of *French Drawings, Eighteenth Century,* by Per Bjurström. *Master Drawings* 22, no. 1 (1984), pp. 64–70.
——. 1984. *See also* exhibitions, Paris, Musée du Louvre, 1984.
Rosenberg, P., and B. Brejon de Lavergnée. *Saint-Non, Fragonard, Panopticon Italiano: Un diario di viaggio ritrovato, 1759–1761.* Rome, 1986.
Rosenberg, P., and I. Compin. "Quatre Nouveaux Fragonard au Louvre." *Revue du Louvre,* no. 3 (1974), pp. 183–92; no. 4–5 (1974), pp. 263–78.
——. 1974. *See also* exhibitions, Paris, Musée du Louvre, 1974.
R[osenberg], P., and M.-A. D[upuy]. *See* exhibitions, Toulon, 1985.
Rosenberg, P., and U. van de Sandt. *Pierre Peyron, 1744–1814.* Paris, 1983.
Rosenblum, R. *Transformations in Late Eighteenth Century Art.* Princeton, 1967.
Roskamp, D. "*Der Philosoph* von Jean-Honoré Fragonard." *Jahrbuch der Hamburger Kunstsammlungen* 6 (1961), pp. 72–78.
Ross, T. "Notes on Selected French Old Master Drawings from the Permanent Collections." *Record of The Art Museum, Princeton University* 42, no. 1 (1983), pp. 4–42.
Roth, G. *See* Diderot, D. 1964.
Röthlisberger, M. "Quelques tableaux inédits du XVIIIᵉ siècle français: Lesueur, Claude Lorrain, La Fosse." *Revue de l'art,* no. 11 (1971), pp. 82–84.
Rouchès, G. "L'Interprétation du *Roland Furieux* et de la *Jérusalem délivrée* dans les arts plastiques." *Études italiennes,* no. 4 (Oct. 1920), pp. 193–224.
——. "L'Interprétation du *Roland Furieux* par la gravure." *L'Amateur d'estampes,* July 1925, pp. 107–12; Oct. 1925, pp. 145–53.
Roux, M. *Inventaire du fonds français: Graveurs du XVIIIᵉ siècle.* Paris, Bibliothèque Nationale, Cabinet des Estampes, vol. I, 1930–31; vol. II, 1933; vol. III, 1934; vol. IV, 1940; vol. V, 1946; vol. VI, 1949.
Roux, M., and E. Pognon. *Inventaire du fonds*

français: Graveurs du XVIII' siècle. Paris, Bibliothèque Nationale, Cabinet des Estampes, vol. VII, 1951; vol. VIII, 1955.

Rubin, J. R. "Le Poète inspiré: Le Portrait de Lebrun-Pindare par Jean Bernard Restout." *Revue du Louvre,* no. 2 (1980), pp. 77–79.

Rubinstein-Bloch, S. *Catalogue of the Collection of George and Florence Blumenthal, New York.* Vols. IV and V. Paris, 1930.

Rudrauf, L. "Imagination matérielle et imagination formelle chez Fragonard." *Les Cahiers techniques de l'art,* Jan.–Apr. 1947, pp. 5–20.

Rueppel, M. C. "Fragonard and America: A Loan of French Paintings to Dallas." *Connoisseur,* no. 656 (Oct. 1966), pp. 88–89.

Rusk Shapley, F. *See* Shapley, F. Rusk.

Ryszkiewicz, A. "Vanloo et Pierre (sur quelques tableaux avec 'Turqueries' dans les collections polonaises)." *Bulletin du Musée National de Varsovie,* no. 1 (1975), pp. 13–27.

S

Sahut, M.-C. *See* exhibitions, Paris, 1984–85.

Saint-Cloud. Château. *Notice des tableaux placés dans les appartements du château de Saint-Cloud.* Paris, 1831.

Saint-Groux, A. de. "La Collection Ch. Sedelmeyer." *Les Arts,* no. 64 (Apr. 1907), pp. 33–40.

Saint-Non, Abbé de. *Fragments choisis dans les peintures et les tableaux les plus intéressans des palais et des églises de l'Italie....* [Paris, 1770–75].

——. *Voyage pittoresque; ou, Description des Royaumes de Naples et de Sicile.* 5 vols. Paris, 1781–86. See especially vols. I–IV.

——. *Journal. See* Rosenberg, P., and B. Brejon de Lavergnée, 1986.

——. *Recueil de Griffonis.... See* Cayeux, J. de, 1964. *See also* Rosenberg, P., and B. Brejon de Lavergnée, 1986.

Saint-Victor, P. de. "Exposition de tableaux anciens." *Beaux-Arts,* Oct. 19, 1860, unpaged.

Salgues, Y. "La Vie passionnée de Fragonard." *Jours de France,* no. 598 (Apr. 30, 1966), pp. 68–76.

Salinger, M. *The Metropolitan Museum of Art: Miniatures.* New York, 1956.

Sánchez Cantón, F. J. *La colección Cambó.* Barcelona, 1955.

Sandoz, M. "Études et esquisses peintes ou dessinées de Jean-Baptiste Deshays." *Gazette des Beaux-Arts,* Apr.–June 1951, pp. 129–46.

——. *Gabriel François Doyen, 1726–1806.* Paris, 1975.

——. *Jean-Baptiste Deshays, 1729–1765.* Paris, 1978.

——. *Jean-Simon Berthélemy.* Paris, 1979.

——. *Nicolas-Guy Brenet.* Paris, 1979.

——. *Louis-Jacques Durameau, 1733–1796.* Paris, 1980.

——. *Les Lagrenée.* Paris, 1983.

Sardou, J. B. *Inventaire sommaire des Archives Communales antérieures à 1790, Ville de Grasse.* Paris, 1865.

• Sauerländer, W. "Über die ursprüngliche Reihenfolge von Fragonards *Amours des bergers.*" *Münchner Jahrbuch der bildenden Kunst* 19 (1968), pp. 127–56.

Saunier, Ch. "Une Collection de dessins de maîtres provinciaux: Le Musée Xavier Atger à Montpellier." *Gazette des Beaux-Arts,* Mar. 1922, pp. 35–50, 161–80.

Schiaffino, E. *La pintura y la escultura en Argentina.* Buenos Aires, 1933.

Schidlof, L. R. *La Miniature en Europe aux XVI', XVII', XVIII', XIX' siècles.* 4 vols. Graz, 1964.

Schmidt, J. von. "Le Baiser à la dérobée." *Tableaux célèbres des galeries d'Europe.* Paris, 1909.

Schmidt Degener, F. "Het genetische problem von de Nachtwacht." *Onze Kunst* 1917, pp. 97–100.

Schnapper, A. *See* exhibitions, Lille, 1985.

Schneider, P. *Louvre Dialogue.* New York, 1971. French translation, *Les Dialogues du Louvre.* Paris, 1971.

Schneider, R. *L'Art français, dix-huitième siècle.* Paris, 1926.

Schneider-Maunoury, M. "La Vie heureuse de Frago." *Arts,* Aug. 4–10, 1954, p. 80.

Schommer, P. "L'Exposition de Carnavalet: Le Théâtre à Paris, XVII' et XVIII' siècles." *Le Figaro, supplément artistique,* no. 227 (Apr. 4, 1929), pp. 413–14.

Schönberger, A., and H. Soehner. *L'Europe du XVIII' siècle.* Paris, 1960.

Schönbrunner, J., and J. Meder. *Handzeichnungen alter Meister aus der Albertina und anderen Sammlungen.* 13 vols. Vienna, 1896–1908.

Schrey, R. "Zeichnungen aus dem Kupferstichkabinett des Hessischen Landesmuseums zu Darmstadt." *Stift und Feder,* July 1929.

Schulz, B. "Observations Concerning a Rediscovered Drawing by Fragonard in Darmstadt." *Master Drawings* 22, no. 4 (1984), pp. 440–43.

Sciolla, G. C. *I disegni di maestri stranieri della Biblioteca Reale di Torino.* Turin, 1974.

Scott, B. "Madame Geoffrin, a Patron and Friend of Artists." *Apollo,* Feb. 1967, pp. 98–103.

——. "Madame du Barry, a Royal Favourite with Taste." *Apollo,* Jan. 1973, pp. 60–71.

Seligman, G. *Oh! Fickle Taste.* New York, 1952.

——. *Merchants of Art: 1880–1960.* New York, 1961.

Seligman, G., and J. Ethlyne. "The Myth of the Fragonard Portraits at Chantilly; or, the Re-discovery of Jean-Marie Ribou." *Art Quarterly,* Spring 1958, pp. 23–38.

Senior, E. "Drawings Made in Italy by Fragonard." *British Museum Quarterly* 11, no. 1 (1936), pp. 5–9.

Sentenac, P. *Hubert Robert.* Paris, 1929.

Serbat, L. "Le Voyage d'Italie et les dessins de l'architecte J.-J. Huvé." *Bulletin de la Société de l'Histoire de l'Art Français* 1924, pp. 40–56.

Sérieys, A., ed. *Lettres du père Paciaudi au comte de Caylus.* Paris, 1802.

Sérullaz, A., and N. Volle. "Dessins néoclassiques: Bilan d'une exposition." Part 2, "Dessins inédits de Fragonard, David, et Drouais." *Revue du Louvre,* no. 2 (1976), pp. 77–81.

Sérullaz, M., L. Duclaux, and G. Monnier. *Dessins du Louvre: École française.* Paris, 1968.

Seznec, J. "Fragonard, interprète de l'Arioste: La Lettre et l'esprit." *Bulletin des études françaises,* Nov.–Dec. 1945, pp. 27–38.

——. 1945. *See also* Mongan, E., Ph. Hofer, and J. Seznec.

——. "Voltaire and Fragonard: Notes on a Legend." *Journal of the Warburg and Courtauld Institutes* 10 (1947), pp. 109–13.

——. *Diderot Salons.* Vol. II, *1765.* 2d ed. Oxford, 1979.

Seznec, J., and J. Adhémar. *Diderot Salons.* Vol. II, *1765.* Oxford, 1960; Vol. III, *1767.* Oxford, 1963; Vol. IV, *1769, 1771, 1775, 1781.* Oxford, 1967.

Shackelford, G. T. M. "Master Drawings." *Museum of Fine Arts, Houston, Bulletin* 9, no. 1 (Fall 1983).

Shapley, F. Rusk. *See* exhibitions, Washington, D.C., 1950.

Sheriff, M. D. "*Au génie de Franklin,* an Allegory by J.-H. Fragonard." *American Philosophical Society* 127, no. 3 (1983), pp. 180–93.

——. "On Fragonard's Enthusiasm." In *The Eighteenth Century: Theory and Interpretation.* 1986.

——. "For Love or Money? Rethinking Fragonard." *Eighteenth-Century Studies* 19, no. 3 (Spring 1986), pp. 333–54.

——. "Invention, Resemblance, and Fragonard's *Portraits de Fantaisie.*" *Art Bulletin* 69 (Mar. 1987), pp. 77–87.

Shestack, A. *See* exhibitions, New Haven, 1984.

Sidoroff, A. A. "Handzeichnungen alter Meister im Moskauer Museum der Schönen Kunst." *Zeitschrift für bildende Kunst* 1929–30, p. 224.

——. *Risunki starykh masterov: Tekhnika, teoriya, istoriya* (Drawings of the old masters). Moscow and Leningrad, 1940.

Simches, S. O. *Le Romantisme et le goût esthétique du XVIII' siècle.* Paris, 1964.

Simpson, J. G. *Le Tasse et la littérature et l'art baroque en France.* Paris, 1962.

Singer, H. W. "Der Vierfarbendruck in der Gefolgschaft Jacob Christoffel Le Blons." *Monatshefte für Kunstwissenschaft,* no. 8–9 (1917), pp. 301–14.

Singer-Lecocq, Y. *Un Louvre inconnu: Quand l'État y logeait ses artistes.* Paris, 1985.

Siple, E. S. "Recent Acquisitions in America." *Burlington Magazine,* no. 347 (Feb. 1932), pp. 109–16.

Sizer, Th. *See* Trumbull, J.

Sjöberg, Y., and F. Gardey. *Inventaire du fonds français: Graveurs du XVIII' siècle.* Paris, Bibliothèque Nationale, Cabinet des Estampes, vol. XIII, 1974; vol. XIV, 1977.

Slatkin, R. "The New Boucher Catalogue." *Burlington Magazine,* no. 911 (Feb. 1979), pp. 117–23.

Slive, S. "A Fragonard Landscape after Jacob Van Ruisdael's *Wooded Landscape with a Pond.*" In *The Shape of the Past: Studies in Honor of Franklin D. Murphy,* pp. 268–76. Los Angeles, 1981.

Sollers, Ph. *Le Coeur absolu.* Paris, 1987.

Soulier, G. "Tribune des arts: Un Fragonard à Rome." *Les Arts,* no. 186 (1920), pp. 19–22.

Stampfle, F. *Seventh Annual Report to the Fellows of the Pierpont Morgan Library* 1957, pp. 76–79.

Standen, E. *See* exhibitions, Paris, Grand Palais, 1986–87.

Stanton, D. "A Drawing by Fragonard." *Bulletin of The Art Institute of Chicago,* no. 6 (Nov. 1936), pp. 77–79.

Starobinski, J. *L'Invention de la liberté.* Geneva, 1964.

Stein, H. "La Société des Beaux-Arts de Montpellier, 1779–1787" (Mélanges offerts à Henry Lemonnier). *Archives de l'art français* 1913, pp. 365–403.

Steinberg, L. "Deliberate Speed." *Art News,* Apr. 1967, pp. 42–47.

Stenger, G. *La Société française pendant le Consulat.* Paris, 1907.

Sterling, Ch. "L'Art français aux États-Unis." *Musées de France,* suppl. 1949, pp. 7–15.

——. 1955. *See* Metropolitan Museum of Art, New York, 1955.

——. *Musée de l'Ermitage: La Peinture française de Poussin à nos jours.* Paris, 1957. English translation, *Great French Painting in the Hermitage,* New York [1958].

• ——. *Portrait of a Man (The Warrior), Jean-Honoré Fragonard: An Unknown Masterpiece by*

Fragonard. Williamstown, 1964.
Sterling, Ch., et al. *The Thyssen-Bornemisza Collection*. 2 vols. Castagnola, 1969.
Sterling and Francine Clark Art Institute, Williamstown, Mass. *See* Sterling, Ch. 1964; *see also* Haverkamp-Begemann, E. 1964.
Stern, J. *Mesdemoiselles Colombe*. Paris, 1923.
Stockho, T. R. "French Paintings of the Seventeenth and Eighteenth Centuries." *Saint Louis Art Museum Bulletin*, n.s., 16, no. 1 (1981), pp. 22–23.
Stuffmann, M. "Französische Malerei." In *Die Kunst des 18. Jahrhunderts*. Berlin, 1971.
———. *See* exhibitions, Frankfurt am Main, 1986–87.
Sutton, D. 1980. *See* exhibitions, Tokyo–Kyoto, 1980.
———. "Frivolity and Reason." *Apollo*, Feb. 1987, pp. 80–91.
———. "Jean-Honoré Fragonard: The World as Illusion." *Apollo*, Feb. 1987, pp. 102–13. (New version of the preface to the exhibition catalogue, Tokyo, 1980.)
[Swarzenski, G.]. *Aquarelle von Jean-Honoré Fragonard im Besitz des Kupferstich Kabinetts des Städelschen Kunstinstituts*. Frankfurt am Main, n.d.
Szambien, W. *Les Projets de l'an II*. Paris, École des Beaux-Arts, 1986.

T

Tasset, J. M. "Faux Fragonard: Féroce bataille entre experts." *Le Figaro*, Mar. 10, 1978.
Tavernier, L. "Fragonard in Italia: Il giardino della villa d'Este a Tivoli." *Atti del convegno "Artisti e scrittori europei a Roma e nel Lazio: Dal Grand Tour ai romantici,"* pp. 39–57. Rome, 1984.
Terver, P. *Le Dernier Prince de Conti à l'Isle-Adam*. Pontoise, 1987.
Thiébault-Sisson, F. "Autour de Fragonard." *Le Temps*, Nov. 9, 1913, p. 3.
———. "Le Salon de la Correspondance." *Le Temps*, Nov. 27, 1913, p. 3.
Thieme, U., and F. Becker. *Allgemeines Lexikon der bildenden Künstler von der Antike bis zur Gegenwart*, vol. XII, pp. 275–76. Entry by R. Graul. Leipzig, 1916.
Thiéry, L. V. *Guide des amateurs et des étrangers voyageurs à Paris*. 2 vols. Paris, 1786–87.
Thirion, H. *La Vie privée des financiers au XVIIIᵉ siècle*. Paris, 1895.
Thoré, Th. [W. Bürger, pseud.]. "Galeries particulières. Collection de M. de Cypierre: Les Peintres au XVIIIᵉ siècle." *Le Constitutionnel*, no. 275 (Oct. 1, 1844), pp. 1–3.
———. "Vente de tableaux composant le cabinet de M. Saint." *Bulletin des arts*, May 10, 1846, pp. 369–71.
———. "Exposition de tableaux de l'école française ancienne tirés de collections d'amateurs." *Gazette des Beaux-Arts*, Sept. 1, 1860, pp. 258–77; Sept. 15, 1860, pp. 333–58; Nov. 15, 1860, pp. 228–40.
———. "Galerie de MM. Péreire." *Gazette des Beaux-Arts*, Mar. 1, 1864, pp. 193–213.
———. "Les Collections particulières." *Paris guide* 1867.
Thuillier, J. 1964. *See* Châtelet, A., and J. Thuillier.
• ———. *Fragonard*. Geneva, 1967.
———. "Le Langage de Fragonard." *Bulletin de la Société des Amis du Musée de Dijon* 1967–69, pp. 51–52.

———. 1974. *See* exhibitions, Paris, Musée du Louvre, 1974.
———. "Fragonard." In *Larousse des grands peintres*. Paris, 1976.
———. "Fragonard." In *Petit Larousse de la peinture*, vol. I. Paris, 1979.
———. "La Peinture en Provence au Musée de Toulon." *Revue du Louvre*, no. 1 (1987), pp. 9–12.
Thyssen-Bornemisza Collection, Lugano. *See* Sterling, Ch., et al. 1969.
Timken Art Gallery, San Diego. *See* Mongan, A. and E.
Tintelnot, H. *Die barocke Freskomalerei in Deutschland*. Munich, 1951.
Tinti, M. "Il Parmigianino." *Dedalo* 1 (1923), pp. 304–26.
Toledo Museum of Art. *European Paintings*. Toledo, Ohio, 1976.
Tornézy, M. A. 1895. *See* Bergeret de Grancourt, P. J. O. 1895.
Tourneux, M. 1875–77. *See* Diderot, D. 1875–77.
———. 1877–82. *See* Grimm.
———. "Les Portraits de Diderot." *L'Art* 1 (1878), pp. 121–30.
———. *L'Âge du romantisme*. Paris, 1887.
———. *Les Tableaux historiques de la Révolution et leurs transformations*. Paris, 1888.
———. "L'Exposition Chardin-Fragonard." *Gazette des Beaux-Arts*, Aug. 1907, pp. 89–102.
Trumbull, J. *The Autobiography of Colonel John Trumbull*. Edited by T. Sizer. New Haven, 1953.
Tuetey, A. "L'Émigration de Madame Vigée-Lebrun." *Bulletin de la Société de l'Histoire de l'Art Français* 1911, pp. 169–82.
Tuetey, A., and Jean Guiffrey. "La Commission du Muséum et la création du Musée du Louvre (1792–1793)." *Archives de l'art français*, n.s. 3 (1909).
Tuetey, L. "Procès-Verbaux de la Commission des Monuments." *Nouvelles Archives de l'art français* 17 (1901); 18 (1902).
———. *Procès-Verbaux de la Commission Temporaire des Arts*. Paris, vol. I, 1912; vol. II, 1917.
Tuzet, H. "Une Querelle littéraire en 1785: L'Abbé de Saint-Non et ses collaborateurs." *Revue de littérature comparée*, no. 83 (July–Sept. 1947), pp. 428–36.

V

Valentiner, W. R., and P. Wescher. *Catalog of the Collection of Mrs. Lucius Peyton Green (Mildred Browning Green)*. Los Angeles, 1956.
Vallery-Radot, J. "Notes sur le peintre liégeois Léonard Defrance." *Bulletin de la Société de l'Histoire de l'Art Français* 1924, pp. 233–42.
———. "Quelques dates dans l'oeuvre de Léonard Defrance, de Liège." *La Revue d'art* (Antwerp) 27, no. 5–6 (1926), pp. 23–39.
———. "Fragonard aquafortiste." *Arts*, Jan. 11, 1956, p. 12.
Valogne, C. "Fragonard, mon grand-père, par Théophile Fragonard." *Les Lettres françaises*, Feb. 17, 1955, pp. 1, 7, 9.
Valori, Mme C. T. de. *Greuze; ou, L'Accordée du village*. Preceded by "Notice sur Greuze et sur ses ouvrages," pp. 1–28. Paris, 1813.
Van der Elst, J. *Six contes ... six tableaux*. Paris, 1950.
Van Regteren Altena, J. Q. "Bajocco." In *Festschrift E. Trautschol[dt]*, pp. 136–42. Hamburg, 1965.
Varshavskaya, M. *Kartiny Rubensa v Ermitazh;*

Rubens' paintings in the Hermitage Museum (in Russian; captions and introduction also in English). Leningrad, 1975.
Vatel, Ch. *Histoire de Madame du Barry*. Versailles, 1883.
Vaudoyer, J.-L. "L'Orientalisme en Europe au XVIIIᵉ siècle." *Gazette des Beaux-Arts*, Aug. 1911, pp. 89, 102.
———. "Un Fragonard quitte la France." *Plaisir de France*, no. 267 (Jan. 1961), pp. 22–23.
V[auxcelles], L. "Un Chef-d'oeuvre de Fragonard retrouvé." *Le Carnet des artistes*, Feb. 15, 1917, pp. 9–11.
Vayer, L. *Meisterzeichnungen aus der Sammlung des Museums der Bildenden Künste in Budapest (14–18 Jahrhundert)*. Budapest, 1956.
Vergnet-Ruiz, J. "Une *Sainte Famille* de Fragonard." *Bulletin des musées de France*, no. 3 (Mar. 1934), p. 60.
Vergnet-Ruiz, J., and M. Laclotte. *Petits et Grands Musées de France*. Paris, 1962.
Verly, P.-L. "Honoré Fragonard, Anatomiste, premier directeur de l'école d'Alfort." Thesis, Maison-Alfort, 1963.
Vermeule, C. *European Art and the Classical Past*. Cambridge, Mass., 1964.
Versini, C. "Fragonard à l'exposition des tableaux de l'École française de l'Ermitage au Louvre." *Les Cahiers de l'Académie Anquetin* 20 (Aug. 1974), pp. 61–67.
———. "Fragonard: Présentation de ses oeuvres au Musée du Louvre." *Les Cahiers de l'Académie Anquetin* 20 (Aug. 1974), pp. 69–74.
———. "La Vie de Fragonard." *Les Cahiers de l'Académie Anquetin* 20 (Aug. 1974), pp. 75–93.
Vigée Le Brun, Mme E. *Souvenirs de Madame Vigée Le Brun*. 3 vols. Paris, 1835–37.
Vigier, J. "Le Cousin Pons à Bordeaux: Il y trouve un auteur Fragonard inconnu." *Le Cousin Pons*, no. 110 (June 15, 1925), pp. 10–11.
Villain, J. *Fragonard*. Paris, 1949.
———. 1975. *See* exhibitions, Brussels, 1975.
———. 1977. *See* exhibitions, Troyes–Nîmes–Rome, 1977.
———. 1980-81. *See* exhibitions, Sydney, 1980-81.
Villiers, P. *Manuel du voyageur aux environs de Paris*. Vol. I. Paris, 1802.
Villiers, S. de. "*Le Billet doux* de Fragonard." *La Vie des arts*, Nov. 3, 1937, p. 9.
Villot, F. *Notice des tableaux exposés dans les galeries du Musée Imperial du Louvre*. Paris, 1855. Many subsequent editions published.
———. *Hall, célèbre miniaturiste du XVIIIᵉ siècle*. Paris, 1867.
Vindry, G. "Les Fresques de la Villa Fragonard." *Grasse expansions* 1972.
Virch, C. *Master Drawings in the Collection of Walter C. Baker*. New York, 1962.
Vivant-Denon, D. *See* Denon, D. Vivant.
Volle, N. *Jean-Simon Berthélemy*. Paris, 1979.

W

W. *See* Wildenstein, G. 1960.
W. and M. *See* Wildenstein, D., and G. Mandel.
Wakefield, D. *Fragonard*. London, 1976.
———. 1978. *See* exhibitions, London, Agnew & Sons, 1978.
———. "Fragonard's Drawings for Ariosto's Orlando Furioso." *Connoisseur*, no. 803 (Jan. 1979), pp. 131–34.
———. *French Eighteenth Century Painting*. London, 1984.

Walch, P. "Foreign Artists at Naples, 1750–1799." *Burlington Magazine,* no. 913 (1979), pp. 247–52.

Wallace Collection, London. *See* Reynolds, G.

Wallraf-Richartz-Museum, Cologne. *See* Röbels, H.

Watelet, J. "L'Orient dans l'art français, 1650–1800." *Études d'art* (Musée National des Beaux-Arts d'Alger), no. 14 (1959), pp. 126–28.

Watson, F. J. B. "Fragonard, the Definitive Book." *Connoisseur,* no. 591 (Mar. 1961), pp. 38–39.

———. *Jean-Honoré Fragonard.* I maestri del colore, no. 163. Milan, 1966.

———. "Eighteenth Century Painting and Decorative Arts." *Apollo,* Dec. 1967, pp. 454–65.

———. "Fragonard: Painterly and Non-Painterly in the France of Louis XVI." *Art News Annual* 37 (1971), pp. 75–88.

Watson, F. J. B., and G. Dardel. "Fragonard dans son musée à Grasse." *Chefs-d'oeuvre de l'art: Grands peintres,* no. 67 (Sept. 26, 1967).

Wavrin, I. de. "Faux Fragonard et règlement de comptes." *La Vie française,* Mar. 20, 1978, p. 7.

Weinshenker, A. B. "*The Lover Crowned* in Eighteenth-Century French Art." *Studies in Eighteenth-Century Culture* 16 (1986), pp. 271–94.

Wells-Robertson, S. 1974–75. *See* exhibitions, Paris, Grand Palais, 1974–75.

———. "Marguerite Gérard." Ph.D. diss., New York, 1978.

———. "Marguerite Gérard et les Fragonard." *Bulletin de la Société de l'Histoire de l'Art Français* 1977 (1979), pp. 179–89.

[Welu], J. A. "*Sleeping Endymion,* by Nicolas-Guy Brenet." *Worcester Art Museum Bulletin,* Nov. 1974, pp. 5–7.

Wentzel, H. "Jean-Honoré Fragonards *Schaukel.*" *Wallraf-Richartz-Jahrbuch* 26 (1964), pp. 187–218.

Wescher, P. "Les Maîtres français du XVIIIᵉ siècle au cabinet des dessins de Berlin." *Gazette des Beaux-Arts* 1934, 1st semester, pp. 351–69.

Wildenstein, D. "*Le Verrou* du Louvre est un faux." *Le Quotidien de Paris,* Oct. 9, 1974.

———. "Sur *Le Verrou* de Fragonard." *Gazette des Beaux-Arts,* Jan. 1975, pp. 13–24.

Wildenstein, D. and Guy. *Louis David: Recueil de documents complémentaires au catalogue de l'oeuvre de l'artiste.* Rouen, 1973.

• Wildenstein, D., and G. Mandel. *L'opera completa di Fragonard.* Milan, 1972.

Wildenstein, Georges. "L'Exposition Fragonard au pavillon de Marsan." *Revue de l'art français,* no. 7 (July 1921), pp. 356–63.

———. "Deux Tableaux de Fragonard au musée d'Angers." *Beaux-Arts,* no. 8 (1923), pp. 120–22.

———. "Un Souvenir de voyage de Fragonard: *La Petite Fille assise sur ses talons* de la Bibliothèque de Besançon." *Les Trésors des bibliothèques de France* 1 (1925), pp. 22–26.

———. "Fragonard et les expositions de son temps." In *Mélanges,* pp. 5–23. Paris, 1926.

———. 1926. *See also* Hourticq, L. et al.

———. "L'Exposition de l'art français de Londres: Le XVIIIᵉ Siècle." *Gazette des Beaux-Arts,* Jan. 1932, pp. 55–76.

———. "Quatre Fragonard inédits." *Gazette des Beaux-Arts,* May 1935, pp. 271–74.

———. "J.-H. Fragonard et la douceur de vivre (à propos de l'exposition de Berne)." *Arts,* Aug. 4–10, 1954.

• ———. *Fragonard, aquafortiste: Etudes et documents pour servir à l'histoire de l'art français du dix-huitième siècle.* Paris, 1956.

———. "Richesse et unité de l'oeuvre de Fragonard (à propos de l'exposition de Besançon)." *Beaux-Arts,* Aug. 19–25, 1956, p. 9.

———. "Fragonard et la formation des collections du Musée du Louvre." *Gazette des Beaux-Arts,* Oct. 1959, pp. 191–202.

• ———. "L'Abbé de Saint-Non: Artiste et mécène." *Gazette des Beaux-Arts,* Nov. 1959, pp. 225–44.

• ———. *The Paintings of Fragonard.* Aylesbury, 1960; French ed. [Paris], 1960 (with a more complete biography).

———. "*La Fête de Saint-Cloud* et Fragonard." *Gazette des Beaux-Arts,* Jan. 1960, pp. 45–50.

———. "Fragonard, Dorat, et les *Baisers.*" *Gazette des Beaux-Arts,* Apr. 1961, pp. 249–52.

• ———. "Un Amateur de Boucher et de Fragonard, Jacques-Onésyme Bergeret (1715–1785)." *Gazette des Beaux-Arts,* July–Aug. 1961, pp. 39–84.

Wilenski, R. H. *French Painting.* Boston, 1931; rev. ed., Boston, 1949; 3d rev. ed., New York, 1973; reprint, 1979.

Wilhelm, J. "Fragonard, illustrateur." *Le Portique,* Jan. 1945, pp. 90–102.

———. "Fragonard." In *Les Peintres célèbres,* edited by B. Dorival. Vol. IV, pp. 232–33. Geneva, 1948.

———. "Fragonard as a Painter of Realistic Landscapes." *Art Quarterly* 11 (Fall 1948), pp. 297–304.

———. 1948. *See also* Bergeret de Grancourt, P. J. O. 1948.

———. 1950. *See* exhibitions, Paris, Musée Carnavalet, 1950.

• ———. "Fragonard." Unpublished monograph written 1950–60.

———. "Fragonard eut-il un atelier?" *Médecine de France,* no. 25 (1951), pp. 17–28.

———. "A Berne, l'exposition Fragonard." *Combat-Art,* no. 9 (Sept. 6, 1954), p. 2.

———. "In Search of Some Missing Fragonard Paintings." *Art Quarterly,* Winter 1955, pp. 364–76.

• ———. "Deux Dessus de portes de Fragonard provenant du château de Louveciennes." *La Revue des arts,* no. 4 (1956), pp. 215–22.

———. "Où étaient-ils sous le Second Empire?" *L'Œil,* no. 18 (June 1956), pp. 10–17.

———. "David et ses portraits." *Art de France* 4 (1964), pp. 158–73.

———. "Le Salon du graveur Gilles Demarteau peint par François Boucher et son atelier avec le concours de Fragonard et de J.-B. Huet." *Bulletin du Musée Carnavalet,* no. 1 (1975), pp. 6–20.

———. "La Coupole peinte par Antoine Callet pour la salon de compagnie des petits appartements du palais Bourbon." *Bulletin de la Société de l'Histoire de l'Art Français* 1979 (1982), pp. 167–77.

Wille, J.-G. *Mémoires et journal de Jean-Georges Wille.* Edited by G. Duplessis. 2 vols. Paris, 1857.

Williams, E. 1978. *See* exhibitions, Washington, D.C., 1978.

———. "Rescuing Fragonard from a Kind of Limbo." *Art News,* no. 5 (May 5, 1979), pp. 74–78.

———. "A Pair of Portrait Miniatures by Jean-Honoré Fragonard." In *Art at Auction: The Year at Sotheby's, 1981–82,* pp. 210–12. London, 1982.

———. 1984. *See* exhibitions, Cambridge, Mass., 1984.

Williams, H. W., Jr. "Portrait of a Lady with a Dog by Fragonard." *Bulletin of The Metropolitan Museum of Art,* 33, no. 1 (Jan. 1938), pp. 14–16.

Willk-Brocard, N. *François-Guillaume Ménageot.* Paris, 1978.

Wilson J. M. *The Painting of the Passions in Theory, Practice, and Criticism in Later Eighteenth Century France.* New York and London, 1981.

Wise, S. *Catalogue des peintures françaises de Chicago.* Forthcoming.

Wolff, E. "The Fragonard Plates for the *Contes* et *Nouvelles* of La Fontaine." *Bulletin of the New York Public Library,* Mar. 1949.

Worcester Art Museum. *European Paintings in the Collection of the Worcester Art Museum.* 2 vols. Worcester, Mass., 1974.

Wright, B. S. "New (Stage) Light on Fragonard's *Corésus.*" *Arts Magazine* 60, no. 10 (June 1986), pp. 55–59.

Wrigley, R. "Pierre-François Delauney, Liberty, and Saint Nicholas." *Burlington Magazine,* no. 945 (Dec. 1981), pp. 745–47.

Wurth Harris, M. A. *See* Harris, M. A. W.

Y

Yussupov Gallery, Leningrad. *Musée du prince Youssoupoff contenant les tableaux, marbres, ivoires, et porcelaines qui se trouvent dans son hôtel à Saint-Petersbourg.* Saint Petersburg, 1839.

———. *Iusupovskaia galeria: Frantsuzskaia* (The Yussupov Gallery: French School; in Russian and French), by S. Ernst. Leningrad, 1924.

Z

Z. C. "Franklin Portraits: The Rockefeller Collection." *Philadelphia Museum Bulletin* 44, no. 220 (Winter 1948), pp. 19–31.

Zafran, E. *See* exhibitions, Atlanta, 1983–84.

Zick, G. "Der zerbrochene Krug als Bildmotiv des 18. Jahrhunderts." *Wallraf-Richartz-Jahrbuch,* Nov. 1969, pp. 149–204.

Zolotov, Y. K. "Les Lettres des artistes français du 18ᵉ siècle dans les archives soviétiques." *Revue d'histoire de la civilisation mondiale,* no. 5 (Sept.–Oct. 1958), pp. 146–56.

———. *Fragonard* (in Russian.) Moscow, 1959.

———. "Eighteenth-Century French Art." In *Universal History of Art,* vol. IV (in Russian). Moscow, 1963.

———. *Frantsuzskiĭ portret vosemnadtsatogo veka* (French portraits of the 18th century). Moscow, 1968.

Index of Names

Listed below are the names of individuals mentioned in the catalogue, with the exception of those cited in the Acknowledgments (page 13), the Family Tree (pages 36–37), and in the Bibliography, as well as the references to works by A. Ananoff, G. Wildenstein, D. Wildenstein and G. Mandel, and those proper names that figure in the titles of works. Numbers refer to page numbers.

R

Rabasse, 393
Radix de Sainte-Foy, 456
Radziwill collection, 483
Randon de Boisset, 178, 195, 216, 272, 274, 420, 451, 452, 472
Raoux, Jean, 209
Raphael, 38, 61, 64, 120, 124, 295, 302, 587, 590
Raphaël, Marquis de Ferrari, 50
Raphaël le Jeune (Daudet de Jossan), 296, 300
Rapilly, 310, 462
Ratouis de Limay, P., 22, 278, 284, 296, 429, 537
Ravai, Francesco, 378
Réau, L., 40, 48, 52, 68, 81, 82, 161, 178, 181, 184, 192, 234, 240, 261, 272, 276, 278, 286, 310, 314, 323, 346, 352, 356, 376, 390, 442, 496, 501, 549, 575
Reber, 493
Reboul, 401
Récamier, Mme, 303
Récipon, G., 161
Recouvreur, A., 218
Regenstein, Helen, 172
Regnault, N. F., 310, 429, 431, 483, 546, 548, 573, 574, 577, 589
von Rehling-Quistgaard, Waldemar, 272
Reinach, S., 155
Reinhart, Oskar, 403
Reininghaus collection, 100
Rembrandt, 34, 58, 92, 150, 163, 168, 172, 178, 180, 182, 183, 202, 204, 206, 207, 208, 209, 216, 225, 236, 254, 266, 270, 295, 296, 405, 456, 476, 484, 505, 587, 590
Rémusat, Abel, 484
Rémy, B., 48, 229, 296, 297, 302, 323, 418, 428, 472
Renaud, François, 237, 246, 381, 406, 408, 410, 411, 412, 413, 440, 544
Reni, Guido, 62, 67, 123, 136, 202, 591
Renou, Antoine, 296, 297, 302, 316, 355, 430, 475, 510, 582
Renouvier, Jules, 31, 256, 562, 584
Restout, J., 34
Reutschler, George A., 206
Revenez, 495
Rey, 88
Rhodes, Margaret E., 572
Ribeiro da Cunha, Mr., 334
Ribera, G., 121, 123, 421, 423, 588
Ribou, Jean-Marie, 423, 424
Ricasoli, Baron, 465
Riccardi, Marquis, 131
de Ricci, Seymour, 120, 122, 123, 133, 149, 219, 306
Rich, D. Catton, 193
Richard, Jean-Pierre, 276
Richardson, J., 236
Richomme, Joseph-Théodore, 216
Riggieri-Romboccoli, Marie-Catherine, 495
Riggieri-Romboccoli, Marie-Madeleine, 496
Riggieri-Romboccoli, Marie-Thérèse, 424, 496, 497
de Rigny, 573
Rinaldo, 160, 516
Ripa, C., 272
Robert, Hubert, 31, 64, 65, 67, 76, 79, 84, 89, 90, 94, 96, 97, 100, 103, 104, 105, 109, 111, 113, 118, 120, 125, 126, 145, 146, 147, 176, 177, 238, 239, 240, 278, 299, 342, 343, 349, 385, 419, 420, 429, 478, 537, 554, 571, 582, 589, 590, 591, 592
Robespierre, M., 587
Robillard, Hippolyte, 222
Robin, 585, 587
de Roche Bousseau, Marquis, 303

Rochefort, H., 164, 234
Rochoux, 393
Rodriguès, Eugène, 376
Roederer, Louis, 509, 511, 517, 518, 520
Roettiers, 286
Roger, Baron, 248
Rogers, M. R., 88, 544
Rohan-Chabot, L. A. A. de, see de Chabot, Duc
Roland, Henri, 146
Roland (Minister of the Interior), 581, 583
Roland (Orlando), 507, 508–9, 518
Roland Michel, Marianne, 177, 248, 323, 412, 433, 434, 475, 485, 505, 506, 508, 532
Romanet, Antoine-Louis, 222, 431, 456, 458
Romano, Giulio, 587
Romney, George, 503
de la Roncière, 573
Roos, J., 295, 300
Rosa, S., 124
Rosebery, Lord, 573
Rosebery, seventh Earl of, 54
Rosenbach, A. S. W., 509, 511, 517, 518, 520
Rosenbaum, A., 48
Rosenberg, P., 57, 67, 68, 94, 97, 117, 118, 122, 127, 130, 131, 133, 134, 137, 138, 203, 228, 260, 278, 314, 315, 370, 405, 419, 459, 476, 481, 525, 531, 566, 575
Rosenberg & Stiebel, Inc., 46
Rosenwald, Edith G., 517
Roslin, Alexander, 256, 530
Ross, B. T., 545
Rossignol, 250
Roth, G., 300
de Rothschild, Alain, 308
de Rothschild, Alphonse, 46, 235, 284, 286
de Rothschild, Edmond, 328, 346, 352, 449, 481, 486, 487, 492
de Rothschild, Édouard, 284, 286, 299, 312, 495
de Rothschild, James Edmond, 246
de Rothschild, Maurice, 46, 252, 492
de Rothschild, Mayer Amschel, 54
de Rothschild, Nathaniel, 46
de Rothschild, Robert, 308
Rothschild collection, 167, 284
Rouart, Henri, 57, 187
Rousseau, Jean-Jacques, 302, 312, 336, 343, 460
Roussel, Mme Eugène, 463
Roustain de la Barolliere, Pierre, 429
Roux, M., 48, 73, 74, 82, 97, 192, 211, 222, 234, 242, 243, 247, 407, 481, 486, 492, 587
Rubens, Peter Paul, 64, 81, 120, 124, 128, 135, 164, 165, 167, 179, 182, 183, 202, 208, 227, 228, 247, 248, 250, 258, 274, 286, 288, 296, 310, 311, 316, 369, 400, 402, 423, 449, 484, 544, 587, 591
de Ruble, Baronne, 172, 446, 530, 531, 532, 534
Rucellaï, Giuseppe, 463
Ruggieri, 216
Ruggiero, 511–15, 517, 521, 522
Ruisdael, J., 180, 184, 185, 194, 195, 197, 198
Ruotte, Louis-Charles, 416, 584
Ryszkiewicz, A., 575

S

Sabatier d'Espeyran, 279
Sabatté, F., 205
Sachs family, 437
Sage, B. G., 484
Sahut, M.-C., 212
de Saincy, L.-R. Marchal, 342, 344
Saint Anne, 474, 476, 477
Saint, D., 235, 238, 239, 240, 357, 389, 522, 552, 562

de Saint-Aubin, A., 278, 410, 522
de Saint-Aubin, G., 38, 46, 48, 52, 63, 76, 77, 90, 95, 106, 107, 127, 129, 131, 151, 160, 161, 163, 164, 169, 178, 181, 182, 188, 189, 211, 212, 229, 230, 255, 282, 340, 342, 355, 357, 419, 420, 422, 559
de Saint Félix, M., 427, 481, 483, 484
Saint Herman, 183
Saint Jerome, 205, 207, 499
Saint Joseph, 468, 471, 478, 479
de Saint-Julien, Baron Baillet, 46, 48, 50, 226, 227, 349
Saint-Lambert, 442
de Saint-Marc, Marquis, 332
Saint-Maurice, 82
de Saint Morys, Chevalier, 182, 404, 455, 528
de Saint-Non, Abbé, 57, 63, 65–70, 76, 77, 89, 94–97, 100, 106, 108, 111, 117–42, 144–47, 149–51, 153, 155, 156, 157, 176, 177, 203, 205, 211, 225, 227, 228, 229, 242, 246, 247, 255, 257, 270, 272, 276, 278, 279, 299, 300, 301, 332, 334, 344, 349, 357, 362, 388, 393, 394, 400, 405, 410, 411, 418, 420, 421, 422, 429, 431, 449, 474, 476, 488, 489, 549, 565, 566, 583
Saint Peter, 205, 207
de Saint-Priest, Viscomte, 180, 423, 424
de Saint-Sauveur, Mme, 195
Saint Sebastian, 142
Saint Teresa, 550
de Saint-Victor, Bruno, 470
de Saint-Victor, Paul, 85, 161, 163, 165, 241, 276, 304, 316, 473, 544, 562
de Saint-Victor, Robert, 188, 194, 195, 472
Salavin, 57
Salamon, Agustoni & Algranti, 76, 164
Samson collection, 352
Sandoz, M., 171, 542
Santamarina, Constanzo, 551
Santerre, Jean-Baptiste, 209, 591
Sappho, 544
Sardou, J.-B., 424
Saulnier, Adam, 338
Saunier, C., 502
Sauerländer, W., 323
Sauvage, Pieter Joseph, 205, 496
Sauvageot, Charles, 211, 449
Sauzay, 440
Saxe-Teschen, Prince Albert of, 107, 170, 171, 172, 384, 440, 498, 500, 524, 525, 565
de Sayve, Marquis, 355
Scellier, 587, 588, 590
Schall, Frédéric, 555
Schedoni, B., 123, 421, 423
Schiff, John M., 541
Schiff, Mortimer, 219, 357, 358, 508, 541
Schlageter, François, 469, 470
de Schlichting, B., Baron, 460, 546
Schnapper, A., 184
Schneider, P., 216
Schulz, Barbara, 432, 436
Schulze, Christian Gottfried, 449
Schuman, Mme Jacque, 413
Schuman, Robert, 588
Schut, Cornelis, 295
Schwiter, L. A., Baron, 175
Sciolla, G. C., 78
Scipion, 302
Sedelmeyer, Galerie, 82
Seilern collection, 390, 568
Seligmann, Arnold and Rey, 88
Seligmann, Germain, 192, 237, 423, 460
Seligmann, Jacques, 335
Semele, 236
Senez, 591
Sentout, Pierre, 217

de Vogüé, Comte Arthur, 545, 570
de Vögué, Comtesse Charles, 263
Volaire, J.-A., 369
Volland, Sophie, 266
Volle, N., 103, 112, 211, 212, 229, 314, 515
Volpeto, 303
Voltaire, 118
Vouet, S., 160
de Voyer, Marquis, *see* d'Argenson, Marc-René
Vuillard, É., 272

W

Wable, E., 422
de Wailly, 61, 225, 227, 228, 590, 592
Waldeck-Rousseau collection, 455
Walferdin, Hippolyte, 84, 90, 92, 158, 164, 172,
 174, 192, 193, 195, 198, 211, 220, 232, 235,
 238, 245, 249, 250, 252, 260, 263, 311, 316,
 329, 331, 352, 379, 386, 389, 401, 441, 445,
 460, 471, 472, 474, 476, 480, 481, 488, 489,
 492, 509, 511, 514, 517, 518, 520, 522, 528,
 539, 540, 543, 549, 552, 554, 555, 557, 560,
 561, 562, 570, 571
Walker, Dean, 401
Wallace, Richard, 467
Wallet, Eugène, 270, 272, 278
Watel, Mme, 260, 329
Watel-Dehaynin, 260

Wâtelet, L.-E., 537
Watson, F., 197
Watteau, J.-A., 85, 258, 272, 316, 343, 344, 346,
 355, 357, 413, 435, 544, 575
Weil, André, 534
Weiroter, Franz-Edmund, 153
Weisweiller, Alec, 261
Weisweiller, Arthur, 250
Wells-Robertson, Sally, 416, 419, 549, 564, 573,
 574–75, 577, 595
Wentzel, H., 346
Wertheimer, Charles, 116, 320, 541
Whatley, Mrs. Spencer, 125
Wicar, J.-B.-J., 584, 585, 587
Wickes, Forsyth, 357, 358
Wildenstein, D., 79, 82, 89, 279, 290, 332, 481,
 482, 483, 485, 578, 583, 584
Wildenstein, Georges, 35, 40, 50, 167, 169, 187,
 188, 237, 238, 239, 241, 243, 252, 255, 266,
 279, 282, 302, 303, 304, 308, 337, 344, 348,
 352, 355, 357, 359, 432, 437, 446, 451, 453,
 462, 463, 467, 472, 473, 474, 484, 495, 522,
 541, 544, 545, 549, 553, 573, 582
Wildenstein, Nathan, 167
Wilenski, R. H., 481
Wilhelm, Jacques, 158, 172, 178, 184, 195, 205,
 263, 299, 310, 312, 314, 327, 328, 331, 335,
 336, 362, 424, 448, 472, 475, 478
Wille, J.-G., 70, 149, 152, 211, 425
Willems, Joseph-Benoit, 438
Williams, E., 65, 84, 85, 89, 96, 111, 117, 133,

155, 173, 199, 219, 220, 238, 245, 282, 309,
 318, 331, 332, 432, 433, 466, 508, 522, 531,
 535, 539, 546, 559, 564, 568, 569, 573, 575
Willk-Brocard, N., 220
Woodner, Ian, 106, 135, 316, 486, 573
von Wrangell, Baronne, 469
Wright, Beth S., 216
Wrightsman, C. and J., 119
de Würtemberg, Duc, 585
Wurth, Mary Ann, 332, 564
Wu Zhen, 357
Wynants, Jan, 185

Y

Yon de St. Pierre, Mme, 247
Yussupov, Prince, 79, 430, 431, 565

Z

Zafran, Eric, 398
Zarine, 192, 332
Zeffirelli, Franco, 164
Zick, G., 306
Zolotov, Y., 431

List of Plates and Subjects

Numbers refer to catalogue numbers.

627

List of Lenders

Numbers refer to catalogue numbers.

List of Works Exhibited in New York

Several works have been added to the "Fragonard" exhibition in New York that are not discussed in the catalogue. For the convenience of visitors to the exhibition, these works have been given sequential numbers:

66 A Fragonard
Le Petit Parc
Gouache on vellum, 20 x 24.4 cm.
Collection Mr. and Mrs. Eugene V. Thaw
For this gouache see pages 153–54 and figure 6.

124 A Fragonard
The Education of a Small Child
Oil on panel, 22.2 x 19.1 cm.
Collection Mr. and Mrs. Eugene V. Thaw
The painting is not otherwise mentioned in this catalogue. It was most recently published by J.-P. Cuzin, *Jean-Honoré Fragonard*, 1987, p. 302, no. 216, ill.

148 A Fragonard
The Love Letter
Oil on canvas, 83.2 x 67 cm.
Inscribed (on letter): A Monsieur/[?] Mon Cuvillere
The Metropolitan Museum of Art, New York, The Jules Bache Collection, 49.7.49
The painting is not otherwise mentioned in this catalogue. It was most recently published by J.-P. Cuzin, *Jean-Honoré Fragonard*, 1987, p. 324, no. 335, ill.

161 A Fragonard
Les Charlatans
Oil on canvas, 49 x 38.7 cm.
Private collection
For this sketch see page 340 and figure 3.

161 B Fragonard
The Toy Seller
Oil on canvas, 40.6 x 34 cm.
Private collection
For this sketch see page 340 and figure 2.

219 A Fragonard
Sultana
Oil on canvas, 97.2 x 78.7 cm.
Private collection
For this painting see pages 451–52 and figure 1.

283 A Fragonard
The Fountain of Love
Oil on canvas, 47 x 37.5 cm.
Private collection
The sketch is not otherwise mentioned in this catalogue. For the completed work to which it relates. see page 548 and figure 4.

284 A Fragonard
The Sacrifice of the Rose
Oil on canvas, 65 x 54.2 cm.
Collection Mr. and Mrs. Stewart Resnick
For this painting see page 549 and figure 1.

121 A Carel Fabritius
Mercury and Argus
Oil on canvas, 73.5 x 104 cm.
Richard L. Feigen & Company
For this work, which was closely copied by Fragonard, see pages 249–50 and figure 1.

Works with the following catalogue numbers have been exhibited in New York only:

24, 25, 28, 32, 34, 42, 43, 44, 46, 48, 49, 55, 58, 61, 64, 77, 79, 83, 84, 88, 137, 138, 166, 172, 175, 178, 181, 184, 185, 191, 203, 204, 209, 210, 266, 268, 270, 277, 288, 289, 292, 293, 295, 297, 299.

Works with the following catalogue numbers have been exhibited only at the Grand Palais, Paris:

12, 14, 15, 16, 17, 19, 27, 29, 30, 31, 33, 35, 39, 40, 45, 47, 50, 51, 52, 53, 56, 57, 59, 60, 62, 63, 66, 67, 68, 69, 70, 71, 71 A, 73, 78, 82, 89, 93, 103, 104, 108, 118, 129, 134, 144, 148, 154, 155,168, 173, 174, 176, 182, 189, 193, 196, 212, 217, 218, 220, 221, 222, 230, 235, 239, 240, 241, 242, 244, 247, 249, 250, 253, 255, 257, 263, 265, 267, 272, 273, 281, 282, 283, 284, 285, 286, 287, 290, 291, 294, 296, 304, 305.

Works with the following catalogue numbers were not exhibited: 97, 107, 280.

Photograph Credits

Numbers refer to catalogue numbers.

Amiens, Musée de Picardie, 124
Amsterdam, Rijksmuseum, Rijksprentenkabinet, 42, 184, 203, 204, 272, 273
Angers, Musée des Beaux-Arts, 105
Annecy, Musée-Château d'Annecy, 86

Barcelona, Museu d'Art de Catalunya, 129
Berlin-Dahlem, Staatliche Museen Preussischer Kulturbesitz, Kupferstichkabinett, 242, 263
Besançon, Musée des Beaux-Arts, 25, 27, 29, 32, 33, 34, 172, 173, 178, 185, 295
Boston, Museum of Fine Arts, 115
Brussels, Musée d'Ixelles, 208
Buenos Aires, Museo Nacional de Arte Decorativo, 285

Cambridge, Harvard University Art Museums (Fogg Art Museum), 41, 113, 156, 215, 225, 278, 303
Chicago, The Art Institute of Chicago, 19, 79, 128, 193, 266
Cleveland, The Cleveland Museum of Art, 282

Detroit, The Detroit Institute of Arts, 1, 2, 3, 4
Dijon, Musée des Beaux-Arts, 260
Dizengoff, "Mula" Photography Studio, 245, 246

Fort Worth, Kimbell Art Museum, 112
Frankfurt am Main, Städelsches Kunstinstitut, 14, 15, 176, 191, 277

Grasse, J. Mayer, 239

Hamburg, Kunsthalle, 101, 238

Jerusalem, The Israel Museum, 202

Karlsruhe, Staatliche Kunsthalle, 65, 180

Langres, Musées de Langres, 259
Le Havre, Musée des Beaux-Arts, 211
Leningrad, The Hermitage, 108
Lisbon, Museu Calouste Gulbenkian, 114, 168
Lisbon, Museu Nacional de Arte Antiga, 158
London, British Museum, 43, 44, 45, 46, 47, 48, 49, 50, 55–56, 57, 58, 59, 60, 61, 62, 64
London, Dulwich Picture Gallery, 103
London, National Gallery, 9
Los Angeles, The Armand Hammer Foundation, 224, 227, 232
Los Angeles, Los Angeles County Museum of Art, 7
Lugano, Thyssen-Bornemisza Collection, 6
Lyons, Musée des Arts Décoratifs, 88, 189

Malibu, J. Paul Getty Museum, 119
Marseilles, Yves Vallois, 36

Minneapolis, The Minneapolis Institute of Arts, 286
Montclair, Helga Photo Studio, 76
Montpellier, Musée Atger, Faculté de Médecine, 11, 179, 197, 198, 200
Moscow, Pushkin Museum, 17, 250
Muncie, Ball State University Art Gallery, 219
Munich, Bayerische Staatsgemäldesammlungen, 110

New Haven, Yale University Art Gallery, 194, 228
New York, The Brooklyn Museum, 243
New York, The Metropolitan Museum of Art, 18, 38, 139, 151, 157, 207, 271, 274
New York, The Pierpont Morgan Library, 95, 106
Nice, Musée des Beaux-Arts Jules Chéret, 99
Norfolk, The Chrysler Museum, 10

Orléans, Patrice Delatouche, 206

Paris, Bibliothèque Nationale, 5, 66, 67, 68, 69, 70, 240
Paris, Bulloz, 31, 82, 97, 248, 251
Paris, CNMHS Marc Jeanneteau/Spadem for Getty, 85
Paris, École Nationale Supérieure des Beaux-Arts, 8
Paris, Giraudon, 183
Paris, Institut Néerlandais, 290
Paris, Musée des Arts Décoratifs, 205
Paris, Réunion des Musées Nationaux, 12, 13, 20, 23, 24, 26, 28, 30, 35, 37, 39, 40, 51, 53, 54, 71, 71A, 72, 73, 74, 75, 80, 81, 83, 84, 88, 89, 91, 92, 93, 94, 96, 98, 99, 102, 104, 109, 118, 121, 122, 123, 125, 126, 127, 130, 131, 132, 133, 134, 141, 143, 144, 145, 148, 150, 153, 154, 155, 161, 167, 170, 174, 175, 177, 187, 188, 190, 195, 196, 209, 212, 214, 217, 218, 221, 223, 229, 230, 235, 236, 241, 244, 253, 254, 255, 258, 264, 265, 270, 275, 276, 279, 281, 283, 284, 287, 288, 289, 291, 292, 293, 294, 296, 301, 305
Paris, Studio Lourmel, 252, 300
Philadelphia, Philadelphia Museum of Art, 146
Philadelphia, The Rosenbach Museum and Library, 262

Quimper, Musée des Beaux-Arts, 149

Rome, Soprintendenza per i Beni Artistici e Storici, 87
Rotterdam, Museum Boymans-van Beuningen, 120, 171, 201, 213, 269
Rouen, Bibliothèque Municipale, 100
Rouen, Musée des Beaux-Arts, 22

Sacramento, Crocker Art Museum, 302
Saint-Jean-Cap Ferrat, Musée "Ile de France," Fondation Ephrussi de Rothschild, 111
Saint Louis, The Saint Louis Art Museum, 21, 233
Saint Petersburg, Florida, Museum of Fine Arts, 160

San Diego, Timken Art Gallery, 166
São Paulo, Museu de Arte, 226

Toledo, The Toledo Museum of Art, 5
Toulon, Musée de Toulon, 152

Vienna, Graphische Sammlung Albertina, 77, 78, 181, 182, 210, 247, 249, 267, 268, 297

Washington, D.C., National Gallery of Art, 117, 162, 163, 164, 165, 261
Williamstown, Sterling and Francine Clark Art Institute, 116, 135
Worcester, Worcester Art Museum, 90